MAC OS X

IN A NUTSHELL

*Jason McIntosh, Chuck Toporek,
and Chris Stone*
with contributions by Scott Gever, Dave Carrano,
and Leon Towns-von Stauber

O'REILLY®

Beijing • Cambridge • Farnham • Köln • Paris • Sebastopol • Taipei • Tokyo

Mac OS X in a Nutshell

by Jason McIntosh, Chuck Toporek, and Chris Stone

Copyright © 2003 O'Reilly & Associates, Inc. All rights reserved.
Printed in the United States of America.

Published by O'Reilly & Associates, Inc., 1005 Gravenstein Highway North, Sebastopol, CA 95472.

O'Reilly & Associates books may be purchased for educational, business, or sales promotional use. Online editions are also available for most titles (*safari.oreilly.com*). For more information, contact our corporate/institutional sales department: 800-998-9938 or *corporate@oreilly.com*.

Editor:	Chuck Toporek
Production Editor:	Mary Brady
Cover Designer:	Emma Colby
Interior Designer:	David Futato

Printing History:

January 2003:	First Edition.

ISBN: 0-596-00370-6
[M]   [3/03]

Table of Contents

Part II. System Configuration

MAC OS X

IN A NUTSHELL

Related Mac OS X Titles from O'Reilly

Essentials

AppleScript in a Nutshell
Building Cocoa Applications:
  A Step-by-Step Guide
Learning Carbon
Learning Cocoa with Objective-C
Mac OS X Pocket Guide
Macintosh Troubleshooting Pocket
  Guide
Objective-C Pocket Reference
REALbasic: The Definitive Guide

Missing Manuals

AppleWorks 6: The Missing Manual
iMovie 2: The Missing Manual
iPhoto: The Missing Manual
Mac OS 9: The Missing Manual
Mac OS X: The Missing Manual
Office 2001 for Macintosh:
  The Missing Manual

Unix Essentials

Using csh & tcsh
Unix in a Nutshell
Unix Power Tools
Learning GNU Emacs
Learning the vi Editor
Learning Unix for Mac OS X

Related Programming

CGI Programming with Perl
Developing Java Beans™
Java™Cookbook
Java™in a Nutshell
Learning Java™
Learning Perl
Perl Cookbook
Perl in a Nutshell
Practical C Programming
Programming with Qt

Mac OS X Administration

Apache: The Definitive Guide
Essential System Administration
sendmail

Part III. System and Network Administration

Part IV. Scripting and Development

Part V. Under Mac OS X's Hood

Preface

Although Apple Computer ushered in the PC revolution in 1980 with the Apple II computer, the inventions that are most synonymous with the company are the Macintosh computer and its ground-breaking graphical operating system, both released in 1984. Let's think of this operating system as Mac OS 1, though Apple wouldn't coin the term "Mac OS" to describe its operating system until the 1990s. The early Mac made its mark in a world where all other popular computer interfaces were obscure.

In the years following the Mac's release, much has changed. Both bad and good things have happened, and some company in Washington called Microsoft started to take over the world. By 1996, Apple knew it needed to modernize the Mac OS (and make it more worthy competition to Windows) from the bottom up, but previous attempts and partnerships to bring this about had ended in failure. So, it made an unusual move and purchased NeXT. This company had made a nice Unix-based operating system called NeXTSTEP, in which Apple saw the seeds of its own salvation. As it happened, NeXT's leader was the ambitious Steve Jobs, one of Apple's founders, who left the company after a political rift in the 1980s. To make a long and interesting story short, Jobs quickly seized control of Apple Computer, stripped it down to its essentials, and put all its resources into reinventing the Mac. Five years later, the result was Mac OS X: a computing platform based around an entirely new operating system that merged the best parts of the old Mac OS, NeXTSTEP, and nearly two decades of user feedback on the Mac OS.

Mac OS X initially may seem a little alien to long-time Mac users; it is, quite literally, an entirely different operating system than Mac OS 9 and earlier versions (even though Mac OS X retains most of its predecessor's important interface idioms, such as the way the desktop and the user interface works, as covered in the first two chapters of this book). However, the Mac is now winning more converts than ever, not just from Windows, but from other Unix systems such as Linux, Solaris, and FreeBSD (from which Mac OS X's Unix core is derived).

Mac OS X brings all of the great things from earlier versions of the Mac OS and melds them with a BSD core, bringing Unix to the masses of the world. Apple has created a rock-solid operating system to compete both on the user and enterprise level. In days gone by, the Mac was mostly looked at as a system for "fluffy-bunny designers."* It's now becoming the must-have hardware (for example, the TiBook) and operating system of geeks and designers everywhere.

With Mac OS X, you can bring home the bacon and fry it up in a pan. Your Mac can be used not only for graphic design and creating web pages, but also as a web server. Not into flat graphics? Fine, Mac OS X sports Quartz Extreme and OpenGL. Want to learn how to program? Mac OS X is a developer's dream, packing in Perl, Python, Ruby, C, C++, Objective-C, compilers, and debuggers; if you're an X jockey, you can also run X Windows on top of Mac OS X if you really want or need to. In addition to the standard programming languages, Mac OS X comes with a powerful set of frameworks for programming with Cocoa, Mac OS X's native language (adopted from NeXT).

The Layers of Mac OS X

As mentioned earlier, Mac OS X is a multilayered system, as shown in Figure P-1. At its core is the *Kernel Environment*, or Darwin (*http://opensource.apple.com/ darwin*), Apple's own open source operating system, which is based on the Mach 3.0 microkernel and BSD 4.4 Unix. Darwin gives Mac OS X its Unix core, along with features such as a protected memory environment, support for multi-threaded applications, and stability that just wasn't attainable in earlier versions of the Mac OS.

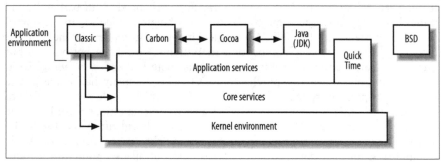

Figure P-1. The layers of Mac OS X

Next up, we have the *Core Services* layer. The Core Services provide a set of application program interfaces (or APIs), which allow applications to speak with and take instructions from the kernel. Unless you're a developer, the Core is something that you'll never have to touch or deal with. For programmers, though, the Core provides access to such things as Core Foundation, Core Graphics, Core Audio, CFNetwork, Carbon Core, and Apple Events, to name a few.

---

* A quote from Nat Torkington.

The *Application Services* layer gives Mac OS X its slick Aqua interface. The components in this layer include Quartz Extreme (which replaces QuickDraw from earlier versions of the Mac OS), QuickTime, and OpenGL. Quartz Extreme draws and renders graphics, performs anti-aliasing, and provides services for rendering and printing PDF. Quartz actually has two components: the Quartz Compositor and Quartz 2D. The *Quartz Compositor* is the window server, while *Quartz 2D* provides a set of APIs for rendering and drawing two-dimensional shapes.

OpenGL—the work horse of the graphics community—provides services for three-dimensional (3D) graphics. If you've played any of the games created in the last 10 years or so, chances are they were based on OpenGL. QuickTime is used in the OS to handle multimedia, such as streaming graphics and movies. Quartz, OpenGL, and QuickTime work together to render all you see in the graphical world of Mac OS X.

On top of it all, we have the *Application Environment*. This final layer is where you do all your work, and is where the applications are run. Apple provides two native APIs for applications to run on Mac OS X: Carbon and Cocoa. *Carbon* applications are older C and C++ applications that have been *Carbonized* to run natively on Mac OS X. *Cocoa* is Mac OS X's "pure" environment: Cocoa applications rely only on the frameworks provided by the system, and not on an older code base.

The application environment contains a pure Java system—not a *virtual machine*, as in older Mac systems—which allows you to run 100 percent–pure Java applications on Mac OS X. The current implementation is J2RE SE 1.3.1_03-69; however, as Jaguar proved, things will change, so you should expect Apple to improve the Java implementation as time goes by.

If you have an older Mac application that hasn't been Carbonized and isn't Cocoa- or Java-based, you're not out of luck. If your system also has Mac OS 9 installed (9.2.2 to be exact), you can run older Mac applications in the *Classic Environment* (or just Classic). When you're running Classic, you're basically running a watered-down implementation of Mac OS 9 *on top of* Mac OS X. Classic is covered in Chapter 3.

Also running at the application layer is the Terminal application (*/Applications/ Utilities*), which is your command-line interface to the Unix shell. For users, the default shell is *tcsh*, and in Jaguar, the default shell for handling shell scripts is *sh* (the default for shell scripts in earlier versions of Mac OS X was *zsh*).

This multilayered architecture gives Mac OS X its power and elegance. Each layer—and in some cases, the components within each layer—is independent from the other, resulting in a system that hardly ever crashes.

Audience for This Book

No book can be everything to everyone, especially at the first edition stage. But *Mac OS X in a Nutshell* does have an audience: one that first needs some clarification.

A question that came up a while back is "Why do I need a Nutshell book if I already have the Missing Manual?" We explain some of the reasoning and the audiences for both books here.

The *Missing Manuals* (co-published by Pogue Press and O'Reilly & Associates, Inc.) are a series of books aimed at the beginner- to intermediate-level user. The books are written in friendly prose and cover everything that a user would want to know and more.

O'Reilly's *Nutshell* series is the opposite of that. These books take a more terse approach to the topic. They give you what you need to know in as few words as possible, while at the same time covering things that are useful not only to beginners, but also advanced users.

The resulting package—the combination of the Missing Manual and the Nutshell book—provides you with the depth and coverage not attainable in a single book (unless, of course, you don't mind lifting weights).

So, to get back to the original question, the answer is: to truly master Mac OS X, you probably do need both the Missing Manual *and* the Nutshell book. Each book takes a different approach to covering Mac OS X, and each offers you something the other cannot.

Who This Book Is for

Due to the unusual pedigree of Mac OS X, readers might meet it in a number of ways. This book is aimed at folks with a more technical bent than the average user—the *poweruser*. This book will come in handy as a quick reference guide for those who are curious about what happens under Mac OS X's hood (and how one might tinker with it), and will be useful to those who are using Mac OS X as a server or development platform.

 It's important to note that this book doesn't cover Mac OS X Server; it covers only the client version, Mac OS X Jaguar. For more information on Mac OS X Server, see Apple's online documentation at *http://www.apple.com/macosxserver*.

Who This Book Isn't for

This book focuses mainly on topics that are not likely to strike the interest of people who use Mac OS X primarily to run applications, such as word processing, graphic design, browsing the Web, and so on. These users might be better served by more user-friendly volumes, such as *Mac OS X: The Missing Manual* (Pogue Press/O'Reilly & Associates, Inc., 2002), or the *Mac OS X Pocket Guide* (O'Reilly, 2002), both of which were recently revised for Jaguar.

How This Book Is Organized

This book is broken down into 5 parts, 25 chapters, and 1 appendix:

Part I, *Lay of the Land*

Chapter 1, *Using Mac OS X*
We begin our exploration of Mac OS X at its surface, by describing and documenting Aqua, the system's liquid-themed graphical user interface. This chapter covers the visual metaphors and window features that every native Mac OS X application uses, as well as onscreen objects that are available from every program, such as the Dock and the menu bar.

Chapter 2, *Using the Finder*
The Finder is Mac OS X's graphical file navigation application, which presents your computer's filesystem through the familiar visual metaphor of folders and files. This chapter explores this application, including a wealth of subtle tips and tricks.

Chapter 3, *Mac OS 9, Mac OS X, and Classic*
Meant especially for longtime Mac veterans, this chapter covers the major differences between Mac OS X and its predecessors, of which Mac OS 9 was the final version.

Chapter 4, *Task and Setting Index*
This chapter provides a quick index of common operating system activities in a question-and-answer format.

Part II, *System Configuration*

Chapter 5, *System Preferences*
This chapter covers the System Preferences application as it appears in Mac OS X Version 10.2, and details how it works as a frontend to the file-based preferences system.

Chapter 6, *Applications and Utilities*
Mac OS X comes with a wealth of core applications, more than any Mac OS before it. This chapter lists the contents of a fresh Mac OS X installation's Applications folder and discusses the system's unique approach to application integration, as well as ways to install new programs onto your Mac.

Chapter 7, *Networking*
This chapter covers the user's part in establishing and using a network connection with Mac OS X centering on the system's Network preferences pane and touching on the programs one uses to take advantage of an active connection.

Chapter 8, *Printer Configuration and Printing*
This chapter details the Mac OS X printing system. It covers printing documents through the standard Print dialogs (as well as through a handful of command-line programs), and discusses configuring the printing system.

Chapter 9, *Filesystem Overview*

> Like any Unix system, much of Mac OS X's functionality is based on its filesystem layout. This chapter tours the various folders found on a typical Mac OS X volume, including the Unix-centric directories that the Finder usually keeps out of sight.

Chapter 10, *Running Java Applications*

> This chapter covers the various ways one can run Java programs in Mac OS X, either as full-fledged Aqua applications, JAR files that provide their own interfaces, or even command-line programs.

Part III, *System and Network Administration*

Chapter 11, *System Administration Overview*

> Now that Macs are actually Unix machines at the core, it pays to know the fundamentals of administrating a multiuser system (even if you're the only human user on it). This chapter also covers the basics of monitoring and maintaining your Mac's network connections, whether they are to a LAN or the world-wide Internet.

Chapter 12, *Directory Services and NetInfo*

> This chapter details the ways Mac OS X stores and accesses its administrative information, ranging from the NetInfo system of network-linked databases to the "old-school" file-based system familiar to Unix administrators.

Chapter 13, *Running Network Services*

> Mac OS X's suite of open source Unix software includes a full complement of network services programs (what the Unix wizards call daemons). This chapter details the major categories of services Unix supplies, including web servers, file sharing, and mail servers. This chapter also covers the control that Mac OS X gives you through either the Sharing preferences pane or the command line.

Chapter 14, *Web Publishing with a DAMP System*

> This chapter shows you how to set up and configure a web-publishing system using DAMP: Darwin, Apache, MySQL, and Perl/PHP/Python.

Part IV, *Scripting and Development*

Chapter 15, *Development Tools*

> Mac OS X is a developer's dream come true, and each new Mac and system comes with Apple's own Developer Tools. This chapter provides a basic overview of the applications and tools that ship as part of the Developer Tools, including Project Builder and Interface Builder, the integrated development environment (IDE) for programming Cocoa-based applications for Mac OS X.

Chapter 16, *AppleScript*

> The Mac's native scripting language, AppleScript, gives you control over the environment and the applications on your system. This chapter introduces you to AppleScript, describing Apple Events and showing you how to use the Script Editor to write AppleScripts.

Chapter 17, *Text Editing on Mac OS X*

Like all Unix systems, Mac OS X is driven by text files. Between various programs' text-based configuration and preference files (often rendered in XML), program source code, the Makefiles, and source code of freshly downloaded software, it pays to know your options with opening, editing, and creating text files. This chapter covers Mac OS X's attitude toward text files and the many editors it includes to help you create and edit them.

Chapter 18, *Using CVS*

CVS, the *concurrent versions system*, gives users and developers an easy way to manage changes made to project files. Under CVS, each person working on a project gets their own "sandbox" copy of every file involved, which they can modify and experiment with however they please; a central, untouchable file repository keeps the canonical files safe. This chapter introduces you to CVS and includes both the administrator and user commands.

Part V, *Under Mac OS X's Hood*

Chapter 19, *Using the Terminal*

With Mac OS X, there's only one way to gain access to the Unix core: the Terminal application. This chapter introduces you to the Terminal application and shows you how to issue commands and tweak its settings.

Chapter 20, *Pattern Matching*

A number of Unix text-processing utilities let you search for, and in some cases change, text patterns rather than fixed strings. These utilities include editing programs like *vi* and *Emacs*, programming languages like Perl and Python, and the commands *grep* and *egrep*. Text patterns (formally called *regular expressions*) contain normal characters mixed with special characters (called *metacharacters*).

Chapter 21, *Shells and Shell Programming*

This chapter covers the shells included with Mac OS X, with the focus placed on *tcsh*, the default user shell. Also included in this chapter is an overview of *tcsh*'s commands, for use in programming the shell to perform various system-related tasks.

Chapter 22, *The Defaults System*

Like the old saying goes, there's more than one way to skin a cat. In this case, the cat we're skinning is Jaguar. When you configure your system or an application to your liking, those preferences are stored in what's known as the *defaults database*. This chapter describes how to gain access to and hack these settings via the Terminal application and the *defaults* command.

Chapter 23, *Running the X Windows System*

As most Unix developers quickly learn, the X in Mac OS X doesn't stand for the X Window System. This chapter describes how to install OroborOSX and XDarwin (a version of XFree86) on top of Mac OS X.

Chapter 24, *Installing Unix Software*

> While Mac OS X is Unix-based, most Unix applications need a little help to get them installed and running. This chapter describes some of the issues you'll run into when installing a Unix application on Mac OS X, and guides you through what's needed to make them run.

Chapter 25, *Unix Command Reference*

> This final chapter lists descriptions and usage terms for nearly 300 of the Unix commands found in Mac OS X. The commands have been painstakingly run and verified against the manpages for accuracy; this is the most complete and accurate Mac-based Unix command reference in print.

The book also has one appendix:

Appendix A, *Resources*

> This appendix is a listing of resources for Mac users, including books, web sites, and mailing lists applicable to Mac OS X users, developers, and administrators.

Conventions Used in This Book

The following typographical conventions are used in this book:

Italic

> Used to indicate new terms, URLs, filenames, file extensions, directories, commands and options, program names, and to highlight comments in examples. For example, a path in the filesystem will appear as */Applications/ Utilities*.

Constant Width

> Used to show the contents of files or the output from commands.

Constant Width Bold

> Used in examples and tables to show commands or other text that should be typed literally by the user.

Constant Width Italic

> Used in examples and tables to show text that should be replaced with user-supplied values.

Menus/Navigation

> Menus and their options are referred to in the text as File → Open, Edit → Copy, etc. Arrows are also used to signify a navigation path when using window options—for example, System Preferences → Login → Login Items means that you would launch System Preferences, click the icon for the Login control panel, and select the Login Items pane within that panel.

Pathnames

> Pathnames are used to show the location of a file or application in the filesystem. Directories (or *folders* for Mac and Windows users) are separated by a forward slash. For example, if you see something like, " . . . launch the Terminal application (*/Applications/Utilities*)" in the text, this means the Terminal application can be found in the *Utilities* subfolder of the *Applications* folder.

Relatedly, a tilde character (~) refers to the current user's Home directory, so ~/*Library* refers to the Library folder within your own Home folder.

↵

A carriage return (↵) at the end of a line of code is used to denote an unnatural line break; that is, you should not enter these as two lines of code, but as one continuous line. Multiple lines are used in these cases due to printing constraints.

%, #

The percent sign (%) is used in some examples to show the user prompt for the *tcsh* shell; the hash mark (#) is the prompt for the root user.

Menu Symbols

When looking at the menus for any application, you will see some symbols associated with keyboard shortcuts for a particular command. For example, to open a document in Microsoft Word, you could go to the File menu and select Open (File → Open), or you could issue the keyboard shortcut, ⌘-O.

Figure P-2 shows the symbols used in the various menus to denote a keyboard shortcut.

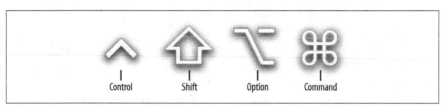

Figure P-2. Keyboard accelerators for issuing commands

Rarely will you see the Control symbol used as a menu command option; it's more often used in association with mouse clicks or for working with the *tcsh* shell.

 Indicates a tip, suggestion, or general note.

 Indicates a warning or caution.

Comments and Questions

Please address comments and questions concerning this book to the publisher:

O'Reilly & Associates, Inc.
1005 Gravenstein Highway North
Sebastopol, CA 95472
800-998-9938 (in the U.S. or Canada)
707-829-0515 (international/local)
707-829-0104 (fax)

There is a web page for this book, which lists errata, examples, or any additional information. You can access this page at:

> *http://www.oreilly.com/catalog/macosxian*

To comment or ask technical questions about this book, send email to:

> *bookquestions@oreilly.com*

For more information about books, conferences, Resource Centers, and the O'Reilly Network, see the O'Reilly web site at:

> *http://www.oreilly.com*

Acknowledgments

The authors would like to acknowledge the masses who helped make the book possible, and also would like to thank the authors of other O'Reilly books, from which some portions of this book were derived; including:

- AppleScript in a Nutshell (Bruce M. Perry)
- CVS Pocket Reference (Gregor N. Purdy)
- Essential System Administration (Æleen Frisch)
- Linux in a Nutshell (Ellen Siever, Stephen Spainhour, Stephen Figgins, and Jessica P. Hekman)
- Mac OS X Pocket Guide (Chuck Toporek)
- Mac OS X for Unix Geeks (Brian Jepson and Ernest E. Rothman)
- DNS & BIND (Paul Albitz and Cricket Liu)
- SSH, The Secure Shell: The Definitive Guide (Daniel J. Barrett and Richard E. Silverman)
- Unix in a Nutshell (Arnold Robbins)

Acknowledgments for Jason McIntosh

Chuck Toporek provided great guidance and insight as an editor, and knew when to step in and help write once my life changed in unexpected ways (i.e., I suddenly stopped being unemployed); this book is much better for his active efforts. Chris Stone took on the command reference chapter before any of us realized the magnitude of that task, and yet he and his cohorts did a smashing job. I mean, just *look* at that thing.

John Keimel and Andrew "Zarf" Plotkin tech reviewed this book. Jim Troutman and Andy Turner at Arcus Digital in Waterville, Maine hosted my email, web, and CVS server, which was crucial to this project (and my life). They also tossed me some freelance programming jobs to gnaw on, and pitched in with tech reviewing. Karl von Laudermann and Derek Lichter assisted with last-minute fact-checking. The filler text in several examples is excerpted from Erik T. Ray's *The Lambda Expressway* and used with permission.

Derrick Story at the O'Reilly Network let me write some Mac OS X articles for *macdevcenter.com*, helping me stave off financial ruin until Erik Brauner and the

Institute for Chemistry and Cell Biology at Harvard Medical School hired me into a wonderful job midway through this book's production. They showed great patience with me as I pulled odd and antisocial office hours in order to complete the book on time.

Reprising their roles from my work on *Perl & XML* (with Erik T. Ray, published by O'Reilly & Associates, 2002), Julia "Cthulhia" Tenney acted as my personal principal gadfly, and the 1369 Coffee House in Cambridge and the Diesel Cafe in Somerville again served as my alternate offices.

Mary Agner, Denis Moskowitz, and the whole regular crowd at the House of Roses game nights made sure I got my biweekly ration of sanity-maintaining game-playing.

My housemates Melissa Kibbe and Noah Meyerhans (and, before them, Charles Peterman and Carla Schack) continually encouraged me to hurry up and finish the book, if only so I'd stop moping about it.

If you've made a web page (or even posted to a mailing list) about Mac OS X, I've probably read it and used its information somehow. Thanks.

Mike Scott at the University of Maine first introduced me to Macintosh computers back when System 7 was brand new. Andy England of Mac Advantage in Bangor and Jeff Wheeler of the Town of Hermon gave me my first Mac-centric, post-college jobs. Jason Lavoie and Andy Turner of the late Maine InternetWorks got me into Unix (by way of Linux and Perl) with my first programming job. O'Reilly & Associates then hired me, after which they unhired me, but not before getting me irrevocably entangled with technical writing. This is more or less how I got here.

I did all my work on this book on my iBook running Mac OS X. The text is courtesy the Emacs text editor, working in raw DocBook XML, and the screen shots come from Apple's Grab application. The Omni Group's OmniOutliner application helped me organize my thoughts and notes for every chapter I wrote.

All remaining thanks go to my parents Dorothy and Richard, my brothers Peter and Ricky, my aunt Jan, and all of my friends both local and remote, whose network of love and support I relied heavily upon throughout this project, and upon which I shall no doubt continue to draw for whatever silly thing I do next. *Yay!*

Acknowledgments for Chuck Toporek

Also acting as editor for the book, I would like to first thank Jason for taking on this beastly project. Mac OS X is a complex operating system, requiring a broad range of knowledge and experience. Jason had all the geeky qualities needed for someone to write *Mac OS X in a Nutshell*.

So, why did the editor get involved as a coauthor, you ask? Well, after Apple's Worldwide Developer Conference (WWDC) in May, 2002, a lot of things changed. Jason was working ahead on some of the more complex chapters in the book, and by the time he was given access to a prerelease of Jaguar, I was tasked with editing and rewriting a lot of the earlier material Jason had written based on

Mac OS X 10.1.*x*. With pressure looming to make the book right and to get it out within a reasonable time after Jaguar officially released, I too jumped in.

Next, I have to thank my wife Kellie Robinson for putting up with her "geek" of a husband while I took on yet another project. My DIY attitude often gets me in trouble, and you'd think that after having spent four years in the U.S. Navy, I would have learned that "NAVY" stands for "Never Again Volunteer Yourself"— but I didn't. Thanks, Kellie, for putting up with the long nights at the air-conditioned Starbuck's in Arlington Center, for my long nights and weekends of working at home, and for supporting me when I needed it. Thanks, too, to Max, our insane kitty, for occasionally sitting on my laptop's keyboard in his constant quest for affection.

Thanks to the many people at O'Reilly for their involvement in this project, including David Chu, my faithful editorial assistant, Claire Cloutier and Mary Brady in production, and Julie Hawks for her most-excellent and masterful indexing skills. We also owe quite a bit of thanks to Chris Stone, Scott Gever, Dave Carrano, and David Brickner for jumping in and taking on the un-Godly task of certifying the Unix command reference. Other folks here who deserve some level of recognition include Lorrie LeJeune for drawing Vinny, the dog on the cover of this book and the *Mac OS X Pocket Guide*, Erik Ray, Lenny Meullner, Joe Wizda, Mike Sierra, Emma Colby, Ellie V., David Futato, Linda Mui and Robert Denn for walks to The Spa, and last but not least, Paula Ferguson, for giving me a much-needed pep talk after a particularly hard editorial group meeting.

Thanks to our great friends at Apple Computer, not only for giving us a killer operating system to work with, but also for their assistance, guidance, and input on some of the technical details we couldn't find answers to.

And last, but not least, I'd like to thank Tim O'Reilly for getting "The Mac Religion," backing all the work I'm doing, and for making O'Reilly a truly awesome place to work.

Acknowledgments for Chris Stone

The *Unix Command Reference* (Chapter 25) couldn't have been completed without the help and support of a lot of great people. For helping with the writing, I can't thank the contributors Scott Gever, Dave Carrano, Leon Towns-von Stauber, and David Brickner enough. Thanks also to Bob Amen, Fred Coffman, Brian Jepson, and David Lents for their technical expertise. Thanks to Chuck, Laurie, Derrick, Bob, CJ, and the other IS folks—Marlene, Larry, and Kirk—for helping to make it all work out. Thanks and apologies to my friends and family, who kindly allowed me to cancel plans: Craig, Junichi, Takashi, Okaasan, Fumiko-san, Mom, Dad, and of course Miho, Andy, and J.J.

Lay of the Land

As any newcomer can attest, Mac OS X's user interface can be over-whelming at first glance. This first part sets the stage for the rest of the book, in that you'll learn the lay of the land for the Mac that sits before you. This part introduces you to Mac OS X's landscape, providing you with details about the user-interface elements, such as the windows, buttons, and various controls, along with information on using the Dock and Finder. For Mac OS 9 users who are coming over to Mac OS X, Chapter 3 will be of interest to you. This part wraps up with a *Task and Setting Index*, which includes over 250 hints, tips, and tricks for using and configuring your Mac OS X system.

The chapters in this part include:

Chapter 1, *Using Mac OS X*

Chapter 2, *Using the Finder*

Chapter 3, *Mac OS 9, Mac OS X, and Classic*

Chapter 4, *Task and Setting Index*

Using Mac OS X

There are actually two interface layers to Mac OS X. One is *Aqua*, the system's native *graphical user interface* (GUI); the other is a *command-line interface* (CLI), which is most commonly accessed via the *Terminal* application (*/Applications/ Utilities*). This chapter provides a quick overview of Mac OS X's Aqua environment; later chapters in the book will introduce you to the Terminal and the BSD Unix side, with a full examination of these deeper OS layers in Part V, *Under Mac OS X's Hood*.

Mac OS X offers a feature-rich graphical user environment that makes it easy for people to interact with the operating system. This chapter starts out with a discussion of Mac OS X's Desktop, and introduces things like the menu bar, the Dock, and basic window controls. Chapter 2 covers the Finder, Mac OS X's file manager.

The Mac Desktop

When you first log on to your Mac, you are presented with the *Desktop*, as shown in Figure 1-1. By "Desktop," we're referring to the entire screen and all of its interface elements, including the menu bar, the Dock, the Desktop, disk and file icons, and the various windows used by the Finder and other applications.

The Menu Bar

Regardless of which application you're using, Mac OS X's menu bar is always located across the top of the screen. This is different from Microsoft Windows or Linux GNOME or KDE Desktop environments, where the menu bar is attached to each individual window. There are some standard items that you'll always find in the menu bar, but as you switch from application to application, you'll notice that the menu names and some of their options change according to which application is active. Figure 1-2 shows the menu bar as it appears when the Finder is active.

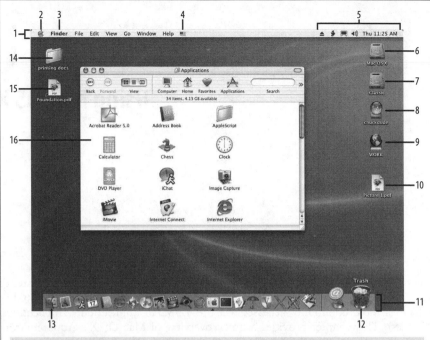

1. The **Menubar** provides access to application-specific menus, as well as the Apple Menu.
2. The **Apple Menu** gives you access to system functions.
3. **Application Menu** gives you access to an application's preferences and other Services provided to that application by other applications.
4. The **Input Menu** lets you switch between keyboard layouts for different languages (configured via System Preferences→International→Input Menu).
5. **Menulets** include the system clock, the Script Menu, and other system controls.
6. **Local disk icon**, partition for Mac OS X.
7. **Local disk icon**, partition for Mac OS 9 (Classic).
8. A mounted **iDisk**.
9. A mounted **Network volume**.
10. A **file icon** (this for a screenshot).
11. **The Dock** holds icons for frequently-used and currently-running applications.
12. Drag items to the **Trash** to delete them from the filesystem.
13. The **Finder** gives you access to everything on your filesystem, and allows you to connect to other machines, network drives, and more.
14. A **folder**, used for organizing files.
15. An **alias**, used to provide a shortcut to a file, folder, or application elsewhere on the system.
16. An open **Finder window** shows directories and the files within.

Figure 1-1. The Mac OS X Desktop

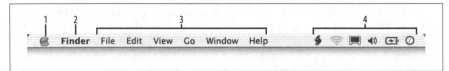

Figure 1-2. The Mac OS X menu bar (with the Finder active)

As Figure 1-2 shows, the following menus and items can be found in the menu bar.

- The Apple menu (see the section "The Apple Menu")
- The Application menu (see the section "The Application Menu")
- A default set of application menus (see the section "Standard Application Menus")
- Menu extras (see the section "Menu Extras")

Active and Inactive Applications

A running application can have one of two possible states: *active* or *inactive*. An active application is the application you're currently using—in other words, the application that receives any input you generate through the keyboard or mouse (with the exception of clicks or keystrokes that switch between applications). An inactive application has been launched, but is running in the background.

You'll typically run many applications at once, using the Dock to track and manage them as described later in "The Dock." For example, you might wish to browse the Web with Internet Explorer while you have *Mail* running in the background. If it alerts you to the arrival of new mail, you can make *Mail* the active application to work with it directly, causing Explorer to slip into the background until you switched back to it for further web browsing.

Menu Basics

All Aqua menus work the same: click once on a word or symbol in the menu bar, and the appropriate menu appears beneath it. The menu closes when you select something from it, pull down a different menu from the menu bar, or click somewhere outside the menu.

Menus can contain two types of things: *commands* and *submenus*.

Commands

Every row that's not a submenu heading is a command. Mousing over a command highlights it; clicking on a menu option closes the menu and invokes the command.

Commands that end in an ellipse (...) require more information from the user before they can do anything. Typically, these menu items summon a dialog box requiring the user to do something else. For example, if you select File → Open..., the Open dialog box appears, prompting you to select a file to open. If you decide that you don't want to open a file (or if you've selected the wrong menu item), click on the Cancel button to close the window.

Most menu commands have keyboard shortcuts (also known as *key bindings*). The keyboard shortcuts, if available, are on the right edge of the menu, and act as an alternate way to invoke a menu command without requiring you to use the mouse to select the menu item. A common example involves saving files, during which you could either select the menu option of File → Save, or issue the ⌘-S shortcut.

Bindings for common commands, such as ⌘-S for saving a file, are the same across all applications. This is in accordance with Apple's Aqua Human Interface Guidelines, more commonly known among developers as "the HIG." The HIG specifies the default key bindings for standard menu options, and should be the interface design Bible of every Macintosh developer. If you've installed the Developer Tools on your system, a copy of the HIG can be found in */Developer/ Documentation/Essentials/AquaHIGuidelines* in both HTML and PDF form. The HIG can also be accessed online at *http://developer.apple.com*.

Submenus

Submenus appear as menu choices with little gray triangles at the right edge of the menu. Mousing over a submenu heading causes another menu to pop up beside the first, as seen in Figure 1-3. Submenus can contain additional menu items or more submenus.

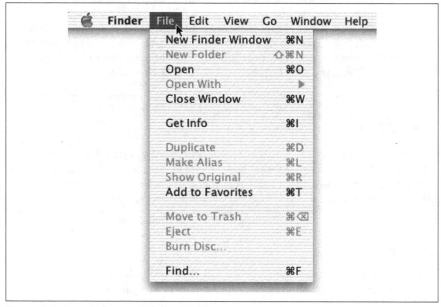

Figure 1-3. A typical menu with key bindings

Contextual Menus

Some objects in the Mac OS X desktop secretly keep *contextual menus* (shown in Figure 1-4), which are special lists of commands and submenus that appear only when you Control-click the objects. In web browsers such as Internet Explorer, hypertext links have contextual menus that let you copy their addresses to the clipboard or open them in separate windows (see Figure 1-5). In the Finder, icons have contextual menus with commands for quickly moving them to the Trash or getting info about them.

Figure 1-4. A contextual menu in Finder

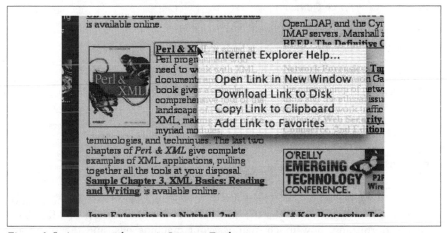

Figure 1-5. A contextual menu in Internet Explorer

When you're in the Finder (or on the Desktop) and you Control-click an item, the mouse pointer's shape will change to include a menu image next to it, as shown in Figure 1-6.

Figure 1-6. The Finder's contextual menu cursor

The Apple Menu

The Apple menu, shown in Figure 1-7, is displayed as a blue apple symbol (),
and is always the left-most item in the menu bar.

If you've used an earlier version of the Mac OS, you'll notice that the Apple menu is now completely different. You can no longer store aliases for files, folders, or applications there. Its new purpose is to provide you with information about your system, and to give you quick access to system preferences, network locations, and recently used files and applications, as well as a means to log out, put your system to sleep, or shut down.

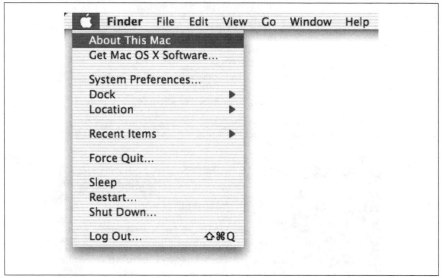

Figure 1-7. The Apple menu

The items you'll find in the Apple menu are listed here:

About This Mac

This window, shown in Figure 1-8, provides you with useful information about your Mac. Here you'll find details about the version of Mac OS X you're running, how much memory your machine has, and the speed and type of processor in your computer. Clicking on the More Info button launches the Apple System Profiler application (*/Applications/Utilities*), which reveals specific details about your hardware, as well as its devices, applications, and extensions. The Apple System Profiler is covered in Chapter 6.

In earlier versions of the Mac OS, the About box would change depending on which application was active. For information about the application, you now have to use the application menu (located to the right of the Apple menu) and select the About option.

When you first select → About This Mac, the window shown on the left side of Figure 1-8 shows you the currently installed version number of Mac OS X. However, if you want to find out which build of Mac OS X you're using, click on the version number and that text will change to show you the versions' build number (center image). Mine, for example, shows that I'm running Build 6C115. Click the build number and you'll see the serial number for your machine.

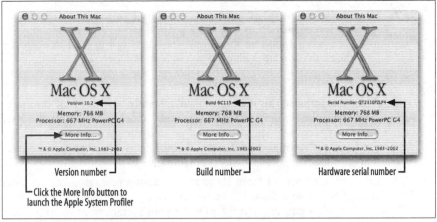

Version number ┘   Build number ┘   Hardware serial number ┘

└ Click the More Info button to
launch the Apple System Profiler

Figure 1-8. The About This Mac window

This provides you with quick access to basic information about your system. The information in the About This Mac window comes in handy when you're on the phone with Apple's customer support, trying to troubleshoot a problem. It also gives you a quick way to launch the Apple System Profiler.

Get Mac OS X Software

Selecting this option takes you to Apple's Mac OS X page (*http://www.apple. com/downloads/macosx*) in your default web browser.

System Preferences

This menu option launches the System Preferences panel. (You can also launch System Preferences by clicking on the light switch icon in the Dock, or by locating and double-clicking on its icon in the Finder. System Preferences allow you to configure the settings on your computer, and includes panels for setting your screen saver or configuring your network connection. You will learn about System Preferences in greater detail in Chapter 5.

Dock

This menu offers a quick way to change settings for the Dock (see the later section "The Dock").

Location

This allows you to quickly change locations for connecting to a network and/ or the Internet. This is similar to the Location Manager Control Panel from earlier versions of the Mac OS.

Recent Items

This menu option combines the Recent Applications and Recent Documents options from Mac OS 9's Apple menu into one convenient menu. The Clear Menu option allows you to reset the recent items from the menu, giving you a clean slate to work from.

Force Quit

This window lets you target any running Aqua application for a force quit. See the section "Force-quitting applications," later in this chapter.

Sleep, Restart, Shutdown, and Log Out have moved from Mac OS 9's Special menu into Mac OS X's Apple menu. If you're looking for a menu option for the Empty Trash option, you need to be in the Finder (Finder → Empty Trash or Shift-⌘-Delete).

Sleep

Just as its name implies, this menu item will instantly put your Mac into sleep mode. Selecting this option will result in your screen going dark; the hard drive on your system will spin down and go into energy saver mode. This is different from the settings you dictate in the Energy Saver preference pane (see Chapter 5 for more on auto-sleep functionality).

To "wake" your computer from sleep mode, simply press any key, or click the mouse if you have a desktop system. However, clicking the mouse on an iBook or PowerBook as an attempt to wake your system from sleep mode is useless; it won't do anything. Instead, you need to press one of the keys on the keyboard (or the Power-On button) to revive your laptop. Opening a sleeping and closed Mac laptop will also wake it up.

If you are connecting your Mac to an overhead projector to give a presentation, put your Mac to sleep, and then wake your Mac up after the projector has been connected.

Restart

This option will open a window (Figure 1-9) to restart your Mac. All active applications will automatically quit; however, you are first prompted to save changes for any files that were open with unsaved changes.

Figure 1-9. The Restart window

System administrators can remove the Restart and Shut Down items from the Apple menu, as described in Chapter 5.

Network Users: Heed This Warning

If other users are connected to your system when you select Restart or Shut-down, no warning will be issued to them to log off. Their only clue is an alert message that pops up on their screen, saying that the server (i.e., your machine) has closed down, and your disk's icon will vanish from their desktop. Worse, if they're directly logged in and using the system through *ssh* or the like (see Chapter 13), they'll find that their shell process, and any programs they were running through it, were unceremoniously terminated.

This is not like other systems, as well as earlier versions of the Mac OS, where you could specify a time limit (in minutes) to restart or shut down and warn connected users.

While this might not seem like a problem for the average user, the lack of any notice will surely wreak havoc for users who work in a networked environment and rely on file servers and other devices. There's nothing like having a file server shut down on you—without warning—particularly when your last save was 30 minutes ago. Our best advice to you is standard: save now and save often. Don't get pinched.

Shutdown
Selecting this option pops up a window (shown in Figure 1-10) for shutting down your Mac. You can also shut down by pressing the Power-On button, which will open the dialog box shown in Figure 1-11 with the options for restarting, shutting down, or putting your Mac to sleep.

Figure 1-10. The Shutdown window

Log Out
This option pops open the window shown in Figure 1-12 to log out of your system. This window takes you back to a login screen. The keyboard shortcut for the Log Out menu option is Shift-⌘-Q.

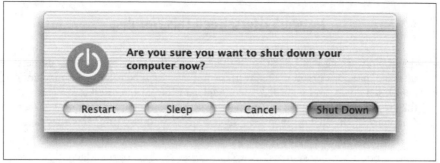

Figure 1-11. The Shutdown window is displayed after pressing the Power-On button

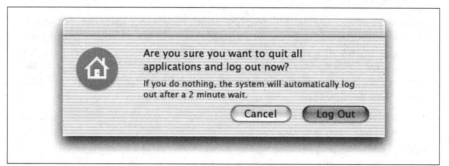

Figure 1-12. The logout window

Force-quitting applications

As in previous versions of Mac OS, if an application hangs—ceasing to respond to any user input—you can send it a Force Quit command. This causes it to quit immediately. Unlike a normal Quit operation, the application won't give you a chance to save any changes to document windows or perform any other clean-up activity; the application simply and ungraciously becomes inactive.

In Mac OS 9 and earlier, force-quitting an application tended to throw the whole system off-kilter, prompting users to save all their work and restart the machine before continuing. Mac OS X's protected memory scheme makes force-quitting a lot safer, affecting nothing but the application itself. Veteran Mac users trained to be hesitant about force-quitting can now do so with impunity with Mac OS X.

However, force-quitting a Classic application can spell trouble to any other Classic applications running at the same time, due to the Classic environment's emulation of Mac OS 9's unprotected memory handling. See Chapter 3.

Thanks to Mac OS X's protected memory, you don't have to restart the entire system if an application crashes or freezes. Instead, you can open the Force Quit window (shown in Figure 1-13). This lists the applications that are running on your system. To force-quit a stuck application, simply click on the application name, then click on Force Quit.

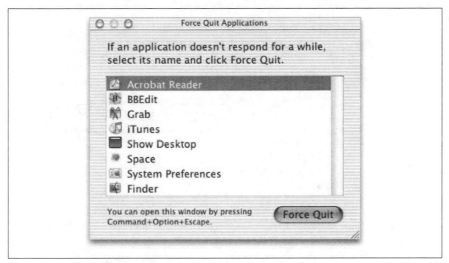

Figure 1-13. The Force Quit window

 Under the hood, Mac OS X sends a *KILL* signal to the application's process, which is equivalent to running *kill -9* on it from the Terminal.

To quit the troublesome application, follow these steps:

1. Select the application name in the Force Quit Applications window.
2. Click on the Force Quit button.
3. A warning sheet, shown in Figure 1-14, will appear, alerting you that force-quitting the application will cause you to lose any unsaved changes.
4. If you're sure you want to quit the application, click on the Force Quit button; otherwise, click on the Cancel button (or hit ⌘-.).

When you've forced the offending application to quit, click the red Close window button in the titlebar to close the Force Quit Applications window.

 You can also force-quit an application by holding down Control-Option and clicking on its icon in the Dock. This pops open the application's context menu, from which you can select Force Quit; however, this quits the application without a warning message, and any unsaved changes will be lost.

The Application Menu

Immediately to the right of the Apple menu in the menu bar is the Application menu, shown in Figure 1-15. As the Apple menu holds commands relevant to the whole system, the Application menu, which is rendered in boldface and named after the active application, holds commands relevant to the active application itself and not any of its windows or documents.

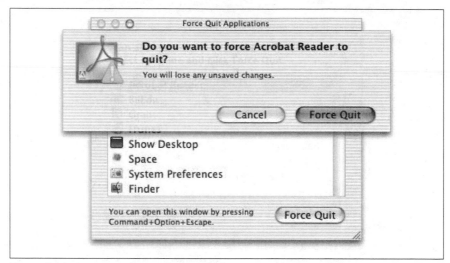

Figure 1-14. A warning sheet will appear before you can force an application to quit

Figure 1-15. The Finder's Application menu

The following are some of the typical Application menu commands:

About Application Name
Displays a small window that typically features the application's name, icon, version number, authors, copyright information, web links, and whatever else the developers felt appropriate.

Preferences...
Calls up the application's preferences window.

Services
Brings up the Services submenu, covered later in "Services."

Hide Application Name
Makes the application and all its windows (including minimized windows on the Dock) invisible to Aqua, and brings the next active application to the foreground. Clicking this application's Dock icon (or bringing forth any of its individual windows through its Dock menu) reveals it once again.

Hide Others
> Hides all running Aqua applications besides the current one.

Show All
> Reveals all hidden applications.

Quit Application Name
> Quits the application. When selected, every open window belonging to that application receives the signal to close. Windows with unsaved changes* will alert the user with a dialog sheet (as seen in Figure 1-33). Hitting Cancel on any of these sheets dismisses that sheet and keeps the window open, cancelling the application's Quit request.

> The one exception to this rule is the Finder. The Finder lacks a Quit option in its application menu, since the Finder is constantly running. However, if the Finder is frozen or otherwise acting up, you can force it to relaunch; see Chapter 2.

Standard Application Menus

In addition to the Application menu, each application (including the Finder) has at least four additional menus in the menu bar:

* File
* Edit
* Window
* Help

The following list touches on the common menu commands found in many Mac OS X applications.

File
> This menu contains commands for working with documents on disk:

> *New (⌘-N)*
>> Opens a new, empty document window.

> *Open... (⌘-O)*
>> Summons a dialog box for selecting a document from the filesystem. Once selected, its content appears in a new window.

> *Open Recent*
>> Contains the names of the last few documents that this application worked with. Selecting one quickly opens it into a new window.

> *Close (⌘-W)*
>> Asks to close the foremost window; this is equivalent to hitting the window's red titlebar button. Some menus also offer Close All (Shift-⌘-W), which is equivalent to Option-clicking the window's Close button.

---

* This includes windows that are reluctant to close for other reasons, such as Terminal windows whose shells still have active child processes.

Save (⌘-S)

If the foremost window represents an existing file (i.e., its titlebar has a real title and a proxy icon), it resynchs its contents with the file, writing all changes made since the last save. Otherwise, it presents the user with a sheet for creating a new file.

Save As... (Shift-⌘-S)

Presents the user with a file-creation sheet, regardless of whether the window already has a file associated with it. After saving, the system reassociates the window with this new file, though the previous one continues to exist in the state in which it was last saved.

Page Setup... (Shift-⌘-P)

This command sets up how the window will present its contents to a printing device.

Print... (⌘-P)

Prepares a document for printing. Chapter 8 covers document printing in more detail.

Edit

The Edit menu almost always holds the all-important clipboard controls and text-editing commands.

Undo action (⌘-Z)

This handy command undoes the last action you performed in this application, be it typing, moving stuff around, drawing a circle, and just about anything else. (This is within limits—it can't, for example, unsend an emotional email you find yourself suddenly regretting.) If you invoke this command repeatedly, then you can undo a whole sequence of actions.

Redo action (Shift-⌘-Z)

This command is simply the antidote of Undo, restoring the last thing you undid, should you change your mind (or go one step too far while performing a multiple Undo). Note that this command is available only immediately after you perform an Undo.

Cut (⌘-X)

Copies the selected text or images onto the system's clipboard, and then deletes it from the window.

Copy (⌘-C)

Copies the selected text or images onto the system's clipboard, leaving it in place in the window.

Paste (⌘-V)

Tries to copy the current clipboard contents to the cursor's current position in the window.

Delete
Clear

Erases whatever's selected. Usually equivalent to hitting the Delete key.

Select All (⌘-A)

Selects all the text or objects in the window.

Find, Spelling

These submenus usually hold some standard interfaces for finding text and using the system's built-in spellchecker.

Window

Like the application's Dock menu, the Window menu usually holds a list of all the windows currently open; selecting one brings it into focus. The menu also often holds the Minimize Window option (⌘-M), which, when selected, minimizes the window to the Dock. You can also minimize a window by clicking on the yellow button in the window's titlebar, or by double-clicking on the titlebar. To bring the window back into focus, simply click on its icon in the Dock.

Some applications also assign keyboard shortcuts to open windows. For example, the Terminal application assigns a Command-*number* keyboard shortcut for each open Terminal window (see Figure 1-16). This allows you to quickly switch back and forth between windows when you need to.

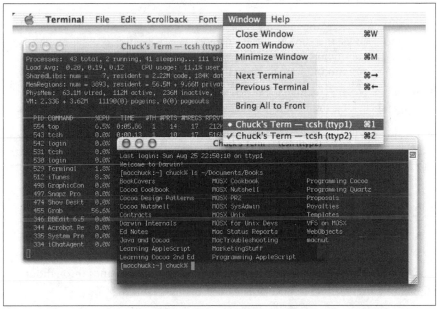

Figure 1-16. The Terminal's Window menu offers keyboard shortcuts to open windows

Help

This menu varies greatly among applications. Some offer just a single command, Application Help (⌘-?), which usually displays the application's documentation in Help Center or your web browser. Other applications fill this menu with commands that let you browse various pieces of documentation and tutorials.

Menu Extras

Mac OS X programs and services can place menu extras on the right side of the menu bar. Like the Apple menu, these little symbols remain constant on the menu bar, regardless of which application you're using.

Menu extras' appearance typically reflects their function, and they often carry menus loaded with commands, just like the other menus. Figure 1-17 shows the menu extra for the Clock.

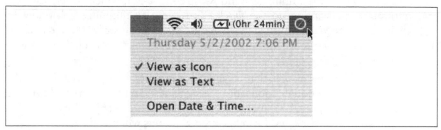

Figure 1-17. The Clock menu extra

By default, the Clock menu extra is located on the far right edge of the menu bar. The clock shows the day and the current time. Clicking on the clock, as in Figure 1-17, summons a menu where you can read the date, change the clock's appearance, or go to the Date & Time preferences panel.

You can move the menu extras to a different location in the menu bar by Command-clicking the icon and dragging it left or right. As you move the menu extra around, the other menu extras will move out of the way to make room for the menu extra you're moving. When you let go of the mouse button, the menu extra will take its new place in the menu bar. To remove a menu extra from the menu bar, Command-click on the icon, drag it off the menu bar, and let go of the mouse button.

 For reference, executables for most of the standard menu extras can be found in */System/Library/CoreServices/Menu Extras* as folders with *.menu* extensions.

As we cover various Mac OS X applications and preference panes throughout this book, we'll make note of the ones that offer menu extras.

The Dock

One of Mac OS X's most visually distinctive features is its Dock, a highly customizable strip of icons found (by default) along the bottom of the screen. Even if you choose to temporarily hide or change its location, the Dock remains active and always available.

As Figure 1-18 shows, the Dock can contain many different kinds of icons, including:

1. The Finder icon
2. Application icons
3. An active application
4. An inactive application
5. The Divider

6. A Finder folder

7. Minimized windows

8. The Trash icon

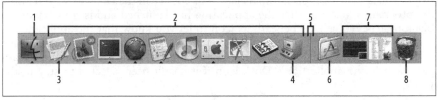

Figure 1-18. The Dock

The icons found in the Dock allow you to quickly launch and maneuver among applications, as well as provide shortcuts to frequently used folders and documents. These icons also sometimes act as applications in their own right. The Dock is the new home of the Trash, which used to reside at the lower-right corner of the Desktop in earlier versions of the Mac OS.

Application Icons

Application icons live to the left of the Dock's divider bar. Each one represents an application, either one that is currently running or one that's idle but "docked" (meaning that you've chosen to let its icon have a permanent home on the Dock).

Not Every Program Gets an Icon

Like any other Unix system, Mac OS X is usually running dozens of programs—more correctly known as *processes*—at any given time. Many of them, however, receive no representation in the Dock. These programs have no Aqua-based user interface, and some have no UIs at all.

Processes in this class include all the little daemons and low-level Unix programs that support network services and core OS-level functionality. Additionally, command-line programs that have only console-based UIs—nearly every shell or Perl script and AppleScripts you encounter, for example—won't appear in the Dock when running, even though you may be interacting with them through the Terminal or some other interface.

You can get a glimpse of the true layout of active processes through the Process Viewer (*/Applications/Utilities*). Each line in its window represents an active process. Some you may recognize as belonging to running Aqua applications, while others have more esoteric names.

To launch an application whose icon is in the Dock, just click on the icon. If an application's icon doesn't reside in the Dock, you can launch an application (or open a file) by locating it in the Finder and performing one of the actions in the following list.

- Double-clicking its icon
- Selecting the icon and selecting File → Open from the menu bar
- Selecting the icon and hitting ⌘-O

When you launch an application, its icon will bounce in the Dock to let you know the program is loading. After the application has launched and is ready to use, a black triangle will appear beneath its icon to let you know that the application is active. (The Finder will always have a black triangle under its icon because it's always available.) When you quit the application, the black triangle will disappear, as will the application's Dock icon if it hasn't been selected to stay in the Dock.

When you have more than one application running, you can bring another application forward by clicking once on that application's icon. That application and all of its open windows will come to the foreground. You can also cycle forward through active applications by holding down the Command key and pressing the Tab key while in the Finder; holding down Shift-⌘ and pressing Tab will cycle backward through the active applications.

Interactive Dock Icons

While most applications identify themselves with a single icon, some change their icons to different images, or even redraw themselves on the fly, as part of their interfaces. For example, CPU Monitor (*/Applications/Utilities*) can turn its Dock icon into a scrolling bar graph representing system load; when *Mail* is running in the background, it posts the number of new messages you have in your Inbox in its icon, as seen in Figure 1-18. (The number of new messages will not be displayed in Mail's icon if it is the active application.)

When a background application needs your attention, its Dock icon will bounce frantically. To see the application, bring it to the foreground by clicking on its Dock icon.

Adding and removing applications from the Dock

The Dock gives you two ways to permanently add application icons:

- You can drag any application's icon onto the Dock from the Finder. The original icon will stay where it is, and the Dock creates a pointer to it, much like an alias.
- If you are running an application that isn't fixed on the Dock, Control-click on the application icon to reveal its Dock menu. Select "Keep In Dock" from the menu to make the icon stay there after the application quits, as described in the next section.

To remove an item from the Dock, simply drag an inactive application's icon off the Dock and release the mouse button. The icon will disappear in a puff of smoke. This has no effect on the actual application; it simply removes the application's icon from the Dock.

You can also remove an active application from the Dock by dragging it off, although the effect is less obvious because it will snap back into place (since all active applications' icons must appear on the Dock). However, the system will remember your action, and quietly remove the icon from the Dock once the application quits (unless, of course, you change your mind by choosing "Keep In Dock" from its Dock menu).

The Dock Is an Application

While it doesn't work like other Aqua applications, the Dock is in fact an application that lives in */System/Library/CoreServices*. As such, it maintains its own registry in your machine's preferences system, described in Chapter 5.

The curious can find a record of all the applications kept on the Dock, as well as other interesting information, in *~/Library/Preferences/com.apple.dock.plist*. A crafty user can tweak this file to control the Dock's behavior. (But, as Chapter 22 states, you shouldn't modify this file unless you're willing to risk the possibility of rendering the Dock unusable. If this happens, you'll have to delete the *.plist* file to reset the Dock.)

Dock Menus

Every active application icon has a *Dock menu*, which you can call up by either Control-clicking the icon or clicking and holding on it. This produces a menu that is attached to the icon and is shaped a bit like a comic strip's word balloon; see Figure 1-19.

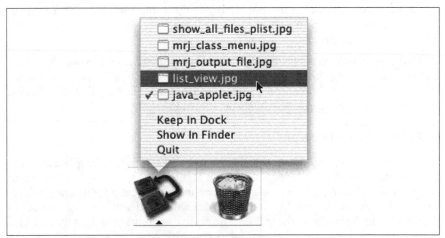

Figure 1-19. A typical Dock menu

Dock menus contain, as commands, the titles of all the windows an application has open, each marked with a little "window" symbol. Select one to bring it forth, along with its parent application. The top window will have a checkmark next to it; there is no distinction for minimized windows.

Classic applications will only have a basic Dock menu without the window list (see "Applications" in Chapter 2). Instead, a Classic application's Dock menu will only give you the options of Show in Finder and Quit (or Force Quit).

Every application's Dock menu typically contains at least a couple other commands, including:

Quit

> Quits the application, even if it's not in the foreground. The application will react as if you had selected File → Quit from its application menu, so any windows representing unsaved documents will raise dialog sheets as seen in Figure 1-33 and described later in the section "Dialogs: windows and sheets."

If you hold down the Option key while looking at an application's Dock menu, Quit changes to Force Quit. Choosing it will instantly kill that application.

The Finder's icon lacks a Quit or Force Quit option. (In fact, all it has is a list of open Finder windows.) If you need to restart the Finder for some odd reason, do so by hitting Option-⌘-Esc or selecting Apple → Force Quit. Then select the Finder and click on the Relaunch button, as described earlier in "The Apple Menu."

Show In Finder

Opens a Finder window, showing the location of the application on your system.

Keep In Dock

This option appears only for icons whose applications aren't permanently docked. Normally, the icon of an undocked application vanishes once that application exits. Select this option to give the application a permanent home in the Dock, where it will remain as an inactive application icon once its corresponding program has quit.

Beyond these basic selections, an application can put whatever it would like in its Dock menu. Among the standard Apple suite, for example, iTunes is notable for cramming a basic audio control panel in its Dock menu, including information about the song that's currently playing, as shown in Figure 1-20.

Disk, Folder, and File Icons

Beyond applications, documents, folders, and disks can also be placed in the Dock to the right of the divider, as shown in Figure 1-21. Clicking on a document in the Dock will open the file using the appropriate application; disks and folders will open a new Finder window bearing their contents. If you click on a folder in the Dock and hold down the mouse button, its contents will be revealed in a Dock menu, allowing you to select from its contents.

One folder you might consider placing in the Dock is your Home folder, which will give you rapid access to everything stored within. To add your Home folder to the Dock, follow these steps:

Figure 1-20. The Dock menu for iTunes

1. Open a Finder window by clicking on its Dock icon.

2. Select Go → Home (Shift-⌘-H) from the menu bar.

3. As shown in Figure 1-22, drag the folder's proxy icon (the little house in the window's titlebar) into the Dock, to the right of the divider. (Proxy icons are covered later in this chapter in "Document Windows.") Your home folder's icon now appears in the Dock.

4. As Figure 1-23 shows, you can now Control-click (or click and hold) on this icon at any time to see your entire Home folder represented as a hierarchical Dock menu. Selecting any file or application opens it, just as if it had been double-clicked from within the Finder.

You can follow these basic steps to add other folders to your Dock, depending on which ones you need access to more often.

Minimized Windows

Aqua offers a number of ways to minimize windows, including the yellow Minimize button on most windows' titlebars, and the Window → Minimize (⌘-M) command, which most native Mac OS X applications recognize.

When a window is minimized, a miniaturized version of the window is placed in the Dock immediately to the left of the Trash icon. (The most recently minimized window will appear next to the Trash.) There's not much you can do with minimized windows except click on them. This pops them back out and places them at the top of the window stack. Hiding an application makes its minimized windows fade away, but they'll return when the application is made active again.

	Apple Help Indexing Tool	
	Extras	▶
	FileMerge	
	icns Browser	
	IconComposer	
	Interface Builder	
	IORegistryExplorer	
	JavaBrowser	
	MallocDebug	
	MRJAppBuilder	
	ObjectAlloc	
	OpenGL Info	
	OpenGL Profiler	
	OpenGL Shader Builder	
	PackageMaker	
	PEFViewer	
	Pixie	
	Project Builder	
	Property List Editor	
	Quartz Debug	
	Sampler	
	Thread Viewer	

Applications	▶
Documentation	▶
Examples	▶
Headers	▶
Java	▶
Makefiles	▶
Palettes	▶
ProjectBuilder Extras	▶
Tools	▶
Show In Finder	

Figure 1-21. Disks, folders, and files can be located to the right of the divider in the Dock

Figure 1-22. Placing the Home folder in the Dock

When a window is minimized, its icon—which is really a miniaturized version of the window—is placed on the Dock, as seen in Figure 1-24. Even while on the Dock, the window will continue to visually update as it normally would. For example, a movie that's playing in the QuickTime Player will continue to play, or a web page set to refresh every minute will continue to do so in a minimized Internet Explorer window. Despite this, you can't use a minimized window's controls. The only way you can interact with a minimized window is by unminimizing it.

Minimized windows feature a tiny icon of the application to which they belong. By the little icons attached to them, we can tell at a glance that the windows seen in Figure 1-24 are from the Terminal, Mail, and Internet Explorer applications, respectively.

Figure 1-23. Accessing your Home folder from the Dock

Figure 1-24. Minimized windows in the Dock

The Finder

As mentioned earlier, the Finder is located on the far-left edge of the Dock. Unlike other applications, the Finder's icon cannot be removed from the Dock. (The same applies to the Trash icon.) The Finder also has a limited Dock menu, which displays only the Finder's current window list. Chapter 2 covers the Finder in detail.

The Divider

In its basic form, the Dock's divider bar is used to segregate application icons to the right, (quick links, folders, minimized windows, etc.) and the Trash to the left. However, if you place the mouse pointer over the divider bar, you'll see that the pointer changes shape, providing you with the ability to:

Resize the Dock
> If you click-drag the divider up or down, you can make the Dock larger or smaller.

Access the Dock's context menu
> If you Control-click on the divider, as shown in Figure 1-25, you'll see a boiled-down, textual version of the Dock's System Preferences panel (see Chapter 5) pop up as a contextual menu.

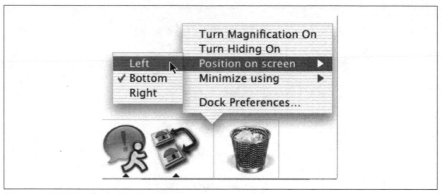

Figure 1-25. The Dock Divider's Dock menu

Relocate the Dock

If you Shift-click on the divider bar and hold down on the mouse button, you can drag the mouse to the left or right edge of the screen to quickly relocate the Dock there.

These are just shortcuts to things you do in the Dock's preferences panel, detailed in Chapter 5.

Trash

The Trash icon is one of the few remnants of the original Mac desktop metaphor that still looks like what it does. Like the Finder icon on the Dock's opposite end, the Trash icon is a permanent fixture in the Dock, ignoring any of your attempts to drag it elsewhere.

Deleting files

The Trash serves many functions, all having to do with removing stuff from your filesystem. You can mark files for deletion in one of the following ways:

- Dragging an item from a Finder window onto the Trash icon in the Dock.
- Selecting an item and hitting ⌘-Delete.
- Selecting an item in the Finder and selecting File → Move to Trash.
- Control-clicking an item and selecting Move to Trash from its context menu.

To see the contents of the Trash, click on the Trash icon to open a Trash window with the Finder. To rescue an item from the Trash, simply drag its icon from the Trash to the Desktop or to another location in a Finder window. If you move a file to the Trash and decide that you don't want to delete it, you can select the file and hit ⌘-Z (Undo) to move the file back to its original location in the filesystem. However, this works only with the most recently trashed item. If you trash a second item and decide that you want to move the first trashed item back, the Undo command won't help you out.

You cannot open files that have been trashed. If you can't remember what you trashed and want to look at it before you empty the trash, you'll have to drag the item out of the trash and onto the Desktop (or anywhere else in the filesystem). Once you're sure this is the file you want to dump, select the file and press ⌘-Delete to move it back into the Trash.

To permanently erase files, you must *empty the trash*. The Trash's Dock menu provides an Empty Trash option, seen in Figure 1-26, which deletes all the files and folders it contains. In the Finder, you can also hit Shift-⌘-Delete to accomplish the same thing.

Figure 1-26. The Trash's Dock menu Empty Trash option

The Trash icon acts as a graphical frontend to the .*Trash* folder in your Home directory. As with all "dotfiles" (a file or folder whose name begins with a period, or *dot*), you can't normally see the .*Trash* file in the Finder, but you can access it with the Terminal.

Unmounting disks

If you drag a disk image (CD, DVD, FireWire drive, or a mounted disk image file) to the Trash, the Trash icon will change to an Eject icon. However, rather than retaining the disk image in the Trash, the image is ejected, or unmounted, from the system. You can also unmount or eject disks while in the Finder by selecting their icons and hitting ⌘-E.

Removing other stuff

Many applications let you drag an object to the Trash. For example, Apple's Mail application lets you drag email messages to the Trash, and Internet Explorer lets you remove favorites from its toolbars by dragging them to the Trash. As with every other drag-and-drop activity, the Trash icon highlights (darkens) when you drag something deleteable over it.

Dock Shortcuts

Table 1-1 contains a listing of keyboard shortcuts for use with the Dock and when clicking on an application's Dock icon:

Table 1-1. Dock shortcuts

Keyboard shortcut	Description
Option-⌘-D	Quickly toggle the Dock's state between visible and hidden.
⌘-drag	Force docked icons to stay put when dragging other icons onto them.
⌘-click	Show this icon in the Finder.

Table 1-1. Dock shortcuts (continued)

Keyboard shortcut	Description
Control-click	Quickly summon an icon's Dock menu (or the divider's Dock preferences menu).
Option-click	Hide the foreground application before bringing this application forward; Option-clicking the same application icon again will bring the previous application forward.
Option-⌘-click	Bring the clicked application forward, and hide all other applications.
⌘-Tab	Select the next active application.
Shift-⌘-Tab	Select the previous active application.

Windows

Nearly every Aqua application centers its interface around windows. Windows can represent either abstract areas of user interactivity, such as with web browser or Terminal console windows, or they can represent the contents of real files or folders on disk.

This section will introduce you to the basic features present in most windows and to the various types of windows you'll encounter while using Mac OS X.

Window Controls

Windows in Mac OS X have an entirely different set of controls than those from earlier versions of the Mac OS. These window features are highlighted in Figure 1-27.

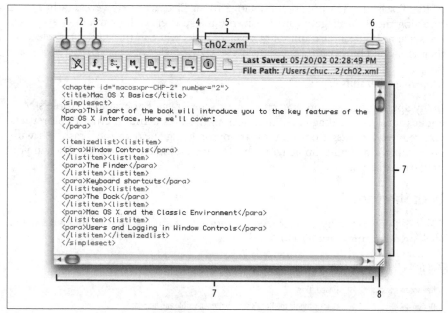

Figure 1-27. A typical window (from BBEdit)

The controls are listed as follows:

1. Close button (red)
2. Minimize button (yellow)
3. Zoom button (green)
4. Proxy icon
5. Filename or title
6. Toolbar button (not available on all windows)
7. Scrollbars and scroll arrows
8. Resize window control

The top part of the window is known as the *titlebar*. The titlebar is home to the three colored window control buttons used for closing (red), minimizing (yellow), and zooming (green) the window. Mousing over the buttons will change their state to be either an X, a minus sign (−), or a plus sign (+), respectively. These are visual cues of the function the button performs.

With some applications, you'll notice that the red Close window button has a dark-colored dot in its center. This means that the document you're working on has unsaved changes; if you save the document (File → Save, or ⌘-S), the dot will go away.

A window's *titlebar* runs across the top edge and, as its name implies, features the title or name of that window. Window names are usually unique within a single application. For example, word processor windows are named for the documents they represent, while web browser windows take their titles from the web pages they display.

 In earlier versions of the Mac OS, double-clicking the titlebar invoked the *windowshade* feature. Everything below the titlebar would hide, leaving you with just the titlebar, which you could leave in place or drag around as needed. The only Mac OS X application that still retains the windowshade feature is Stickies (found in */Applications*). However, if you miss this feature, you can download a third-party application called WindowShade X (*http://www. unsanity.com*).

Titlebars are a window's simplest control. You can move a window around just by dragging its titlebar, and double-clicking the titlebar will cause the window to minimize to the Dock. Beyond this built-in functionality, however, the titlebar is home to several other controls, such as the close, minimize, and maximize window buttons, the proxy icon, and in certain circumstances, a toolbar button.

Document Windows

A window's titlebar gains a couple of special properties if it represents something in the filesystem:

Path view and selection
Command-click the window's title (the actual text in the middle of the titlebar) to produce a pop-up menu showing the object's path (as seen in

Figure 1-28), with one menu row for each enclosing folder or disk. Selecting any of these folders or disks opens that object's window in the Finder.

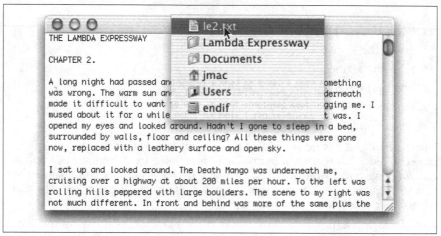

Figure 1-28. The titlebar path menu exposed by Command-clicking on the proxy icon or title

The final item in this pop-up menu is always a disk icon (most often that of a hard disk, or a disk partition); selecting it opens a Finder view of that disk's *root*. See "Files, Folders, and Disks" in Chapter 2 for more about disk icons in the Finder.

 This also works with Finder windows, as a rapid way to navigate to any point in an open folder's path.

Proxy icon

Any window that represents a file, folder, or disk gets a miniature version of its Finder icon to the left of its title in the titlebar, as seen in Figure 1-28; this is its *proxy icon*. (New document windows don't get a proxy icon until the first time they are saved.) While this can be useful for visually determining a document's file type, it's more than a mere label.

You can click and drag this icon and get the same effect as if you were dragging its "real" Finder icon around. Hence, you can drop its icon into another document window, onto another application's icon, place it in the Dock, and so on. In all cases, you'll receive the same effect as if you performed the same action from the Finder. (There are some exceptions to this—you usually can't drag an open document window's proxy icon into the Trash, for example!)

Modifier keys for moving, copying, and making aliases all apply when dragging a proxy icon, as detailed in "Moving, Copying, and Renaming Objects" in Chapter 2.

Some nondocument windows put proxy icons to other clever uses. Internet Explorer, for example, puts a little @-shaped proxy icon in the titlebar of web pages. Dragging it is equivalent to dragging the page's URL string, letting you quickly paste it into an email message or drop it on the Desktop as a "Web Internet Location" document.

If the window is not in sync with its document (i.e., it contains unsaved changes), then the proxy icon is grayed out and untouchable. Saving the document returns it to its opaque and interactive state.

Toolbars

Some applications assign a *toolbar* to its windows, giving you quick access to various commands. As seen in Figure 1-29, every Finder window has a toolbar, which you can use to store links to folders or commands you use frequently.

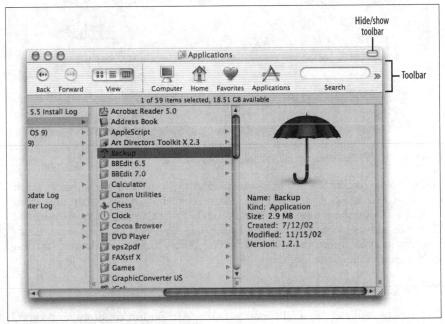

Figure 1-29. The Toolbar button

Windows with toolbars have a transparent button on the right side of their title-bars, as shown in Figure 1-29. If you click on the toolbar button, the toolbar disappears; click on it again, and the toolbar reappears.

Most applications that use toolbars make them customizable by way of a "Customize Toolbar..." option in their menu bar. Selecting this summons a large dialog box that presents you with a palette of all the buttons you can place in that particular window's toolbar (including a predefined default set, at the bottom) as well as options to control their appearance and organize them into groups. You can now make the toolbar look just how you want. Figure 1-30 shows the Finder's Customize Toolbar window.

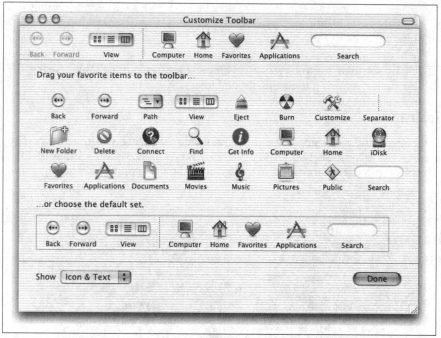

Figure 1-30. The Finder's Customize Toolbar window

You can also customize a toolbar to some extent without using this dialog. If you hold down the ⌘ key, you can drag toolbar icons left or right to rearrange them, or drag and drop them from the toolbar to make them go away in a puff of smoke. (You can add them back again later by visiting the Customize Toolbar... dialog box.) Some applications, such as System Preferences and the Finder, let you drag icons onto and off of the toolbar.

Window Types

Widgets are standard Aqua UI elements that appear within windows and control their content. "Widgets" is a generic term for what Mac OS X programmers call *views*, discussed in Chapter 2. These include all the buttons and controls that help give the Aqua interface its name, as well as some special interface features unique to Mac OS X, such as sheets and drawers.

Dialogs: windows and sheets

Dialogs are a common sight in any GUI. When an application requires you to make a decision or otherwise needs your attention, it interrupts its activities to display a special window. Thereafter, it won't let you perform any other activities within that application until you give it due attention, whether that involves making a choice, or merely acknowledging or dismissing the dialog.

A common example of a dialog window, or *box*, is what you see when you select File → Open in any document-editing application, as shown in Figure 1-31.

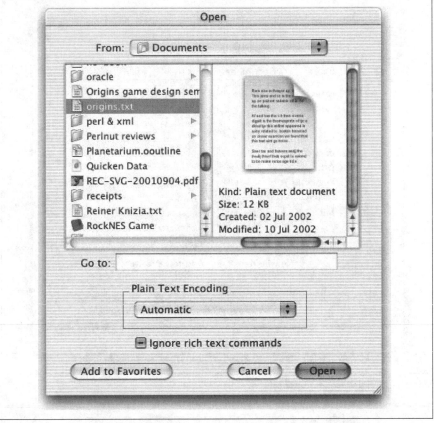

Figure 1-31. The Open window

The open window's view is similar to the Column View in the Finder. It offers a way to navigate to a specific file to open with that application. When you locate the file you wish to open, either select the file and hit the Open button, or dismiss the dialog through its Cancel button.

A *sheet* is a special kind of dialog that slides out from beneath the window's titlebar, partially covering its content; see Figure 1-32. Cocoa applications (see "Applications" in Chapter 2) tend to use sheets whenever possible, while Carbon and other application types often use separate dialog windows instead.

A window loses most of its interactivity when displaying a sheet; the sheet requires your input on some decision (even if it's just to dismiss the sheet through its Cancel button), although you can still use window controls to move, resize, and minimize the window. However, you can continue using other windows, even those belonging to that application.

The sheet you'll see most often is the Save As sheet, seen when you first save a new document to disk or whenever you choose Save As... from an application's File menu.

You'll also often see the sheet that appears when you try to close the window of an unsaved document, as with Figure 1-33.

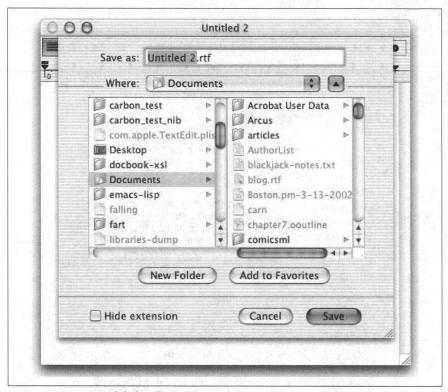

Figure 1-32. A Typical dialog sheet

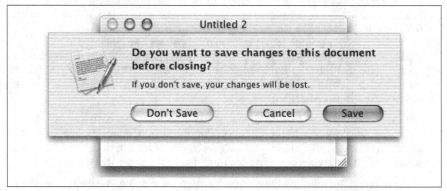

Figure 1-33. This sheet appears when you attempt to close a window with unsaved changes

Typically, clicking Save or pressing Return saves the document (summoning a new Save sheet if it doesn't already have a filename), clicking Don't Save or pressing ⌘-D closes the window and discards all changes, and clicking Cancel or pressing Esc or ⌘-. dismisses the sheet and leaves the window open (and unsaved).

Drawers

Windows can choose to hide parts of themselves in *drawers*, modular subwindows that contain information and controls secondary to the window's main function. When summoned, a drawer slides out of a window's left or right side. One such application that uses drawers is Mail, shown in Figure 1-34. Mail uses a drawer to hold a list of all the accounts and mailboxes you use for email.

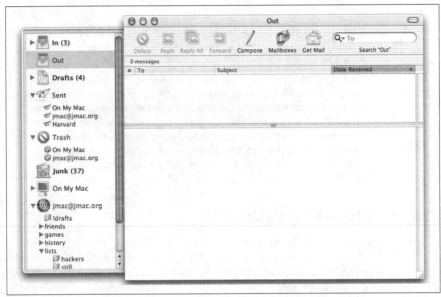

Figure 1-34. The Mail application's mailbox drawer

As with sheets, a drawer remains attached to its window, even if you move or resize the parent window. You can change the width of a drawer by clicking and dragging on one of its edges. (You can also close it entirely by dragging it to the window's edge, but usually it or its window provides faster ways to close it.)

Interleaving windows

Unlike previous versions of the Mac OS, Aqua windows can *interleave* freely. This means that windows belonging to a given application don't insist on sticking together; bringing one window of an application into focus doesn't automatically pop all other windows of that application to the top of the stack. This can prove useful when working with two applications side by side. You can arrange the windows so that you can see the contents of both without having to wrestle with any other open windows belonging to either application.

> If you do want to bring all of an application's windows to the top of the window stack, just click once on that application's icon in the Dock.

Mac OS X windows follow the usual behavior of forming into a single stack, with one window at a time possessing focus and ready for user interaction. Aqua uses subtle visual cues to make the top window visually distinct, giving it an opaque titlebar with red, yellow, and green control buttons (see "Window Controls" earlier in this chapter), as well as a drop-shadow.

Most of the time, you'll bring a window into focus by clicking on it, which makes it snap to the top of the stack. You can also call it forth by selecting its name from the Dock menu of its parent application's Dock icon, or choosing it from its application's Window menu, if it offers one.

 You can use ⌘-` to cycle through all of the application's open windows. (That's the "backtick" key, located in the upper-left corner of your keyboard.)

You can interact with a background window (not in focus) by holding down the ⌘ key while using its various controls and widgets. You can always move, resize, or scroll it by ⌘-dragging its various controls—if it uses standard Cocoa interface widgets, you can even press buttons and select text without losing focus from the top window! Similarly, you can also access the close, minimize, and zoom window control buttons by just mousing over them; no keypress required.

Opening and Saving Documents

Nearly all applications that let you create and edit documents, and that make use of Mac OS X's Aqua interface, use the same dialogs for opening and editing files. They give you a variety of ways to navigate through the filesystem folder by folder until you find the place or object you're seeking, or simply specify a known location in a single step.

This section will discuss the open and save dialogs, showing you how to navigate through the maze of disks, folders, and files on your Mac.

The Open Window

The centerpiece of every Open dialog window, as shown in Figure 1-31, is a columnar view of some place in your filesystem. In fact, it has the same function as the Finder's Column View (see "Column View" in Chapter 2). Through it, you can select the file you'd like to open. Some applications might let you choose folders and disks to open as well.

Above that window floats a From pull-down menu. Its first (and default) option is always set to the right-most disk or folder selected in the window's path of columns. Pulling down and selecting something else from the menu instantly zaps the columnar window to a folder elsewhere on your filesystem. Its selections are similar, but not identical, to those of the Finder's Go menu:

Desktop (⌘-D)
   Switches the location to your Desktop folder.

Home (Shift-⌘-H)
   Switches the selected location to your Home directory.

iDisk

This submenu points to the various top-level folders on your iDisk, if you have a .Mac account. The Open dialog knows what the default folders of your iDisk are, even if it isn't mounted on your Desktop.

 If your iDisk isn't mounted and you select one of its folders, the iDisk will be mounted for you, using the settings you've specified in the Internet System Preferences panel.

To open a file on your iDisk, select one of the top-level folders (Backup, Documents, Movies, Music, Pictures, Public, Sites, or Software) and then select the file you wish to open.

Favorite Places

Beneath this grayed-out label is a list of all the folders and disks you've marked as favorites (see "Favorites" in Chapter 2). Note that any files that you've similarly marked don't show up here. Likewise, your Home directory, Desktop, or iDisk won't show up in this list either if you've marked them as favorites.

Recent Places

Beneath this grayed-out label are the five most recent folders from which you've opened or saved files.

Near the bottom of the open dialog lies a text field labeled Go to:. Similar to the Finder's Go → Go to Folder... (Shift-⌘-G) command, you can type a Unix path here, and then hit the Return key (or click the window's Go button) to be taken to that location in the filesystem. If you typed the name of a folder, the Column View will take you to that location. If you typed the name of a file the application is capable of opening, it will do so (closing the Open window in the process). If you type a filename that the application isn't capable of opening, the open dialog will close as if you had clicked its Cancel button. If you type in a path to something that doesn't exist, it'll tell you so by playing the alert sound.

At the bottom of the open dialog, you typically get the following three buttons:

Add to Favorites

Adds an alias to the selected object (i.e., whatever's highlighted in the next-to-last column) into your Favorites folder.

Cancel

Dismisses the window without opening any files. You can also use ⌘-. to invoke the Cancel button.

Open

At first, this button is grayed out until you select a folder or file in the Column View. If you enter something into the "Go to" field, the Open button will change to Go. After you've selected something in the Column View to open, click this button (or hit Return) to open the file.

The Save Window

Because it's usually attached to a document window, you'll usually see the file-saving dialog as a sheet that rolls out from under the window's titlebar. The Save window appears when you first try to save an unnamed document, or if you select File → Save As... at any time.

The dialog's interface looks and works a lot like that of an Open window, with some key differences: its purpose is not to get you to choose a file, but to get you to name the file and choose a location in the filesystem where the file will be saved.

Choosing a filename

Two controls at the top and bottom of the sheet help you indicate the name you'd like to give this file. Enter the filename you want to use in the Save as: text field at the top of the window.

If the window also features a Hide Extension checkbox at the bottom, leaving it unchecked will let the application choose and assign the file extension (e.g., *.txt*, *.doc*, *.html*, etc.). If you opt to use your own file extension, the application may refuse to accept your replacement or simply ignore you, tacking its own extension on the end anyway. (More polite applications will warn you with a dialog box.)

The default state of the Hide Extension checkbox depends on what you've specified in the Finder's preferences via the "Always show file extensions" checkbox. If it's unchecked, then Hide Extension *is* checked, and vice versa.

Choosing a location

The two "Where:" controls let you choose the disk or folder into which the application will write the file. The controls consist of a pull-down menu and a columnar file-navigation view that operate exactly like the From: menu and view found in the Open window, with a couple of differences.

First, the menu has an arrow button to its right, stamped with a black triangle. Clicking the arrow button toggles the navigation view between hiding and revealing itself. The view itself differs from its file-opening counterpart as it lets you choose only disks or folders on your filesystem; all files are grayed out and cannot be selected.

If you find that the folder you'd like to save this file to doesn't exist yet, you can create a new one by clicking on the New Folder button. A window will pop up, prompting you to enter a name for the new folder. After naming the new folder, click the Create button and the sheet will disappear; the location to where the file will be saved is now set to the new folder you've just created.

Finally, hit the Cancel button to dismiss the dialog without writing anything to disk, or choose the default Save to create a new file with the name and location you've specified. If the filename matches the name of a file already in the selected folder, a dialog box will appear, asking whether you want to continue with the save and replace the like-named file with the file you're saving, or whether you want to cancel the save and assign a different name to the file.

Services

The Services submenu can be found under most any Aqua program's application menu. It allows the foreground application to invoke functions of other applications, usually while passing along user-selected text or objects to them.

The Service menu's contents depend on the applications installed on your Mac. When installed, some applications like Mail and BBEdit can place entries in the Services menu. If an application provides more than one service, those items will be placed into a submenu named after that application.

As seen in Figure 1-35, Mail provides two services under Application → Services → Mail → Send To.

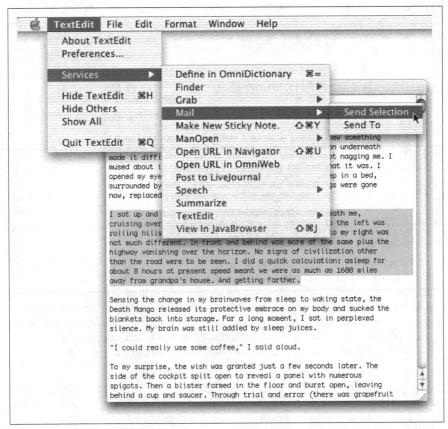

Figure 1-35. The Services menu

If you have some text or images selected in the foremost application and select Mail Text, the Mail application creates a new email message whose body consists of that selection. Selecting an email address in any application and then choosing Mail's Mail To service will also create a new email message, this time pre-addressed to the selected address. In both cases, the Mail application launches (if it wasn't already active) and makes itself the active application.

Some services make themselves especially easy to invoke through key bindings, which remain omnipresent throughout your use of the OS. The Make Sticky service turns any text you've selected into a new sticky note, and is bound to the key combo Shift-⌘-Y.

 Applications define the services they offer through the *Info.plist* files found within their bundles. See Chapter 22 for more information.

Of course, an application might have its own idea about what Shift-⌘-Y means! An application's own key bindings always trump those in the Services menu. Services know when the current application has a binding that conflicts with theirs and might try to offer alternative keystrokes, changing its binding indicator in the Services menu to reflect this. If all of its bindings raise conflicts, it stops trying altogether, and can only be used through the Services menu for that particular application.

Logging Out and Shutting Down

When you're done using your Macintosh, there are two ways to bring your session to a close: shutting down, and logging out.

Because Mac OS X is a multiple-user system and a server platform, you should choose to shut down the computer *only* if nobody else on your local network is using it or the services it provides. This includes both the other human users on the system, who might be logged into it remotely (see the section "Remote Logins" in Chapter 7) or using network-shared volumes (see the section "File Sharing Services" in Chapter 13), as well as people or programs using any running network services (described in Chapter 7).

For example, if you are using printer sharing (as described in Chapter 8) to let other computers in your home or office use the printer connected to your Macintosh, then shutting down the Mac will also make that printer invisible to the other machines. The same goes for any web, mail, or other network services the machine may be running. On the flip side, if you are the sole account holder of your Mac, connect through the Internet via dial-up, and do not run any public network services, then it won't hurt to shut down when you're all done for the day.

Logging out is the better option for Macs that are shared by many users, or that act as network servers. When you log out (via ⌘ → Log Out, or Shift-⌘-Q), then all the programs you launched since you logged in will terminate (Aqua applications all quit in the usual way, giving you a last chance to save changes), and you'll be dropped back to the login screen. Behind that placid-looking screen, though, the computer remains busy because every other process—including those owned by the system itself, as opposed to you or any other human user—continues to work. So, if you activate printer sharing and then log out, printer sharing still works, so long as the computer stays on and connected to the printer (or until you or another user with admin privileges deactivates printer sharing). This is because the internal programs that make printer sharing (and web serving, mail delivery, and all other core network services) work belong to the system—the root user—not to any individual user.

If, for some reason, you have active logins to the machine from other computers on the network, they (and the programs running under them) won't be affected by logging out of your account locally.

Actually, you have *three* choices (sort of). If you would like to remain logged in to the machine while you're away, but prevent random people from sitting down and using your account, you can use a password-protected screen saver, as described in the section "Screen Effects" in Chapter 5.

Note, however, that this isn't considered very polite if multiple people have accounts on the machine, since nobody will be able to get past the screen saver and log in as themselves without knowing your password. In this case, it's probably better to avoid the spite of your friends, family, or coworkers and just log out.

If this *does* happen, a Unix-savvy user with admin privileges can circumvent the screen saver by *ssh*-ing into the Mac from some other computer and forcibly killing the screen saver. *sudo killall ScreenSaverEngin* will do the trick nicely (yes, that's spelled correctly—Darwin commands have a 16-character limit), or even the forgetful user's entire login session. But this is also rather impolite. Again, better to avoid the issue entirely.

Starting Up and Logging In

When you turn on your Mac (or restart it), it spends a couple of minutes or so initializing various processes to ready the machine for user login, as well as whatever network service it may provide (see Chapter 7). Unix veterans are used to seeing this phase as a cascade of messages spilling down a text console, but Mac OS X hides all this information behind a plain white screen with a plain gray Apple logo on it.

You *can* see all that startup text if you really want to, by booting into single-user mode, as described in Chapter 11. This can be a useful diagnostic tool for hardcore Unix-heads who know what they're doing, or a way for the merely curious to watch the strange sight of their Mac rolling out of bed and stumbling around in pure-Unix mode before it puts on its Mac OS face. Use the *exit* command at the single-user shell to resume the normal Mac OS X boot process.

You may also view some of the machine's startup messages after the fact by looking at the file */var/log/system.log*. (Note that only users with admin access can read the file.)

Eventually the system either settles on the login screen, or goes ahead to log in a specific user, depending upon the machine's configuration. In the former case, you've got to provide your username (either by choosing it from a list or typing it in—again, based on configuration settings in the Accounts preference pane) and password before you can continue into the Finder, whereupon you can actually start using the operating system.

Logging in is necessary because of Mac OS X's Unix-based file permissions system; before you can interact with the system in any way, the machine has to know who you are so that it can tell what files and folders you're allowed to access, and to what degree. Generally speaking, everything in your Home folder (which you can always go to through the Finder's Go → Home (Shift-⌘-H) option) belongs to you, and you are unrestricted in how you read, modify, create and delete the files and folders within it (and the files and folders within those folders, and so on). Everything *outside* your Home folder is another matter. For example, all users can run the applications stored in the */Applications* folder, but only admin users can modify that folder's contents; and no user, admin or otherwise, has full access to any other user's Home folder.

See Chapter 9 for more information on the structure of Mac OS X's filesystem and permissions. Logging in also sets up all of your personal system-interaction preferences, as stored in your Library folder; see Chapter 9.

Startup and Shutdown Keys

For most users, starting and shutting down your Mac is fairly routine: press the Power-on button to start, and go to ⌘ → Shut Down to turn off the machine at night. But there are times when you need to do more, for whatever reason. Table 1-2 lists some of the additional keys you can use when starting, restarting, logging out, and shutting down your system.

 Some of the keyboard shortcuts listed in Table 1-2 will work only on newer hardware. If you are using an older Mac, these keyboard shortcuts may not work.

Table 1-2. Shortcuts for starting, restarting, logging out, and shutting down

Key command	Description
C	Holding down the C key at startup will boot from a CD (useful when installing or upgrading the system software).
T	Holding down the T key at startup will boot from a FireWire drive, if it has a bootable System folder.
X	Holding down the X key at startup will force the machine to boot into Mac OS X, even if Mac OS 9 is specified as the default startup disk.
⌘-S	Boots into single-user mode.
⌘-V	Boots into verbose mode, displaying all the startup messages onscreen. (Linux users will be familiar with this.)
Shift	Holding down the Shift key at startup invokes *Safe Boot* mode, turning off any unnecessary kernel extensions (*kexts*), and ignoring anything you've set in the Login Items preferences panel.
Option	Holding down the Option key at startup will take you to the Startup Manager, which allows you to select which OS to boot into.
Mouse button	Holding down the mouse button at startup will eject any disk (CD, DVD, or other removable media) that may still be in the drive.
Shift-Option-⌘-Q Option + ⌘ → Log Out	Logs you off without prompting you first.

Table 1-2. Shortcuts for starting, restarting, logging out, and shutting down (continued)

Key command	Description
Option-Power-on Option + 🍎 → Shut Down	Shuts down your system without prompting you first.
Option + 🍎 → Restart	Restarts your machine without prompting you first.
Control-⌘-Power-on button	Forces an automatic reboot of your system; this should be used only as a last resort as it could mess up your system. (Mostly, you'll just wait forever at the gray Apple startup screen while an *fsck* happens in the background.)

2

Using the Finder

The Finder is the application that gives you access to your entire filesystem, network drives, and any externally mounted drives, including USB and FireWire drives and devices, such as an iPod. With Jaguar, the Finder's capabilities have been expanded to include the ability to search for files on your system and to be used as an ad hoc FTP application.

This chapter will cover the use of the Finder, along with tips and tricks to make you a more efficient Mac user.

Finder Overview

In earlier versions of the Mac OS, the Finder was located in the application menu at the far-right edge of the menu bar. The Finder was the application responsible for displaying the contents of a drive or folder; when it was double-clicked, a window would open, displaying either an Icon or List View of the contents. Mac OS X's Finder really isn't that different from Mac OS 9's Finder. It still displays the contents of drives and folders; however, now it is much more powerful, particularly in Jaguar. To open a new Finder window, click on the Finder icon, located at the far left of the Dock.

The Finder Toolbar

Near the top of the Finder window is a toolbar (shown in Figure 2-1), which offers a quick way to access files and directories on your system, and also to switch between the View modes discussed in the next section.

The Finder toolbar has the following controls and icons by default:

Back
> Takes you to the previous view in the same Finder window.

Forward
> If you've gone backward in a Finder window, clicking the Forward button will take you forward in the view.

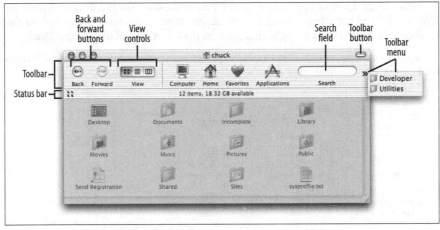

Figure 2-1. The Finder toolbar

View

The three Finder View buttons let you switch from Icon View, List View, or Column View, respectively, from left to right.

Computer

Clicking this icon is the same as invoking the Go → Computer (Shift-⌘-C) menu option, which takes you to a view listing of the drives (local, networked, and partitions) and external storage devices connected to the Mac.

Home

Clicking this icon is the same as invoking the Go → Home (Shift-⌘-H) menu option, which takes the user to their home directory (~/ or */Users/username*).

Favorites

Clicking this icon is the same as invoking the Go → Favorites (Shift-⌘-F) menu option, which opens the Finder view to *~/Library/Favorites*.

Applications

Clicking this icon is the same as invoking the Go → Applications (Shift-⌘-A) menu option, which opens the Finder view in the Applications directory (*/Applications*).

Search

The Search field offers the user a way to perform context-based searches on the filesystem. See "Searching for and Locating Files" later in this chapter for more information on using this field.

In looking at Figure 2-1, you'll notice another menu off to the side of the Search field. This side menu is created when you've added additional icons to the Finder toolbar and haven't resized the window to make them visible. If you see the double-arrow (>>) icon at the right edge of the Finder toolbar, click on it to reveal its contents.

To remove an icon that shows up in the side menu, you need to resize the Finder window to make your icons appear. Then you can click on the undesired icon and drag it off the toolbar and resize the Finder window, if you'd like.

To add a file, folder, or application to the Finder toolbar, simply drag and drop its icon to the toolbar from a Finder view. Application icons that get added to the toolbar will launch with a single click, just as they do when placed in the Dock.

Located at the upper-right corner of the Finder window is a clear, elliptical button that can be used to hide the Finder's toolbar, as shown in Figure 2-2.

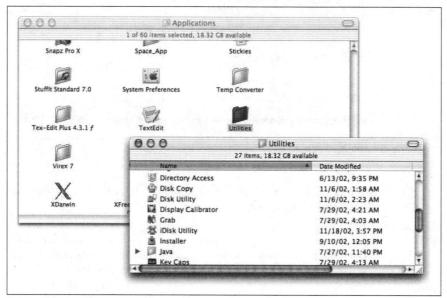

Figure 2-2. A Finder window with its toolbar hidden

If you are in Icon or List View with the toolbar hidden, the Finder performs just like the windows in Mac OS 9. Double-clicking a folder icon will open a new window for that folder, displaying its contents. Column View will function normally.

Customizing the Toolbar

In addition to hiding the toolbar, users can customize the Finder's toolbar in a variety of ways. As mentioned earlier, the easiest way to customize your Finder's toolbar is to drag and drop icons in the toolbar. To remove an icon, drag it away from the toolbar and it will disappear.

Another way to customize the Finder's toolbar is to switch to the Customize Toolbar window, shown in Figure 2-3, by selecting View → Customize Toolbar or Shift-clicking on the toolbar button.

Here you can choose from a plethora of icons to place in the Finder's toolbar, along with an option to revert back to the default set. At the lower left of the Customize Toolbar window is a pop-up menu with Show next to it. This menu is used to set how the icons will appear in the toolbar. By default, Show is set to "Icon & Text". Other options available are "Icon Only" and "Text Only". When finished customizing the Finder toolbar, click the Done button to go back to the previous Finder view (but with the newly customized toolbar, if you've made any changes).

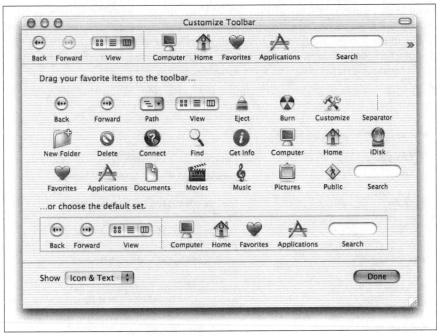

Figure 2-3. The Customize Toolbar window

Finder Views

The Finder serves as a graphical file manager, which offers three ways (or Views) to look at the files, folders, applications, and other filesystems mounted on your system. The Finder also sports a toolbar at the top of the window, which gives you quick access to frequently used files and directories, along with a built-in Search field for context-based searches.

More on the Finder toolbar and how to search for files later; for now, let's look at the three Views available to the Finder: Icon, List, and the new Column View. To select any of these views for a Finder window, click on the View menu and select "as Icons" (⌘-1), "as List" (⌘-2), or "as Columns" (⌘-3), respectively.

Depending on the View you've selected for your Finder window, you can also tweak the settings for that view by selecting View → Show View Options (⌘-J). The View Options for each View will be discussed in the sections that follow.

Icon View

This shows the contents of a directory as file, folder, or an application icons, as shown in Figure 2-1. In this view, every Finder object appears as an icon of a variable size. Icons can be arbitrarily arranged within a window by dragging and dropping them to different locations. If you find that icons are overlapping or out of order, you can clean up the view by selecting View → Clean Up, or View → Arrange (by Name, Date Created, Date Modified, Size, or Kind).

Double-clicking on an icon will do one of three things, depending upon its type: launch an application, open a file, or display the contents of a double-clicked folder in the Finder window. If the Finder window's toolbar is hidden when you double-click on a folder, the contents of that folder will be displayed in a new Finder window, rather than the same Finder window.

Table 2-1 lists some keyboard shortcuts for navigating within the Finder's Icon View.

Table 2-1. Icon View's keyboard shortcuts

Key command	Description
Left Arrow	Select item to the left of the currently highlighted icon.
Right Arrow	Select the item to the right of the currently highlighted icon.
Up Arrow	Select the item above the currently highlighted icon.
Down Arrow	Select the item below the currently highlighted icon.
⌘-Up Arrow	Used to go backward in the filesystem (e.g., if an application is highlighted and you hit ⌘-Up Arrow, the view will switch to */Applications*).
⌘-Down Arrow	Used to launch a highlighted application icon, or to open a folder in the view.
Letter or Number keys	Selects the item in the list that begins with that letter or number.

Icon View's options

With a Finder window in Icon View, you can select from the following options by selecting View → Show View Options (⌘-J), as shown in Figure 2-4.

Icon size
> This slider is used to control the size of all the window's icons. If dragged all the way to the right, the icons will resize to 128 × 128 pixels. Dragging the slider all the way to the left reduces them in size to 16 × 16 pixel (which happens to be the same size as the Column View icons, or the smaller List View icons). The default size is 32 × 32 pixels.

Text size
> A pop-up menu for choosing the size of the icon's text label.

Label position
> Lets you select where an icon's label will be placed: Bottom (the default) or Right.

Snap to grid
> With this option selected, the icons will stick to a strict grid layout. Dropping an icon in the window will make it appear in the nearest empty spot of this grid, unless you've selected one of the options from the "Keep arranged by" pop-up menu.

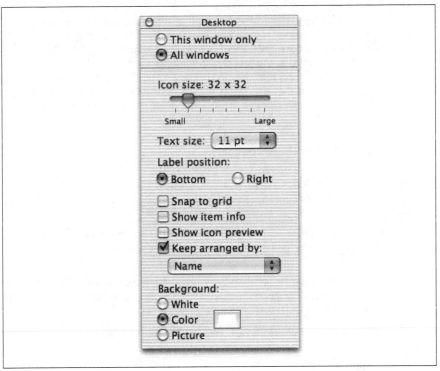

Figure 2-4. Icon View's View Options palette

Show item info
> If selected, the Finder displays a very brief piece of information about certain kinds of items beneath their labels. Folders display how many files and folders are contained within, disks will show their capacity, and images display their dimensions in pixels.

Show icon preview
> If this checkbox is selected, document icons that offer a simple preview display (such as image files) will use this preview (scaled to the selected icon size) in place of their ordinary Finder icon.

Keep arranged by
> If selected, a pop-up menu will become active, allowing you to select how the icons in the view will be arranged. The available options in the pop-up menu include:

Name
> Sorts the icons alphabetically, by name.

Date Modified
> Sorts files based on the date they were last modified, oldest first.

Date Created
> Sorts files based on the date they were created, oldest first.

Size
> Sorts files by their file size, smallest first.

The "Keep arranged by size" option can cause some visual confusion in a window containing lots of folders. Determining the total size of a folder and everything inside it can take a while. As the Finder works on the problem, it arranges all the icons based on the information it's received up to that second. Thus, the Finder usually ends up shuffling everything in the window several times while you watch (which can frustrate your attempts to select something).

Kind
> Sorts by the type of object.

Background
> By default, the background for Finder windows is set to White; however, there are two other options available:

Color
>> If you select Color, a box will appear next to this label, which when clicked on opens a color picker that you can use to select a color.

Picture
>> If you select Picture, click on the Select button to be taken to your Pictures folder (~/Pictures) so you can select a picture to use as the background.

In addition to these options, there are two additional options at the top of the window:

This window only
> Applies the view options only to the open Finder window, based on the folder or drive the window is for.

All windows
> Applies the view options you've set to all present and future Finder windows.

By default, the settings you apply to a view will apply to "All windows". If you select "This window only," the options you've set will apply to that particular folder or drive every time you open that window in Icon View in the Finder. This gives you the option of color-coding folders by setting the background color (or image) for individual folders.

List View

This view, as shown in Figure 2-5, displays the contents of a folder or drive in a table list, with one row for each file or folder and one column for each bit of information about the object.

Next to each folder in a List View is a black disclosure triangle. To view the items within the folder without opening a new Finder window, click on the disclosure triangle to view the folder's contents. Another way to navigate through the icons and folders in the Finder's List View is by using the keyboard, as noted in Table 2-2.

Figure 2-5. The Finder in List View

Table 2-2. List View's keyboard shortcuts

Key command	Description
Down Arrow	Move down through the list of items.
Up Arrow	Move up through the list of items.
Right Arrow	Open a folder's disclosure triangle to reveal its contents.
Left Arrow	Close a folder's disclosure triangle to hide its contents.
Option-Right Arrow	Open a folder and any subfolders to reveal their contents.
Option-Left Arrow	Close a folder and any subfolders to hide its contents.
Letter or Number keys	Selects the item in the list that begins with that letter or number.

To open all the folders in the View, select all the View's contents (⌘-A) and use Option-Right Arrow (likewise, Option-Left Arrow to close them again). To open all the folders in the View including subfolders, add the Shift or Command key (e.g., Shift-Option-Right Arrow or Option-⌘-Right Arrow to open, Shift-Option-Left Arrow or Option-⌘-Left Arrow to close).

Sorting a List View

A List View is sorted alphabetically by the name of the file or folder by default. This corresponds to whichever of the column headings is highlighted. If you click on a different column heading, that one takes on the highlight, and all the view's rows rearrange themselves according to this new sort criteria.

Clicking the highlighted column a second time will reverse the sort order. A little triangle on the right side of the highlighted header suggests the sort order. When pointing up, the window sorts the data in alphabetical (A–Z), numerical (0–9), or chronological order (oldest to most recent). Click on the column head again to reverse the sort order.

List View's options

With a Finder window in List View, you can select from the following options by selecting View → Show View Options (⌘-J), as shown in Figure 2-6.

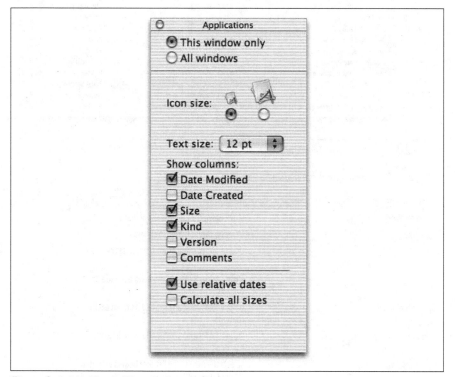

Figure 2-6. List View's View Options palette

Icon size
Choose between small (16 × 16) or large (32 × 32) size. The default is small.

Text size
Select the size of the text in the view. The range is 10-16 point type, with 12 point being the default size.

Show columns
These six checkboxes, listed here, let you specify which columns the Finder should display in the List View. Note that the Name column will always appear in the List view.

Date Modified
The date and time the file was last modified.

Date Created
The date and time the file was created.

Size
Shows the file size.

Kind
Displays the file type (e.g., Alias, Application, Folder, etc.).

Version
If applicable, this will display the version number for the file or application.

Comments
Displays any comments attached to the file (typically entered via the file's Get Info window).

Use relative dates
In a List View, the dates are typically displayed using the date and time format specified in the System Preferences (International → Date → Short Date, and International → Time); for example, 12/13/02, 8:57 a.m. However, if you select "Use relative dates", the date for newly created or recently edited files will change to Yesterday or Today, as applicable.

Calculate all sizes
If checked, the Finder will dig through each folder in the view, calculating its total size, and then displaying it in the view's Size column. This box is unchecked by default because it takes the system a fair amount of time (and processor power) to calculate the size of the folder's contents. If left unchecked, every folder's size shows up simply as "−−". However, you can always find out the size of a folder (or file) by selecting it and going to File → Get Info (⌘-I).

In addition to these options, List View's options palette also has "This window only" and "All windows" options at the top of the window. These act in the same manner as described in the "Icon View's options" section.

Arranging columns in List View

When you select an item in the "Show columns" section of List View's Options, you'll notice that the columns appear in the order in which the buttons are listed in Figure 2-6. But what if you wanted the Version column to appear next to the name column without turning all of the other columns off? To do this, click on the column header you'd like to move and hold down on the mouse button. You'll notice that the column header will turn gray. Now drag that column left or right and drop it where you would like it to appear; the other column(s) will move out of its way.

The only column you can't move is the Name column. By default, the Name column will always be the left-most column in the List View display; you cannot place another column to the left of the Name column.

Column View

Column View, shown in Figure 2-7, displays a directory's contents in column form. This is similar to List View, except that when you click on an item, a new pane opens to the right and either exposes the contents of a folder or displays some information about a file, including its name, type, and file size.

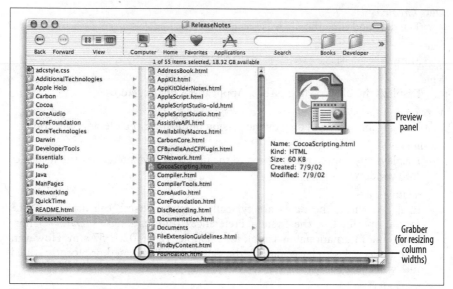

Figure 2-7. The Finder's Column View

Column View divides a Finder window into several columns, similar to the frames on a web site, each with its own vertical scrollbar (if needed). As Figure 2-7 shows, drives and folders will have a gray arrow at the right edge of their column. Clicking on a drive or folder will reveal its contents in the next column to the right, ending with a selected object in the Preview column. The Preview column displays some basic information about the file or application, including its name, size, date created and modified, and version number if it is an application icon.

The advantage to using Column View is its ability to rapidly scroll back and forth through the filesystem. It allows you to use a combination of the scrollbars and the titlebar's proxy icon (see "Document Windows" in Chapter 1) to quickly switch to a different location. (Remember, if you ⌘-click on the proxy icon, a context menu will pop up, showing you where you are in the filesystem.)

Column View's options

Unlike Icon and List View, the Finder's Column View only has three items in its Show View Options window:

Text size
> Select the size of the text in the view. The range is 10–16 point type, with 12 point being the default size.

Show icons
> This option decides whether icons will be displayed in the Column View along with their appropriate text label. "Show icons" is enabled by default; if you deselect this checkbox, the icons in the Column View will disappear, leaving you with text labels only.

Show preview column
> The far right column shown in Figure 2-6 is known as the Preview column. If you disable this option, file and application icons won't be displayed in the Column View.

Table 2-3 lists the keyboard shortcuts that can be used within the Finder's Column View.

Table 2-3. Column View's keyboard shortcuts

Key command	Description
Right Arrow	Move to the next column
Left Arrow	Move to the previous column
Up Arrow	Select the above item in the column
Down Arrow	Select the next item down in the column
Letter or Number keys	Selects the item in the next column that begins with that letter or number

Resizing column widths

Between each column is a vertical bar with what looks like a sideways equals sign at the bottom, which is known as a *grabber*. To adjust the width of all the columns, click and hold on the grabber and drag the mouse left or right to make the column width decrease or increase, respectively. However, if you only want to adjust the width of a single column, hold down the Option key when you click and drag the grabber. To reset the columns so they're all the same width, simply double-click on any available grabber.

Finder Preferences

As with most other applications, the Finder keeps its preferences command in the application menu under Finder → Preferences. This command brings forth the Finder's preferences window (Figure 2-8), which contains the following options:

Show these items on the Desktop
This category gives you three checkboxes for controlling the types of disk icons to be displayed on your Desktop:

- Hard disks
- Removable media (such as CDs)
- Connected servers

By default, all three are checked, which means icons for those disk types will be displayed on your Desktop. Uncheck an item, and its icon will disappear from your Desktop, but you can still see them in the Finder's Computer window (Go → Computer, or Shift-⌘-C).

New Finder Window shows
This pair of options lets you select the default location that new Finder windows will open up to: either Home (your home directory) or Computer.

Always open folders in a new window
If checked, any folder you double-click on in a Finder view will open in a new Finder window (rather than appear in the same Finder window). This is how Mac OS 9's Finder reacted when a folder was double-clicked. If you leave this item unchecked, you can open a folder in a new window by holding down the Command (⌘) key when double-clicking a folder icon.

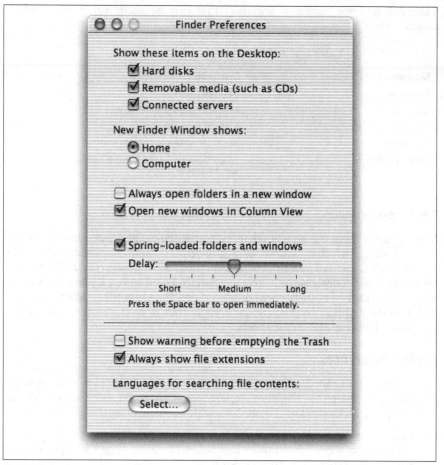

Figure 2-8. The Finder's preferences window

Open new windows in Column View

If you select this checkbox, all new Finder windows will open in Column View (described earlier).

Spring-loaded folders and windows

This determines how folders and windows will react when you drag an item over its location. If unchecked, dragging an item to another folder or window will just place that item there. However, if this option is checked, the location where the item has been dragged will open in a new Finder window.

You can use the slider to specify the Delay before the new Finder window appears. By default, the Delay is set to a Medium time frame. If you have the Delay set for Long, but you're sure of where you're moving the file, hold down the Spacebar to open the new location immediately.

Show warning before emptying the Trash

When checked, the Finder makes emptying the Trash a two-step process, displaying a dialog box asking you to confirm the deletion of files in the Trash. If you don't want to be bothered by that warning note, uncheck this box.

Always show file extensions

>This item is not checked by default, although we recommend that you check it. Leaving it unchecked allows the Finder to chop off file extensions (e.g., *.doc*, *.xls*, *.psd*, *.txt*, *.html*, etc.) when displaying filenames, while checking this option will append the appropriate file extension.

>Apple prefers to hide extensions from nontechnical users so they can't accidentally break the association between documents and their assigned applications. This is much easier to do in Mac OS X than in previous versions of the Mac OS, since it is now based on easy-to-edit file extensions and not more arcane creator codes (see Chapter 9).

Languages for searching file contents

>The lone item for this option is a Select button, which, when clicked, pops open a window that lists the languages supported by Mac OS X. The fewer languages you select in this window, the faster your content indexing and searching will be.

Menus and Keyboard Shortcuts

On the Mac (as with Windows and Linux desktops), you have two ways of invoking commands in the GUI: by using the menus or by issuing shortcuts for the commands on the keyboard. Not every menu item has a keyboard accelerator, but for the ones that do—the more common functions—using the keyboard shortcuts can save you a lot of time.

Aside from its application menu, the Finder has the following menus in its menu bar:

- The Finder's application menu
- File
- Edit
- View
- Go
- Window
- Help

The commands found in these menus will are highlighted in Tables 2-4 through 2-10. While most of these commands function the same across all applications, the functions of some, such as ⌘-B and ⌘-I, can vary between programs, and others may only work when the Finder is active. For example, ⌘-B in Microsoft Word turns on boldface type or makes a selection bold, while in Project Builder, ⌘-B builds your application. Likewise, ⌘-I in Word italicizes a word or selection, while hitting ⌘-I after selecting a file, folder, or application in the Finder opens the Get Info window for the selected item. Table 2-11 contains a listing of keyboard shortcuts that should work across most applications.

The Finder's Application Menu

As with other applications, options found in the Finder's application menu (Table 2-4) give the user access to its Preferences and the Services menu, and provides information about the Finder, options for hiding and showing windows, and options for emptying the Trash.

Table 2-4. The Finder's application menu

Menu option	Keyboard shortcut	Description
About Finder	None	Displays the Finder's About Box
Preferences	None	Opens the Finder's preferences window
Empty Trash	Shift-⌘-Delete	Empties the Trash
Services	None	Gives you access to Services provided by other applications on the system
Hide Finder	⌘-H	Hides all open Finder windows
Hide Others	Shift-⌘-H	Hides the windows for other open applications
Show All	None	Brings all Finder windows to the forefront

The File Menu

The Finder's File menu lacks the usual Open, Save, and Print commands found in most other applications. Instead, the commands for the File menu, listed in Table 2-5, contain commands for dealing with files and folders.

 If you've been using the Mac OS prior to Mac OS X, you'll notice that the keyboard shortcut for creating a new folder has changed; ⌘-N now opens a new Finder window, while Shift-⌘-N creates a new folder.

Table 2-5. The File menu

Menu option	Keyboard shortcut	Description
New Finder Window	⌘-N	Opens a new Finder window.
New Folder	Shift-⌘-N	Creates a new folder.
Open	⌘-O	Opens a file or folder; can also be used to launch applications.
Open With	None	If the selected item is a file, this submenu will display Mac OS X and Classic Mac applications you can use to open the selected file.
Close Window	⌘-W	Closes the window.
Get Info	⌘-I	Opens the Get Info window for the selected item.
Duplicate	⌘-D	Creates a duplicate copy of a selected item. This command adds the word "copy" to the filename before the file extension.
Make Alias	⌘-L	Creates an alias of the selected file.
Show Original	⌘-R	Opens a Finder window that takes you to the original of an alias.
Add to Favorites	⌘-T	Adds the selected item to your Favorites list (~/Library/Favorites).

Table 2-5. The File menu (continued)

Menu option	Keyboard shortcut	Description
Move to Trash	⌘-Delete	Moves the selected item to the Trash.
Eject	⌘-E	Ejects or unmounts the selected disk.
Burn Disc	None	Opens the Disk Utility (*/Applications/Utilities*) for use with creating CDs and DVDs.
Find	⌘-F	Opens a Find window for searching through the file-system.

The Edit Menu

Commands found in the Edit menu, listed in Table 2-6, allow you to perform actions on a file in the Finder window.

Table 2-6. The Edit menu

Menu option	Keyboard shortcut	Description
Undo	⌘-Z	Undoes the previously issued command
Cut	⌘-X	Deletes the selected item or text and copies it to the clipboard
Copy	⌘-C	Copies the selected item or text to the clipboard
Paste	⌘-V	Pastes the contents of the clipboard at the currently selected location
Select All	⌘-A	Selects all of the items within the Finder view or text document
Show Clipboard	None	Displays the contents of the clipboard

The View Menu

The items in the View menu, listed in Table 2-7, offer shortcuts for changing the Finder's view.

Table 2-7. The View menu

Menu option	Keyboard shortcut	Description
as Icons	⌘-1	Changes the Finder to Icon View.
as List	⌘-2	Changes the Finder to List View.
as Columns	⌘-3	Changes the Finder to Column View.
Clean Up	None	Aligns the items within the Finder view.
Arrange	None	Only an available option in Icon View. Grayed out if the View Option's "Keep arranged by" option is checked; otherwise, it lets you arrange the icons in the view by Name, Date Modified, Date Created, Size, and Kind.
Hide Toolbar	⌘-B	Hides the Finder's toolbar.
Customize Toolbar	None	Used for customizing the Finder's toolbar.
Hide/Show Status Bar	None	Hides or shows the status bar in the Finder view.
Show View Options	⌘-J	Opens the Finder view's View Options window.

The Go Menu

The Finder's Go menu offers a number of shortcuts (listed in Table 2-8), some hardcoded and some user-definable, to various folders and disks on your system. This menu also contains commands to mount disks via a network connection, and for users willing to speak a little Unix, a quick way to view the contents of any folder in the filesystem in the Finder.

Table 2-8. The Go menu

Menu option	Keyboard shortcut	Description
Back	⌘-[	Goes backward in the Finder view.
Forward	⌘-]	Goes forward in the Finder view.
Computer	Shift-⌘-C	Shows which volumes are mounted on the computer.
Home	Shift-⌘-H	Takes the user to their home directory (*/Users/ username*).
iDisk	Shift-⌘-I	Mounts the user's iDisk based on the settings made in System Preferences → Internet → .Mac. If the user doesn't have a .Mac account, a window will appear to let the user mount another .Mac user's iDisk Public folder.
Applications	Shift-⌘-A	Takes the user to the Applications folder (*/Applications*) in the Finder view.
Favorites	Shift-⌘-F	Gives the user access to the items they've specified as Favorites, stored in *~/Library/Favorites*.
Favorites (submenu)	None	This submenu displays the items saved as a Favorite so the user can quickly select one.
Recent Folders	None	This submenu displays a list of the recently accessed folders.
Go to Folder	Shift-⌘-G	Displays a sheet that lets the user quickly change the Finder's view to the location of a specific folder.
Connect to Server	⌘-K	Lets the user connect to another computer on the network via AppleTalk, AFP, Samba, IP, and WebDAV.

The Window Menu

Items found in the Window menu (Table 2-9) give you access to the open Finder windows.

Table 2-9. The Window menu

Menu option	Keyboard shortcut	Description
Zoom Window	None	Resizes the window, making it either larger or smaller, depending on its last resize
Minimize Window	⌘-M	Minimizes the window to the Dock.
Bring All to Front	None	Brings all of the Finder windows to the front of the window stack.
[List of Open Windows]	None	All open Finder windows will be listed at the bottom of this menu, allowing you to quickly select a Finder window based on its title.

The Help Menu

The Finder's Help menu (as with most, but not all applications) gives you access to the Mac's Help Viewer application. Some applications' Help menus, such as Microsoft Word, include quick links to the product's web site or a means for checking for software updates. The Finder's lone Help menu item is listed in Table 2-10.

Table 2-10. The Help menu

Menu option	Keyboard shortcut	Description
Mac Help	⌘-?	Opens the Help Viewer

Basic Keyboard Shortcuts

Table 2-11 lists some additional keyboard shortcuts that will work the same across most applications on Mac OS X.

Table 2-11. Additional keyboard shortcuts for Mac OS X

Keyboard shortcut	Description
Option-⌘-Escape	Open the Force Quit window
⌘-Tab	Cycle forward through active applications in the Dock
Shift-⌘-Tab	Cycle backward through the active applications in the Dock
⌘-. (Command-period)	Cancel operation
⌘-B	Bold the selected text in most text editing applications, such as TextEdit, Word, etc.
⌘-C	Copy selection
Option-⌘-D	Turn Dock hiding on/off
⌘-I	Italicize the selected text in most text editing applications, such as TextEdit, Word, etc.
Option-⌘-M	Minimize all open windows for an application
⌘-N	Create a new document, depending on the application
⌘-O	Open a file
⌘-P	Print a file
⌘-Q	Quit application (you cannot quit the Finder)
⌘-S	Save the current file
⌘-V	Paste items that have been copied to the clipboard
Option-⌘-W	Close all open windows for an application
Shift-⌘-Z	Redo (not available in all applications)
Shift-⌘-3	Take a screenshot of the entire display (saved as a PDF file to the Desktop)
Shift-⌘-4	Take a screenshot of a selected area of the display (saved as a PDF file to the Desktop)

Keyboard Navigation

When working with Finder windows, you can perform almost all the navigation you need via the keyboard, speeding up things considerably.

Selecting icons

You can select a file by starting to type its name. When looking at a Finder window, typing (for example) "S" will select the first file in the view whose name begins with the letter "S." If you quickly follow that with an "H," then the first file whose name begins with "SH" will be highlighted, and so on.

Alternately, you can change the selection via the arrow keys, which switches the selection depending on their icons' window position, or with Tab, which selects the next alphabetical icon. Shift-Tab selects the previous alphabetical icon in the view.

Opening icons and navigating folders

Once you've selected the file, folder, or application you want to open, just hit ⌘-O, which has the same effect as double-clicking on the icon or choosing Open from the File menu (File → Open).

Note that you can do this with folders to drill down through your filesystem. If you find yourself too deep, use the keyboard shortcut ⌘-Up Arrow or ⌘-[to go backward in the view.

Files, Folders, and Disks

Your machine's *filesystem* refers to all the disks, both local and remote, that your computer is able to see and work with. The definition also includes the machine's installed hard disk(s); any removable media such as CDs, Zip disks, or digital cameras; mounted, in-memory disk images; and any filesystems (or parts thereof) that make themselves available over a network, mounted on your machine through AppleShare or SMB, for example.

The Finder gives you visual cues to let you know which of these you're working with, and it gives you the same methods to navigate through all of them.

Disks

The Finder lists all the machine's available disks in the Computer window, which you can summon through Go → Computer (Shift-⌘-C).

As Figure 2-9 shows, this window contains one icon for each disk the Mac can see, as well as a special Network icon that leads to any directories mounted over the *network filesystem* (NFS, covered in Chapter 11).

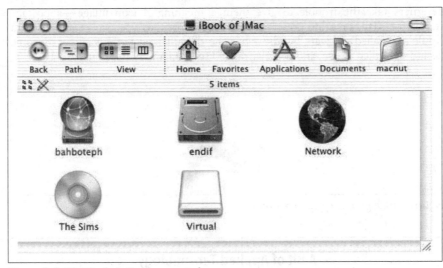

Figure 2-9. The Finder's Computer window

 The contents of the Computer window don't reflect any actual folder on your machine. The window is just an abstract container the Finder uses to visually represent all the machine's mounted volumes that contain all the real files and folders. As Chapter 11 covers in more detail, each disk has a "real" location, or *mount point*, somewhere on the physical filesystem—but you don't need to know this in order to use the Finder.

Disk icons also appear on the Desktop unless you've set the Finder Preferences to behave otherwise, as detailed later in "Finder Preferences."

As shown in Figure 2-9, disk icons can have a variety of shapes. Volumes based on local media, such as hard drives, CDs, and iPods, have icons shaped like the devices they're on. Network-mounted disks usually look like a standard disk icon supporting a blue sphere. "Virtual" disks mounted via Disk Copy have icons resembling generic disk drives.

Opening a disk icon—by double-clicking it, or choosing File → Open (⌘-O) while it's selected—produces a window displaying the files and folders stored within it.

Files

A file is the basic unit of filesystem currency in any modern operating system. The following discusses some of the flavors of files you find in Mac OS X.

Applications

Applications live in the filesystem as bundles of executable files and the code libraries, pictures, sounds, and other resources they need to run. Most application designers take the trouble to give them a meaningful icon image—a postage stamp for Mail, or a life preserver for Help Center, to use two examples from Apple's installed software bundle—but the default icon is the vaguely Masonic design of a ruler, brush, and pencil arranged to form an "A" (see Figure 2-10).

Figure 2-10. A generic application icon

A Bit of Applied Terminology

In a general computer–use context, "application" can mean any computer program, especially one that works with documents in some way. This book, however, uses it specifically to refer to programs that run within Mac OS X's Aqua workspace—i.e., programs with icons that you can launch from the Finder or the Dock, and (except for Classic applications) have all the window and menu bar behaviors described in Chapter 1. This distinguishes them from the hundreds of programs that run solely in Darwin, the BSD-based Unix operating system at the core of Mac OS X. (To continue to use the Apple parlance, Darwin's programs are further divided into *tools* for interactive programs you run via the Terminal application, and into *system services* for things that tend to lack an interface and spend all their time managing tasks in the background. This book often calls the latter category of the programs, covered extensively in Chapter 13, *daemons*, which is the more traditional Unix terminology.)

Double-clicking an application's icon in the Finder will launch it. (If you're already running that application, it will simply step into the foreground, becoming the active application.)

Mac OS X applications come in four flavors:

Cocoa

These applications are built with Apple's Cocoa programming API and take full advantage of all the functionality the Aqua interface offers.

Cocoa applications get their power by forsaking their past: they run solely on Mac OS X, and not Mac OS 9. As time passes and Mac OS X soaks up more of the market share among Macintosh users, Cocoa applications will likely take their place as the favored flavor for new applications.

Carbon

These applications use Apple's Carbon API, which lets them use Aqua's basic features when running in Mac OS X, as well as run on Mac OS 9 systems (so long as they have a copy of Apple's CarbonLib extension installed). In a sense, they're actually polite Mac OS 9 applications that can adapt to Mac OS X's Aqua interface on request.

During these transitional times, Carbon is a popular choice among commercial application developers, who want both Mac OS X and Mac OS 9 users to be able to buy and use their products.

Classic

These applications are built for Mac OS 9 or lower, and are completely unable to run within the Aqua interface. However, you can still run Classic applications on Mac OS X using the *Classic environment*, a watered-down version of Mac OS 9 that runs within an emulator. Classic is covered more thoroughly in Chapter 3.

Java

As with Classic, Java applications run in their own workspace: the Java runtime environment. Thanks to the Java Swing GUI libraries, Java applications can look and act a lot like any other Aqua application, and Mac OS X gives Java programs packaged into the usual application bundle directories the same user-interface benefits it gives other application types, such as Dock icons.

Mac OS X can also run Java applets, as well as raw classes and JAR files, but it won't treat them as full Aqua applications per se. See Chapter 10.

You don't necessarily need to know about these distinctions when using Mac OS X. The Finder treats all three types of applications the same.

Documents

Documents are files that you read from, write to, and otherwise manipulate through applications. A document can, but doesn't have to, associate itself with an application residing elsewhere on your Mac. If it does, then it usually displays its allegiance by changing its icon somehow. The generic document icon is a blank white piece of paper with a dog-eared upper-right corner, and most applications decorate their documents' icons by sticking to this shape while stamping some art onto the "paper" that suggests its contents, as shown in Figure 2-11.

Figure 2-11. A generic Finder document icon, and a few application-specific ones

Double-clicking a document's icon directs the Finder to *try* to open the file with an appropriate application. It tries to find this application by examining the document's extension, if it has one, and its resource fork, if it has one of those. If the file lacks one of these, the Finder displays the dialog seen in Figure 2-12.

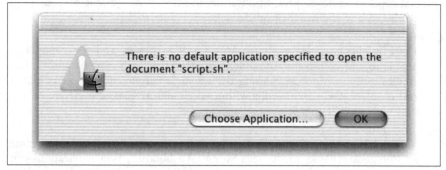

Figure 2-12. Double-clicking a file with no file type

Binding documents to applications

If the Finder can decide on a document's "owner," it assigns it a "Kind" attribute and an icon image defined by the owning application. Otherwise, it leaves the document with a "generic" icon, and double-clicking it causes the Finder to display the dialog shown in Figure 2-12. Clicking the Choose Application button will display a dialog window similar to Figure 2-13.

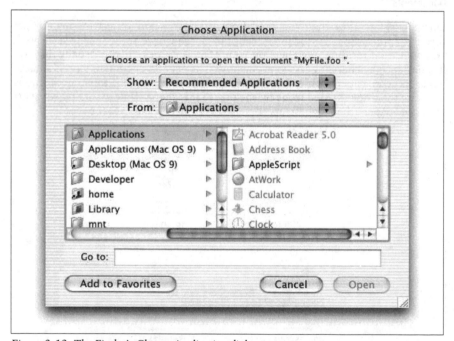

Figure 2-13. The Finder's Choose Application dialog

Through this dialog, which works like a standard Open window (see "The Open Window" in Chapter 1), you can choose an application that will try to handle your future attempts to open this file and all files like it—based on filename extension (or the lack thereof) and its resource fork (if it has one)—from the Finder.

Folders

Folders, also referred to as *directories* (especially in a Unix context), give disks a hierarchical structure. A disk can hold any number of files and folders, and these folders can contain more files and other folders, ad infinitum.

Folders' icons usually look like a blue file folder, though some applications like to fashion folders for themselves that add a touch of custom art to this design. However, the default folders in a user's Home directory have icons to suggest their intended use.

Double-clicking a folder icon in the Finder causes its contents to appear in a Finder window. If the folder icon was on the Desktop, it opens a new window for itself; otherwise, it takes over the current window, putting itself in the titlebar and filling the view up with its own contents. (You can step back to its parent folder or disk by the window toolbar's Back button, or by typing either ⌘-↑ or ⌘-[.)

You can have a folder display its contents in a new Finder window, keeping the old one onscreen, by Command-double-clicking its icon. (This again keeps to the browser-like nature of Finder window navigation, since many Mac web browsers also open a new browser window if you Command-click a link.)

Bundles

Under the hood, folders are actually Unix directories. However, not all Unix directories on the filesystem are folders—some are bundles, holding application resources or special multiple-file document types that the Finder doesn't think you really need to know about. Most of the Cocoa and Carbon programs in the Applications folder are bundles, though they may appear to be single files in the Finder. The same goes for any *.rtfd* files (RTF with attached images) you might create with TextEdit.

The Finder will give up a bundle's secrets if you specifically ask for them. Control-clicking on an application's icon will display, as with every other Finder icon, its contextual menu, within which you'll find the command "Show Package Contents." Selecting this menu command opens a new Finder window containing the files and folders this icon covertly contains.

Naturally, the other way to slip into a bundle involves grabbing a command line in the nearest Terminal window and just *cd*-ing into the bundle, since it's really just an ordinary directory from Unix's point of view.

Mac OS X's Application-to-Document Map

The system determines a document's *kind* in one of two ways. First it sees if the document has an *attribute fork*, a data attachment possessed by documents created by Classic and Carbon applications that provides information about the document's type (among other things). If the file lacks a resource fork, then it looks to the document's filename extension; Mac OS X maintains a system-wide map between these extensions and recognized document types.

The system's map that binds particular filename extensions to certain Aqua applications is made from two sorts of files. Each application's *Info.plist* file (see Chapter 22) can define the filename extensions that its documents use. For example, Terminal application files have the extension *.term*, and it says as much in its Info file (located, for the curious, at */Applications/Terminal.app/ Contents/Info.plist*. If only one application lays claim to a particular file extension (as is the case with *.term*, at least in a fresh Mac OS X installation), then the system will recognize a binding between that application and all files with that extension; double-clicking these documents in the Finder will open them through that application.

These claims, however, may be overruled by the contents of another file: *com. apple.LaunchServices.plist*, which is another XML property list file that exists in your Home folder's */Library* folder (see Chapter 9). It lists the preferences that you have stated (through the Finder's Show Info window, and other means) regarding what applications to use with which files, or classes of files.

If the Finder encounters an ambiguity due to two or more applications recognizing the same file extension (as is the case with Acrobat Reader and Apple's Preview application with *.pdf* files), then the system again looks to this file, seeing if the user has a stated preference. If not, then it will favor a Carbon or Cocoa application over a Classic one and, failing that, an application with a more recent modification time on the filesystem.

Based on this attached information, a document's icon gets its image, its "Kind" label (as it appears in List view; see "List View" later in this chapter), and knowledge of which application it will activate when double-clicked. You can, however, adjust any of these connections through the document's Info window, as detailed in "The Get Info Window."

See Chapter 9 for further detail on how Mac OS X manages its files.

Bundles carry the icons of either applications or documents, depending upon the role they play. Double-clicking a bundle icon in the Finder will have one of the other double-click effects we've already covered, depending upon what sort of bundle it is. An application's bundle will launch the application it contains, and a document-flavored bundle will try to open itself inside another application, just like any other document.

Bundles are yet another subtle point of Mac OS X's GUI that works transparently unless you know where to look. Most users of this OS probably have no reason to explore the depths of any bundles, instead taking what they offer at face value.

Aliases

An *Alias* is a special file that acts as a pointer to some other file, folder, or disk elsewhere in the filesystem. Opening the alias has the same effect as opening its target file. Through aliases, you can create shortcuts to various files wherever you'd like (in your home directory, for example) without having to actually move the originals around.

An alias's icon matches that of its original, with the addition of a small arrow in its corner, as seen in Figure 2-14.

Figure 2-14. A PDF file and its alias

Aliases and symlinks

Aliases are similar, but not identical, to the Unix concept of *symbolic links*, better known as *symlinks*. Like aliases, symlinks (created through the Unix *ln* command) are shortcuts between distant parts of a filesystem.

Symlinks, however, are pointers to paths, not to actual filesystem objects. A symlink, when opened, will resolve to whatever happens to reside at its pointed-to path at that moment—which might be nothing at all. Mac OS X aliases, on the other hand, always refer to a specific file, folder, or disk, and are able to keep their links alive even if the original object moves elsewhere in the filesystem. (An alias will break if its original is deleted or unmounted, of course.)

In this way, aliases act more like Unix *hard links*, but that's the limit of their similarity; unlike aliases, hard links are completely indistinguishable from their originals, and can't refer to files on different volumes.

The Finder is aware of Unix symlinks, and displays their icons as aliases. This allows you to work with both the Mac and the Unix notions of filesystem short-cuts from the Finder. However, when working with Mac OS X's Unix side through the Terminal, only Unix symlinks will work as shortcuts—aliases show up as meaningless binary files. (In truth, they contain the filesystem ID number of the objects they point to, but your Mac's Unix side can't use this information by itself.)

Moving, Copying, and Renaming Objects

Moving a file or folder in Finder is as easy as dragging its icon. Some rules apply to what you can move and where you can move it, however, and you can perform more specific actions—such as copying files or creating aliases—through modifier keys.

File Permissions

First of all, due Mac OS X's strict, Unix-style file permissions, you might not be able to move or otherwise modify a file or folder. Anything in your home folder is generally malleable, and if you're in the system's *admin* group, you can choose to modify certain system-level folders, such as */Applications*.

Otherwise, you may see a dialog box like the one in Figure 2-15, informing you that you lack the credentials to perform some action with the filesystem. If you still need it done, contact an administrator of this Mac. If you *are* an administrator (or the Mac's sole user!) and see this dialog, then you may be trying to manipulate *root*-owned files that the system doesn't want people messing with, such as those in the */System* folder. Refer to Chapter 5 for more information about these and other special folders.

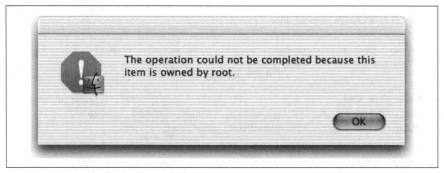

Figure 2-15. A permission-denied dialog box

Exactly what fate befalls a file when you drag it depends upon where you drop it, and if you were holding down modifier keys at the time.

See Chapter 5 for detailed information about Mac OS X's file permissions system and user accounts.

Moving and Copying Objects

To move an object, just click and drag it. Its destination depends on where you drop it.

If you drop an icon in the same window that it started in, its position in the filesystem doesn't change at all.

Dropping an icon into a different folder on the same disk moves the file, while dropping it onto a folder located on a different disk *copies* it, keeping the original file in place while creating a duplicate in the destination folder.

Finder gives you a visual cue to let you know which action would happen: when dragging an icon over an icon or window that would result in its copying, rather than its moving, the cursor gains a little plus-sign icon, as seen in Figure 2-16.

Figure 2-16. The file-copying cursor

Force Finder to copy rather than move an object by holding down Option when you drop the icon(s). You can also copy a file into the same folder via File → Duplicate (⌘-D).

Creating Aliases

While you can make an alias to a selected object appear through File → Make Alias (⌘-L), you can make an move and alias in one step by dragging an icon to the icon or window where you'd like to place its alias, and then holding down Option-⌘ as you drop it. Finder will signal this planned action by sticking an arrow onto the cursor as you drag, as seen in Figure 2-17.

Figure 2-17. The alias-creation cursor

Renaming Objects

To rename an object in the Finder, select its icon, and then click on its actual text label. If you have write permission to this object, the label transforms into a text field (as shown in Figure 2-18), letting you type what you wish. Once you've modified the filename, press Return or click elsewhere to make it permanent.

Figure 2-18. Renaming a file in the Finder

You can also make the selected icon's label editable simply by pressing Return.

Filename Rules

Mac OS X limits filename length to 256 characters, and Finder displays a polite refusal in a dialog box, if you attempt to go over this limit while renaming an icon.

In the interest of saving screen real estate, Finder also abbreviates long filenames when displaying icons in windows, replacing a variably sized swath of characters from its middle with an ellipse (...), as shown in Figure 2-19.

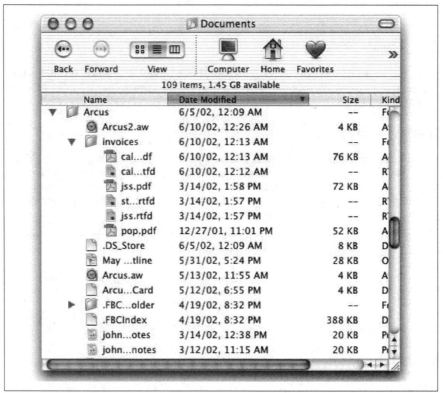

Figure 2-19. A long filename in a short window

You can view the entire filename by mousing over the label; after a second, the full name appears in a floating tooltip.

Finder can't have any colon (:) characters in filenames, and will in fact display a hyphen character (-) if you try to add a colon to a filename.

Finder (and many other applications) won't let you precede a file with a period (making *.my file* an illegal name, for instance). This would turn it into a Unix dotfile, thus making it vanish from sight, since Finder hides all such things! (See "Hidden Files" in Chapter 9.) Of course, this isn't exactly a feature if you actually *want* to turn something into a dotfile. Alas, you'll have to use Terminal and the *mv* command for that.

Moving Objects to the Trash

Finder gives you several ways to toss things into the Trash:

- Drag icons into the Trash icon, located on the Dock.
- Select Move to Trash from an icon's contextual menu.
- Press the window toolbar's Delete button (if available).
- Select File → Move To Trash (⌘-Delete).

See "Trash" in Chapter 1 for more about the Trash.

Since filesystem navigation is a task common to every disk-based operating system, including the Unix which Mac OS X relies upon, every task the Finder can perform has equivalent command-line commands. Double-clicking a folder and seeing its contents in a focused window is the same as *cd*-ing to it and then running *ls*; ejecting a CD by dragging its icon into the Trash is the same as *umount*-ing it in the Terminal.

It pays to master both of Mac OS X's two built-in interfaces, Aqua and command-line. This is discussed further in Chapter 19.

The Get Info Window

Get Info gives you access to all sorts of information about the files, directories, and applications on your system. To view the information for an item, click on its icon in the Finder and either go to File → Get Info or use its keyboard shortcut, ⌘-I. The Get Info window, shown in Figure 2-20, has six different panes, which offer different kinds of information about the file.

To reveal the content of one of these items, click on its disclosure triangle to expand the pane. The panes of the Get Info window include the following:

General
> This pane tells you the basics about the file, including its kind, size, where it's located in the filesystem, and when it was created and last modified. The General section also includes two controls for attaching the following special properties to an object:

Stationary Pad
> This checkbox only appears in a file's Info window. One of the most obscurely useful Finder commands that survived the transition to Mac OS X, this checkbox signals applications to treat this file as a template instead of an editable file. If opened with an application capable of working with stationary pad files, it will copy the files' contents into an untitled new document window, leaving the original file as is on disk.

Locked
> When checked, the object becomes hard to modify or delete. Applications will read from, but won't change, a locked document. Locked folders will let you explore them, but you cannot add or remove anything from them. The Trash will not allow you to add a locked item to it. A locked object will get a tiny padlock added to the corner of its icon, which is a visual clue to you that the file is locked.

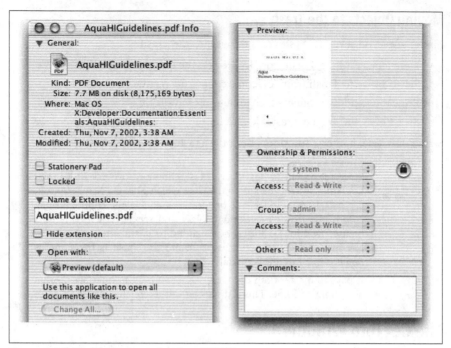

Figure 2-20. The Get Info window for a PDF file

 Locking an object protects it against accidental user damage, but offers no real security, since unlocking it is as easy as unselecting this checkbox. User the Ownership and Permissions section of the Get Info Window to make a file truly write-protected.

If you don't have write permission for the object in question, the controls are grayed out.

Name & Extension

This pane displays a text box with the name of the file or directory.

Content index

This pane is only available when you use Get Info on a folder or drive (not with individual files); it tells you whether its contents have been indexed. Indexing stores information about the files contained within that directory or drive in an information database used by the Find command when searching for files on your system. To index a folder, click on the Index Now button; this may take some time, depending on how many files or folders are contained within.

Open with

This option is only available if you select a file (i.e., not a folder or an application). Here you can specify which application will open this file or all similar files.

Preview

Depending on the file type, you can view the contents of the file here (this also works for playing sounds and QuickTime movies).

Changing the Preview Icon

If you have a single object selected, you can change its icon through the Get Info window. You can invoke clipboard commands on it. Edit → Copy (⌘-C) will copy the icon image, at its full size, to the clipboard. Edit → Paste (⌘-V) will change the object's icon to whatever image (if any) is in the clipboard.

You can also set the icon by simply dragging an image file's icon onto the Get Info window's displayed icon.

Ownership & Permissions
> This displays the name of the owner and the name of the group to which the file belongs. It also allows you to set access privileges to that file for the Owner, Group, and Others on the system (see "The File Permissions System" in Chapter 9).

Comments
> This field can contain some basic information about the file, folder, or application. If you have your Finder set to List View, you can opt to have the Comments displayed within the view.

The Get Info window for applications has the General Information, Name & Extension, and Ownership & Permissions options mentioned previously (although the Ownership & Permissions options are disabled by default), as well as one or both of the following options:

Languages
> Shows the languages supported by that application.

Plug-ins
> If applicable, this lists the available plug-ins for the application. (iPhoto's Info window has a Plug-ins section.)

Noticeably missing from a Mac OS X application's Get Info window is the Memory option. Because memory for applications is assigned dynamically by virtual memory, you no longer have to specify how much memory an application requires. However, if you use Get Info on a Mac OS 9 application, the Memory option will be there.

Favorites

Mac OS X's *Favorites* concept provides yet another way, along with Finder window toolbars and the Dock, to build shortcuts to frequently accessed folders and files. It can prove especially handy to make favorites out of folders you use frequently, since all the objects you've marked as Favorites show up as selections in the From: menu of the standard Open dialog box, and in the Where: menu of the standard Save dialog. This lets you quickly access these folder from inside most any application—see "Opening and Saving Documents" in Chapter 1.

Aqua gives you several ways to create a new favorite:

- In the Finder, select the object(s), then choose File → Add To Favorites.
- Drag an object onto the heart-shaped Favorites icon in a Finder window's toolbar.
- Click the Add to Favorites button (see Figure 1-32) on any application's Open or Save dialog after selected an object within it.
- Add aliases of the objects to ~/Library/Favorites (see the earlier section "Creating Aliases").

All of these methods add aliases of selected objects to ~/Library/Favorites directory. You can visit this folder in any of the usual ways, or by clicking once on the Favorites icon in a Finder window's toolbar.

Searching for and Locating Files

Mac OS X gives you five ways to find files—two easy-to-use methods through the Finder, and three more as Unix commands you can invoke through the Terminal.

Finding Files Through the Finder

Selecting File → Find (⌘-F) in the Finder brings up the window shown in Figure 2-21. You can also open the Find window by clicking on the word "Search" below the Search field in the Finder's Toolbar.

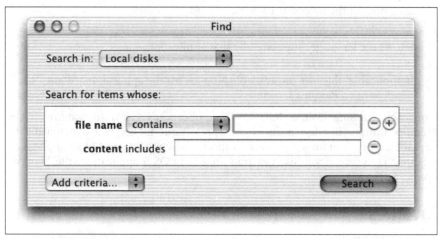

Figure 2-21. The Finder's file-finding interface

 Mac OS Versions 8.5 through 10.1 launched the separate Sherlock application at this Finder menu command. Sherlock still exists in the latest versions of Mac OS X (see "Applications" in Chapter 6), but it has been demoted to work solely as a web-searching interface. Aqua-based file-finding functions have been placed back in the Finder's realm.

The "Search in" pop-up menu lets you define the domain of your search. It contains the following choices:

Everywhere
> The search will include every disk mounted on the filesystem, including network-mounted volumes.

Local disks
> The search will include every disk mounted on the filesystem, except for network-mounted volumes.

Home
> The search will limit itself to your Home folder.

Specific Places
> Selecting this summons a filesystem browser, which lets you add disks to include in the search, as well as individual folders within any mounted disk.

> You can also add folders to the search by dragging and dropping them into the list, as Figure 2-22 shows.

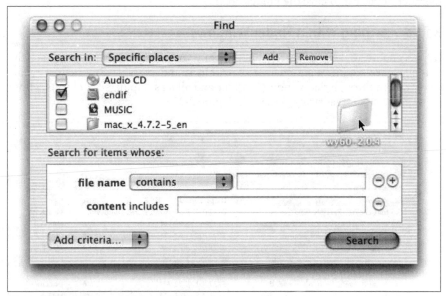

Figure 2-22. Adding a folder to a Specific places search

Under "Search for items whose," arrange criteria for the search. You can add new criteria by selecting them from the "Add criteria" pop-up menu, which includes the following:

file name
> The file's name.

content
> Text strings that appear within the file itself. See the later section "Finding Files by Content."

date modified
> The last time this file was modified.

date created
> The time this file was created.

kind
> The kind of Finder object this file is (a document, a folder, an application, etc.)

size
> The total size of this file.

visibility
> Whether this file is visible to the Finder. See Chapter 6 for more information.

extension
> The filename extension this file uses (such as *txt* or *html*).

Each kind of criteria you add introduces its own pop-up menus or text areas for defining your search parameters. When you're ready to perform the search, click the Search button. The Finder opens a separate results window, and displays every object that matches your criteria as it encounters them. Double-click any member of this list to have the Finder open it.

Rapid Searching Within Finder Windows

If you choose to keep a Search field within your Finder window toolbar (the default), then typing some characters within it and pressing Return will recursively search through that window's folder and all its subfolders for objects whose filenames contain that string, as seen in Figure 2-23.

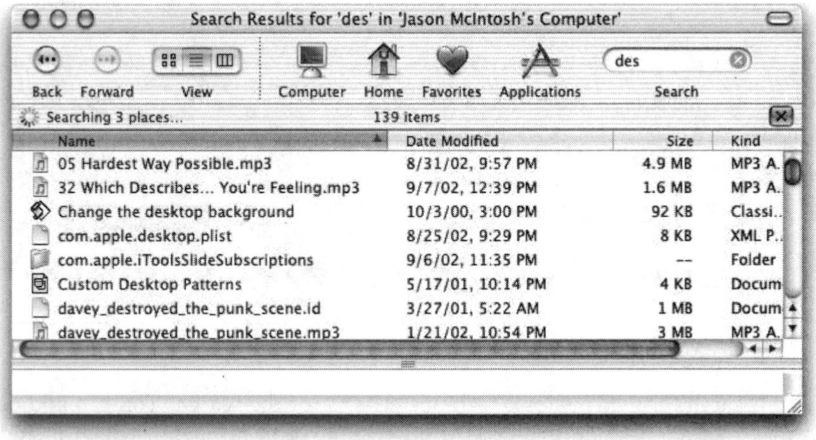

Figure 2-23. Using the Finder's toolbar search field

Finding Files by Content

When you add the "content includes" criteria to your Finder file search, Finder goes an extra step in its search by looking not just at the names and attributes of files, folders, and disks, but opening up files within the search domain and scanning their text contents.

When you perform a by-content search, the Finder launches an invisible application called *ContentIndexing*,[*] which proceeds to crawl through the disks and folders you defined as the search domains. The first time *ContentIndexing* searches through a folder, it creates a Finder-invisible dotfile (see Chapter 9) called *.FBCIndex*, holding (in an opaque binary format) an index of various words and strings. On its next pass through, if the folder hasn't changed, then *ContentIndexing* will (very quickly) learn about the folder's contents from that existing index file. Otherwise, it crawls the folder again and updates the index.

If the text in the files you work with tends to be in only one or two languages, you can speed up content indexing by selecting Finder → Preferences, and then clicking the "Languages for searching file contents" button at the bottom of that dialog. This results in a list of languages, shown in Figure 2-24. When performing content indexing, the system scans for word stems and language constructs appropriate to any of the checked languages. By unchecking some, you decrease the complexity of *ContentIndexing*'s job, and increase its speed.

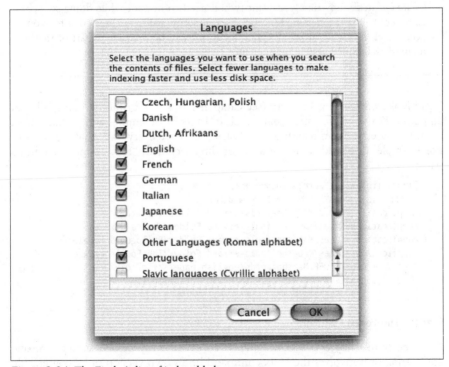

Figure 2-24. The Finder's list of indexable languages

---

[*] For certain values of "invisible," anyway. In one example, using a 500 MHz G3 computer, *ContentIndexing* causes a notable, general slowdown while it runs, as it monopolizes the hard disk for the many minutes it takes to crawl through all the necessary directories.

Finding Files with the Terminal

As with all Darwin command-line programs, you can find a quick and complete reference to these in Chapter 25.

The locate command

The *locate* command finds files not just by filename, but by full path. It's also *very* fast—easily the fastest method for finding files—because it reads from a database that it builds as a result of an earlier filesystem crawl.

The locate Database

Building the *locate* database—a single file found at */var/db/locate.database*—takes a while. You can manually run the database-updating script (*/usr/libexec/locate.updatedb*) any time you want (you'll need to be root while doing so; see Chapter 9), but the default Mac OS X *cron* setup will run this script for you every week (every Saturday at 4 a.m. local time, to be precise) as part of *root*'s regularly scheduled system maintenance tasks.

You invoke *locate* using a pattern (see Chapter 15), and it instantly returns a list of all paths across the filesystem that match it. In its most simple (and perhaps most common) use, you can feed it a literal string and see every path that contains it. For example, to quickly scan for a file or directory with "fool" somewhere in its path:

```
[jmac@wireless251 /etc]% locate fool
/Applications/Games/MAC-the-fools-errand Folder
/Applications/Games/MAC-the-fools-errand Folder/.DS_Store
/Applications/Games/MAC-the-fools-errand Folder/Fool's Puzzles
/Applications/Games/MAC-the-fools-errand Folder/Prologue & Finale
/Applications/Games/MAC-the-fools-errand Folder/The Fool's Errand
/Users/jmac/OLDSTUFF/Martha/words/english papers/fool bib
/Users/jmac/Sites/jmac_web/cgi-bin/nomic/voting/foolib
[jmac@wireless251 /etc]%
```

Searching file content with grep

As its entry in Chapter 25 shows, *grep* is an enormously flexible command; one application of it involves the Unix command line's own version of by-content file searching. Through the syntax grep *pattern files*, you can search fairly rapidly through text files for a certain string or regular expression (see Chapter 15).

Useful *grep* options for file searching include the recursive *-r* flag, the case-insensitive *-i* flag, and the *-l* option, which lists only filenames, suppressing *grep*'s default behavior of printing out every line in which it finds a match.

For instance, you can search through your entire home directory for the string "rutabaga" (or "Rutabaga") with this command: *grep -ril rutabaga ~*.

Note that this can take a long time, since, unlike the Finder, *grep* doesn't use content indexing. (Nor should it, really; it's meant to be a general-purpose tool for not just file searching but also filtering out interesting lines from large volumes of program output, through the clever application of Unix pipes. But that's a topic for another chapter—specifically, Chapter 21.)

find

Finally, Darwin's *find* command is roughly equivalent to the interface described earlier in "Finding Files Through the Finder," but ten times as sophisticated and one-tenth as easy to use. Generally speaking, you run *find* with a list of paths, options, arguments, and operators (of which there is a bewildering variety), and it outputs a list of filenames that match your criteria. While useful for simply finding files, a veteran Terminal user can then pipe this output into other programs to use as input, but this is again a topic for Chapter 21.

Chapter 25 sorts out the complexities of the *find* command.

Relaunching the Finder

The Force Quit window (see "Force-Quitting Applications" in Chapter 1) is the quickest way to restart the Finder if it seems to be stuck, or if you want to apply some change you've made by hacking the Dock's preferences (see Chapter 5).

To restart the Finder, go to  → Force Quit (Option-⌘-Esc), select the Finder, and click on the Relaunch button. As with force-quitting other applications, a warning sheet will slide down from the window's titlebar asking you to confirm the operation. If you still want to restart the Finder, click on the Relaunch button; if not, click on the Cancel button or hit ⌘-. (Command-period) to cancel the operation.

3

Mac OS 9, Mac OS X, and Classic

Mac OS X is way ahead of its time. When Apple developed this hybrid operating system, they knew it would take a while for application developers to Carbonize their applications to run on Mac OS X. Rather than locking out older software entirely, Apple made it possible to run both Mac OS 9 and Mac OS X on the same system, and took it a step further by building a Mac OS 9 *virtual machine* into Mac OS X, called *The Classic Environment*, or just Classic.

This chapter covers some of the changes between Mac OS 9 and Mac OS X, and introduces you to Classic.

Changes to Mac OS X from Mac OS 9

There are many noticeable changes in the user interface from earlier versions of the Mac OS to Mac OS X, while others may not be so apparent. Two of the biggest changes from Mac OS 9 to Mac OS X can be found in the Apple menu and the Control Panels.

The Apple Menu

The Apple menu, displayed as an apple symbol () in the menu bar, is completely different. For Mac OS 9 users, the thing that will probably impact you most is that you can no longer store aliases for files, folders, or applications here. Here's what you'll find in Mac OS X's Apple menu:

About This Mac
> This option pops open a window that supplies you with information about your Mac. Aside from telling you that you're running Mac OS X on your computer, the window shows you which version of Mac OS X is installed, how much memory you have, and the speed and type of processor in your computer. Clicking on the More Info button will launch the Apple System Profiler (*/Applications/Utilities*), which gives you a greater level of detail about your computer.

As mentioned in Chapter 1 and shown in Figure 1-8, clicking on the version number in the About This Mac window will reveal the build number of Mac OS X; clicking it again will show the hardware serial number for your computer. These small details are important to have when contacting Apple Customer Service and when reporting a probable bug.

In earlier versions of the Mac OS, the About box would change depending on which application was active. For information about the application, you now have to use the Application menu (located to the right of the Apple menu) and select the About option.

Get Mac OS X Software

Selecting this option takes you to Apple's Mac OS X software page (*http://www.apple.com/downloads/macosx*) in your default web browser.

System Preferences

System Preferences replaces most of the Control Panels from earlier versions of the Mac OS. See Chapter 5 for more details.

Dock

This menu offers a quick way to change settings for the Dock (described later).

Location

This is similar to the Location Manager Control Panel in earlier versions of the Mac OS; it allows you to change locations quickly for connecting to a network and/or the Internet.

Recent Items

This menu option combines the Recent Applications and Recent Documents options from Mac OS 9's Apple menu into one convenient menu. A Clear option allows you to reset the recent items from the menu.

Force Quit

Thanks to Mac OS X's protected memory, you don't have to restart the entire system if an application crashes or freezes. Instead, you can come here (or use Option-⌘-Esc) to open a window that lists the applications running on your system. To force-quit an application, simply click on the application name, then click on Force Quit.

Unlike applications, you cannot force-quit the Finder by Control-clicking on its icon in the Dock. Instead, you need to restart it from here. When you select the Finder, the Force Quit button changes to Relaunch; click this button to restart the Finder.

Sleep

Selecting this option will immediately put your Mac into sleep mode. This is different from the settings you dictate in System Preferences → Energy Saver for auto-sleep functionality. To "wake" your computer from sleep mode, simply press any key.

If you close the lid (or display) on your iBook or PowerBook while it is running, the computer will go into sleep mode. Opening your laptop will wake up your system automatically.

Restart

This will restart your Mac. If any applications are running, they will be automatically shut down, and you will be prompted to save changes for any files that were open.

Shutdown

This shuts your Mac down. You can also shut down your Mac by pressing the Power-On button, which will open a dialog box with the options for restarting, shutting down, or putting your Mac to sleep.

Log Out

This option logs you out of your system, taking you back to a login screen. The keyboard shortcut to log out is Shift-⌘-Q.

As you can see, Sleep, Restart, Shutdown, and Log Out have all moved from Mac OS 9's Special menu into Mac OS X's Apple menu. In addition, if you're looking for a menu option for Empty Trash—which also used to be in the Special menu—you need to be in the Finder (Finder→ Empty Trash, or Shift-⌘-Delete).

Think System Preferences, Not Control Panels

One of the most notable changes in Mac OS X is the Control Panels (⌘→ Control Panels) aren't in the Apple menu. The Control Panels of old are now replaced by System Preferences. Table 3-1 lists the Control Panels from Mac OS 9 and shows you their equivalents in Mac OS X.

Table 3-1. Mac OS 9's Control Panels and their disposition in Mac OS X

Mac OS 9 control panel	Equivalent in Mac OS X
Appearance	System Preferences → Desktop System Preferences → General
Apple Menu Options	System Preferences → General
AppleTalk	System Preferences → Network → AppleTalk
ColorSync	System Preferences → ColorSync
Control Strip	Gone; replaced by the Dock
Date & Time	System Preferences → Date & Time
DialAssist[a]	System Preferences → Network → Show → Internal Modem
Energy Saver[a]	System Preferences → Energy Saver
Extensions Manager	Gone. With Mac OS X, you no longer need to manage your extensions. To view the extensions on your system, launch the Apple System Profiler (*/Applications/Utilities*), and click on the Extensions tab.
File Exchange	Gone
File Sharing	System Preferences → Sharing
File Synchronization	Gone
General Controls	System Preferences → General
Infrared	System Preferences → Network → Show → infrared-port
Internet	System Preferences → Internet
Keyboard	System Preferences → Keyboard System Preferences → International → Input Menu
Keychain Access	Applications → Utilities → Keychain Access

Mac OS 9 control panel	Equivalent in Mac OS X
Launcher	Gone; replaced by the Dock
Location Manager	System Preferences → Network → Location (This only applies to network settings, unlike Location Manager.) → Location
Memory[a]	Gone
Modem[a]	System Preferences → Network → Show → Internal Modem
Monitors	System Preferences → Displays
Mouse	System Preferences → Mouse
Multiple Users[a]	System Preferences → Accounts
Numbers	System Preferences → International → Numbers
Password Security[a]	Available on new machines via open firmware
QuickTime Settings	System Preferences → QuickTime
Remote Access[a]	Applications → Internet Connect
Software Update	System Preferences → Software Update
Sound	System Preferences → Sound
Speech	System Preferences → Speech
Startup Disk	System Preferences → Startup Disk
TCP/IP	System Preferences → Network
Text	System Preferences → International → Language
Trackpad[a]	System Preferences → Mouse

[a] Not available under Classic.

See Chapter 5 for additional information about Mac OS X's System Preference panels.

Other Missing Items

Some other things you'll find missing from Mac OS X include:

Apple CD Audio Player
> This has been replaced by iTunes.

The Chooser
> To configure a printer in Mac OS X, you will need to use the Print Center (*/Applications/Utilities*). To connect to a server or another computer on your network, you will need to use Go → Connect to Server (⌘-K).
>
> The Chooser still exists for printing and networking from the Classic environment (described later).

Put Away (⌘-Y)
> This command had two functions: to eject a disk (floppy or CD), or to move an item out of the Trash back to its place of origin. Instead, ⌘-E can be used to eject a CD or unmount a networked drive.

On newer iBooks and PowerBooks, pressing the F12 key will eject a CD or DVD.

Graphing Calculator
> Gone; at present there is no equivalent replacement for Mac OS X.

Note Pad and SimpleText
> These have been replaced by the much more versatile TextEdit application. However, if you installed the Developer Tools, SimpleText can be found in */Developer/Applications/Extras*, but isn't available otherwise.

Scrapbook
> Gone; at present there is no equivalent replacement for Mac OS X.

SimpleSound
> This has been replaced by the Sound panel, which can be accessed from System Preferences → Sound → Alerts.

Now that we've shown you what's changed between Mac OS 9 and Mac OS X, it's time to learn more about Classic so you can run your Mac OS 9 applications *on top of* Mac OS X.

What Is Classic?

To help bridge the application gap between Mac OS 9 and Mac OS X, Apple has built a *virtual machine* that enables you to run older Mac software under Mac OS X in the Classic Environment, or just Classic. Classic is an emulator that looks and feels just like Mac OS 9, and, in fact, it is—just slightly watered down.

Classic allows you to run most older Mac applications on Mac OS X without requiring you to boot directly into Mac OS 9. The big difference is that Classic applications won't benefit from the features of Mac OS X, such as protected memory and its advanced printing capability. Meaning, if a Classic application crashes, it could bring down everything else running under Classic; just as a crash under Mac OS 9 could affect your entire system.

Additionally, some Control Panels (⌘ → Control Panels), such as Control Strip, Memory, and Remote Access, are disabled. However, if you boot into Mac OS 9 instead of Mac OS X, you will be using a full version of the OS. See the section "Dual-Booting with Mac OS 9" later in this chapter for details on how to choose your Startup Disk.

If you want Mac OS 9 and Mac OS X on separate partitions, you will need to partition your hard drive and reinstall both systems. In most cases, the biggest benefit to installing Mac OS 9 and Mac OS X on separate partitions is being able to choose which version of the OS to boot at startup by holding down the Option key. Otherwise, you can choose which OS to boot using the Startup Disk Control Panel (Mac OS 9) or System Preferences → Startup Disk (Mac OS X).

At the time of this writing (January, 2003), Apple will reportedly make it impossible for you to boot into Mac OS 9. This would mean that the only way you will be able to run Mac OS 9 applications on new Macintosh computers will be via Classic.

Until all Mac applications are Mac OS X–compliant, you will need to install a version of Mac OS 9 (9.2.2, to be exact) if you want to run older Mac applications. Most new Apple hardware will ship with Mac OS 9 and Mac OS X preinstalled on the same disk partition. However, the boxed release of Mac OS X Jaguar doesn't include a copy of Mac OS 9. If you find yourself in need of Classic, you can probably find a copy of Mac OS 9 on eBay at *http://www.ebay.com*. (Apple no longer sells this version of Mac OS.)

Starting Classic

When Classic is started, it doesn't actually boot Mac OS 9. Instead, it launches the Classic Startup process, found in */System/Library/CoreServices*. In turn, the Classic Startup process looks for a Mac OS 9 system folder on the system. If one is found, Classic will start; if not, you will receive an error message, letting you know that Classic cannot be started because there isn't a valid Mac OS 9 system folder on your computer.

There are three ways to launch Classic:

Launch a Classic application
> When you launch any Classic application (one of the three application flavors the Finder recognizes; see Chapter 2), Mac OS X will automatically start Classic if it isn't running already.

The Classic preferences panel
> Go to System Preferences → Classic → Stop/Start, and click on the Start button to launch Classic.

> The table view under "Select a system folder for Classic:" lists every disk or partition on the filesystem that holds a Mac OS 9 System Folder. (If you've gone the usual route of installing Mac OS 9 and Mac OS X on the same disk or partition, then you'll see just one choice here.)

Starting Classic when you log on
> Select the checkbox next to "Start Classic when you login" to have the Classic environment launch automatically when you log in to your account.

Savvy Unix users will quickly see that there's a fourth way to launch Classic: from the command line. If you launch the Terminal (*/Applications/Utilities*), you can launch the Classic Startup process (*Classic Startup.app*) by switching directories to */System/Library/CoreServices* and issuing either of the following commands:

```
% open Classic\ Startup.app
% open "Classic Startup.app"
```

Whichever route you take to launch the Classic Startup application, you'll see a window containing the virtual Mac's startup sequence, as shown in Figure 3-1.

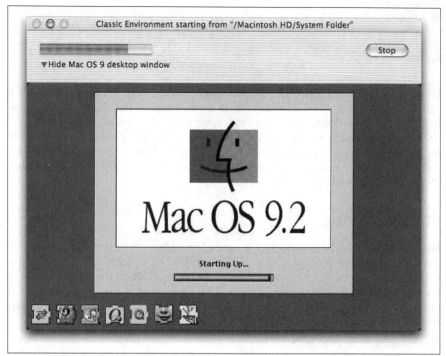

Figure 3-1. Classic Startup's window

While Classic is starting, you will see Classic's icon bouncing in the Dock; once Classic has finished loading, the icon will disappear. To verify that Classic is running, you can go to System Preferences → Classic → Start/Stop and look for a bolded message that says "Classic is running on /Macintosh HD/System Folder."

 If you would like a quicker way to launch Classic, there is a process that keeps the Classic icon in the Dock. As Classic is launching, Control-click on Classic's Dock icon and select "Keep In Dock" from its Dock menu. However, after Classic starts, its Dock icon won't have a black triangle beneath it, and its Dock menu offers only "Show In Finder" as an option (i.e., there is no option to Quit or Force Quit Classic from its Dock menu).

Controlling Classic

Classic's preference panel, shown in Figure 3-2, has three tabs, or panes, from which you can control its settings and monitor its activities. To launch the Classic preference panel, go to System Preferences → Classic.

The three tabbed panes found in the Classic preference panel include:

Start/Stop
>	This pane, shown in Figure 3-2, provides controls for starting, stopping, restarting, and force-quitting Classic. A bolded message near the top of this pane will let you know whether or not Classic is running, and the text box below it will look for and display a valid Mac OS 9 System Folder.

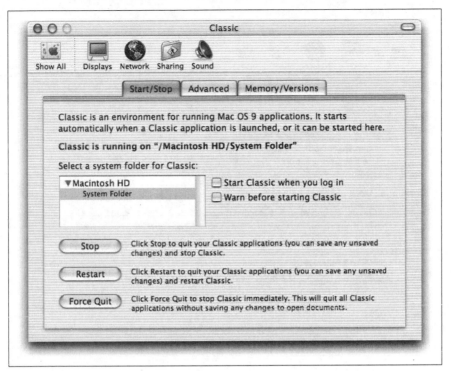

Figure 3-2. The Classic preference panel

OS 9, OS X, & Classic

Advanced

This pane, shown in Figure 3-3, gives you more granularity and control over how Classic will run on your system.

The controls found in the Advanced pane include:

Startup Options

This pop-up menu can be used to specify whether Mac OS 9's extensions will be turned off by default, or whether to open the Extension Manager as Classic starts up, which allows you to select which extensions to load. A third item in this menu is "Use Key Combination," which lets you specify a keyboard shortcut (up to five characters) for stopping and restarting Classic.

Restart Classic

When clicked, this button will restart Classic.

Use preferences from home folder

Selecting this checkbox will force Classic to use the preferences you've set for Mac OS X.

Sleep timer

This slider allows you to set the amount of time Classic is inactive before its process is put into sleep mode. By default, this is set to five minutes. Move the slider left or right to specify the delay before Classic will be put to sleep (from two minutes to never).

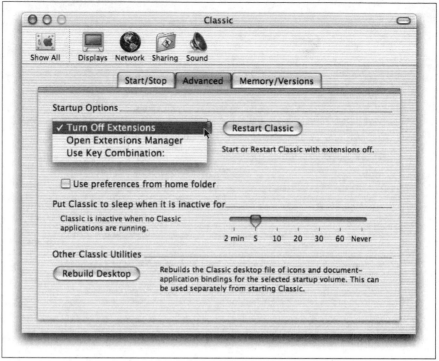

Figure 3-3. Classic's Advanced pane

> *Rebuild Desktop*
> For Mac OS 9 users, rebuilding the Desktop is something of a regular occurrence: once or twice a week you hold down Option-Command during the startup process to rebuild the desktop database. However, clicking this button will do the same thing for you, without forcing you to boot into Mac OS 9.

Memory/Versions
This pane, shown in Figure 3-4, lets you keep track of the processes running in the Classic environment.

By default, the checkbox next to "Show background processes" is unchecked. To view the Active Processes running under Classic, check this box. When Classic is running, there will always be two running processes: Classic Support and the Queue Watcher.

The bottom of this window shows details about the version and build of Classic, as well as the Mac OS version it's using.

Managing Classic Applications

Mac OS X's Finder manages your Classic applications just like any other; the only difference is that they are stored in */Applications (Mac OS 9)*, rather than */Applications*. When Classic is running, you won't work with the old Mac OS 9 Finder; however,

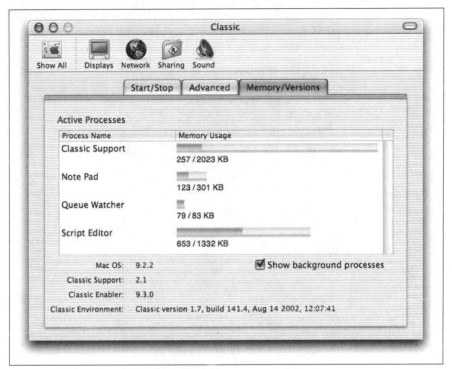

Figure 3-4. Classic's Memory/Versions pane

when a Classic application is running in the foreground, the menu bar changes to that of Mac OS 9. Similarly, the Dock provides space for the icons of Classic applications and even lets you keep them in the Dock.

You can easily identify a Classic application in the Dock, as its icon will have a Mac OS 9–style (32 × 32 pixel) icon, which will look "chunky" if viewed at a higher resolution.

Classic Applications and Memory

As mentioned earlier, Mac OS 9 applications don't benefit from Mac OS X's protected memory space or its dynamic memory allocation. In Classic, a Mac OS 9 application is still a Mac OS 9 application, requiring you to assign memory the old way: via the Get Info window. Figure 3-5 shows the Get Info window for Mac OS 9's Script Editor (*/Applications (Mac OS 9)/Apple Extras/AppleScript*).

The Memory section of the Info window (available only for Classic applications) lists the following three items:

Suggested Size
> This number represents the amount of RAM (in kilobytes) that the application's developers suggest to get optimum performance from the application. This number will always remain constant, and cannot be changed.

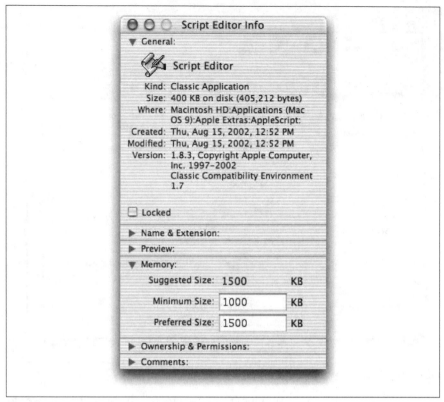

Figure 3-5. Mac OS 9's Script Editor's Info window, showing the Memory section

Minimum Size

> This field holds the minimum amount of memory the application needs before it can launch.

Preferred Size

> This field holds the amount of RAM that this application will use when it is running. By default, this number is set to match the applications' Suggested Size. You can make this number larger or smaller, but the Preferred Size shouldn't be smaller than the Minimum Size.

Normally, the only time you should modify these is if the Classic application in question complains about a lack of memory, either during runtime or by failing to launch altogether. For more information about memory allocation for Classic applications, see Chapter 5 of *Mac OS 9: The Missing Manual* (Pogue Press/ O'Reilly & Associates, Inc., 2000).

Using Classic Applications

Classic is unlike other OS emulators in that the emulated applications, though running in their own separate environment, visually integrate with the Mac OS X workspace. You use the Finder and the Dock with Classic application icons just as you would with any other.

Some concessions do have to be made, however, because Classic applications don't know how to interact at all with the Aqua environment. (If they did, they would be true Carbon applications and wouldn't rely on Classic.) While we certainly won't cover everything about Mac OS 9 applications here, we will cover some of the more noticeable differences you'll have to work with.

Classic's Menu Bar

As mentioned earlier, when a Classic application is running in the foreground, Mac OS X's menu bar is replaced with a Mac OS 9–style one, as shown in Figure 3-6.

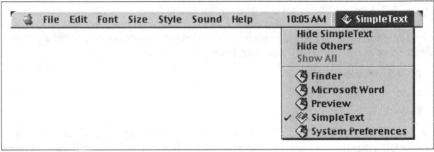

Figure 3-6. A typical Classic application's menu bar

Mac OS 9's menu bar is structurally quite different from Aqua's (which you'll see again as soon as you switch back to an Aqua application or click on the Desktop). Here's a brief rundown of what you'll find in Mac OS 9's menu bar:

- The rainbow-colored Apple menu contains the application's About box, as well as all the objects within */System Folder/Apple Menu Items* on the Classic startup volume, including a path to Mac OS 9's Control Panels.
- Standard application menus, such as File, Edit, and Help. Note the lack of a Mac OS X–style application menu here.
- The only menu extra you'll see when in Classic mode is the Clock.
- The application menu, which is located to the right of the Clock. Mac OS 9's application menu is entirely different from the one you'll find in Mac OS X. This menu contains a list of all active applications (including Aqua ones, as shown in Figure 3-6), and options for hiding the current or other applications, as well as a Show All option to unhide any hidden applications. As such, it mixes some of the functionality of Mac OS X's application menu and Dock.

One function that some Mac OS 9 users might miss while in Classic mode is the Applications palette, which you can get in Mac OS 9 by clicking on the Application menu and slowly dragging it away from the menu bar. While this works if you boot into Mac OS 9, it isn't available under Classic; however, you can still use the Dock to switch back and forth between running applications.

Classic Application Windows

Classic application windows use Mac OS 9's "Platinum" theme for their look, as shown in Figure 3-7.

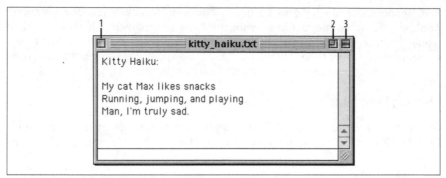

Figure 3-7. A typical Classic window (this is from SimpleText)

Most of their controls are analogous to Aqua windows; however, there are a few differences listed here as they appear, from left to right:

1. Close window button
2. Zoom window button
3. Windowshade button

The windowshade button collapses the window into its titlebar, which remains in place. Clicking this button again brings the full window back into view. Try as you might, you cannot minimize a Classic window to the Dock, as you can with the yellow minimize button on Aqua windows.

Some other oddities you'll find with Classic application windows include:

- Compared to Aqua applications, fewer document-centric Classic applications offer proxy icons in their titlebars, as noticed in Figure 3-7. When they do appear, however, you can use them in all the ways detailed in Chapter 1.

- Although they look different, Classic windows share the window stack with all open Aqua windows; however, they don't interleave. This means that when a Classic application is running in the foreground, all of its windows are in the foreground. If you bring an Aqua application to the front, either by its Dock icon or by clicking on one of its windows, that application comes to the foreground as well, and the Classic application windows are placed in the background.

- Classic applications also lack certain windowing features common to Mac OS X applications, such as sheets and drawers. Since Mac OS 9 doesn't use threaded processing, when a Classic application's dialog box appears, you cannot do anything else in Classic until you give the window the attention it deserves. (You can still step out and use other Aqua applications while Classic waits for a dialog box response, of course.)

The Dock and Classic

Active Classic applications' icons appear on your Dock like any other, and nearly all the tricks covered in Chapter 1 apply to them.

The biggest difference is that Classic icons on the Dock receive only a limited Dock menu, containing just the three basic items:

- Keep In Dock
- Show In Finder
- Quit (or Force Quit, if you hold down the Option key)

Noticeably missing in a Classic application's Dock menu is a listing of its open windows. Unlike Aqua applications where you can interleave windows, Classic forces you to bring all of its windows forward when you click on an application's Dock icon.

If a Classic application is running in the background (i.e., you're using an Aqua application in the foreground) and it needs your attention, its Dock icon won't bounce. Instead, the Classic application will interrupt what you're doing to display its dialog boxes.

Force-Quitting Classic Applications

Although they put on airs of equality with Aqua applications, appearing side by side with them in the Finder and on the Dock, Classic applications get much different treatment from Mac OS X.

The Process Viewer (*/Applications/Utilities*), or running *ps -awux* in the Terminal, reveals that Classic applications aren't given their own, separate Unix process ID, as with Cocoa and Carbon applications. All Classic applications run within the opacities of the *TruBlueEnvironment* process. (As mentioned earlier, if you want to see which Classic applications are running, go to System Preferences → Classic → Advanced, and look in the Active Processes window.)

Despite this, all active Classic applications still appear as choices in Mac OS X's Force Quit window (which you can make appear even when a Classic application is in the foreground by using the Option-⌘-Esc key combo).

Should you quit a Classic application this way, though, you run the risk of pulling down the entire Classic environment with it, especially if the application you are trying to force-quit has crashed. Mac OS 9's lack of memory protection means that applications can corrupt memory that belongs to other applications, or to the Classic system itself. The Force Quit window pops up a sheet to remind you of this whenever you attempt to force-quit a Classic application. (You can get around this warning by Control-Option-clicking the Classic application's Dock icon and selecting Force Quit there.) Before force-quitting a Classic application, you should save all your work in other active Classic applications, if you can.

Since it's just another Mac OS X application, if the whole Classic environment does crash, it doesn't affect any Classic or Carbon applications, or any other part of the Mac OS X system. You can just "Reboot" the Classic machine through the Classic preference pane, or by opening a Classic application from the Finder or Dock.

Printing from Classic

While we cover printing in Chapter 8, we note here that the interface for printing from a Classic application works entirely differently than printing from Aqua.

In Classic, as in Mac OS 9, you use an application called the Chooser to connect to file servers, manage printers, and perform other network-related tasks. In Classic, most of this is moot, since Mac OS X handles Classic's networking needs. However, if you want to print from a Classic application, you need to use the Chooser to select and configure a printer.

The Chooser, shown in Figure 3-8, can be found in the Apple menu of any Classic application (assuming that you haven't moved the Chooser icon out of */System Folder/Apple Menu Items*).

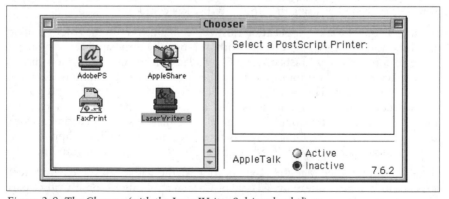

Figure 3-8. The Chooser (with the LaserWriter 8 driver loaded)

 If your printer driver isn't available, you need to boot into Mac OS 9 and install the printer's drivers (which you can usually download for free from the printer vendor's web site, if you don't have the printer's bundled software CD). Then restart and boot back into Mac OS X.

Use the following steps to configure your printer using the Chooser; these depend on the type of connection between your Mac and the printer:

USB (non-PostScript) Printers

These steps apply to USB-connected, non-PostScript printers, such as most inkjets or low-end laser printers.

1. With a Classic application active, choose → Chooser.

2. In the upper-left section of the Chooser, select your printer type.

3. In the field to the right, select the printer name or printer port (either may appear, depending on the printer driver).

4. Close the Chooser.

AppleTalk Printers

Follow these steps to connect to a printer available over a legacy AppleTalk network.

1. With a Classic application active, choose → Chooser.

2. In the upper-left section of the Chooser, select your printer type.

3. If AppleTalk Zones appear on your network, select one from the lower-left section of the Choose.

4. In the field to the right, select the printer by name.

5. Close the Chooser.

LPR or PostScript USB

These steps apply when connecting to a printer over TCP/IP, or to a USB-connected printer that uses PostScript.

1. Open the Desktop Printer Utility (*/Applications (Mac OS 9)/Utilities*).

2. Select the printer type "LPR" to connect to a printer via IP address, or "USB" to connect via direct USB connection.

3. Click OK.

4. Click the upper Change button to select a PPD file, and then click Select.

5. Click the lower Change button to select your printer. USB users choose the printer from a list. LPR users select the printer by entering its DNS name or IP address for the printer in the Printer Address field. Then click OK.

6. Click Create to make the printer connection.

Dual-Booting with Mac OS 9

There are times when you may need to use Mac OS 9 as an actual operating system, rather than just in Classic mode. In these situations, you can still opt to boot into Mac OS 9 by selecting a startup disk in the Startup Disk preferences panel (System Preferences → Startup Disk), shown in Figure 3-9.

To boot into Mac OS 9, select its system folder and click the Restart button. When your Mac restarts, and every time thereafter, it will boot into Mac OS 9. To reset your computer so it will boot into Mac OS X, you need to use Mac OS 9's Startup Disk Control panel (→ Control Panels → Startup Disk). As with the Mac OS X's

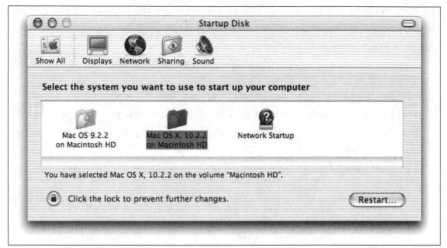

Figure 3-9. The Startup Disk preference panel

System Preferences panel, select Mac OS X's system folder and click Restart to boot back into Mac OS X.

If you have Mac OS X and Mac OS 9 installed on separate partitions (or drives), you can subvert the process of going through the System Preferences and Control panels by using the following startup keyboard shortcuts:

Option
> Holding down the Option key at startup opens the Startup Manager, which detects the System Folders on any partitions or drives connected to your Mac, allowing you to select which one to boot into.

T
> Holding down the "T" key at startup forces your Mac to boot from a connected FireWire drive if it finds a System Folder there. This option allows you to keep Mac OS 9 on an external drive, rather than on your internal drive.

> If you have two Macs connected to each other via FireWire and you hold down the "T" key while rebooting one Mac, its hard drive will mount as a FireWire drive on the other Mac.

X
> Holding down the "X" key at startup forces your Mac to boot into Mac OS X, even if Mac OS 9 is selected as the default startup disk.

4

Task and Setting Index

After rooting through all of the System Preferences and looking at the Applications and Utilities that come with Mac OS X, you'll quickly find that there are literally hundreds of ways to configure the settings for your system. Finding all these items in the interface can sometimes be a challenge.

This chapter provides a comprehensive listing of settings and tasks that can be performed with the System Preferences, Applications, Utilities, and from the command line in the Terminal application. In some cases, we've provided instructions for how to perform tasks using the GUI tools and by issuing Unix commands in the Terminal. It's up to you to decide which is faster or easier to use (but you're likely to realize quickly that the power of Unix is unmatchable by most GUI tools).

The tasks in this chapter are sorted alphabetically by their function, rather than by the application or utility name. Headings show major functional groupings (like "Accessibility" or "Display"). These group miscellaneous entries up until the next functional grouping.

This section provides shorthand instructions to help you configure and use your Mac OS X system as quickly as possible. Each task is presented as the answer to a "How do I..." question (for example, "How do I change the color depth of my display?"), followed by the shorthand way to execute the answer (e.g., System Preferences → Displays).

If you're new to Mac OS X, or if you just want to jog your memory when you can't quite remember where a particular setting is located, then this is the place to start.

Accessibility

Change the settings for a person with disabilities?
    System Preferences → Speech

    System Preferences → Universal Access

    System Preferences → Keyboard → Full Keyboard Access

Enable full keyboard access so I can navigate through and select menu items without using a mouse?

    System Preferences → Keyboard → Full Keyboard Access → select the checkbox next to "Turn on full keyboard access"

Enable Universal Access keyboard shortcuts?

    System Preferences → Universal Access → select the checkbox next to "Allow Universal Access Shortcuts"

Set the voice for my system?

    System Preferences → Speech → Default Voice → Voice

Change the rate at which the default voice speaks?

    System Preferences → Speech → Default Voice → Rate (move the slide control left or right to make the voice speak slower or faster, respectively; click on the Play button to test the speed)

Turn on speech recognition?

    System Preferences → Speech → Speech Recognition → On/Off → Apple Speakable Items is → On

View the speakable items?

    System Preferences → Speech → Speech Recognition → Open Speakable Items Folder

Where does an application store its speakable items?

    In ~/Library/Speech/Speakable Items/Application Speakable Items/application

Enable accessibility devices to be used with the system?

    System Preferences → Universal Access → select the checkbox next to "Enable access for assistive devices"

Change the display settings for person with a visual impairment?

    System Preferences → Universal Access → Seeing

Provide a visual alert cue for a user with a hearing impairment?

    System Preferences → Universal Access → Hearing → select the checkbox next to "Flash the screen whenever an alert sound occurs"

Place the scrollbar controls together so they're easier to access?

    System Preferences → General → Place scroll arrows → Together

Change the display from color to grayscale?

    System Preferences → Universal Access → Seeing → Set Display to Grayscale

Change the display so everything is white on black?

    System Preferences → Universal Access → Seeing → Switch to White on Black

Use the numeric keypad instead of the mouse?

    System Preferences → Universal Access → Mouse → Mouse Keys → On

Have the system "read" an email message to me?

    Select the text in the email message, or select all with Edit → Select All. Then go to Mail → Services → Speech → Start Speaking Text

Allow menu bar commands to be spoken and recognized?

    System Preferences → Speech → Commands → select the checkbox next to Menu Bar commands

Accounts and User Management

Add another user to the system?

    System Preferences → Accounts → New User (requires administrator privileges)

    Unix administrators might be tempted to use the *useradd*, *userdel*, and *usermod* commands to add, remove, and modify a user, respectively, from the Terminal. However, this isn't possible, since those commands don't exist on Mac OS X.

Remove a user from the system?

    System Preferences → Accounts → *username* → Delete User

    While logged in, you can't remove yourself from the system. If you want to remove your user account from the system, you will have to log out and log back in as another user.

Configuring my login?

    System Preferences → Accounts → Login Options

Change my login password?

    System Preferences → My Account My Password → Change

    System Preferences → Accounts → Users → *username* → Edit User

    Use the *passwd* command in the Terminal.

    When choosing a password, you should avoid using dictionary words (i.e., common, everyday words found in the dictionary) or something that could be easily guessed. To improve your security, we recommend that you choose an alphanumeric password. Remember, passwords are case-sensitive, so you can mix upper- and lowercase letters with your password as well.

Give a user administrator privileges?

    System Preferences → Accounts → Users → *username* → Edit User → Allow user to administer this computer (requires administrator privileges)

Restrict which applications a user can use?

    System Preferences → Accounts → Users → *username* → Capabilities. Click on the checkbox next to "Use only these applications," and then use the lower-half of the window to pick and choose which applications the user can have access to.

    Keep this in mind if you have a user you'd like to restrict from issuing Unix commands. You can cut off their access to using the Terminal application by clicking the disclosure triangle next to Utilities, and then unchecking the box next to the Terminal.

Keep a user from changing his password?

    System Preferences → Accounts → Users → *username* → Capabilities; uncheck the box next to Change password

Turn off automatic login?
> System Preferences → Accounts → uncheck the box next to "Log in automatically as *username*"

On a multiuser system, specify which user will be automatically logged on?
> System Preferences → Accounts → Users → *username* → Set Auto Login... → enter the user's password and click the OK button

Require users to type their username and password when logging in?
> System Preferences → Accounts → Login Options → Display Login Window As → select the radio button next to "Name and password"

Allow a user to log into my Mac from a Windows system?
> System Preferences → Sharing → Services; check the box next to Windows File Sharing

Set a password hint?
> System Preferences → Accounts → *username* → Edit User; select the text in the Password Hint field, type in a new hint, and click OK to accept the change

Find out which users have admin privileges?
> System Preferences → Accounts; users with administrator privileges will have Admin next to their name in the Type column.
>
> Launch NetInfo Manager (*/Applications/Utilities*). In the Directory Browser pane, select / → groups → admin. In the lower-half of the window, look at the Property value next to users; you will see something like (root, *username*) in the Value(s) column. (Requires administrator privileges.)

Add a new group?
> Launch NetInfo Manager (*/Applications/Utilities*), and follow these steps:
>
> 1. Click on the padlock icon in the lower-left corner of the window, and enter the administrator's password. This will allow you to make changes.
> 2. In the Directory Browser pane, select / → groups.
> 3. From the menu bar, go to Directory → New Subdirectory (⌘-N). (Requires administrator privileges.)
> 4. In the Directory pane below, select the new_directory name by double-clicking on it, and type in a new group name (e.g., *editorial*) and press Return.
> 5. Go to Domain → Save Changes. A message window will appear, asking if you want to save the changes; click on the "Update this copy" button. The name of the new group will appear in the Directory Browser pane.
> 6. Click on the padlock to prevent further changes from being made, and quit NetInfo Manager.

 As with the user-related Unix commands, Unix users will notice that the various group commands (*groupadd*, *groupdel*, *groupmod*, *gpasswd*, *grpconv*, and *grpunconv*) are missing from Mac OS X. You will need to use NetInfo Manager to manage groups.

Enable the root user account?
> Follow these steps to enable the root user account from NetInfo Manager:
>
> 1. Launch NetInfo Manager.
> 2. To make changes to the NetInfo settings, click on the padlock in the lower-left corner of the NetInfo window. You will be asked for the administrator's name and password; enter those, and click OK.

3. In the menu bar, select Security → Enable Root User.

4. You will be asked to enter a password for the root user. In earlier versions of Mac OS X, the root password had to be eight characters or less; however, in Jaguar, the root password must only be more than five characters in length.

5. Click OK, and then enter the password again to confirm the password for the root user account. Click on the Verify button to confirm the password and enable the root account.

6. If you have no further changes to make in NetInfo Manager, click on the padlock at the lower-left of the window to prevent further changes from being made, and quit the application (⌘-Q).

7. To enable the root user account using the Terminal, enter the following command:

```
[macchuck:~] chuck% sudo passwd root
Password: *******
Changing password for root.
New password: ********
Retype new password: ********
[macchuck:~] chuck%
```

The first time you're asked for a password, enter your own. Once you're verified by the system to have administrator privileges, you will be asked to enter and confirm a new password for the root user account.

The asterisks shown in this example won't appear onscreen when you enter the passwords; actually, nothing will happen onscreen. If you make a mistake while entering the password, you can always hit the Backspace or Delete key to go back over what you typed; then just re-enter the password.

Once the root account has been assigned a password, you can use it to log in with the username *root*.

Restrict a non-admin user to using the Simple Finder?
System Preferences → Accounts → Users → *username* → Capabilities → select the checkbox next to Use Simple Finder

AirPort

Find the MAC address for my AirPort card?
System Preferences → Network → TCP/IP; the Airport ID should appear at the lower-left of the panel

System Preferences → Network → AirPort; the AirPort ID should appear at the top of that window

Applications → Utilities → Apple System Profiler → System Profile tab → Network Overview section → Airport → Ethernet address

Configure an AirPort Base Station?
Applications → Utilities → AirPort Admin Utility

Configure my AirPort settings for wireless networking?
Follow the steps for connecting to an Ethernet network first, and then use the AirPort Setup Assistant (*/Applications/Utilities*). The settings you've applied for your regular network will be applied to your AirPort settings.

Quickly switch to an AirPort network after disconnecting the Ethernet cable from my iBook?

System Preferences → Network → Show → Active Network Ports. Click on the checkboxes next to the network ports you want to enable, and drag the ports in the list to place them in the order in which you're most likely to connect to them. (The Automatic location should do this for you, but it doesn't always work.)

Share my modem or Ethernet connection with other AirPort-equipped Macs?

System Preferences → Sharing → Internet panel; click on the Start button to turn Internet sharing on.

Display the AirPort strength meter in the menu bar?

System Preferences → Network → AirPort → select the checkbox next to "Show AirPort status in menu bar"

Enable a computer to set up AirPort networks?

System Preferences → Network → AirPort → select the checkbox next to "Allow this computer to create networks"

AppleScript

Find out which version of AppleScript I'm using?

Applications → AppleScript → select the Script Editor → ⌘-I (or File → Get Info)

Enable the Script Menu in the menu bar?

Applications → AppleScript → double-click on "Script Menu.menu"

Remove the Script Menu from the menu bar?

Command-click on the icon and drag it off the menu bar

Locate the scripts found in the Script menu?

Finder → Macintosh HD → Library → Scripts

Create a place for my AppleScripts in the Script menu?

Save your scripts to ~/Library/Scripts

Go to the Scripts folder (/Library/Scripts) and create a new folder (File → New Folder) to place your scripts in

Find out which Scripting Additions are on my system?

Look in /Library/ScriptingAdditions

Background Images

Change my Desktop image?

System Preferences → Desktop

Control-click on the Desktop itself and select Change Desktop Background from the context menu

Have the pictures on my Desktop change automatically?

System Preferences → Desktop → Click on the checkbox next to "Change picture" and select an interval from the pull-down menu.

Use one of the Mac OS 9 background images for my Desktop instead of the (boring) ones that come with Mac OS X?

System Preferences → Desktop → Collection → Choose Folder. A Finder sheet will slide down; use this to navigate to Mac OS 9 System Folder → Appearance → Desktop Pictures. Then select one of the following folders, and click the Choose button: 3D Graphics, Convergency, Ensemble Photos, or Photos. The images in that directory will appear as part of your Desktop Collection.

Add a new background pattern, making it available to all users?
   Create or save the image to either the Abstract, Nature, or Solid Colors folder in
   /Library/Desktop Pictures

Change the background of a Finder window to a different color or to an image?
   Finder → View → as Icons; then use View → Show View Options (⌘-J); select
   either Color or Picture for the Background option

Classic

Find out what version of Mac OS 9 I'm running?
   In the Classic environment, use → Apple System Profiler → System Profile
   panel; look in the System overview section.

See whether Classic is running?
   System Preferences → Classic → Start/Stop; look for a bolded message that says
   "Classic is not running" or "Classic is running on...(path to Mac OS 9's System
   Folder)"

Launch Classic?
   System Preferences → Classic → Start/Stop → click on the Start button

Quit Classic?
   System Preferences → Classic → Start/Stop → click on the Stop button

Restart Classic?
   System Preferences → Classic → Start/Stop → click on the Restart button

   System Preferences → Classic → Advanced → click on the Restart Classic button

Set a keyboard shortcut for starting and restarting Classic?
   System Preferences → Classic → Advanced → Startup Options → select "Use Key
   Combination:" from the pop-up menu and enter a keyboard shortcut (up to five
   keys) in the text field

Keep the Classic icon in the Dock?
   Control-click on the Classic icon while Classic is starting up and select Keep In
   Dock from its context menu

Start Classic automatically when I start up my computer?
   System Preferences → Classic → Start/Stop → select the checkbox next to "Start
   Classic when you log in"

Rebuild Classic/Mac OS 9's Desktop without booting into Mac OS 9?
   System Preferences → Classic → Advanced → click on the Rebuild Desktop button

See how much memory a Classic application is using?
   System Preferences → Classic → Memory/Versions → Active Processes

Allocate memory to a Classic application?
   Finder → Select the drive or partition → Applications (Mac OS 9) → Select the
   application icon → File → Get Info → Memory → Change the value for Preferred
   Size to a larger number

View the background processes running under Classic?
   System Preferences → Classic → Memory/Versions → select the checkbox next to
   "Show background processes"

Configure a printer so I can print from a Classic app?
   From Mac OS 9's → Chooser → select the printer

Colors

Find the 8-bit hexadecimal value for a color from an image?
> Open the image with Preview (*/Applications*) → Launch DigitalColor Meter (*/Applications/Utilities*) → select "RGB As Hex Value, 8-bit" from the pull-down menu → move the mouse pointer over an area in the image → Shift-⌘-H (for Hold Color) holds the RGB value in the application window

Copy an RGB color value from an image and paste it into an HTML document?
> Open the image with Preview → Launch DigitalColor Meter → select "RGB A Hex Value, 8-bit" from the pull-down menu → move the mouse pointer over an area in the image → Shift-⌘-C (for Copy Color) → switch to the text editor you're using to edit the HTML page → ⌘-P to paste in the hex value (e.g., "#2C61B9")

Date and Time

Change the date/time?
> System Preferences → Date & Time → Date & Time

Specify how the date and time will appear in the menu bar?
> System Preferences → Date & Time → Menu Bar Clock

Specify the date and time settings for another country while I'm traveling?
> To change the date: System Preferences → International → Date panel → select a country from the Region pull-down menu
>
> To change the time: System Preferences → International → Time panel → select a country from the Region pull-down menu

Use a network time server to set my clock's time?
> System Preferences → Date & Time → Network Time → click on the checkbox next to "Use a network time server" → select an NTP Server in the scroll list → click on the Set Time Now button

 You must be connected to the Internet to use a network time server. One helpful hint is to first use the network time server to set an accurate time for your system, then uncheck the "Use a network time server" box.

Set my time zone?
> System Preferences → Date & Time → Time Zone

Display the current date and time from the command line?
> Use the *date* command:
>
> ```
> [macchuck:~] chuck% date
> Mon Nov  4 15:34:25 EST 2002
> ```

Display the time in military time?
> System Preferences → Date & Time → Menu Bar Clock → select the checkbox next to "Use a 24-hour clock"

Disks

Find out how much disk space I have left?

Applications → Utilities → Disk Utility → select hard drive or partition (e.g., Macintosh HD) → Information

Launch the Finder and look in the status bar, just below the toolbar. You will see something that says how many items are in that directory, and how much space is available on your hard drive.

In the Finder, select the the hard drive icon in the Computer view and select File → Get Info (⌘-I).

Issue the *df -k* command in the Terminal

Find out whether a drive is formatted with HFS?

Applications → Utilities → Disk Utility → Select the drive or partition → Information

Create a disk image?

Launch Disk Copy (*/Applications/Utilities*), then go to File → New → Blank Image (⌘-N). Enter a name for the disk image in the "Save as" field (a *.dmg* extension will be appended), select where you would like it saved to, enter a name for the volume, its size and format, and choose whether the disk image will be encrypted or not. Click the Create button to create the disk image, which will be mounted on your Desktop. Double-click on the disk image to open its Finder window, then drag and drop the items you would like included in the disk image, close the Finder window, and Eject the image (⌘-E) to complete the process.

To create a disk image from an actual disk, such as your hard drive or a CD, choose File → New → Image from Device (Option-⌘-I) or Image from Folder or Volume (⌘-I). Specify the details for the disk image and where you would like it to be saved, and then click the Image button.

Display the contents of a shared folder on another volume in my network?

Finder → *volume* → *folder*

From your home directory in the Terminal:

```
[macchuck:~] chuck% ls -la /Volumes/volume/folder
```

Partition a new hard drive?

Applications → Utilities → Disk Utility → Select the new drive → Partition

Partition an existing drive?

Follow these steps:

1. Back everything up, because partitioning the drive requires a reinstall of the system and reformatting of the hard drive (don't skip this step).

2. Insert the Mac OS X installation CD.

3. Restart the computer and hold down the C key to boot from the CD.

4. Select Installer → Disk Utility.

5. Select the hard drive and specify the partition sizes, names, and the format of the partition (HFS+ is recommended).

6. Click on the Partition button.

7. When that's completed, finish installing Mac OS X and then load your data back on from the backup.

Unmount an external drive or partition?
    Drag the disk icon from the Desktop to the Trash

    Applications → Utilities → Disk Utility → select the drive or partition → Options → Unmount (this may require you to enter the administrator's password)

Erase a CD-RW disc or hard drive?
    Applications → Utilities → Disk Utility → select the CD or disk → Erase

Create a RAID (redundant array of independent disks) for my system?
    Applications → Utilities → Disk Utility → select the drives → RAID

Hide the hard disk (or partition) icons on my Desktop?
    Finder → Preferences → Show these items on the Desktop → uncheck the box next to "Hard disks"

Display

Change my Desktop size/resolution, or the color depth of my display?
    System Preferences → Displays → Display panel

Get a menu extra in the menu bar for changing my display's settings?
    System Preferences → Displays → select the checkbox next to "Show displays in menu bar"

Configure the settings for a second monitor?
    System Preferences → Displays → Detect Displays

    Click on the Displays icon in the menu bar → Detect Displays

Change the display from color to grayscale?
    System Preferences → Universal Access → Seeing → click on the "Set Display to Grayscale" button

Enlarge the display?
    System Preferences → Universal Access → Turn On Zoom → use Option-⌘-+ to zoom in and Option-⌘- – to zoom out

The Dock

Change the Dock's preferences?
    ⌘ → Dock → Dock Preferences

    System Preferences → Dock

    Control-click on the Dock's divider bar and select Dock Preferences from the context menu.

Quickly resize the Dock without launching its System Preferences panel?
    Place the mouse over the divider bar in the Dock; the pointer will change from an arrow to a horizontal bar with arrows pointing up and down. Click on the divider bar and move the mouse up or down to make the Dock larger or smaller, respectively.

Add a program to the Dock?
    Drag and drop an application's icon in the Dock from a Finder window.

    After launching an application that isn't normally in the Dock, Control-click on that application's icon, and select "Keep in Dock" from the pop-up menu.

Remove a program from the Dock?
Drag the application icon from the Dock, and drop it anywhere.

Change the Dock's location from the bottom of the screen to the left or right side?
System Preferences → Dock → Position on screen (Left or Right)

 → Dock → Position on (Left or Right)

Control-click on the Dock's divider and select Position on screen → (Left or Right)

Shift-click on the Dock's divider and move the pointer to the left or right edge of the screen

Control the magnification of icons in the Dock?
System Preferences → Dock → Magnification

 → Dock → Turn Magnification (On/Off)

Control-click the Dock's divider and select Turn Magnification (On/Off)

Make it so the Dock hides when I'm not using it?
Option-⌘-D

System Preferences → Dock → Automatically hide and show the Dock

 → Dock → Turn Hiding (On/Off)

Control-click the Dock's divider and select Turn Hiding (On/Off)

Stop application icons from bouncing when a program is launched?
System Preferences → Dock → Animate opening applications

Files and Folders

Create a new folder?
File → New Folder (in the Finder)

Control-click → New Folder (in a Finder window or on the Desktop)

Shift-⌘-N

In earlier versions of the Mac OS, ⌘-N was used to create new folders; now ⌘-N is used for opening a new Finder window.

Rename a file or folder?
Click once on the icon and hit Return, type in the new name, and then hit Return to accept the new name.

Click once on the icon, and then click once on the name of the file to highlight it (or press Return). Type in the new name for the file or folder, and hit Return to accept the new name.

Click on the icon, and then use ⌘-I to open the Get Info window. Click on the disclosure triangle next to Name & Extension, and enter the new file or directory name.

In the Terminal, use the following command:

```
[macchuck:~] chuck% mv myFile.txt yourFile.txt
```

The *mv* command will change the name of *myFile.txt* to *yourFile.txt*.

Change the program associated with a particular extension?

Click on a file, and then use File → Get Info (or ⌘-I). Click on the disclosure triangle next to "Open with" and select one of the applications from the pull-down menu, or choose Other to select a different program. If you want to specify that application as the default for opening files with that particular extension, click the Change All; otherwise, close the Info window to save the changes.

Change the permissions for a file or directory?

Click on a file or directory, and then use File → Get Info (or ⌘-I). Click on the disclosure triangle next to "Ownership & Privileges" to change the access for the Owner, Group, and Others.

Use the *chmod* command. To learn more about *chmod* and its options, see its manpage (*man chmod*).

Copy a file to the Desktop instead of moving it or creating a shortcut?

Select the file, then Option-drag the icon to the Desktop (notice a plus sign will appear next to the pointer in a green bubble), and release the mouse button.

In the Finder, select the file → Edit → Copy *filename* → Home → double-click on the Desktop icon → Edit → Paste item.

Find out where an open file exists in the filesystem?

Command-click on the proxy icon in the titlebar. This will pop open a context menu, showing you where the file exists. Selecting another item (such as a hard drive or a folder) from the proxy icon's context menu will open a Finder window taking you to that location.

Quickly create a directory and a set of numbered directories (such as for chapters in a book)?

```
[macchuck:~] chuck% mkdir -p NewBook/{ch}{01,02,03,04,05}
[macchuck:~] chuck% ls -F NewBook
ch01/ ch02/ ch03/ ch04/ ch05/
```

Try doing that in the Finder—you can't! After issuing the first command, *ls -F NewBook* is used to list the folders within the *NewBook* directory, which shows us that five separate subdirectories have been created.

Quickly delete a directory (and its subdirectories) without sending it to Trash?

Issue the following command in the Terminal:

```
[macchuck:~] chuck% rm -rf directory_name
```

Make the Trash stop asking me if I'm sure I want to delete every file?

Finder → Preferences; uncheck the option next to "Show warning before emptying the Trash"

Empty the trash of locked items?

Shift-Option-⌘-Delete. The addition of the Option key forces the deletion of the contents of Trash.

Give a file or folder a custom icon?

Open an image file, and copy it with ⌘-C. Select the icon → File → Get Info (⌘-I). Select the file icon in the General section, and then paste (⌘-V) in the new image.

 The proper image size for an icon is 128 × 128 pixels.

Quickly create an alias of an open file, or move it, depending on the app (e.g., Word)?

Click and drag the file's proxy icon to a new location (i.e., the Desktop, Dock, Finder, etc.). The file must first be saved and named before an alias can be created.

 Dragging a folder's proxy icon from a Finder window's titlebar will move that folder to the new location instead of creating an alias. If you want to create an alias for a folder, you should select the folder in the Finder, then Option-⌘-drag the folder to where you'd like the alias to be. As a visual cue to let you know you're creating an alias, the mouse pointer will change to a curved arrow.

Finder

Hide the Finder toolbar?

View → Hide Toolbar (⌘-B)

Click on the transparent button in the upper-right corner of the titlebar.

Customize the Finder toolbar?

Finder → View → Customize Toolbar

Shift-click the toolbar button.

Control-click within the toolbar and select Customize Toolbar from the context menu.

Shift-clicking on the toolbar button again will close the Customize Toolbar window and return you to the previous Finder View.

Always open the Finder in Column View?

Finder → Preferences → select the checkbox next to "Open new windows in Column View"

From Icon View, open a folder in a new Finder window?

Command-double-click the folder icon.

Force folders to open in a new Finder window when they're double-clicked?

Hide the Finder toolbar (only works in Icon or List View).

Quickly switch to my home directory?

Go → Home (Shift-⌘-H)

Quickly go back or forward in a Finder view?

Use ⌘-[or ⌘-] to go back or forward, respectively.

 This also works in most web browsers, including Internet Explorer, Netscape Communicator, Mozilla, and Chimera.

Only show the icons or text labels of items in the toolbar?

View → Customize Toolbar → Show; select Icon Only or Text Only from the pull-down menu

Control-click on the toolbar and select Icon Only Mode or Text Only Mode from the context menu.

Speed up Finder searches?
> Open the Finder's preferences panel (Finder → Preferences). Click on the Select button at the bottom of the window; this pops open a window that lets you select the languages to use when searching a files' contents. The fewer languages you select here, the faster your search.

Locate a specific folder in the Finder?
> Go → Go to Folder (or ⌘-~)

Where is the database file saved for use with context searches from the Finder?
> It is saved in ~/Library/Indexes/FindByContent/00001/.FBCIndex.

Fonts and Font Management

Share fonts with other users on my system?
> If you are the administrator, move the font from /Users/username/Library/Fonts to /Library/Fonts.

Where can I store new fonts I've purchased or downloaded from the Internet?
> Save them to /Users/username/Library/Fonts for your personal use, or to /Library/Fonts to allow everyone on the system access to them.

Why aren't my bitmap fonts working?
> Mac OS X does not support bitmapped fonts—it supports only TrueType, Open-Type, and PostScript Level 1 fonts.

Make my Mac OS X fonts available in Classic Applications?
> Open two Finder windows. In Window #1, go to Mac OS 9 → System Folder → Fonts; in Window #2, go to Mac OS X → Library → Fonts. In Window #2, select all of the Fonts (⌘-A), then Option-drag the Mac OS X fonts into the Mac OS 9 Fonts folder in Window #1.

What does the .dfont extension mean on some of my Mac OS X fonts?
> The extension stands for "Data Fork TrueType Font." Basically, this just tells you that this is a TrueType font.

Turn off font antialiasing?
> You can't, but you can adjust the minimum font size to be affected by font smoothing in System Preferences → General → "Turn off text smoothing for font sizes x and smaller" (8 points is the default setting).

Create a Font Collection?
> In TextEdit, go to Format → Font → Font Panel (⌘-T), and select Edit Collection from the pull-down menu at the bottom of the window. The title on the window will change to "Font – Collections." Click on the plus sign (+) at the lower-left to add a new item in the Collections column; double-click on the name (New-1), enter a different name (such as BookFonts), and hit Return. Select a font in the All Families column, and then click on the << button to add that typeface to your Family column. When you have added all of the fonts, click on the Done button.

Where are my Font Collections stored, in case I want to share them with another user?
> They are stored in /Users/username/Library/FontCollections.
>
> If you want to share a collection, place a copy of the collection in the Shared folder. All font collections have a .fcache file extension.

Groups

Add a group?
> See "Accounts and User Management."

Internet, Web, and Email

Change the default email client and web browser from Mail and Internet Explorer, respectively?

To select a different email client, go to System Preferences → Internet → Email panel, and choose a different client in the Default Email Reader pull-down menu.

To select a different web browser, go to System Preferences → Internet → Web panel, and choose a different browser in the Default Web Browser pull-down menu.

Specify where files downloaded from the Internet will be saved?

System Preferences → Internet → Web panel. Click on the Select button next to "Download Files To."

Change my browser's default home page?

System Preferences → Internet → Web; enter the new URL in the Home Page text box.

Turn on web sharing?

System Preferences → Sharing → Services pane; click on the checkbox next to Personal Web Sharing to start this service. Enabling this service will allow others to access your Sites folder (*/Users/username/Sites*) from the Internet.

Register my license number for QuickTime Pro?

System Preferences → QuickTime; click on the Registration button and enter your license number.

Listen to an Internet radio station?

Dock → iTunes → Radio Tuner; click on the Radio Tuner option in the Source pane to the left, and the right pane will change to show you a list of different music genres from which to choose. Click on the disclosure triangle next to a music type to reveal the available stations.

Use my own stylesheet for viewing web pages in Internet Explorer?

Internet Explorer → Explorer → Preferences → Web Browser → Web Content; select the checkbox next to "Use my style sheet," then click on the Select Style Sheet button, and then locate and select the Cascading Style Sheet (CSS) you want to apply.

Connect to an FTP site?

Finder → Go → Connect to Server (⌘-K) → enter the address for the FTP site (e.g., *ftp://ftp.oreilly.com*), and it will mount on your Desktop

Create shortcuts on my Desktop for web sites I visit often, or for people I email frequently?

Open the TextEdit application, and enter a URL (such as *http://www.oreilly.com*) or an email address (such as *chuckdude@mac.com*), then triple-click on the address to select the entire line and drag that to your Desktop. This creates an icon on your Desktop for whatever you drag there. When you double-click on the icon, your default web browser will open that URL, or your email client will create a new message window with the address specified by the shortcut.

You can take this a step further by adding these shortcuts to your Favorites folder (open the Finder and click on the Favorites heart icon in the toolbar, or press ⌘-T).

.Mac Accounts

Set up a .Mac account?
    System Preferences → Internet → .Mac → Sign Up (you must be connected to the Internet to set up a .Mac account)

Find out how much space I have available on my iDisk?
    System Preferences → Internet → iDisk

Require a password from others before they can access my iDisk's Public folder?
    System Preferences → Internet → iDisk; click on the checkbox next to "Use a Password to Protect your Public Folder," and then click on the Password button to set a password

Menu Extras

Remove a menu extra from the menu bar?
    Command-click on the icon and drag it off the menu bar.

Switch the position of a menu extra with another?
    Command-click on the icon and drag it left or right; the other menu extra icons will move out of the way, giving you room to drop the icon where you want it to be.

Change the settings for the clock's menu extra?
    System Preferences → Date & Time → Menu Bar Clock

    Click on the clock menu extra → View as (Icon/Text)

Remove the clock from the menu bar?
    Command-drag the clock off the menu bar.

    System Preferences → Date & Time → Menu Bar Clock → deselect the checkbox next to "Show the date and time in the menu bar"

Add a menu extra to show the status of my iBook's battery?
    System Preferences → Energy Saver → select the checkbox next to "Show battery status in the menu bar"

    In the Finder, go to */System/Library/CoreServices/Menu Extras* and double-click on the *Battery.menu* folder.

Add a menu extra for controlling the displays connected to my Mac?
    System Preferences → Displays → select the checkbox next to "Show displays in menu bar"

    In the Finder, go to */System/Library/CoreServices/Menu Extras* and double-click on the *Displays.menu* folder.

Add an AirPort menu extra?
    System Preferences → Network → AirPort → select the checkbox next to "Show AirPort status in menu bar"

    In the Finder, go to */System/Library/CoreServices/Menu Extras* and double-click on the *AirPort.menu* folder.

Add a menu extra for the different keyboard language types?
    System Preferences → International → Input Menu → select the languages you would like to turn on by clicking on their checkboxes

Access the Character Palette from the menu bar?
System Preferences → International → Input Menu → select the checkbox next to "Character Palette" to make this accessible through the Input Menu

Add an eject button for my CD/DVD drive to the menu bar?
In the Finder, go to */System/Library/CoreServices/Menu Extras* and double-click on the *Eject.menu* folder.

Add a sound control to the menu bar?
System Preferences → Sound → select the checkbox next to "Show volume in menu bar"

In the Finder, go to */System/Library/CoreServices/Menu Extras* and double-click on the *Volume.menu* folder.

Get that little lock icon in my menu bar for quickly locking and unlocking my keychain?
Applications → Utilities → Keychain Access → View → Show Status in Menu Bar

Control-click on Keychain Access (*/Applications/Utilities*) → select "Show Package Contents" → change the Finder view to Column View (⌘-3) → Contents → Resources → double-click on the *Keychain.menu* folder

Add the Script Menu to the menu bar?
In the Finder, go to */Applications/AppleScript* and double-click on the *Script Menu.menu* folder.

Add a menu extra for iChat?
iChat (*/Applications*) → Preferences → Accounts → Status Settings → click on the checkbox next to "Show status in menu bar"

In the Finder, go to */System/Library/CoreServices/Menu Extras* and double-click on the *iChat.menu* folder.

Add a menu extra for Bluetooth?
System Preferences → Bluetooth → Settings → select the checkbox next to "Show Bluetooth status in the menu bar"

In the Finder, go to */System/Library/CoreServices/Menu Extras* and double-click on the *Bluetooth.menu* folder.

Display the modem status in the menu bar?
System Preferences → Network → Show → Internal Modem → Modem → select the checkbox next to "Show modem status in menu bar"

In the Finder, go to */System/Library/CoreServices/Menu Extras* and double-click on the *PPP.menu* folder.

Add a menu extra for my PPPoE (Point-to-Point Protocol over Ethernet) connection?
System Preferences → Network → PPPoE → select the checkbox next to "Show PPPoE status in menu bar"

In the Finder, go to */System/Library/CoreServices/Menu Extras* and double-click on the *PPPoE.menu* folder.

Add a menu extra for use with an infrared port?
In the Finder, go to */System/Library/CoreServices/Menu Extras* and double-click on the *IrDA.menu* folder.

Add a menu extra for viewing the status of the PCMCIA card in my PowerBook?
In the Finder, go to */System/Library/CoreServices/Menu Extras* and double-click on the *PCCard.menu* folder.

Mice, Trackpads, and Scrollwheel Mice

Change the double-click speed of my mouse?
System Preferences → Mouse → Mouse panel

Change the scrolling speed for my scrollwheel mouse?
System Preferences → Mouse → Mouse panel → Scrolling Speed

Change the settings on my iBook's trackpad so it can emulate mouse clicks?
System Preferences → Mouse → Trackpad panel → Use trackpad for (Clicking, Dragging, Drag Lock)

Modems and Dial-Up Networking

Configure a modem for dialing into my ISP?
System Preferences → Network, and follow these steps:

1. Select New Location from the Location pull-down menu. Enter a name for the new location (for example, My ISP), and click OK.
2. Select Internal Modem from the Show pull-down menu.
3. In the TCP/IP panel, select Using PPP from the Configure pull-down menu.
4. Fill in the blanks on the PPP panel.
5. Select your modem type from the Modem panel.
6. Click the Apply Now button.

Show the modem status in the menu bar?
System Preferences → Network → select Internal Modem from the Show pull-down menu → Modem pane → click on the checkbox next to "Show modem status in menu bar"

Make sure my modem is working?
Applications → Utilities → Internet Connect

Set my computer to wake up from sleep mode when the modem rings?
System Preferences → Energy Saver → Options → Wake Options → click on the checkbox next to "Wake when the modem detects a ring"

Find out the speed of my dial-up connection?
Applications → Utilities → Internet Connect; the bottom section of the window tells you the speed of your connection.

Disable call waiting on my phone when using the modem?
System Preferences → Network → PPP; insert *70 at the beginning of the telephone number you're dialing (e.g., *70, 1-707-555-1212).

Where are my modem configuration files stored?
They are stored in /Library/Modem Scripts.

Specify how many times my modem will redial if it detects a busy signal?
System Preferences → Network → Show → Internal Modem → PPP panel → PPP Options → Session Options

Networking

Find the MAC (media access control) address for my Ethernet card?
Finder → Applications → Utilities → Apple System Profiler → System Profile → Network Overview → Built-in → Ethernet address

System Preferences → Network → TCP/IP panel; toward the bottom of the window, look for a sequence of numbers and letters next to Ethernet Address

Configure my system to connect to an Ethernet network?

Go to System Preferences → Network, and follow these steps:

1. Select New Location from the Location pull-down menu. Enter a name for the new location (for example, ORA-Local), and click OK.

2. Select Built-in Ethernet from the Show pull-down menu.

3. From the Configure pull-down menu in the TCP/IP panel, select Using DHCP if your IP address will be assigned dynamically, or Manually if your machine will have a fixed IP address. (In most cases, particularly if you have a broadband Internet connection at home, your IP address will be assigned via DHCP.)

4. If you're on an AppleTalk network, select the Make AppleTalk Active option in the AppleTalk panel, and select your Zone (if any).

5. Click the Apply Now button.

Change my Rendezvous name from my full name to something else?

System Preferences → Sharing → enter the new name in the Rendezvous Name text box. Your Rendezvous name will have a *.local* extension—for example, *MacChuck.local*.

Find out the speed of my network connection?

Applications → Utilities → Network Utility → Info panel; look next to Link Speed in the Interface Information section.

Find out what's taking a site so long to respond?

Applications → Utilities → Network Utility → Ping panel; enter the network address for the location (e.g., *www.macdevcenter.com*, or an IP address, such as *10.0.2.1*).

Use the *ping* command as follows:

```
[macchuck:~] chuck% ping hostname
```

Trace the route taken to connect to a web page?

Applications → Utilities → Network Utility → Traceroute panel; enter the URL for the location.

Use the *traceroute* command as follows:

```
[macchuck:~] chuck% traceroute hostname
```

Restrict access to my computer so others can get files I make available to them?

System Preferences → Sharing → File & Web panel; click on the Start button in the File Sharing section to give others access to your Public folder (*/Users/ username/Public*).

The Public folder is read-only, which means that other people can only view or copy files from that directory; they cannot write files to it.

Where can my coworkers place files on my computer without getting access to the rest of my system?

With file sharing turned on, people can place files, folders, or even applications in your Drop Box, located within the Public folder (*/Users/username/Public/Drop Box*).

View what's inside someone else's iDisk Public folder?

Go → Connect to Server; at the bottom of the dialog box, type *http://idisk.mac. com/membername/Public*. Click Connect, or press Return; the Public iDisk image will mount on your Desktop.

 Not all iDisk Public folders are created equal. An iDisk's owner can choose to make their Public folder read-only, or read-write (which allows others to place files in their Public folder). The Public folder can also be password protected, which means you need to enter a password before you can mount the Public folder.

Connect to a networked drive?

Finder → Go → Connect to Server (⌘-K)

If the server to which you want to connect is part of your local area network (LAN), click on the Local icon in the left pane, and select the server name to the right. If the server is part of your local AppleTalk network, click on the Apple-Talk Network icon in the left pane, and select the server or computer name to the right.

Connect to an SMB share?

Finder → Go → Connect to Server (⌘-K)

If you need to connect to a Windows server, you must specify the Address in the text box as follows:

    smb://hostname/sharename

After clicking the Connect button, you will be asked to supply the domain to which you wish to connect as well as your username and password. You can speed up this process by supplying the domain and your username, as follows:

    smb://domain;username@hostname/sharename

Where *domain* is the NT domain name; *username* is the name you use to connect to that domain; and *hostname* and *sharename* are the server name and shared directory that you have or want to access. Now when you click on the Connect button, all you will need to enter is your password (if one is required), and the networked drive will appear on your Desktop.

 Before pressing the Connect button, press the Add to Favorites button first. This will save you time in the future if you frequently need to connect to the same drive, since you won't have to enter that address again .

Printer Configuration and Printing

Configure a printer?

Print Center (*/Applications/Utilities*) → click on the Add button in the Printer List window, or select Printer → Add Printer From the menu bar. Select how the printer is connected using the pull-down menu (AppleTalk, Directory Services, IP Printing, or USB).

- If you select AppleTalk, select the zone (if any) using the second pull-down menu, choose the printer in the lower pane, and then click the Add button.
- If you select Directory Services, you can choose between printing via Rendez-vous or to a printer listed in the NetInfo Network. Select the printer name, and then click the Add button.
- If you select IP Printing, you need to fill in the IP address of the printer. Select the printer model and click the Add button.
- If you select USB, choose the name of the printer and the printer model, then click the Add button.

View the jobs in the print queue?
  Print Center → double-click on the name of the printer to see the print queue

Cancel a print job?
  Print Center → double-click on the printer name → click on the name of the print job → click on the Delete button

Halt a print job?
  Print Center → double-click on the printer name → click on the name of the print job → click on the Hold button. (Click on the Resume button to start the job where it left off.)

Share the printer that's connected to my Mac with another user?
  System Preferences → Sharing → Services; click on the checkbox next to Printer Sharing.

View a list of available AppleTalk printers on my network?
  From the command line, use the *atlookup* command.

If you're on a large AppleTalk network, *atlookup* will show you everything: printers, servers, computers ... *everything*. You will have to look through the output to find the item you're looking for.

Screensavers

Adjust the amount of time my system needs to be idle before the screensaver kicks in?
  System Preferences → Screen Effects → Activation

Quickly activate my screensaver when I know I'll be away from my desk for a while?
  System Preferences → Screen Effects → Hot Corners; mark a corner of the screen with a check mark to activate the screensaver when the mouse is moved to that corner. Likewise, you can place a minus sign in a Hot Corner to disable the screensaver when the mouse is moved there.

Protect my system from prying eyes while I'm away from my computer?
  System Preferences → Screen Effects → Activation → select "Use my user account password" to require a password when waking the system from the screensaver

Screenshots

Take a screenshot of everything on my display?
  Shift-⌘-3

Take a screenshot of a certain portion of my display?
  Shift-⌘-4; the mouse pointer will change to a set of crosshairs, which you can use to drag-select the area you desire

Quickly take a screenshot of just the Dock without taking a screenshot of the entire display?

Shift-⌘-4-Spacebar (this will change the pointer from a set of crosshairs to a camera) → move the camera over the Dock (the Dock will become gray, as if it were selected) → click the mouse button

Convert a PDF screenshot into a JPEG image?

Applications → Preview → File → Open → select the file and click on the Open button → File → Export → Format → select JPEG from the pull-down menu → click on the Save button

Take a screenshot of the topmost window, including its shadow?

Shift-⌘-4; position the crosshairs outside the upper-left corner of the window and drag-select the window, including its drop shadow

Take a screenshot and copy it to the pasteboard without actually creating a screenshot file?

Shift-Control-⌘-3 to take a screenshot of the entire display, or Shift-Control-⌘-4 to select a screenshot area, and then use ⌘-P to paste the screenshot from the clipboard into another document

Get my regular mouse pointer back after hitting Shift-⌘-4 without taking a screenshot?

Click the mouse once without drag-selecting an area with the crosshairs

Searching for and Locating Files

Find a file when I don't know its name?

Finder → enter a keyword in the Search field in the toolbar → hit Return to start the search

Finder → File → Find (⌘-F)

Index my hard drive to allow for content-based searching?

Finder → Computer → Macintosh HD → File → Get Info → click on the disclosure triangle next to "Content index" → click on the "Index Now" button.

The Finder does not index filenames—only the contents of files. However, you can still search for filenames.

Find a file when I can't remember where I saved it?

Use the *locate* command in the Terminal. However, you must first update the *locate* database as follows:

```
[macchuck:~] chuck% cd /usr/libexec
[macchuck:/usr/libexec] chuck% sudo ./locate.updatedb
```

If you haven't built the *locate* database yet, this command could take a few minutes to run; afterwards, you will be returned to the command line.

The *locate.updatedb* command is executed weekly by default, as noted in the */etc/weekly* file. However, you might want to issue this command shortly after installing Mac OS X.

Now you can use the *locate* command; for example:

```
[macchuck:/usr/libexec] chuck% locate temp98.doc
/Users/chuck/Books/Templates/temp98.doc
[macchuck:/usr/libexec] chuck%
```

In this example, we used *locate* to search for the file *temp98.doc*; in return, the command tells us where the file is located.

 Indexing your hard drive via Get Info allows you to do context searches, while building the *locate* database helps speed things up when you're searching for a filename. Use both the Finder and the command line to your advantage.

Where is the locate database stored?
It is stored in */var/db/locate.database*.

How can I speed up my Finder searches?
Finder → Preferences → Languages for searching file contents; click on the Select button, and choose the checkboxes for the languages you want to base your searches on. Unless you're working in a multilingual environment, you should select only your primary language.

Clear the Finder's search field?
Click on the X at the right edge of the search field.

Security

Manage keychains?
Applications → Utilities → Keychain Access

Enable the firewall on my system?
System Preferences → Sharing → Firewall → click the Start button

Allow people access to my Public folder?
System Preferences → Sharing → Services → click on the checkbox next to Personal File Sharing

System Information

Find out how much memory I have?
 → About This Mac

Find out what version of Mac OS X I'm running?
 → About This Mac

 → About This Mac → click on the version number (e.g., 10.2.3) to reveal the build number (e.g., 6G30).

Finder → Applications → Utilities → Apple System Profiler → System Profile panel; look in the System overview section to see the exact build of Mac OS X.

Find out what processor my Mac has?
 → About This Mac

Finder → Applications → Utilities → Apple System Profiler → System Profile → Hardware Overview

What type of cache do I have and how big is it?

Applications → Utilities → Apple System Profiler → System Profile → Memory Overview

Find out what programs (or processes) are running?

Finder → Applications → Utilities → Process Viewer

From the command line, using the *ps -aux* command.

From the command line, using the *top* command.

Display the status of the computer's used and free memory?

From the command line, using the *top* command. The *top* command gives you a real-time view of the processes running on your system, as well as processor and memory usage. To stop the *top* command from running, hit Control-C or ⌘-. (Command-period).

View the hardware connected to my system?

Finder → Applications → Utilities → Apple System Profiler. This information can be gathered from System Profile → Hardware Overview, and from the Devices and Volumes panel.

Quickly generate a report about my system so I can submit it to Apple along with a bug report?

From the Terminal, issue the following command:

```
[macchuck:~] chuck% AppleSystemProfiler > sysprofile.txt
```

The *AppleSystemProfiler* command launches the Apple System Profiler application (*/Applications/Utilities*). It redirects the output (with the > symbol) that would normally print in the Terminal and saves it in the *sysprofile.txt* file in your home directory. Now you can open, view, and print the file using TextEdit, or copy and paste this into a bug report.

System Status

Find out how long my system has been running?

Use the *uptime* command:

```
[macchuck:~] chuck% uptime
3:34PM  up  10:09, 2 users, load averages: 0.09, 0.12, 0.09
```

The *uptime* command displays, in the following order: the current time, how long the system has been running (up 10:09, or 10 hours 9 minutes), the number of users logged in to the system, and the load averages on the processor.

Display the battery status for my PowerBook in the menu bar?

System Preferences → Energy Saver → select the checkbox next to "Show battery status in menu bar"

Display a volume control in the menu bar?

System Preferences → Sound → select the checkbox next to "Show volume in menu bar"

Change the name of my computer?

System Preferences → Sharing → enter the new name for your computer in the Computer Name text box

Automatically check for updates to the system?

System Preferences → Software Update → Update Software → select the checkbox next to "Automatically check for updates when you have a network connection," and then select the frequency (Daily, Weekly, Monthly) from the pull-down menu

Have an application start up automatically after I log in?

> System Preferences → Login Items → click the Add button, and then use the Finder to select the applications you would like to have started after you log in

> Drag an application icon from the Finder to the window in the Login Items panel

Display the process meter in the Dock?

> Applications → Utilities → CPU Monitor → Preferences → Application Icon → select either "Display the standard view in the icon" or "Display the extended view in the icon"

Terminal Settings

This section offers advice on how to configure the settings for the Terminal application (also covered in Chapter 19). Previously, you would use Terminal → Preferences to configure the Terminal's settings. However, with Jaguar, you need to use File → Show Info and change the settings from the Terminal Inspector window via the pull-down menu at the top of the window.

Change the style of the cursor?

> Display & Cursor Style → (Block, Underline, Vertical Bar)

Stop the cursor from blinking?

> Display → Cursor Style → Deselect Blinking Cursor

Change the background color and font colors of the Terminal window?

> Color → click on the color selection boxes next to Background, Cursor, Normal Text, Bold Text, and Selection to open another window with the color wheel. This allows you to change and select a different color and even the transparency of the Terminal window.

Assign a different title to the Terminal window?

> Window → Title

Assign a different title to the current Terminal window?

> With an open Terminal window, select File → Set Title (Shift-⌘-T). The Terminal Inspector window will open with Window selected in the pull-down menu. Enter a new title for the window in the Title field and hit Return or Tab to change the title of the current window.

Specify the number of lines a Terminal window can contain in the scrollback buffer?

> Buffer → Buffer Size. You can either specify a number of lines in the field provided (10,000 lines is the default), or select either an unlimited scrollback or no scrollback at all.

Set the Terminal's emulation mode to VT100?

> Emulation → Strict VT-100 keypad behavior

Close the Terminal window after I've exited?

> Shell → When the shell exits → select from either "Close the window" or "Close only if the shell exited cleanly"

Where is the history file for the shell?

> It is in ~/.tcsh_history.

Where is the shell's configuration file located?

> It is located in /usr/share/tcsh/examples/rc.

Create a customized shell environment that's different from the one used by other users on the system?

> Read and follow the instructions in the *README* file located in /usr/share/tcsh/examples.

Troubleshooting and Maintenance

Force quit an application that's stuck?

Option-⌘-Escape opens a window showing all of the running applications. Select the troublesome application, and click the Force Quit button.

Option-click the application's icon in the Dock. A pop-up window will appear next to the icon with the Force Quit option; move the mouse over and release it on that option.

Applications → Utilities → Process Viewer → select the process that's causing the problem → Processes → Quit Process

Restart my computer automatically after a power failure?

System Preferences → Energy Saver → Options pane → select the checkbox next to "Restart automatically after a power failure"

Turn on crash reporting so I can see why an application crashed?

Applications → Utilities → Console → Preferences → Crashes panel → select both options. Now when an application crashes, the Console application automatically launches and displays the cause of the crash.

Where are crash logs kept?

It is kept in *~/Library/Logs*.

Fix a disk that won't mount?

Applications → Utilities → Disk Utility → select the disk that won't mount → First Aid.

Restart my system when it has completely frozen?

Hold down the Shift-Option-⌘ keys, and press the Power-On button.

Make sure that my system is okay after it has completely frozen?

Follow these steps:

1. Do a hard restart of your system by pressing Control-⌘-Power-On (or Eject).

2. Log back into your system.

3. Launch the Terminal (*/Applications/Utilities*).

4. Enter the following command and hit Return:

   `[macchuck:~] chuck% sudo shutdown now`

This forces an automatic shutdown of your system and takes you into single-user mode. Your screen will go black and you'll be faced with a text prompt.

5. At the prompt, enter the following command:

   `sh-2.05a# fsck -y`

The *fsck* command will perform a filesystem check and will report back its findings:

```
bootstrap_look_up( ) failed (ip/send) invalid destination port
bootstrap_look_up( ) failed (ip/send) invalid destination port
bootstrap_look_up( ) failed (ip/send) invalid destination port
** /dev/rdisk0s2
** Root file system
** Checking HFS Plus volume.
** Checking Extents Overflow file.
** Checking Catalog file.
** Checking multi-linked files.
```

```
** Checking Catalog hierarchy.
** Checking volume bitmap.
** Checking volume information.
** The volume MacChuck appears to be OK.
sh-2.05a#
```

If *fsck -y* reports that the disk has been modified, you need to run the command again until the filesystem checks out OK.

If everything is fine, enter *reboot* at the command prompt and hit Return to reboot your system.

Access command-line mode and bypass Aqua?

There are three ways you can access the command-line interface:

1. Hold down ⌘-S when starting up the system; this is known as *single-user mode*.

2. At the login window, type >*console* as the username, don't enter a password, and click on the Login button. This is known as *multiuser mode* and is just like being in the Terminal, except that your entire screen is the Terminal.

3. From the Terminal, type **sudo shutdown now**, and hit Return; this also places you in single-user mode.

When you've finished diagnosing your system, type **reboot** and press Return to reboot your system into Aqua.

Rebuild Classic's Desktop?

System Preferences → Classic → Advanced panel. There is no need to rebuild Mac OS X's Desktop; holding down Option-⌘ keys at startup is futile.

All of the icons on my system look funny. Is there an easy way to fix this problem?

Even though Mac OS X is more reliable than earlier versions of the Mac OS, icons and such can still go haywire. The quick fix for this problem is to delete the three "LS" files (*LSApplications*, *LSClaimedTypes*, and *LSSchemes*) in *~/Library/ Preferences*.

There is a question mark icon in the Dock. What is this?

A question mark icon in the Dock or in one of the toolbars means that the application, folder, or file that the original icon related to has been deleted from your system. Just drag the question mark icon away from the Dock or toolbar to make it disappear.

I have a dual-processor G4 machine. Can I see how efficiently the processors are distributing the workload?

Applications → Utilities → CPU Monitor; each processor will have its own meter bar.

View a log of software updates?

System Preferences → Software Update → Show Log

Connect an external monitor or projector to my PowerBook without restarting?

Select → Sleep to put your laptop to sleep, plug in and turn on the display, and then hit the Escape key to wake your system and the display. You can then use the Display System Preference (System Preferences → Display) to turn display mirroring on or off as needed.

Windows

Open a new window?
> File → Open (⌘-O)

Close a window?
> File → Close (⌘-W)

Close all open windows for an application?
> Option-click on the close window button.

 If there are changes that need to be saved in any of the windows being closed, you will be prompted to save. Either hit Return to save the changes, or enter ⌘-D to invoke the Don't Save button.

Minimize a window?
> Window → Minimize Window (⌘-M)
>
> Double-click on the window's titlebar.

Minimize all open windows for a single application?
> Option-⌘-M

 With some applications, Option-⌘-M may function differently. For example, issuing Option-⌘-M in Microsoft Word (Office v.X) will open the Paragraph format window (Format → Paragraph). Instead, you can minimize all of Word's windows by holding down the Option key and double-clicking on a document's titlebar.

To be safe, you should save changes to the file before trying to minimize all of the application's windows with Option-⌘-M.

Slow down the genie effect while minimizing a window to the Dock?
> Shift-click on the minimize button in the window's toolbar. (This works in reverse, too; shift-clicking a minimized window icon in the Dock opens it up slowly.)

Really slow down the genie effect while minimizing a window the Dock?
> Shift-⌘-click on the minimize button.

Hide the windows for other active applications?
> Option-⌘-click on the Dock icon for the application you're using; the open windows for all other active applications will instantly hide. To bring another application's windows to the front, click on that application's Dock icon. To unhide all the other windows, select Show All from the application menu (e.g., Finder → Show All).

System Configuration

Now that you've learned your way around Mac OS X, it's time to configure your system. This part of the book provides an overview of the System Preferences (the applications and utilities that come with Mac OS X), and shows you how to configure your system printing and networking. If you plan to run Java applications on your Mac, Chapter 10 provides an overview of Mac OS X's Java environment.

The chapters in this part include:

Chapter 5, *System Preferences*

Chapter 6, *Applications and Utilities*

Chapter 7, *Networking*

Chapter 8, *Printer Configuration and Printing*

Chapter 9, *Filesystem Overview*

Chapter 10, *Running Java Applications*

5

System Preferences

After figuring your way around the Mac's interface, the next thing you'll want to do is configure your system to suit your needs. The primary way to do this is with Mac OS X's System Preferences application. By using the System Preferences and the panels within, you can configure and customize your system and how you interact with it. You can perform actions like set your Desktop image, configure your network settings (including those for your .Mac account), and manage user accounts if your system has more than one user.

This chapter covers the use of the System Preferences application and describes all the individual panes that Mac OS X ships with. It also explains how the application works, including ways to add panes of your own to its display.

Using System Preferences

The System Preferences application, as seen in Figure 5-1, contains many individual *preference panels*, each represented by its own icon in the application's main display window.

To launch the System Preferences application, you can choose one of three ways:

- Click on its icon in the Dock; the System Preferences icon is the one that looks like a light switch with a gray Apple logo next to it.
- Select → System Preferences.
- Double-click on its icon in the Finder (found in */Applications*), as shown in Figure 5-2.

Long-time Mac users will recognize that most of the panels in the System Preferences application are similar to the Control Panels found in earlier versions of the Mac OS. For a listing of the differences between Mac OS X and earlier versions of the Mac OS, see Chapter 3.

Figure 5-1. The System Preferences application

Each panel is really a separate application, found in */System/Library/ PreferencePanes*; however, they are designed to work exclusively within the System Preferences window, rather than as standalone programs. To open a panel, click once on its icon, or select its name from the View menu. This causes the System Preferences window to change into an interface for that particular panel. To return to the main System Preferences window, click the Show All icon in the upper-left corner of the window's toolbar, or select View → Show All In Categories (⌘-L).

The Toolbar

As seen in Figure 5-1, the System Preferences window has a toolbar at the top of its window. It can contain the icon of any preference panel. The toolbar remains visible—unless you choose to hide it—even when a particular preference panel is active within the window. This allows you to switch between panel displays quickly.

Unlike the Finder's toolbar, you cannot customize the System Preferences toolbar. (You can customize the Finder's toolbar by Control-clicking on the toolbar itself and selecting Customize Toolbar from the context menu.) You can add and

Figure 5-2. The System Preferences application, as found in the Finder

remove icons from the System Preferences toolbar by dragging an icon onto or off of the toolbar. When you drag an icon off the toolbar, it will disappear, similar to what happens when you remove an icon from the Dock. You can also change the size of the icon and the text labels for the icons by Command-clicking on the toolbar button as follows:

Command-click #1
    Reduces the size of toolbar icons and the text labels.

Command-click #2
    Removes the text labels and displays the icons at the normal size.

Command-click #3
    Reduces the size of the toolbar icons without the text labels.

Command-click #4
    Removes the panel icons and replaces them with large text labels.

Command-click #5
    Reduces the size of the text labels without the panel icons.

Command-click #6
    Returns the icons and text labels for the panels in the toolbar to their normal, original size.

> If you add the Shift key to any of these ⌘-click combinations, you'll go backward through the cycle to the previous setting.

You can move the icons in the toolbar around by click-dragging them to a different position. The only icon you can't remove from the toolbar is the Show All icon, which is permanently fixed to the far left of the toolbar. Additionally, you can't place anything to the left of the divider bar in the toolbar.

By default, the System Preferences toolbar contains four panel icons: Displays, Sound, Network, and Startup Disk. These are Apple's best guess at the four items you'll need the most. However, after using Mac OS X for a while, you may find that having Displays in the toolbar is useless, since you can make its controls available via a menu extra. For example, system administrators might find having Login Items, My Account, Accounts, Software Update, and Sharing as a useful set of toolbar icons for System Preferences. The next section covers the System Preference panels in greater detail.

The System Preference Panels

System Preferences breaks the different panels down into four categories, each of which appears as its own row of icons in the program's main display window. The four categories are:

- Personal
- Hardware
- Internet & Network
- System

If you or another application needs to add panels to the System Preferences window (see "Adding Panes to System Preferences" later in this chapter), they will appear in a separate category row called Other.

> The changes you make to the various panels in the System Preferences is saved as XML data in the form of a *property list*, or *plist*. These plists can be found in your *~/Library/Preferences* directory, and can be further tweaked and manipulated using a text editor, or using the Property List Editor application if you've installed the Developer Tools. Look for filenames that begin with *com.apple. something.plist* in this directory.

The panels found in System Preferences are discussed in the sections that follow.

Personal

These panels allow you to configure various aspects of the Aqua "look and feel" of your system, such as the placement and behavior of the Dock, window appearance, language preferences, and the ability to customize some features of user accounts.

The panels included in the Personal section include:

- Desktop
- Dock

- General
- International
- Login Items
- My Account
- Screen Effects

These Preference panels are explained further here.

Desktop

The Desktop panel, shown in Figure 5-3, lets you change the background image that appears on your Desktop. You can choose from several pre-installed collections, or use an image you've saved in your Pictures folder (*~/Pictures*) or elsewhere on your system.

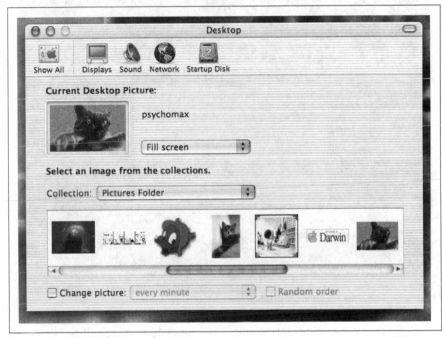

Figure 5-3. The Desktop panel

New features added to the Desktop panel in Jaguar include:

- A pull-down menu that allows you to specify whether an image will fill the screen, stretch to fill the screen (thus changing the proportional size of the original image), center the image on screen, or tile the image (if needed).
- The ability to change the Desktop picture automatically. For example, if you have a bunch of JPEG images saved in your Pictures folder, you can specify that as the target source for your background image, and then select the checkbox at the bottom of the Desktop window. Clicking on the "Change picture" checkbox will enable the pull-down menu, which lets you set the timing rotation of the images.

- If you Control-click (or right-click) on the Desktop itself, a context menu will appear with an option to Change Desktop Background. Selecting this menu item opens the Desktop panel.

If you have more than one display connected to your system, selecting the Desktop panel opens a separate panel in each display, as shown in Figure 5-4. This panel allows you to set a separate Desktop picture for the other display. If you look closely at Figure 5-4, you'll notice that the Desktop panel window on the second display doesn't have a toolbar. For more information on running a dual-headed system, see the later section "Displays."

Figure 5-4. The Desktop panel as displayed on a second monitor

 At the time of this writing, we discovered a slight bug. If you have two monitors connected to your system and enable the "Change picture" feature on the main monitor, that change will apply to the second monitor whether you like it or not. Even after we unchecked the box next to "Change picture", the Desktop picture on the second monitor continued to change on its own, even after resetting the Desktop picture for that monitor a number of times.

Dock

The Dock panel lets you control the Dock's appearance and behavior, including its size, icon magnification, and screen position. As Figure 5-5 shows, you can also dictate the animation style used for minimizing windows (choose between the Genie Effect or the Scale Effect).

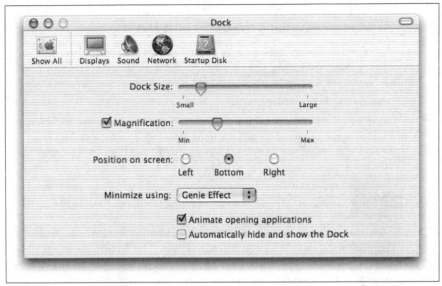

Figure 5-5. The Dock preferences panel

The checkbox next to "Animate opening applications" is checked by default, which causes an application icon to bounce in the Dock as it starts up. If you uncheck this box, the icon won't bounce, but the black triangle beneath the icon will pulse instead to indicate that the application is launching.

If you find that the Dock takes up too much space on your screen, you can check the box next to "Automatically hide and show the Dock" to make it hide when you don't need it. When you need to launch an application, use the Finder, or unminimize a window, just move your mouse to where the Dock should be and it will reappear.

> As Chapter 1 states, abbreviated versions of the Dock panel appear in the Apple Menu submenu, and the Dock divider's Dock menu, shown in Figure 1-25.
>
> Don't forget that you can always quickly toggle the Dock's hidden/shown state by pressing Option-⌘-D.

The plist file for Dock preferences is saved as *~/Library/Preferences/com.apple.dock.plist*.

General

The General pane, seen in Figure 5-6, lets you select the color to use for text high-lighting, configure window scrollbar appearance and behavior, specify the number of entries the Apple Menu should keep under its Recent Items submenu, and control text smoothing (antialiasing) throughout the system.

The ability to select font smoothing based on your monitor type is new with Jaguar. For example, if you're using an iBook or PowerBook, you should set your "Font smoothing style" to "Medium-best for Flat Panel."

Hacking the Dock's plist File

Suppose you wanted your Dock to appear at the top of the screen, beneath the menu bar. While this isn't one of the positions available (as shown in Figure 5-5), you *can* do this by hacking the Dock's *plist* file.

To do this, follow these steps:

1. Open the *com.apple.dock.plist* file (*~/Library/Preferences*) by double-clicking on its icon in the Finder. This will open the file using the Property List Editor if you have installed the Developer Tools; otherwise, the file will open in TextEdit.
2. Click on the Dump button.
3. Click on the disclosure triangle next to Root, and look for a key item named "orientation."
4. Change the value of "orientation" from "bottom" (or "left" or "right," depending on where you have it placed) to "top," hit Return to accept the change, then save the file and quit the Property List Editor.
5. Logout (🍎 → Log Out), and then log back in.

When you log back in, the Dock will appear at the top of the screen, below the menu bar. To move it back, you can either edit the *plist* file again, or use the Dock's preferences panel to select Left, Right, or Bottom as its location [🍎 → Locate at (Bottom, Left, or Right)].

The General pane's Appearance pull-down menu lets you select from either Blue (the default) or Graphite as the color Mac OS X uses for its interface elements, such as buttons, scrollbars, and menus.

International

The international pane, shown in Figure 5-7, is Mac OS X's user interface to its localization features. Through it, you can set your preferred language, as well as the date, time, and number formats most appropriate to the part of the world you live in.

Mac OS X uses a fairly elegant strategy for implementing system-wide *localization*, letting the system and its various applications modify their text and interfaces depending on the user's native language. For example, a person from the United States would probably prefer to use an English-language system, whose controls and text flow from left to right and top to bottom. Likewise, a person from Saudi Arabia would benefit from applications with Arabic-language interfaces and a right-to-left flow of text and controls.

There are five panes to the International preferences panel, whose functions are as follows:

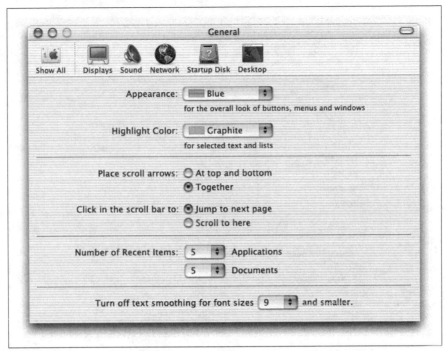

Figure 5-6. The General preferences pane

Language

This pane is used to select the languages you prefer to use in your application menus and dialogs. The language at the top of the list is your default language, which is established when you install Mac OS X. To change your preferred language, click on another and drag it to the top of the list (the mouse pointer will change to a hand symbol).

If you don't see a language in this list, or if you would like to make it shorter, click on the Edit button. A sheet will slide down, containing a checkbox list of the more than 50 languages supported by Mac OS X. You can also use this listing to reduce the number of languages that appear in the Languages window by deselecting their checkboxes.

The lower portion of the Languages pane allows you to specify the text behaviors for each script. As with the Languages section, these are set to your default language.

Date

The Date pane lets you specify how the system date will appear in the menu bar clock. At the top of this pane is a pull-down menu that lets you select your region. Any additional changes or tweaks to the format for the Region you've selected can be made in the middle portion; the area at the bottom of the window shows how the Long and Short Date will be displayed.

Figure 5-7. The International preferences panel

Time

    As with the Date pane, this pane lets you select your Region from a pull-down menu, and also lets you specify the format for your clock.

Numbers

    The Numbers pane includes a Region pull-down menu, along with controls for specifying the Separators numbers (Decimal and Thousands), the symbol to be used for Currency, and whether your Measurement System will be standard or metric. Typically, you won't have to change the items under Separators, Currency, or Measurement System, as their defaults are based on the Region you select from the pull-down menu.

Input Menu

    This pane is used to select the keyboard layout for your system, based on the language you've specified as the default. Initially, you will only have one language selected here. However, if you select other languages by clicking on their checkboxes, the Input Menu will appear in your menu bar.

    If you decide to switch keyboard layouts (say from U.S. to Polish), you will need to log out and log back into your account for the change to take effect.

    One item you'll want to add to your Input Menu is the Character Palette, especially if you frequently need to add international characters or mathematical symbols to your documents. If you select the Character Palette from the

Input Menu, the palette will open in a separate window. To add a character to a document, find the symbol you're looking for and drag it to where you would like it inserted.

Clicking on the Options button opens a sheet with Input Menu Shortcuts (keyboard shortcuts for switching the default keyboard layout or input method), and an option to synchronize the font and keyboard scripts.

Mac OS X has the textual base covered by making Unicode its native text-encoding architecture. To make localized user interfaces, application developers can build groups of interface widgets or text strings to use depending upon the user's local settings. These resources are built into *.lproj* folders found within the application's */Resources* folder.

When a user launches an application, that application looks up the user's language and localization preferences, as defined by the International panel. It then uses the *.lproj* resource folder that provides the resources highest on the user's list of preferred languages and scripts (as seen in Figure 5-8).

Figure 5-8. The International panel's Language preferences

Third-party applications you download from the Internet or install from CD can support many different languages at once; depending upon the vendor, you may be able to select and install only the language support that you need. Apple defines lots of localization bundles for Mac OS X's core applications (the ones covered in Chapter 6); the interfaces they make available depend on the language support you chose to install from the Mac OS X system CDs (or have added since then via the CDs or the System Update application).

Login Items

The Login Items panel, shown in Figure 5-9, lists applications and/or filesystem objects (files, folders, and disks) that you would like to open when you log into your account. For Mac OS 9 users, the Login Items panel is similar to dragging an application alias to the */System Folder/Startup Items* folder.

Figure 5-9. The Login Items panel

The interface for the Login Items panel is fairly self-explanatory. To add an item to launch or mount upon startup, you can drag an item from the Finder or click the Add button. To remove an item, select it with the mouse and click on the Remove button. You can also specify the order in which the items will launch by dragging them up or down in the listing.

My Account

The My Account panel, shown in Figure 5-10, lets you change your account password, as well as the picture that appears on the login window (if the system is configured to automatically list users' names there; see the section "Accounts" later in this chapter).

Features of this panel include:

- You can change your user accounts' password by clicking on the "Change..." button. A sheet will slide out of the panel's titlebar, prompting you to enter your current password before you can change it to something else.

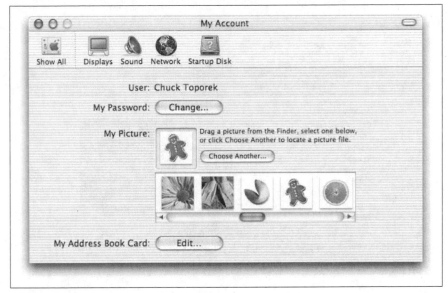

Figure 5-10. The My Account preferences panel

- If you decide that the standard set of login image icons don't suit your taste, you can click on the "Choose Another..." button to select a different image. A Finder sheet will slide out of the panel's titlebar, allowing you to navigate through your system to find the image you want to use.

- Clicking on the "Edit" button next to "My Address Book Card" will open your card in the Address Book application, allowing you to make changes to your address information. You may notice that some information is already in your record; this data came from the information you provided when you first installed Mac OS X on your system.

Screen Effects

The Screen Effects panel, shown in Figure 5-11, lets you configure the system's built-in screen saver.

The Screen Effects panel has three tabbed panes:

Screen Effects

This pane, shown in Figure 5-11, lets you select which screen saver to use. Some screen effects allow you to alter their settings by clicking on the Configure button.

If you have a .Mac account, clicking on the Configure button will let you select the Public Slide Show. You can also set this to use another .Mac user's public slide show by entering their Membership Name in the field provided.

Clicking on the Open Energy Saver button will open the Energy Saver preferences panel, described in the later section "Hardware."

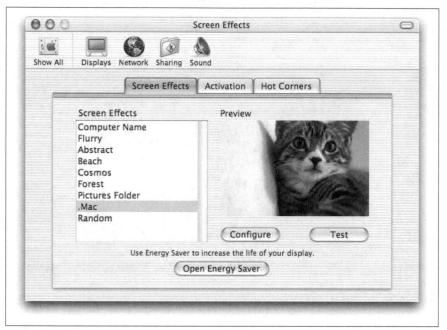

Figure 5-11. The Screen Effects preferences panel

Activation

This pane, shown in Figure 5-12, lets you specify the amount of time your system must be idle before the screen saver kicks in. Using the radio buttons below the time slider, you can opt whether to require your user account's password to deactivate the screen saver.

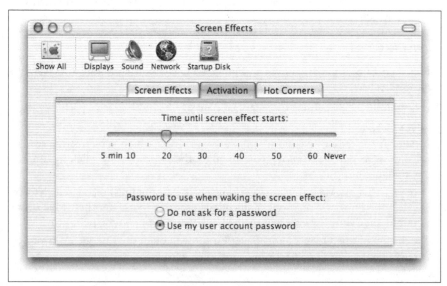

Figure 5-12. The Activation pane of the Screen Effects preferences panel

Hot Corners

This pane, shown in Figure 5-13, lets you specify which corners of your screen to use to quickly enable/disable the screen saver.

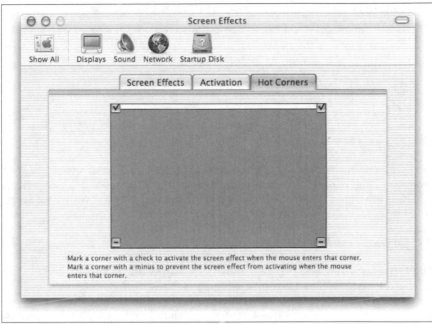

Figure 5-13. The Hot Corners pane of the Screen Effects preferences panel

This is a handy feature, as it allows you to immediately activate the screen saver, rather than waiting for the time you've specified in the Activation pane.

 Selecting the "Use my user account password" radio button (Figure 5-12) is a quick way to improve your account's security, if your Mac is in an office or other setting where you'd rather not risk prying eyes when you need to leave the keyboard for a little while. On the other hand, it's an effective way to accidentally "hog" a shared machine, since if you forget to log out before leaving for the day, the Mac won't let anyone else on until you return and provide your password. However, a skilled system administrator can log in to the machine remotely and end your session forcefully, if needed.

The options you set in the Screen Effects panel take effect only when you are logged in; your settings won't work for another user or when the machine is idle at the login screen after starting your Mac. To configure the machine's *real* screen-saving setup, use the Energy Saver panel, described later in "Hardware."

Screen savers are essentially a collection of JPEG image files, bundled together and saved in */System/Library/Screen Savers*. If you have a .Mac account, you can download an application called Mac Slides Publisher, available in */Software/Apple*

Software, and create screen savers from your own images. To create and publish your screen saver using Mac Slides Publisher, follow these steps:

1. Make sure you're connected to the Internet.
2. Using the Finder, mount your iDisk (Go → iDisk, or Shift-⌘-I).
3. Locate the images you'd like to use in the screen saver (either in iPhoto or the Finder).
4. Drag the images onto the Mac Slides Publisher icon in the Dock.

 Don't launch Mac Slides Publisher before dragging the image files onto its icon; if you do, nothing will happen. Additionally, it's worth noting that you can only use JPEG images as part of a slide show.

After dragging the images onto the icon, Mac Slides Publisher creates the screen saver slides and publishes them to your iDisk in your */Pictures/Slide Shows* folder. You can then opt to use the slide show you just created as your own screen saver. Other .Mac users can use it as well, as long as they know your username.

Hardware

Apple has used the term "digital hub" as a marketing slogan to describe its computers' zero-configuration plug-and-play abilities with various devices. The Hardware preference panels let you control your Mac's behavior when you connect or insert various kinds of media or devices (such as a digital camera or iPods), or insert a CD or DVD.

The standard set of panels in the Hardware section include:

- CDs & DVDs
- ColorSync
- Displays
- Energy Saver
- Keyboard
- Mouse
- Sound

In addition to the standard set of Hardware preference panels, there are two more that you might find, depending on additional hardware or peripherals you have attached to your system. These include:

- Bluetooth
- Ink

The standard set of Hardware preference panels, along with Bluetooth and Ink are discussed in the following sections.

CDs & DVDs

The CDs & DVDs preferences panel, shown in Figure 5-14, lets you determine what action (if any) will be taken when you insert a CD or DVD.

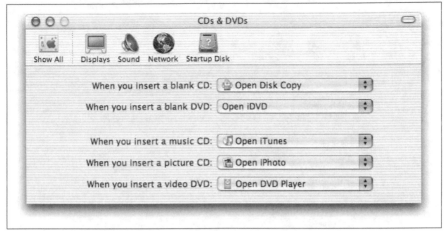

Figure 5-14. The CDs & DVDs preferences panel

The items in the CDs & DVDs panel all share the same basic interface: a pull-down menu that lets you choose what the Mac does when it mounts various kinds of disks. You can choose to have it simply open the new media volume as a Finder window, launch an appropriate application (such as iTunes for music CDs and Disk Copy for blank discs), run a script, or prompt you for some other action to take. The pull-down menus ask you what action to take when you perform one of the following actions:

Insert a blank CD
Insert a blank DVD
> Specifies the Mac's behavior when you insert a blank, recordable CD or DVD. By default, both of these are set to "Ask what to do." However, you might want to change the action for these to either "Open Finder" or "Open Disk Copy."

Insert a music CD
> Specifies the Mac's behavior when it mounts an audio CD (including an MP3 CD). The default is to open the CD with iTunes.

Insert a picture CD
> Specifies the Mac's behavior when it mounts a picture CD; the default is to open the CD with iPhoto.

Insert a video DVD
> Specifies the Mac's behavior when it mounts a DVD with a movie on it; the default is to open it with the DVD Player.

ColorSync

The ColorSync panel, shown in Figure 5-15, is used to define the ColorSync color-matching method (CMM) you prefer, as well as the default ColorSync profiles that applications should use for documents that lack embedded profiles. You can separately define defaults for RGB, CMYK, and grayscale documents.

This panel is mostly important to high-end graphic designers, where ColorSync helps on-screen colors approximate print colors as closely as possible. If you never

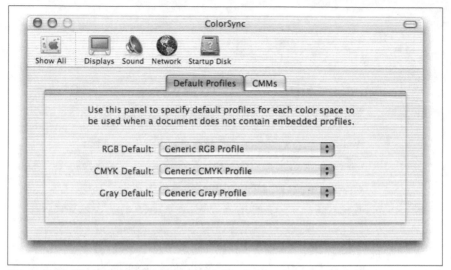

Figure 5-15. The ColorSync preferences panel

knowingly use ColorSync technology, you can safely ignore this panel (as well as the other ColorSync utilities that ship with Mac OS X).

The default ColorSync profiles are saved in */System/Library/ColorSync/Profiles*, while any custom profiles you create using the Display Calibrator application (*/Applications/Utilities*) are saved in *~/Library/ColorSync/Profiles*. You can also launch the Display Calibrator from the Displays preferences panel by clicking on the Calibrate button in the Color tab.

Displays

The Displays panel configures the resolution, color depth, and refresh rates available to the currently connected monitor (see Figure 5-16.)

The Color tab contains controls for associating and calibrating a ColorSync profile with the current display. As mentioned earlier, clicking on the Calibrate button launches the Display Calibrator application, which allows you to create a custom ColorSync calibration for your particular monitor and needs.

 It's wise to leave the "Show modes recommended by display" item checked, as it will keep you from selecting a screen resolution that may not be supported by your monitor.

If you check the "Show displays in menu bar" checkbox, the Displays menu extra shown in Figure 5-17 will appear in the menu bar.

If you connect more than one display to your computer, you'll notice some differences in the some of the System Preference panels, described in the next list.

- An Arrangement tab, shown in Figure 5-18, is added to the Displays preferences panel. This tab allows you to select the placement of the second monitor in relation to the primary display.

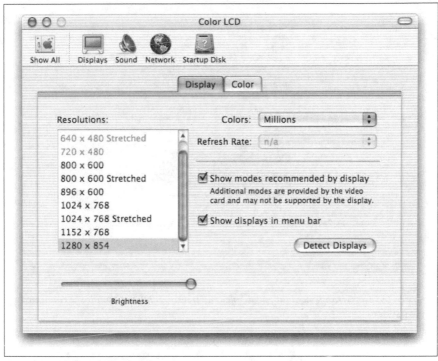

Figure 5-16. The Displays preference pane

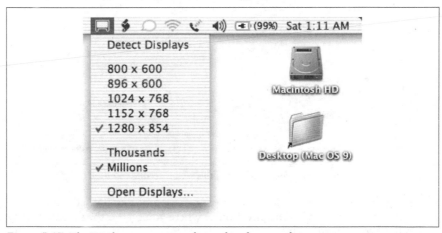

Figure 5-17. The Displays menu extra, located in the menu bar

If you select the Mirror Displays checkbox, the second monitor will mirror the main display. This is particularly useful when you connect your computer to an overhead projector to give a presentation.

• A watered-down version of the Displays panel will appear on the second monitor, as shown in Figure 5-19.

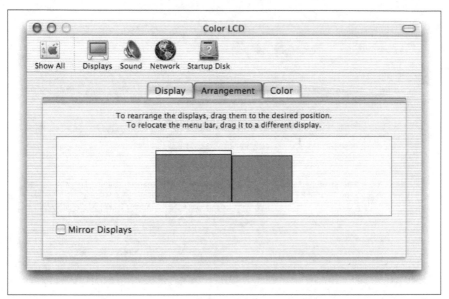

Figure 5-18. The Arrangement tab; available only if more than one monitor is connected to your system

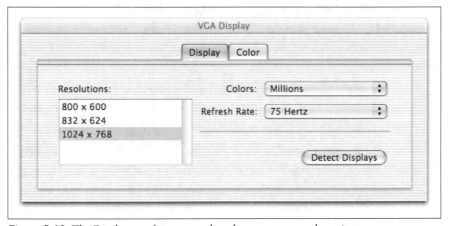

Figure 5-19. The Displays preference panel as shown on a second monitor.

To interact with this window, move your mouse over to the second monitor by moving the cursor in the direction of where you placed the second display in the Arrangements tab.

If you click on the Show All icon in the System Preferences toolbar on the main display, the Displays panel disappears from the second monitor.

• You can set the Desktop pictures for both displays independent of each other. To do so, click on the Desktop panel and a similar panel (again, without the toolbar) appears on the second display. Select the Desktop pattern you would like to see on the second display, and then click on the Show All toolbar icon in the main display to make the window on the second display disappear.

- You can set Hot Corners for the second display in the Screen Effects panel, as shown in Figure 5-20.

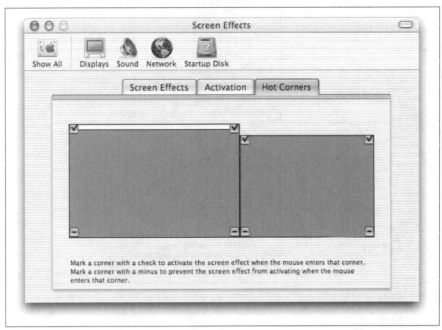

Figure 5-20. Setting the Hot Corners for the second monitor from the Screen Effects panel

 While at first glance this might seem like you can enable the screen saver on the second monitor independently from your main display, you can't. If you move the mouse into the Hot Corner to enable the screen saver, both monitors will display the screen saver simultaneously. (Maybe that's something Apple can work on for a future revision of Mac OS X?)

- The Displays menu extra in the menu bar allows you to control both displays from the same menu, as shown in Figure 5-21.
- When you minimize a window in the second display, you can watch as it's whisked away to a place in the Dock on the primary display. Likewise, when you unminimize that window, it will spring back to its former placement on the second display.

The advantage of using two displays is you have additional screen real estate to work with. For example, you could use the second display to have various Finder windows open so you can drag and drop text and image files into a dynamic web page builder (like Dreamweaver MX), which you're running on your main display.

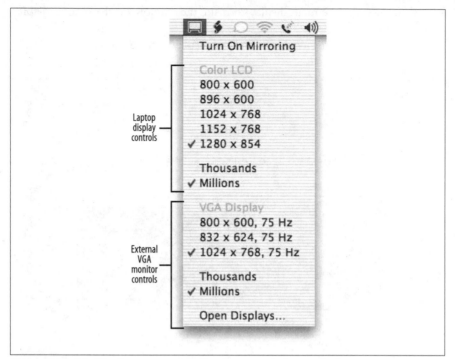

Figure 5-21. The Displays menu extra, showing controls for two displays

Energy Saver

The Energy Saver panel is used to specify the machine's idle time before it enters sleep mode, and defines special conditions (such as network or modem access) under which it awakens itself. Depending on which machine you have, the Energy Saver panel you see may be different. If you have a Desktop system like an iMac or a G4 tower, the Energy Saver panel you'll see is shown in Figure 5-22; if you have an iBook or PowerBook, the panel you'll see is shown in Figure 5-23.

This panel allows you to specify the amount of time your system is inactive before your computer or monitor is put to sleep. If you want your monitor to go to sleep sooner than the computer, click on the checkbox next to "Use separate time to put the display to sleep." Another option, "Put the hard disk to sleep when possible," allows you to put your Mac into the ultimate Energy Saver mode, where the hard disk spins itself down, reducing the power consumption even more.

 Because the settings defined by the Energy Saver panel take effect for the entire system (and not just while your login is active, as with the Display Effects preferences pane), you must open the pane's authentication lock (see "The authentication lock" in Chapter 6) before making any changes here.

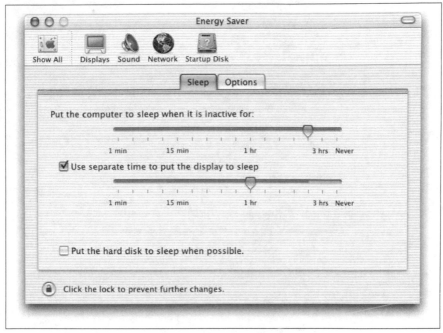

Figure 5-22. The Energy Saver preferences panel as displayed on a G4 tower

As noted earlier, iBook and PowerBook users will see the Energy Saver panel shown in Figure 5-23. The reason for this change is to give laptop users the ability to set the sleep time for when they're plugged in, or when they're operating on battery power. Note the two pull-down menus at the top of the window:

> At some point, Apple removed the ability to configure the hard drive spindown time in Energy Saver: the value is stuck at 10 minutes. This can be changed by editing */var/db/SystemConfiguration/ com.apple.PowerManagement.xml*, or by using the command *pmset -a spindown n* (where *n* is a number in minutes) to write the config value. See *man pmset* for more information.

Optimize Energy Settings
    This menu allows you to select one of six settings: Automatic, Highest Performance, Longest Battery Life, DVD Playback, Presentations, or Custom. You can alter the sleep settings for each of these or go with their defaults, based on what Apple thinks will give you the most bang for your battery's buck.

Settings for
    This menu lets you select from two options: Power Adapter or Battery Power. You can have separate, independent Energy Saver settings for when you're plugged in, or for when you're unplugged and running on battery. It's in your best interest to enter settings for both of these based on your own habits, although the presets, based on what you select in the "Optimize Energy Settings" pull-down menu, should work just fine for most people.

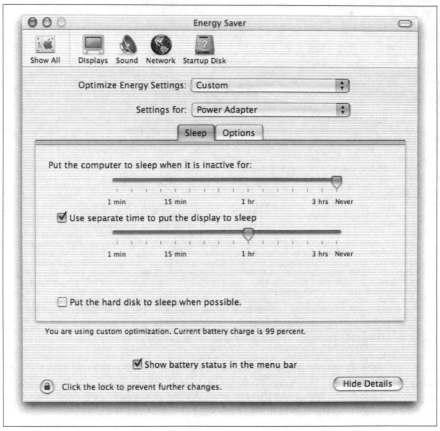

Figure 5-23. The Energy Saver preferences panel as displayed on a PowerBook G4

Additionally, if you have a laptop, you should check the box next to "Show battery status in the menu bar" so you can keep track of how much life your battery has. (Desktop systems do not have this option in their Energy Saver panel.) The battery menu extra, shown in Figure 5-24, gives you the following information:

- The icon in the menu bar shows whether the computer is plugged in, running on battery, or if the battery is charging:
  - If you are plugged in, the battery icon has a plug symbol inside.
  - The battery icon displays a progress meter to show the amount of life remaining in your battery. As the energy in the battery depletes, the indicator bar moves to the left.
  - The battery icon has a small lightning bolt inside it when the battery is charging.
- When your battery is below 25 percent, the progress meter inside the battery turns red, alerting you to the fact that you should plug in somewhere (and soon).

You will receive one final warning when your battery hits 8 percent, telling you that you are running on reserve power. If you get this warning and you fail to plug in soon, your computer *will* be put to sleep automatically to preserve the contents of memory.

- The menu extra allows you to select how the time remaining on your battery will be displayed next to the battery icon in the menu bar. You can choose from Show Time, Show Percent, or Show Neither; the menu also has an option to open the Energy Saver preferences panel. Show Time displays the time remaining on your battery in hours and minutes (e.g., 2:36 is the equivalent of 2 hours and 36 minutes); Show Percent displays the percentage of your battery's life; and Show Neither displays only the battery icon with its progress meter in the menu bar.

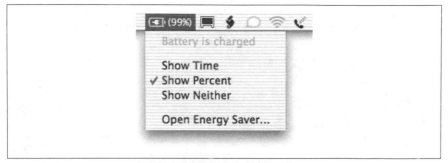

Figure 5-24. The battery menu extra, found in the menu bar

Depending on which item you select in the menu extra, Show Time or Show Percent, the opposite will be shown as gray text as the first item in the menu extra. For example, if you select Show Percent, the percentage will be shown in the menu bar, while the time remaining on your battery will be displayed as gray text at the top of the menu extra. If you select Show Neither, the time remaining will be shown as hours and minutes in gray text at the top of the menu extra.

Keyboard

The Keyboard panel, shown in Figure 5-25, controls the repeat rate when you depress a key and hold it down. You can specify the speed of the repeat (from slow to fast) and the delay between the time the key is first depressed until the repeat option kicks in (from long to short). If you select the Off option for Delay Until Repeat, the repeat feature will be disabled entirely.

If you click on the Full Keyboard Access tab (Figure 5-26) and opt to "Turn on full keyboard access," you can use the Control key with either Function keys, Letter keys, or Custom keys instead of using the mouse. These key combinations and their functions are listed in Table 5-1.

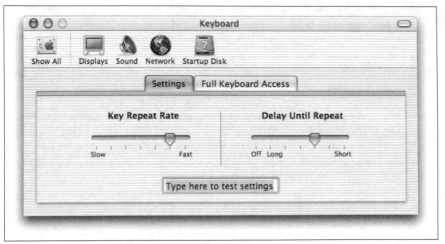

Figure 5-25. The Keyboard preferences panel

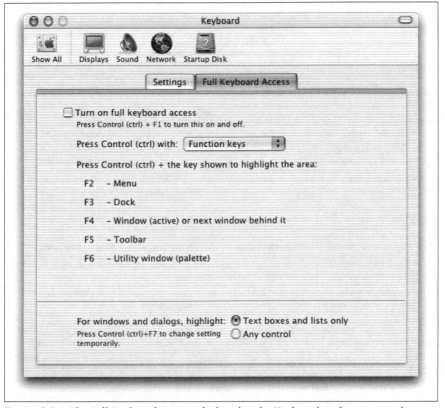

Figure 5-26. The Full Keyboard Access tab, found in the Keyboard preferences panel

Table 5-1. Keyboard Access key combinations

Function keys	Letter keys	Description
Control-F1	Control-F1	Enable/disable keyboard access
Control-F2	m	Control the menu bar
Control-F3	d	Control the Dock
Control-F4	w	Activate the window or the window behind it
Control-F5	t	Control an application's toolbar
Control-F6	u	Control an application's utility window (or palette)
Control-F7	Control-F7	Used for windows and dialogs to highlight either text input fields and lists, or for any window control
Esc	Esc	Return control to the mouse, disabling the Control-Fx key combination
Spacebar	Spacebar	Perform the function of a mouse click

If you are using an iBook or PowerBook, you need to use Control plus the *fn* key along with the Function or Letter key for keyboard access—for example, Control-fn-F2 to access menus. The *fn* key is at the bottom-left corner of your keyboard, next to the Control key (and below the Shift key).

The *fn* key is used on laptop models to invoke the actions of the function keys (F1-F12) instead of their other functions, including contrast controls (F1 and F2), volume controls (F3-F5), number lock (F6), display mirroring (F7), and eject (F12).

Mouse

The Mouse panel, shown in Figure 5-27, lets you specify the speed of the mouse, as well as the delay between double-clicks.

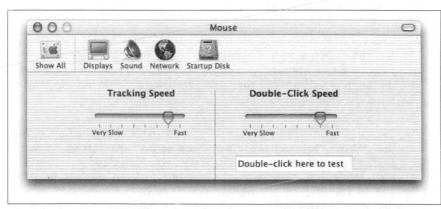

System Preferences

Figure 5-27. The Mouse preferences panel

If you're using an iBook or PowerBook, the Mouse preferences panel will have an added section for setting the controls for your trackpad, as shown in Figure 5-28.

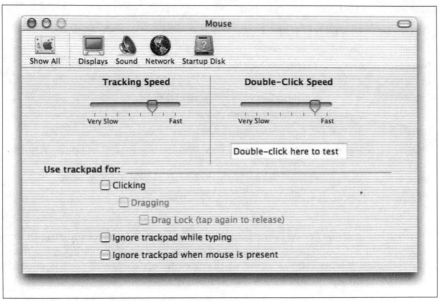

Figure 5-28. The Mouse preferences panel, with options to control the trackpad

The options for use with a trackpad include:

Clicking

Checking this box lets you use the trackpad to perform mouse clicks, instead of using the trackpad's mouse button. To click with the trackpad, just tap your finger once for a single-click, and twice for a double-click. If you select the Clicking option, you can opt to use the trackpad for Dragging and Drag Lock, which are explained here:

Dragging

This option allows you to use the trackpad to drag-select items, either in the Finder or on your Desktop. To drag-select, tap twice with your finger, hold your finger down on the second tap. Then move your finger on the trackpad to select the items. To deselect the items, tap once to release.

Drag Lock

This option allows you to drag-select (as with the Dragging option) and drag the files to another location (such as over the Trash icon in the Dock). To use Drag Lock, tap twice with your finger and hold down on the second tap and move your finger on the trackpad to select the items, and then tap once to end the selection. With the items selected, tap your finger on the trackpad twice to "grab" them, and then drag the items to where you want to move them. To "let go" of the items, tap your finger on the trackpad once; to deselect the items, move the pointer elsewhere and tap the trackpad once.

Ignore trackpad while typing
> Selecting this item disables input to the trackpad while you're typing. This is particularly useful if you have a tendency to move or rest your hands next to the trackpad while typing.

Ignore trackpad when mouse is present
> Checking this box disables the trackpad if a mouse is connected to your laptop, forcing you to use the mouse instead of the trackpad. This also works for wireless mice, like the scrollwheel mouse that comes with Wacom's Graphire 2 graphics tablet (*http://www.wacom.com*).

Sound

The Sound panel, shown in Figure 5-29, offers three panes: one for configuring Sound Effects (or alert sounds), one for sound Output (such as speakers), and one for sound Input.

Figure 5-29. The Sound preferences panel

The three Sound preferences panes are described as follows:

Sound Effects
> The Sound Effects pane lets you select the alert sound your Mac will emit when an error occurs. It also offers a slider control for setting the volume level for the alert sound.

Output

The Output pane lets you choose a device for sound output (typically, the built-in audio controller) and includes a slider for controlling the left-right balance.

Input

The Input pane lets you specify the sound input device, or microphone, for your computer. If you have a laptop, the internal microphone will be selected by default. If you're using an external microphone, you will need to select the Line In option.

All three panes include the same lower portion, with a slider control for setting your computer's Output volume. The volume you set here applies to all sound output, including system sounds and the audio content you play via iTunes. There is also a checkbox for enabling a sound volume slider as a menu extra in the menu bar. The number of "sound waves" in the menu extra's icon corresponds to the current system's volume setting.

All newer Macs have sound controls on the keyboard, which allow you to decrease, increase, or mute the sound level. On laptops, you can use F3 to mute the sound, F4 to decrease it, and F5 to increase the output sound level. If you're using a Desktop system with an extended keyboard, the output sound controls are located across the top of the number pad.

Bluetooth

Bluetooth is a short-range wireless technology for communicating with devices, such as cellular phones, PDAs, keyboards, mice, and other computers. At present, the only way to add Bluetooth for your Mac is via a USB dongle. However, knowing Apple, it won't be long before Bluetooth is built in to future hardware, just as Infrared was a few short years ago.

The Bluetooth panel has the following four tabbed panes:

Settings

This pane is used to control the settings for how your computer will be recognized via Bluetooth, whether authentication is required, if 128-bit encryption should be used for transmitting data over Bluetooth, and if your computer will support connections to older Bluetooth phones. This pane also tells you that the Bluetooth Device Name is the same as the Computer Name set up in the Sharing preferences, and offers an option to place a Bluetooth menu extra in the menu bar.

Receiving Files

This pane is used to configure what to do with the files you receive, and where to store them.

Serial Ports

This pane shows the Bluetooth ports on your computer for incoming and outgoing connections to Bluetooth devices. To disable a port, deselect the checkbox in the On/Off column. To change the settings of a port, click on the Edit button; a sheet will slide down allowing you to edit the port's name.

The sheet also has options for enabling authentication and encryption over the port.

Paired Devices

If there are any Bluetooth devices within range of your computer and you're able to connect to them, they will appear in the Paired Devices area.

Ink

One of the newer panels and features added to Mac OS X is an application called Inkwell, whose actions and controls are managed by the Ink preferences panel. Ink allows you to take input from a graphics pen and/or tablet (such as the Graphire 2 from Wacom), and either write directly into that application or to the InkPad, which is accessible through a small floating palette on your Desktop.

 For long-time Mac users, Ink is similar to Newton in many ways, including its infancy.

In order to use Ink (and Inkwell), you must first install the drivers and connect the tablet to your computer (typically via one of its USB ports).

At the top of Ink's panel is a radio button that allows you to turn handwriting recognition on or off. The three panels for Ink offer the following settings:

Settings

The Settings pane, shown in Figure 5-30, is used to control how Inkwell will handle your handwriting.

The panel has the following controls:

Allow me to write:

This pop-up menu lets you select from Anywhere or only in InkPad. If you opt to write "Anywhere," you can write anywhere onscreen into what looks like a yellow, lined sheet of paper, as well as to the InkPad, if you have it open. If you select "Only in InkPad," you will be restricted to writing and drawing in the InkPad via its floating palette.

My handwriting style is:

Here you have a slider control, which you can move left or right, depending on how closely or widely spaced your writing is, respectively.

InkPad font:

This menu lets you select the font to use when writing in the InkPad; the default is Apple Casual. (Next to this control is a checkbox, giving you the option to "Play sound while writing.")

Options...

Clicking this button reveals a sheet that gives you finer control over how your handwriting is recognized.

When you first start using Ink, this panel will be your friend. Here you can set the delay for how quickly recognition begins after you've stopped writing, how far the pen must move before the writing begins, and how long the pen

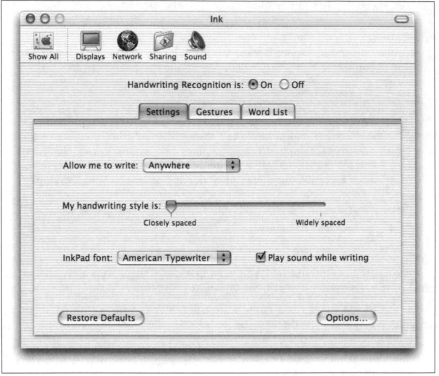

Figure 5-30. Ink's Settings pane

must be still to be used as a mouse. We strongly encourage you to play around with these settings to tune Ink to your writing style.

Gestures

The Gestures pane, shown in Figure 5-31, shows you the handwriting gestures that you can use to perform certain actions while writing, such as add a space, insert a carriage return (or "Vertical Space"), etc.

When you click on an Action to the left, the gesture will be drawn in the little box to the right to show you how you should enter that gesture while writing.

 If you plan to use Ink often, you might want to take a screenshot of the Gestures tab and keep that handy until you have memorized the gestures.

Word List

The Word List panel, shown in Figure 5-32, allows you to add common words to Ink's dictionary.

The button controls to the right of the text field are fairly self-explanatory; click Add to add a word, click Edit to change the spelling of a word, click Delete to remove a word, etc. If you try to add a word that's already in Ink's dictionary, you will be alerted as such.

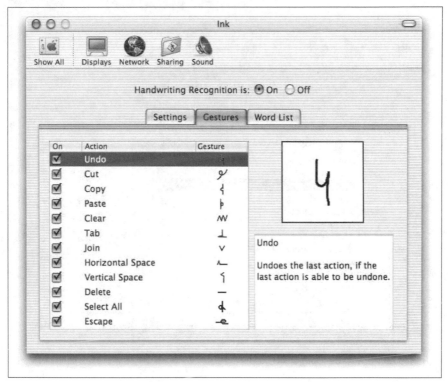

Figure 5-31. Ink's Gestures pane

The only downside to Ink is that it's still (obviously) very much a work in progress. For example, you can't add your own gestures to the Gestures panel, and while you can add words to Ink's repertoire, you cannot add a gesture for them either. That said, the mere fact that Apple has included Ink with Jaguar shows that they have bigger and better things in mind for it someday.

Internet & Network

Through these panes, users can set up and manage their .Mac accounts, set up their email account, select a default web browser, and configure how QuickTime handles incoming streaming media. System administrators can further use the Sharing panel to activate file sharing, web serving, and remote login services.

The standard set of panels in the Internet & Network section include:

- Internet
- Network
- QuickTime
- Sharing

These panels are explained in the sections that follow.

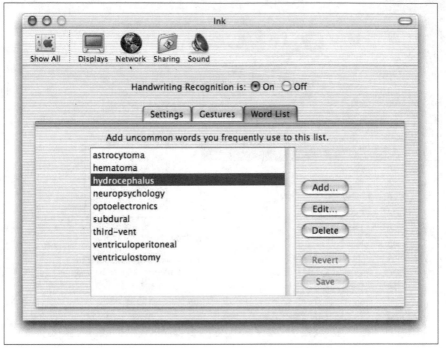

Figure 5-32. Ink's Word List pane

Internet

The Internet panel is where you can go to configure your settings for your .Mac account and the applications you use to access the Internet. There are four tabbed panes to the Internet preferences.

.Mac

The .Mac panel, shown in Figure 5-33, is where you go to set up your .Mac account.

If you already have a .Mac account, you can just enter your .Mac member name and password; if you don't, you can sign up for a .Mac account by clicking on the Sign Up button.

 .Mac is Apple's subscriber service, which replaced the free iTools account. The annual cost of a .Mac account is $99. See *http://www. mac.com* for more information about what services and software are included with a .Mac account.

iDisk

This pane, shown in Figure 5-34, gives you information about your iDisk, if you have a .Mac account.

The top-half of the window shows you how much space you've used on your iDisk. If you need more space and wish to purchase some, click on the Buy More button.

Figure 5-33. The .Mac pane

  Clicking on the Buy More button will take you to .Mac's Upgrade storage page, where you can purchase additional space for your iDisk and your .Mac email account and additional *mac.com* email-only accounts.

The lower half of this window allows you to specify the permissions for your iDisk's Public folder. The three options for your Public folder include:

Read-Only

Allows others to view and download the contents of your Public directory.

Read-Write

Allows others to view, download, and save files to your Public directory.

Password Protect

Allows you to set a password for your Public folder, which means that anyone who tries to access your Public folder would have to supply a password before they're given access. Note that the Read-Only and Read-Write options still apply the same, even if password protection is turned on.

Email

The Email pane, shown in Figure 5-35, is where you configure the settings for your default email account.

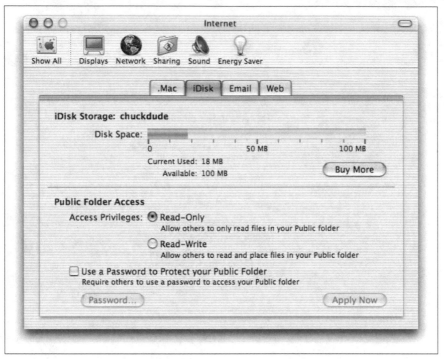

Figure 5-34. The iDisk pane

At the top of the window is a pull-down menu that lets you select the Default Email Reader, which is initially set to Apple's Mail application. If you have another email client installed on your system, Mac OS X should recognize and place it in this menu. If it doesn't, you can choose the Select option and locate the application you'd like to use for reading and sending email.

The other fields in this window are used for entering the settings for your email account, such as your email address, incoming and outgoing mail server, user account ID and password, and the type of email account (POP or IMAP). If you will be using your .Mac email account as the default, you can select the checkbox next to "Use .Mac Email account" and all of the fields below will fill in automatically.

 If your .Mac account is secondary to a primary email account, such as the one you use for work, you *should not* select the checkbox next to "Use .Mac Email account," as it will wipe out your mail settings in *Mail.app*.

Web

The Web pane, shown in Figure 5-36, is used to select your default web browser, home page, and for designating where files you download from the Internet will be saved.

As with the Email pane, Mac OS X should automatically detect any web browsers you've installed and place them in the Default Web Browser pull-

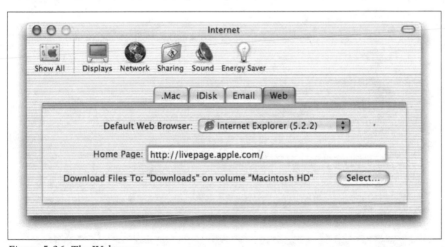

Figure 5-35. The Email pane

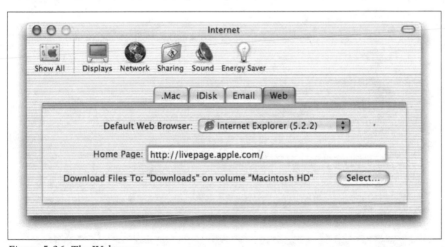

Figure 5-36. The Web pane

down menu. If you've installed some obscure web browser and don't see it in there, choose the Select option from the menu.

The URL shown in the Home Page field is the page that opens automatically when you launch the default web browser. By default, this is set to *http:// livepage.apple.com*, as shown in Figure 5-36.

By default, your Mac is set up to download files to your Documents folder. However, if you'd like to change the location, click on the Select button and choose another folder.

 One way to keep track of the files you've downloaded from the Internet is to have them download to your Desktop, or to a Downloads folder you create on your Desktop (see Figure 5-36).

Network

The Network panel, shown in Figure 5-37, is the interface to the Mac's basic network interfaces, including Ethernet, AirPort, and dialup modems. At least one of these interfaces has to be configured properly to get the Mac into a network environment or onto the Internet. The Network preferences panel is described in detail in Chapter 7.

Figure 5-37. The Network preferences panel

QuickTime

The QuickTime panel, shown in Figure 5-38, lets you specify the preferences for the QuickTime Player, as well as how multimedia is handled on your system.

Figure 5-38. The QuickTime preferences panel

There are five tabbed panes to the QuickTime preferences panel.

Plug-In

This pane is used to configure the settings for the QuickTime plug-in for your web browser. Clicking on the MIME settings button reveals a sheet (shown in Figure 5-39) that gives you access to how your browser will handle various file types, including streaming media, audio, MPEG movies, MP3 files, image files, and miscellaneous multimedia.

To select all of the types for a category, click on the checkbox so a check appears. If a category box has a minus sign in it, that means that one of the options inside is unchecked. To reveal all of the file types for a category, click on the disclosure triangle.

Connection

This is where you specify the speed of your network connection. Clicking on the Instant-On button reveals a sheet that lets you choose whether streaming media will be played automatically as it starts to download, and if so, you choose whether to set the delay period. The Transport Setup button reveals a sheet for setting the transport protocol (UDP or HTTP) and their respective ports.

Music

Used to specify the default synthesizer for playing music and MIDI files. The QuickTime Music Synthesizer is selected by default.

Media Keys

Used to authorize access to secured or password-protected media files.

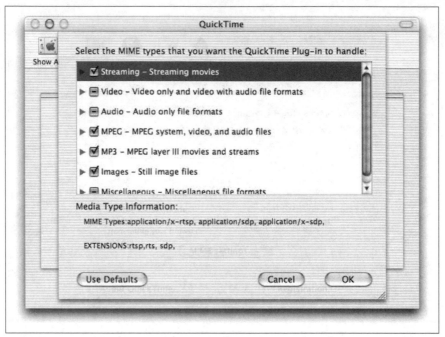

Figure 5-39. The QuickTime panel's MIME settings sheet

Update

Used to check for updates to QuickTime itself, as well as third-party Quick-Time software.

At the bottom of the QuickTime panel are the following two button controls:

About QuickTime

Clicking this button reveals a sheet that tells you which version of Quick-Time is installed on your system.

Registration

If you've purchased a registration key for QuickTime Pro, you need to click on this button to enter your registration number. For more information about QuickTime Pro, see Apple's QuickTime web site (*http://www.apple.com/quicktime*).

Sharing

The Sharing panel provides some simple controls to activate various *network services* (programs that other computers can connect to over a network or the Internet).

There are two text fields at the top of the Sharing panel for specifying your Computer Name and Rendezvous Name. By default, these are set to your username (e.g., Chuck Toporek's Computer) after installation; however, you can change these to whatever you'd like (for instance, MacChuck).

The name you specify in the Computer Name field will be used as your machine's hostname.

In addition to these basic text fields, the Sharing panel has three tabbed panes, described as follows:

Services

The Services pane, shown in Figure 5-40, is for allowing others (including yourself from a remote machine) access to your computer. These services include:

Personal File Sharing

When active, the Mac's disks become available for mounting on other machines over the network.

Windows File Sharing

Lets you to share folders on your computer with Windows users via SMB and CIFS.

Personal Web Sharing

Used to turn on the Apache web server so people on the outside world can view web pages stored in your ~/*Sites* directory.

Remote Login

Controls *sshd*, which allows users to connect remotely to your Mac via the secure shell (SSH).

FTP Access

Controls the machine's FTP server.

Remote Apple Events

Allows applications on other Mac OS X systems to send Apple Events to applications on your system via AppleScript.

Printer Sharing

Activates USB printer sharing, letting other computers on the network use the printer connected to your Mac.

Firewall

The Firewall pane, shown in Figure 5-41, lets you activate and configure the firewall on your Mac. For more information on the Firewall pane, see Chapter 11.

Internet

The Internet pane, shown in Figure 5-42, lets you share your Internet connection with other Macs on the same network, even via AirPort. Enabling Internet sharing lets you turn your Mac OS X machine into a router.

System

This final category of preinstalled preference panes lets system administrators manage the machine's user accounts, adjust the system clock, and set the Mac's startup disk. It also serves as the main interface for obtaining system software

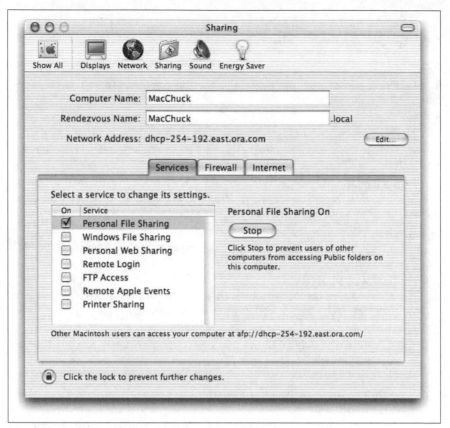

Figure 5-40. The Services pane

updates from Apple. Some of these panes involve system-wide settings, and require administrator privileges.

The standard set of panels in the System section include:

- Accounts
- Classic
- Date & Time
- Software Update
- Speech
- Startup Disk
- Universal Access

These panels are explained in the sections that follow.

Accounts

The Accounts panel lets users with administrator privileges create and delete users from the system, as well as manage the user accounts. The Accounts panel has the following tabbed panes:

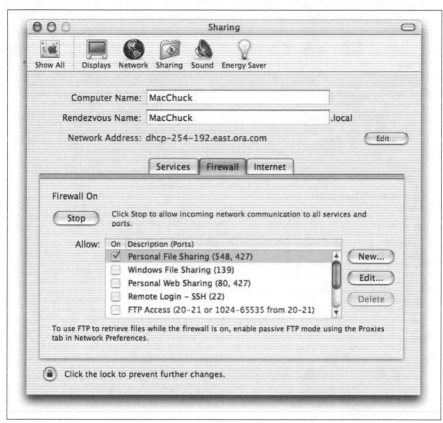

Figure 5-41. The Firewall pane

Users

The Users pane, shown in Figure 5-43, provides the administrator with access to managing individual user accounts on the system.

As Figure 5-43 shows, there are two users with Admin privileges on this system, and one regular user (Max). Users with Admin privileges are allowed to do pretty much anything they want on the system, as long as they provide the proper administrator's password when prompted. Regular users, however, are restricted somewhat from installing and updating the system software, as well as from changing vital settings on their system.

You can further clip a normal user's wings by selecting the user's name and clicking on the Capabilities button. The sheet shown in Figure 5-44 will appear.

The user Capabilities sheet gives an administrator greater control over what a user can do on the system, as well as restrict them from using certain applications and utilities. For example, if you have a user whose exposure to Unix is minimal, you can restrict them from using the Terminal application by clicking on the disclosure triangle next to Utilities and unchecking the box next to Terminal.

Figure 5-42. The Internet pane

You can also select Use Simple Finder to restrict what a user can do. Selecting this option unchecks the items listed under "This user can:", in effect keeping them from doing too much damage to their system preferences.

To remove a user from the system, select their name in the Users window and click on the Delete User button. You will receive a warning to confirm whether this is what you want to do; if it is, click the OK button to delete the user. The contents of the users home directory will be packaged up and placed in */Users/Deleted Users*.

Login Options

The Login Options pane, shown in Figure 5-45, determines how the users of a multiuser Mac OS X system will be greeted when logging into the system.

If you select "Name and password," users will be required to enter their username and password before they can log in. If you select "List of users," users will see a list of the users for that system. All they need to do to log in is click on their name, enter their password, and press Return.

Figure 5-43. The Users pane of the Accounts preferences panel

Classic

The Classic panel lets you manually start, stop, and configure the Classic environment that runs Mac OS 9 applications within Mac OS X. Use of the Classic panel
is described in Chapter 3.

Date & Time

If you have administrator privileges, the Date & Time panel, shown in
Figure 5-46, lets you set the system clock and time zone, as well as select an NTP
(Network Time Protocol) server.

The Date & Time panel has four tabbed panes, described as follows:

Date & Time
> The Date & Time pane is where you set the date and time for your system. If
> you opt to use an NTP server, the date and time controls won't be visible on
> this pane.

Time Zone
> The Time Zone pane provides you with a map of the continent you live in so
> you can select your time zone, either from the pull down menu or by drag-
> ging the time zone bar left or right.

Network Time
> If you opt to use an NTP server for setting your system's time and date, the
> Network Time pane allows you to select one of three Apple-run time servers

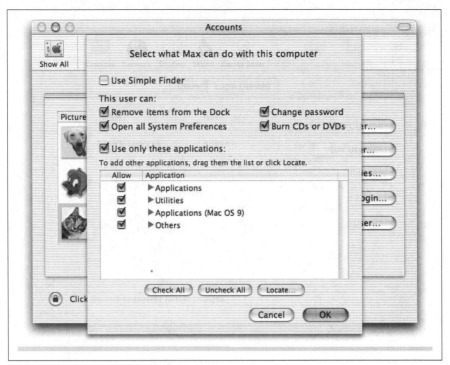

Figure 5-44. *The user capabilities sheet*

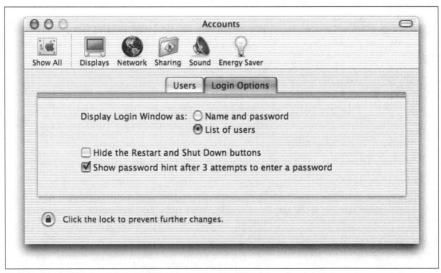

Figure 5-45. *The Login Options pane*

(Apple Americas, Apple Asia, or Apple Europe). You can type in the address for a third-party NTP server as well.

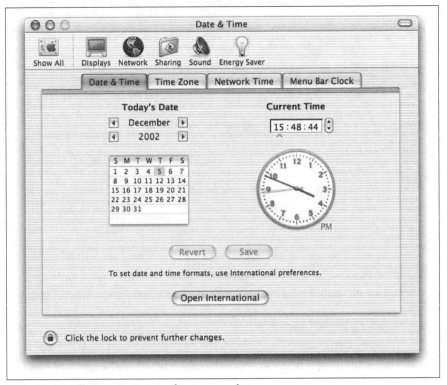

Figure 5-46. The Date & Time preferences panel

Menu Bar Clock

The Menu Bar Clock pane lets you determine whether the date and time will show up in the menu bar, as well as the manner they appear there.

Software Update

The Software Update panel, shown in Figure 5-47, lets you contact servers at Apple to check for updates to Mac OS X system software, updates to security, and updates to the iApps. There are two tabbed panes for Software Update:

Update Software

The Update Software pane is used to check for updates and to configure your system to automatically check for updates (Daily, Weekly, or Monthly) when your system is connected to the Internet. To check for available updates, click on the Check Now button.

Installed Updates

The Installed Updates pane lists the updates you've installed on your system. This list is stored in */Library/Logs/Software Update.log*. You can view the *Software Update.log* file by clicking on the Open as Log File button, which opens the log file in the Console application (*/Applications/Utilities*).

If Software Update detects an available update when you click on the Check Now button, a separate window will pop up, showing you the available updates (as

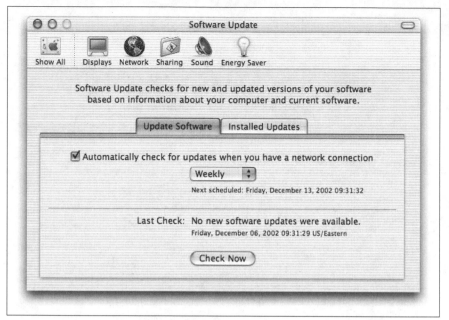

Figure 5-47. The Software Update panel

shown in Figure 5-48). To find out more information about the update, click on its name; its description will appear in the text field below the listing of updates.

To install an available update, select the checkbox next to the package and click on the Install button (administrator privileges are required for most updates). Some other tips for using Software Update include the following:

- If there is an update you want to install at a later time, unselect its checkbox and install the other updates (or quit Software Update with ⌘-Q). The next time you run Software Update, the update you deferred will show up as an available update.

- If there is an update that you feel you will never install, such as a foreign language update, click on the update's name and choose Update → Make Inactive. The next time Software Update is run, that update won't appear in the list of available updates. However, if you decide later that you do want to install it, you can do so by selecting Update → Make Active.

- To view a list of Inactive updates, go to Update → Show Inactive Updates.

- To save an update rather than install it (say, for archive purposes), place a checkmark in the box next to the update and then select Update → Download checked items to Desktop.

- Apple maintains a listing of available updates for Mac OS X on their web site, *http://www.apple.com/downloads/macosx/apple*.

- You can tell Software Update to check immediately by holding down the Option key as you click its icon in the System Preferences Window. Also, you can run */usr/sbin/softwareupdate* from the command line if you really want to (to apply an update remotely via SSH, for example).

Figure 5-48. Software Update's window lists available updates

Speech

The Speech panel lets you set the preferences regarding Apple's speech recognition system, as well as the voice that your Mac uses when reading text to you.

For more details about the Speech panel, see the later section "Speech Recognition and Speakable Commands."

Startup Disk

The Startup Disk panel lists the available icons for detected Mac OS X and Mac OS 9 system folders. This panel is used to select which operating system will boot when you start or restart your Mac.

Use of the Startup Disk panel is described in Chapter 3.

Universal Access

The Universal Access panel lets you activate and configure many options to make Mac OS X easier to use by persons with disabilities or physical limitations. There are four tabbed panes, described as follows:

Seeing
  The Seeing pane, shown in Figure 5-49, is used for controlling the display. It has three main functions, which are described in the following list.

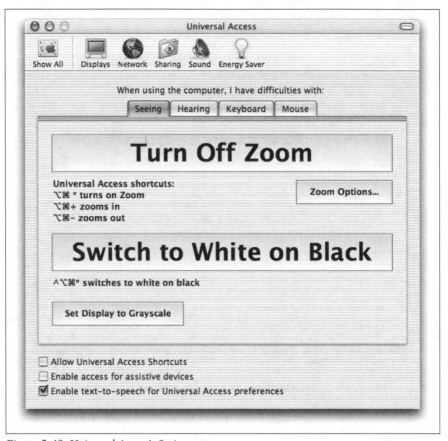

Figure 5-49. Universal Access's Seeing pane

- Enable/disable the Zoom feature, which allows you to zoom in and out of the viewable display. When Zoom is enabled, clicking on the Zoom Options button gives you more control over the Zoom feature. There are slider controls for specifying the maximum and minimum zoom range, a checkbox for adding a preview rectangle to the display as a target area for zooming in, and an option for smoothing images.

The size of the preview rectangle is based on the Maximum Zoom setting, and takes the shape of your display. If you enable the preview rectangle, your mouse pointer is placed at the rectangle's center. When you zoom in, the area defined by the preview rectangle is the focus of the display. The keyboard shortcuts for Zoom are shown in Table 5-2.

Table 5-2. Keyboard shortcuts for using Zoom

Shortcut	Description
Option-⌘-*	Toggle Zoom on/off
Option-⌘-+	Zoom in
Option-⌘-–	Zoom out
Option-⌘-\	Toggle display smoothing on/off

- Switch the screen mode to White on Black, and vice versa (essentially giving the user a view that looks similar to a black-and-white film negative).
- Set the display to grayscale (clicking the button a second time returns your display to full-color mode).

Hearing

The Hearing pane, shown in Figure 5-50, offers a checkbox that, when activated, causes the screen to flash (with a single white pulse) instead of playing an alert sound.

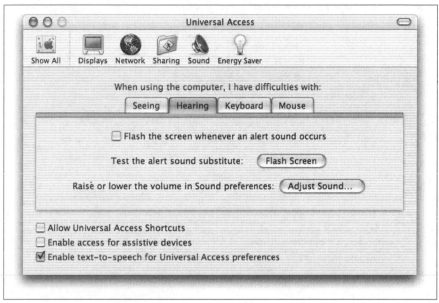

Figure 5-50. Universal Access's Hearing pane

System
Preferences

Starting with Mac OS X 10.2.*x*, the display flashes (regardless of this setting) if the system tries to play an alert sound and the sound is muted, or if there is no sound output device connected to the Mac.

Clicking the Adjust Sound button changes the System Preferences window to the Sound panel, described earlier in this chapter in the "Hardware" section.

Keyboard

The Keyboard pane, shown in Figure 5-51, assists users who have trouble pressing more than one key at a time, and/or difficulty with repeating keystrokes (for example, if they tend to hold down on a key too long while pressing it).1

There are two sections to the Keyboard pane: Sticky Keys and Slow Keys, described as follows:

Sticky Keys

Switching on the Sticky Keys radio button causes Mac OS X to treat key combinations as individual key sequences. For example, the keyboard shortcut Option-⌘-W is used to close all the open windows for an application. Typically, these keys are pressed together, or by holding

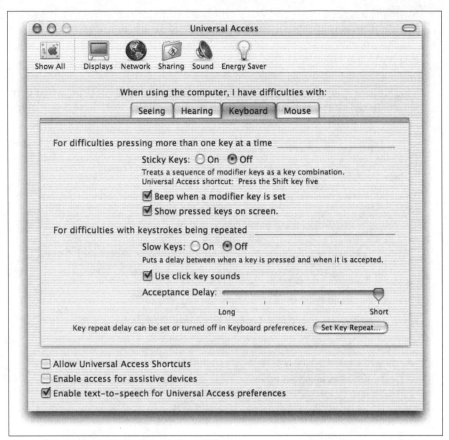

Figure 5-51. Universal Access's Keyboard pane

down Option-⌘ and then pressing W. However, with Sticky Keys enabled, you can press these keys one at a time to invoke the command.

If you press a modifier key (Control, Shift, Option, or Command) twice, the key will be *super-sticky*, so that it remains active after you issue a key combination. This is useful when you want use the same modifier key but invoke a different command—for example, when using Word, you might want to make some text bold (⌘-B) and italic (⌘-I). Typing a modifier key three times removes it from the current key combination's list of modifier keys. If you remove all the modifier keys from the combination you are constructing, then the keyboard returns to its usual typing mode.

 If you check the Allow Universal Access Shortcuts option at the bottom of the window, you can press the Shift key five consecutive times to turn Sticky Keys on or off.

Slow Keys

In Mac OS X 10.2.x, these controls are an addendum to those found in the Keyboard preferences panel (see the *Hardware* section earlier in this chapter). If you enable Slow Keys, the slider lets you set a delay between key presses. Using this feature along with the Keyboard preferences panel can reduce accidental letter repetition while typing.

Pressing the Set Key Repeat button opens the Keyboard preferences panel. In earlier versions of Mac OS X, this button was the only control available for Slow Keys.

Mouse

If you have trouble using the mouse, you can enable Mouse Keys via the Mouse pane (shown in Figure 5-52). Mouse Keys allows you to use your keyboard's number pad instead of the mouse.

By holding down the number keys as detailed in Table 5-3, you can move the mouse pointer in eight different directions, and use the 5 and 0 (zero) keys as the mouse button. (Conversely, the keypad ceases to function as a device for typing numbers; you need to turn off Mouse Keys to enter numbers.)

Table 5-3. Mouse Keys numeric mouse controls

Number key	Action
1	Move pointer down and to the left
2	Move pointer down
3	Move pointer down and to the right
4	Move pointer left
5	Mouse click
6	Move pointer right
7	Move pointer up and to the left
8	Move pointer up
9	Move pointer up and to the right
0	Mouse click

Mouse Keys can come in handy if the Mac's mouse breaks or goes missing. You may want to enable the Allow Universal Access Shortcuts checkbox, even if you don't normally use the Universal Access options regularly. If you enable this checkbox, you can press the Option key five consecutive times to turn on Universal Access.

Speech Recognition and Speakable Commands

Mac OS X's built-in speech recognition software lets you execute various system and application commands by speaking them (assuming that you have a microphone attached to or built into your Macintosh). The system includes many

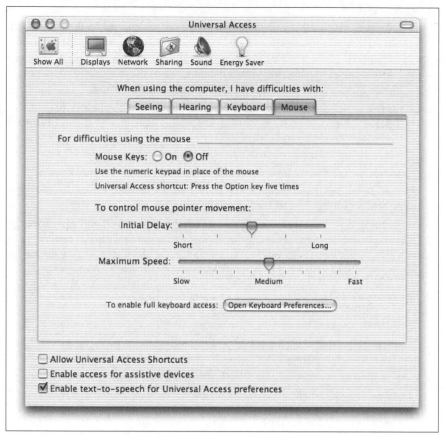

Figure 5-52. Universal Access's Mouse pane

commands. Application developers can also define spoken commands that work within their own programs, and users can expand the machine's speakable repertoire by writing and installing scripts.

The speech recognition system is primarily useful for defining voice-activated macros and shortcuts. It doesn't let you use your microphone as a complete alternative to the keyboard and mouse. The system can't, for example, take dictation into a word processor. For that level of functionality, you need a third-party application, such as IBM's ViaVoice (*http://www.ibm.com/software/speech/mac/osx/*).

Activating Speech Recognition

You can configure and activate the speech recognition through the three tabbed panes of the Speech preferences panel, shown in Figure 5-53.

To turn speech recognition on, set the "Apple Speakable Items is" radio button to On. This causes the speech systems' round "listener" window (Figure 5-54) to appear. Note that the listener floats over all your active windows, but you can drag it anywhere you like. It remains visible until you switch the Apple Speakable Items button back to Off.

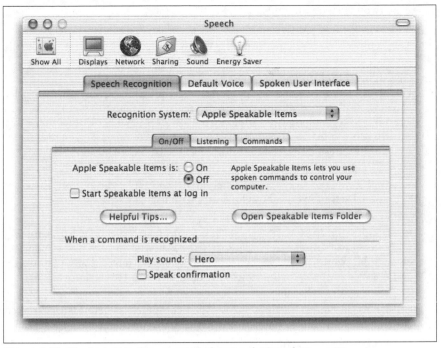

Figure 5-53. The Speech preference panel, showing the Speech Recognition pane

Figure 5-54. Speech's microphone

The system doesn't try listening for commands until you put it into listening mode via the Speech panels' Speech Recognition → Listening tab. By default, the listening key is set to Esc (the Escape key). Until you press the Esc key, the microphone will be grayed out; however, when the Esc key is pressed, the listener will look similar to Figure 5-54, complete with a sound input indicator (the blue-, green-, and red-colored bars) and indicator arrows showing that sound is being received by the microphone. If you don't want to have the Esc key as the default key for listening, click on the Change Key button and enter a new key or key combination (e.g., ⌘-Esc).

If you use the Terminal and Speech Recognition together, you should change your listening key to something other than Esc, since that key has a special meaning and functionality when running programs from the command line.

There are two Listening Methods:

Listen only while key is pressed
This setting is an on-demand mode, which listens only when the Esc key is pressed

Key toggles listening on and off
Under this setting, pressing and releasing the listening key (Esc) toggles listening mode on or off. Since this means the computer's microphone will actively receive and analyze sounds over longer stretches of time, you must set two more controls to help it discriminate the commands you speak from background noise (or other things you might say while sitting at your computer).

If you have selected the "Key toggles listening on and off" radio button, there are some additional settings you should look at, including:

Name
By default, this is set to the Star Trek-esque Computer, which means you must first say "Computer, ..." before issuing a spoken command. You can change the Name—however, you should choose a name that's easy to say and unlikely to appear in any conversation that your Mac might overhear.

Name is
This pop-up menu defines how the computer differentiates spoken commands from other sounds. The options in this menu are:

Optional before commands
When this setting is selected, the machine doesn't listen for its Name and tries to interpret everything it hears as a potential command. For example, in order to check your mail and then switch to iTunes, you only need to say, "Get my mail. Switch to iTunes."

 This setting is actually rather dangerous because if you are in listening mode, anything you say that the computer hears can be interpreted as a command.

Required before each command (the default)
This setting has the speech system listen for the name defined in the Name field before interpreting every command. For example, to hear a knock-knock joke, you could say "Computer, tell me a joke." (If you try this, remember that you need to say "Computer, ..." before each step of the joke. For example, "Computer, who's there?", and "Computer, Thea who?".)

Required 15 seconds after last command
Required 30 seconds after last command
These settings also require that you speak the Name that you chose in the Name text field. Once you have said it, however, the machine will continue to interpret sounds as possible commands until either 15 or 30 seconds have elapsed without recognizing a command. Thus, you can launch multiple commands like this: "Computer, get my mail. Switch to iTunes."

The last two items at the bottom of the Listening pane allow you to specify which microphone to use (Line In or Internal microphone) and to set the volume for the microphone's input. Pressing the Volume button pops open a window that lets you test and adjust the volume level by having you say some sample commands.

Speakable Items

To see which commands are available to you at any time, click on the triangle at the bottom of the listener window, as shown in Figure 5-55.

Figure 5-55. Clicking on the listener's triangle opens its context menu

The Speech Commands window, shown in Figure 5-56, has two parts:

- The top section shows a log of the speech commands issued.
- A Commands section (at the bottom of the window), which shows a list of available commands, collapsed into categories with disclosure triangles to reveal the speakable commands.

Figure 5-56. The Speech Commands window

By default, there are two categories in the Commands section:

Speakable Items
> This is a catch-all category for commands you can invoke throughout the system.

Application Switching
> This lists the special commands for switching (and launching) between applications, based on the application icons in the Dock.

Applications such as the Finder, Mail, and Internet Explorer define their own speakable items when they are the active (i.e., frontmost) application. When that application is active, its list of speakable items shows up in the Commands section.

Customizing Speakable Items

If you click on the Open Speakable Items Folder button located on the Speech → Speech Recognition → On/Off pane, a Finder window pops open, listing the speakable items on your system. The speakable items available exist as files in */Library/Speech/Speakable Items*. Files residing within that folder directly represent system-wide items. Those inside the *Application Speakable Items* folder are specific to various applications on your system.

Each speakable item is either a property list (*.plist*) file, an AppleScript, or some other type of Finder object. Property lists simply execute the commands predefined by the system or speech-friendly application. AppleScripts are executed by the system.

In other words, users can make their own voice-activated commands by writing (or finding on the Internet) an AppleScript that performs a particular task or series of tasks, giving that script a pronounceable name. The AppleScript can then be placed into the *~/Library/Speech/Speakable Items* directory.

Finally, any other Finder object—arbitrary files, folders, disks, or aliases to one of these—acts as if it was double-clicked in the Finder when its name is spoken.

Adding Panes to System Preferences

Preference panes are really just slimmed-down Mac OS X applications, and as such, can be installed from a source disk (or a freshly downloaded disk image) to your local hard drive with a simple drag-and-drop procedure (see Chapter 6). They can even be launched like other applications; double-clicking a *.prefPane* file's icon while in the Finder causes it to open within System Preferences (launching that application first, if it wasn't already running).

However, the System Preferences application won't display preference panes' icons as part of its main view (Figure 5-1) unless you add them into one of the filesystem's Library folders. Placing a *.prefPane* file in the *~/Library/PreferencePanes* folder located within your own Home folder causes it to appear listed among the System Preferences' pane icons for you alone. If you want to let all users of the

TinkerTool

One third-party preference pane that quickly gained popularity in the Mac OS X community is Marcel Bresnik's TinkerTool (*http://www.bresink.de/osx/index. html*). TinkerTool provides a friendly interface to many obscure System Preferences, which are adjustable by virtue of having entries in the underlying *defaults* system (as detailed in Chapter 22), but for which no Apple-authored preference panes or application preference windows exist.

For example, one of the pane's several pages allows you to position the Dock in places that the official Mac OS X Dock preference pane doesn't, such as along the top of the screen or attached to a corner rather than centered along a side. These options are fully supported by the operating system, but the operating system does not provide an obvious way to get to them. (The non-obvious way involves opening up the file *~/Library/Preferences/com.apple.dock.plist* in the Property List Editor application and modifying the values of the pinning and orientation keys.)

machine use the pane (and you have admin privileges), you can place it in */Library/ PreferencePanes*. (Note that this shares only the interface; unless the pane explicitly sets system-wide preferences, it will read from and write to only the appropriate preference file within the */Library* folder of any user who uses it.)

See Chapter 9 for more information about how the Mac OS X Library folders.

6

Applications and Utilities

Apple has included a set of native applications and utilities for Mac OS X, including the famous iApps (iMovie, iPhoto, and iTunes; future releases will most likely include iCal and iSync as well).

There are applications for such things as viewing and printing PDF files, basic word processing, sending and receiving email, creating movies, and utilities to help you manage your system.

Use the Finder to locate the Applications (*/Applications*) and Utilities (*/Applications/ Utilities*) on your system. You can quickly go to the *Applications* folder by clicking on the Applications icon in the toolbar, or by using the Shift-⌘-A keyboard shortcut. Because there is no keyboard shortcut to the Utilities, you might consider dragging the Utilities folder to the Finder toolbar.

These aren't the only programs that Mac OS X ships with. The underlying Darwin system involves hundreds of command, tool, and system service programs (also known as *daemons*), which run either behind the scenes to make the operating system work, or are invoked as command-line programs through the Terminal. In Apple parlance, however, *application* specifically refers to a program that runs in the Aqua graphical interface (or in the Classic Environment). Chapter 25 covers command-line tools and system daemons.

If you've installed the Developer Tools, then you have access to another suite of applications that is located in */Developer/Applications*. These programs all focus on the process of creating Mac OS X applications yourself; they (especially the key Project Builder and Interface Builder applications) are described in Chapter 10.

This chapter provides a basic overview of the Applications and Utilities that ship with Mac OS X 10.2, and also covers installing applications from disk images (*.dmg* files), uninstalling applications, and use of StuffIt Expander for uncompressing application archives.

Applications

This section very briefly touches on Mac OS X's standard-issue productivity and utility applications, even though some of them (such as iMovie) are sophisticated enough to have entire books written on them already.

Acrobat Reader

> This Adobe program lets you browse PDF files. Note that Apple's Preview application is the system's default application for opening PDF files. Acrobat Reader, however, contains more PDF-specific features, such as the ability to follow in-document hyperlinks or search for text within the document.
>
> If you prefer to use Acrobat Reader instead of Preview, then call up any PDF file's Info window in the Finder (see "The Get Info Window" in Chapter 2), set Acrobat Reader 5.0 as its application (as shown in Figure 6-1), and then click the window's "Change All..." button.

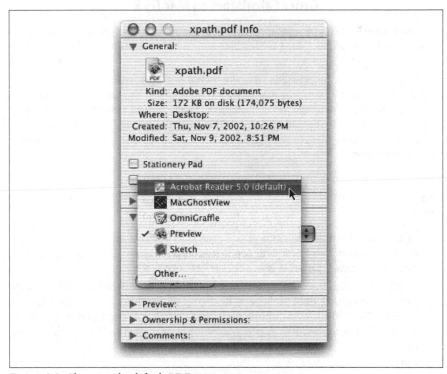

Figure 6-1. Changing the default PDF viewer

AppleScript

> This folder contains applications for creating and running AppleScripts, as well as subfolders holding example scripts. See Chapter 11 for more on AppleScript.

Address Book
> A simple frontend to the current user's Address Book database, which stores email addresses and associated information. This database is primarily used by Apple's Mail application, but other applications run by the same user can read from and write to it as well. (The actual database exists as binary files in *~/Library/Addresses*.)

Calculator
> The Calculator application that ships with Jaguar has a fully functional scientific calculator, compared to the simple four-function calculator that shipped with earlier versions of the Mac OS. Calculator also has a Paper Tape sheet that allows you to view the math functions, which you can copy and paste into a document.

Other Calculators on Mac OS X

If you have Mac OS 9 installed, than you can use the Graphing Calculator, found in */Applications (Mac OS 9)*, which lets you plot equations and watch the results in 2D or 3D space.

Through the Terminal, you can run a command-line program called *bc*, which is the GNU project's calculator that ships with Mac OS X. You can use it either as an interactive calculator or a complete mathematical scripting language involving variable substitution, Boolean logic operations, binary and hexadecimal computation, and many other features. Consult *bc*'s manpage for complete documentation.

Chess
> An implementation of the GNU project's chess program, a staple of many other Unix distributions, and good enough to consistently crush the authors of this book at its easiest skill level. It features 2D and 3D modes, and can document games' progress using chess notation.
>
> Apple also uses this application to demonstrate its speech recognition technology. Activating the Use Speech Recognition checkbox under the Chess → Preferences... window summons the circular speech recognition microphone window (as described in Chapter 5), letting you play chess by speaking your moves.

DVD Player
> If your Mac has a DVD drive, use this application to play DVDs. When active, you can use menu commands and a control panel window to navigate through the active disc and its features. You can also activate the DVD's own menu selections simply by pointing to and clicking on them.

iCal
> iCal is a calendaring application (similar to Entourage, if you're a Windows convert) that allows you to manage and publish your calendar to any WebDAV-enabled server (including your .Mac account). You can also

subscribe to other calendars (such as a listing of holidays, the schedule for your favorite sports team, or that of another user). iCal didn't release in time to make it on the CDs for Jaguar; however, you can download it from Apple at *http://www.apple.com/ical.*

iChat

This is the new chat client. iChat allows you to chat with other .Mac members, as well as with AOL Instant Messenger (AIM) users. iChat also supports messaging via Rendezvous for dynamically finding iChat users on your local network. To learn more about iChat, go to Apple's page at *http://www.apple.com/jaguar/ichat.html.*

Image Capture

This application automatically activates when you plug a digital camera into your Mac's USB port. By launching it manually, you can configure its behavior upon activation, such as setting the location to which it downloads pictures from the camera, having it automatically build web pages from them, or launching other applications like iPhoto.

iMovie

This application lets you create digital movies by sequencing and combining video and audio sources (either from on-disk files or from devices such as a digital video camera), and gives you basic tools for working with title overlays, scene transitions, and other effects. It's capable of exporting your creations to the cross-platform QuickTime (*.mov*) file format.

Internet Connect

This application can act as an interface to your modem, if you use dial-up services to connect to the Internet (see Chapter 7). It also displays information about your current Internet connection—such as throughput speed—no matter what network interface you're using.

Internet Explorer

Microsoft's web browser, and the only (obvious) one that ships with Mac OS X. As such, it is the default application for handling local HTML files that you open in the Finder, as well as HTTP or FTP URLs that you open through other applications. See Chapter 7 for more about your Mac OS X web-browsing options.

iPhoto

iPhoto allows you to download, organize, and edit images taken with a digital camera. iPhoto is much more powerful than Image Capture, described earlier. To learn more about iPhoto, see *iPhoto: The Missing Manual* (Pogue Press/O'Reilly & Associates, Inc.), or Apple's iPhoto page at *http://www.apple.com/iphoto.*

iSync

iSync can be used to synchronize data—contact information from your Address Book, your iCal calendars, music, etc.—from your computer to another device such as a cellular phone, PDA, iPod, or another computer. iSync is a late addition to Jaguar and is available for download from Apple's web site at *http://www.apple.com/isync.*

iTunes

iTunes can be used to play CDs, listen to Internet radio stations, import (rip) music from CDs, burn CDs from music you've collected, and to store and play MP3 files. If you have an iPod, you can also use iTunes to synchronize your MP3 files. To learn more about iTunes, see Apple's page at *http://www. apple.com/itunes*.

Mail

Mail is the default email client for Mac OS X. It supports multiple accounts per user, which can be either local Unix mail accounts or remote mail accounts updated through the POP or IMAP mail protocols.

Preview

Preview is a simple image viewer that lets you open and export files that have been saved in a variety of image formats, including PICT, GIF, JPEG, and TIFF, to name a few. Preview is the default viewer for opening PDF files (the default file format for screenshots taken with Shift-⌘-3 or Shift-⌘-4).

QuickTime Player

The default viewer for QuickTime files (both locally stored and network-streamed) as well as a handful of other video formats (such as MPEG and AVI). QuickTime Player can also play audio formats such as MP3, but it lacks the sophisticated audio-friendly cataloguing features of iTunes.

Sherlock

Unlike previous versions of Sherlock, which you could use to index and search for items on your system, Sherlock 3 is Apple's venture into web services. (As mentioned in Chapter 2, the search functionality is built into the Finder, and indexing is now done via the Get Info window for drives, partitions, and folders.) To use Sherlock under Jaguar, you must have a connection to the Internet. Sherlock 3, shown in Figure 6-2, can be used to conduct searches on the Internet for:

- Pictures
- Stock quotes
- Movie theaters and show times
- Locating a business in your area (based on the address information you provide in Sherlock's preferences), along with driving directions and a map to the location
- Bidding on eBay auction items
- Checking the arrival and departure times of airline flights
- Finding the definition or spelling for a word in the dictionary
- Searching in AppleCare's Knowledge Base to solve a problem you're having with your computer
- Getting a quick translation from one language to another

Stickies

A standard part of the Mac OS since Version 7.5, this application lets you cover your workspace in virtual stick-on notes containing reminders, phone numbers, images, and so on.

Figure 6-2. Sherlock's web-searching interface (with the Apple channel selected)

System Preferences
> A frontend to all the system's preference panels, as described in Chapter 5.

TextEdit
> Like most applications that come with Jaguar, TextEdit also received a bit of an upgrade. TextEdit now sports a ruler bar with text formatting buttons for changing the alignment, leading, and indentation of text. By default, TextEdit documents are saved as rich text format (*.rtf* and *.rtfd*), but you can also save documents as plain text (*.txt*) via the Format → Make Plain Text menu option. TextEdit replaces the SimpleText application from earlier versions of the Mac OS.

Apple recently released Sherlock's API so user could extend Sherlock's services. One web site that tracks these extensions is Sherlockers (*http://www.sherlockers. com*).

Utilities

The tools found in the Utilities folder (*/Applications/Utilities*) can be used to help manage your system:

AirPort Admin Utility
> Lets you set up and configure AirPort Base Stations that are visible to your machine (either via direct connection or over a network).

AirPort Setup Assistant

A "wizard" program that helps you configure the machine to join an AirPort (or other 802.11b wireless) network. It's basically a hyper-friendly version of the Network system preferences pane (described in the section "The Network Pane" in Chapter 7).

Apple System Profiler

Generates reports on the hardware and software installed on this machine. Its interface is a simple window with multiple tabs, as follows:

System Profile

An overview of this machine's core hardware, system software, and network interfaces, as seen in Figure 6-3.

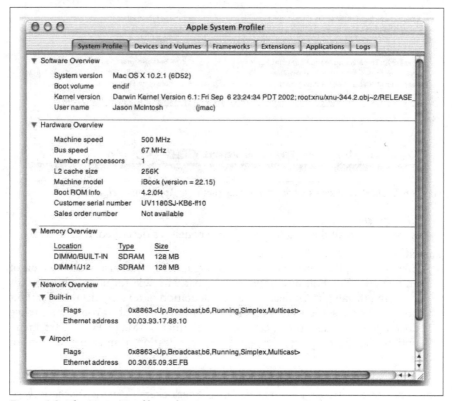

Figure 6-3. The System Profile application

Devices and Volumes

A visual map of every disk volume mounted on the computer, as well as devices attached to its external ports (such as USB) and internal slots (such as PCI). See Figure 6-4.

Frameworks

Displays all the frameworks (dynamic code libraries) installed on the system. Apple System Profiler obtains this information by searching through all the filesystem's */Library/Frameworks* folders (see Chapter 9).

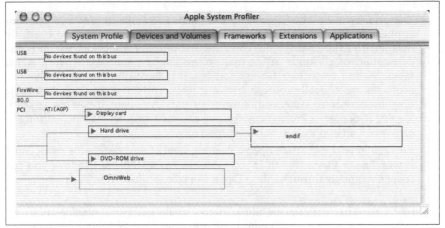

Figure 6-4. System Profile's Devices and Volumes tab

Extensions
> A list of drivers and low-level kernel extensions, as found in */System/Library/Extensions*.

Applications
> Lists all the applications installed throughout the filesystem.
>
> If you wish, you can expand this report's results to include other disks beyond the machine's startup volume. Call up the Commands → Search Options (⌘-F) window, and activate the checkboxes of other disks.

> The reports generated by the Frameworks, Extensions, and Applications tabs all feature an "Is Apple" column. Each component is marked "Yes" if it's Apple-authored, and "No (*Vendor*)" if it's from a known third-party vendor. It is left blank if the software component comes from an unknown source.

Audio MIDI Setup
> This utility is used to add, set up, and configure devices with a Musical Instrument Digital Interface (MIDI).

Bluetooth File Exchange
> This utility allows you to exchange files with other Bluetooth-enabled devices, such as cellular phones, PDAs, and other computers. To exchange a file, launch this utility, and then drag a file from the Finder to the Bluetooth File Exchange icon in the Dock. A window will appear, asking you to select a recipient (or recipients) for the file.

ColorSync Utility
> This utility has three significant features. By pressing the Profile First Aid icon, it can be used to verify and repair your ColorSync settings. The Profiles icon keeps track of the ColorSync profiles for your system, and the Devices icon lets you see which ColorSync devices are connected, as well as the name and location of the current profile.

Console

The primary use of the Console application is to log the interactions between applications on your system as well as with the operating system itself. By default, Console displays the contents of */var/tmp/console.log*, which is the destination of all kinds of internal system chatter, such as network status messages and crash logs for applications that have quit unexpectedly. The messages are typically too esoteric to interest end-users, but are invaluable diagnostic tools for system administrators and developers. If you enable crash logging (Console → Preferences → Crashes), the Console will open automatically when an application quits unexpectedly.

You can have the Console open a running view of any system log by opening it with File → Open (⌘-O). If you close the main Console window, you can reopen it quickly through File → Open Console (Shift-⌘-O).

 Then again, many administrators would know that running *tail -f* on a file in the Terminal does the same thing that this application does.

CPU Monitor

Lets you view a continuously updating bar graph of the machine's CPU usage and system load, either in its own window or on the CPU Monitor's Dock icon. If you have a dual-processor machine, there will be two meters.

DigitalColor Meter

This small application is used to view and copy the color settings for any pixel on your screen.

Directory Access

This utility controls access for Mac OS X systems to Directory Services, such as NetInfo, LDAP, and Active Directory. For more information on NetInfo and Directory Services, see Chapter 12.

Disk Copy

Creates, manages, and mounts disk images, which are files that act like folders, except that they mount onto the filesystem as separate disk volumes.

You'll likely launch this program manually only when you wish to create disk images (*.dmg* files). Otherwise, it will most often launch automatically in order to mount freshly downloaded images containing new appllications, as described later in "Disk Images."

Disk Utility

Analyzes, repairs, and initializes disks. Its interface window features the following tabs:

Information

Lists various information (inlcuding capacity, format, mount point, and manufacturer) about all the storage devices (including mounted disk images) currently residing on the machine's filesystem.

First Aid

Searches for and attempts to repair any problems a disk might have. You can't scan or repair the startup volume, however—to do this, restart using a Mac OS X system CD, and then run the Disk Utility application (from either disk). Disk Utility can alse be used to repair permissions problems, even on a boot volume.

If you don't have a system CD (or other alternate bootable disk) handy and you're desperate to repair your startup volume, you can boot into single-user mode and run the *fsck* command. See the section "Single-User Mode" in Chapter 11.

Erase
Lets you wipe out a storage device and all its volumes (partitions), replacing it with a single, large, empty volume.

Partition
Displays how a connected storage device is split into separate partitions (each of which appears as a separate disk volume in the Finder), and lets you redefine them if you have sufficient priveleges.

RAID
Allows you to bind several disks together to form a single RAID device.

To perform any actions to a disk with this application, you must open the authentication lock at the bottom of the window (see "The authentication lock" later in this chapter).

Display Calibrator
Helps you calibrate your display and create ColorSync profiles.

Grab
The Grab utility can be used to take screenshots of your system. Two of its most useful features include the ability to select the pointer (or no pointer at all) to be displayed in the screenshot, as well as the ability to start a 10-second timer before the screenshot is taken. The timer function is handy, as it gives you time to set up the shot, pop open menus, etc. Screenshots taken with Grab are saved as TIFF files, unlike those taken with Shift-⌘-3 or Shift-⌘-4, which are saved as PDF. To take a screenshot of an application window, follow these steps:

1. Select Grab's Capture → Selection (Shift-⌘-A) command.

2. Use ⌘-Tab to cycle through the active applications in the Dock to bring the application whose window you want to take a snapshot of to the front.

3. Click and drag over the target window to take the screenshot.

4. Grab will open a window with the screenshot, which you can then save to a location on your filesystem.

Installer
This application launches whenever you open a software installer document (see the later section "Software Installers"). If you launch it manually, you just get a standard Open dialog box, prompting you to find an installer document.

Java
This folder contains the following applications, which are specific to running Java software on your Macintosh (see Chapter 10).

Applet Launcher
Allows you to open and launch Java applets outside of a web browser, as described in Chapter 10.

Quick Screenshots with the Keyboard

Just as with older versions of the Mac OS, Mac OS X gives you several keystrokes to quickly grab the screen and save it to a prenamed file, available anytime (unless the active application overrides them). They are described in the following list:

Shift-⌘-3
> Captures the entire screen.

Shift-⌘-4
> Lets you select a rectangle, then captures it.

These key combos save their results in your Desktop folder, in files named *Picture Number.pdf*, where *Number* is a unique number. These files are PDFs, not the TIFF files that Grab generates.

To convert TIFF or PDF files into some other format, open them in the Preview application, and select File → Export. This displays the Export dialog shown in Figure 6-5. You can choose a different file format from the Format pop-up menu, and (for some formats) click the Options button to set some relevant options (such as compression level with JPEG images).

If you need *lots* of variety and flexibility in your image conversion work, see GraphicConverter, an excellent shareware application from Lemke Software (*http://lemkesoft.com/us_gcabout.html*).

Java Plugin Settings
> Lets you define settings and preferences regarding Java's presence in your web browsers. (These work independently of any Java-related preferences you might declare in your browser's preferences.)

Java Web Start
> Java Web Start (JWS) can be used to download and run Java applications on your system.

Key Caps
> This application's window lets you preview a font by mapping its characters onto an image of the keyboard connected to your Mac. Use the application's Font menu to browse the various fonts available to you.
>
> As Figure 6-6 shows, you can also use it to view a typeface's special characters by holding down modifier keys (and combinations thereof). Pressing these keys while running Key Caps (or clicking and holding on their on-screen representations) results in the window's keys displaying the characters they would now type.
>
> Keys with thick white borders represent "sticky" glyphs that can combine with others to make accented characters. In most Latin-alphabet fonts, for example, typing Option-U followed by a vowel results in that vowel with an umlaut character inserted into the active text field.

Figure 6-5. Preview's Export dialog

Figure 6-6. The Key Caps display (with the Option key held down)

Keychain Access

A frontend to your personal keychain databases (which exist in *~/Library/ Keychains*). Internet services and applications that require authorization to work can store the username and password you use as encrypted text in these keychain files. Figure 6-7 shows an example of an application asking permission to decode a keychain entry that it made earlier.

Through Keychain Manager, you can browse, view, and manage these keychain files.

Figure 6-7. The Mail application working with Keychains

NetInfo Manager

Provides a graphical interface to all the NetInfo databases of administrative information available to this machine. Chapter 12 describes NetInfo in more detail, as well as the NetInfo Manager application.

Network Utility

This utility is a graphical frontend to a standard set of Unix tools such as *netstat, ping, traceroute, whois,* and *finger*. It also lets you view specific information about your network connection and scan the available ports for a particular domain or IP address.

ODBC Administrator

This tool allows you to connect to and exchange data with ODBC-compliant data sources. ODBC, which stands for Open Database Connectivity, is a standard protocol, supported by most database systems such as FileMaker Pro, Oracle, MySQL, and PostgreSQL. You can use ODBC Administrator to add data sources, install new database drivers, trace calls to the ODBC API, and configure connection pooling.

Print Center

The Print Center is the utility that configures and controls the printers connected to your computer, either locally or on a network via AppleTalk, Directory Services (via IP or Rendezvous), IP Printing, or USB. For users who are coming over from Mac OS 9, the Print Center replaces the Chooser (discussed in Chapter 3) for managing printers. For more information about the Print Center utility, see Chapter 8.

Process Viewer

Basically a friendly graphical interface to the Unix *top* command, which displays a list of all the machine's active processes. As seen in Figure 6-8, the Process Viewer places this list into a table view. Clicking on a column header sorts the list by that criteria. By default, Process Viewer sorts by % CPU (the total percent of the processor's time that this process currently uses), so that the processes using the most processor resources appear first.

Note the distinction between processes and applications here: Process Viewer's list includes not just your active applications with Dock icons, but every active command-line tool, helper application, and low-level system service as well. (You can view these categorically through the Show: pull-down menu, in the window's upper-right corner.)

You can quickly force-quit a process that you own by double-clicking its row in Process Viewer's list. You'll immediately get a dialog box giving you the chance to kill that process. (If you don't own the process, you'll be told as much, and not given the option to kill it.)

StuffIt Expander

StuffIt Expander is the popular utility for expanding, or decompressing, files. To launch StuffIt Expander, simply double-click on the compressed file. StuffIt Expander can open files saved as *.bin*, *.hqx*, *.sit*, *.zip*, *.tar*, *.tar.gz*, and *.tgz*, to name a few. For more information about its typical use, see the "File Compression" section later in this chapter.

Terminal

The Terminal application is the command-line interface (CLI) to Mac OS X's Unix core. For more information about the Terminal, see Chapter 19.

Installing Applications

Since each Mac OS X Cocoa application tidily keeps itself and all its required resources and files inside a single bundled folder (as described in "Applications" in Chapter 2), installing them onto a local hard disk is often just a manner of dragging an application icon from its original medium (such as a CD-ROM or a mounted disk image) into a local destination folder.

This can be anywhere on the filesystem, but the system's application database won't automatically register it unless you place it in one of the system's predefined Applications folders (as Chapter 9 further details). Basically, if you have admin privileges and wish to make an application available to all the Mac's users (or if you are the Mac's sole user), you should drag the application icon into

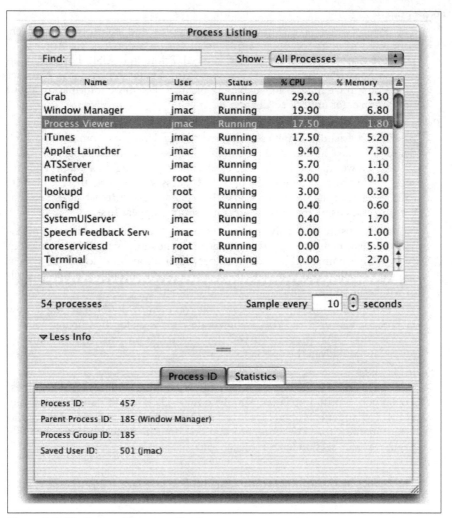

Name	User	Status	% CPU	% Memory	
Grab	jmac	Running	29.20	1.30	
Window Manager	jmac	Running	19.90	6.80	
Process Viewer	jmac	Running	17.50	1.80	
iTunes	jmac	Running	17.50	5.20	
Applet Launcher	jmac	Running	9.40	7.30	
ATSServer	jmac	Running	5.70	1.10	
netinfod	root	Running	3.00	0.10	
lookupd	root	Running	3.00	0.30	
configd	root	Running	0.40	0.60	
SystemUIServer	jmac	Running	0.40	1.70	
Speech Feedback Serv	jmac	Running	0.00	1.00	
coreservicesd	root	Running	0.00	5.50	
Terminal	jmac	Running	0.00	2.70	

Figure 6-8. The Process Viewer application

the */Applications* folder (the one that the Finder's Applications toolbar button leads to). To make an application accessible to you alone, place it in the Applications folder within your Home folder (creating it first, if necessary).

Software Installers

Some software packages, particularly those that update core system software or install several applications at once, require the use of special installer applications to get them onto a machine's local disk. Using these applications is as simple as launching them and then following the prompts.

Many (perhaps most) software installers, especially if they plan on writing any files outside of your Home folder, require that you have admin privileges before they do anything. If you do, these installers have an authentication lock (see "The authentication lock"), which automatically prompts you for your username and password after the installer loads.

Uninstalling applications

Uninstalling the majority of applications is easy: just drag their Finder icons into the trash (or *rm -rf* their *Application-name.app* directories within the Terminal). If you used an installer application, however, it may be more complicated, since the application may have placed other files acorss the filesystem.

As in previous versions of Mac OS, applications do tend to leave a legacy behind in the form of preference files. If you've run an application at least once, chances are good that it wrote a *.plist* file in your */Library/Preferences* folder (see Chapter 22), as well as performed other actions, such as create a folder for itself in */Library/Application Support*.

These files are usually negligible in size (especially if you have a multigig hard drive) and have no effect on the system by their mere presence if their creator application no longer exists. They're arguably even useful at times: if you ever reinstall the software (or other software that shares or imports the other application's preferences), it will remember your old settings. If you are still concerned about clutter, you can manually sift through your Preferences folder every so often, or use a utility like Aladdin Systems' Spring Cleaning to do it for you.

If you used a package installer, though, things can get trickier, since it's not obvious how many files it wrote and where they were written. Fortunately, Mac OS X does feature a rudimentary package management system. *.pkg* installers, when run, write an "invoice" of their contents to */Library/Receipts*, under a bundle directory with the same name (and *.pkg* extension) as the original installer. These bundles silently stick around even after you trash the original installer package.

To actually do something with the information contained therein, install the OSXGNU project's *pkgInstall* utility (*http://www.osxgnu.org*). This command-line tool knows how to read these receipt files, and (if run as root or under the *sudo* command) act upon it to seek out and *rm* all the files that the package installed. The same organization also offers the OS X Package Manager, a graphic utility that lets you select and delete installed packages with a single click. See Chapter 24 for more about software package management on the Darwin side of things.

 Don't uninstall packages unless you know exactly what they are. (Opening the bundle and browsing its *Info.plist* can give you clues, if you really have forgotten.) Among the bundles in */Library/ Receipts* are installers of your Mac's Developer Tools, printer drivers, Darwin software, and other things you probably wouldn't want to see go away.

The authentication lock

Many Mac OS X applications and their functions require administrator intervention. For example, only users in the machine's admin group can add new users to the system, or install software from a CD-ROM into the machine's */Applications* folder. Before you can perform these sorts of actions, you must *authenticate* yourself to prove that you're a user with administrative priveleges.

Figure 6-9 shows a typical example of the Mac OS X *authenticaion lock* button in action. When you first visit this panel, this button bears an image of a closed padlock and the message "Click the lock to make changes". (Unfortunately, it displays this rather vague message even if you're installing software or doing other things that one doesn't normally associate with "making changes," often leading to confusion among new users.) If you're a member of the system's admin, you can authenticate yourself by clicking this button, which summons the dialog shown in Figure 6-10.

Figure 6-9. The Users preference panel, with a closed authentication lock

You can enter your real name or username in the top field (the Mac actually places your real name there for you) and your account password in the bottom field. Clicking OK completes the authentication and results in an open padlock

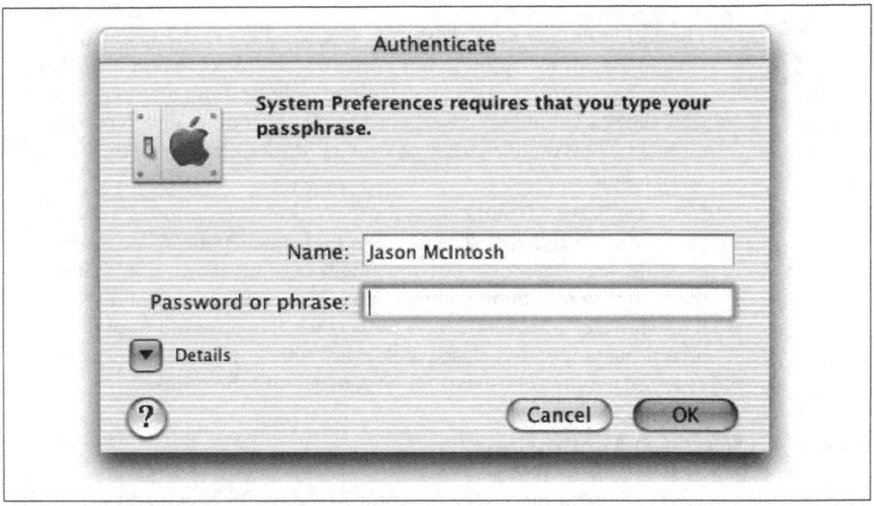

Figure 6-10. The lock's authentication challenge

and previously grayed-out commands and controls becoming available, as shown in Figure 6-11. Clicking the padlock button again closes it once more and locks out the commands that require authentication.

Figure 6-11. The Users preference panel, with an open authentication lock

Applications
and Utilities

The lock asks for your account's password even though you've already used it to log into your current Mac OS X session. This is just to make sure you're who you claim to be and not an interloper who slipped behind your keyboard to cause trouble while you left for lunch. This double-checking strategy works similarly to the Terminal's *sudo* command.

Some applications' authentication locks, however, choose to be a bit less security-strict. The System Preference panels' locks, for example, stay open between your login sessions if you don't close them after you're done making changes. On the other hand, NetInfo Manager's authentication lock takes the opposite approach, presenting you with a closed lock every time you launch the application, regardless of its state when you last quit the utility.

Installing Mac OS 9 Applications

Thanks to the Classic Environment (see Chapter 3), Mac OS X can run most Mac OS 9 applications without a hitch. However, due to philosophical differences between the two operating systems, installing Mac OS 9 software within Mac OS X doesn't always work as smoothly.

Since Mac OS 9 is a single-user system, software installers treat the whole root volume the same way that Mac OS X treats the current user's Home folder, and often try writing software directly under the *root* folder. Even if you do have write permission to the *root* directory (as all admin users do, by default), you likely won't want arbitrary applications cluttering that space, so you'll need to move the results into */Applications* (or wherever it should go) once the installer exits.

Furthermore, even if you are an admin user, you might not have write permission to the */System Folder* directory, which many Mac OS 9 software installers add files to.

Worse, since Mac OS 9 has no concept of user permissions, that system's installers assume that the person behind the keyboard has full write access to the Mac OS 9 System Folder sitting under *root*. In Mac OS X, this usually isn't true, since System Folder is owned by root. Even admin users will see an error dialog if the installer wants to add files to it.

While Mac OS X also has a */System* folder of its own, it is a sacred space that not even software installers can modify (except for Apple's own system software updaters). Modern Mac applications and their installers instead use the filesystem's various */Library* folders to store auxilliary, system-dependent files. See Chapter 9 for more information.

You can skirt these issues by modifying your filesystem's permissions, by making the System Folder writeable by the *admin* group, through a command like this:

```
% sudo chgrp -R admin "/System Folder"
% sudo chmod -R g+w "/System Folder"
```

However, if you seldom install new Mac OS 9–only applications (an increasingly likely condition as Mac software developers switch their focus to creating Carbon and Cocoa applications), you may be better off simply booting into Mac OS 9 just to perform these installs, and otherwise leaving your Mac OS X filesystem as it is.

Disk Images

While the concept of disk images exists in both Mac OS 9 and Unix, Mac OS X uses it more than either system as a standard software installation idiom. Quite often, a freshly downloaded file will decompress into a single *disk image* file with a *.dmg* extension, represting an entire, compressed disk volume.

When opened with Disk Copy (or just double-clicked from the Finder), the system spends a moment verifying that the image's data integrity and then mounts it as a disk volume, so that it appears under the Finder's Computer window as well as on the Desktop (if you've chosen that option under Finder Preferences; described in "Finder Preferences" in Chapter 2).

 If you *don't* have the "Removable media (such as CDs)" checkbox under Finder → Preferences... checked, then nothing obvious happens as a result of mounting a disk image, unless the Computer window happens to be open. You'll need to open the Computer window to see (and work with) the new volume's Finder icon.

Once a disk image is mounted, it behaves like any other Finder disk, even though it exists entirely in the computer's memory, rather than as a physical device. You can open files and applications on the disk, and they work as expected. However, you'll need to copy any files and folders you wish to permanently keep off the mounted image and onto a more stable location (such as the Applications folder of your machine's hard drive) if you'd like to permanently keep them, as the disk image's contents will go away once you unmount it. (You can always choose to mount the same image later, of course.)

A downloaded disk image often contains little more than the application icon, ready for dragging onto a hard disk, along with some optional or informational files, such as a README file.

 If you have your */Applications* folder represented in your Finder windows' toolbar, then you can quickly install an application from a disk image by dragging the application's icon onto the Finder toolbar's Applications button. (You may have to click the disk image window's toolbar button (see Figure 1-29) first.)

File Compression

Applications downloaded over the Internet are nearly always available only in some compressed file format. Through file compression, several files can be melded into a single file, which itself is shrunk through reversible compression algorithms to a compact size. This makes for much smaller network transfer times.

Mac OS X supports both the StuffIt (.sit) and Binhex (.hqx) file compression formats that were ubiquitous with Mac OS 9 file sharing, and can handle the tar (.tar) and gzip (.gz) formats often seen in the Unix world, as well as the PKZip (.zip) format usually seen in Windows.

To the end user, all these compression formats work the same way: double-clicking the compressed file's icon launches StuffIt Expander, and its uncompressed original file or folder appears beside it a few seconds later. (Many web browsers and other Internet applications that download files are smart enough to launch StuffIt Expander for you upon downloading the compressed file.)

By default, StuffIt Expander leaves the compressed files alone once it has expanded them, which can lead to a cluttered Desktop or downloads folder in short order—especially when dealing with .tar and .gz files that are both compressed and encoded, which leaves behind an extra, intermediate file. By launching StuffIt Expander and checking the file-deletion boxes under StuffIt Expander → Preferences, you can direct the application to delete compressed files once it finishes expanding them into usable files or folders.

Cleaning Up

Once your new software is in the /Applications folder, you'll have a bit of cleanup to do.

You can safely delete the .gz and .tar files that might be lying around after a successful download-and-install procedure. You can also get rid of installer applications and .pkg packages; Mac OS X's package manager doesn't need these original files to track the packages' presence on your system, as the earlier section "Uninstalling applications" details.

Disk images can be a little confusing, since they require a two-step process to be deleted. Once you're done using a mounted disk image, you can unmount it through the Finder by either dragging its icon to the Trash, or selecting it and then choosing File → Eject (⌘-E), just as you would with removable media or network-mounted volumes.

However, the original disk image file will remain on your filesystem. You can stash it away somewhere if you think you may want to remount the disk image sometime later, but if it's already delivered its payload, then you may as well delete it.

7

Networking

These days, using a computer and using a network are nearly synonymous concepts. Since Unix has always been a network-oriented operating system, Mac OS X supports networking (and Internetworking) at its core, and provides many friendly interfaces to let users take advantage of this.

This chapter covers the basics of getting a Mac OS X machine connected to a network, particularly the Internet, from a user's perspective. Chapter 11 covers network administration in more detail.

Networking Basics

Connecting to a network basically involves telling your Mac where on the network it belongs by giving it a network IP address (which might belong to the Internet, or maybe just the local area network) and telling it where it can find its router (which lets it speak to the network outside of the immediate subnetwork). Depending upon your network's configuration, you might have to enter this and other information manually, or you can have a network server configure your network setup for you through DHCP, as described later in this chapter in "Configuring TCP/IP."

In any case, Mac OS X's main interface for setting and displaying all this information is the Network preference pane, described in the next section. Network administrators can also use *ifconfig*, *route*, and other command-line tools to fine-tune a machine's network settings, as covered in "Configuring TCP/IP."

Mac OS X networking primarily involves TCP/IP, the family of protocols upon which the Internet is built. When configuring a Mac's network connection, you'll often work with IP addresses. These are dot-notated numbers, such as 192.168.0.1 or 66.101.11.57, which (with an exception or two) are unique for every computer that belongs to a network. Chapter 11 describes this concept in detail.

Mac OS X machines are also capable of using AppleTalk, the legacy communication protocol more often found on networks of older Macs. You may see AppleTalk used in Mac-centric local area networks. A Mac OS X machine can communicate through TCP/IP and AppleTalk simultaneously, though AppleTalk isn't active by default.

The Network Pane

As Figure 7-1 shows, the Network pane has three main elements: a Location menu (whose function we describe later in this chapter in "Locations"), a Show menu, and a large tabbed view. The Show menu contains one item for every active network interface within your machine (such as Ethernet, AirPort, or modems), and its current selection dictates the tabbed view's content. In Figure 7-1, the tabbed view displays configuration information relevant to an Ethernet interface.

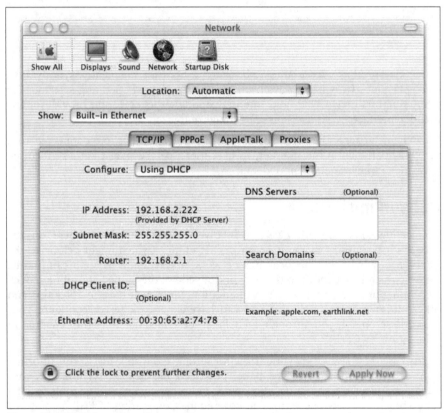

Figure 7-1. The Network preferences pane

Choosing network interfaces

The final (and ever-present) option of the Network pane's Show menu is Active Network Ports. When selected, the pane's view changes to look like Figure 7-2. The Active Ports table lists all the network interfaces available to this machine. The checkbox to the left of each indicates whether it's active or inactive.

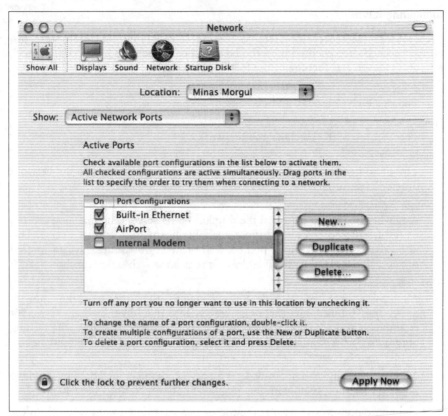

Figure 7-2. Activating interfaces through the Network pane

If your machine has more than one interface active, it can take advantage of *multi-homing*, surveying the network interfaces available to it and choosing the most preferable one, whenever it needs to connect to a network. To show your order of preference among several interfaces through the Network pane, drag the contents of the Active Ports table into the order you'd like. With the setup shown in Figure 7-2, the machine will first try to establish a network connection through its Ethernet port. If it can't (because, perhaps, no Ethernet cable is plugged into it at the moment), it will try connecting through AirPort instead. If that fails, it will give up because no more interfaces are active. (Checking that final "Internal Modem" item would instead have the machine turn to its dial-up connection as a last resort.)

 To see a precise (and more technical) summary of your machine's network interfaces' current status and configurations, consult the Info tab of the Network Utility application, as described in Chapter 11.

Configuring TCP/IP

Since all Mac OS X network interfaces use the TCP/IP communication protocols, every interface's representation in the Network pane includes a TCP/IP tab view, as seen in Figure 7-1. It contains the following text fields:

IP Address
> The machine's network address, unique across the network.

Subnet Mask
> The IP mask of the machine's subnetwork.

Router
> The IP address of the machine's router, which gives it access to the network outside of its subnet.

Domain Name Servers
> A newline-separated list of all the domain name servers the machine can use to resolve IP addresses into human-readable hostnames, and vice versa. This allows you to, for example, point a web browser at www.oreilly.com instead of 209.204.146.22, the raw IP address of that same web server machine.

Search Domains
> A newline-separated list of domain names that the machine can try appending to hostnames that don't resolve into IP address by themselves. For example, if you access machines in the morgul.net domain often, then listing morgul.net as a search domain will let you refer to spider.morgul.net as spider, cricket.morgul.net as cricket, and so on.
>
> This is basically a domain-wide way to accomplish machine-by-machine aliasing that you can do with the */machines* entry in NetInfo; see Chapter 7.

The Configure pull-down menu at the top of this view determines who fills in the values of these various fields: you the admin-allowed user, or an automatic, network-based configuration system. The menu's contents depend on the selected interface, but here are the more common options:

Manually
> All the IP text fields are editable and contain no values by default, leaving it up to you to set them all.

Using DHCP
> DHCP is the Dynamic Host Configuration Protocol, which allows network servers to tell client machines how they ought to be configured. When you select this option, the machine will, when trying to establish a network connection, search for a DHCP server by broadcasting a request to the whole network.
>
> None of the text fields are editable; the DHCP server fills in their values once a connection is established.

Manually Using DHCP Router
> This is the same as Using DHCP, but you specify your machine's IP address manually. This information is used to seek a specific DHCP server, which in turn supplies a router address you can use.

Using BootP

This option works just like Using DHCP, except that it uses the BootP protocol, intended especially for network-booting computers.

Using PPP

PPP, the Point-to-Point protocol, lets TCP/IP run over a serial link, usually a dial-up modem connection. Commonly, a PPP server also provides IP configuration information to a client upon connection, just as DHCP can do through Ethernet.

When selected, no fields are editable; the PPP server fills in all values for you.

Finally, if the selected interface is an Ethernet card (as depicted in Figure 7-1) or an AirPort card, the interface's *hardware address*, also known as a MAC address or Ethernet address, appears in the lower-left corner of the TCP/IP tabbed view. (It will be labeled AirPort ID on an AirPort interface.) This is a colon-notated hexadecimal number assigned to the hardware interface itself. It is globally unique, and cannot be modified, generally speaking.*

Other configurations

The TCP/IP tab contains the most important information for any network interface's setup. Other tabs contain configuration information specific to different interfaces.

AppleTalk

Controls whether AppleTalk is active (along with TCP/IP), and defines the current AppleTalk zone.

Proxies

If your location requires the use of proxies for different kinds of Internet traffic, you can define them in this tab. See Figure 7-3.

This is also where you'll find the checkbox that lets you activate passive FTP mode; see "Passive FTP Mode," later in this chapter.

AirPort

Here, you can specify settings particular to AirPort usage.

The "After restart or wake from sleep" radio button lets you define how the network will seek and choose 802.11b wireless network whenever its AirPort card activates one of the following:

Join network with best signal

Of all the wireless networks available, try to join the one with the strongest signal.

---

* Those with sufficient inclination can use network analysis/sniffer tools like *ettercap* (*http:// ettercap.sourceforge.net*, also available though Fink; see Chapter 24) or even the system's built-in *ifconfig* command to "spoof" different MAC addresses different from the ones their network interfaces actually possess. This sort of thing is far beyond the realm of ordinary network use, though. (On the other hand, it falls well within the concern of system administrators trying to run a secure network, but that's another topic.)

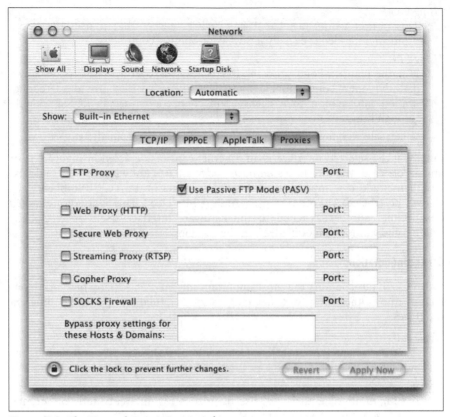

Figure 7-3. The Network Pane's Proxies tab

Join most recently used available network
> The default setting. Of all the wireless networks available, try to join the one most recently used. You can also activate the Remember network password checkbox to resend the password you last used.

Join a specific network
> Join the network named in the Network pop-up menu.

Activate the Show AirPort status in the menu bar checkbox to display the AirPort menu extra (Figure 7-4), which doubles as a handy signal-strength indicator.

PPP
> See "Connecting Through Dialup," later in this chapter, for an explanation.

Modem
> Specifies the modem configuration to use when making dial-up connections. The Modem pop-up menu contains references to all the configuration files in */Library/Modem Scripts*.

Activate the Show modem status in the menu bar checkbox to reveal the modem menu extra.

Figure 7-4. The AirPort menu extra

PPoE

If your network uses PPP over an Ethernet connection (as with a DSL connection), use this tab to configure your account information as described in "Connecting Through Dialup."

When the Show PPPoE status in menu bar checkbox is active, the PPoE menu extra appears. Just as with dialup-based PPP, this menu extra lets you quickly make and break your PPPoE connection.

Locations

The Network pane (Figure 7-1) is actually a frontend that lets you create and manage several independent profiles of network configuration information, which are called *locations*. The default location is called *Automatic*; if your machine isn't the traveling type, you can just leave it be. Otherwise, you'll need to create a list of locations.

Mac OS 9 users may recall the Location Manager control panel. Its functionality is wholly part of Mac OS X's Network pane, as well as the Location submenu under the Apple menu.

Adding and using locations

To create a new location, select New Location... from the Location menu. A sheet prompting you with a text field will appear. Fill it out with an appropriate name ("Home," "Office," "Steve's house," and so on), and click OK.

That location will now appear as a selectable choice in the Network pane's Location menu, as well as in the Apple menu's Location submenu. Selecting a location in either of these ways will adjust your Mac's network settings.

Selecting a location from the Apple menu will apply its network settings immediately. Selecting one from the Network pane won't change the Mac's behavior until you click the pane's Apply Now button. This behavior lets you adjust a location's setting before (or even independently of) they take effect.

Changes to your network settings via the Network pane also change the currently selected location. If you, for example, change the Configure menu from Using DHCP to Manually, and then switch to some other location, then the next time you select the original location, the Configure menu will snap back to Manually.

 Even if your Mac does travel among different networks, it's likely that it uses DHCP to dynamically fetch its IP address from each one. In this case, you can get away with sticking to the Automatic location. You really only need to switch locations if the *way* that your machine receives its network identity differs from place to place.

Editing and removing locations

Selecting Edit Locations from the Location menu displays the sheet shown in Figure 7-5. It offers controls for modifying the list of network locations stored on your Mac. (To change the actual *settings* under a particular location, just select that location from the Network pane's Location menu and make the necessary changes.)

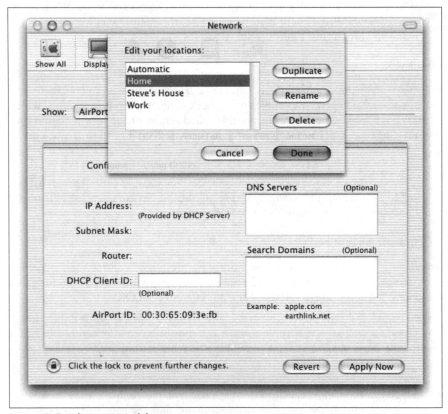

Figure 7-5. Editing network locations

Duplicate

Clicking this button duplicates the selected location. This can be handy if you'd like to base a new location off an existing one that's different by only one or two settings, or if you'd like to make a backup copy of a location that you're about to modify.

Rename

This button will make the selected location's name editable.

Delete

Click this to remove the selected tab from the list.

Connecting Through Dialup

Compared to the immediacy of Ethernet or AirPort-based network connections, connecting to a network through a modem requires the additional step of the computer dialing up a server through a phone line. You can choose to have your computer perform this step automatically, or only when you request it, but either way you need to set up some additional configuration information under the Network pane's PPP tab, seen in Figure 7-6.

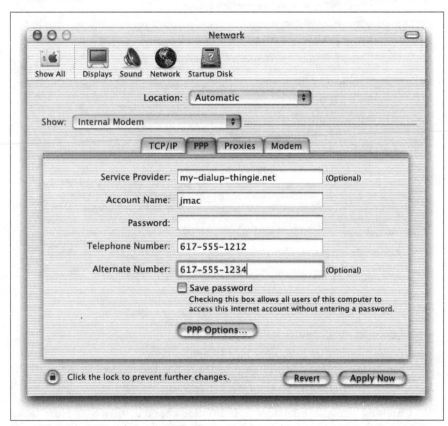

Figure 7-6. The Network pane's PPP tab

Type the PPP server's telephone number into the Telephone Number field. Provide the service provider's name and an alternate phone number in the appropriate fields, if you wish. You can *try* supplying a PPP account name and password into the last two text fields; your Mac's PPP client will try to guess when to supply them to the server. It usually gets it right, but if it doesn't, you can connect through a terminal window.

Clicking the PPP Options button displays the sheet shown in Figure 7-7, which contains two sets of checkboxes. Session Options controls when, how, and for how long the machine makes dial-up connections, and Advanced Options manages some miscellaneous connection preferences.

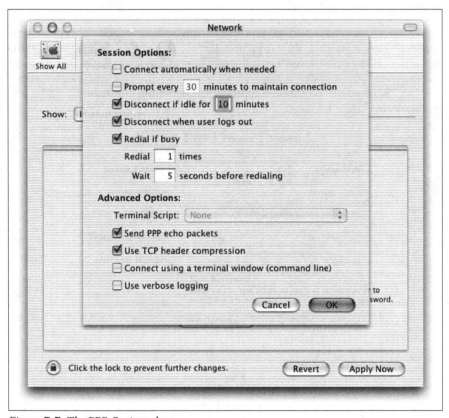

Figure 7-7. The PPP Options sheet

Two checkboxes are of particular interest:

Connect automatically when starting TCP/IP applications
> When checked, the Mac will automatically use the modem to dial into the PPP server when any program wishes to use the network (for an explanation of what to do if any other active network interface fails to work, see "Choosing network interfaces"). If it's not checked, then you must use a program like the Internet Connect application and launch the dial-up process yourself.

Connect using a terminal window (command line)
   If checked, then the Mac will present you with a simple terminal window (with no affiliation to the Terminal application) that lets you manually log in and authenticate with the PPP server. If you leave it unchecked, Mac OS X will use the username and password you supplied in the Network pane's PPP tab to try authenticating itself.

You'll need to resort to this option only if connecting through an office's custom in-house PPP setup, or the like; almost all ISPs keep their PPP authentication protocol simple enough to let Mac OS X's PPP software work without user assistance.

If you are experiencing problems when dialing into your ISP, you can try connecting via the PPP terminal to see what its authentication process looks like. If it's something more complicated than a username prompt followed by a password prompt, you might have to connect through the terminal; talk to your ISP about it.

Mounting Network Disks

Mac OS X gives you a number of ways to mount a remote filesystem (or a segment of one) as a disk accessible through the Finder. The remote system need not run under Mac OS; you can, for example, use SMB to connect to Windows machines, and NFS to mount filesystems on Unix computers.*

Mounting Through the Finder

The Finder's Connect to Server (⌘-K) command gives you a simple interface for mounting remote disks locally. As Figure 7-8 shows, the Connect to Server window contains three ways to specify the server you'd like to mount:

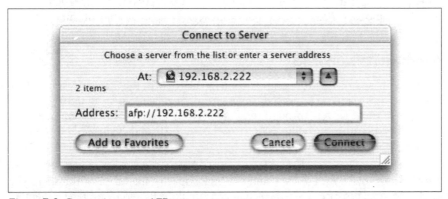

Figure 7-8. Connecting to an AFP server

---

* On the other hand, Mac OS X isn't unique in offering cross-platform file sharing options, so it's quite possible to find yourself connecting to Unix machines via SMB, for example.

At menu

This menu contains a list of the last few servers you've connected to through the Finder, as well as servers you've placed among your Favorites (see "Favorites" in Chapter 2). Selecting one and then clicking the window's Connect button will connect to it.

Network browser

If your machine is part of a network that uses the Rendezvous or the SLP protocol to advertise available network services, then you can use this column view to browse through them. Selecting a disk or server in this table and then clicking Connect will initiate a connection.

Clicking the triangle button to the right of the At menu hides the network browser.

Address text field

Here you can type in the URL that points to the disk you wish to mount. The Finder knows what type of disk it is (and which network protocol to use) by the URL's prefix, such as afp:// or smb://; if you don't use a prefix at all, the Finder assumes AFP.

Using this field overrides the server names displayed in the At list or the network browser. Clicking Connect when it contains a URL will connect to the shared disk to which it points.

The next few sections cover the kinds of remote filesystems the Finder recognizes.

Connecting to AFP shares

AFP is the Apple Filing Protocol,* the native file-sharing protocol for Macintosh computers since Mac OS 8.5. It works over both TCP/IP and the much older AppleTalk protocol. When you share folders or disks through the Mac OS X's Sharing preferences pane (see "File Sharing Services" in Chapter 13), you're using AFP. Other operating systems, including Mac OS Versions 8.5 through 9.2, as well as Windows 2000 and Windows NT, are also capable of running AFP services. See Figure 7-9.

Connecting to SMB/CIFS shares

Windows-based file servers communicate through SMB, the Server Message Block protocol. (It's also known as the *Common Internet File System* (CIFS)). You can connect to these servers through the Finder's Connect To Server command, just as described in the previous section. As Figure 7-10 and Figure 7-11 show, the process differs only slightly:

The URL you type into the Address text field takes the form smb://*host*/*share-name*. It must start with smb://, and you must specify the name of the share you wish to connect to after a slash (/) character; unlike AFP, you won't get a menu of shares to choose from.

---

* Available online at *http://developer.apple.com/techpubs/macosx/Networking/AFP/AFP3.0.pdf,* or if you have installed the Developer Tools, this document can be found on your system in */Developer/ Documentation/Networking/AFP.*

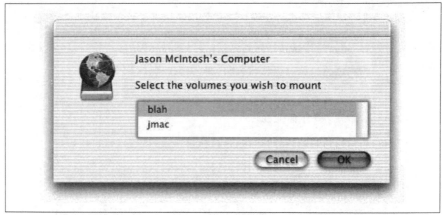

Figure 7-9. Choosing a volume from an AFP server

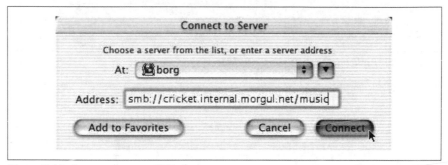

Figure 7-10. Connecting to an SMB share

Once you connect and authenticate, the SMB share shows up as a disk in the Finder, and you can use it like any other.

Mounting WebDAV sites

The *Web-based Distributed Authoring and Versioning system* (WebDAV; *http://www.webdav.com*) extends HTTP (the protocol upon which the Web runs) with version-control commands (much like RCS), allowing several web developers to simultaneously and safely work on the same set of files over a network connection, rather than edit them locally and then FTP them to a server (thus eliminating the risk of conflicting changes).

To mount a WebDAV site, call up the Connect to Server (⌘-K) window and type in its URL, prefixed with http://, as shown in Figure 7-12.

NFS

For many years, the *Network File System* (NFS) protocol has let Unix machines transparently share directories over a network. While Apple doesn't include any easy-to-use frontends for either serving or using NFS mount points with Max OS X, its underlying Darwin system does feature full NFS support. This book covers NFS in depth in Chapter 11.

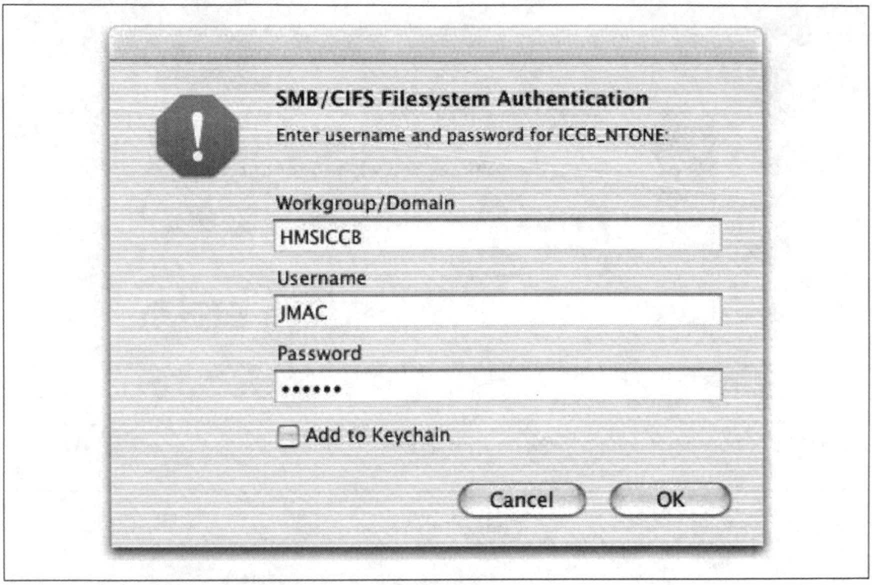

Figure 7-11. Authenticating with an SMB share

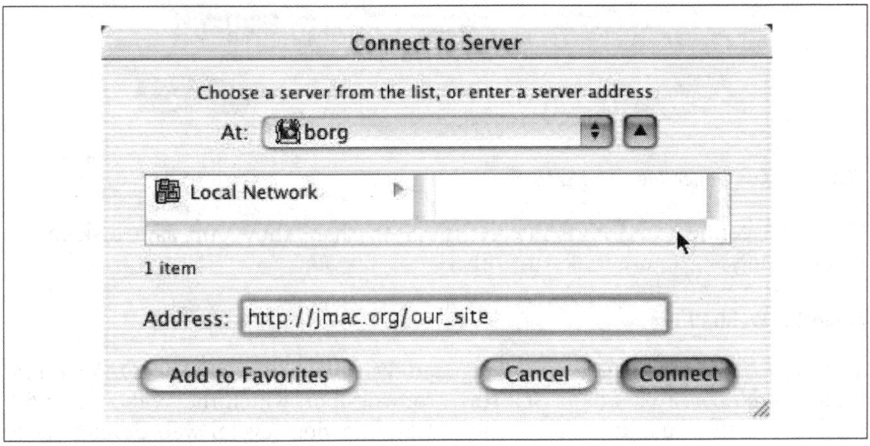

Figure 7-12. Connecting to a WebDAV site

Mounting Disks Through the Terminal

Advanced users who wish to have finer control over mounting these remote file-systems can instead use the *mount* command, or one of the *mount_fstype* Terminal commands, to graft them to arbitrary points in the filesystem, or specify special arguments to pass to the mounting programs.* Table 7-1 lists both the

---

* If you only want a mounted disk to appear at some arbitrary place in the local filesystem, you can simply mount it as described earlier in "Mounting Through the Finder," and then make an alias of it (see "Aliases" in Chapter 2), placing it wherever you wish.

specific *mount_fstype* commands for each kind of remote filesystem you can mount. Use *mount* (with a -t argument appropriate to the target filesystem) if you've defined mount points through NetInfo, as described in the section "NFS through automount" in Chapter 11.

Table 7-1. Remote filesystem types

mount-t argument	Handler program	Filesystem type
smb	*mount_smbfs*	SMB share
afp	*mount_afp*	AFP (AppleShare) shared disk
webdav	*mount_webdav*	WebDAV site
nfs	*mount_nfs*	NFS export

Refer to Chapter 25 for the proper arguments for each of these commands. For example, to mount the SMB share from Figure 7-10 into the local directory *~/mnt/ music*:

```
% mount_smbfs
//jmac@cricket.internal.morgul.net/music ~/mnt/music
Password: myBigSecretPassword
```

If *~/mnt/music* is already defined as an SMB mount point through NetInfo, you could just run this command:

```
% mount ~/mnt/music
Password: ********
```

Web Browsing

Web browsing on Mac OS X is as easy as launching Microsoft's Internet Explorer, which ships with Mac OS X. You can find it in */Applications*, and the Dock displays its icon (a big, blue lowercase "e") among its default icons for new users.

Alternative Browsers

Internet Explorer is a fine browser, but curious users may want to investigate some of the alternative browsers available for Mac OS X. They all serve the same basic function of letting you view HTML files on the World Wide Web, but each has its own style and set of unique, fine-tuned features.

iCab
> This browser, available from *http://www.icab.de*, has a relatively small memory footprint and features built-in HTML validity checking and error-reporting, which can be useful for web designers. (It also may be the only currently popular browser that still offers new versions for ancient, pre-PowerPC Macintoshes running System 7!)

Mozilla
Chimera

The much-heralded Mozilla is an open source, cross-platform, and very feature-heavy web browser (as well as an email client and Usenet news reader) project originally launched by Netscape in 1998. It hit Version 1.0 in 2002; the latest Carbon version is available from its web site, *http://www.mozilla.org.*

The separate Chimera project (*http://chimera.mozdev.org*) is a true Cocoa port of Mozilla.

OmniWeb

The Omni Group's shareware web browser, which concentrates on having a very streamlined, Cocoa-based user interface. This is available at *http://www.omnigroup.com/applications/omniweb/.*

Opera

The impressively speedy piece of shareware called Opera (*http://www.opera.com/mac*) has long been a popular alternative browser on Windows machines, and has more recently offered a Carbon version.

Network Disks and Security

All these remote disk-mounting methods are great for safely sharing information with other computers located elsewhere on a closed intranet, when you and they are all tucked safely behind a firewall or grouped together through a virtual private network (VPN). When sending information (including the passwords you use to connect to these network services) over the world-wide Internet, however, the packets that make up this information must potentially pass through many points unknown. A malicious eavesdropper sitting somewhere in between and running a network packet-sniffing program could intercept your passwords and other sensitive information, which would be Bad. When possible, consider using a secure Internet protocol, such as *ssh* for remote logins or *sftp* for file transfers. Unfortunately, this precludes the connections that the Finder makes super-easy. Express due paranoia when appropriate.

This warning counts *double* for AirPort-enabled Macs, by the way; the Airport protocol, 802.11b (the same used by nearly all popular IP-over-radio devices, Apple or otherwise, at the time of this writing), has been shown to be easily crackable at any level of its built-in encryption, giving network snoops another potential door into your network. SSH, SSL, and other secure connection layers work just as well as they do over a wired network, though; so use them (through the *ssh* program, the "Use SSL" checkbox in the Mail application's preferences, and so on) where your servers allow them.

Changing the Default Browser

By default, Mac OS X uses Internet Explorer to view any URLs you open through other applications (such as Mail). If you find that you prefer using a different browser, visit the Internet pane of the System Preferences application and then choose its Web tab, giving you the view seen in Figure 7-13.

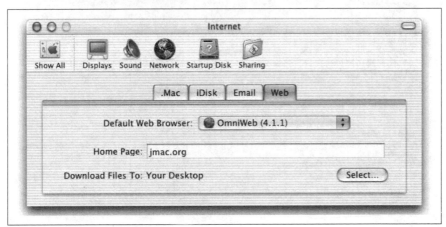

Figure 7-13. The Internet pane's Web tab

Pull down the Default Web Browser menu and choose Select... to bring up an Open dialog window. Choose the application you'd rather use for web browsing (the window will already display the contents of */Applications*) and click its Select button to lock in your selection.

If you wish, you can also choose a separate application for handling local HTML files that you open through the Finder. This involves using any HTML file's Info window to change the file type's default application (as described in "The Get Info Window" in Chapter 2). Otherwise, the browser you define in the Internet pane will handle local files, as well.

Browsing in the Terminal

Finally, *lynx* deserves special mention. It is an all-text, console-based web browser and one of the first web browsers ever written, in the early 1990s at the University of Kansas. It allows you to surf the Web *very* quickly (if not very prettily) from within the Terminal application (Figure 7-14), using the arrow keys and Return instead of the mouse to follow links, and the space bar to scroll though web pages.

Lynx's home page is at *http://lynx.browser.org*, and you can find an easy-to-install package prepared by the OSXGNU project at *http://www.osxgnu.org/software/Networking/lynx/*, or through the Fink system (see Chapter 24).

A more recent text-based browser, *links*, is also worth investigating; it can render HTML tables within a Terminal window and display pages while it loads them, much like a graphical browser.

Networking

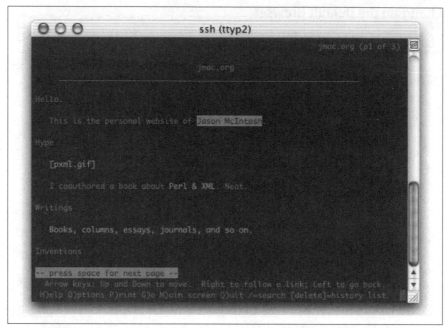

Figure 7-14. Lynx in action

Using FTP

The *File Transfer Protocol* (FTP) is one of the oldest Internet protocols for file sharing that is still in use. It consists of a simple command set for getting lists of available files from servers, as well as for performing file downloads and uploads. (To learn about Mac OS X's more modern and Finder-friendly notions of file sharing, see the earlier section "Mounting Network Disks.")

The most common FTP transactions occur through anonymous, read-only logins to an FTP server, letting you browse through world-readable directories and download the files found therein. Internet Explorer (or any other web browser; see the earlier section "Alternative Browsers") handles this sort of functionality seamlessly; pointing it at a URL with an ftp prefix, such as ftp://ftp.gnome.org, begins an anonymous FTP session with that location. You can also put a username and password into the URL like this: ftp://*username:password@host* (but see the warning below).

To do anything more sophisticated in an FTP session than merely browsing available files, you'll have to use an FTP client. Mac OS X does not ship with any FTP client Aqua applications, but it does ship with *ftp*, a rather minimalist command-line program (documented in Chapter 25). For a more sophisticated FTP client program, consider the feature-rich, open source Terminal program *ncftp*, available at *http://www.ncftp.com*.

Popular third-party Aqua FTP applications include the shareware programs Fetch (available from *http://fetchsoftworks.com/*) and Transmit (available at *http://panic.com/*).

Using FTP non-anonymously represents a security risk, since your username and password travel over the network as cleartext, quite visible and vulnerable to eavesdroppers. Consider using the *sftp* or *scp* commands instead, which encrypt your file transfer sessions. See Chapter 25 for more information about them.

Passive FTP Mode

If a firewall lies between you and the Internet, then you'll have to use *passive mode*. Turning on passive mode for Aqua applications is simple: in the Proxies tab of the Network pane (pictured in Figure 7-3), activate the "Use Passive FTP Mode (PASV)" checkbox. Like all settings performed through the Network pane, this state is associated with the current location file, so the FTP mode will automatically switch between passive and active modes as you switch locations (once you've specified which locations require passive mode).

When using Terminal-based programs, you may need to specify passive mode through a command-line argument or an interactive command. For example, you need to issue a *passive* command when connected to a site via the *ftp* program to enter passive mode.

Remote Logins

Through the Terminal application, you can log into other (usually Unix or Mac OS X) machines over a network and run command-line programs on them through a shell, just as Terminal lets you normally do with your own machine.

Programs you can use for this include *telnet* and *ssh*. You can find references to both in Chapter 25, but the general way to run them is to simply use *telnet* (or *ssh*) *-l username host*. If *host* accepts the connection, you'll be prompted for a password. Once authenticated, the remote machine will greet you with a shell prompt of its own. For example, the following example is the user jmac using *ssh* to connect from his local machine (named endif) into another Mac OS X machine on his local network (named borg):

```
[jmac@endif /Users/jmac]% ssh borg
jmac@borg's password: *****
Last login: Sat Jun 29 23:00:58 2002 from 192.168.0.251
Welcome to Darwin!
[borg:~] jmac%
```

Note the different prompts, due to different shell configurations this user has on the two machines. Note also that configuring one's shell to display the current hostname within one's prompt can be a good idea, since it acts as a constant reminder of which machine you're working with!

If your username on the remote machine is not the same as the one you use locally, use the *ssh* command's *ssh username@host* or *ssh -l host* syntax.

 If you have X Windows installed on your Mac, you can run other Unix machines' GUI software on your machine, as described in Chapter 23. You can also use VNC to log into other Mac OS X machines and enjoy their full Aqua interfaces; see Chapter 23.

While their basic interfaces are the same, a very important difference lies between the two programs. *telnet* sends and receives all of its data as cleartext, while *ssh* works solely with encrypted data. This means that *any use of telnet* can constitute a security risk, since network eavesdroppers can capture all your activities, including your username and password. Consider using only *ssh* whenever possible.

Virtual Network Computers

Through the Virtual Network Computer (VNC) system, you can log into a remote Mac OS X machine from another computer, launch an application on the remote Mac OS X machine, and have the application display on your local machine. The local machine can be running the X Window System, Microsoft Windows, or another platform supported by VNC.

VNC consists of two components: a VNC server (which must be installed on the remote machine) and a VNC viewer (which is used on the local machine to view and control applications running on the remote machine). The VNC connection is made through a TCP/IP connection.

The VNC server and viewer may not only be on different machines, but can also be installed on different operating systems. This allows you to, for example, connect from Solaris to Mac OS X and launch and run Aqua applications on Mac OS X, but view and control them from your Solaris box. VNC can be installed on Mac OS X with the Fink package manager (look for the *vnc* package), but that version (the standard Unix version of the VNC server) supports only running X11 programs, not Aqua applications. VNC translates X11 calls into the VNC protocol. All you need on the client machine is a VNC viewer.

Alternatively, OSXvnc is an Aqua-aware VNC server, available from *http://www. osxvnc.com*. OSXvnc is installed by downloading, unpacking, and mounting the disk image, and then dragging the OSXvnc folder to the */Applications* folder.

Of the two, OSXvnc is more experimental, since it hooks into Mac OS X at a low level. The standard Unix version of the VNC server is more robust, since it does not interact with your display, but instead intercepts and translates the X11 network protocol. (In fact, the Unix version of the server is based on the XFree86 source code.) Applications that you run under the Unix server are never displayed on the server's screen. Instead, they are displayed on an invisible X server that relays its virtual display to the VNC viewer on the client machine.

Launching VNC

If you installed VNC via Fink, you can start the VNC server by issuing the *vncserver* command.

You need to enter a password when you connect from a remote machine. (This password can be changed using the command *vncpasswd*.) You can run several servers; these are identified by the name of the machine on which the VNC server is running with a :number appended. For example, suppose you start the VNC server twice on a machine named abbott; these servers will be identified as *abbott:1* and *abbott:2*. You need to supply this identifier when you connect from a client machine. By default, the VNC server runs the *twm* window manager. So, when users connect, they will see an X11 Desktop instead of the Mac OS X Desktop. (You can specify a different window manager in *~/.vnc/xstartup*.) To terminate the VNC server, issue a *vncserver -kill :display* command. For example, to terminate *abbott:1*, issue the following command while logged into abbott as the user who started the vncserver:

```
vncserver -kill :1
```

To start the OSXvnc server, double-click the application in the Finder, enter a password, and click Start Server. A remote user that is connecting to OSXvnc will see your Mac OS X Desktop.

 There is a derivative of VNC, called TightVNC, which is optimized for bandwidth conservation. It can also be installed with Fink. TightVNC also includes automatic *ssh* tunneling on Unix and backward compatibility with the standard VNC.

Connecting to the Mac OS X VNC Server

To connect to a Mac OS X machine that is running a VNC server, you need a VNC viewer. Viewers are available for a variety of platforms, including Solaris, Linux, Windows, and even Palm devices. See *http://www.uk.research.att.com/vnc* to obtain a VNC viewer. To connect, start your viewer, specify the hostname and display number (such as *abbott:1* or *abbott:2*). If all goes well, you'll be asked for your password and connected to the remote Mac OS X Desktop.

Mac OS X VNC Viewers

If you want to connect to a VNC server from your Macintosh, there are several VNC viewers for Mac OS X, including VNCViewer (*http://homepage.mac.com/ kedoin/VNC/VNCViewer*), VNCthing (*http://webthing.net/vncthing*), and VNCDimension (*http://www.mdimension.com/Community*).

8

Printer Configuration
and Printing

From a user's perspective, Mac OS X's printing system contains two major parts: a list of printers that your machine knows about, which you can access and modify through the Print Center application, and the standard dialog that shows up when you select File → Print (⌘-P) in nearly any application.

How Printing Works

Mac OS X ships with a suite of software known as the *Common Unix Printing System* (CUPS)[*], which acts as the operating system's *print server*. Whenever you ask an application to print a document (using either the Aqua interface described later in "The Print Dialog" or the Terminal commands listed later in "Command-Line Tools"), it in turn makes a request to the print server. This maintains one or more *queues*, each of which represents a printer device and its first-in, first-out list of *jobs*. Jobs are the documents in the print server's memory, which wait their turn to go to a printer and be made into hardcopy.

Mac OS X's print server is actually a network service that is able to receive and process print requests from other machines, but its default configuration refuses any request that does not come from the same Mac that it's running on. In other words, unless you turn on printer sharing (detailed later in "Printer Sharing"), printer queues you set up on your Mac through the Print Center will be for your machine's own private use. This is probably what most computer users expect.

Generally printers come in two varieties:

USB
> Printers directly connected to your Mac via USB cabling are always visible to your machine alone, unless you have printer sharing activated.

---

[*] You can find information about CUPS, including full user and administrator documentation, at *http://www.cups.org*.

Network

Printers accessible over a network are attached to print servers, which might be (on high-end models) in the printer itself or running on another computer to which that printer is connected. (The computer could be a Mac OS X machine with its own printer-sharing features activated, or any other machine running a print server that understands the LPR or IPP printing protocols.)

CUPS handles either case with equal finesse. See "Adding and configuring printers," later in this chapter, for more about adding printers to your machine's own list of available printers.

The Print Dialog

Almost every Mac OS X application supports a File → Print (⌘-P) menu command. When selected, a print dialog (Figure 8-1) appears, usually as a sheet attached to the foremost document window.

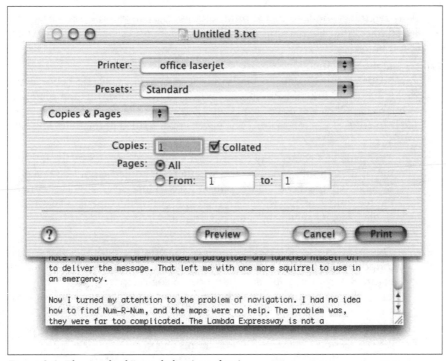

Figure 8-1. The standard Print dialog (as a sheet)

The dialog contains three menus. The first two are always available:

Printer

This menu, shown in Figure 8-2, contains the name or IP address of every printer you have defined through the Print Center application. An additional choice, Edit Printer List..., will launch Print Center and summon its printer list editing window for you (see "The Printer List," later in this chapter).

Figure 8-2. Print Center's printer list window

The menu's default selection—appearing in the menu after you call up the dialog through File → Print (⌘-P))—is whichever printer you've named as default through Print Center.

Presets

This menu lets you load sets of print settings that you've previously used and saved. See the later section "Saving Your Printing Settings" for more information.

Printer Output Menu and Panes

An unlabeled third menu on the Print dialog lets you navigate between the dialog's various functionality panes. When you first open up the dialog, it displays the Copies & Pages pane (which contains the controls you're most likely to adjust from job to job). The panes are described in the following list:

Copies & Pages

This pane lets you specify the number of separate copies of the job that the printer should produce, and whether the copies should be collated. By clicking the From radio button (see Figure 8-1), you can print a limited range of pages, rather than the entire document. (To print a single page, just enter the same page number in both fields.)

Layout

This pane gives you an easy interface for printing multiple pages, each proportionally scaled down in size, onto a single physical page. As Figure 8-3 shows, you can tile up to 16 logical pages onto a physical page, choose the order in which they appear, and specify a border to put around each.

This pane doesn't control the way content is laid out over a single page; see the section "Page Setup," later in this chapter.

Duplex

If your printer can handle duplex printing, activating this pane's Print on Both Sides checkbox takes advantage of it. You can also use the Binding control to have a page's reverse side be printed upside down, which makes vertical binding feasible.

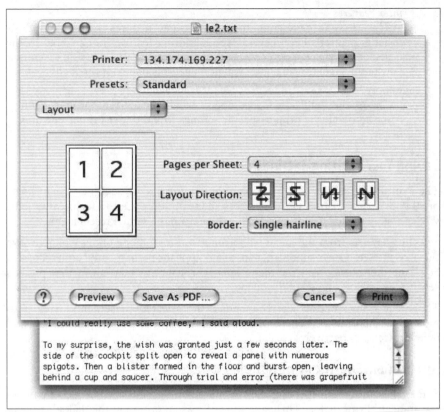

Figure 8-3. The Print dialog's Layout pane

Paper Feed

Selects which of the printer's paper trays to use for the printout. The default selection, Auto Select, will have the printer choose a tray based on the logical page size.

By selecting the "First page from" radio button, you can split the job's paper source between two trays, both of which you specify separately. This can be useful if, for example, a report's cover page needs to be printed on a heavy stock stored in one tray, and the body pages all use more standard paper that is kept in another.

Error Handling

This pane, available only with PostScript printers, lets you set the level of error reporting you want to see should a PostScript error occur, and specify the system's behavior if the initial paper tray runs out of paper before a job is complete.

Application-specific options

If the active application offers printing options of its own, they will appear in the menu under a heading named after that application. See "Application-Specific Print Options" later in this chapter.

Printer Features
> This catch-all pane contains any additional features defined by a Post-Script printer's PPD file. Any special printer features not covered by the standard Print dialog controls show up here. If you are using a printer with the Generic PPD, then you don't get this pane option at all.

Summary
> This pane simply lists a summary of all the current printer settings, including all the printer-specific settings found under Printer Features, if any.

Saving Your Printing Settings

The Print dialog's Presets pop-up menu lets you create presets (i.e., "snapshots" of all your chosen printer settings) across all the option panes. In future print jobs, you can recall these settings by selecting them from the same Presets menu.

Selecting Save As from the menu will prompt you for a name under which to save the new preset. Once supplied, that name appears permanently under Presets. Selecting that name from the menu later will instantly snap all of that preset's settings into place, across all the dialog's panes.

The menu's Save option lets you update the selected preset, modifying it to include all the dialog's current settings. Rename and Delete let you rename and delete presets, respectively.

Application-Specific Print Options

Some applications can specify their own print settings and add them to a pane in the standard Print dialog. This pane shows up as an option in the dialog's navigation pop-up menu. Figure 8-4 shows Internet Explorer's custom Print settings, which contain controls specific to printing web pages.

The Simplified Print Sheet

Some applications that aim for an especially easy user interface use a simplified print sheet like that seen in Figure 8-5. It takes several of the controls from different panes of the standard Print dialog and places them into a single pane.

Clicking a simplified print sheet's Advanced Options button transforms the dialog into the standard print sheet.

Print Center

The Print Center Application (*/Applications/Utilities*) lets you define the list of printers available for use from your machine, as well as obtain queue and status information for each of them. Print Center acts as the UI for printing once the application has finished rendering all the pages and sent them off to the print server.

Print Center has two views: an editable list of all the printers the computer knows about and an interactive look into the print queue for each one.

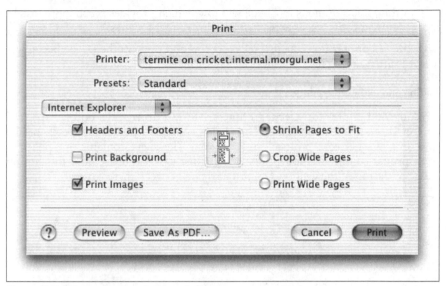

Figure 8-4. Internet Explorer's Print dialog pane

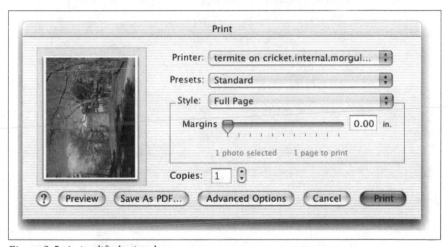

Figure 8-5. A simplified print sheet

The Printer List

Figure 8-2 shows a typical Printer List window. The default printer—the one that appears already selected in the standard Print dialog's Printer menu (Figure 8-1)— is in boldface. To change the default printer, select a different one by clicking on its row, then choosing Printers → Make Default (⌘-D).

The window has just three columns: Name holds the printer's network name or IP address, Kind describes the type of network connection between the computer and this printer, and Status shows a very brief summary of the printer's current state, with regard to any print jobs you've sent it. Double-clicking on any printer's

Printing

row in this table summons its queue window, which provides much more insight into its current activities, as explained later in "Printer Queues."

To remove a printer from the list, select its row and then hit the Delete button (or select Printers → Delete).

Adding and configuring printers

Clicking Add Printer (or selecting Printers → Add Printer) calls up the lists' Add Printer sheet, seen in Figure 8-6. This dialog contains controls for specifying the new printer's network protocol and location. The sheet contains one pane for each printer communication protocol that Mac OS X can use, and the pop-up menu at the top of the window lets you navigate between these panes:

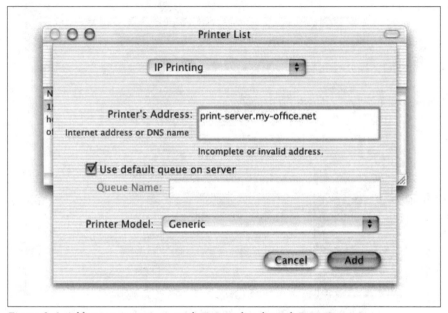

Figure 8-6. Adding a printer queue to the printer list through Print Center

AppleTalk
    If your local network uses the legacy AppleTalk protocol, use this pane to locate its printers.

    This pane gives you another menu to switch between different AppleTalk zones and a column view to browse the currently selected zone (the local one, by default).

IP Printing
    This pane lets you set up connections to any Unix (or Mac OS X) print server—LP, LPR, or CUPS—through IP. This server can be another computer running a print server, or it can be a printer itself (very full-featured printer models have an Ethernet card, can take an IP address, and run software to act as their own print servers). Because of TCP/IP's flexibility, this server can be elsewhere on your machine's subnet, or at some antipodal point over the Internet.

Enter the server's Internet hostname or IP address into the Printer's Address text field. (The dialog provides some running commentary below the text field to let you know whether the address is a valid one, even performing DNS lookups while you type.) If you want to use the server's default (or only) printer, leave the "Use default queue on server" checkbox active. Otherwise, uncheck it and then type the printer's name in the Queue Name text field.

 To investigate the printers queues that a given server makes available, use the *lpstat* command with the *-h* (hostname) and *-p* (printer listing) options, like so:

```
% lpstat -h my-print-server.my-office.com -p
printer room_501_laserjet disabled since Jan 01 00:00 -
printer color_laser_room_623 is idle.  enabled since Jan 01
00:00
```

In this example, room_501_laserjet and color_laser_room_623 are the queues that the server recognizes, and therefore are valid values in the Queue Name text field. (We also see that the former of the two printers seems to be disabled, but we'd have to talk to the office network administrator to find out the reason for that.)

USB
This pane simply displays a selectable list of all the printers visible to your machine via direct USB connection.

Directory Services
This pane lets you browse and select all the printers defined by the various directory services your computer uses. See Chapter 12.

Modifying list entries

Internally, there's not much to a printer list entry; just a network location and (maybe) a printer model type associated with it. Once you've added a printer to the printer list, you can change its settings (such as the driver it uses) by selecting it, and then choosing Printers → Get Info (⌘-I.) You can also use the CUPS web interface, described later in "Web-Based Print Administration."

This is not to be confused with the Configure Printer button (and command, under the Printers menu), which lets you perform remote configuration on the actual printer itself, if that model supports it.

Printer Queues

The print server maintains a *queue*, a list of pending print jobs, for each printer it knows about. Double-clicking a row in the printer list window reveals that printer's queue window (see Figure 8-7), which lists that printer's queue as well as some basic status information, such as whether the printer is active or idle, or whether it is accepting new jobs or not.

Printing

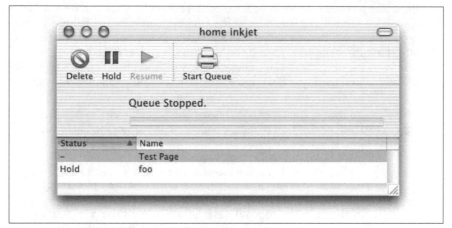

Figure 8-7. Print Center's printer queue detail window

Page Setup

The Page Setup dialog, which you can summon with most applications through File → Page Setup (Shift-⌘-P), lets you define paper size, orientation, and scale options. These options apply for the current application; at the start of the printing process, it consults them in order to figure out the dimensions of the rectangle that it will draw to for each page. The system remembers them until the application quits—the next time you launch that application, Page Setup's values will return to their defaults.

The standard dialog contains the following controls, as seen in Figure 8-8:

Settings
> This pop-up menu switches the dialog's view between the Page Attributes control panel and a summary of all its current settings. The summary includes a detailed rundown of the selected paper size's dimensions, including margins.

Format for
> This menu specifies the printers that the Page Setup dialog's settings affect. The default choice is Any Printer, but you can click on the menu to select any other single printer in your printer list (see the earlier section "The Printer List"). Page Setup can store several sets of options in parallel, one for each printer, as well as the Any Printer set (which acts as default for any printers whose Page Setup options you don't specifically change).

Paper Size
> Clicking this menu reveals all the paper sizes available through the printer selected under the "Format for" menu. These sizes are defined by the printers' PPD files; you'll get a limited list for printers using the "Generic" driver or if Format for is set to Any Printer.

Orientation

These buttons let you choose between portrait (the default) and landscape page layout; with the latter, you can choose whether the page's logical top is on the physical page's right or left side.

Scale

Express, as a percentage, with 100 percent being a normal-sized printout.

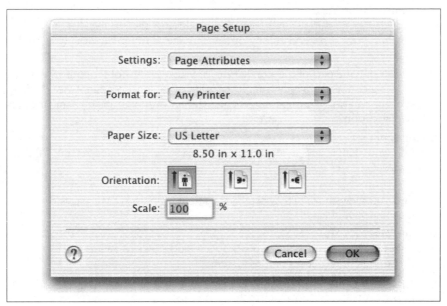

Figure 8-8. The Page Setup dialog

The Page Setup dialog controls only page-level scaling and layout. For dozens of other printing-related controls, see the Print dialog, described earlier in "The Print Dialog."

Alternative Printer Interfaces

Print Center is Apple's fully Aqua-integrated print management application, but it's really just one possible frontend to Mac OS X's printing system. CUPS (and therefore Mac OS X) ships with several command-line programs for creating and tracking print jobs, as well as administrating the machine's print server. You can also access the CUPS server through a web browser to track jobs and perform administrative tasks.

Web-Based Print Administration

Since CUPS uses the IPP protocol—an extension of HTTP—it's quite capable of handling ordinary HTTP requests from a web browser. Load *http://localhost:631* in a browser to see your print server's web interface. Depending on how permissive you've set CUPS to be (see the section "Sharing Through cupsd.conf" later in

Printing

this chapter) you may also be able to connect to your machine's CUPS web interface remotely, over the local network or even the Internet. By default, if Printer Sharing is activated (see the later section "Printer Sharing Through the Sharing Pane"), then any machine that can see your Mac's IP address can also connect to its CUPS server.

The web interface's main page features the following subpages:*

Do Administration Tasks
> Provides some simple interfaces for modifying the printer list, managing pending print jobs, and setting up *classes* (see "Printer Classes" later in this chapter).
>
> This is the one part of the site that has any access control set on it by default, allowing connections only from IP 127.0.0.1 (the local machine). See the later section "Sharing Through cupsd.conf" for information on customizing this configuration.

Manage Printer Classes
> Lets you define and manage printer classes (see the later section "Printer Classes").

On-Line Help
> Lets you view the CUPS system's documentation as HTML pages or download it as PDF files.

Manage Jobs
> Takes you to a page where you can view and manage pending print jobs in the various print queues on this system.

Manage Printers
> Lets you create, edit, and delete the printer list.

Download the Current CUPS Software
> Whisks you off to the CUPS web site where you can download the most recent CUPS source and binary distributions. (Note that, since CUPS is officially a part of Mac OS X, Apple makes security patches and other important updates to the CUPS software available through Software Update, as they are released.)

Command-Line Tools

While the commands listed below are all part of the CUPS project, several of them borrow their names and syntax from old-school Unix commands for backwards compatibility (with both existing scripts that might call these commands and Unix-veteran humans who have used these commands for years). This explains, for example, the presence of both *lp* and *lpr*, which do the exact same thing with different syntaxes.

---

* Those wishing to hack their own CUPS web site may find its document *root* at */usr/share/doc/cups*, and its *cgi-bin* directory at */usr/libexec/cups*. You can modify these files through *cupsd.conf*'s *DocumentRoot* and *ServerBin* directives, respectively. You must have admin privileges to modify any of these files.

lpr
lp

> These commands both create new print jobs and send them to a print server. Along with the *lpoptions*, they serve as the Terminal's equivalents to Aqua's Print dialog.

lpadmin

> An all-around print server administration tool. It lets you modify your machine's printer list, much like Print Center, but provides even more control through setting user print quotas, individual printer access control, and more.

enable

> Stops a queue. The print server will continue to accept and remember jobs for this printer, but won't send them to the printer until the queue is started again.

disable

> Starts a stopped queue.

reject

> Sets a queue to reject all further print jobs.

accept

> Sets a queue to start accepting new print jobs.

lpoptions

> Displays, and lets you set, printer options and defaults. *lpoptions* gives you a command-line interface to the various printer options you set through the Print dialog's various configuration panes (see the section "Printer Output Menu and Panes" earlier in this chapter).

cancel
lprm

> These commands remove pending jobs from a queue.

lpinfo

> Lists the printer drivers and hardware/network interfaces that the current CUPS configurations recognizes.

lpstat

> Lists printer queues currently available to the system and fetches details about pending print jobs.

Printer Classes

CUPS' web interface and *lpadmin* command both let you set up lists of *printer classes*. A printer class is simply a queue that has more than one printer associated with it.

When a class receives a print job, it chooses a single physical printer to receive and process it. If any printers are idle, one of them gets the job; otherwise, the print server holds the job in the class queue until one of the class's printers becomes available. In effect, a class acts like a queue capable of printing several jobs in parallel. This can make it an effective tool in high-throughout printing environments.

At the time of this writing, the Print Center application lacks commands to configure classes; you'll have to use one of the other CUPS interfaces already described.

Printer Sharing

You can configure your Mac's CUPS print server to listen for incoming print jobs over the network. This lets other computers use your machine as their print server, printing out documents on the printers connected to it. These client machines can run any OS that can speak the CUPS, LP, or LPR protocols—e.g., Windows, Unix, or other Mac OS X machines (the latter of which would access your printers by adding an IP Printing printer entry into their own printer lists, as described earlier in "Adding and configuring printers," pointing it at your computer's IP address).

Printer Sharing Through the Sharing Pane

The easiest way to activate this feature involves bringing up the Sharing preferences pane's Services tab (Figure 8-1) and activating the USB Printer Sharing checkbox. This automatically modifies the relevant part of the */etc/cups/cupsd.conf* file and then restarts the print server for you.

If the Sharing pane finds */etc/cups/cupsd.conf* in an unexpected state (such as the result of your performing manual edits on it), then the Sharing pane will refuse to modify the file further; the Printer Sharing checkbox will lock into a checked state, even if you try unchecking it.

Should you find yourself in this situation and wish to make this simple interface available again, remove the existing */etc/cups/cupsd.conf* file (backing it up somewhere first, if you wish), and then copy */etc/cups/cupsd.conf.old* in its place. If *both* files get corrupted somehow, you'll have to fall back to your OS X installation CDs to get fresh copies, or download the files anew (along with every other part of CUPS) from cups.org.

This simple interface lets any machine that can see your machine via IP use all the printers attached to it. This may be acceptable behavior if your Mac is not connected to the Internet or hidden behind a firewall, and therefore has an IP address that only other machines on the subnet can see (typically 192.168.X.X or 10.10.X.X). However, if your Mac has an IP that the whole world can see through the Internet, use this option with care, lest you allow anyone anywhere on Earth to send their documents to your printer! Consider manually configuring your CUPS server instead, as detailed in the next section.

Configuring CUPS

CUPS, an open source project initiated and headed by Easy Software Products, was adopted by Apple as Mac OS X's internal printing system starting with OS Version 10.2.0.

For decades, the majority of Unix systems (including earlier versions of Mac OS X) have used a patchwork of different vendors' printing systems, usually a mix of Berkeley Unix's LPD/LPR and System V's LP, which trace their roots back to the 1970s. As its name suggests, CUPS provides a printing system intended to work on any Unix-based system. It uses more recent technologies, particularly the Internet Printing Protocol (IPP), which layers printing-specific commands onto HTTP.* This allows, among other things, a CUPS-based print server to use HTTP-style authentication and access control, and to accept web client connections (as covered earlier in "Web-Based Print Administration").

Sharing Through cupsd.conf

For more sophisticated control and greater security over your computer's role as a network-accessible print server, use a text editor (such as *TextEdit*, *Emacs*, or *vi*) to manually modify the CUPS server's configuration file, found at */etc/cups/cupsd.conf*.

This file purposely looks and works like Apache's configuration file (described in Chapter 13). Just like *etc/httpd/httpd.conf*, */etc/cups/cupsd.confd* works simply by listing many key-value pairs of server directives, either standing alone (where they affect the whole server) or enclosed in XML-like block tags (where they affect a limited scope or location). The default file contains lots of chatty comments to help you figure out which directives belong to what.

Of particular interest are the *Location* directive blocks, which you can find at the end of the file, after the comment that reads *Security Options*. CUPS maps its various features into a directory system accessible by URI, each of which can have its own security settings. Table 8-1 lists these locations.

Table 8-1. Security locations on a CUPS system

Location	Description
/classes	All classes (groups of printers) this system defines
/classes/*name*	The class named *name*
/printers	All printers this system defines
/printers/*name*	The printer named *name*
/admin	All this print system's administrative functions

Within each of these locations, you can place authentication and access-control directives, as listed in Table 8-2.

Table 8-2. CUPS access-control directives

Directive	Description
AuthType	HTTP authentication style—can be *None*, *Basic*, or *Digest* (choosing *None* still lets you use address-based authorization)
AuthClass	Authorization class—can be *Anonymous*, *User*, *System* (meaning any user in the group defined by the separate *System-Group* directive—*admin* by default), or *Group*
AuthGroup	The group name, if an *AuthClass* of *Group* is used

---

* For another Mac OS X–friendly technology that builds on HTTP, read about WebDAV in Chapter 7.

Table 8-2. CUPS access-control directives (continued)

Directive	Description
Order	The order of Deny/Allow processing—either *Deny, Allow* or *Allow,Deny*
Allow	An address, domain, or subnet from which connections are allowed
Deny	An address, domain, or subnet from which connections are denied

You can find full documentation for configuring and administering CUPS online at cups.org, or by following the *Documentation* link from your machine's own CUPS web interface (see "Web-Based Print Administration").

Printer Drivers

Mac OS X supports PostScript Printer Description (PPD) files for PostScript printers and its own driver format for non-PostScript printers. All these files go into the */Printer* folders of the system-wide *Library* hierarchy, as described in Chapter 9.

Apple chooses to make the Local/System domain difference a little fuzzy with the printer drivers it includes with Mac OS X. Drivers for Apple-branded printers go into */System/Library/Printers*, and other vendors' drivers go into the less-protected */Library/Printers* directory—despite the fact that Apple's installer software puts both kinds of drivers into place, and that Apple itself hasn't sold printers in years.

Generally speaking, you probably don't have to worry too much about having the right printer drivers, since Apple includes dozens of drivers for several vendors' printer models with Mac OS X, and regularly adds to the list (and updates existing drivers) via the System Update application.

Saving as PDF

Every Mac OS X application that uses the system's standard print system renders its pages via PDF before sending them to the print server. While the most common destination thereafter is a printer (by way of CUPS-defined PDF-to-PostScript and PDF-to-raster filters), you can interrupt the print process to preview this internal PDF document, and even save it to disk in PDF format in lieu of actually printing it.

Clicking the Preview button on the standard Print dialog (Figure 8-1) launches the Preview application, which opens the document to be printed in a separate window of its own. While this displays an accurate preview of the proposed printed output, showing margins and page breaks as a real printer would produce them. Select File → Save As PDF to save the preview to disk, as is, as an independent PDF file.

Alternately, you can skip a step and just tell the Print dialog to print to a file instead of a printer, simply by hitting the standard dialog's Save As PDF button. You can also save any document in raw PostScript format: under the Print dialog's Output Options pane (Figure 8-9), activate the Save As File checkbox, and select a file format from the Format pop-up menu (either PDF or PostScript).

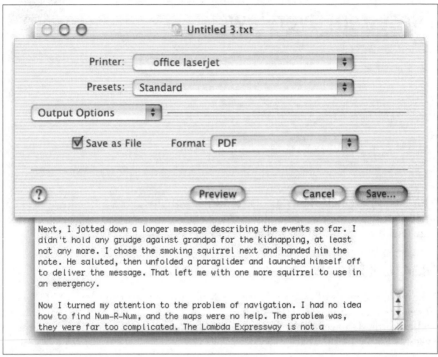

Figure 8-9. The Print dialog's Output Options pane

Because every modern operating system can read PDF documents (through Apple's Preview, Adobe's Acrobat Reader, the open source Ghostscript, or other applications), Mac OS X's ability to instantly turn any document into a PDF file represents a quick and easy way to share documents that other people are guaranteed to be able to read no matter what operating system they might use. Here's a quick way to attach an arbitrary document from any Mac OS X application to an outgoing email:

1. Select File → Print (⌘-P), then click the Print dialog's Preview button. This launches Preview, which in turn displays the document as a PDF in a separate window.

2. Create a Mail message, addressed and with appropriate introductory text.

3. Drag the PDF document window's proxy icon from its titlebar into the body of the Mail message. (The pointer will sport a plus sign as you hover over the message window, to signal that it's a legal drop-spot.)

Your message, with its PDF attachment, is now ready to send. When you're done, you may close the Preview window to dismiss that PDF, or you can save it to disk somewhere.

9

Filesystem Overview

This chapter examines how Mac OS X works with files, both in the lower level of its filesystems, and more generally in the specific directory layouts it uses to organize its most important files and keep track of installed applications.

Mac OS X Filesystems

Like earlier versions of Mac OS, Mac OS X filesystems favor the *Mac OS Extended Format*, better known as *HFS+* (Hierarchical File System),* but they also work well with the Universal File System (UFS) that most other Unix-based operating systems use as their primary filesystem.

Most Mac OS X volumes use HFS+ as their format because it allows backward compatibility with legacy Mac files. They also use it because it supports multiple file forks (see the later section "File Forks"). Through strong UFS support, a Mac OS X machine can work seamlessly with other Unix volumes, such as network-mounted ones that may be accessible over NFS.

Differences Between HFS+ and UFS

Among the most noticeable differences between the HFS+ and UFS file formats are the following:

- UFS is case-sensitive in its file path interpretation, while HFS+ is not. The paths */tmp/foo*, */tmp/Foo*, and */TMP/FOO* all point to the same location on an HFS+ system, but to three different ones on a UFS filesystem.

---

* Mac OS 8.1 and later used HFS+, while versions prior to 8.1 used the older Mac OS Standard Format, known as just HFS (without the plus).

Some software from the UFS world might assert case-sensitivity despite HFS+'s permissiveness. The Tab-completion feature of the *bash* or *zsh* shell command lines, for example, is case-sensitive, even if the filesystem they're working with is not.

- UFS uses slashes (/) as its path separator, while HFS+ uses colons (:). However, various Mac OS X applications accept slash-using path notation, no matter the underlying filesystem format. The Finder's Go → Go To Folder (Shift-⌘-G) command lets you type a path to travel to that point on the computer's filesystem. On the other hand, the Finder's Get Info window displays the real, colon-based path of the selected Finder object if it's on an HFS+ system.

  The two filesystems have a different concept of "root," or what the path / or : means, respectively. A UFS system's *root* directory is the top level of some designated disk volume, while the *root* to an HFS+ filesystem contains no data, but has a list of available volumes. This is why absolute filenames expressed in HFS+ terms always lead in with a volume name, such as *Volume:tmp:foo*. (It's also philosophically similar to the filesystem *root* as the Finder displays it, through its Go → Computer (Shift-⌘-C) command.)

 Mac OS X often expects absolute paths to act as they would look on a UFS system. In the Terminal, *cd /* takes you to the top level of the boot volume, not to the HFS+ *root*. (Other volumes are accessible from */Volumes*.)

- HFS+ stores two time-related pieces of metadata with each file: its creation date, and its modification date. UFS stores only modification dates.

File Forks

HFS+ is perhaps most distinctive among filesystems by how it allows files to store information in multiple *forks*. A typical non-Carbonized application for Mac OS 9 stores its executable binary code in a *data fork* and supplemental information—such as icons, dialogs, and sounds—is stored in a *resource fork*. Each of these forks is a separate subsection of the file. Documents also have both data and resources forks, which applications can read from and write to as they see fit.

However, Mac OS X is based on Unix, which was built to work with single-forked files, holding nothing except their own data. Modern Mac OS applications eschew all use of resource forks, instead taking one of two paths. They either store all their resources in a separate file with an *.rsrc* extension, or simply keep their resources as separate files and bundle them as parts of the application package. Carbon applications usually take the former, single-file route for their resources, and Cocoa applications favor the latter.

In order to support Classic applications (as well as the files they produce), Mac OS X recognizes files' resource forks.

Attribute forks

HFS+ files can store metainformation in a third fork, called an *attribute fork*. Most commonly, this fork, if used, holds the file's application and creator codes.

As with resource forks, Mac OS X supports this fork and its codes, but considers them deprecated. Modern Mac applications link files to themselves through file-name extensions, not creator codes. As a user, you can also modify these application-document links as you wish, through the "Open with application" page of the Finder's Get Info window (as described in "The Get Info Window" in Chapter 2).

Other Supported Filesystem Formats

Mac OS X can recognize and work with several local filesystem formats beyond UFS and HFS+, as listed in Table 9-1.

Table 9-1. Mac OS X's supported filesystem formats

Filesystem type	Description
HFS+	Mac OS Extended Format. The standard filesystem format for Mac OS Versions 8.1 and later (including Mac OS X).
HFS	Mac OS Standard Format. Used by Mac OS versions prior to 8.1.
UFS	Universal File System, used by most Unix-based systems.
UDF	Universal disk format, used by DVDs.
ISO 9660	Used by CD-ROMs.
MS-DOS	Used primarily by DOS and Windows, sometimes other media (such as some digital cameras).
NFS	The Network File System (see Chapter 11).

This list doesn't include the remote filesystems that Mac OS X can mount as network-shared volumes. See "Mounting Network Disks" in Chapter 7.

Filesystem Organization

Mac OS X defines several folders across the filesystem as holding special significance to the system. Individual applications, as well as the system software itself, consult these directories when scanning for certain types of software or resources installed on the machine. For example, a program that wants a list of fonts available to the whole system can look in */Library/Fonts* and */System/Library/Fonts*. Font files can certainly exist elsewhere in the filesystem, but relevant applications aren't likely to find them unless they're in a predictable place.

Domains

You might also have a */Library/Fonts* folder inside your home folder, and perhaps yet another inside */Network*. Each of these *Fonts* folders exists inside a separate *domain*, Mac OS X's term for the scope that a folder resides in (in terms of both function and permission from the current user's point of view). The system defines four domains.

The term "domain" is a contender for the most overloaded word used to describe Mac OS X. While reading this section, try not to confuse the concept of filesystem domains with that of Internet domain names (such as "oreilly.com") or NetInfo domains (as covered in Chapter 12). None of these have anything to do with each other.

User

Contains folders that are under complete control of the current user. Generally speaking, this includes the user's Home folder and everything inside it.

Local

Holds folders and files usable by all users of this machine, which may be modified by system administrators (users in the admin group), but are not crucial to the operating system.

Folders directly under the *root* directory (/) that don't belong to other domains fall into the Local domain. On most systems, these include the */Library* and */Applications* folders.

Network

Works like the Local domain, except that its folders are accessible to all users of a network and modifiable by network administrators. Usually, this domain extends to cover all the folders found within the */Network* directory.

System

Contains folders and files that exist to support the computer's operating system and are not intended for direct human use. Nobody except the root account has permission to modify anything in the */System* domain.

The */System* folder contains a typical Mac OS X machine's System domain.

 Not every folder on the system lies in a domain. Other users' Home folders, for example, are always out of reach, even for administrative users, and the system has no special use for them. From the current user's point of view, they have no relevance; hence, they have no domain.

When an application needs to scan a system-defined folder for information, it usually seeks the folder in each of these four domains and scans its content, if it exists. The search order it uses is usually as follows:

1. User
2. Local
3. Network
4. System

An individual application can use a different order if it wishes, but the above order suffices for most. It starts at the User domain (the scope where the current user has the most control), continues through the Local and Network domains (where system administrators might have put files for users' shared use), and ends at the System domain (where files critical to the operating system live and whose presence is usually a decision of Apple's).

For example, a program that wishes to find a particular font knows that it would find that font's file in a */Library/Font* folder. This folder can exist in any of the four domains, so it scans the following directories, in order:

1. */Users/username/Library/Fonts/*
2. */Library/Fonts/*
3. */Network/Library/Fonts/*
4. */System/Library/Fonts/*

If it finds the font, it stops its search. If that same application wishes to build a list of all fonts available to the user, then it would scan all the above folders in their entirety. In the case of duplicates—for example, Courier is defined in both the User and System domains—then the earlier domain in the search order (User, in this case) takes precedence.

Special Folders

There are two *root* directories on MacOS X: one that you can see from the Finder, and a Unix *root* directory that's mainly accessible from the Terminal. For more information on accessing the Unix *root* directory from the Finder, see "Exploring root" later in this chapter.

When you click on the Computer icon in the Finder toolbar (or select Go → Computer (Shift-⌘-C) and click on the hard drive icon, you will see the folders listed in Table 9-2. These folders contain essential system files, applications, and the directories for all of the system's users.

Table 9-2. Special folders in the root directory

Directory	Domain	Description
Applications	Local, System[a]	Holds applications available to all users of this machine.
Library	Local	Contains resources available to all users of this machine, such as fonts, plug-ins, and documentation.
System	System	This is the system folder for Mac OS X.
System Folder	System	This is the system folder for Mac OS 9. Present only if Mac OS 9 is also installed on this volume.
Documents	-	Miscellaneous files from a previous Mac OS 9 installation.
Applications (Mac OS 9)	-	Applications from a previous Mac OS 9 installation.

[a] This folder exists in both the local and system domains. Most of its content belongs to the admin group, but some applications, such as Print Center, can't be modified by even admin-group users.

User directories

Once created, each user is provided with a series of subdirectories in the Home directory (*/Users/username*). These directories, listed here, can be used for storing anything, although some have specific purposes.

Desktop

This directory contains the items found on your Desktop, including any files, folders, or application aliases placed there.

Documents

While it isn't mandatory, the */Documents* directory can be used as a repository for any files or folders you create.

Library

This directory is similar to the */System/Preferences* directory found in earlier versions of the Mac OS; it contains resources used by applications, but not the applications themselves.

Movies

This is a place where you can store movies you create with iMovie or hold QuickTime movies you create or download from the Internet.

Music

This directory can be used to store music and sound files, including *.aiff*, *.mp3*, and so on. This directory is also where the iTunes Library is located.

Pictures

This directory can be used as a place to store photos and other images. iPhoto also uses the */Pictures* directory to house its iPhoto Library directory, which contains the photo albums you create.

Public

If you enable file or web sharing (System Preferences → Sharing), this is where you can place items you wish to share with other users. Users who access your */Public* directory can see and copy items from this directory. Also in the */Public* directory is the Drop Box (*/Public/Drop Box*), which is a place where other users can place files for you.

Shared

If your system has more than one user on it, a */Shared* directory will be created. Because users are allowed to add or modify files only within their own home directories, the */Shared* directory is a place where you can drop items to be shared with other users on the system.

Sites

If you enable Personal Web Sharing (System Preferences → Sharing → Services), this is the directory that will house the web site for your user account.

The Library folder

Every domain contains a Library folder. Applications searching for additional resources and software available to it scan through the Library folders in the order noted earlier in "Domains."

Library folders hold system-specific application resources. Unlike the application-specific icons, sounds, and other resource files found within an application's package, Library resources are either shared among many applications (as fonts are) or are specific to both individual applications and the current system (as user preference files are).

A running application has access to the resources in all the Library folders within the domains that the current user can see. Thus, if the user *jmac* is running an application, the application combs through */Users/jmac/Library*, */Library*, */Network/ Library*, and */System/Library* for resource files. If searching for a particular resource, such as a font or a configuration file, it looks through the folders in the usual User → Local → Network → System domain search order, unless the application specifies a different order for some reason.

Anything a user places in his own User domain's Library folder, either directly or through an application, is available to that user alone. For example, all applications on the system are stored in */Applications*; however, a user's preferences for an application are stored in */Users/username/Library/Preferences* as *plist* files. This separation allows multiple users on the system to use the same applications, and yet have a different set of preferences to suit their needs. A system administrator can place resources in the Local domain's Library folder to allow all users of that computer access to them, and a network administrator can place files in the Network domain's Library so that all users of all computers across a network can use them. Nobody should ever need to modify the System domain's Library folder; leave that up to Apple's own system software installer and updater applications.

Mac OS X's Library folders are somewhat analogous to the *lib* directories found in key places around a typical Unix system, such as */usr/lib* and */usr/local/lib*. Unix *lib* directories usually hold code libraries and modules and Mac OS X Library folders hold frameworks (the dynamic code libraries that Cocoa applications can link to in their Frameworks subfolders; see Chapter 15). As this section illustrates, though, Library folders also hold all manner of other application resources.

It's worth noting that a typical Mac OS X system does, in fact, have a number of more traditional Unix *lib* directories in the usual places, which the underlying Darwin OS uses when compiling software.

The following list briefly describes the folders often found in Library folders. Unless otherwise noted, they might be found in any domain.

Application Support
> This folder acts as a "scratch pad" for various applications. By convention, each application creates its own subfolder in this one, within which it can write whatever files it wishes.

Assistants
> Programs that assist with the configuration of other applications or services (also known as *wizards*).

> Sloppier applications can, however, place folders for themselves directly underneath the Library folder, rather than in */Library/Application Support*. (For example, Apple's iTunes application tends to do this.)

Audio
> Audio-related resources, including system alerts and audio plug-ins for various applications' use.

ColorPickers
> Programs for choosing a color according to various models. The available color pickers appear as choices when an application displays a color well panel (Figure 9-1). Mac OS X's default pickers, including the color wheel, slider, and image-based ones, live in */System/Library/ColorPickers*.

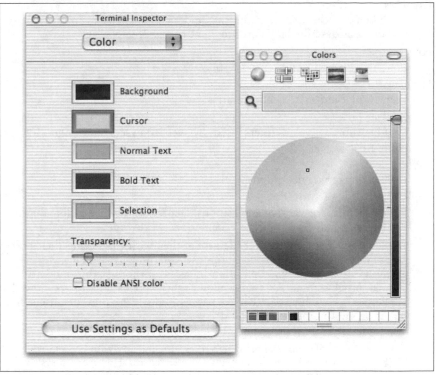

Figure 9-1. A color well panel

ColoSync
    ColorSync profiles and scripts.

Components
    Miscellaneous components and extensions. This folder tends to exist solely in the System domain.

Documentation
    Documentation files. Can be in Apple Help format, plain text files, collections of HTML, or just about anything else.

    As with */Library/Application Support,* applications usually place their files within their own, eponymous subfolders.

Extensions
    Device drivers and kernel extensions. Appropriate only in the system domain.

   Don't confuse the */System/Library/Extension* folder with Mac OS 9's */System Folder/Extensions* folder. The two are somewhat analogous in that both contain device drivers and low-level system extensions, but Mac OS 9's */Extensions* folder often contains all the sorts of things that Mac OS X's Library folders now hold, in one big, unsorted directory.

Favorites

Found only in the User domain, this folder contains aliases to files, folders, and disks, as described in "Favorites" in Chapter 2.

Fonts

Font files, for both printing and display.

Frameworks

Frameworks and shared code libraries.

Internet Plug-ins

Plug-ins, libraries, and filters used by web browsers and other Internet applications.

Keyboards

Keyboard mapping definitions.

Preferences

Preference files for various applications. Depending upon the domain, these can be for an individual user, or system- or network-wide.

Applications can use whatever file format they wish for storing their preferences. Many modern Mac applications use XML property list files, with a *.plist* extension; this allows its application to access it through the standard user-defaults programming APIs, and allows other applications to see how that application is configured. (Unix's permission system prevents users from spying on one another's config files!)

 The files in */Library/Preferences* usually apply to system-wide things, such as login window preferences. However, a system administrator can place an individual application's preferences file here to override individual users' preferences for that application.

See Chapter 22 for more information about Mac OS X's preferences system known as the *defaults database*.

Printers

Printer drivers and PPD plug-ins, organized by printer vendor.

Setup for individual printers doesn't go here; see Chapter 8 to learn how that works.

QuickTime

QuickTime components and extensions.

Scripting Additions

AppleScript extensions (see Chapter 16).

Scripts

Scripts to display under the Script menu extra (see Chapter 16). The menu extra's content is an aggregation of all the filesystem domains' */Library/Scripts* folders. Subfolders show up as submenus.

WebServer

/Library/WebServer is the default document *root* of the Apache web server that ships with Mac OS X. See Chapter 13 for more on running Apache.

Hidden Files

By default, the Finder hides many files and folders from view, including the entirety of Darwin's diretory layout, under the philosophy that most Mac OS X users will never need to access the system's Unix underpinnings. Savvier users, on the other hand, have a number of ways to see and work with all the filesystem's files.

Seeing Hidden Files

There are two ways to see files that don't appear in the Finder. The most direct way involves simply viewing a folder's contents by dropping into the Terminal and running the *ls* command on it. The Terminal sees the world simply as a tree of directories and files, and nothing more; files that have special, Mac-specific system roles appear like any other file. (However, you'll have to run *ls* with the *-a* flag.)

The other way involves changing the Finder preference that keeps these files hidden from sight. (Apple gets points for making this a user-adjustable preference, albeit not a very obvious one.) You'll need to add a value to the Finder preferences' file. You can accomplish this by operating the *defaults* command-line program on your com.apple.finder user defaults domain (described in Chapter 22), or by directly editing your */Users/username/Library/Preferences/com.apple.finder.plist* file with the Property List Editor application, as shown in Figure 9-2.

To add a value to the *com.apple.finder.plist* file, follow these steps:

1. Launch the Property List Editor (*/Developer/Applications*).
2. Open the *com.apple.finder.plist* file located in */Users/username/Library/ Preferences*.
3. Click on the disclosure triangle next to Root to reveal the values and keys for the Finder's preferences.
4. Select Root by clicking on it once.
5. Click on the New Child button.
6. In the first column, enter AppleShowAllFiles.
7. Change its class to Boolean.
8. Change its value to Yes.
9. Save the changes to the *plist* file (File → Save or ⌘-S).
10. Quit the Property List Editor (⌘-Q).

Your work's almost over. To make the changes take effect, you need to relaunch the Finder, as follows:

1. Go to → Force Quit (or Option-⌘-Esc).
2. Select the Finder.
3. Click the Relaunch button.

There will be a short pause while the process for the Finder quits and restarts, after which the changes you made will take effect.

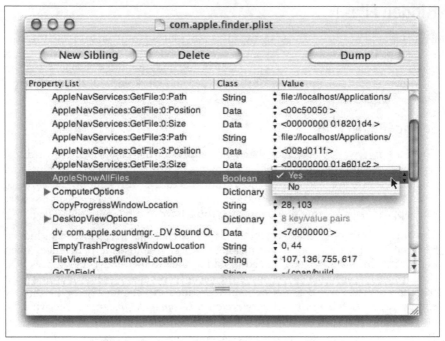

Figure 9-2. The Finder's preferences, as seen in Property List Editor

 If you already know about a Finder-hidden folder's existence, you can view its contents in the Finder by choosing Go to Folder (Shift-⌘-G) and then typing the path to that folder. Typing /bin, for example, reveals the contents of that directory (for all the good it will do, since it mainly contains programs that only the Darwin layer knows how to run).

Dotfiles

Following the traditional Unix model, the Finder hides all *dotfiles*, which are simply files (or folders) whose names begin with a period (dot) character. Applications can access dotfiles like any other file.

Your Mac's filesystem will likely accrue many dotfiles over time, particularly in users' Home folders, since this is the typical location for legacy Unix applications to store preference and configuration files. (Mac OS X–specific applications prefer to store this sort of information in Library folders, as described earlier in "The Library folder.") The following list covers some of particular interest.

.Trash
Found in users' Home folders, this directory contains all the files and folders that a user has sent to the Trash (through either the Dock's Trash icon or the Finder's Move to Trash (⌘-Delete) command), but not yet deleted. This folder's contents appear in a special Finder window labeled Trash when a user clicks once on the Dock's Trash icon.

This knowledge is useful for accessing users' Trash folders from the Terminal, or doing it programatically through Perl or a shell script.

 Mac OS 9, if present, also keeps its systemwide Trash can as a hidden folder, separate from the Trash folder in each Mac OS X user's Home folder. See "Hidden Mac OS 9 files," later in this chapter.

.FBCIndex
.FBCLockFolder

The Finder creates these dotfiles in each directory that it indexes by content. *.FBCIndex* is a binary file that acts as an index to the content of all the folder's files. When performing a by-content search via a folder or disk's Get Info window, the Finder quickly reads from these index files, rather than picking through all the individual files again.

Exploring root

The *root* directory of a Mac OS X boot disk has the most to hide, from the Finder's point of view; it may play *root* to as many as three separate operating systems' filesystems, all at once! Beyond holding the lowest-level directories of the Mac OS X filesystem, such as the */System* and */Library* folders, the *root* directory also contains the basic directories that Darwin—the pure Unix system running at Mac OS X's core—needs. These include the directories that any Unix user would recognize, such as */etc* and */tmp*. Compare Figure 9-3 with Figure 9-4.

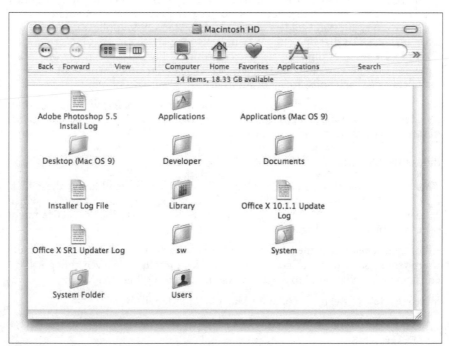

Figure 9-3. A typical Finder view of the boot disk's root

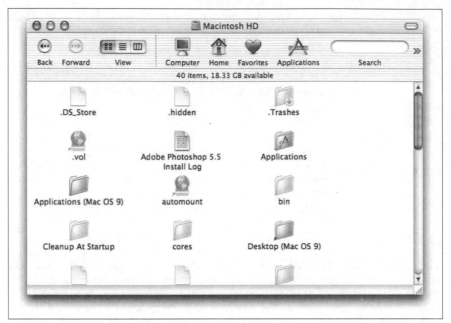

Figure 9-4. The same view, with hidden files revealed

Furthermore, if Mac OS 9 is installed on the boot disk, then its System Folder appears under the *root* directory, as do several Mac OS 9 configuration files. Other arbitrary files and folders created by the Mac OS 9 application might also exist at *root*, since that operating system lacks Mac OS X's permission system and doesn't view the *root* directory as "sacred ground." For example, many Mac OS 9 software installers create new folders directly under *root*, where Mac OS X installers place their software in locations like */Applications/Library*.

Mac OS X's Finder, when displaying the boot disk's *root* folder, will show most of the low-level Mac OS X and Mac OS 9 filesystems' folders, but keep several special files hidden from sight, and it won't show any of Darwin's directories at all.

Hidden Mac OS 9 files

This isn't a book about Mac OS 9, so we won't go into detail about these files' functions. However, it's worthwhile to point out their presence on disks on which Mac OS 9 and Mac OS X are both installed, as their mysterious existence might otherwise prove confusing.

All of these exist under the boot volume's *root* directory (/). Mac OS 9 is a single-user system, so it finds no fault in writing files directly to /, even though that's considered sacred ground to any Unix system, including Mac OS X.

Here are a few of the more common Mac OS 9 hidden files:

- Cleanup At Startup
- Desktop DB
- Desktop DF

- Temporary Items
- TheFindByContentFolder
- TheVolumeSettingsFolder
- Trash

As a rule of thumb, if you see mysterious, hidden files lurking directly under the *root* directory, then they're probably the doings of Mac OS 9.

Hidden Darwin files

This book frequently mentions "traditional Unix systems" when comparing Mac OS X to other Unix-based operating systems. The truth is that Darwin (already noted) *is* a rather traditional Unix system, when considered all by itself. It has its own directory structure that subtly shares disk space with the more visible Mac OS X structure covered earlier in "Filesystem Organization."

All of these files and directories exist under the *root* directory (/). (This may make them sound like the hidden Mac OS 9 files described in the previous section, but they're quite different, serving as the core of the Darwin system, and hence of Mac OS X itself, in a way.)

mach
mach.sym
mach_kernel
    These files make up the Mach kernel, the heart of Darwin and Mac OS X.

etc
private/etc
    The */etc* directory holds Darwin's system configuration files. While many of these files, such as */etc/hosts /etc/passwd*, have roles superceded by Mac OS X's Directory Service technologies (see Chapter 12), others, such as */etc/ hostconfig*, are central to the whole operating system's configuration, especially during the startup process.

tmp
private/tmp
    The usual Unix *tmp* directory is readable and writeable by all users and processes, despite the fact that it's squirreled away in the invisible */private* directory. Lots of command-line programs and utilities use this directory as a scratch pad to write temporary files to disk. (Modern Mac OS X applications are more likely to use users' *Library* folders.)

var
private/var
    The */var* directory holds logs, spools, PID files, and other file-based resources used by active processes.

bin
    Core Terminal commands, such as *cd* and *mkdir*. (As with all Unix command-line functions, all these commands, even the seemingly simple ones such as *ls*, are executable program files.)

sbin

Command-line utilities to perform basic filesystem and other administrative operations, such as mounting, unmounting, configuring, and diagnosing disks. Since these commands affect the whole system, they must usually be run as *root* (see the section "Acting as Root" in Chapter 11).

automount

The system uses this directory when mounting networked volumes over NFS; see Chapter 11.

dev

Device files, each a pointer to some kind of Unix device the system supports, are both real (such as disks and their partitions) and virtual (such as */dev/null*).

Volumes

This is the default mount point Mac OS X uses for the filesystems of disks and partitions other than the boot volume. One subdirectory appears here for every disk (except for the boot disk and Network icon) that the Finder would show in its Computer window (see "Disks" in Chapter 2).

The File Permissions System

Mac OS X uses the Unix file permission system to control who has access to the filesystem's files, folders, and disks, and what they can do with them.

Ownership and permissions are central to security. It's important to get them right, even when you're the only user, because odd things can happen if you don't. For most users' interaction with Mac OS X, the system will do the right thing, without their having to think much about it. (Things get a little trickier when viewing the system as an administrator, though.)

Permissions refer to the ways in which someone can use a file. There are three such permissions under Unix:

Read

Allows you to look at a file's contents.

Write

Allows you to change or delete a file.

Execute

Allows you to run a file as a program. (This isn't so important when using Mac OS X's GUI, though; see the sidebar "What About the Execute Bit?" later in this section.)

When each file is created, the system assigns some default permissions that work most of the time. For instance, it gives you both read and write permission, but most of the world has only read permission. If you have a reason to be paranoid, you can set things up so that other people have no permissions at all.

There are times when defaults don't work, though. For instance, if you create a shell script or Perl program in the Terminal, you'll have to assign executable permission so that you can run it. We'll show how to do that later in this section, after we get through the basic concepts.

Permissions have different meanings for a directory:

Read
> Allows you to list the contents of that directory.

Write
> Allows you to add or remove files in that directory.

Execute
> Allows you to list information about the files in that directory.

Don't worry about the difference between read and execute permission for directories; basically, they go together. Assign both or neither.

If you allow people to add files to a directory, you are also letting them remove files. The two privileges go together when you assign write permission. However, there is a way you can let users share a directory and keep them from deleting each other's files.

There are more files on Unix systems than the plain files and directories we've talked about so far. These are special files (devices), sockets, symbolic links, and so forth—each type observes its own rules regarding permissions. But you don't need to know the details on each type.

Owners and Groups

Now, who gets these permissions? To allow people to work together, Unix has three levels of permission: *owner*, *group*, and *other*. The *other* covers everybody who has access to the system and who isn't the *owner* or a member of the *group*.

The idea behind having groups is to give a set of users, like a team of programmers, access to a file or set of applications. For instance, a programmer creating source code may reserve write permission to herself, but allow members of her group to have read access through a *group* permission. As for *other*, it might have no permission at all.

Each file has an *owner* and a *group*. The *owner* is generally the user who created the file. Each user also belongs to a default *group*, and that *group* is assigned to every file the user creates. You can create many groups, though, and assign each user to multiple groups. By changing the *group* assigned to a file, you can give this level of access to any collection of people you want.

Mac OS 9 had something similar to this system with its "Users & Groups" Control panel, but this was relevant mainly to configuring who could mount your machine's hard drive over a network. Mac OS X's permission system also applies itself to this use, but is far more pervasive, affecting every user's interaction with every part of the filesystem, whether they are logged in locally or over a network.

Viewing and Modifying File Permissions

The permissions system is another part of Mac OS X with two distinct interfaces: you can either use the traditional Unix command-line tools through the Terminal to view and change a file's permissions, or you can use the Finder's Get Info window for a graphical interface to the same task.

Figure 9-5 shows the Finder's interface to the permission system, a section of the Finder's Info window (see "The Get Info Window" in Chapter 2).

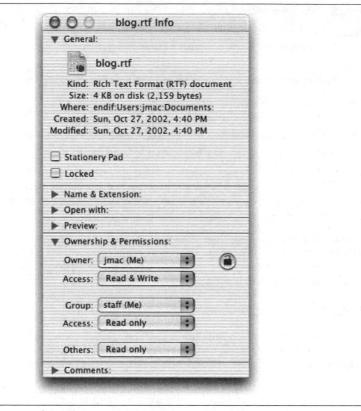

Figure 9-5. The Get Info window's Ownership & Permissions view

The pop-up menus display the object's current owner and group, as well as the owner, group, and other access permissions.

If you are the file's owner, you can modify the three permission menus, setting them to Read & Write, Read Only, or No Access for that type of user. If you have administrative priveleges, you can also modify the object's owner and group.

What About the Execute Bit?

Unix veterans will note that the Finder offers no interface to any of a file's "execute" bits, which determine whether someone is allowed to try launching a file as a program. Simply put, this type of distiction doesn't exist in Mac OS X's Aqua layer, where the Finder recognizes only certain kinds of files or directories as launchable, including *.app* application bundles and *.jar* Java archive files.

Furthermore, directories created in the Finder—through File → New Folder (Shift-⌘-N)—always have their execute bits set, and there's no way to unset them in the Finder. Again, you'll have to use *chmod* for that.

If you run the *ls* command with the *-l* option, it lists the requested files in a tabular format, with columns specifying the group, owner, and permissions of each file. Here is the Terminal's view of the same file depicted in Figure 9-5:

```
[jmac@wireless251 Documents]% ls -l blog.rtf
-rw-r--r--  1 jmac  staff  2159 Oct 27 16:40 blog.rtf
```

The code of letters and dashes in the first column lists the permissions. The first hyphen means it's a plain file (as opposed to a directory, which would be designated with a *d*). The next three characters list the read, write, and execute bits for the file's owner; rw- means that the read and write permissions are active, but the execute permission is not. (If it were, you'd see rwx instead.) Then there are three characters showing the group permissions (read-only, in this case) and three more for "other" permission (read-only, again).

After this, we see the file's owner (jmac) and group (staff), followed by the file's size in bytes, a timestamp, and finally, the file's name.

To change permissions, you must use the *chmod* command, while the *chown* and *chgrp* commands change a file or directory's owner and group, respectively. Consult Chapter 25 or your Mac's manpages for more information on these commands. You may also wish to consult the *ls* command's documentation to see other ways you can list files in the Terminal.

10

Running Java Applications

Java is Sun Microsystems' popular "write once, read anywhere" software technology, whose applications can run on many different operating systems without the need for porting (modifications may be necessary due to OS differences). Java is unusual specifically because a single compiled Java program can run as is on many different operating systems. It's not the only portable programming language that Mac OS X ships with, though; Perl, for example, is an interpreted language, so a Perl program also can run on many different machines, since it's compiled every time it's run. Apple considers Java support among Mac OS X's core features; Java is one of the four types of Aqua-environment applications (as listed in the section "Applications" in Chapter 2). This chapter describes the process of running Java programs on Mac OS X.

How Java Works

Like Classic applications, compiled Java applications must run in their own environment, as they're not in a binary format native to Mac OS X. Launching a Java program also launches the Java environment program, known as a *virtual machine*, or VM. As its name implies, its an entirely software-based "computer" that runs within the confines of the real computer's operating system, and is capable of executing Java programs. The interpreter—the one OS-specific part of any system's Java installation—takes care of translating the running program's Java commands into Mac-friendly system calls, all on the fly.

 Mac OS X uses Sun's Hotspot software as its Java VM. Its compiler comes in two "flavors." This doesn't have all the runtime optimizations that the server compiler does, but it makes up for it with a faster startup time and a smaller memory footprint.

You can invoke the machine's Java interpreter manually through the *java* Terminal command, which is covered later in this chapter in the section "Java on the Command Line." However, a properly packaged GUI application can be launched from the Finder and run within Aqua like any other Mac OS X application, as the following section describes.

Running Standalone Applications

While Java programs are meant to be run on any operating system for which a Java VM exists, developers can make them easier to run on Mac OS X in particular by packaging them up as applications. A standalone Java application looks and works in the Finder like any other kind of Mac OS X application (as described in the section "Applications" in Chapter 2), particularly in that you can double-click it to launch it. (This may not seem like much, but it is considerably more convenient than fussing with class paths and Jar files, which running Java programs from the command line can entail.)

Mac OS X ships with a pair of this sort of standalone Java application: Applet Launcher, and MRJAppBuilder (on the Developer Tools suite). As it happens, they're themselves utilities for Java users and developers, and their use is covered later in this chapter.

Running Applets

A *Java applet* is a Java program that has a graphical interface, but not a full application interface with a menu bar, Dock icon, and so on. Instead, it runs within a "wrapper" application. Most of the world's Java applets live embedded in web pages, and most web browsers can act as their wrappers. You can also use Mac OS X's Applet Launcher application to run applets that exist on your local machine.

Applets in a Web Browser

Most modern web browsers (including Microsoft's Internet Explorer, the browser that ships with Mac OS X) feature Java applet support. If you load a web page containing an applet,[*] your browser renders it within a rectangle right on the page, just as it does with images (or other embedded media, such as QuickTime movies or Flash animations). See Figure 10-1. This rectangle serves as the applet's entire interface; using it involves clicking or typing into it, as appropriate.

If you need to change the browser's applet-running behavior (including switching off its Java support altogether), call up the appropriate part of its preferences window. In Internet Explorer, select Explorer → Preferences (⌘-;), and then choose the Java page, as shown in Figure 10-2. (This section makes specific reference to Internet Explorer's Java settings, but other popular Mac OS X web browsers, such as OmniWeb or iCab, have their own similar preference windows.)

---

[*] Applets can appear in web pages through the <embed>, <object>, or <applet> HTML tags.

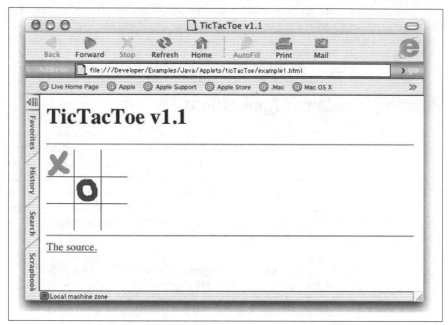

Figure 10-1. A Java applet running in Internet Explorer

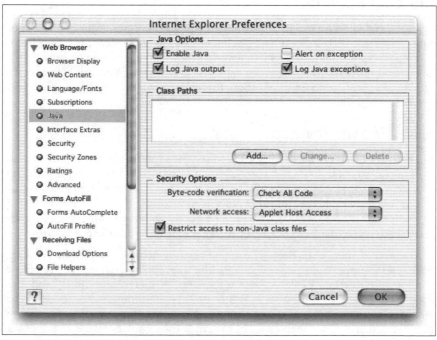

Figure 10-2. Internet Explorer's Java preferences window

When adjusting your web browser's preferences, don't confuse Java with the unfortunately named JavaScript, which is a programming language that can be embedded in web pages (usually in a <script> tag) to enable dynamic features. Beyond its chummy relationship with the Web, JavaScript has nothing at all to do with Java or Java applets.

Here's a rundown of some controls you'll find within the window:

Enable Java
While checked (as it is by default), the browser loads applets it finds embedded in web pages. Uncheck it to have the browser ignore all Java applets. (This also grays out every other control in this window.)

Alert on exception
When checked, the browser displays a dialog box every time a Java applet that is running raises an exception (a runtime error).

Class paths
Because they rely on the presence of client-side software, the majority of Java applets use classes that are common to most machines' and browsers' Java distributions. However, some applets might require that you download and install additional classes or Jar files; if so, you may need to alert the browser to their existence by adding them to the list of class paths.

For more about class paths, see the section "Class Paths," later in this chapter.

Byte-code verification
This pull-down menu specifies whether the browser performs on applet classes before running them. (You can choose to check all code, check only remotely stored classes, or not to check any code at all.) If verification fails, the browser displays an error message and the applet won't load.

Applets in Applet Launcher

Applet Launcher (itself a Java application) lets you run Java applets outside of a web browser. Its interface, seen in Figure 10-3, is quite simple; type a URL pointing to a remote file existing somewhere on the Web (with an http://*prefix*), or a file on the local filesystem (and have a file://*prefix*).

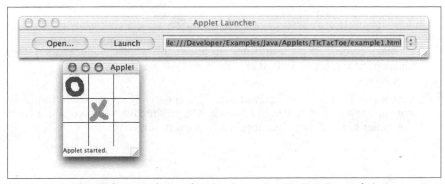

Figure 10-3. The Applet Launcher application (running a Tic-Tac-Toe applet)

You can navigate to local files through the Open button, but you must manually type in or paste remote URLs. In either case, clicking the Launch button loads the page, analyzes it for embedded applets, and launches each of them in its own window.

 You can quickly recall URLs previously visited with Applet Launcher by clicking the button to the right of the text field, which expands into a pull-down menu of recent URLs. (You can clear the application's history, or cease its record-keeping altogether, through Edit → Preferences.)

This program is basically a GUI version of Sun's *appletviewer* command-line tool, which also comes with Mac OS X. See Chapter 25 for the full list.

Applet Launcher treats the Mac OS X menu bar a little oddly. When you have the main Applet Launcher window focused, you get an Applets menu that acts as an alias to */Developer/Examples/Java/Applets/*. Focusing on a running applet's window instead gives you an Applet menu, containing the following commands:

Restart
Stops and restarts the applet.

Reload
Stops the applet, reloads it into memory from its original source file (either local or remote), and runs it anew.

Stop
Stops the applet, but keeps its window open (so you can continue selecting Applet menu commands on it).

Save
Calls up a file-navigation dialog, which lets you serialize the applet (save it and its current state information as a file). The resulting file has a *.ser* extension, and can be referenced by the HTML <applet> tag's "object" attribute

Start
Starts the applet, if it's been stopped.

Clone
Launches another instance of this applet, running in its own window.

Tag
Displays the HTML tag that references this applet.

Info
Displays embedded meta-information about this applet (such as its author and copyright information), if any.

Edit
This menu item is always greyed out. The underlying *appletviewer* tool does not yet support this command (which will presumably allow you to modify the applet's HTML tag), but apparently plans to someday.

Character Encoding
Displays the HTML file's character encoding in the applet window's status line.

Print
Summons a standard Mac OS X Print dialog window.

Properties
Lets you set preferences on the underlying *appletviewer* program, including HTTP proxies and Java class access restrictions.

Close
Stops and closes the applet. (Closing the window with the red titlebar button has the same effect.)

Java

Java on the Command Line

You can run Java programs from the command line through the *java* command. Generally, you invoke it in one of two ways:

`java options class argument1 argument2...`
Loads the specified class and runs its *main* method. If it has no such method, or if it's of the wrong format,[*] then the class will fail to launch.

You should have a class path defined so that the Java interpreter will know where on the filesystem to search for the specified class. See "Class Paths."

`java options -jar jarfile arguments`
In this case, the *-jar* option tells the Java interpreter to launch a program encapsulated in a Jar (Java Archive) file.[†] This works only if the Jar file knows its own *Main-class*, which defines the *main* method.

Jar files, like Mac OS X applications, are self-contained and ignore the user's class path definitions.

 This section involves using the Terminal. If you are completely unfamiliar with this application, or with using a Unix command line in general, you may want to skip ahead to Chapter 19 first.

You can find a full list of Java's options under its manpage, but here are some of the more useful ones:

`-cp`
Lets you define the class path for one command invocation. See the later section "Class Paths."

`-Dproperty=value`
Sets a system property value.

`-verbose`
Displays information about each loaded class.

---

[*] To be invokable like this, a Java class's *main* method must have the signature `public static void main(String[ ] args)`.

[†] Jar files are created through the *jar* utility, one of several standard Java tools that come with Mac OS X; see Chapter 25.

If the Java program you wish to run from the command line happens to be a self-contained Mac OS X application (of the sort described earlier in "Running Standalone Applications"), then you can simply run the command *open Application*, just as you can with any Cocoa, Carbon, or Classic application.

Class Paths

When you launch a Java program from the command line by invoking its class, you must have *class paths* defined. This is a list of filesystem paths pointing to directories and Jar files that the Java interpreter can search in order to locate the referenced class definition, as well as any classes that it might reference in turn.

There are two ways you can set class paths. If you're using the *java* command in the Terminal, you can feed it the *-cp* flag followed by a colon-delimited list of paths. For example, this command would include both the current directory (abbreviated as "."") and the */Library/Java* folder located in your Home folder into the class path while invoking the *MyClass* class:

```
% java -cp .:~/Library/Java/ MyClass
```

You can set class paths in a more permanent fashion through the CLASSPATH environment variable (see "Environment Variables" in Chapter 21).

 Some Java programs intended to run on the command line make things easier for users by including a shell or Perl script that acts as its frontend. Quite often, this script's job involves setting up class paths properly before running the Java interpreter on the program's main class.

Other applications' Java-related configuration might also deal with class paths. Internet Explorer, for example, lets you specify additional class paths that Java applets can use (see "Applets in a Web Browser" earlier in this chapter).

Other Command-Line Tools

Mac OS X ships with Sun's full suite of Unix command-line Java tools, which includes the *java* command. However, the rest—such as *javac*, the Java compiler, and the documentation browser *javadoc*—are primarily of interest to Java developers. This book covers these in Chapter 25.

Building Applications with MRJAppBuilder

If you have the Developer Tools software suite installed on your Mac, then you can use the *MRJAppBuilder* application, found in */Developer/Applications*, to bundle Java files into Mac OS X–style applications. This program is intended for use by Java developers to make their programs more Mac-friendly, but Mac users who know a thing or two about Java can also use it in order to assert friendliness upon Java programs they encounter.

Figure 10-4 shows *MRJAppBuilder*'s main interface. As you can see, the most important information you need to provide is the name of the Java class that contains the *main* method, which you can type into the "Main classname" field. Alternately, you can click the Choose... button to navigate through your file-system and find the *.jar* or *.class* file that contains this class. Once selected, *MRJAppBuilder* presents you with a menu of all the classes that file defines, as Figure 10-5 shows.

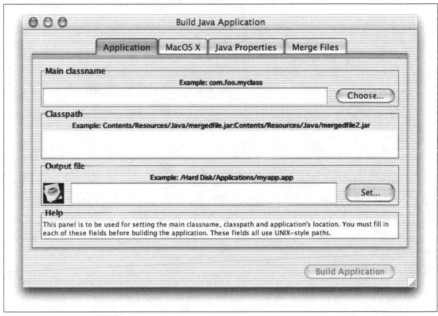

Figure 10-4. MRJAppBuilder

You can then supply the application-to-be's class path by placing it as a colon-separated list in the Classpath text view. (Unfortunately, there's no file browser for this operation; you have to type or paste the class path in manually.)

Finally, you must choose a name for the application you're building, including a file path. You can type a path into the "Output file" text field, or use the Set... button to browse the filesystem for a suitable destination directory and then supply an appropriate application name, as shown in Figure 10-6. To follow Mac OS X application conventions, it should have a *.app* extension.

In many cases, the information under this Application tab is all you'll need to supply in order to build a simple, working application from existing Java files. The *MRJAppBuilder* window's other three tabs serve the following functions:

Figure 10-5. MRJAppBuilder's class menu

Mac OS X

This page's table of key-value pairs will become the application's *Info.plist* file, containing metadata that defines its version number, icons, file extentions, and other information as described in Chapter 15. You can ignore this if you're just building a simple application for your own use.

Java Properties

This key-value table sets Java runtime properties. Perhaps the one of most interest is the *parameters* property, to which you can provide a text string that will be passed as arguments to the main class's main method. It's equivalent to the parameter string you'd provide on the command line after the class name, when using the *java* command (see the earlier section "Java on the Command Line").

Set the *main* and *classpath* properties by filling in the Application tab's text fields, as described earlier in this section.

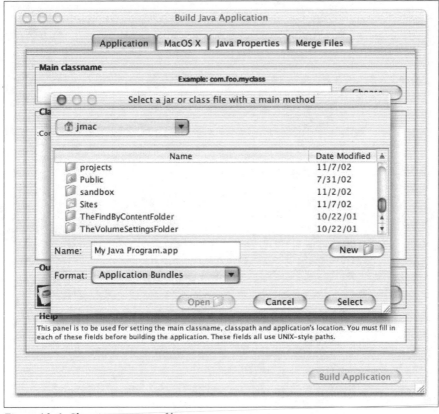

Figure 10-6. Choosing an output file

Merge Files

This page simply holds a list of files that *MRJAppBuilder* will bundle into the final application package. All the files that you name under the Application tab already appear in this list, but you can use the Add button to specify additional resource files the application might use.

System and Network Administration

Now that you have your Mac set up the way you want it, it's time to dive deeper into the operating system. This part of the book introduces you to the basic concepts of system administration, and includes coverage of Directory Services and NetInfo, and the various network services and daemons that run on Mac OS X. The part wraps up with an example of how to build a web-publishing system with DAMP (Darwin, Apache, MySQL, and Perl/PHP/Python).

The chapters in this part include:

11

System Administration Overview

Since Mac OS X has Unix at its heart, performing some system administration tasks is unavoidable, even for the most casual users. For this reason, the system lets you approach many administrative duties from two different angles. Fundamental tasks such as user account management (you'll need at least one user on the system, after all) and network setup may be performed though the friendly frontends of System Preference panes, while a more experienced admin can perform more subtle and sophisticated tasks through the Terminal's command line.

As such, much of this chapter assumes knowledge of the Terminal application and Darwin's Unix command line. See Chapter 19 first if you need to.

Many administrative tasks also require looking up and modifying information stored in the machine's NetInfo database. See Chapter 12 for complete coverage of NetInfo and its available user interfaces.

Acting as Root

Like all Unix systems, Mac OS X has a concept of a special user named *root*. Root can read from and modify any part of the filesystem, execute any program, and send signals (including the terminate signal) to all running programs and processes, regardless of who might own them. Root doesn't correspond to any one user; instead, a user with proper access privileges can become root temporarily in order to perform tasks that the Unix file and process permission systems wouldn't otherwise allow, such as launching or reloading system services or installing software on the Darwin side of things (see Chapter 24).

Mac OS X offers a couple of well-known ways to step into root's shoes via the Terminal, and a somewhat obscure way to perform the more dangerous act of logging into the system as the root user.

Using sudo

All admin users who work with the Terminal application (detailed in Chapter 19) should be aware of the *sudo* command (short for "superuser do," and pronounced "sue-doo"), which can precede any Terminal command to run it as root. For example, if I have a file in my current directory that I wish to copy to */usr/local/bin*, I could try this command:

```
[jmac]% cp my_script.pl /usr/local/bin
cp: /usr/local/bin/my_script.pl: Permission denied
[jmac]%
```

A peek at the target directory's permissions reveals the reason:

```
[jmac]% ls -ld /usr/local/bin
drwxr-xr-x  76 root  wheel  2584 Aug 27 01:18 /usr/local/bin
[jmac]%
```

The directory is writable by root only. So, here is precisely where *sudo* comes in handy. I'll try the command again, this time preceding it with *sudo*. The system will ask me for my password, just to confirm I'm not an intruder who is at my keyboard while I'm not looking:

```
[jmac]% sudo cp my_script.pl /usr/local/bin
Password: mybigsecretpassword
[jmac]%
```

The system executed the command without complaint.

When performing several root-level commands in a row, you don't need to provide your password each time; *sudo* keeps an internal timer, so running a *sudo* command within a few minutes of a previous one will forgo the password prompt. You can also run a shell under *sudo* in order to make it "sticky," with all subsequent commands run as root:

```
[jmac]% sudo zsh
Password: *****
[root@jmac]#
```

(This example assumes that I prefer the *zsh* shell; I could have used *bash* or *tcsh*, as covered in Chapter 21.) The prompt character changes from % to #, which tips you off that every command you type now will come from root's mouth. Furthermore, this particular shell is set to show the username within the prompt, making the change more obvious, but not all prompts feature this information—see Chapter 21 to learn more about configuring shell prompts through Terminal. To step back from the ledge and become an ordinary user again, issue the *exit* command, or just hit Control-D, to pop back to your previous shell.

 This convenience can go wrong for you if you forget that the root user is all-powerful, turning typos into tragedy. Even though it takes more work, consider making a habit of manually prefacing every root-run command with *sudo*, if only to remind yourself, with each such command, of what you're getting into. See the following section for more about casual root abuse.

The Root User Account

Mac OS X lets you log in as root right at the login screen, whereupon you can not only use Terminal commands without any need for further authentication, but you can also do just about anything in the Finder and other system-affecting Aqua applications without any of them complaining about permission problems. As you might imagine, this is somewhat dangerous, so Apple has turned to the security-through-obscurity model, forcing you to follow some very deliberate steps before you can do this.

1. First, you must activate the root user. Launch NetInfo Manager (/*Applications/ Utilities*); after authenticating yourself (through either clicking on the window's authentication lock button or selecting Security → Authenticate), select Security → Enable Root User.

2. Now give the root user a password. It should really be something different than your account password, and it should go without saying that it be something very hard to crack. In NetInfo Manager, select Security → Change Root Password to define this password.

3. If you wish, you can now log out (→ Log Out) and try the root user on for size. In any case, when you next see the login window, you can log in with username root. As Figure 11-1 shows, if you've set the login window to display a list of users rather than a simple pair of username/password text fields (see "Managing Users Through the Accounts Pane," later in this chapter), a mysterious "Other" option rounds out the user list, providing a text entry field. Here, you can type "root."

Managing Users and Groups

Mac OS X stores user and group information in the NetInfo database, under /*users* and /*groups*, respectively. (This is different than how most other Unix systems do it; see Chapter 9.)

Managing Users Through the Accounts Pane

While direct manipulation of NetInfo gives you the most control over user accounts, the Accounts preference pane, seen in Figure 11-2, contains controls for creating and deleting user accounts, as well as editing various properties associated with them.

The table on the left side of the Users tab page lists the system's users, showing their name, login picture, and type (which is either normal user or admin). Double-clicking on a user's row in this table lets you edit it.

The buttons down the pane's right side affect the currently selected user or modify the list as a whole.

New User
This summons the sheet seen in Figure 11-3. You must provide a value for every field except for Password Hint. The sheet will choose a random picture for the new user; you can leave this be and allow the user to set his own picture through the My Account preferences pane.

Figure 11-1. The login window, with the root user enabled

The Name text field holds the user's real, full name. Short Name is for the user's actual username.

Clicking OK adds the user to the machine's local NetInfo database and creates a new Home folder for them as well.

You should use this procedure only when creating accounts intended for use by actual human users. See the next section for information about creating accounts for daemons and other processes.

Edit User

Lets you edit the selected user through the same sheet that appears for the New User... button, except that it's already filled out with the user's current information.

Delete User

Deletes the selected user from the NetInfo database, preventing further logins. The user's Home folder remains in place, however; its ultimate fate (compressing and mailing it, perhaps, or simply trashing it) is up to you.

Figure 11-2. The Accounts preference panel

Set Auto-Login

Sets the selected user to automatically log in after the system starts up (provided that you can successfully provide that user's password). Only one user on a given Mac can hold this privilege.

Consider using this feature only if you're the sole person with physical access to this computer.

The Login Options tab (Figure 11-4) leads to some controls relevant to the appearance and behavior of the login window.*

Display Login Window as:

Lets you choose whether the login window displays a list of all the machine's users, or simply provides a text field for typing in a username (or a user's full name). In either case, the user logging in must still type in her password.

Disable Restart and Shut Down buttons

This checkbox controls whether the Restart and Shut Down buttons appear as part of the login window. (This has no effect on the computer's physical restart button or power switch.)

---

* The login window is actually an application unto itself, found at */System/Library/Core Services/ loginwindow*. Its *.plist* file, which the Accounts panel lets you modify, is found in */Library/com. apple.loginwindow.plist*.

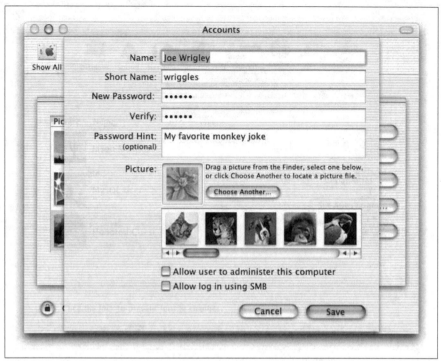

Figure 11-3. The Login Options tab of the Accounts preference pane

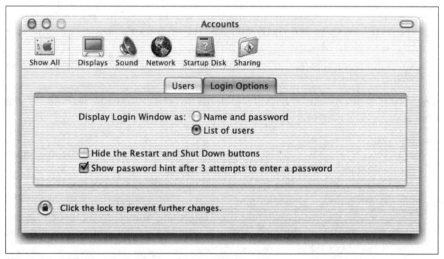

Figure 11-4. The Login Options preference panel

Show password hint after 3 attempts to enter a password

When this checkbox is active, the login window displays the user's password hint after three login attempts with a valid username but an incorrect password.

For maximum security, deactivate the "Show password hint" option. It will save you the worry of users setting their password hints to dangerously obvious values.

Nonhuman User Accounts

Some user accounts are intended for use only by programs, for the sake of system security; they typically have no login shell and have permissions limited to the programs they work with, so that if a malicious hacker should compromise the account, the possible damage is minimal. For example, Mac OS X's default Apache configuration has its web server running via the "www" user.

Since a nonhuman user doesn't need things like a Home folder or a place in the login window's user list, the Accounts pane's New User... might be overkill for creating one. Consider just duplicating and then modifying an existing nonhuman user directory (such as *www*) already in your NetInfo database.

Managing Groups

Mac OS X provides no special interface for managing groups; making changes to the machine's groups setup entails using NetInfo Manager or other tools to modify the NetInfo */groups* directory.

You can, however, indirectly control the membership of some groups through the Accounts panel. The real effect of granting a user admin privileges, by checking the Allow user to administer this computer checkbox in the Accounts preference pane (see Chapter 5), is simply to add that user to the *admin* group. Belonging to this group gives users a little more leeway in what the parts of the filesystem they're allowed to read from and write to—for example, the */Applications* folder belongs to the *admin* group and is group-writable (which lets admin users install system-wide Aqua applications), and the system logs that you can find in */var/log* are set readable to *admin* group members.

Furthermore, the *admin* group has global *sudo* privileges, letting them use the powerful command described earlier in "Acting as Root." For this reason, you should only check that checkbox for users you trust with the entire system.

All human users should have their *gid* property set to 20, that of the staff group. The Accounts pane's New User function takes care of this for you. (You can modify *gids* manually through the NetInfo utilities; see Chapter 12.) Human users that do not belong to staff may face some unfortunate challenges navigating the filesystem!

Network Administration

Networks connect computers so that the different systems can share information. For users and system administrators, Unix systems have traditionally provided a set of simple but valuable network services, which let you check whether systems are running, refer to files residing on remote systems, communicate via electronic mail, and so on.

For most commands to work over a network, each system must be continuously running a server process in the background, silently waiting to handle the user's request. This kind of process is commonly called a *daemon*.

Most Unix networking commands are based on Internet protocols. These are standardized ways of communicating across a network on hierarchical layers. The protocols range from addressing and packet routing at a relatively low layer to finding users and executing user commands at a higher layer.

The basic user commands that most systems support over Internet protocols are generally called TCP/IP commands, named after the two most common protocols. You can use all of these commands to communicate with other Unix systems besides Linux systems. Many can also be used to communicate with non-Unix systems, as all modern operating systems support TCP/IP.

Mac OS X includes several applications that bring graphical interfaces to these commands. Some, such as Network Utility, are little more than Aqua-window wrappers to the basic command-line tools. Others, like the Network preferences pane, bundle them into programs of their own.

Overview of TCP/IP

TCP/IP is a set of communication protocols that define how different types of computers talk to one another. It's named for its two most common protocols: the Transmission Control Protocol and the Internet Protocol. The Internet Protocol moves data between hosts—it splits data into packets, which are then forwarded to machines via the network. The Transmission Control Protocol ensures that the packets in a message are reassembled in the correct order at their final destination and that any missing datagrams are re-sent until they are correctly received.

IP addresses

The *IP (Internet) address* is a 32-bit binary number that differentiates your machine from all others on the network. Each machine on a given network must have a unique IP address.

Gateways and routing

Gateways are hosts responsible for exchanging routing information and forwarding data from one network to another. Each portion of a network that is under a separate local administration is called an *autonomous system* (AS). Autonomous systems connect to one another via exterior gateways. An AS also may contain its own system of networks, linked via interior gateways.

Configuring TCP/IP

Mac OS X expects you to configure your machine's network connection through the Network preference pane, described in "Configuring TCP/IP" in Chapter 7. You can also use traditional Unix command-line tools such as *ifconfig* to view and set the machine's TCP/IP configuration.

---

ifconfig

The network interface represents the way the networking software uses the hardware—the driver, the IP address, and so forth. To configure a network interface, use the *ifconfig* command. With *ifconfig*, you can assign an address to a network interface, setting the netmask, broadcast address, and IP address at boot time. You can also set network interface parameters, including the use of ARP, the use of driver-dependent debugging code, the use of one-packet mode, and the address of the correspondent on the other end of a point-to-point link. For more information on *ifconfig*, see Chapter 25.

Troubleshooting TCP/IP

Mac OS X not only includes the standard Unix suite of tools to troubleshoot and diagnose TCP/IP connections, it also gives them a graphic interface through the Network Utility application (Figure 11-5), found in the */Applications/Utilities* folder. You can also run them as command-line tools within the Terminal.

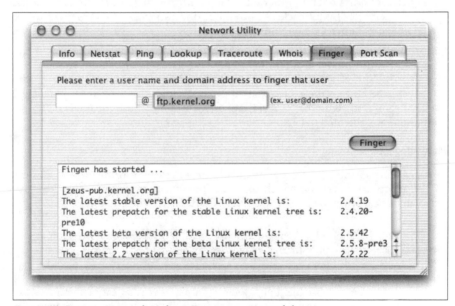

Figure 11-5. Using Network Utility's Finger on a network host

Table 11-1 lists these commands by their Terminal command-line name and their Network Utility name. You can find details of these programs under their respective entries in Chapter 25.

 If you're new to system administration (or perhaps just a curious user), feel free to try the various Network Utility tools on different Internet addresses, whether they lead to machines you control. (Try them on *www.oreilly.com*, for example, or hit your own machine by providing 127.0.0.1 as an address.) Watching the results can show you a lot about how TCP/IP packets behave at the low level.

Table 11-1. TCP/IP troubleshooting tools

Terminal program	Network Utility tab	Purpose
ifconfig	Info	Get information on network interfaces (Ethernet ports, Airport cards, etc.)
netstat	Netstat	Show current network status
ping	Ping	See if a machine at a certain address is alive
nslookup (or *dig*)	Lookup	Get DNS information about a domain or host
traceroute	Traceroute	Details the host-to-host relay route of packets between this and another machine.
whois	Whois	Get administrative DNS information about a domain or host
finger	Finger	Ask a host for information about one of its users
portscan[a]	Port Scan	Investigate a host's open TCP/IP ports

[a] Mac OS X doesn't have a *portscan* command by default; see "More about port scanning" later in this chapter.

Some network hosts offer information through *finger* that's not tied to any specific user. For example, Linux hackers know that one can finger *ftp.kernel.org* to see the latest Linux kernel version numbers.

Unfortunately, the Network Utility's Finger pane doesn't make this possibility obvious; if you fill in its host text field but leave its user field blank, you'll get an error dialog. You can trick the system, however, by typing a space character into the user field. Hitting the Finger at this point performs a finger on the machine itself, as shown in Figure 11-5. (Alternatively, you can just use the *finger* Terminal command, documented in Chapter 25.)

More about port scanning

Port scanning is the act of programatically probing many or all of a machine's TCP/IP ports to determine which ones accept outside network traffic. You can perform this on any machine through Network Utility's Port Scan tab.

It's considered bad form to use the Port Scan tool on hosts without their administrators' knowledge. Since a Port Scan reveals potential weak points in a machine's public network interface, it's both a useful security tool and the first thing that black-hat hackers often use to "case the joint," seeing if a machine is an easy target for a break-in. Port Scanning indiscriminately can lead to you or your system administrator receiving accusatory emails from the alarmed owners of these other machines, who have noticed your curiosity in their system logs! Administrative tools like Snort (*http://www.snort.org*) can automatically alert system administrators about port scanning attempts on their machines.

Mac OS X doesn't ship with a command-line version of Network Utility's port-scanning tool, but you can create one easily enough, simply by running this command:

```
sudo cp /Applications/Utilities/Network\ Utility.app/Contents/↵
Resources/stroke /bin/portscan
```

That *stroke* file is a simple program that Network Utility uses to perform its port scans, but it works fine all by itself as well. (You don't have to name it *portscan*, but it may make it easier to remember.)

NFS

The Network File System (NFS) is a distributed filesystem that allows users to mount remote filesystems as if they were local. From the Finder's point of view, an NFS-mounted filesystem appears as a disk, usually (but not necessarily) appearing under the special */Network* folder.

NFS uses a client-server model, in which a server exports directories to be shared, and clients mount the directories to access the files in them. NFS eliminates the need to keep copies of files on several machines by letting the clients all share a single copy of a file on the server. NFS is an RPC-based application-level protocol.

Both mounting and serving filesystems through NFS involve setting up configuration information in NetInfo, and then running command-line programs or launching (or reloading) daemons. For more about NetInfo, see Chapter 12.

You must also have user and group IDs in agreement among all the machines involved in an NFS connection. If your username and UID are jmac and 501 on your machine, then you should also have UID 501 on any machine whose directories you have mounted. Discrepancies can lead to confusion with filesystem permissions.

NFSManager

Unfortunately, Mac OS X doesn't include any friendly interface to its own NFS abilities; you must manually set NetInfo values and run Terminal commands as this section describes. A third-party alternative solution is NFSManager, a shareware application written by Marcel Bresnik, available at *http://www.bresink.com/ osx/NFSManager.html*. It provides a graphical interface to modify the appropriate parts of NetInfo and runs the *mount* and *umount* commands for you.

Mounting NFS

There are two ways to mount NFS filesystems in Mac OS X: *static mounting* and *automounting*.

Static NFS mounting

Static mounting simply binds another machine's exported filesystem to a local directory. Depending upon the exported system's setup, you might have to be root (or use the *sudo* command) to perform this mount. In any case, use the *mount* command with the *-t* flag set to *nfs*; this directs the *mount* program to use *mount_nfs* to plug the filesystem into the proper place. For example, if the

---

machine borg exports its */Users/Shared* directory, and you want it grafted onto your machine's filesystem at */mnt/shared/*, you'd *mkdir* on that directory if it didn't already exist and then run this command:

```
% mount -t nfs borg:/Users/Shared /mnt/shared
```

To unmount the remote system, simply *umount* the directory:

```
% umount /mnt/music
```

Use the *showmount* command with the *-e* flag to see what directories a certain host offers for export, as well as the slice of network it exports to. For example:

```
[jmac@endif /Users/jmac]% showmount -e cricket
Exports list on cricket:
/mnt/data                    192.168.2.0/255.255.255.0
/home                        192.168.2.0/255.255.255.0
```

This informs you that the host cricket exports two of its directories, */mnt/data* and */home*, but only to the 192.168.2.0 subnet.

NFS through automount

A daemon named *automount*[*] reads and acts on NFS-mounting information stored in NetInfo. It mounts these remote filesystems whenever the need arises, and then unmounts them once they fall idle.

To set up a mount point in this way, create a new directory under the NetInfo */mounts* directory, containing the following properties:

name
> The remote host, followed by a colon, and then the remote directory to mount.

vfstype
> The type of filesystem this entry represents; set it to *nfs*.

dir
> The local directory to which the remote filesystem should be grafted.

opts
> Options passed to *mount_nfs* when mounting.

If you list *net* among the values under the directory's *opts* property, then *automount* ignores the value you provided under *dir* and mounts the directory as a disk under */Network/Servers*. Otherwise, it appears under the location you specify with the *dir* property.

Once you set up NetInfo, send a *kill -HUP* to the automount process to have it reread the NetInfo database and act accordingly.

---

[*] With all its options and arguments, it runs as *automount -m /Network/Servers -fstab -m /automount -static*.

Daemons

NFS server daemons, called *nfsd daemons*, run on the server and accept RPC calls from clients. NFS servers also run the *mountd* daemon to handle mount requests. On the client, caching and buffering are handled by *biod*, the block I/O daemon. The *portmap* daemon maps RPC program numbers to the appropriate TCP/IP port numbers.

Exporting filesystems

Each directory on your machine that you wish to share with other machines via NFS must have its own directory under NetInfo's */exports* directory, as shown in Figure 11-6. (The */exports* directory doesn't exist in a fresh NetInfo distribution, so you may have to create it first.) Each of these directories has the following properties:

name
> The local filesystem directory to be exported via NFS.

clients
> A list of hostnames or IP addresses of machines able to mount this directory. If this list has any values, then *only* those machines can NFS-*mount* this directory. Otherwise, *mountd* uses other means (such as the *network* and *mask* options) to determine client eligibility.

opts
> Options read by *mountd*. Each option takes the form of *key=value*. The full list of options appears under the 5 manpage, but here are the more common ones:

> *maproot*
>> The credential of the specified user is used for remote access by root. The credential includes all the groups to which the user is a member on the local machine. The user may be specified by name or number.

Figure 11-6. Defining an NFS export point through NetInfo

network
mask

> The network subnet and network mask, respectively, that define the network slice you're willing to export this directory to. If you don't have an explicit client list defined under this directory's *clients* property, then *mountd* uses these options. If *neither* the property nor these options are defined, then the directory offers itself to world-wide export, which is probably asking for trouble; see the next section.

Once you set up NetInfo, send a *killall -HUP* to the *mountd* process to have it reread the NetInfo database and act accordingly.

NFS and network security

NFS offers wonderful convenience and ease of use when properly configured, but all of its traffic is insecure and unencrypted. We recommend that you NFS-export directories only to the local physical subnet, rather than to the whole world. (Also consider not using NFS at all over a wireless (Airport) connection, which introduces security flaws of its own.)

If you do want to share a filesystem with a broader slice of the Internet, then consider setting up a shared disk over AFP or Samba, which at least offer password-based authentication. Also consider sharing the information as a web site through Apache, or an FTP site through *ftpd*, as described in Chapter 13.

Mac OS X's Firewall

A *firewall* is a program running on a system that sits between an internal network and an external network (i.e., the Internet). It is configured with a set of rules that it uses to determine what traffic is allowed to pass and what traffic is barred. While a firewall is generally intended to protect the network from malicious or even accidentally harmful traffic from the outside, it can also be configured to monitor and measure traffic leaving the network. As the sole entry point into the system, the firewall makes it easier to construct defenses and monitor activity.

The firewall can also be set up to present a single IP address to the outside world, even though it may use multiple IP addresses internally. This is known as *network address translation (NAT)* or *masquerading*. Masquerading can act as additional protection hiding the very existence of a network. It also saves the trouble and expense of obtaining multiple IP addresses.

Mac OS X uses *ipfirewall*, a.k.a. *ipfw*, a firewall package originally developed for FreeBSD. Its main user interface is the command-line program *ipfw*; in Mac OS X versions prior to 10.2.*x*, this is the only way to configure firewall behavior without using third-party software. Starting in Version 10.2.*x*, the Sharing preference pane lets you define basic firewall functionality; see the later section "Through the Sharing pane."

Conceptually, *ipfw* is fairly simple: TCP/IP packets passing through the machine are each subjected to a ordered list of rules. Each of these rules examines some aspects of the packet, such as its point of origin, its direction (incoming or outgoing), and the protocol it uses, and then compares it to a value. If the rule matches the packet, then the firewall applies an action—also defined by the rule—to the packet. Common actions include allowing the packet to pass, denying it further passage, or rerouting it to another destination. Once this action happens, the firewall moves on to the next packet. Only one rule can match each packet.

If none of the rules match the packet in question, then *ipfw* falls back to its immutable *default rule*. On Mac OS X, the default rule simply allows the packet to pass by unmolested.

A popular third-party *ipfirewall* frontend for Mac OS X is Brick-House, a shareware application by Brian Hill (*http://personalpages. tds.net/~brian_hill/brickhouse.html*). While the Sharing pane's firewall controls (described later in "Through the Sharing pane") duplicate much of its basic functionality, it does allow more precise editing of the machine's *ipfw* rule set, and attempts to simplify the process of IP sharing.

Using the ipfw command

You can view all your machine's current rules by entering *ipfw l* in a Terminal window. For example:

```
[jmac@endif /Users/jmac]% sudo ipfw l

00100 deny tcp from script.kiddiez.com to localhost 80
01234 deny all from 123.45.67.0/24 to any
65535 allow ip from any to any
```

In this (very) simple configuration, all packets passing through the machine pass through these rules, in this order:

1. (Rule 0100) The firewall turns away TCP connection attempts to port 80 (the web server) on this machine that originate from the host *script.kiddiez.com*.

2. (Rule 01234) The firewall refuses all packets of all kinds originating from the entire 123.45.67.0 subnetwork.

3. (Rule 65535) Finally, the default rule: none of the earlier rules match, so we let the packet pass through.

Chapter 25 details the *ipfw* command. In brief, you use it to add, edit, and delete rules from the firewall's list. *ipfw* knows where in the list to insert new rules by the number you attach to each one, with lower numbers applying sooner. The default rule, which matches all packets, always has number 65535; no rule can have a higher number (or lower priority) than that.

Through the Sharing pane

Calling up the Sharing pane under System Preferences and then clicking its Firewall tab results in the page shown in Figure 11-7. This control panel gives you a very simple way to view and edit *ipfw*'s current *allow* and *deny* rules.

If the Mac's firewall isn't running—that is, if *ipfw* has no rules defined except for the default *allow ip from any* to *any*—then clicking the Start button immediately applies all the checked rows in the Allow table, and ties them off with the penultimate rule *deny tcp from any* to *any*, so that the firewall turns away all TCP traffic outside of the specified ports.

If the firewall is running, clicking Stop simply runs *ipfw flush*, removing all the firewall's rules outside of the default. The Allow table remains intact, however, so you can edit rules "offline," and later click the Start button to reapply them all.

If the firewall has been activated by any means other than the Sharing pane (such as by adding rules through the *ipfw* Terminal command), then the Sharing pane grays out all these controls and keeps them unavailable until you deactivate the firewall (*ipfw flush* accomplishes this nicely) and restart the System Preferences application.

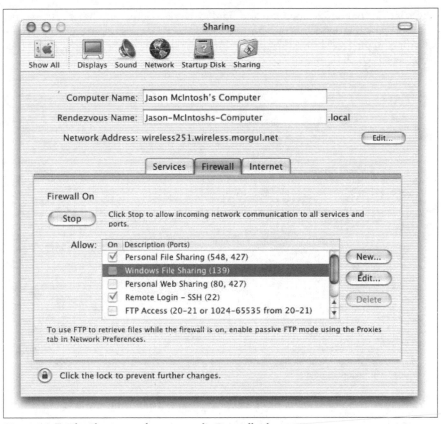

Figure 11-7. The Sharing preference panel's Firewall tab

 The Sharing panel's firewall interface uses its own preference file (found at */Library/Preferences/com.apple.firewall.sharing.plist*) to keep track of filters you set up. This list can become out of sync with reality if you, for example, set some custom filters in the Sharing pane and then remove them via *ipfw*.

If you need to configure your firewall for tasks more sophisticated than the basic port-blocking you can do through the Sharing pane, consider using *ipfw* alone, or split the difference through a shareware product such as BrickHouse.

Internet sharing

Because firewalls have the ability to redirect packets at will, you can use them for *IP sharing*, also known as *IP masquerading*. On Mac OS X, this process involves using *ipfw* together with the Network Address Translation Daemon (*natd*), a system service that rewrites packets to make them appear to originate from the current machine.

The specifics of configuring *ipfw* and *natd* to work together are hairy and arcane, but Mac OS X provides a one-button interface to set everything up for you—specifically, the Start button inside the Internet tab view of the Sharing preference pane, as shown in Figure 11-7.

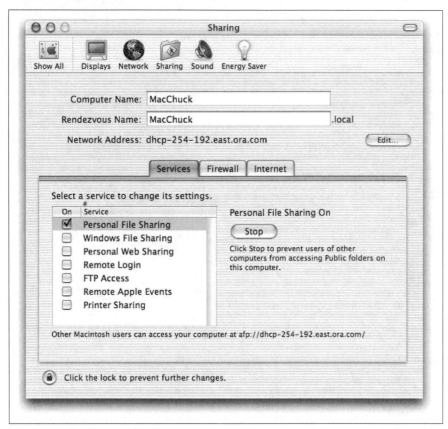

Figure 11-8. The Internet Sharing pane

Before you can activate Internet Sharing, your Mac must have either an Ethernet-based connection to both the Internet and the machines with which it will share its connection (as is the case if your Mac, a cable modem, and the other machines were all connected to the same Ethernet hub), or to two separate network interfaces, one of which is configured to receive Internet traffic in the usual fashion (as described in "The Network Pane" in Chapter 7). The other acts as the interface to all the machines that will use your Mac as their Internet gateway. For example, if you have a modem and an Ethernet port, you can connect to your ISP through dial-up, and then share the connection via Ethernet with your local network. Or, if you have Ethernet and an AirPort card, you can share incoming Ethernet-based traffic with nearby machines that also have 802.11b wireless capability.

With your machine acting as gateway and firewall, all the computers appear to have the same IP address to the outside world, so all incoming packets will have the same destination address. However, your Mac will know (through binding packets to MAC addresses) which incoming packets are supposed to go to which machines and forward them as appropriate. The whole process works transparently for any Internet task that does not require a unique IP address.

When you click the pane's Start, your Macintosh assigns itself an additional IP address for every outgoing interface you selected in the Sharing pane's checkbox list, binding each IP and interface together. (If you are using a single Ethernet interface for both your external Internet connection and internal sharing, then your Ethernet interface will have two IP addresses.) The system then launches a DHCP server visible to the sharing interface's subnetwork. Any machine located there that is configured to use DHCP will recognize the server, receive its own internal IP address, and start using the Internet.

Do *not* activate Internet Sharing if another DHCP server already exists on the subnetwork! Otherwise, confusion can result as your Mac happily intercepts traffic intended for the other server, which probably isn't going to make the other computers (or their users) very happy. Depending upon your network's location and topology, it might adversely affect the connectivity of other customers of your ISP, or other machines on your office LAN.

In short, don't turn on this feature unless you have total control over your subnetwork. Furthermore, consider not using it at all on laptops that you carry between home and work, lest you forget to deactivate it one morning and subsequently wreak havoc on the office network.

Sharing over AirPort

You can set up what Apple calls a *Software Base Station* by sharing incoming modem- or Ethernet-based Internet traffic via your AirPort card. If you choose AirPort as a sharing interface, the Sharing pane makes an AirPort Options button available. Clicking it makes the sheet shown in Figure 11-9 appear. Its controls, listed here, let you configure your Mac's AirPort-sharing abilities.

Network Name
> This string will be the network name that your Mac will broadcast. Other wireless-equipped computers will see your shared network's presence by this name—Mac OS X users will see it as an option under their AirPort menu extras, for example.

Channel
> Select a number to restrict your card's broadcasting to a specific wireless channel. Otherwise, select "Automatic" (the default option).

Enable encryption
> To add a little bit of security to your wireless network, check this box to activate the sheet's remaining controls. (See the warning at the end of this section about AirPort security.)

Password
> If you enter (and confirm) a password here, users will have to provide the same password in order to share your Internet connection.

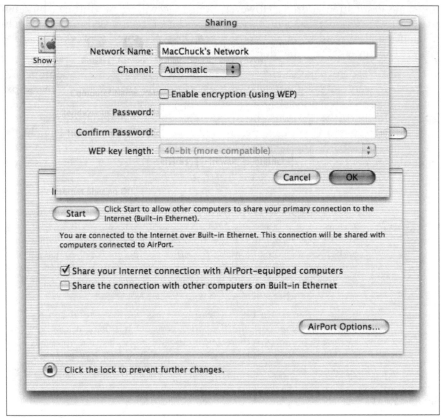

Figure 11-9. The Sharing pane's AirPort configuration options

WEP key length
> You can choose a WEP key length of 40- or 128-bits. (Some client devices might not be able to handle 128-bit encryption.)

 Finally, yet another security note: an AirPort network, like all 802.11b-based wireless networks, is inherently insecure. Placing WEP encryption or a password on your network stops casual snoopers and would-be freeloaders (respectively), but if a determined outsider really wants to eavesdrop or use your AirPort connection, there's little you can do, short of limiting physical access to the network's covered area.

Single-User Mode

Like other Unix systems, Mac OS X has an unadvertised feature known as *single-user mode*, which lets you boot the system under the most minimal terms. As the name implies, it allows only one user access—that user is whatever human seated at the keyboard directly plugged into the machine. No daemons run, the network interfaces lie dormant, and not even the root filesystem is mounted.

You will seldom, if ever, use your Mac in single-user mode. Some low-level diagnostic activities might require it—this is where you can manually and safely run /sbin/fsck -y to check and repair filesystem errors, for example.

Because the one user who logs in during single-user mode happens to be root, you can also change all the system's user passwords, including that of the root account itself. Thus, you can consider single-user mode an emergency back door into the system, should your passwords become lost and you don't have a system CD available.

Mac OS X also lets you log in through a plain Unix text console after the machine has started up. See Chapter 21.

Booting into Single-User Mode

You can activate single-user mode only during system startup. To enter single-user mode, hold down ⌘-S during startup, while the Apple logo is displayed. After a moment, instead of the blue Mac OS X startup screen, everything goes black, and startup console messages start spilling down the screen in plain white text, finally ending at a command prompt.

As this point, you can run whatever commands you'd like as root. As the prompt suggests, you can *fsck* the filesystem for problems, and you can *mount* it to work with individual files if you need to. (Specifically, run the command *mount -uw /* to get the permissions and mount point correct.)

If you want to change any passwords or perform other administrative tasks, you must stir up some NetInfo daemons so that you can access the NetInfo database. Run the *SystemStarter* command, and now you can, for example, use the *passwd* command at will.

Note the human behind the keyboard during single-user mode has power over the entire system, since that user is always root. Obviously, you'd prefer that this human is yourself or a trusted ally, and not some random interloper who knows about the ⌘-S trick.

You can put some defenses in place to thwart this behavior (a popular solution at the time of this writing is Secureit, a Perl script available free for download at *http://users.ez-net.com/~jasonb/index.html*, which lets you assign a separate single-user mode password to the system), but the upshot is that you should always be aware of who has physical access to your Mac. A single reboot by a malicious and knowledgeable person can compromise all the machine's security.

Exiting Single-User Mode

You have three commands to leave single-user mode via various routes.

reboot
    Restarts the computer.

exit

Continues the normal Mac OS X boot process. If you've manually run *SystemStarter* or otherwise changed or activated features that the system would expect to activate itself during the boot process, consider running *reboot* instead.

shutdown -h now

Safely shuts down the computer.

Cron Tasks

Through the Unix *cron* utilities, you can have your Macintosh run scripts and other programs at scheduled times or regular intervals. While this is a pretty neat feature that offers convenience to users and crucial maintenance-program scheduling for system administrators, Mac OS X does not ship with any friendly, GUI frontend to the *cron* utilities. That said, if you can use a text editor (such as any of those described in Chapter 17), then you can set up cron tasks for yourself or (if you have the right credentials) the whole machine.

Cron works courtesy of a clock-watching daemon named *crond*. When this loads, it reads all of the *cron tables* defined in some standard filesystem locations, which contain entries representing lists of times or repeating intervals, with a Darwin command to execute for each entry. On Mac OS X, these tables exist in two locations:

/etc/crontab

This is the *cron* table for the whole system. Each entry in this table represents a command that root will run at the given time. The file is world-readable, but only root may edit it.

/var/cron/tabs/

This directory contains one file for each user on the machine who uses the cron system. You actually don't interact directly with these files (whose permissions prevent it anyway); you must use the *crontab -e* command to edit your own file. You cannot read or change other users' cron tables.

The *cron* tables' format is tricky and hard to remember (unless you're a system administrator who must update them regularly), but as it happens, the system-wide crontab file contains a quick-reference guide to itself. Here's an excerpt from a typical */etc/crontab* file:

❶	❷	❸	❹	❺	❻	❼
#minute	hour	mday	month	wday	who	command
#						
#*/5	*	*	*	*	root	/usr/libexec/atrun
#						
# Run daily/weekly/monthly jobs.						
15	3	*	*	*	root	periodic daily
30	4	*	*	6	root	periodic weekly
30	5	1	*	*	root	periodic monthly
10	*	*	*	*	root	/sw/sbin/anacron -s

As the commented-out lines at the top suggest, each entry in the table (i.e., each line in the file) is broken up into tab-delineated fields representing time intervals, arranged in this order:

❶ Minute.

❷ Hour.

❸ Day of the month.

❹ Month.

❺ Day of the week.

❻ User to run this command as. (Only for the system-wide crontab; an individual user's crontab file lacks this field, since all commands are always run as that user.)

❼ Command to run.

Each of the first five fields can hold either a number or an asterisk character. Asterisks mean that column doesn't have influence over when the command runs. So, we see from this table that the command *periodic monthly* runs at 5:30 A.M. on the first day of every month. If the month (fourth) column held the number 6 instead of an asterisk character, then it would run at 5:30 A.M. on June 1st only.

See the cron(5) manpage (type *man 5 cron* in the Terminal) for a more exhaustive reference to cron table files, which allow for some pretty sophisticated syntax.

Cron works great when your computer runs all the time (as *crond*, like all good system daemons, continues to run regardless of which human users—if any—are logged into the machine, as Chapter 1 describes). If you have an iBook or Power-Book, however, then its runtimes become less dependable, since laptops, like cats, spend much of their lives in sleep mode, and are likely to doze through scheduled tasks. Furthermore, there might be some tasks you wouldn't want a laptop to run when it's on battery, such as the hard-disk-intensive */usr/libexec/locate.updatedb*.

The latter problem is the simpler to solve: if you precede a command with *@AppleNotOnBattery*, then the cron daemon won't run the command if the machine is running on battery power when the time comes. So, the following line will run a (notional) *update_everything* program every ten minutes, but only when the machine is plugged in:

```
10       *       *       *       *       @AppleNotOnBattery /usr/local/
bin/update_everything
```

If you need your laptop to check its cron backlog every time you open it up, so that it executes all the tasks that it slept through, investigate *anacron* (*http:// sourceforge.net/projects/anacron*), a cron replacement, whose main purpose involves this very feature. You can easily install it onto you system via Fink (see Chapter 24).

12

Directory Services and NetInfo

Mac OS X machines use *directory services* to get information about their users and available network services. These are various programs and protocols that run on both your local machine and on other computers and devices networked to it, which accept queries about administrative information or broadcast the availability of network services.[*] Mac OS X abstracts the usage and configuration of all these directory services into a single system called *Open Directory*.

This chapter introduces the fundamentals of Open Directory and the tools that Mac OS X makes available to work with it. It puts special emphasis on the NetInfo system, which Mac OS X uses to store and retrieve administrative information. Later chapters about administrative tasks (such as user account maintenance and setting up shared printing services) will cover specific applications of the NetInfo database and other Open Directory services.

Open Directory Overview

Open Directory is a Mac OS X technology that acts as a wrapper around various other protocols, some of which are particular to Macintosh computers, but all of which serve one of two general functions:

Administrative and user information
> Your Mac needs an administrative database in order to know about the users that can access it, as well as what permissions they possess for running programs and owning files. On most Unix machines, this information lives in text files stored in out-of-the-way places like the */etc* directory. Mac OS X can use these files too (and sometimes it has to), but most of the time, it relies on *NetInfo*. This is a network service program that runs on every Mac, providing it with its own administrative information, which is able to query other NetInfo servers running on other machines.

---

[*] The word *directory* here has nothing to do with Unix filesystem directories, and everything to do with directory services' role as network-based information lookup tables for your computer, just as telephone directories are book-based phone number lookup tables for you.

Since NetInfo is a core technology for Macintosh setup and administration, much of this chapter is dedicated to exploring it. Note, however, that fiddling with NetInfo is of interest only to "power users," and sophisticated configuration of database binding and inheritance isn't relevant to anyone beyond administrators of school or corporate networks.

Service Discovery

Your Mac can learn about printers, file servers, and other interesting things sharing the local network through *service discovery*. The Open Directory system can use various protocols, including SMB for Windows-based services or Rendezvous for services running on other Macs, to listen for local network services' announcing their presence and availability.

Using Open Directory for service discovery works quite transparently; any application with reason to look for network services will automatically do so when appropriate, and then display the results for you. Examples of these applications include iChat, with its Rendezvous window that scans for other iChat users on your local network; the Finder's disk-mounting features (described in "Mounting Network Disks" in Chapter 7); and the system-wide Print dialog sheet, which scans the network for available printers and makes them available as hardcopy destinations alongside the printers you've defined manually (see Chapter 5 for more information).

Directory Access

Users with admin access can use the Directory Access application (which is located in */Applications/Utilities*) to configure whether and how the Mac interacts with the various protocols that Open Directory supports. The application provides a set of GUI interfaces for activating and configuring service-listening protocols, as well as for setting up *search policies* for performing user authentication and contact information lookups.

Services

Directory Access' Services tab lists all the protocols Open Directory supports, with a checkbox next to each, as Figure 12-1 shows. Open directory will use every checked protocol when listening for network services or performing directory service lookups. As of Mac OS X Version 10.2.0, the following services are available:

AppleTalk

This is Apple's legacy protocol, which is useful when your local network contains older Macintosh file servers.

BSD Configuration Files

When checked, your Mac will read administrative information from the filesystem, in the manner of traditional Unix machines. Note that this "protocol" is not checked by default; Mac OS X machines usually fetch this info from their NetInfo databases.

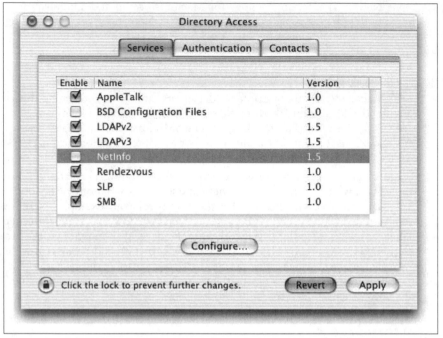

Figure 12-1. The Directory Access Services list

LDAPv2
LDAPv3

The Lightweight Directory Access Protocol, Versions 2 and 3. This is an open protocol that is more cross-platform than NetInfo and hence more likely to be used on heterogeneous networks. Windows and Unix servers have their own LDAP implementations, all of which work with Open Directory's.

NetInfo

This is Apple's own directory services protocol, which is part of the NetInfo system that every Mac uses to store basic administrative information. It tends to be used to its full extent only on all-Mac OS X networks.

Rendezvous

This is Apple's more modern, IP-based protocol for discovering file, print, and other network services.

SLP

The Service Location Protocol, an open network services discovery protocol that is popular with many Unix servers.

SMB

This is Microsoft's Server Message Block protocol for Windows file and print services.

Disabling a service under Directory Access doesn't mean that the protocol won't work anywhere else in the operating system or that your machine will stop serving it (if it was already doing so). For example, if the NetInfo checkbox is unchecked, then Open Directory won't use NetInfo for directory service lookups, but your Mac will continue to run its local NetInfo domain and still use NetInfo to perform user authentication.

Some of the protocols offer further configuration options through the window's Configure button (see "Building a NetInfo Hierarchy" later in this chapter).

Authentication and Contacts

The Directory Access applications' other two tabs let you define your machine's search policies for user authentication and contact information lookup. A search policy is simply an ordered list of directory service sources that your machine consults when looking for information. Both tabs have a Search pull-down menu for selecting a lookup style from three possible options:

Automatic
> This uses the local directory domains, bound NetInfo domains (see the later section "Building a NetInfo Hierarchy"), and shared LDAP domains via DHCP. This is the default selection, and is probably exactly what you want.

Local
> When selected, lookups are restricted to the machine's local domains.

Custom path
> This choice gives you additional controls (Add and Remove buttons, to be precise) for editing a list of available directory service nodes, such as NetInfo servers, LDAP, or even BSD files (if you've activated them through the Services tab). These constitute the directory sources your machine will use for lookups.

The first member of both lists is always */NetInfo/Root*; you cannot change this. These types of lookups will always consult the machine's NetInfo database first, even if that database involves only the local NetInfo domain.

NetInfo Concepts

Mac OS X keeps all its administrative information in NetInfo. Understanding how NetInfo works is important to performing all but the most basic administrative tasks in Mac OS X.

Every Mac OS X machine, whether a solitary home computer or part of a local network, has access to a NetInfo database. NetInfo functions as a directory service. Processes running on your Mac can query NetInfo for information about the machine's users, printers, network services, mounted filesystems, and so on. Processes owned by users with administrative credentials can also modify NetInfo.

Literally speaking, the database runs through a process running locally called *netinfod*, which acts as an interface to some on-disk binary files. NetInfo's real strength lies in the fact that this daemon can be bound to others running on different machines, creating a distributed NetInfo database. Network administrators can use this feature to create sophisticated hierarchies of shared administrative information among many Macs.

To see how this works, we'll examine the concept of a NetInfo domain.

NetInfo Versus Flatfiles

Most Unix systems store administrative information in world-readable, root-writable *flatfiles* that are stored in traditional spots around the machine, especially in the */etc/* directory. One can usually find a list of the machine's users in */etc/passwd*, for example, and a description of global mail aliases in */etc/alias*. A default Mac OS X system also has many of these files, as a glance in its own */etc/* will show, but under normal circumstances the system never reads from or writes to them. NetInfo replaces their functionality.

As the comment blocks prepended to many of these files state, they are still used should you ever run the machine in single-user mode (see "Single-User Mode" in Chapter 11), but otherwise the system makes no effort to keep its flatfiles in sync with the "real" information in its NetInfo database. In short, when you think system administration, think NetInfo.

NetInfo Domains

A Mac's NetInfo database is spread across some number of *domains* (not to be confused with Internet domain names). Domains come in two varieties: local and shared. Every Mac OS X machine hosts a local domain for itself, which it runs as a single *netinfod* process. If configured for it, a machine can also run any number of shared domains, each with their own, separate *netinfod* process.

Local domains

Every Mac OS X machine runs its own private NetInfo domain, which it calls *local*. Information stored within this domain is visible only to processes running on that one Mac; no matter how else the NetInfo network is set up, other machines can't access the information within one another's local domains.

Shared domains

Shared domains collect information for more than one computer's benefit. A shared domain acts as parent domain to other shared or local domains, which can run on the same machine or on machines elsewhere along the network. All the information that a shared domain contains becomes accessible to these child domains. Through shared domains, an administrator can set up user accounts that apply to several machines at once or make shared printers available to select groups of computers.

A Mac neither hosts nor connects to any shared domains unless specifically directed to do so, via the tools described later in "NetInfo User Interfaces." Shared domains are often hosted on machines with Mac OS X Server installed, since its Server Admin application makes creating and maintaining shared domains easier.

As seen in the section "Building a NetInfo Hierarchy," shared domains are key to setting up hierarchical information networks.

Directories

A NetInfo domain organizes its information into *directories* (not to be confused with the directories on the filesystem, which have little to do with NetInfo's operation despite some shared terminology). When a process wishes to learn some information that NetInfo holds, it needs to specify both the domain and the proper directory within it.

The easiest way to browse directories involves using NetInfo Manager, as described later in "NetInfo Manager." We also cover some typical directories later in "Exploring Common Directories."

Building a NetInfo Hierarchy

You construct a NetInfo-based information hierarchy across a network (which can be as small as a private LAN or as large as the Internet) by defining *bindings* between NetInfo domains. Bindings are established "upstream," from child to parent. On startup, a domain seeks out its parent domain, if it has one defined. Parent domains do not seek their children, but instead passively listen for binding attempts, much like any network service listens for connections.

While NetInfo domain initialization and binding often occurs as part of the system startup process, binding is resolved individually for each domain on the machine and not for the machine itself. A server might host three domains, for example, with its local domain binding to one parent, a shared domain binding to a different parent, and a third domain binding to nothing at all.

Binding styles

NetInfo gives you three ways to perform bindings. In all cases, the binding attempt happens through the *nibindd* process, usually during system startup, after it's done spawning all the machine's *netinfod* server processes.

Broadcast binding
> This style works best for LANs and other private subnets. It's the default binding style.
>
> Under broadcast binding, a domain will seek its parent by broadcasting its request across the machine's subnet. If an available domain chooses to respond, then the bind is made.

Static binding

> With this method, the child domain permanently stores the static IP address of the machine hosting its parent domain, so that *nibindd* makes a beeline for this machine rather than broadcasting the request throughout the network.
>
> Note that this style can work to bind the domains on any two machines connected to the Internet.

DHCP binding

> DHCP binding works the same as static binding except that on startup, the domain asks a DHCP server for the current IP address of its parent domain's machine, rather than storing a permanent and static IP address.

Configuring bindings

The Directory Access application (see the earlier section "Directory Access") contains a friendly interface for defining parental bindings for your Mac's local NetInfo domain, through the dialog sheet shown in Figure 12-2. Call it up by clicking the Configure... button in the application's Services tab while you have the NetInfo service highlighted.

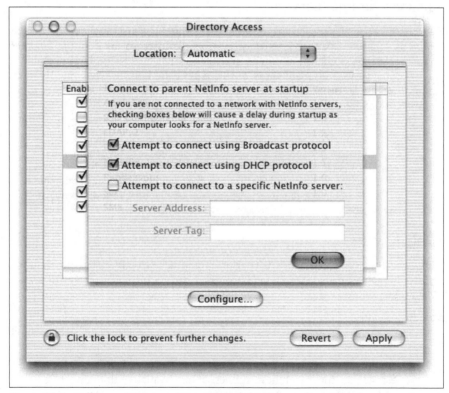

Figure 12-2. Calling up Directory Access' NetInfo binding configuration sheet

Note that the configuration sheet gives you checkboxes for selecting a binding style, implying that you can choose more than one. If you do so, then *netbindd* will follow this order for seeking the domain's parent:

1. Static
2. DHCP
3. Broadcast

Note also that it has room for defining only one parent for the local domain. While shared NetInfo domains can have any number of children, local and shared domains can have exactly one parent, or none at all.

Domain replication

A shared domain can *replicate* itself to both improve its availability and back up its data. Through replication, machines can declare that they host *clones* of a certain domain on some other machine. These clone domains act as mirrors to the original (known as the *master* domain in this context), automatically keeping themselves in sync with all modifications made to it. A NetInfo domain can bind itself as a child to a clone, and it works as well as binding to the original master domain.

NetInfo User Interfaces

Mac OS X gives you many ways to modify the information inside NetInfo.

NetInfo Manager
> This application, which you can find under */Applications/Utilities*, provides a bare-bones view into the machine's NetInfo database, displaying raw administrative information of directories full of key-value pairs without much in the way of documentation or explanation. Any user can run this application to browse the database, but only members of its admin group can make modifications to it.
>
> See "NetInfo Manager," later, for more about using this application.

Command-line utilities
> Apple provides a suite of command-line utilities for working with NetInfo. You can use them interactively from the Terminal, or you can write Perl or shell scripts that invokes them and works with their plain-text output.

System Preferences
> Several of the standard System Preference panes act as friendly interfaces to very specific sections of the NetInfo database. For example, the Login pane allows a user to modify his own account information as recorded in NetInfo. The Users pane lets an authenticated administrator similarly modify all the machine's user accounts.
>
> However, any changes made through them could also be made by using NetInfo Manager to directly manipulate the database's */users/* directory. The panes simply provide friendly interfaces.

Apple's Server Admin application provides another interactive view into NetInfo, which is similar to System Preferences except it is aimed specifically at network administration tasks. However, this application is available only through the Mac OS X Server software package, which Apple sells separately from Mac OS X.

As with the System Preference panes, Server Admin doesn't provide any functionality that a knowledgeable sys admin couldn't perform through NetInfo Manager or the command-line tools; it just puts a friendlier face on common admin tasks. As such, this book does not cover it in detail.

Using NetInfo from Within Programs

Programmers have a number of options when it comes to working with NetInfo-stored information from within programs.

The command-line utilities listed in the next section work well for things like shell and Perl scripts, since their output is consistent and easy to parse.

Mac OS X includes a C library, *netinfo/ni.h*, which provides a full programmatic API into NetInfo. You can find its documentation under *man netinfo*.

Finally, the *lookupd* daemon allows programs using legacy Unix lookup methods to unwittingly talk to NetInfo. It quietly intercepts and translates all POSIX-compliant information requests (such as the gethostbyname or getpwuid functions, in C or Perl) into NetInfo queries, and returns the results in a format that the program expects.

Command-Line NetInfo Tools

You can find more information about the following tools under their respective manpages, as well as in Chapter 25.

nicl
> This program is basically a command-line version of NetInfo Manager that allows you to browse a domain's directories and modify them if you have permission.
>
> *nicl* offers an interactive mode, with commands like its own *cd* and *pwd* to navigate through a domain's directories, and *auth* to become a different user. Enter interactive mode simply by running *nicl* with no arguments.

niutil
> This is another general-purpose, console-based NetInfo browser like *nicl*, but older, dating from NeXT's heyday. It has fewer commands and lacks an interactive mode, but it's still around for backward compatibility in case legacy scripts wish to invoke it.

---

nidomain

This command acts as a frontend to the *netbindd* daemon, and can query the *netbindd* process on any machine, local or networked. Through *nidomain*, you can learn which NetInfo domains a given host serves. If you have administrative authority, you can also create and destroy domains, as well as set up clones of existing domains (see the earlier section "Domain replication").

nidump

This utility dumps the content of the specified NetInfo directory into standard output. It differs from *nicl* or *niutil* by its ability to format its output into legacy Unix flatfile formats.

For example, the following command presents the system's user account information in the standard Unix *passwd* format:

```
% nidump passwd .
```

niload

The inverse of *nidump*, this command can accept a variety of Unix administrative files as input, importing its information into the proper directory of a specified NetInfo domain. You can choose to have it override or try to intelligently merge properties with the same name between the file and the existing NetInfo directory.

The following command loads a Unix passwd-style file named *users* into the machine's local domain:

```
% niload passwd . < users
```

nigrep

This command searches through a domain for a given string or regular expression. Its output is similar to the filesystem's *grep* command, including a list of NetInfo directories that contain it (with their ID numbers), followed by the key-value property pair that holds the string. For example:

```
% nigrep jmac .
154 /users/jmac:  _writers_passwd jmac
154 /users/jmac:  name jmac
154 /users/jmac:  _writers_picture jmac
154 /users/jmac:  home /Users/jmac
10 /groups/wheel:  users jmac
25 /groups/admin:  users jmac
163 /machines/jmac.localhost:  name jmac.localhost
171 /machines/jmac.org:  name jmac.org
165 /afpuser_aliases/jmac:  name jmac
```

nifind

Like *nigrep*, except that it searches for directories rather than for property values. By default, it searches the machine's own NetInfo hierarchy, starting at its local domain and then climbing up its binding path through the root domain, reporting on all the matches it makes. You can limit the search by specifying a domain on this path, or expand it to include the entire hierarchy, including subtrees that the current machine's local domain isn't a member of. For example:

```
[jmac@endif /Users/jmac]% nifind /users/jmac
/users/jmac found in /, id = 154
```

NetInfo Manager

NetInfo Manager gives you a GUI without guidance to your machine's NetInfo hierarchy. It lets you easily traverse, browse, and (if qualified) modify the database. Figure 12-3 shows the main NetInfo Manager interface window.

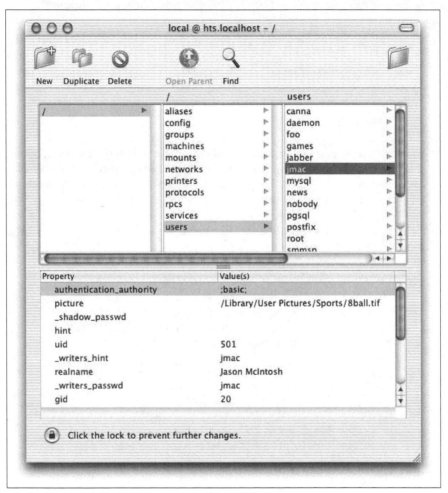

Figure 12-3. NetInfo Manager's main window

When you first launch the application, the columnar *directory browser* in the middle of the window displays the contents of your local NetInfo domain's top-level directory (unless you've changed this behavior, as described later in "NetInfo Manager Preferences").

The directory browser works like the Finder's column view (see "Column View" in Chapter 2), except that it displays only directory names. If the selected directory contains subdirectories of its own, they appear in the right-most column, but any properties it holds appear as key-value pairs in the property browser underneath it.

The left-most column always displays "/", which is the root directory of this domain (not to be confused with the root domain of the whole NetInfo hierarchy, also known as "/"). "Exploring Common Directories," later in this chapter, lists the directories typically found under the root.

The following sections deal with modifying the NetInfo database. You've got to authenticate yourself via the window's lock button before any of these commands become available (see "The authentication lock" in Chapter 6).

That said, you should avoid changing NetInfo information unless you're sure of what you're doing. Changing or deleting key pieces of information can disable your system.

Creating new directories

NetInfo Manager gives you two ways to create a new directory. Choosing Directory → New Subdirectory (⌘-N) creates a new, empty directory within the directory that is currently selected inside the directory browser.

However, since the subdirectories within a given directory almost always share the same structure, you may find Edit → Duplicate (⌘-D) a more convenient choice. This makes a recursive copy of the selected directory, copying over all the original's properties and subdirectories as well. You can than modify the values of the copy's contents without having to refer to how the original directory was set up.

By default, NetInfo Manager displays a confirmation dialog (such as that seen in Figure 12-4) every time you attempt any modification to any directory or property. You can make the application act a little less cautious by selecting "Never" from the Preferences window's Confirm Modifications radio button (Figure 12-5).

Figure 12-4. NetInfo Manager's confirmation dialog

Modifying properties

The property browser is a standard Aqua table view. Double-click on a key or value to make it editable, and type in your changes. You can tab (or Shift-tab) between these fields to edit several consecutively.

Directory Services

To add a new key-value pair, select Directory → New Property (Shift-⌘-N) or Directory → Insert Property (Shift-⌘-I). To add more than one discreet value to the selected key, select Directory → New Value (Option-⌘-N) or Directory → Insert Value (Option-⌘-I).

NetInfo Manager Preferences

Selecting NetInfo Manager → Preferences. brings up the window shown in Figure 12-5, which contains the following sections:

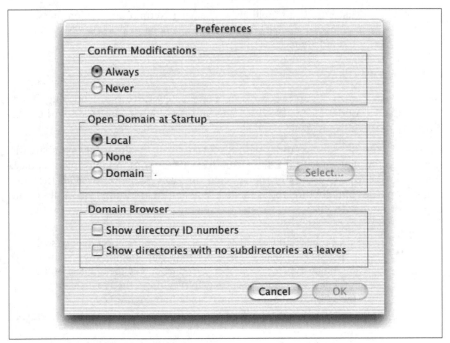

Figure 12-5. NetInfo Manager's Preferences window

Confirm Modifications
> This pair of radio buttons lets you choose whether NetInfo Manager displays a confirmation dialog whenever you attempt to modify any directory or property.
>
> If you use NetInfo Manager just to browse directories, this choice has no effect.

Open Domain at Startup
> These radio buttons control the application's startup behavior. The default selection, Local, directs NetInfo Manager to show the machine's local domain in its directory browser after it launches. You can instead choose to have it show no domains (None), requiring you to manually pick one through Domain → Open (⌘-O) or open a different domain hosted by your machine.

Domain browser
> Check the "Show directory ID numbers" checkbox to have the directory browser display directories' ID numbers as well as their names.
>
> Leave the "Show directories with no subdirectories as leaves" box unchecked to have the browser show disclosure triangles next to every directory, as in Figure 12-3. Checking it causes the browser to not show triangles for directories lacking subdirectories.

Exploring Common Directories

This section explores several important directories that most every Mac OS X machine has in its NetInfo database. For solitary Macs, these all live in the local NetInfo domain. Macs living as leaves in a more complicated tree of bound NetInfo domains might find directories at different levels of the information hierarchy. For example, a lab might have all its Macs's local domains bound to a server domain that holds all login information in a single */Users* directory.

aliases
> Defines aliases used by this machine's mail server (usually sendmail). See Chapter 13 for more about running a mail server on Mac OS X.
>
> This directory replaces the old Unix */etc/aliases* flatfile.

config
> Stores miscellaneous system config information. The Date & Time preference panel, for instance, keeps the address of the selected NTP host inside this directory.

groups
> Replaces the Unix */etc/groups* flatfile, listing the system's groups with their names, GIDs, and member users.

machines
> Replaces */etc/hosts* by assigning hostnames to machines via their IP or Ethernet (MAC) addresses. *localhost* is usually defined here, for example, pointing at 127.0.0.1, the network loopback address. Your computer consults the */machines* directories of visible domains to find hosts that DNS can't locate. (All this work occurs transparently to you, courtesy of the *lookupd* daemon.)
>
> Domains' */machines* directories also play a special role in setting up NetInfo hierarchies, as described in the next section.

mounts
> Contains references to network-hosted NFS filesystems that are currently mounted on the system.

networks
> The properties listed in this directory assign names to Internet network and subnet addresses.

printers

Contains information about print services that this domain makes available. Note that this directory, even in the local NetInfo domain, is distinct from a Mac's internal printer list, which is managed by its own CUPS-based printing system, as Chapter 8 details.

protocols

Lists the network transport protocols that this machine recognizes.

services

Pairs the common names of network services with their default port numbers and communication protocols. It replaces the */etc/services* flatfile.

users

Holds one subdirectory for every user on the system. Each of these is equivalent to one line of a standard Unix */etc/passwd* flatfile, containing information about the user's name, UID, password (stored via one-way encryption), shell, and so forth. You can also find nontraditional information here, such as a path to the user's login-screen picture, if one is selected.

 Note that the list of users is larger than that seen under the Users preference panel. Like most any Unix system, Mac OS X keeps UIDs for "virtual" users who aren't real people, but rather system concepts that can claim ownership of certain files and processes for convenience and security. See "Nonhuman User Accounts" in Chapter 11.

The Machines Directory

As noted earlier in "Exploring Common Directories," the */machines* directories within a NetInfo hierarchy play a special role in defining it. They describe the domains that make up a NetInfo hierarchy by mapping machines to the domains that they host.

A */machines* directory contains one subdirectory for every machine (a single computer somewhere on the visible network) that it defines. Figure 12-6 shows an example as seen in NetInfo Manager, with the *localhost* subdirectory selected. (Every Mac's local NetInfo database should contain */machines/localhost*, as it defines the local machine's role in hosting its own NetInfo domain.)

Along with the name and address properties that make each such subdirectory work similarly to a line in the old Unix */etc/hosts* config file, each of these machine-specific directories contains a *serves* property, whose value indicates the NetInfo domain hosted on this machine. In Figure 12-6, we can see that the machine called localhost serves the domain tagged *local*.

Figure 12-6. A local domain's /machines directory

For More Information

You can also find detailed instructions for configuring various parts of the Open Directory system through the Help Viewer application; select Help → Directory Access Help (⌘-?) from the *Directory Access* application to get started.

13

Running Network Services

A *network service* is a program running on a local machine that other machines can connect to and use over a network. Common examples include web, email, and file-transfer servers.

This chapter builds on the network administration fundamentals covered in Chapter 11 to describe how network services work in general, and how several of the more popular services work on Mac OS X. For information on using these services client-side, consult Chapter 7.

Network Services Overview

Generally, a network service operates through a *daemon* program that listens for incoming connections on a certain port—web servers usually listen on port 80, for example, and *ssh* connections typically happen on port 22. (The precise way it accomplishes this is implementation-specific; it might choose to handle the whole connection itself, or fork off another process to handle it so the daemon can get back to listening.)

Running Services in Mac OS X

Like so many other administrative tasks in Mac OS X, you have two ways to run the network services. The classic Unix way involves invoking the daemon on the command line, either manually through the Terminal or with a script. The Sharing preference pane, though, provides a very simple on/off switch for many network services.

Running Services Through the Sharing Pane

The Sharing pane contains three tabbed panes shown in Figure 13-1.

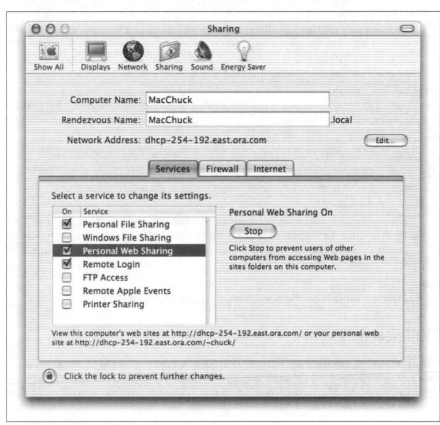

Figure 13-1. The Sharing preference panel's Services pane

Services
> Lists several service daemons that you can control.

Firewall
> Contains controls for the system's built-in firewall. (See "Mac OS X's Firewall" in Chapter 11.)

Internet
> Lets you enable/disable Internet sharing.

Every item in the Services list is visually paired with an On checkbox and is (behind the scenes) associated with a daemon program. Generally, when you check a checkbox, the related daemon launches; unchecking the checkbox kills the daemon, making the service unavailable. In some cases, the system service remains running in either state, but toggling the checkbox causes the system to rewrite its configuration file and then restart it.

Personal File Sharing

When active, other computers can mount disks and folders on your file-system via AFP. See "File Sharing Services," later in this chapter.

Windows File Sharing

The same as Personal file sharing, but uses the SMB protocol to share disks and folders, making access easier for users of Microsoft Windows machines—though other operating systems, including Mac OS X, can also mount SMB shares easily. See "File Sharing Services."

Personal Web Sharing

Checking this launches the computer's Apache web server. See "Web Services," later in this chapter.

Remote Login

Launches the Mac's SSH server. See the later section, "The Secure Shell."

FTP Access

Runs the FTP server, as described later in "File Transfer Protocol (FTP)."

Remote Apple Events

When activated, every active application that responds to Apple Events (i.e., is controllable by AppleScript) also becomes a web service that responds to the SOAP protocol, accessible from anywhere on the Internet. Chapter 16 covers Apple Events in more detail.

Printer Sharing

Activates printer sharing. See "Printer Sharing" in Chapter 8.

Mail Services

Email-related daemons can be put into two categories: *mail transport agents* (MTAs), which send new email messages to their destination machines, and *mail delivery agents* (MDAs), which send mail that's landed in a user's mailbox to that user's personal computer.

Mail Transport Agents (sendmail)

A mail transport agent sends email to other computers, most often via the SMTP protocol. Mac OS X ships with *sendmail*, the most common mail-serving program on the Internet.

Run *sendmail* only if you need to provide mail-sending services to yourself or your network. You don't need to run this service to simply send email, so long as there is an SMTP server that will accept connections from your machine; most ISPs provide mail services on their own servers, for example.

Using sendmail

Mac OS X has no easy interface for running *sendmail* as a daemon, but it doesn't take too much work to get it going, since most of the setup has already been done for you. Just edit */etc/hostconfig*, changing the line `MAILSERVER=-NO-` to

MAILSERVER=-YES-. This line is read by the startup script at *System/Library/StartupItems/Sendmail/Sendmail*, which cleans up the mail queue and starts the sendmail daemon by issuing the command *sendmail -bd -q1h*. See "Configuring Startup Items" later in this chapter for more information on how this works. When you restart the machine, sendmail should start along with it. (You can also test it by simply running the script from the command line.)

From there, *sendmail* runs quite well without any further intervention. If you change its configuration file (at */etc/mail/sendmail.cf*) or your machine's mail alias list (in NetInfo's */aliases* directory), you can simply *kill -HUP* the *sendmail* process to have the changes take effect without interrupting mail services.

Chapter 25 contains a complete list of *sendmail*'s command-line arguments. If you need to customize your Mac's *sendmail* setup, you should read a good reference book on the topic, such as *sendmail* (O'Reilly & Associates, Inc., 2003), or the online materials found at *http://www.sendmail.com*.

Alternative mail agents

While a robust, popular, and well-supported piece of software, *sendmail* is also famous for its extremely opaque *.cf* configuration files (located in */etc/mail/sendmail.cf*). For this and other reasons, many Unix system administrators prefer other MTAs, such as *postfix* and *exim* (see *http://www.postfix.org* and *http://www.exim.org*, respectively).

At the time of this writing, though, no easy-to-install MTA alternative exists for Mac OS X, though you can try downloading and building some from source. Anyone but the most adventurous Mac OS X administrators should probably stick with *sendmail*.

Mail Delivery Agents

Most email users don't read mail directly from their mailhosts; instead, they download their mail from the host to their personal computers. A daemon running on the mailhost called a *Mail Delivery Agent* (MDA) facilitates this by supporting a mail-delivery protocol, and individual mail clients (including Apple's Mail application, Microsoft's Entourage, Qualcomm's Eudora, and countless other programs) connect to this service to check for and download new messages.

The two most common MDA protocols are the *Post Office Protocol* (POP) and the *Internet Message Access Protocol* (IMAP). POP, the older and more commonly supported of the two, comprises a very simple command set, allowing users to do little besides download their mail and delete it from the server. IMAP represents a newer and more sophisticated protocol that lets users store and organize all their mail on the server-side. This offers much greater convenience to users, but at the cost of more server resources; consider using the *quota* command (see Chapter 25) to set users' storage capacities if you support IMAP.

Unfortunately, Mac OS X ships with neither *popd* nor *imapd*, the daemons that give you POP and IMAP services, respectively. You can cover both these bases by installing the UW IMAP server, available as a source code tarball (*http://www.imap.org*). From there it takes some work to configure IMAP properly for Mac OS X's particular filesystem setup, but there is an excellent article on the topic by Graham Orndoff at *http://www.stepwise.com/Articles/Workbench/eart.2.0.html*.

Web Services

Mac OS X comes with Apache, an open source web server responsible for more than half of all the Internet's web sites.* At its most basic level, Apache runs as a daemon named *httpd* that supports HTTP, the Hypertext Transfer Protocol, listening to web surfers' requests (on port 80, by default) and replying with response codes and web pages.

Apache Configuration

Apache's configuration information lies in the */etc/httpd* directory, mainly in the file */etc/httpd/httpd.conf*. This file sets up options through lists of directives and values, often mapped to filesystem directories and other criteria. Many of its options are highly specific to Mac OS X, so that Apache works "out of the box"; turning on web services with a single click in the Sharing pane (see the earlier section "Running Services Through the Sharing Pane") launches a full-featured web server on a fresh Mac OS X installation. Here are some highlights (and variances from the defaults you'd see in a platform-independent Apache installation):

- The DirectoryRoot directive defines the location of the server's default location for HTML files and other web-servable documents; in other words, what you'd see if you pointed your web browser to *http://localhost/*. Mac OS X sets this directive to */Library/WebServer/Documents/*.

- Following the usual Unix tradition, Mac OS X Apache lets a host's individual users build personal web sites in their own Home folders, accessible by pointing a web browser to *http://network_address/~username*. To find your network address, go to the Sharing preferences panel, as shown in Figure 13-1. Most Unix systems define users' personal document roots at *~username/public_html*; Mac OS X Apache sets it to *~username/Sites*.

  An Include directive at the bottom of the file reads in several additional Apache configuration files located in */etc/httpd/users/*. One *username.conf* file exists for every user created through the Accounts pane (see "Managing Users Through the Accounts Pane" in Chapter 11). Each one defines Apache options and directives for serving that user's */Sites* folder over the Web, thus allowing an administrator to set different options on different users' personal web sites.

- Apache keeps two log files, *access_log* and *error_log*, in the */var/log/httpd/* directory. The *access_log* file keeps a record of the files served (graphics, web pages, etc.), and to whom the files were served by displaying the IP address of the machine that accessed the server. The *error_log* file reports any errors from people who have attempted to access a file on the web server that doesn't exist.

---

* Netcraft tracks the changing popularity levels of Apache and other web servers on its web site at *http://www.netcraft.com/survey/*

Apache Modules

Apache modules are code libraries that extend Apache's abilities beyond fundamental HTTP serving. Apache lets you install modules two ways: *static* modules are "baked in" to the *httpd* program at compile time, while *dynamic* modules are separate files that *httpd* can load and include into its functionality without any recompiling needed.

Mac OS X's Apache setup uses the latter of these strategies. To enable an existing but inactive module, simply locate the LoadModule and AddModule directives within */etc/httpd/httpd.conf* and remove the # characters from the start of both lines, turning the lines from comments into actual directives. To disable an active module, just insert a # at the start of both lines, commenting them out. Then restart the web server.

To install new modules, place their *.so* files (compiling them first, if necessary) into the */usr/libexec/httpd/* directory, and then add new LoadModule and AddModule lines to */etc/httpd/httpd.conf*.

File Transfer Protocol (FTP)

FTP services run courtesy of the *ftpd* daemon. It allows the machine's users to remotely access the filesystem, so that they can browse directory listings and transfer files to and from the machine. It obeys the filesystem permissions just as a login shell does.

Enabling Anonymous FTP

First, create a user named *ftp*, under which all anonymous FTP activity will occur. Since this account doesn't represent an actual person, you should use the account creation method described in "Nonhuman User Accounts" in Chapter 11.

Create a home directory for *ftp*. (Be sure that *ftp*'s NetInfo directory correctly refers to this directory as its home.) The FTP server forbids an anonymous user from accessing anything on the filesystem outside of the *ftp* user's home directory.

You can now populate this directory with whatever you'd like anonymous users to be able to browse and download. To make a typical FTP site, add a *pub/* folder containing all the downloadables, as well as an introductory blurb in a *welcome. txt* file; many FTP clients automatically look for a text file with this name upon connecting to a site, and automatically display it if present.

For security's sake, consider changing the ownership of all these files and folders to root using the *chown* command, and using *chmod* to make them read-only for all users. This will prevent anonymous FTP users from uploading (and perhaps overwriting) files as well as keep the directory safe from tampering by local users. (A */pub/incoming* directory, writeable by the FTP user, is the typical spot for anonymous file uploads, if you'd like to allow that to a limited degree.)

Remote Login Services

There may come a time when you need to log into your Mac from another machine, or log into another Mac (or Unix system) from your machine. For this, Mac OS X offers remote login services such as the Secure Shell, Telnet, and the remote shell.

The Secure Shell

The Secure Shell (SSH), is a protocol for using key-based encryption to allow secure communication between machines. As its name suggests, it is most commonly used for interactive sessions with shells on remote machines, so that one can use the *ssh* command as described in "Remote Logins" in Chapter 7.

Mac OS X ships with the OpenSSH (*http://www.openssh.com*) client and server software. This includes the *ssh* command, which you use to open SSH connections to other machines, and the *sshd* daemon program, which you run to allow other machines to SSH into your Mac.

As with FTP (see "File Transfer Protocol (FTP)"), running an SSH service (the *sshd* daemon) on Mac OS X is easy: just activate the Remote Login checkbox in the Sharing pane.

Telnet

Mac OS X versions prior to 10.1.0 shipped with *telnetd*, a daemon that runs the Telnet protocol. Telnet is a decades-old method for getting a virtual terminal on a remote machine through a network. However, it's inherently insecure, since all of its transmissions are *cleartext*, lacking any sort of encryption, and hence easily readable by malevolent entities monitoring the traffic that enters and leaves your network. Use of Telnet has, in recent years, fallen out of favor for Internet-based remote logins now that tools like SSH are freely available.

If you must, you can run *telnetd* on your Mac OS X machine. You'll find it in */usr/libexec/telnetd*, and can either invoke it directly or write a Startup Item for it (see the later section "Configuring Startup Items")—but consider carefully configuring your firewall to allow Telnet connections only from other machines on the local subnetwork. Incoming Telnet traffic from the global Internet can be snooped by outside eavesdroppers, even if connections are limited to trusted machines. Logging into a machine through Telnet is tantamount to shouting your password across a crowded roomful of strangers so that your friend down the hall can hear it. Whenever possible, use *ssh* instead of *telnet*.

The Remote Shell

The *remote shell*, or RSH, is used to issue commands on another system. The *rsh* command allows you to quickly login and execute a command on a remote host; however, like Telnet, *rsh* is insecure and has been disabled under Mac OS X. You should use SSH instead for remote access to other machines.

File Sharing Services

Mac OS X's native file-sharing method is the Apple Filing Protocol (AFP). As with related technologies like SMB and NFS (see "NFS" in Chapter 11), it lets users of other computers (often, but not necessarily, other Macs) mount volumes of your local filesystem onto their own.

Both the command-line and GUI interfaces for administering AFP are very simple. To turn on AFP, activate the Personal File Sharing checkbox in the Sharing preference pane's Services tab. This simply launches the *AppleFileServer* daemon (which resides in */usr/sbin*). *AppleFileServer* takes no arguments; it makes all your machine's volumes and User folders available for mounting on other computers, as described in "Mounting Through the Finder" in Chapter 7. The program keeps its configuration information (including the location of log files, whether it allows Guest access, and so on) under the NetInfo database's */config/AppleFileServer* directory.

Toggling this checkbox in the Sharing pane also modifies the AFPSERVER line in */etc/hostconfig*, read by the startup script */System/Library/StartupItems/AppleShare/AppleSahre* (see the next section).

The AFP server handles user authentication through NetInfo, just like Mac OS X generally does when handling user logins. When working with a mounted volume, that disk's permission system applies just as if that same user were logged into the machine and accessing the filesystem directly. If a user mounts a volume as Guest (and the server is set to allow Guest access), then the server grants that user the same permissions as the system's special nobody user; in other words, that user can see only those files, folders, and disks that are world-readable, and write only to ones that are world-writable.

> Technically, you can change this behavior by *chown*ing files and folders to nobody, but that isn't recommended. (If you're coming from a Unix system where nobody ran the web server and had an excuse to own several files and directories, note the presence of Darwin's www user, instead.)

Configuring Startup Items

Starting up all the various system service daemons by hand every time the machine starts up would be quite a chore. As part of its coordination of the startup process, the *SystemStarter* application scans and runs special scripts kept in */Library/Startup Items/*. To have a daemon launch at startup and be owned by the root user (so that it is running when the first user logs in, and continue to run until the machine is shut down or it's explicitly killed), add to this collection of startup items or modify an existing one, if applicable. (More startup scripts are in */System/Library/Startup Items/*, but, like everything else in the */System/* folder, are not meant to be messed with.)

Each object under *Startup Items* is a folder named after its function. Inside it lay two important files: a parameter list of options in *StartupParameters.plist* (see the later section "StartupParameters.plist") and the script itself, which must have the same name as the folder.

For example, this is the entirety of */System/Library/StartupItems/SSH/SSH*:

```
#!/bin/sh     ❶

. /etc/rc.common     ❷

##
# Start up secure login server
##

if [ "${SSHSERVER:=-NO-}" = "-YES-" ]; then     ❸

    ConsoleMessage "Starting Secure Login Server"     ❹

    if [ ! -f /etc/ssh_host_key ]; then     ❺
        echo "Generating ssh host RSA1 key..."
        ssh-keygen -t rsa1 -f /etc/ssh_host_key -N "" -C "$(hostname)"
    fi
    if [ ! -f /etc/ssh_host_rsa_key ]; then     ❺
        echo "Generating ssh host RSA key..."
        ssh-keygen -t rsa -f /etc/ssh_host_rsa_key -N "" -C "$(hostname)"
    fi
    if [ ! -f /etc/ssh_host_dsa_key ]; then     ❺
        echo "Generating ssh host DSA key..."
        ssh-keygen -t dsa -f /etc/ssh_host_dsa_key -N "" -C "$(hostname)"
    fi

    /usr/sbin/sshd     ❻

fi
```

Here's what it does, in order:

❶ Its "shebang" line (`#!/bin/sh`) marks this file as a shell script.

❷ It uses the shell's . (dot) command to execute the shell script at */etc/rc.common*. This script sets up many environment variables useful to startup scripts.

❸ If the SSHSERVER environment variable (set by *rc.common*, after it reads the */etc/hostconfig* file) has a value of -YES-, then it continues with the next step. Otherwise, the script exits cleanly.

❹ The *ConsoleMessage* command (defined by *rc.common*) dumps a status message to the console, which passes it along to the startup screen.

❺ It checks for the presence of local SSH host keys in the */etc* directory. If any of the three types that the SSH software might need are missing, it uses the *ssh* command to generate a key and prints a message to the console.

❻ Finally, it launches *sshd*, the SSH daemon. The machine is now ready to accept SSH connections!

Manually Running StartupItems

Much like their counterparts, the */etc/rc.init* scripts found on Linux and BSD systems, *StartupItems* can also be run on the command line. When available, it's generally a better idea to use a daemon's *StartupItem* rather than invoking it directly (i.e., by using */System/Library/StartupItems/SSH* instead of directly calling */usr/sbin/sshd*), since the script is "safer," making sure that the machine's software and network environment is set up correctly for the daemon's use.

Typically, you must run *StartupItems* as root (or under the auspices of the *sudo* command), and provide one of three standard arguments:

start
> Launch the service this *StartupItem* represents. It usually fails if it's already running.

stop
> Kill this service.

restart
> Equivalent to stop-ing and then start-ing the service; often it actually sends a HUP (hangup) signal to the service's process. This causes it to reread its configuration files and act appropriately, allowing it to reconfigure itself without suffering any downtime.

The /etc/hostconfig File

Many *StartupItems* must make a choice about whether they're supposed to perform their stated function. If you don't want your machine to accept SSH connections, for example, then you won't want the SSH startup script to launch the *sshd* daemon. You could modify or remove the */System/Library/StartupItems/ SSH* file, but that's a messy solution that would probably lead to confusion if you (or, worse, another administrator on the machine) want to activate SSH later on.

A better solution, and the one that Mac OS X intends you to use, involves modifying the */etc/hostconfig* file. This file, which is nothing more than a newline-separated list of key-value pairs (as well as a few comments), is loaded by */etc/rc. common*, a shell script which itself is run as an initial step by most startup scripts. This means that all the variables it sets become accessible to scripts that load *rc. common*, such as the SSH startup item. Thus, if you simply set *hostconfig*'s SSHSERVER key to -NO-, the SSH startup script will know that you don't want *ssh* services activated on startup, and quietly exits rather than launching the *ssh* daemon. (This is, in fact, exactly what happens when you deactivate the Sharing preference pane's Remote Login checkbox. Many other System Preferences controls have the effect of modifying lines in */etc/hostconfig*, as well.)

StartupParameters.plist

The *StartupParameters.plist* file (an example of a property list XML file, detailed in Chapter 22) can contain the following keys:

Description
> A brief description of this startup item's function, such as "Apache web server" or "Secure login server."

Provides
> A list of keywords that name the services that this startup item provides, when run.

Requires

A list of keywords that name the services that must already be running before this startup item can be launched.

Uses

A list of keywords that names the services that this startup item might make use of, but doesn't absolutely require.

Messages

A dictionary of status messages that get sent to the console (and the startup screen, if it's visible) when the startup item starts or stops.

The *SystemStarter* program determines the order to run all the system's startup items by scanning all their *StartupParameters.plist* files and then comparing the values of their Provides, Requires, and Uses keys. It then determines an order where items that provide other items' Required services run first, so that later items' prerequisites will be met.

14

Web Publishing with a DAMP System

DAMP is an acronym for *Darwin, Apache, MySQL, and PHP/Perl/Python*, the components necessary to create a powerful and scalable open source web-publishing platform on a Mac OS X system. It's actually a play on the older term *LAMP*, where the L stands for Linux.

The idea is quite simple. The site's content is stored in an SQL database running alongside the web server. Except for a handful of static pages that don't need to change (such as the site's splash page or the company's "About us" page), every web page on the site is built on the fly through programs that output HTML based on information pulled from the database. This can be done through a sophisticated template system, simple CGI scripts, or anything in between. This chapter details the elements involved in setting up a system like this on Mac OS X.

Elements of a DAMP System

Mac OS X ships with every technology that this section mentions, short of a database server. Fortunately, MySQL, the software that puts the "M" in DAMP, is easy to obtain and install; see the next section.

Darwin
> We refer specifically to Darwin in this chapter, since running a DAMP platform means running a collection of network services (see Chapter 13) and software that runs solely on the Unix layer of Mac OS X. It doesn't use any of the application or user interface layers that make up the top half of the operating system's architecture as depicted in Figure P-1.

Apache
> Through the Apache web server's module system (see "Apache Modules" in Chapter 13), you can enable extensions to the default web server. These embed Perl, PHP, or Python interpreters into the server, letting you use and write software in these languages that runs very fast and has access to Apache's internal information and variables.

MySQL

To be truly robust and scalable, a dynamic web site—be it an e-commerce site, an online journal, or a research results catalog—should keep all of its content in a database.

MySQL is a very popular open source database system from the Swedish company MySQL AB (*http://www.mysql.com*). It's fast, scales well, and has enjoyed years of support as the favorite of the open source programming community. MySQL is free to use for projects that run on your own servers, but you do have to purchase licenses for it if you bundle it as part of a packaged, commercial solution.

> You don't have to run MySQL per se to run a DAMP (or at least DAMP-like) system; any SQL database that your language of choice can work with will do. This can include other open source database systems like PostgreSQL, or commercial packages like Microsoft SQL Server or Oracle.
>
> Due to its advantage of community support and the fact that it comes preinstalled with recent Mac OS X versions, the rest of this chapter covers the MySQL configuration specifically.

PHP, Perl, Python

These are three interpreted, portable languages well known for their ability to serve up dynamic web pages. All are open source, with online support communities several years old, and all come standard with recent versions of Mac OS X. (Older versions included only Perl.) See "Choosing a Language" for a brief comparison between these languages.

Whichever language (or combination thereof) you go with, its function within a DAMP system is the same, acting as a glue between Apache and MySQL. Specifically, upon receiving a request, the web server will (instead of simply fetching an HTML file and returning it to the client) run a separate computer program that itself generates an HTML page, built by combining templates with information that it fetches from the database. There are many, many ways you might go about this, from simple CGI scripts to intricate templating and content management systems.

Setting Up DAMP

This section will help you decide on the language for your DAMP system (the P port), how to install and configure MySQL, and how to further configure Apache to use Perl and PHP.

Choosing a Language

You should probably have some proficiency in at least one of the "P" languages, even if your site is going to run code written by others. The following is a very brief rundown on the individual strengths of these languages.

PHP

PHP is the only language of the three designed entirely with web programming in mind; it boasts web-page embedability among its core features. It is arguably the best of the three for building very simple database-backed web applications, and may be the fastest to pick up and learn, given its ability to immediately show results in a web browser.

However, it's very hard to extend, since adding new functionality means recompiling the PHP software itself; it isn't modular, as Perl and Python are.

Perl

Perl is a general-purpose programming language that excels at handling text—since any web page is really just a long string of text, Perl has been a natural choice for crafting dynamic web sites for as long as the Web has existed.

Perl is the oldest of the three languages, with a history going all the way back into the 1980s. Without a doubt, it enjoys the most support. Anyone can extend Perl through writing modules (in either Perl or C), and the famous Comprehensive Perl Archive Network (CPAN, headquartered at *http://www. cpan.org*) serves as a globally shared repository of these modules, most of which have an object-oriented interface.

The language's "love it or hate it" features include a "there's more than one way to do it" philosophy (which lets you express most fundamental—and, by extension, all higher-level—program structures in a variety of ways), and its punctuation-heavy syntax (an amalgamation of the many older, Unix-based languages that Perl borrows from with the designer's ideas about natural language). Many programmers feel that these make Perl an extremely flexible language that's a joy to work with; others think that the language's very broad range of allowable programming styles makes the typical Perl program look like unreadable garbage. In truth, you can (and probably should) write readable, well-documented, and easily maintainable Perl programs and modules, but you can also write horrible and opaque code. Perl won't complain if you really want to act that way (if you specifically ask it not to complain by deactivating its built-in warning and strictness compiler pragmas).

Python

Like Perl, Python is a general-purpose language that is strong in text processing, so it too works well for cranking out HTML pages. Python quickly earned a lot of support as an alternative to Perl due to its own design philosophies, which in some ways are the reverse of Perl's: it uses a much cleaner syntax and limits the number of ways a programmer can express fundamental structures. Python's fans think that this leads to much more readable code than Python's peers have.

Python is also extensible through user-written modules, though its support community isn't quite as vast as Perl's. Still, it's managed to earn a reputation over the years as a good first programming language, balancing power with clarity and its insistence on good programming practices.

Preparing the Language for Database Connections

The language you choose will need a way to connect to your SQL database and pass queries to it.

PHP

PHP features various built-in commands to connect to databases, with different commands for different kinds of database servers.

Perl

Perl uses a common API called DBI (for *database interface*) for all its database connections. Connecting to an SQL database in Perl requires at least two pieces of software: the DBI module and a database driver (DBD) module that is specific to a certain kind of database system.

You can fetch DBI.pm and the MySQL/mSQL DBD module by downloading them from CPAN. Visit *http://www.cpan.org* or use Perl's interactive CPAN module, like this:

 If you haven't configured CPAN on your system before, issuing the first command in this example can do this for you. Just use the defaults—the items within brackets ([...])—and then you're ready to go.

```
% sudo perl -MCPAN -e shell
Blah blah blah
cpan> install DBI
[... lots of build, test, and install
output ...]
cpan> install DBD::MySQL
[... yet more build, test, and install
output ...]
cpan> bye
```

Python

Python uses a different, single module for each kind of database. While they don't use a common superclass's API, as with Perl's DBI module, database modules must adhere to a specific API (defined at *http://www.python.org/ topics/database/modules.html*) in order to receive the Python community's blessing.

Python's "official" MySQL module is from SourceForge, at *http://sourceforge. net/projects/mysql-python*.

Setting Up MySQL

Once installed, MySQL requires no special setup for use on a DAMP system; it doesn't have to be aware of the other components, as does Apache and your language of choice. So long as it's ready to receive connections and queries from your code, it's good to go.

Installing MySQL

Unless you are running Mac OS X Server, you must download and install MySQL yourself. Fortunately, since it's such a popular database solution, others have already wrapped it up into easy-to-install packages for you. The following is a list of options that exist at the time of this writing.

- A MySQL distribution available through the Fink package manager. Once you set up Fink on your machine as described in Chapter 24, you can install its MySQL package through the Terminal command *apt-get install mysql*. As is Fink's way, it will probably also take the opportunity to install a handful of other packages that it depends upon, once it gets your permission to do so.

- A Finder-launchable installation package built and maintained by Marc Liyanage, available at *http://www.entropy.ch/software/macosx/*. (You'll note a PostgreSQL package available on the same page as well, should you want to try SQL databases other than MySQL, or already have a preference for PostgreSQL.)

- You can get a "raw" binary distribution at *http://www.mysql.com*.

Starting the database

In the Terminal, *cd* to the directory created by the install (*/usr/local/mysql*, unless you used Fink with its default */sw/* working directory, in which case you'll go to */sw/mysql*). Run the following commands as root (we'll use the *sudo* command to achieve this):

```
./scripts/mysql_install_db
chown -R mysql /usr/local/mysql/*
./bin/safe_mysqld --user=mysql &
```

Now test it, by requesting to start an interactive Terminal session with the server's test database:

```
% mysql test
Welcome to the MySQL monitor.  Commands end with ; or \g.
Your MySQL connection id is 2 to server version: 3.23.51-entropy.ch

Type 'help;' or '\h' for help. Type '\c' to clear the buffer.
mysql>
```

Now you get to configure it! If you already know MySQL, from this point on everything will work as you expect. Otherwise, you have a bit of a learning curve to overcome. You can read MySQL's excellent online documentation about this (and every other) topic at *http://www.mysql.com/documentation/index.html*,[*] or you might turn to a third-party application for help, such as the free and open source web-based mysqltool, found at *http://dajoba.com/projects/mysqltool/*. (A CGI-based program written in Perl, this software gives you the bonus of being a DAMP application itself, when running on Mac OS X.)

Generally, with a new MySQL install, you should follow these steps:

1. Assign a password to the MySQL root user (not to be confused with the system root user).

2. Create a database that your DAMP application will use.

3. Create a user within the MySQL system that's able to access that database, can connect from *localhost* only, and can't do anything else. This is the user that your programs will use when working with the database to build web content.

---

[*] You'll also find a link to a print version of the same work, published by O'Reilly & Associates, Inc. as the *MySQL Reference Manual*.

Setting Up Apache

The */etc/httpd/httpd.conf* file (see "Apache Configuration" in Chapter 13) contains a few commented-out lines that activate language-relevant Apache modules:

```
#LoadModule perl_module          /usr/libexec/httpd/libperl.so
#LoadModule php4_module          /usr/libexec/httpd/libphp4.so
[ ... later in the file ... ]
#AddModule mod_perl.c
#AddModule mod_php4.c
```

Activating PHP

To use PHP, uncomment the php4_module and mod_php4.c lines. This allows you to start using PHP embedded in web pages right away, such as with the following example, a simple HTML page that looks at the client's user agent:

```
<html>
<h1>What browser are you using?</h1>
<?php
if (strstr($_SERVER["HTTP_USER_AGENT"], "MSIE")) {
?>
<p>You seem to be using Microsoft Internet Explorer.</p>
<?php
} else {
?>
<p>You are using a non-Microsoft browser.</p>
<?php
}
?>
```

Activating mod_perl

If you're going to use Perl with your DAMP system, it will behoove you to activate *mod_perl*, an Apache module that places a persistent Perl interpreter within your web server (*http://perl.apache.org*). This not only makes Perl-based CGI programs run faster (since Apache need not launch a Perl interpreter every time it runs a CGI program), but also lets them access and modify information about the current web server request. This lets you write very sophisticated programs and modules that control server behavior on a deep level, and also opens the door for using many existing Perl modules that use *mod_perl* and packages on your site.[*]

To activate *mod_perl*, uncomment the perl_module and mod_perl.c lines from *httpd.conf*. As with any change to Apache's configuration file, you must restart the web server to have the changes take effect. Either send a HUP signal to its process or just stop and then restart it through the Sharing pane.

Once *mod_perl* is running, you'll typically want to start running all Perl-based CGI scripts (including any that you might already have) through the

---

[*] When browsing CPAN (at *http://www.cpan.org*), note the *Apache* module directory.

Apache::Registry module. This requires adding a block of configuration information to your */etc/httpd/httpd.conf* file, like this:

```
<Location /perl>
   SetHandler perl-script
   PerlHandler Apache::Registry
   Options ExecCGI
</Location>
```

The XML-like <Location> tag is a block-style Apache directive; all the directives that it contains (SetHandler, PerlHandler, and Options, in this case) apply only to the relative path that it defines—here, all the scripts contained within the */perl* directory. Modify this to suit your own site setup; to have it apply across the board, define the location as / instead.

Modules and packages that use *mod_perl* often rely on variables you define in Location or Directory blocks in your */etc/httpd/httpd.conf* file.

Using Web Serving Frameworks

Once you've got the four components of a DAMP system running together (you don't have to do anything for Darwin), you can take advantage of frameworks that use them all together to make dynamic web site creation and maintenance much easier. The following list holds pointers to some of the more popular ones.

AxKit
Maki
> AxKit (*http://www.axkit.org*) and Maki (*http://maki.sourceforge.net*) are XML-based content delivery systems that use Perl and Python, respectively. These systems allow you to serve XML documents by performing on-the-fly transformations to them (usually to HTML), and boast other nifty features such as automatic document caching.

Mason
> Mason (*http://www.masonhq.com*) is a *mod_perl* package that lets you build dynamic web sites through file-based components containing a mix of Perl and HTML. Calls to these components can then be placed into HTML files as if they were ordinary HTML tags.

Template Toolkit
> The Template Toolkit (*http://template-toolkit.org*) is similar to Mason, but with more emphasis on defining different page templates, depending upon context. It features its own simple scripting language, rather than Perl.

Zope
> Zope (*http://www.zope.org*) is a highly ambitious all-in-one solution for content management and application serving. It's written in the Python language.

JaneBuilder
> Not really a framework in the same sense as the rest of these, but deserves mention as a shareware Aqua (Carbon) application that helps you create PHP web pages. It includes support for tying in MySQL databases, both local and remote. Find it at *http://www.seejanecode.com*.

IV

Scripting and Development

Mac OS X is a developer's dream come true. On the Unix side, you have access to all the standard programming languages you'd expect to find, such as C/C++, Java, Perl, Python, and Ruby. Mac developers who have installed Apple's Developer Tools have access to utilities such as Project Builder and Interface Builder for building native applications for their Mac, based on Carbon, Cocoa, and even AppleScript.

The chapters in this part include:

Chapter 15, *Development Tools*

Chapter 16, *AppleScript*

Chapter 17, *Text Editing on Mac OS X*

Chapter 18, *Using CVS*

15

Development Tools

As Chapter 3 notes, Mac OS X maker Macintosh software development far easier than ever before. Not only does Mac OS X ship with a large variety of development tools for free, but the tools themselves—especially the integrated development environment applications Project Builder and Interface Builder—are beautiful pieces of work that help even newcomers start writing Mac OS X applications quickly.

This chapter outlines the tools Mac OS X provides for Aqua application development, and touches on the system resources that make Darwin-level development possible.

Getting the Developer Tools

When first installed onto a machine, Mac OS X actually lacks all the development tools mentioned in this chapter (as well crucial BSD-layer development tools such as gcc). You have to take a few extra steps to install them.

The fastest way into the Developer Tools suite simply involves inserting the Mac OS X Developer Tools CD-ROM, which ships with every boxed set of Mac OS X, and double-clicking its installer icon. This installs the whole */Developer* hierarchy and various Darwin-side libraries and executables that make software development (or even just compiling programs from downloaded source code) possible.

 If you purchased new hardware, you may not have the Developer Tools CD. Instead, you can install the Developer Tools by double-clicking on *Developer.mpkg*, found in */Applications/Installers/Developer Tools*.

We recommend that you follow up by joining the Apple Developer Connection (ADC), at *http://connect.apple.com*. (It costs no money, but you do have to provide some personal registration information.) Through the ADC's web site, you can download updates to Mac OS X Developer Tools as Apple releases them, and also gain access to a searchable, up-to-date archive of documentation and other media (such as QuickTime movies of recent conference presentations) relevant to Mac OS X development.

That said, some of the topics this chapter mentions, in particular, AppleScript, come as part of the main Mac OS X main distribution, as does the Perl programming language (since many bits and pieces of the underlying system rely on its presence).

The Developer Folder

The */Developer* folder contains the following subfolders:

Applications
Aqua applications for development, as detailed further in the next section.

Documentation
This folder holds an immense amount of system documentation in HTML and PDF format, covering the entirety of Mac OS X from a developer's point of view. Topics range from general descriptions of system functionality, to highly specific reference manuals, to the Cocoa and Carbon programming APIs. For more about the documentation that the Developer Tools offer, see the later section "Finding Documentation."

All the documentation found in this folder also exists on Apple's developer web site, *http://developer.apple.com.*

Examples
The */Examples* folder contains a wide variety of application project folders, organized by category. Some are *.pbproj* files and related Aqua interface and localization resources all ready for opening in Project Builder, while others are simple shell scripts or AppleScripts that demonstrate various concepts.

The */Examples/Web Services* folder, for example, contains a source to an Aqua application called *XMethodsInspector*, a couple of AppleScripts (embedded in shell scripts), and a couple of C++ source files. All show different ways of invoking SOAP and XML-RPC web services from your software.

Headers
This folder contains *FlatCarbon* flat header files, which help developers port applications from Mac OS 9 (which had no concept of Frameworks—see "Frameworks," later in this chapter, for the difference). The *FlatHeaderConversion* folder holds *tops* and *perl* scripts to help you convert existing legacy source files' header invocations into Mac OS X–style #include directives. Either of these methods will help you migrate older Macintosh codebases to Mac OS X, but the latter method results in code that compiles faster.

Java
Headers and other resources used by Project Builder's Cocoa-Java bridge (see the Java entry in the later section, "Programming Languages").

Makefiles

Makefiles that Project Builder transparently uses when building applications. Generally speaking, you can leave these be.

Palettes

Interface Builder (described later in this chapter in "Interface Builder") uses *palettes* to hold the basic elements of Aqua applications' interfaces: windows, controls, and views. When designing interfaces through Interface Builder, drag these controls off the available palettes and into the interface that you're designing.

This folder contains extra palettes beyond those built into Interface Builder.

ProjectBuilder Extras

Extra templates, plug-ins, and examples for Project Builder (see the later section, "Project Builder").

Tools

Command-line tools from Apple, specifically useful for Darwin development or working with HFS+ filesystems. Chapter 25 covers them all in detail.

Development Applications

These Aqua applications all exist within */Developer/Applications*.

Apple Help Indexing Tool

A frontend to the system's content indexer, tuned especially for making Apple Help web sites. To use it, drag and drop a folder filled with HTML onto this application's Finder icon; it automatically generates index files and inserts them into the target folder.

Through this tool, you can also specify an HTTP-based remote root, from which the Apple Help application will try to fetch help files that your other help pages reference, but that aren't present. These pages have a three-day time out on the user's machine. In this way, you can transparently give an application's users the most up-to-date Apple Help-based documentation.

Extras

A folder full of curiosities and experimental applications, such as the Mac OS X port of Mac OS 9's SimpleText text editor, Bluetooth traffic monitors, and the amazing, self-destructing "BombApp" application that demonstrates Mac OS X's protected memory in a very direct fashion.

FileMerge

A GUI for the *diff* and *merge* command-line tools, which helps you analyze the differences between two text files and merge them into one. It can be especially useful within a CVS context, as described in Chapter 18.

icns Browser

Lets you view the contents of *icns* resource files, which contain the images and bitmasks that make up Aqua icons. (A single *icns* file can hold several different images, specifying what the icon should look like at various sizes in color depths.)

IconComposer

A tool for building *icns* icon files. You don't actually construct the icons with this application; it just binds images you have made through other means into a Mac OS X–friendly format.

Interface Builder

A tool used to construct the GUIs for your Carbon or Cocoa Aqua applications. It's intended for use alongside Project Builder, as described later in "Interface Builder."

IORegistryExplorer

A graphical browser to the computer's IO Registry system, which is organized like a standard Mac OS X property list, letting you tour the hierarchy of I/O devices available to the OS.

JavaBrowser

A simple, column-view browser that lets you navigate through the various Java classes installed on your machine. You can view their APIs (including methods, fields, and constructors) as well as their documentation and source code, if available.

By default, the browser knows about several dozen class paths across your file-system (largely in the */System* domain). Select JavaBrowser → Preferences to add more class paths.

MallocDebug

Named after C's malloc (memory allocation) function, this application lets you browse the sizes of memory structures within a running application. This can be a great help in detecting memory leaks—the sad state that a program can enter if it allocates more memory than it releases. (Since Objective-C, Mac OS X's lingua franca, does not feature automatic garbage collection, this can come in quite handy for Cocoa developers.)

MRJAppBuilder

This tool lets you bundle Java classes into Mac OS X applications (i.e. *.app* directories). Its use is described in "Building Applications with MRJApp-Builder" in Chapter 10.

ObjectAlloc

Lets you spy on the memory allocation of a running application, much like the *MemoryAlloc* program, but focuses on the higher-level object allocations: Cocoa and Core Foundation. It contains comprehensive documentation under ObjectAlloc → About ObjectAlloc.

OpenGL Info

Displays information about the current machine's OpenGL capabilities.

OpenGL Profiler

Analyzes running OpenGL programs.

OpenGL Shader Builder

A shader tool for use with OpenGL development.

PackageMaker

This application lets you create installer packages, of the sort described in "Software Installers" in Chapter 6. This is useful for distributing software that involves more than a single application bundle.

Command-line (Darwin) programs often ship as an installer package, usable from Aqua, though they themselves aren't Aqua applications.

PEFViewer

Lets you browse PEF (Preferred Executable Format) files, a kind of shared library format. (You can find examples in */System/Library/CFMSupport*.)

Pixie

Presents you with a magnified view of the pixels directly underneath the mouse pointer, which can serve as an aid in designing custom GUI elements.

Project Builder

The central development environment for all Aqua programming, detailed later in "Project Builder."

Property List Editor

While you can create Property List files in any text editor, this application eases the process (and removes any XML-related hassles you may have) by letting you build *.plist* files through a graphical, hierarchical-display format. Buttons and pop-up menus control the adding, modification, and deletion of *.plist* elements.

This application doubles as a browser for existing property lists, serving as Mac OS X's default handler for opening *.plist* files from the Finder.

Chapter 22 covers property lists in more detail.

Quartz Debug

An analysis and debugging tool for Quartz, the PDF-based, 2-D graphics rendering engine that makes Aqua possible. Useful if you're involved in low-level Aqua display hacking, or if you're simply curious as to various application window attributes that the system keeps track of.

Sampler

Another application runtime analysis tool like MallocDebug or ObjectAlloc, except with an emphasis on time, rather than space; it helps you determine which internal functions and routines an application spends its time on while executing, and lets you view and pull apart these call stacks in various ways. This makes it a great tool for analyzing and improving application performance.

Thread Viewer

Displays parallel threads running within a given application as colorful graphs, displaying their relative levels of activity at a glance, and whether any are in loops, locked, or stopped altogether.

Project Builder

The Project Builder application is your center for all Cocoa and Carbon application development. It lets you construct and manage *projects*, which it defines as collections of files—source code, libraries, and resource files—that go into an application. Included in Project Builder are context-aware text editors (featuring syntax highlighting and "smart" indentation), and frontends to the GNU project's gcc compiler* and gdb debugger.

Figure 15-1 shows a typical Project Builder window. The window has two sections: a list on the left and a detail view on the right. The nature of each is

---

* Technically speaking, Mac OS X uses an Apple-modified version of gcc that is more proficient with Objective-C than the GNU project's official version. Details, including source code, are available as part of the Darwin project.

determined by which tab you have currently selected. Describing these views also gives us a brief tour of Project Builder's abilities:

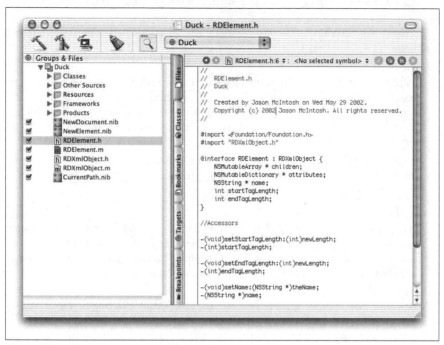

Figure 15-1. The main Project Builder window

Files

This view displays, in the left frame, a list of all the files that a project uses. They are arranged *logically*, not necessarily adhering to the reality of the file-system; you can create folders—through Project → New Group (or Option-⌘-N) and arrange the list's files within them however you like, without affecting their true filesystem locations. Furthermore, while many of the files (especially source code specific to this project alone) will reside in the project's real folder, others (such as shared frameworks) are merely present by reference, residing elsewhere on the filesystem. Project Builder remembers where all the files actually are, but if you would like to know, simply select one and then choose Project → Show Info (⌘-I).

(You're likely to spend most of your Project Builder time under the *Files* tab while you edit source code.)

Classes

This view lets you browse all the object classes available to your file, as a flat list or as a collapsible hierarchy that displays inheritance. The list visually differentiates between classes defined by linked-in frameworks and those you define yourself (by default, classes defined by the project are blue, and imported ones are black).

The Classes tab also gives you a great way to browse reference documentation. See the next section.

Bookmarks

You can add a line of source to a project's bookmark list by selecting View →
Add to Bookmarks (Option-⌘-Down Arrow) while the insertion point is in
that line. This adds a reference to the line to the list of bookmarks that
appears under the Bookmarks tab.

Targets

The list under this tab details the project's *targets*, in the *make* command's
sense of the term: each target represents a single product—such as an application or a plugin—that this project creates. See the later section, "Targets"
for more details.

Breakpoints

While browsing your source code, you can set *breakpoints* by clicking in the
breakpoint gutter (Figure 15-1) to the left of a line of code. A little blue arrow
appears at that point, and the line also shows up among the list of breakpoints visible beneath the Breakpoints tab.

Breakpoints are a central function of using Project Builder's debugger. An
application running within the debugger pauses in its execution when it
encounters an active breakpoint, letting you view the values of variables and
other structures at that frozen moment of runtime. You can then use the
debugging controls to resume execution as if it hadn't stopped at all.

Finding Documentation

You have several ways to look up documentation for specific object classes or
more general Mac OS X programming topics, both through Project Builder and
the Finder.

Class and method documentation

Friendlier frameworks, including all the major, Apple-supplied frameworks that
come with Mac OS X, pack HTML documentation in as part of their resources.
Project Builder contains several ways to access it.

While you're editing code, you can Option-double-click any class or method
name within the editing window to have Project Builder look up its documentation, displaying any that it finds. (If it finds multiple matches, then it first pops up
a contextual menu, letting you narrow the choices.)

To browse available documentation for the classes you're using, click the
window's Classes tab. As Figure 15-2 shows, every class in the hierarchy with
attached documentation has a little blue book icon beside it. Clicking a book
displays the class's HTML documentation in the window's content frame, and
also places a list of all that class's methods into the Members frame, giving
another book icon to each one with its own section within the class's
documentation.

You can also dig manually into the Framework's contents through the Finder and
open up the reference files in a web browser. The */Developer/Documentation*
folder contains aliases into the documentation folders of the frameworks you'll
probably use the most often, such as the Cocoa and Application Kit frameworks.

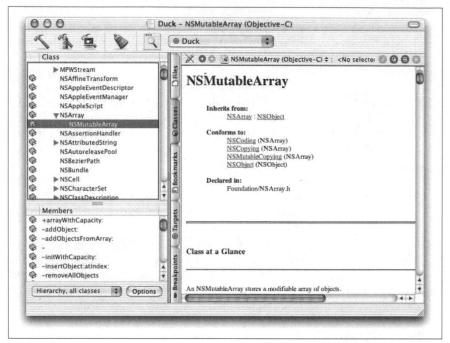

Figure 15-2. Browsing the class hierarchy for documentation

Manualpages

Like any good Unix system, Mac OS X stores much of its documentation in Unix manual page—a.k.a. *manpage*—format. Since manpages tend to deal mainly with C functions and command-line tools, their information isn't always of immediate relevance to most Aqua development projects. However, Project builder gives you a convenient way to read manpages anyway: just select Help → Open man page, and then specify the command, function, or topic you wish to read about. Project Builder renders manpages with hyperlinks, making it easy to follow any embedded cross-references.

You can also read manpages through the Terminal's *man* program or through a third-party application, such as Carl Lindberg's free and open source Aqua application ManOpen, available at *http://www.clindberg.org/projects/ManOpen.html*.

Project Types

When you select File → New Project (Shift-⌘-N), the dialog window shown in Figure 15-3 appears with all the types of projects that Project Builder supports. By selecting one and clicking the Next button, Project Builder creates a new project folder (writing it to the path you specify in the next window) preloaded with resource files, NIB files, and frameworks appropriate to the project's type.

Empty Project
    This starts a new project tied (at first) to an empty folder.

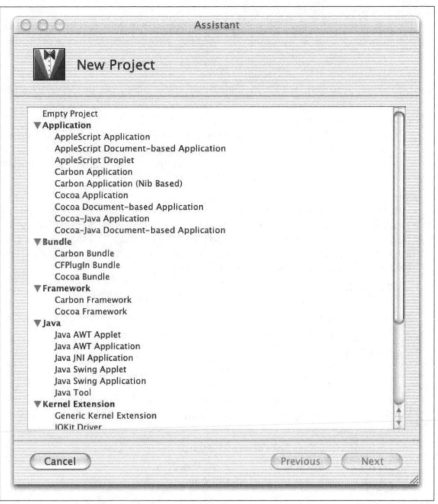

Figure 15-3. Project Builder's New Project window

Application

Projects with the goal of building Cocoa, Carbon, or AppleScript Studio applications.

AppleScript Application

An AppleScript Studio application (see Chapter 16), written primarily with AppleScript (and the merest hint of Objective-C).

Carbon Application

A Carbon application, authored in C++, that uses Resource Manager (*.r* or *.rsrc*) for all its resources. Resource Manager, part of the Core-Services framework, is a library for working with these old-format resource files or file resource forks.

Carbon Application (NIB-Based)
As above, but uses NIB files for its interface resources, letting you use Interface Builder alongside this project, just as with a Cocoa or Apple-Script Studio project.

Cocoa Application
An application written in Objective-C and based on the Cocoa framework, Mac OS X's native API for Aqua application programming.

Cocoa-Java Application
As above, but with hooks into a Java-to-Objective-C language bridge, letting you write your source in Java, even though the application you'll build will be Mac OS X–native. See "Programming Languages" later in this chapter for more about this odd duality.

Bundle
While Applications and Frameworks are also bundles (as described in "Bundles" in Chapter 2), Project Builder lets you build "generic" bundles that, while containing executable code and its associated resources just like any other bundle, serve some other purpose of your own devising. The following describes the three types of bundles:

Carbon Bundle
A bundle that links agaist the Carbon framework.

CFPlugIn Bundle
A bundle that links agaist the Core Foundation framework.

Cocoa Bundle
A bundle that links agaist the Cocoa framework.

Framework
The following project types let you create your own frameworks (see "Frameworks" later in this chapter), against which future projetcs can link in turn.

Carbon framework
A framework that links against Carbon.

Cocoa framework
A framework that links against Cocoa.

Java
The following project styles help you make pure-Java applications, which run within Mac OS X's Java VM (see Chapter 10). These are different projects than the Cocoa-Java ones; see the later section, "Programming Languages" for more about the difference.

Java AWT Applet
An AWT-based Java applet that is built as a Jar file and run using *applet-viewer* or Applet Launcher (see "Applets in Applet Launcher" in Chapter 10).

Java AWT Application
An AWT-based Java application built as an application bundle.

Java Swing Application
A Swing-based Java applet built as a Jar file and run using *appletviewer* or Applet Launcher (see "Applets in Applet Launcher" in Chapter 10)

Java Tool
A library or application built as a Jar file.

Kernel Extension

Project templates for creating kernel extensions (MACH extensions that load at boot-time and live in */System/Library/Extensions*).

Standard Apple Plug-ins

The following templates help you create specific types of plug-ins, bundles meant for loading into a running application. (You can create other sorts of plug-ins through the generic Cocoa or Carbon Bundle templates.)

IBPalette

A custom palette that lets you use Aqua GUI widgets of your own design with Interface Builder (see "Interface Builder).

PreferencePane

A plug-in for the System Preferences application (see Chapter 11).

Screen Saver

A screen saver module for the Screen Effects preference pane; see "Personal" in Chapter 5. (Interestingly, this is an example of a plug-in that works with a plug-in.)

Tool

This final category of project templates help you create command-line (Terminal) programs with Project Builder.

C++ Tool

A command-line tool that links against the stdc++ library.

CoreFoundation Tool

A command-line tool that links against the Core Foundation framework.

CoreServices Tool

A command-line tool that links against the Core Services framework.

Foundation Tool

A command-line tool that links against the Foundation framework.

Standard Tool

A command-line tool that uses C.

Document-based applications

Some things in the list make a distinction between applications and *document-based applications*. In Mac OS X development terms, a document-based application's prime function involves the creation and editing of individual documents, each of which can be saved to, or loaded from, disk. Such an application uses, along with an application controller and window controllers, a *document controller* class that inherits from the *NSDocument* class and manages these user-editable documents.

Starting a document-based project though Project Builder gives you (among other things) a *MainMenu.nib* NIB file whose File menu is already linked to Open, Save, and Save As actions that do exactly what you'd expect: opening up the dialogs described in "Opening and Saving Documents" in Chapter 1. It also creates a document controller class named *MyDocument*, primed with skeletal methods saving and loading the document's data.

Among Mac OS X's application suite (covered in Chapter 17, TextEdit is an example of a document-based application. An "ordinary" application doesn't use documents in this faction; it serves some self-contained purpose, and in many cases, has only a single interface window. Examples include the Address Book or Chess applications.

Building Projects

Building a project is as easy as clicking the Build (hammer) button or selecting Build → Build (⌘-B), but Project Builder takes a lot of information into account when you do so. It looks for new library dependencies that need to be fulfilled and new code it needs to compile or re-compile, as well as examines the project's current *target* and *build style* settings in order to determine what sort of thing it should produce.

Targets

Every Project Builder project has at least one target, representing a "deliverable," something that your project produces. The majority of projects produce only a single executable (either a file or a bundle), and hence have just one target. However, some software projects may find it useful to have more than one target; you may want to build the client and server ends of a client-server package under a single project, for example, or produce a command-line tool that somehow complements your project's main Aqua-application product.

You can add targets to your project through Project → New Target, and edit the settings and *Info.plist* meta-information of any target (including the one you start a new project with) through Project → Edit Active Target (Option-⌘-E). You can view all the targets you've got so far via the Project Builder Window's Targets tab.

The target pop-up menu at the top of the project window displays the current active target and lets you quickly switch to another. While the project window's Files tab lists all of the files that the project refers to, only the ones with active checkboxes beside them are linked into the current target.

Build styles

As with targets, a project has one active build style at any given time. A build style is simply a list of arguments that Project Builder takes into account when compiling the project's targets during the build phase. You can view and edit build styles by selecting them under the Targets tab, and add new build styles through Project → New Build Style.

A new project defines two build styles: *Development* and *Deployment*, with the former as the default. When you're ready to release a project, select Deployment as the build style and then built the project; the products it will build will undergo optimization, removing all the debugging symbols and other bits of binary that made Development-style builds easier to diagnose but slower to run.

Using the Debugger

When you build and run a project in Debug mode (by selecting Build → Build or Debug-⌘-Y, or clicking the hammer-and-spraycan button), then you get access to Project Builder's debug frame, shown in Figure 15-4. These include a set of runtime control buttons and two additional tabbed subviews. The latter of these include Console and Standard I/O, which let you view console messages (including gdb's raw output, which Project Builder parses and arranges into the Debug window for you) and anything that the program might send to the Unix Standard Output filehandle, respectively.

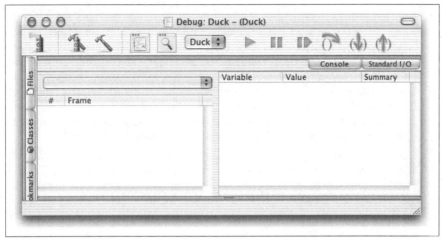

Figure 15-4. Project Builder's debug frame

Programming Languages

As with every operating system, Mac OS X supports as many languages as it has compatible compilers.* Some are described in the following list. Its status as a Unix-flavored system, arguably the most flexible platform for programming, means that it already has a wide support base.

Objective-C
> As C is to a "generic" Unix system, and as C++ is to Mac OS 9, one language lies closest to Mac OS X's heart, in terms of support and programming ease: Objective-C. This elegeant, object-oriented langauge, which adds a handful of syntax rules onto plain-vanilla C, is the lingua franca of Cocoa development.

> In order to better support legacy code, Mac OS X also supports strange notions such as Objective-C++, which allows a programmer to invoke and work with C++ object classes from Objective-C code, and vice versa.

> One important downside to Objective-C programming is the fact that most newcomers to Mac OS X programming have likely never used or even seen it before; in fact, it's hard to find any application of it outside of Mac OS X. The developers most likely to already know Objective-C are those who already have programming experience with NeXTSTEP (Mac OS X's predecessor,

---

* Or compatible virtual machines, in the case of machine-independent languages like Java (see Chapter 10) or Squeak (a Smalltalk-based programming environment found at *http://www. squeak.org*).

whose OpenStep libraries envolved into the Cocoa frameworks we have today). Fortunately, Objective-C does not present large barriers to entry; people with any programming experience can start down this path by reading *The Objective-C Programming Language*, a concise, excellent, and free book found in */Developer/Documentation/ObjectiveC/*.

Java

Java has a dual-faced nature on Mac OS X. Through the Java Bridge software that lurks among the system's Developer Tools, programmers more familiar with Java than with Objective-C can use it to develop Cocoa applications through the Project Builder environment; all of the Cocoa and Foundation classes have Java APIs identical in spirit (if not in syntax) to their Objectice-C interfaces. You can find these documented in the *Java* folders of */Developer/Documentation/Cocoa/Reference/ApplicationKit* and */Developer/ Documentation/Cocoa/Reference/Cocoa*, or by browsing class documentation in a Cocoa-Java project as described earlier in "Finding Documentation."

However, the resulting Cocoa applications will *not* be Java applications! They'll run solely on Mac OS X, just like any other Cocoa program. Project Builder's Java Bridge exists solely as a convenience for new developers who know Java but not Objective-C (a situation far more likely than the opposite). We recommend that Cocoa programmers who do know Java consider learning Objective-C anyway.

Mac OS X also supports pure Java applications, which really do run within the Java VM, as described in Chapter 10. The trade-off is that they don't really use Aqua interface; instead, they must provide a UI of their own. Fortunately, Mac OS X ships with an Aqua-like PLAF (pluggable look-and-feel) plug-in for Java Swing, and even makes it the default swing interface, as predefined in the */Library/Java/HomeLib/swing.properties* file.

While Project Builder bends over backwards to accomodate Java-Cocoa development, it can only do so much with pure Java programming; you can't use Interface Builder at all to help you create Swing UIs, for example. Pure Java developers may wish to also investigate *Emacs* (see Chapter 17) or third-party solutions such as the Java-based, open source NetBeans (*http://www. netbeans.org*).

AppleScript

This scripting language has been a part of Mac OS since System 7.1. It's a rich language tuned specifically to act as glue and gopher between other existing applications. For example, an AppleScript application that comes with Developer Tools called Watson will use Apple's Mail application to search through all of your mailboxes for a user-specified string.

Historically, AppleScript programs run in their own environment, doing whatever they do and then quitting, without any fancy UI. Mac OS X's Developer Tools introduce AppleScript Studio, which allows your AppleScripts to hook into Cocoa interface APIs, turning them into full-fledged Aqua applications with interfaces that you can design with Interface Builder.

See Chapter 16 for more information on AppleScript.

Perl

Perl is a powerful, general-purpose language with a special knack for text processing that can be used for either simple cross-application scripting, high-level object-oriented application development, CGI programming, and just about anything else. Unlike AppleScript or Objective-C, Perl speaks expressly to Mac OS X's Unix side, so you'll probably find Perl programming most comfortable in a text editor such as *Emacs* (see Chapter 17); Mac OS X includes two *Emacs* modes for editing Perl code (the simple perl-mode and the highly configurable cperl-mode).

While Mac OS X ships with Perl (out of necessity, since so much of the distribution depends on Perl to install and run correctly), it doesn't include any connection between it and Aqua; you can write only non-Aqua applications, such as Darwin-based Terminal applications or system daemons, or use Perl/Tk to make GUI programs if you have X Windows installed (as described in Chapter 23). However, the infant Camelbones project (found at *http://camelbones.sourceforge.net*, aims to bridge the worlds of Perl and Cocoa programming.

Python

Python is another open source, Unix-grounded, all-purpose progamming language. Boasting a cleaner syntax and a sizeable support community of its own, Python proves an attractive alternative to Perl for many programmers.

Interface Builder

Because it is so graphically oriented, Aqua applications adhere to a very passive runtime model. In fact, a typical Mac OS X application spends most of its time running in an idle loop, waiting for some sort of user input, such as a keypress or a mouseclick onto one of its buttons. Through the Interface Builder application, you specify the onscreen controls that your application will have, and tie these into handler methods within your code.

Interface Builder helps you generate *.nib* files, which are serialized versions of Cocoa application elements. Typically, an application has one *.nib* file for every window that its interface contains. A very simple text-editing application, for example, might have one such file for its document window (containing the text view where the user actually types), another for the application's Preferences window, and a third for its About panel. All but the most minimal applications also contain a *.nib* that holds its menu bar menus (including its application menu and everything to the right of it, as described in "The Menu Bar" in Chapter 1).

Through Interface Builder, build these windows by dragging template windows, controls, and views off of palettes, as shown in Figure 15-5. Then establish connections between parts of the window and classes belonging to your application. Normally, you define a special class known as a *Window Controller* for every window (and therefore every *.nib* file), and supply it with two types of data: *outlets*, which are pointers to things existing on the window, and *actions*, which are pointers that connect window controls back to methods in the project's source.

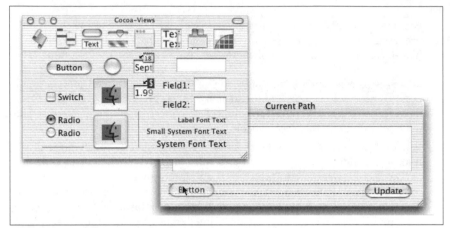

Figure 15-5. Building a window with Interface Builder

Figure 15-6 shows an example window "on the table." We can see a connection between the window's OK button and an object connected to the *.nib* file (represented by a blue cube icon). This object belongs to the controller class for this window. Clicking the button (in the eventual, running application that will incorporate this under-construction *.nib* file) calls a method named insertElement: on the window controller object.

 Before Mac OS X, when Project Builder existed as the IDE for NeXTSTEP, the concepts of NeXT machines and cube shapes were tightly intertwined, so this same cube icon existed, but without its present Aqua-blue tint. You can see another mark of NeXT's legacy in Cocoa's class and function names, which all begin with the namespace-marking letters NS—short for "NeXTSTEP."

Looking at Figure 15-6, we see that the controller object also has connections—outlets—to the window. One, called *menu*, points to the window's sole pop-up menu. Any of the window controller's methods can thus access that menu and all the values it contains (including the one currently selected by the user), through its own *menu* instance variable, which is actually a pointer to an object of the class *NSPopUpButton*.

To summarize: in the running application, the user selects something from the list, and hits OK. This calls insertElement: on the window's controller object, which would, in all likelikehod, call a method on the active *document controller* object, letting it know that the user wishes to insert an element into the frontmost document (and probably passing as an argument the selected contents of that pop-up menu). Having done this, the window controller's mission is complete, so the insertElement: function's final instruction probably closes the window.

This window, by the way, appears when the user selects a menu item from the application's menu bar—itself defined by a separate *.nib* file that lies among the application's internal resources. In this way, we see how an Aqua application's whole interface comprises a web of *.nib* files and callback methods.

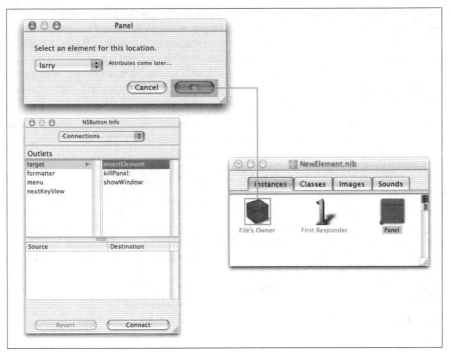

Figure 15-6. Connecting controls and setting outlets on an object

Libraries and Frameworks

Projects you build with Project Builder link against Mach-style dynamic libraries. Rather than #include-ing flat header files, though, projects usually link against *Frameworks*, which include both libraries and related resources.* (See the */Developer/Headers* folder, described earlier in "The Developer Folder," for a fast way to port flat-library-linking legacy code.)

Frameworks

Frameworks are simply dynamic libraries packaged into bundles. Along with the library file itself lives its related resources. Like all bundles, frameworks use a consistently named internal structure of folders, so that programs can easily find what they need within. These resources can include images, plists, and NIB files, just like an application bundle. This not only makes shared code libraries possible, but also complete shared interface libraries. The standard spell checker interface, for example, actually lives as a NIB file within the Application Kit (or AppKit) framework's resources.

Resources particular to framework bundles—and of interest to developers wishing to make use of them in their software projects—include the library's header files

---

* Unix emigrees looking for a lengthy discussion about Darwin's dynamic libraries versus ELF libraries may wish to reference *Mac OS X for Unix Geeks* (O'Reilly & Associates, Inc., 2002).

and class documentation. You can navigate to and open these from the Finder if you'd like, but Project Builder gives you easier ways to browse these framework resources if you've loaded a reference to the framework into your project. Clicking the disclosure triangle next to a framework icon in the Files tab reveals that framework's headers, which you can select to load into the window's content frame. As for documentation, frameworks automatically add any HTML docs they provide to the Class browser—see "Finding Documentation."

The system's search paths for frameworks are the */Library/Frameworks* folders found around the filesystem (see "The Library folder" in Chapter 9), with Apple's core development frameworks (including those that make Cocoa development possible) found in */System/Library/Frameworks*. Project Builder abstracts the task of selecting from these frameworks through its New Project interface (see Figure 15-3), which will set up your new project to link to the appropriate frameworks. Linking in non-Apple frameworks (such as those your might write yourself or download from the Internet) is as simple as selecting Project → Add Frameworks (Option-⌘-A), or just dragging the frameworks' Finder icons into your project's Files list. From there, you can use the frameworks' methods from any source file that #includes its main header file; the documentation included with more socially adept frameworks should guide you from there.

The Info.plist File

Metainformation about your project, which you usually define through Project Builder's Project → Edit Active Target (Option-⌘-E) dialog, is stored in a special *Info.plist* file, which Project Builder writes to the application's */Contents* folder upon building. Every Bundle-style application on your system (that is, every Cocoa application and every Bundle-style Carbon or Java application as well) has one of these files, which are, like all *.plist* files, in Property List XML format (described in Chapter 22).

Taken together, all the *Application/Application.app/Contents/Info.plist* files installed in all the filesystem's domain-level *Application* folders (see "Domains" in Chapter 9) compose a registry of all the applications available to the machine. This lets the system build a database of application information, which lets the Finder assign the correct Kind to application-specific files under its List view and Info windows, the *defaults* program pair preference domains to applications (as Chapter 22 describes), and more. The application itself can also pull information from this file in order to help build its *About* dialog, for example, as well as know what file format its own documents use.

A related file, *version.plist*, can exist in the same directory as *Info.plist*. As its name suggests, it contains information about the applications' version and build numbers, as well as release status.

16

AppleScript

By *scripting*, we mean writing programs that act as "glue," passing information between other existing applications in order to suit some purpose or act as macros, letting a user execute several commands in some program (or across several programs) with a single gesture. In this terminology, scripts are different than full-on applications because they lack a user interface; they just do their job and exit.

The highest-level scripting language on Mac OS X is AppleScript, initially developed by Apple in the early 1990s. AppleScripts enjoy a special dispensation on the Mac because of their native handling of Apple Events, which are simply messages that Mac applications can pass to one another. The majority of this chapter covers AppleScript, as well as AppleScript Studio, which is the Project Builder extension for building complete Aqua applications wrapped around AppleScript cores.

The Script Menu Extra

Apple's Script menu extra (see Figure 16-1) offers perhaps the most convenient way to run scripts, both of the AppleScript and shell script variety. It doesn't appear in your menu bar by default, but installing it is very easy: just run the *Script Menu.menu* program, found in */Applications/AppleScript*. The Script menu extra pops into your menu bar and remains there until you manually remove it (by command-dragging it off of the menu bar).

This menu extra gets its contents from the */Library/Scripts* folders in your machine's various domains, as described in "The Library folder" in Chapter 9. As with every other Library-based resource, you add your personal scripts to *~/Library/Scripts*, and administrators can add scripts for all the machine's users to share under */Library/ Scripts*.

A new Mac OS X installation actually comes with quite a few scripts already installed into */Library/Scripts*, organized into categorical folders (which the script menu extra handles hierarchically). (The folder found at */Applications/AppleScript/ Example Scripts* is actually a symbolic link to this folder.) They are all sample AppleScripts meant to demonstrate some feature of that language; you're free to

Figure 16-1. The Script menu extra

try running a few (none of them do anything permanent or potentially embar-
rassing) as well as open any up in Script Editor to view the source code and
discover how they work. (In particular, check out the Internet Services scripts,
which use SOAP to grab information through web services.)

While all the preinstalled examples are AppleScripts, you can add any kind of inter-
preted-language program, including Perl programs and shell scripts (as shown in
Figure 16-1), into Script menu extra items, just by copying them into a */Library/
Scripts* folder, and turning on their executable permission bits (most easily accomplished through the Terminal command *chmod +x filename*). When selected from
the menu extra, these scripts act as if they were invoked on the command line with
no arguments.

Programming AppleScript

AppleScript is a relatively simple programming language with a forté for gluing
Macintosh applications together. While you can use it to a limited extent as a
general programming language, its real power comes from its native ability to
sling Apple Events around, letting even inexperienced programmers create interapplication scripts, as well as programs that drive a single application through a
certain multistep task.

About Apple Events

An *Apple Event* is simply a message that one application running on a Mac OS X
system sends to another (or itself), running either on the same computer or on

another Macintosh via a network connection. (Technically, the recipient application can even be a program running in a non-Mac OS X environment, if it happens to answer to the Apple Events messaging protocol, but this sort of cross-platform messaging is more often handled by SOAP or XML-RPC.)

On Mac OS X, Apple Events are implemented through Mach kernel messaging, a feature of the operating system's lowest levels. However, for maximum compatibility and maintainability, Apple recommends that developers prefer Apple Events for their software's interapplication functionality. This isn't something you need to think about while writing AppleScripts (which speak strictly in Apple Events), but it is something to keep in mind when writing more sophisticated applications. See "Scripting the Terminal," later in this chapter.

Apple Events do not offer a way to *broadcast* information to other applications, which would let any interested program pick up on its information. Instead, they are always targeted events, with a specific destination application in mind.

To use broadcasting in Cocoa applications, go through the `NSDistributedNotifcationCenter` class; in Carbon code, go through the Core Foundation's `CFNotificationCenter` class (see "Finding Documentation" in Chapter 15).

Most useful AppleScripts compile into a list of Apple Event directives; just about every statement in a `tell` block translates into an Apple Event.

The Five-Minute Guide to AppleScript

While AppleScript is sophisticated enough to warrant books unto itself, it is also simple enough to allow one to quickly create programs just by knowing a few tricks and then blundering around from there. The worst you can do is write ugly programs that don't work. OK, technically, the worst you can do is delete your hard drive, but you'd have to do something like this:

```
tell Finder move all files to trash-object set warns before emptying of
trash-object to false empty trash end tell
```

As you can see, AppleScript's English-like syntax makes it hard to cause this kind of a disaster unless you're really asking for it.

Once you've gotten that far, a bit of tweaking and experimentation should lead you to ugly programs that do exactly what you want. (You can worry about making them prettier as you get better at AppleScripting.)

AppleScript uses simple object-oriented notation to describe its environment. Scriptable applications and the things you can manipulate within them are objects (a.k.a., "nouns"); these objects define methods ("verbs") that causes them to perform various actions. For example, just about every scriptable application's AppleScript object recognizes the verb "quit," which, when issued to it by an Apple Event, causes it to react as if a user had selected *Application* → Quit from within it.

AppleScript

The language also includes a small set of built-in keywords to drive these objects around. One of AppleScript's most important keywords is tell, which turns a program's focus to a certain object for the length of a code block. Most often, this object is an application that the AppleScript script wishes to control. For example, a block of code that fires Apple Events at the Mail application might look like this:

```
tell application "Mail"
    activate -- brings the application (Mail, in this case) to the front
    (* Other commands that would become Apple Events sent to Mail go here *)
end tell
```

To learn what Apple Event–producing statements you can feed an application while a *tell* block is aimed at it, look at that application's scripting dictionary. Either drag its application icon onto the Script Editor's Finder icon, or choose it from the application list window after selecting File → Open Dictionary. You'll see a window like that shown in Figure 16-2. The list of words and phrases in its left frame shows all the keywords that this application's AppleScript object recognizes—verbs (methods) are in plain text, and nouns (objects) are in italics. Click on any word to see the dictionary's documentation about its purpose and use, including syntax and return values (for verbs), and available elements and properties (for nouns).

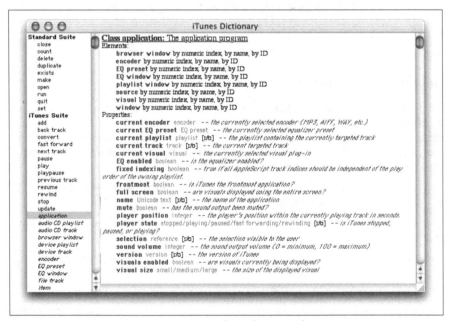

Figure 16-2. iTunes' Script Dictionary, seen through Script Editor

Once you get a feel for AppleScript's syntax and available data types, know how to use tell, and can comfortably navigate applications' dictionaries, you're ready to start scripting. For example, let's write a little glue script between iTunes in Mail. The following AppleScript fetches the current track from iTunes and the content of a signature called "Musical Template" from Mail. Then it assigns the combination of the two to the signature "Musical," as in the following example:

```
set theTrack to "" // Declare variable here, to give it global scope
tell application "iTunes"
  set theTrack to current track
end tell

tell application "Mail"
  set theSig to the content of signature "Musical Template"
  set theSig to theSig & (theTrack's name)
  set the content of signature "Musical" to theSig
end tell
```

You can learn about the iTunes current track method and the name property of the resulting object, from iTunes' scripting dictionary, and likewise with Mail's signature method, with its content property.

Of course, the program assumes, perhaps wrongly, that you've set up "Musical" and "Musical Template" signatures already. By modifying Mail's tell block and making simple use of AppleScript's built-in display dialog function, you can make the script a little more polite:

```
tell application "Mail"
  set requiredSignatures to {"Musical", "Musical Template"}
  repeat with theSignature in requiredSignatures
    if not (exists signature (theSignature as string)) then
      display dialog "Missing signature: " & theSignature
      return
    end if
  end repeat
  set theSig to the content of signature "Musical Template"
  set theSig to theSig & (theTrack's name)
  set the content of signature "Musical" to theSig
end tell
```

Now if either of the script's required signatures fail to exist, Mail will complain with a minimal dialog box, and then the script will quietly exit without having any effect. Of course, an even *better* solution would involve creating those signatures if they don't exist already, or perhaps not relying on a signature-based template and instead place it in a file, which you can access by telling Finder. You get the idea.

AppleScript syntax summary

Since most of AppleScript's functionality involves controlling objects defined by other applications, its own syntax is fairly small and simple, containing only a handful of keywords and very few built-in functions. Tables 16-1 and 16-2 contain its fundamentals.

Table 16-1. AppleScript syntax

Keyword(s)	Purpose	Example
set	Value assignment	set myVar to 4 set theItem to the first item
copy	Value duplication (objects in the value are duplicated rather than referenced)	copy myVar to myOtherVar

The keywords in Table 16-2 can be used in either block style or on one line. For example, a complicated AppleScript if structure looks like this:

```
if condition
    (* Statements to execute if the condition is true *)
else
    (* Statements to execute if the condition is false *)
end if
```

A simple if statement, however, can fit on one line:

```
if condition then true-condition-statement else false-condition-statement
```

Note that the block-ending end if statement becomes unnecessary with this one-line syntax.

Table 16-2. AppleScript flow control keywords

Keyword(s)	Purpose	Example

if *condition* [then] *true-condition-statements* [else *false-condition-statements*] end if	Conditionally run statement block. The else statement block is optional.	`if my first item exists`
		`    return my first item`
		`else`
		`    display dialog "I don't have any items."`
		`end if`

repeat with *variable* in *list*	Looping construct. On each iteration, *variable* is set to the next value of *list*.	`-- tell Mail to synchronize all IMAP accounts`
		`tell application "Mail"`
		`    repeat with theAccount in accounts`
		`        if theAccount's account type is imap`
		`            synchronize theAccount`
		`            -- No "else" is needed here;`
		`            -- we ignore other account types.`
		`        end if`
		`    end repeat`
		`end tell`

try *statements* [on error *statements*] end try	Trap errors, and (optionally) run statements if an error occurs.	`try`
		`    set myPath to theDocument's path`
		`on error`
		`    display dialog "Uh oh, I couldn't get the path of theDocument."`
		`    return`
		`end try`

And there you have a good idea of AppleScript's fundamentals, without even getting into defining functions or calling other scripts and more advanced magic. To continue your path into AppleScript wizardry, see the AppleScript web site, at *http://www.apple.com/applescript*, or Bill Cheeseman's *AppleScript Sourcebook* (*http://www.applescriptsourcebook.com*).

Extending AppleScript

AppleScript is a very extensible language: besides letting applications extend it by defining their own scripting dictionaries, it also recognizes bundles of C or C++ code known as *OSA Extentions*, or, more commonly, *osaxen* (the plural form of *osax*). These software modules extend AppleScript's functionality by defining new functions, which you can invoke at any point.

Osaxen take the form of binary files with *.osax* filename extensions. To install an osax file, simply add it to an appropriate */Library/ScriptingAdditions* folder. The commands that the osax defines become available to users on the machine or network as per the usual Library folder rules (described in "The Library folder" in Chapter 9).

For example, the *XML Tools.osax* file available from Late Night Software Ltd. (*http://www.latenightsw.com/freeware/XMLTools2/index.html*), when installed, makes two new functions available: parse XML, which turns a string of XML into an AppleScript record structure, and generate XML, which performs the opposite transformation.

Online AppleScript and osaxen resources include *osaxen.com*, a web site run by MacScripter.net, which hosts (at the time of this writing) around 200 Mac OS X–compatible osaxen packages, and Late Night Software Ltd. (at *http://www. latenightsw.com*), home of lots of interesting osaxen and other OSA resources.

Script Editor

Apple's Script Editor offers a somewhat atavistic way to create and edit AppleScripts. It's a rather precise port of the Mac OS 9 application of the same name, which itself has changed very little from AppleScript's introduction in the early 1990s. While it does offer niceties like syntax highlighting, you might prefer using the sorts of text editors covered in Chapter 17 over Script Editor's text area. That said, this application certainly offers the easiest way to compile and run AppleScripts, even if you use a different program for editing them.

Creating, compiling, and running scripts

Just start typing into Script Editor's lower text area, or paste or drag text from some other source into it. New text shows up in an orange-colored Courier typeface. While Script Editor features syntax-aware text highlighting and formatting, it doesn't bother applying it until you ask for it by clicking the window's Check Syntax button. This causes Script Editor to compile (but not run) the script; if successful, then it will instantly prettify all that orange text, changing every term's color and text style and every line's indentation level as it sees fit. If it can't compile the script due to a syntax error, it will let you know, and will highlight the point where the compiler got stuck.

AppleScript

The compiler will perform application dictionary lookups as necessary to fetch application-specific keywords (which are colored blue by default). Thus, you can get away with referring to signatures with a tell application "Mail" block, but in other locations—outside of a tell, or within a tell aimed at the Finder, for example—Script Editor would interpret signatures as a variable (and color it green).

To prevent collision from variables and application keywords, consider always using the "studlyCaps" style in your variable names—i.e., preferring variables named theList or myMessages over list or messages.

You can modify Script Editor's choice of text-highlighting colors, fonts, and sizes by choosing Edit → AppleScript Formatting... and then using the Font and Style menus to modify the text in the resulting format window.

To run a script from Script Editor, click the Run button, or select Controls → Run (⌘-R). (Script Editor first tries compiling the script if you've made any changes to it since its last compilation or if it hasn't been compiled at all yet, and won't run the script if the compiler reports any syntax errors.) The script runs until it exits (by finishing execution of all its statements, hitting a return statement, or encountering an untrapped runtime error). You can force a script to stop by clicking the Stop button on its window, or selecting Controls → Stop (⌘-.).

All compiled AppleScripts that you run appear in the system process table under the label System Events. If the script falls into an infinite loop or otherwise gets out of hand while you're running a script through the Script menu extra and thus lack Script Editor's handy Stop button, you can just locate and terminate this process, either through the Process Viewer application or through the Terminal's *ps* and *kill* commands.

Recording scripts

Very few applications are *recordable*, able to automatically generate script statements out of actions that they make. By using Script Editor to record your activities with one of these rare applications, you can quickly generate AppleScript code, either to create a reusable macro, or just to investigate the statements needed to produce certain activities with that application.

Saving scripts

In its most raw state, an AppleScript is just a text file, like any other piece of source code. Script Editor's Save dialog offers a Format pop-up menu with the following choices:

Text

Saves as a plain text file. (It will set the file's resource fork to continue pointing at Script Editor as its creator file, though; use the Finder's File → Get Info (⌘-I) dialog's Open With controls to change its default application to something else, such as TextEdit.)

Compiled Script

The default option, which causes Script Editor to compile the script and save the file in a binary format with a *.scpt* extension. AppleScripts must be compiled before an application such as Script Editor or the Script menu extra will run them.

 The fastest way to start using a new script, once you're happy with how it works, is to save it in compiled form in your *~/Library/ Scripts* folder, where it will immediately appear as an option under the Script menu extra (described earlier in "The Script Menu Extra"). If you write a lot of AppleScripts, consider adding this folder to your Favorites (see "Favorites" in Chapter 2) so that you can quickly access it from the Save dialog's Where: pop-up menu.

Application

Saves the script as a Finder-launchable application file.

Testing scripts

Two special windows help you perform simple testing and debugging with your AppleScripts.

Selecting Show Result (⌘-L) summons the Result window (labeled "the result"). When open, the return value (if any) of scripts you run in Script Editor appear within this window.

To see a more thorough view of values passing through your script, select Open Event Log (⌘-E). The resulting Event Log window will, when you run your script through Script Editor, display a line describing every Apple Event generated by your code (if the window's Show Events checkbox is activated, as it is by default) interspersed with the events' return values (if the Show Event Results box is checked). See Figure 16-3.

AppleScript Studio

AppleScript Studio is a set of software libraries that marries AppleScript with the the Project Builder and Interface Builder development tools (described in Chapter 15), allowing you to build Cocoa applications with full Aqua interfaces that use AppleScript source code.

Starting with Version 10.2, the Developer Tools suite comes with AppleScript Studio. In fact, (by virtue of alphabetical ordering) AppleScript applications show up at the top of the list of project types in Project Builder's New Project window (see "Project Types" in Chapter 15).

You can find a full reference to AppleScript studio programming at */Developer/ Documentation/CoreTechnologies/AppleScriptStudio/index.html*. However, if you already understand how to program Cocoa or Carbon applications with Project Builder and Interface Builder, there isn't a whole lot more to learn. The following describes the basic differences between AppleScript Studio programming and ordinary Cocoa programming.

AppleScript

Figure 16-3. A brief AppleScript and its Event Log

AppleScript source

Instead of Objective-C object classes, AppleScript Studio applications have AppleScripts make up their source code. However, like any other Cocoa application's sources, these script files aren't programs unto themselves; they instead define methods (verbs, through AppleScript's on *verbname* syntax), some of which must bear the responsibility for UI event handlers. As with any Aqua application, a typical AppleScript Studio application spends most of its time in an idle loop, running its methods only when some user-directed event occurs.

Scripts in the source can use AppleScript's script *scriptname* syntax to define subscripts that play the same role as object classes in other Cocoa applications.

Note that there's still a *main.m* file, written in Objective-C—as with ordinary Cocoa development, you can almost always get away with using the *main.m* that Project Builder provides for you, unmodified.

Interface connections

In Interface Builder, you build connections between message-sending interface objects (such as buttons) and the AppleScript handlers they trigger.

However, AppleScript Studio doesn't use the concept of outlets like Objective-C cocoa applications do. Instead of defining outlet objects in the window controller class that represent interface elements (such a pop-up menu it may wish to get information from when the user clicks a button), AppleScript Studio window controllers simply give you access to an entire window object, from which you can access any contained element through the usual AppleScript syntax.

Scripting the Terminal

As Chapter 19 describes, the Terminal application doesn't *do* anything so much as it provides a command-line interface to Darwin, the Unix system running underneath Mac OS X's GUI layers. AppleScript reflects this by offering only one real Terminal-scripting command: do script. If you tell the Terminal application do script *some_command*, then the Terminal acts as if you had invoked *some_command* by typing it on the command line.

For example, here is an alternate way to send someone email through an Apple-Script, going through the Darwin's *mail* command (via the Terminal) instead of the Mail application (assuming that you have a mail server running locally):

```
set theMessage to "Hi, Mom!"
tell application "Terminal"
    do script "echo '" & theMessage & "' | mail mom@jmac.org"
end tell
```

Another level of scripting the Terminal involves using any of the Unix scripting languages that ship with Mac OS X, including Perl, Python, and Ruby. These languages can be used for tasks ranging from simple glue between Darwin programs to acting as full-fledged applications in their own right.

Unfortunately, one can't learn these languages by a little bit of guided stumbling, as one can use to start playing with AppleScript (see "The Five-Minute Guide to AppleScript" earlier in this chapter). That said, they're high-level languages that are not very difficult to pick up, and your Mac includes full documentation for each by way of the Terminal's *man* command. (For example, *man perl*.) It's likely worth your while to gain some fluency in at least one of these interpreted, Darwin-level languages (see "Programming Languages" in Chapter 15 for a little bit of comparative analysis), since they let you write very powerful and general-purpose programs in very little time. (They aren't geared toward writing Aqua applications, though; for that, turn to Project Builder, and the languages it uses, particularly Objective-C. See Chapter 15.)

Note that you can use both kinds of Terminal scripting together. If you write a Perl program to accomplish some task, for example, you can then call it as part of a larger AppleScript script through the Terminal's do script function.

17

Text Editing on Mac OS X

Like all Unix systems, Mac OS X is driven by its text files. Between various programs' text-based configuration and preference files (often rendered in XML), program source code, the Makefiles, and source code of freshly downloaded software, it pays to know your options with opening, editing, and creating text files.

This chapter covers Mac OS X's attitude toward text files and the many editors it includes to help you create and edit them.

Types of Text Files

By *text file*, we usually mean a file that contains text characters and nothing else—not even graphics or formatting information. Every byte found in a text file represents either a text character or (with Unicode or other multibyte character encodings) a piece of one.

Mac OS X makes this notion a little fuzzy by its native handling of RTF, which (at least on the Aqua layer, through the Finder) it handles as smoothly as plain text. In fact, many Aqua applications favor using RTF over plain text unless you specifically request otherwise.

.txt files
> The Finder recognizes *.txt* files, associating them with TextEdit by default (see "TextEdit," later in this chapter).

unlabeled files
> Text files that lack recognizable filename extensions or resource forks fall into this category. The vast majority of text files used by Mac OS X's Unix layer go unrecognized by the topmost Aqua layer; by default, double-clicking one of these file's undecorated icons results in the dialog shown in Figure 17-1.
>
> In one sense, it's rather a moot point, since you'll usually use the Terminal to work with these "Unix-space" files, where Finder icons and file-to-application mappings don't matter. That said, it may still be nice to have the option

Figure 17-1. The Finder lacking a file-to-application mapping

of easily opening these files from the Finder if you want to. You can accomplish this by assigning an application to this file type (or lack thereof) through the Get Info window, as shown in Figure 6-1.

The Finder is smart enough to tell the difference between unlabeled text and binary files, so that, even if you set up this mapping, double-clicking on Unix executables (such as the many programs in */usr/bin*, all of which show up as documents in the Finder) still results in the "There is no default application..." dialog.

.plist files

Property list files, often in XML. The section "Property Lists," later in this chapter, describes these in detail.

.rtf files

RTF stands for *Rich Text Format*, an open standard[*] for formatted text—that is, text mixed with *text attributes* (such as font, size, and color) and *formatting information* (such as margin width and edge justification).

The Finder also recognizes *.rtfd* files, which are actually not files at all but bundled directories that contain RTF documents with image references, as well as the images themselves. Applications that know how to deal with RTFD, such as TextEdit, render them as single documents with inline images.

.html files

HTML files hold web pages, viewable in a browser such as Internet Explorer.

To view (and edit) the underlying source—the raw, tagged-up text—of an HTML file, open it in a text editor instead of a web browser.

---

[*] RTF is currently maintained by Microsoft, who publishes the complete standard at *http://msdn. microsoft.com/library/en-us/dnrtfspec/html/rtfspec.asp?frame=true*.

Text Editing

When in the Terminal, you can use Darwin's *file* command to get information about text files and other documents, like so:

```
[jmac@wireless251 Documents]% file story.sav XSLTquickref.
pdf hackers
story.sav:        IFF data
XSLTquickref.pdf: PDF document, version 1.2
hackers:          English text
[jmac@wireless251 Documents]%
```

It works by examine the file's name, filesystem attributes, and content, comparing what it finds to information found in its configuration file, */etc/magic*. This system is not connected to the Finder's methods for opening files as described in Chapter 2, however. It exists mainly for use by the lower BSD layer of Mac OS X, including scripts that run on this level.

Property Lists

A *property list* is a text file that stores some arbitrary lists of information in a standard format. It's most often used by the Mac OS X defaults system (as described in Chapter 22). Some applications use the format for other purposes; Omni Software's OmniOutliner, for example, uses the property list format for all of its documents (though they have their own extension, *.ooutline*, and hence system identity, apart from *.plist* files).

Most property lists these days are in XML format, adhering to a property list DTD file found at */System/Library/DTDs/PropertyList.dtd*.

Because it's plain text, you can edit a property list with any editor covered in this chapter (and every other plain-text editor, too). Because it's XML, you can open and edit a property list file with any general XML editing program. Under */Developer/Applications* you'll find the Property List Editor application, which lets you browse and edit these files with a hierarchical view, as Figure 9-2 shows.

Property lists may be easy to edit, but watch where you step. Making changes to the sole copy of a file that an application uses for preferences storage, for example, might end up corrupting that file, either through breaking the XML or just inserting values that the application doesn't expect or know how to handle.

Consider using only the *defaults* command, detailed in Chapter 22, to adjust property lists that control application or system behaviors. (This is assuming that you want to make adjustments unavailable through more obvious channels, such as the System Preferences application or individual applications' *Applications* → *Preferences* dialogs.)

Graphical Text Editors

Aqua's default text view, found in nearly every Cocoa application that involves text entry, is laden with a wide and predictable range of features. For a core OS service, the standard Aqua textbox gives you some fairly sophisticated editing tools.

About XML and Mac OS X

XML, the *Extensible Markup Language*, is a very simple and flexible set of rules for marking up electronic documents to lend an extra layer of meaning to the things they contain, mainly through the use of ubiquitous, angle-bracketed tags that most people probably associate with HTML (an older cousin of XML). XML is itself not a markup language, but a way to create markup languages to suit various purposes; the magic comes from the fact that all these languages follow the same standardized rules, and thus make it easy for a computer program to parse, pulling apart into meaningful, labeled chunks for further processing. The fact that XML tags are all in plain English (or some other equally plain language) means that a human reading through a well-designed XML document can also discern its structure with no great difficulty, whether the information stored within the tags is plain text or unreadable binary data.

Mac OS X property lists are an example of an *XML application*, a markup language written according to XML's rules. This book is another, written as it is in *DocBook*, an XML-based language for creating technical documentation. A third is *SOAP*, a protocol for wrapping up interprocess method calls in easy-to-parse XML envelopes before sending them over a network.

First of all, there's a myriad of undocumented keystrokes you can use to quickly move your cursor around, besides the obvious use of the arrow keys, or the even more obvious (and time-consuming) use of the mouse. These have been variously cribbed from Microsoft Word, NeXTSTEP, and even the *Emacs* text editor. (In this table, a "line" means a single row of text as it appears in the window, and a "paragraph" means any number of rows, bound on either end by either a hard carriage return or the start or end of the text area.)

Key command	Action
⌘- ←, Control- ←	Move the cursor to the beginning of the line.
⌘- →, Control- →	Move the cursor to the end of the line.
Control-A	Move the cursor to the start of the paragraph.
Control-E	Move the cursor to the end of the paragraph.
Option-↑	Move the cursor up one paragraph.
Option-↓	Move the cursor down one paragraph.
Option- →	Move the cursor right one word.
Option- ←	Move the cursor left one word.
Control-D	Delete the character to the right of the cursor.
Option-Delete	Delete the word to the left of the cursor.
Control-K	"Kill" (delete but remember) all text from the cursor to the end of the paragraph.
Control-Y	Insert the most recently "killed" lines at cursor's current location.
Control-L	Center the view upon the cursor's current location.

Secondly, text views commonly come paired with some interesting menu options, including the Find, Spelling, and Speech options in the application's Edit menu,

Text Editing

as well as all kinds of goodies inside the Format menu, such as the Font panel and Text alignment options (all of them often stick to the same standards among different applications).

TextEdit

TextEdit is the default graphical text editor for Mac OS X, replacing Simple Text from Mac OS 9. As Figure 17-2 shows, it offers a lot of settings for fine-tuning the application's document-handling behavior.

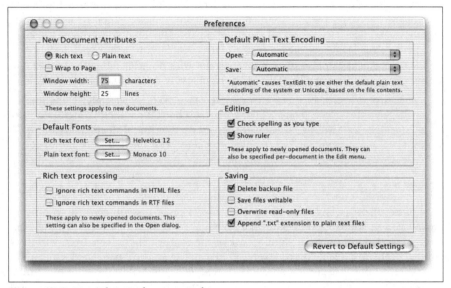

Figure 17-2. TextEdit's Preferences window

If you prefer to work mostly with plain text, consider selecting the Plain text radio button from the application's Preferences window, as well as activating the Ignore rich text commands in HTML files checkbox, which prevents TextEdit from rendering HTML documents that you open, instead displaying them as plain text. Relatedly, if you ever use TextEdit to edit or create anything other than *.txt* files, you may wish to deactivate the "Append ".txt" extension to plain files" checkbox.

Unix Text Editors

For years, two text editors have held equal sway in Unix culture: *vi* and *Emacs*. Not one to take sides, Mac OS X ships with both of them. The following two sections give you a whirlwind tour of both.

You don't have to use one of these editors in order to open a text document from a Terminal window. You can instead use the *open* command with its *-a* (application-specifying) option to send the document to an Aqua text editor, such as TextEdit, like this:

```
% open -a TextExit somefile.txt
```

vi

vi is a *modal* editor, signifying that the meaning of what you type at any point depends entirely on what mode (context) the program is in. *vi*'s modes include *command mode* (see the later section "Command mode"), which performs deletion, cut-and-paste, searching, and other text-editing commands, and *insertion mode*, which adds new text to the document through typing.

Command-line syntax

The three most common ways of starting a *vi* session are:

- vi *file*
- vi +*line-number file*
- vi +/*pattern file*

You can open *file* for editing, optionally at line *n* or at the first line matching *pattern*. (See Chapter 20 for more on pattern matching.) If no *file* is specified, *vi* opens with an empty buffer. See Chapter 25 for more information on command-line options for *vi*.

Command mode

Once the file is opened, you are in command mode. From here, you can:

- Invoke an insert mode
- Issue editing commands
- Move the cursor to a different position in the file
- Invoke ex commands
- Invoke a Unix shell
- Save or exit the current version of the file

Insert mode

In insert mode, you can enter new text in the file. Press the Escape key to exit insert mode and return to command mode. The following commands invoke insert mode:

Key command	Action
a	Append after cursor.
A	Append at end of line.
c	Begin change operation.
C	Change to end of line.
i	Insert before cursor.
I	Insert at beginning of line.
o	Open a line below current line.
O	Open a line above current line.

Text Editing

Key command	Action
R	Begin overwriting text.
s	Substitute a character.
S	Substitute entire line.

Syntax of vi commands

In *vi*, commands have the following general form:

[*n*] *operator* [*m*] *object*

The basic editing *operators* are:

Key command	Action
c	Begin a change.
d	Begin a deletion.
y	Begin a yank (or copy).

If the current line is the object of the operation, the object is the same as the operator: cc, dd, yy. Otherwise, the editing operators act on objects specified by cursor-movement commands or pattern-matching commands. *n* and *m* are the number of times the operation is performed or the number of objects the operation is performed on. If both *n* and *m* are specified, the effect is *n m*.

An object can represent any of the following text blocks:

Object	Action
word	Includes characters up to a whitespace character (space or tab) or punctuation mark. A capitalized object is a variant form that recognizes only whitespace.
sentence	Is up to ., !, or ?, followed by two spaces.
paragraph	Is up to next blank line or paragraph macro defined by the para= option.
section	Is up to next section heading defined by the sect= option.

Examples

Key command	Action
2cw	Change the next two words.
d}	Delete up to next paragraph.
d^	Delete back to beginning of line.
5yy	Copy the next five lines.
y]]	Copy up to the next section.

Status-line commands

Most commands are not echoed on the screen as you input them. However, the status line at the bottom of the screen is used to echo input for these commands:

Key command	Action
/	Search forward for a pattern.
?	Search backward for a pattern.
:	Invoke an ex command.
!	Invoke a Unix command that takes as its input an object in the buffer and replaces it with output from the command.

Commands that are input on the status line must be entered by pressing the Return key. In addition, error messages and output from the CTRL-G command are displayed on the status line.

Movement Commands

A number preceding a command repeats the movement. Movement commands are also objects for change, delete, and yank operations.

Character

Key command	Action
h, j, k, l	Left, down, up, right ($\leftarrow$, $\downarrow$, $\uparrow$, $\rightarrow$).
Spacebar	Right.

Text

Key command	Action
w, W, b, B	Forward, backward by word.
e, E	End of word.
), (	Beginning of next, current sentence.
}, {	Beginning of next, current paragraph.
]], [[	Beginning of next, current section.

Lines

Key command	Action
0, $	First, last position of current line.
^	First nonblank character of current line.
+, -	First character of next, previous line.
Return	First character of next line.
$n\|$	Column n of current line.
H	Top line of screen.
M	Middle line of screen.
L	Last line of screen.
nH	n lines after top line.
nL	n lines before last line.

Text Editing

Screens

Key command	Action
CTRL-F CTRL-B	Scroll forward, backward one screen.
CTRL-D CTRL-U	Scroll down, up one-half screen.
CTRL-E CTRL-Y	Show one more line at bottom, top of window.
z Return	Reposition line with cursor to top of screen.
z.	Reposition line with cursor to middle of screen.
z-	Reposition line with cursor to bottom of screen.
CTRL-R	Redraw screen (without scrolling).

Searches

Key command	Action
/text	Search forward for text.
n	Repeat previous search.
N	Repeat search in opposite direction.
/	Repeat forward search.
?	Repeat previous search backward.
?text	Search backward for text.
/text/+n	Go to line n after text.
?text?-n	Go to line n before text.
%	Find match of current parenthesis, brace, or bracket.
fx	Move search forward to x on current line.
Fx	Move search backward to x on current line.
tx	Search forward to character before x in current line.
Tx	Search backward to character after x in current line.
,	Reverse search direction of last f, F, t, or T.
;	Repeat last character search (f, F, t, or T).

Line numbering

Key command	Action
CTRL-G	Display current line number.
nG	Move to line number n.

Key command	Action
G	Move to last line in file.
:*n*	Move to line number *n*.

Marking position

Key command	Action
m*x*	Mark current position with character *x*.
x	Move cursor to mark *x*.
'*x*	Move to start of line containing *x*.
``	Return to previous mark (or to location prior to a search).
''	Like above, but return to start of line.

Edit Commands

Recall that c, d, and y are the basic editing operators.

Inserting new text

Key command	Action
a	Append after cursor.
A	Append to end of line.
i	Insert before cursor.
I	Insert at beginning of line.
o	Open a line below cursor.
O	Open a line above cursor.
Esc	Terminate insert mode.
CTRL-J	Move down one line.
Return	Move down one line.
CTRL-I	Insert a tab.
CTRL-T	Move to next tab setting.
Backspace	Move back one character.
CTRL-H	Move back one character.
CTRL-U	Delete current line.
CTRL-V	Quote next character.
CTRL-W	Move back one word.

Changing and deleting text

Key command	Action
cw	Change word.
cc	Change line.
C	Change text from current position to end of line.

Key command	Action
dd	Delete current line.
ndd	Delete n lines.
D	Delete remainder of line.
dw	Delete a word.
d}	Delete up to next paragraph.
d^	Delete back to beginning of line.
d/pat	Delete up to first occurrence of pattern.
dn	Delete up to next occurrence of pattern.
dfa	Delete up to and including a on current line.
dta	Delete up to (but not including) a on current line.
dL	Delete up to last line on screen.
dG	Delete to end of file.
p	Insert last deleted text after cursor.
P	Insert last deleted text before cursor.
rx	Replace character with x.
Rtext	Replace with new text (overwrite), beginning at cursor.
s	Substitute character.
4s	Substitute four characters.
S	Substitute entire line.
u	Undo last change.
U	Restore current line.
x	Delete current cursor position.
X	Delete back one character.
5X	Delete previous five characters.
.	Repeat last change.
~	Reverse case.

Copying and moving

Key command	Action
Y	Copy current line to new buffer.
yy	Copy current line.
"xyy	Yank current line to buffer x.
"xd	Delete into buffer x.
"Xd	Delete and append into buffer x.
"xp	Put contents of buffer x.
y]]	Copy up to next section heading.
ye	Copy to end of word.

Buffer names are the letters az. Uppercase names append text to the specified buffer.

Saving and Exiting

Writing a file means saving the edits and updating the file's modification time.

Key command	Action
ZZ	Quit *vi*, writing the file only if changes were made.
:x	Same as ZZ.
:wq	Write and quit file.
:w	Write file.
:w *file*	Save copy to *file*.
:*n,m*w *file*	Write lines *n* to *m* to new *file*.
:*n,m*w >> *file*	Append lines *n* to *m* to existing *file*.
:w!	Write file (overriding protection).
:w! *file*	Overwrite *file* with current buffer.
:w %.*new*	Write current buffer named *file* as *file.new*.
:q	Quit *vi*.
:q!	Quit *vi* (discarding edits).
Q	Quit *vi* and invoke ex.
:vi	Return to *vi* after Q command.
:e *file2*	Edit *file2* without leaving *vi*.
:n	Edit next file.
:e!	Return to version of current file at time of last write.
:e #	Edit alternate file.
%	Current filename.
#	Alternate filename.

Accessing Multiple Files

Key command	Action
:e *file*	Edit another *file*; current file becomes alternate.
:e!	Return to version of current file at time of last write.
:e +*file*	Begin editing at end of *file*.
:e +*n file*	Open *file* at line *n*.
:e #	Open to previous position in alternate file.
:ta *tag*	Edit file at location *tag*.
:n	Edit next file.
:n!	Force next file.
:n *files*	Specify new list of *files*.
CTRL-G	Show current file and line number.

Key command	Action
:args	Display multiple files to be edited.
:rew	Rewind list of multiple files to top.

Interacting with Unix

Key command	Action
:r *file*	Read in contents of *file* after cursor.
:r !*command*	Read in output from *command* after current line.
:*n*r !*command*	Like above, but place after line *n* (0 for top of file).
:!*command*	Run *command*, then return.
!*object command*	Send buffer *object* to Unix *command*; replace with output.
:*n,m*! *command*	Send lines *nm* to *command*; replace with output.
n!!*command*	Send *n* lines to Unix *command*; replace with output.
!!	Repeat last system command.
:sh	Create subshell; return to file with *EOF*.
CTRL-Z	Suspend editor, resume with fg.
:so *file*	Read and execute ex commands from *file*.

Macros

Key command	Action
:ab *in out*	Use *in* as abbreviation for *out*.
:unab *in*	Remove abbreviation for *in*.
:ab	List abbreviations.
:map *c sequence*	Map character *c* as *sequence* of commands.
:unmap *c*	Remove map for character *c*.
:map	List characters that are mapped.
:map! *c sequence*	Map character *c* to input mode *sequence*.
:unmap! *c*	Remove input mode map (you may need to quote the character with CTRL-V).
:map!	List characters that are mapped for input mode.

The following characters are unused in command mode and can be mapped as user-defined commands:

Letters
    g K q V v
Control keys
    ^A ^K ^O ^W ^X
Symbols
    _ * =

Miscellaneous Commands

Key command	Action
J	Join two lines.
:j!	Join two lines, preserving whitespace.
<<	Shift this line left one shift width (default is eight spaces).
>>	Shift this line right one shift width (default is eight spaces).
>}	Shift right to end of paragraph.
<%	Shift left until matching parenthesis, brace, or bracket. (Cursor must be on the matching symbol.)

Alphabetical List of Keys

For brevity, control characters are marked by ^.

Key command	Action
^]	Perform a tag look-up on the text under the cursor.
a	Append text after cursor.
A	Append text at end of line.
^A	Unused.
b	Back up to beginning of word in current line.
B	Back up to beginning of word, ignoring punctuation.
^B	Scroll backward one window.
c	Change operator.
C	Change to end of current line.
^C	Unused in command mode; ends insert mode (stty interrupt character).
d	Delete operator.
D	Delete to end of current line.
^D	Scroll down half window (command mode). Move backward one tab stop (insert mode).
e	Move to end of word.
E	Move to end of word, ignoring punctuation.
^E	Show one more line at bottom of window.
f	Find next character typed forward on current line.
F	Find next character typed backward on current line.
^F	Scroll forward one window.
g	Unused.
G	Go to specified line or end of file.
^G	Print information about file on status line.
h	Left arrow cursor key.
H	Move cursor to Home position.
^H	Left arrow cursor key; Backspace key in insert mode.
i	Insert text before cursor.
I	Insert text before first nonblank character on line.
^I	Unused in command mode; in insert mode, same as Tab key.

Text Editing

Key command	Action
j	Down arrow cursor key.
J	Join two lines.
^J	Down arrow cursor key; in insert mode, move down a line.
k	Up arrow cursor key.
K	Unused.
^K	Unused.
l	Right arrow cursor key.
L	Move cursor to last position in window.
^L	Redraw screen.
m	Mark the current cursor position in register (az).
M	Move cursor to middle position in window.
^M	Carriage return.
n	Repeat the last search command.
N	Repeat the last search command in the reverse direction.
^N	Down arrow cursor key.
o	Open line below current line.
O	Open line above current line.
^O	Unused.
p	Put yanked or deleted text after or below cursor.
P	Put yanked or deleted text before or above cursor.
^P	Up arrow cursor key.
q	Unused.
Q	Quit *vi* and invoke ex.
^Q	Unused (on some terminals, resume data flow).
r	Replace character at cursor with the next character you type.
R	Replace characters.
^R	Redraw the screen.
s	Change the character under the cursor to typed characters.
S	Change entire line.
^S	Unused (on some terminals, stop data flow).
t	Move cursor forward to character before next character typed.
T	Move cursor backward to character after next character typed.
^T	Return to the previous location in the tag stack (Solaris *vi* command mode). If autoindent is set, indent another tab stop (insert mode).
u	Undo the last change made.
U	Restore current line, discarding changes.
^U	Scroll the screen upward half window.
v	Unused.
V	Unused.
^V	Unused in command mode; in insert mode, quote next character.
w	Move to beginning of next word.
W	Move to beginning of next word, ignoring punctuation.

Key command	Action
^W	Unused in command mode; in insert mode, back up to beginning of word.
x	Delete character under cursor.
X	Delete character before cursor.
^X	Unused.
y	Yank or copy operator.
Y	Make copy of current line.
^Y	Show one more line at top of window.
z	Reposition line containing cursor. z must be followed either by: Return (reposition line to top of screen), (reposition line to middle of screen), or (reposition line to bottom of screen).
ZZ	Exit the editor, saving changes.
^Z	Suspend *vi* (only works on systems that have job control).

Setting Up vi

This section describes the following:

- The :set command
- Options available with :set
- Example .exrc file

The :set command

The :set command allows you to specify options that change characteristics of your editing environment. Options may be put in the ~/.exrc file or set during a *vi* session.

The colon should not be typed if the command is put in .exrc:

Key command	Action
:set *x*	Enable option *x*.
:set no*x*	Disable option *x*.
:set *x=val*	Give *value* to option *x*.
:set	Show changed options.
:set all	Show all options.
:set *x?*	Show value of option *x*.

Options used by :set

Table 17-1 contains brief descriptions of the important :set command options. In the first column, options are listed in alphabetical order; if the option can be abbreviated, that abbreviation is shown in parentheses. The second column shows the default setting *vi* uses unless you issue an explicit :set command (either manually or in the .exrc file). The last column describes what the option does when enabled.

Table 17-1. :set options

Option	Default	Description
autoindent (ai)	noai	In insert mode, indent each line to the same level as the line above or below. Use with the *shiftwidth* option.
autoprint (ap)	ap	Display changes after each editor command. (For global replacement, display last replacement.)
autowrite (aw)	noaw	Automatically write (save) the file if changed before opening another file with : n or before giving Unix command with : !.
beautify (bf)	nobf	Ignore all control characters during input (except tab, newline, or formfeed).
directory (dir)	/tmp	Name directory in which ex/*vi* stores buffer files. (Directory must be writable.)
edcompatible	noedcompatible	Remember the flags used with the most recent substitute command (global, confirming) and use them for the next substitute command. Despite the name, no version of ed actually behaves this way.
errorbells (eb)	errorbells	Sound bell when an error occurs.
exrc (ex)	noexrc	Allow the execution of .exrc files that reside outside the user's home directory.
hardtabs (ht)	8	Define boundaries for terminal hardware tabs.
ignorecase (ic)	noic	Disregard case during a search.
lisp	nolisp	Insert indents in appropriate Lisp format. ( ), { }, [[, and]] are modified to have meaning for Lisp.
list	nolist	Print tabs as ^I; mark ends of lines with $. (Use *list* to tell if end character is a tab or a space.)
magic	magic	Wildcard characters . (dot), * (asterisk), and [ ] (brackets) have special meaning in patterns.
mesg	mesg	Permit system messages to display on terminal while editing in *vi*.
novice	nonovice	Require the use of long ex command names, such as *copy* or *read*.
number (nu)	nonu	Display line numbers on left of screen during editing session.
open	open	Allow entry to *open* or *visual* mode from ex. Although not in Solaris *vi*, this option has traditionally been in *vi*, and may be in your Unix's version of *vi*.
optimize (opt)	noopt	Abolish carriage returns at the end of lines when printing multiple lines; speed output on dumb terminals when printing lines with leading whitespace (spaces or tabs).
paragraphs (para)	IPLPPPQP LIpplpipbp	Define paragraph delimiters for movement by { or }. The pairs of characters in the value are the names of troff macros that begin paragraphs.
prompt	prompt	Display the ex prompt (:) when *vi*'s Q command is given.
readonly (ro)	noro	Any writes (saves) of a file fail unless you use ! after the write (works with *w*, *ZZ*, or *autowrite*).
redraw (re)		*vi* redraws the screen whenever edits are made (in other words, insert mode pushes over existing characters, and deleted lines immediately close up). Default depends on line speed and terminal type. *noredraw* is useful at slow speeds on a dumb terminal: deleted lines show up as @, and inserted text appears to overwrite existing text until you press Esc.
remap	remap	Allow nested map sequences.
report	5	Display a message on the status line whenever you make an edit that affects at least a certain number of lines. For example, 6dd reports the message six lines deleted.

Table 17-1. :set options (continued)

Option	Default	Description
scroll	[*window*]	Number of lines to scroll with ^D and ^U commands.
sections (sect)	SHNHH HU	Define section delimiters for [[and]] movement. The pairs of characters in the value are the names of troff macros that begin sections.
shell (sh)	/bin/sh	Pathname of shell used for shell escape (: !) and shell command (:*sh*). Default value is derived from the shell environment, which varies on different systems.
shiftwidth (sw)	8	Define number of spaces in backward (^D) tabs when using the *autoindent* option, and for the << and >> commands.
showmatch (sm)	nosm	In *vi*, when) or } is entered, cursor moves briefly to matching (or {. (If there is no match, the cursor rings the error message bell.) Very useful for programming.
showmode	noshowmode	In insert mode, display a message on the prompt line indicating the type of insert you are making. For example, OPEN MODE or APPEND MODE.
slowopen (slow)		Hold off display during insert. Default depends on line speed and terminal type.
tabstop (ts)	8	Define number of spaces a tab indents during editing session. (Printer still uses system tab of 8.)
taglength (tl)	0	Define number of characters that are significant for tags. Default (zero) means that all characters are significant.
tags	*tags /usr/lib/tags*	Define pathname of files containing tags. (See the Unix *ctags* command.) (By default, *vi* searches the file tags in the current directory and in */usr/lib/tags*.)
tagstack	tagstack	Enable stacking of tag locations on a stack.
term		Set terminal type.
terse	noterse	Display shorter error messages.
timeout (to)	timeout	Keyboard maps time out after one second.[a]
ttytype		Set terminal type. This is just another name for *term*.
warn	warn	Display the warning message, No write since last change.
window (w)		Show a certain number of lines of the file on the screen. Default depends on line speed and terminal type.
wrapscan (ws)	ws	Searches wrap around either end of file.
wrapmargin (wm)	0	Define right margin. If greater than zero, automatically insert carriage returns to break lines.
writeany (wa)	nowa	Allow saving to any file.

[a] When you have mappings of several keys (for example, :map zzz 3dw), you probably want to use *notimeout*. Otherwise, you need to type zzz within one second. When you have an insert mode mapping for a cursor key (for example, :map! ^[OB ^[ja), you should use *timeout*. Otherwise, *vi* won't react to Esc until you type another key.

Example .exrc file

```
set nowrapscan wrapmargin=7
set sections=SeAhBhChDh nomesg
map q :w^M:n^M
map v dwElp
ab ORA O'Reilly & Associates, Inc.
```

Text Editing

Emacs

Mac OS X (as of Version 10.2) ships with Version 21.1 of GNU Emacs, the Free Software extensible text editor; see "Extending Emacs," later in this chapter, to learn more about its many editing modes and its customizability.

To start an *emacs* editing session, type:

```
emacs file
```

Notes on the tables

emacs commands use the Control key and the Meta key—a system-neutral way of describing a function-changing modifier key. On a Mac, this corresponds to the Option key. (This behavior is set through the Terminal applications' preferences—see Chapter 19.)

In this chapter, the notation C- indicates that the Control key is pressed at the same time as the character that follows. Similarly, M- indicates the use of the Meta, or Option key on Mac OS X: either hold Option while typing the next character, *or* press and release the Escape key followed by the next character.

In the command tables that follow, the first column lists the keystroke and the last column describes it. When there is a middle column, it lists the command name. This name is accessed by typing M-x, followed by the command name. If you're unsure of the name, you can type a space or a carriage return, and *emacs* lists possible completions of what you've typed so far.

Because *emacs* is such a comprehensive editor, containing literally thousands of commands, some commands must be omitted for the sake of preserving a quick reference. You can browse the command set by typing C-h (for help) or M-x (for command names).

Absolutely essential commands

If you're just getting started with *emacs*, here's a short list of the most important commands:

Keystrokes	Description
C-h	Enter the online help system.
C-x C-s	Save the file.
C-x C-c	Exit *emacs*.
C-x u	Undo last edit (can be repeated).
C-g	Get out of current command operation.
C-p	Up by line or character.
C-n	Down by line or character.
C-f	Forward by line or character.
C-b	Back by line or character.
C-v	Forward by one screen.
M-v	Backward by one screen.

Keystrokes	Description
C-s	Search forward for characters.
C-r	Search backward for characters.
C-d	Delete next character.
Del	Delete previous character.

Summary of Commands by Group

Reminder: C- indicates the Control key; M- indicates the Meta key.

File-handling commands

Keystrokes	Command name	Description
C-x C-f	find-file	Find file and read it.
C-x C-v	find-alternate-file	Read another file; replace the one read with C-x C-f.
C-x i	insert-file	Insert file at cursor position.
C-x C-s	save-buffer	Save file (may hang terminal; use C-q to restart).
C-x C-w	write-file	Write buffer contents to file.
C-x C-c	save-buffers-kill-emacs	Exit *emacs*.
C-z	suspend-emacs	Suspend *emacs* (use *exit* or *fg* to restart).

Cursor-movement commands

Keystrokes	Command name	Description
C-f	forward-char	Move forward one character (right).
C-b	backward-char	Move backward one character (left).
C-p	previous-line	Move to previous line (up).
C-n	next-line	Move to next line (down).
M-f	forward-word	Move one word forward.
M-b	backward-word	Move one word backward.
C-a	beginning-of-line	Move to beginning of line.
C-e	end-of-line	Move to end of line.
M-a	backward-sentence	Move backward one sentence.
M-e	forward-sentence	Move forward one sentence.
M-{	backward-paragraph	Move backward one paragraph.
M-}	forward-paragraph	Move forward one paragraph.
C-v	scroll-up	Move forward one screen.
M-v	scroll-down	Move backward one screen.
C-x [	backward-page	Move backward one page.
C-x]	forward-page	Move forward one page.
M->	end-of-buffer	Move to end of file.
M-<	beginning-of-buffer	Move to beginning of file.
(none)	goto-line	Go to line *n* of file.
(none)	goto-char	Go to character *n* of file.

Keystrokes	Command name	Description
C-l	recenter	Redraw screen with current line in the center.
M-*n*	digit-argument	Repeat the next command *n* times.
C-u *n*	universal-argument	Repeat the next command *n* times.

Deletion commands

Keystrokes	Command name	Description
Del	backward-delete-char	Delete previous character.
C-d	delete-char	Delete character under cursor.
M-Del	backward-kill-word	Delete previous word.
M-d	kill-word	Delete the word the cursor is on.
C-k	kill-line	Delete from cursor to end of line.
M-k	kill-sentence	Delete sentence the cursor is on.
C-x Del	backward-kill-sentence	Delete previous sentence.
C-y	yank	Restore what you've deleted.
C-w	kill-region	Delete a marked region (see next table).
(none)	backward-kill-paragraph	Delete previous paragraph.
(none)	kill-paragraph	Delete from the cursor to the end of the paragraph.

Paragraphs and regions

Keystrokes	Command name	Description
C-@	set-mark-command	Mark the beginning (or end) of a region.
C-Space	(same as above)	
C-x C-p	mark-page	Mark page.
C-x C-x	exchange-point-and-mark	Exchange location of cursor and mark.
C-x h	mark-whole-buffer	Mark buffer.
M-q	fill-paragraph	Reformat paragraph.
(none)	fill-region	Reformat individual paragraphs within a region.
M-h	mark-paragraph	Mark paragraph.

Stopping and undoing commands

Keystrokes	Command name	Description
C-g	keyboard-quit	Abort current command.
C-x u	advertised-undo	Undo last edit (can be done repeatedly).
(none)	revert-buffer	Restore buffer to the state it was in when the file was last saved (or auto-saved).

Transposition commands

Keystrokes	Command name	Description
C-t	transpose-chars	Transpose two letters.
M-t	transpose-words	Transpose two words.
C-x C-t	transpose-lines	Transpose two lines.
(none)	transpose-sentences	Transpose two sentences.
(none)	transpose-paragraphs	Transpose two paragraphs.

Capitalization commands

Keystrokes	Command name	Description
M-c	capitalize-word	Capitalize first letter of word.
M-u	upcase-word	Uppercase word.
M-l	downcase-word	Lowercase word.
M-; M-c	negative-argument; capitalize-word	Capitalize previous word.
M- M-u	negative-argument; upcase-word	Uppercase previous word.
M- M-l	negative-argument; downcase-word	Lowercase previous word.
(none)	capitalize-region	Capitalize region.
C-x C-u	upcase-region	Uppercase region.
C-x C-l	downcase-region	Lowercase region.

Word-abbreviation commands

Keystrokes	Command name	Description
(none)	abbrev-mode	Enter (or exit) word abbreviation mode.
C-x a i g	inverse-add-global-abbrev	Type global abbreviation, then definition.
C-x a i l	inverse-add-local-abbrev	Type local abbreviation, then definition.
(none)	unexpand-abbrev	Undo the last word abbreviation.
(none)	write-abbrev-file	Write the word abbreviation file.
(none)	edit-abbrevs	Edit the word abbreviations.
(none)	list-abbrevs	View the word abbreviations.
(none)	kill-all-abbrevs	Kill abbreviations for this session.

Buffer-manipulation commands

Keystrokes	Command name	Description
C-x b	switch-to-buffer	Move to specified buffer.
C-x C-b	list-buffers	Display buffer list.
C-x k	kill-buffer	Delete specified buffer.
(none)	kill-some-buffers	Ask about deleting each buffer.

Keystrokes	Command name	Description
(none)	rename-buffer	Change buffer name to specified name.
C-x s	save-some-buffers	Ask whether to save each modified buffer.

Window commands

Keystrokes	Command name	Description
C-x 2	split-window-vertically	Divide the current window into two, one on top of the other.
C-x 3	split-window-horizontally	Divide the current window into two, side by side.
C-x >	scroll-right	Scroll the window right.
C-x <	scroll-left	Scroll the window left.
C-x o	other-window	Move to the other window.
C-x 0	delete-window	Delete current window.
C-x 1	delete-other-windows	Delete all windows but this one.
(none)	delete-windows-on	Delete all windows on a given buffer.
C-x ^	enlarge-window	Make window taller.
(none)	shrink-window	Make window shorter.
C-x }	enlarge-window-horizontally	Make window wider.
C-x {	shrink-window-horizontally	Make window narrower.
M-C-v	scroll-other-window	Scroll other window.
C-x 4 f	find-file-other-window	Find a file in the other window.
C-x 4 b	switch-to-buffer-other-window	Select a buffer in the other window.
C-x 5 f	find-file-other-frame	Find a file in a new frame.
C-x 5 b	switch-to-buffer-other-frame	Select a buffer in another frame.
(none)	compare-windows	Compare two buffers; show first difference.

Special shell characters

Keystrokes	Command name	Description
C-c C-c	comint-interrupt-subjob	Terminate the current job.
C-c C-d	comint-send-eof	End-of-file character.
C-c C-u	comint-kill-input	Erase current line.
C-c C-w	backward-kill-word	Erase the previous word.
C-c C-z	comint-stop-subjob	Suspend the current job.

Indentation commands

Keystrokes	Command name	Description
C-x .	set-fill-prefix	Use characters from the beginning of the line up to the cursor column as the fill prefix. This prefix is prepended to each line in the paragraph. Cancel the prefix by typing this command in Column 1.
(none)	indented-text-mode	Major mode: each tab defines a new indent for subsequent lines.
(none)	text-mode	Exit indented text mode; return to text mode.
M-C-	indent-region	Indent a region to match first line in region.

Keystrokes	Command name	Description
M-m	back-to-indentation	Move cursor to first character on line.
M-C-o	split-line	Split line at cursor; indent to column of cursor.
(none)	fill-individual-paragraphs	Reformat indented paragraphs, keeping indentation.

Centering commands

Keystrokes	Command name	Description
M-s	center-line	Center line that cursor is on.
(none)	center-paragraph	Center paragraph that cursor is on.
(none)	center-region	Center currently defined region.

Macro commands

Keystrokes	Command name	Description
C-x (	start-kbd-macro	Start macro definition.
C-x)	end-kbd-macro	End macro definition.
C-x e	call-last-kbd-macro	Execute last macro defined.
M-n C-x e	digit-argument and call-last-kbd-macro	Execute last macro defined n times.
C-u C-x (	universal-argument and start-kbd-macro	Execute last macro defined, then add keystrokes.
(none)	name-last-kbd-macro	Name last macro you created (before saving it).
(none)	insert-keyboard-macro	Insert the macro you named into a file.
(none)	load-file	Load macro files you've saved.
(none)	*macroname*	Execute a keyboard macro you've saved.
C-x q	kbd-macro-query	Insert a query in a macro definition.
C-u C-x q	(none)	Insert a recursive edit in a macro definition.
M-C-c	exit-recursive-edit	Exit a recursive edit.

Basic indentation commands

Keystrokes	Command name	Description
M-C-	indent-region	Indent a region to match first line in region.
M-m	back-to-indentation	Move to first nonblank character on line.
M-^	delete-indentation	Join this line to the previous one.

Detail information help commands

Keystrokes	Command name	Description
C-h a	command-apropos	What commands involve this concept?
(none)	apropos	What functions and variables involve this concept?
C-h c	describe-key-briefly	What command does this keystroke sequence run?
C-h b	describe-bindings	What are all the key bindings for this buffer?

Text Editing

Keystrokes	Command name	Description
C-h k	describe-key	What command does this keystroke sequence run, and what does it do?
C-h l	view-lossage	What are the last 100 characters I typed?
C-h w	where-is	What is the key binding for this command?
C-h f	describe-function	What does this function do?
C-h v	describe-variable	What does this variable mean, and what is its value?
C-h m	describe-mode	Tell me about the mode the current buffer is in.
C-h s	describe-syntax	What is the syntax table for this buffer?

Help commands

Keystrokes	Command name	Description
C-h t	help-with-tutorial	Run the *emacs* tutorial.
C-h i	info	Start the Info documentation reader.
C-h n	view-emacs-news	View news about updates to *emacs*.
C-h C-c	describe-copying	View the *emacs* General Public License.
C-h C-d	describe-distribution	View information on ordering *emacs* from the FSF.
C-h C-w	describe-no-warranty	View the (non)warranty for *emacs*.

Summary of Commands by Key

Emacs commands are presented below in two alphabetical lists. Reminder: C- indicates the Control key; M- indicates the Meta or Option key.

Control-key sequences

Keystrokes	Command name	Description
C-@	set-mark-command	Mark the beginning (or end) of a region.
C-Space	(same as previous)	
C-]	(none)	Exit recursive edit and exit query-replace.
C-a	beginning-of-line	Move to beginning of line.
C-b	backward-char	Move backward one character (left).
C-c C-c	comint-interrupt-subjob	Terminate the current job.
C-c C-d	comint-send-eof	End-of-file character.
C-c C-u	comint-kill-input	Erase current line.
C-c C-w	backward-kill-word	Erase the previous word.
C-c C-z	comint-stop-subjob	Suspend the current job.
C-d	delete-char	Delete character under cursor.
C-e	end-of-line	Move to end of line.
C-f	forward-char	Move forward one character (right).
C-g	keyboard-quit	Abort current command.
C-h	help-command	Enter the online help system.
C-h a	command-apropos	What commands involve this concept?

Keystrokes	Command name	Description
C-h b	describe-bindings	What are all the key bindings for this buffer?
C-h C-c	describe-copying	View the *emacs* General Public License.
C-h C-d	describe-distribution	View information on ordering *emacs* from FSF.
C-h C-w	describe-no-warranty	View the (non)warranty for *emacs*.
C-h c	describe-key-briefly	What command does this keystroke sequence run?
C-h f	describe-function	What does this function do?
C-h i	info	Start the Info documentation reader.
C-h k	describe-key	What command does this keystroke sequence run, and what does it do?
C-h l	view-lossage	What are the last 100 characters I typed?
C-h m	describe-mode	Tell me about the mode the current buffer is in.
C-h n	view-emacs-news	View news about updates to *emacs*.
C-h s	describe-syntax	What is the syntax table for this buffer?
C-h t	help-with-tutorial	Run the *emacs* tutorial.
C-h v	describe-variable	What does this variable mean, and what is its value?
C-h w	where-is	What is the key binding for this command?
C-k	kill-line	Delete from cursor to end of line.
C-l	recenter	Redraw screen with current line in the center.
C-n	next-line	Move to next line (down).
C-p	previous-line	Move to previous line (up).
C-r Meta	(none)	Start nonincremental search backward.
C-r	(none)	Repeat nonincremental search backward.
C-r	(none)	Enter recursive edit (during query replace).
C-r	isearch-backward	Start incremental search backward.
C-s Meta	(none)	Start nonincremental search forward.
C-s	(none)	Repeat nonincremental search forward.
C-s	isearch-forward	Start incremental search forward.
C-t	transpose-chars	Transpose two letters.
C-u *n*	universal-argument	Repeat the next command *n* times.
C-u C-x (	universal-argument and start-kbd-macro	Execute last macro defined, then add keystrokes.
C-u C-x q	(none)	Insert recursive edit in a macro definition.
C-v	scroll-up	Move forward one screen.
C-w	kill-region	Delete a marked region.
C-x (	start-kbd-macro	Start macro definition.
C-x)	end-kbd-macro	End macro definition.
C-x [	backward-page	Move backward one page.
C-x]	forward-page	Move forward one page.
C-x ^	enlarge-window	Make window taller.
C-x {	shrink-window-horizontally	Make window narrower.
C-x }	enlarge-window-horizontally	Make window wider.
C-x <	scroll-left	Scroll the window left.
C-x >	scroll-right	Scroll the window right.

Keystrokes	Command name	Description
C-x .	set-fill-prefix	Use characters from the beginning of the line up to the cursor column as the fill prefix. This prefix is prepended to each line in the paragraph. Cancel the prefix by typing this command in column 1.
C-x 0	delete-window	Delete current window.
C-x 1	delete-other-windows	Delete all windows but this one.
C-x 2	split-window-vertically	Divide the current window into two, one on top of the other.
C-x 3	split-window-horizontally	Divide the current window into two, side by side.
C-x 4 b	switch-to-buffer-other-window	Select a buffer in the other window.
C-x 4 f	find-file-other-window	Find a file in the other window.
C-x 5 b	switch-to-buffer-other-frame	Select a buffer in another frame.
C-x 5 f	find-file-other-frame	Find a file in a new frame.
C-x C-b	list-buffers	Display the buffer list.
C-x C-c	save-buffers-kill-emacs	Exit *emacs*.
C-x C-f	find-file	Find file and read it.
C-x C-l	downcase-region	Lowercase region.
C-x C-p	mark-page	Mark page.
C-x C-q	(none)	Toggle read-only status of buffer.
C-x C-s	save-buffer	Save file (may hang terminal; use C-q to restart).
C-x C-t	transpose-lines	Transpose two lines.
C-x C-u	upcase-region	Uppercase region.
C-x C-v	find-alternate-file	Read an alternate file, replacing the one read with C-x C-f.
C-x C-w	write-file	Write buffer contents to file.
C-x C-x	exchange-point-and-mark	Exchange location of cursor and mark.
C-x DEL	backward-kill-sentence	Delete previous sentence.
C-x a i g	inverse-add-global-abbrev	Type global abbreviation, then definition.
C-x a i l	inverse-add-local-abbrev	Type local abbreviation, then definition.
C-x b	switch-to-buffer	Move to the buffer specified.
C-x e	call-last-kbd-macro	Execute last macro defined.
C-x h	mark-whole-buffer	Mark buffer.
C-x i	insert-file	Insert file at cursor position.
C-x k	kill-buffer	Delete the buffer specified.
C-x o	other-window	Move to the other window.
C-x q	kbd-macro-query	Insert a query in a macro definition.
C-x s	save-some-buffers	Ask whether to save each modified buffer.
C-x u	advertised-undo	Undo last edit (can be done repeatedly).
C-y	yank	Restore what you've deleted.
C-z	suspend-emacs	Suspend *emacs* (use *exit* or *fg* to restart).

Meta-key sequences

Keystrokes	Command name	Description
Meta	(none)	Exit a query-replace or successful search.
M- M-c	negative-argument; capitalize-word	Capitalize previous word.

Keystrokes	Command name	Description
M- M-l	negative-argument; downcase-word	Lowercase previous word.
M- M-u	negative-argument; upcase-word	Uppercase previous word.
M-$	spell-word	Check spelling of word after cursor.
M-<	beginning-of-buffer	Move to beginning of file.
M->	end-of-buffer	Move to end of file.
M-{	backward-paragraph	Move backward one paragraph.
M-}	forward-paragraph	Move forward one paragraph.
M-^	delete-indentation	Join this line to the previous one.
M-*n*	digit-argument	Repeat the next command *n* times.
M-*n* C-x e	digit-argument and call-last-kbd-macro	Execute the last defined macro *n* times.
M-a	backward-sentence	Move backward one sentence.
M-b	backward-word	Move one word backward.
M-C-	indent-region	Indent a region to match first line in region.
M-C-c	exit-recursive-edit	Exit a recursive edit.
M-C-o	split-line	Split line at cursor; indent to column of cursor.
M-C-v	scroll-other-window	Scroll other window.
M-c	capitalize-word	Capitalize first letter of word.
M-d	kill-word	Delete word that cursor is on.
M-DEL	backward-kill-word	Delete previous word.
M-e	forward-sentence	Move forward one sentence.
M-f	forward-word	Move one word forward.
(none)	fill-region	Reformat individual paragraphs within a region.
M-h	mark-paragraph	Mark paragraph.
M-k	kill-sentence	Delete sentence the cursor is on.
M-l	downcase-word	Lowercase word.
M-m	back-to-indentation	Move cursor to first nonblank character on line.
M-q	fill-paragraph	Reformat paragraph.
M-s	center-line	Center line that cursor is on.
M-t	transpose-words	Transpose two words.
M-u	upcase-word	Uppercase word.
M-v	scroll-down	Move backward one screen.
M-x	(none)	Access command by command name.

Summary of Commands by Name

The *emacs* commands below are presented alphabetically by command name. Use M-x to access the command name. Reminder: C- indicates the Control key; M- indicates the Meta key.

Keystrokes	Command name	Description
(none)	*macroname*	Execute a keyboard macro you've saved.
(none)	abbrev-mode	Enter (or exit) word abbreviation mode.
C-x u	advertised-undo	Undo last edit (can be done repeatedly).
(none)	apropos	What functions and variables involve this concept?
M-m	back-to-indentation	Move cursor to first nonblank character on line.
C-b	backward-char	Move backward one character (left).
Del	backward-delete-char	Delete previous character.
(none)	backward-kill-paragraph	Delete previous paragraph.
C-x Del	backward-kill-sentence	Delete previous sentence.
C-c C-w	backward-kill-word	Erase previous word.
M-Del	backward-kill-word	Delete previous word.
C-x [	backward-page	Move backward one page.
M-{	backward-paragraph	Move backward one paragraph.
M-a	backward-sentence	Move backward one sentence.
M-b	backward-word	Move backward one word.
M-<	beginning-of-buffer	Move to beginning of file.
C-a	beginning-of-line	Move to beginning of line.
C-x e	call-last-kbd-macro	Execute last macro defined.
(none)	capitalize-region	Capitalize region.
M-c	capitalize-word	Capitalize first letter of word.
M-s	center-line	Center line that cursor is on.
(none)	center-paragraph	Center paragraph that cursor is on.
(none)	center-region	Center currently defined region.
C-c C-c	comint-interrupt-subjob	Terminate the current job.
C-c C-u	comint-kill-input	Erase current line.
C-c C-d	comint-send-eof	End-of-file character.
C-c C-z	comint-stop-subjob	Suspend current job.
C-h a	command-apropos	What commands involve this concept?
(none)	compare-windows	Compare two buffers; show first difference.
C-d	delete-char	Delete character under cursor.
M-^	delete-indentation	Join this line to previous one.
C-x 1	delete-other-windows	Delete all windows but this one.
C-x 0	delete-window	Delete current window.
(none)	delete-windows-on	Delete all windows on a given buffer.
C-h b	describe-bindings	What are all the key bindings for in this buffer?
C-h C-c	describe-copying	View the *emacs* General Public License.
C-h C-d	describe-distribution	View information on ordering *emacs* from the FSF.
C-h f	describe-function	What does this function do?
C-h k	describe-key	What command does this keystroke sequence run, and what does it do?
C-h c	describe-key-briefly	What command does this keystroke sequence run?
C-h m	describe-mode	Tell me about the mode the current buffer is in.

Keystrokes	Command name	Description
C-h C-w	describe-no-warranty	View the (non)warranty for *emacs*.
C-h s	describe-syntax	What is the syntax table for this buffer?
C-h v	describe-variable	What does this variable mean and what is its value?
M-*n* C-x e	digit-argument and call-last-kbd-macro	Execute the last defined macro *n* times.
M-*n*	digit-argument	Repeat next command *n* times.
C-x C-l	downcase-region	Lowercase region.
M-l	downcase-word	Lowercase word.
(none)	edit-abbrevs	Edit word abbreviations.
C-x)	end-kbd-macro	End macro definition.
M->	end-of-buffer	Move to end of file.
C-e	end-of-line	Move to end of line.
C-x ^	enlarge-window	Make window taller.
C-x }	enlarge-window-horizontally	Make window wider.
C-x C-x	exchange-point-and-mark	Exchange location of cursor and mark.
M-C-c	exit-recursive-edit	Exit a recursive edit.
(none)	fill-individual-paragraphs	Reformat indented paragraphs, keeping indentation.
M-q	fill-paragraph	Reformat paragraph.
(none)	fill-region	Reformat individual paragraphs within a region.
C-x C-v	find-alternate-file	Read an alternate file, replacing the one read with C-x C-f.
C-x C-f	find-file	Find file and read it.
C-x 5 f	find-file-other-frame	Find a file in a new frame.
C-x 4 f	find-file-other-window	Find a file in the other window.
C-f	forward-char	Move forward one character (right).
C-x]	forward-page	Move forward one page.
M-}	forward-paragraph	Move forward one paragraph.
M-e	forward-sentence	Move forward one sentence.
M-f	forward-word	Move forward one word.
(none)	goto-char	Go to character *n* of file.
(none)	goto-line	Go to line *n* of file.
C-h	help-command	Enter the online help system.
C-h t	help-with-tutorial	Run the *emacs* tutorial.
M-C-	indent-region	Indent a region to match first line in region.
(none)	indented-text-mode	Major mode: each tab defines a new indent for subsequent lines.
C-h i	info	Start the Info documentation reader.
C-x i	insert-file	Insert file at cursor position.
(none)	insert-keyboard-macro	Insert the macro you named into a file.
C-x a i g	inverse-add-global-abbrev	Type global abbreviation, then definition.
C-x a i l	inverse-add-local-abbrev	Type local abbreviation, then definition.
C-r	isearch-backward	Start incremental search backward.
C-r	isearch-backward-regexp	Same, but search for regular expression.

Keystrokes	Command name	Description
C-s	isearch-forward	Start incremental search forward.
C-r	isearch-forward-regexp	Same, but search for regular expression.
C-x q	kbd-macro-query	Insert a query in a macro definition.
C-g	keyboard-quit	Abort current command.
(none)	kill-all-abbrevs	Kill abbreviations for this session.
C-x k	kill-buffer	Delete the buffer specified.
C-k	kill-line	Delete from cursor to end of line.
(none)	kill-paragraph	Delete from cursor to end of paragraph.
C-w	kill-region	Delete a marked region.
M-k	kill-sentence	Delete sentence the cursor is on.
(none)	kill-some-buffers	Ask about deleting each buffer.
M-d	kill-word	Delete word the cursor is on.
(none)	list-abbrevs	View word abbreviations.
C-x C-b	list-buffers	Display buffer list.
(none)	load-file	Load macro files you've saved.
C-x C-p	mark-page	Mark page.
M-h	mark-paragraph	Mark paragraph.
C-x h	mark-whole-buffer	Mark buffer.
(none)	name-last-kbd-macro	Name last macro you created (before saving it).
M- M-c	negative-argument; capitalize-word	Capitalize previous word.
M- M-l	negative-argument; downcase-word	Lowercase previous word.
M- M-u	negative-argument; upcase-word	Uppercase previous word.
C-n	next-line	Move to next line (down).
C-x o	other-window	Move to the other window.
C-p	previous-line	Move to previous line (up).
C-% Meta	query-replace-regexp	Query-replace a regular expression.
C-l	recenter	Redraw screen, with current line in center.
(none)	rename-buffer	Change buffer name to specified name.
(none)	replace-regexp	Replace a regular expression unconditionally.
(none)	re-search-backward	Simple regular expression search backward.
(none)	re-search-forward	Simple regular expression search forward.
(none)	revert-buffer	Restore buffer to the state it was in when the file was last saved (or auto-saved).
C-x C-s	save-buffer	Save file (may hang terminal; use C-q to restart).
C-x C-c	save-buffers-kill-emacs	Exit *emacs*.
C-x s	save-some-buffers	Ask whether to save each modified buffer.
M-v	scroll-down	Move backward one screen.
C-x <	scroll-left	Scroll the window left.
M-C-v	scroll-other-window	Scroll other window.
C-x >	scroll-right	Scroll the window right.

Keystrokes	Command name	Description
C-v	scroll-up	Move forward one screen.
C-x .	set-fill-prefix	Use characters from the beginning of the line up to the cursor column as the fill prefix. This prefix is prepended to each line in the paragraph. Cancel the prefix by typing this command in Column 1.
C-@ or C-Space	set-mark-command	Mark the beginning (or end) of a region.
(none)	shrink-window	Make window shorter.
C-x {	shrink-window-horizontally	Make window narrower.
(none)	spell-buffer	Check spelling of current buffer.
(none)	spell-region	Check spelling of current region.
(none)	spell-string	Check spelling of string typed in minibuffer.
M-$	spell-word	Check spelling of word after cursor.
M-C-o	split-line	Split line at cursor; indent to column of cursor.
C-x 2	split-window-vertically	Divide the current window into two, one on top of the other.
C-x 3	split-window-horizontally	Divide the current window into two, side by side.
C-x (	start-kbd-macro	Start macro definition.
C-z	suspend-emacs	Suspend *emacs* (use *exit* or *fg* to restart).
C-x b	switch-to-buffer	Move to the buffer specified.
C-x 5 b	switch-to-buffer-other-frame	Select a buffer in another frame.
C-x 4 b	switch-to-buffer-other-window	Select a buffer in the other window.
(none)	text-mode	Exit indented text mode; return to text mode.
C-t	transpose-chars	Transpose two letters.
C-x C-t	transpose-lines	Transpose two lines.
(none)	transpose-paragraphs	Transpose two paragraphs.
(none)	transpose-sentences	Transpose two sentences.
M-t	transpose-words	Transpose two words.
(none)	unexpand-abbrev	Undo the last word abbreviation.
C-u *n*	universal-argument	Repeat the next command *n* times.
C-u C-x (	universal-argument and start-kbd-macro	Execute last macro defined, then add keystrokes to it.
C-x C-u	upcase-region	Uppercase region.
M-u	upcase-word	Uppercase word.
C-h n	view-emacs-news	View news about updates to *emacs*.
C-h l	view-lossage	What are the last 100 characters I typed?
C-h w	where-is	What is the key binding for this command?
(none)	write-abbrev-file	Write the word abbreviation file.
C-x C-w	write-file	Write buffer contents to file.
C-y	yank	Restore what you've deleted.

Extending Emacs

Emacs' many modes come courtesy of *elisp* files, programs written in Emacs' own LISP-based language and stored in *.el* and *.elc* files (the latter for compiled files).

Getting into the Elisp language is outside the topic of this book,* but be aware that all the modes you're working with are written in *elisp*.

Darwin's directory for Emacs extensions is */usr/share/emacs/emacs-version-numberlisp*. Generally speaking, installing Emacs extensions that you download is as simple as moving them into this folder or into the neighboring *site-lisp* directory. Some *.el* files need to be compiled in order to work; this involves using the *M-x byte-compile-file* command from within Emacs. Packages that contain many interdependent files, such as the PSGML extension for editing SGML and XML files (*http://www.lysator.liu.se/projects/about_psgml.html*), may make this process easier by including standard Unix *configure* and *Makefile* files (described in Chapter 24), which often just run Emacs in batch mode to compile the files in the right order.

Many modes require you to activate various Emacs variables and settings before they'll work. This usually involves editing your *.emacs* file (see the next section) in some way, and is usually described in the extension's README file, or perhaps in the comment section of the *elisp* file itself.

Many of Emacs' modes and main functions are centered around programming. The *elisp* files that ship with Mac OS X include full-featured (which is to say, many-variabled) major modes for C, Java, Perl, and many other languages. Through Meta-X commands like *compile*, *debug*, and the *compilation-mode* major mode, you can even use Emacs as a complete build-and-debug environment.

That said, there's not much reason to use Emacs as your IDE, unless you're working with a very obscure language that lacks editor support outside of Emacs modes (such as *elisp*!), or with a rapid-development language with a console-based interface that doesn't really need an IDE, such as Perl or shell scripting. For all other Mac OS X programming, investigate what Project Builder can do. See "Project Builder" in Chapter 15.

The .emacs file

You can configure Emacs' default behavior by creating and editing a special *elisp* file named *.emacs* in your Home folder. (As with all "dotfiles," the Finder hides *.emacs* from sight; see "Hidden Files" in Chapter 9.) Emacs executes all the commands in this file whenever you launch the program, so it's a great place to set variables, activate and customize major mode options, and so on.

Even if you don't know *elisp*, it's good to know about *.emacs*, since Emacs extesions that you download from the Internet often require you to. If you use Emacs a lot, you may find your *.emacs* file growing over time. A well-organized *elisp* file maintains scalability through grouping similar commands together into well-commented blocks, so that you'll know what everything does each time you return to add to (or debug) the file.

---

* But there are books on this topic alone, such as *Writing GNU Emacs Extensions* (O'Reilly & Associates, Inc., 1997).

As an example, here's part of the *.emacs* file on a Mac OS X system:

```
; First, adjust my loadpath so I can see me own .el files
(setq load-path (cons (expand-file-name "/Users/jmac/emacs-lisp/") load-
path)
)
; Activate and configure PSGML mode

(autoload 'sgml-mode "psgml" "Major mode to edit SGML files." t )
(custom-set-variables)
(custom-set-faces
 '(font-lock-comment-face ((((class color) (background dark)) (:foreground
"orchid1")))))
;; required for Emacs 21
(setq after-change-function nil)



;; Activate XSL-editing mode
(autoload 'xsl-mode "xslide" "Major mode for XSL stylesheets." t)

;; Turn on font lock when in XSL mode
(add-hook 'xsl-mode-hook
          'turn-on-font-lock)

(setq auto-mode-alist
      (append
       (list
        '("\\.xsl" . xsl-mode))
       auto-mode-alist))

;; Activate the 'time-clock' minor mode, which adds time-tracking
functionality.

    (require 'timeclock)

;; Define some keystrokes to trigger timeclock functions quickly.
    (define-key ctl-x-map "ti" 'timeclock-in)
    (define-key ctl-x-map "to" 'timeclock-out)
    (define-key ctl-x-map "tc" 'timeclock-change)
    (define-key ctl-x-map "tr" 'timeclock-reread-log)
    (define-key ctl-x-map "tu" 'timeclock-update-modeline)
    (define-key ctl-x-map "tw" 'timeclock-when-to-leave-string)

;; The M-x-erase-buffer command will warn you about your rash deed unless
;; you have the following variable set:
(put 'erase-buffer 'disabled nil)
```

You can find plenty of other *.emacs* examples online, including a whole repository just for them at *http://www.dotfiles.com*.

Note the path-extending command, *(setq load-path ...)*, at the top of the above
example. If you're not a member of the machine's *admin* group, and thus lack
the *sudo* powers necessary to write to the */usr/share/emacs/21.1/* directory, you

can define your own space to place *elisp* files, just as I have here with the directory */Users/jmac/emacs-lisp*. This tells Emacs to add that directory to the paths it scans when it seeks extension files.

GUI Emacs

Various solutions exist for running Emacs outside of the Terminal. Unfortunately, none of them are very obvious.

Through X Windows
> If you're running X Windows on your Macintosh (having taken the steps described in Chapter 23), then you can compile Emacs and run it with X support.

XEmacs
> XEmacs (*http://www.xemacs.org*) is a separate project in the Unix world, aiming to maintain a version of Emacs more suited to use in a GUI environment than GNU Emacs. A Carbon version fo XEmacs has existed for about as long as Mac OS X has, thanks to the efforts of Pitts Jarvis; see *http://homepage.mac.com/pjarvis/xemacs.html*.

Mac-patched Emacs
> Finally, you can try using a version of GNU Emacs that's been patched to play nicer with the Aqua interface, such as the one available at *http://www.porkrind.org/emacs/*, courtesy of Andrew Choi and David Caldwell.

Choosing a Default Editor

Emacs and *vi* are the two heavyweights of the Unix text editor world, but there are plenty of others to choose from. Two lesser favorites inlcude *pico* (part of the standard Mac OS X distribution) and *joe* (obtainable through Fink or the GNU Mac OS X project; see), both of which have fans due to their online help systems, which include ever present key-combination guides.

Since all text editors are really different paths to the same destination, most people learn one editor and then tend to use it for everything (at least when working within the Terminal). Because of this, you can set two Darwin environment variables, VISUAL and EDITOR, to the name of your preferred editor. (Specifically, to the command that launches it; so, set its name, along with any command-line arguments you might use.) These let programs know which editor you'd like to use, if the program needs to launch a text editor. (Otherwise, the program gets to choose.)

So, if you're using the Z shell (*zsh*) and prefer to use *Emacs* as your Terminal text editor, add these lines to my *~/.zshrc* file:

```
export VISUAL=emacs
export EDITOR=emacs
```

See Chapter 21 for more about environment variables and shell configuration files.

Why two different variables for the same value? It's because of what we politely call "historical reasons." In a nutshell, Unix culture has, over the years, standardized these two variables as the place that programs should seek a user's default editor, but never settled on which of the two to prefer. So, you're better off just setting both.

Fortunately, it doesn't add up to much of an inconvenience; once you set them in your shell's *rc* file, you can just forget about the oddity.

Text Encodings

At the lowest level, all text files (and strings of individual text within lager files) are just sequences of binary numbers. By knowing about the file's *text encoding*, the operating system can convert these numbers into readable text, which it can then display by applying an appropriate font to them.

Because of its capacity to contain all written languages and common symbols that modern humans use (with room to spare), *Unicode* is considered Mac OS X's native text encoding. Specifically, Mac OS X supports Unicode's UTF-16 (fixed 16-bit) and UTF-8 (variable-length) encodings. (See the next section for a brief introduction to Unicode encodings.)

Mac OS X also ships with support for proprietary text encodings; those available on a given Mac depend on the language bundles selected at install time.

Unicode on Mac OS X

After a couple decades of development, the *Unicode* character-encoding architecture is now being rapidly adopted as a standard by all manner of information technologies, from data format standards such as XML to entire operating systems such as OS X. By its ability to contain all human alphabets, punctuation, ideograms, and other written symbols in a single, very large character set, Unicode makes character encoding relatively simple to implement.

We refer to Unicode as not just a character encoding, but a *character-encoding architecture* because it encompasses a single character set and several ways to encode the characters within it. The set is simply a consistent mapping of hexadecimal numbers (called *code points*) to *glyphs* (which are written symbols). For example, the uppercase Latin letter "A" has a code point of 40, notated as U+0040. The Greek letter "α" has code point U+03B1, and among Unicode's block of miscellaneous symbols, we find "ˇ" at code point U+0263A.

Text that conforms to Unicode is, at the lowest level, made of a sequence of these numbers. It's the computer's job to recognize these numbers and map some font onto them when displaying or printing this text. The main difference between the various Unicode encodings involves the style each uses to represent these numbers. The popular UTF-16 strictly stores every glyph-number as a 2-byte (16-bit) sequence, while the newer and more flexible UTF-8 uses between 1 and 6 bytes for every glyph. Both encodings work with the same character set, though: the millions of potential code points in Unicode's glyph space.

For more information about Unicode (including a searchable reference manual to its character set), visit the Unicode Consortium's web site at *http://www.unicode.org*.

18

Using CVS

CVS, the *concurrent versions system*, gives developers an easy way to manage changes made to project files. Under CVS, each person working on a project gets their own "sandbox" copy of every file involved, which they can modify and experiment with however they please; a central, untouchable file repository keeps the canonical files safe. It lets several developers work on the same set of files without fear of accidentally wiping out other peoples' changes (hence the *concurrent* part of the system's name).

CVS also lets you view and work with all the previous versions of a file, without having to manage a whole archival library yourself. This gives you a great way to track, annotate, and access changes to a file over time.

While CVS is designed with source code in mind, it works with any kind of text file–based project that develops over time, such as web sites[*] and books.

Mac OS X gives you two ways to work with CVS. It ships with the command-line *cvs* program, the same one currently maintained by Cyclic Software (*http://www. cyclic.com*). Through this program, you can both check out CVS-based software located on other machines via a network, or you can set up CVS repositories on your own machine (which then become available for checkout by yourself or others with the right permissions). The next section summarizes the use of this tool.

On that note, Mac OS X's other use of CVS lies within Project Builder, which has integrated CVS functionality, letting you easily manage and review the version histories and logs of a Project Builder project and all its files. The later section "CVS in Project Builder" describes this feature.

---

[*] Philip Greenspun writes about this use of CVS at *http://philip.greenspun.com/wtr/cvs.html*.

Basic Concepts

RCS (Revision Control System) works within a single directory. To accommodate large projects using a hierarchy of several directories, CVS creates two new concepts called the *repository* and the *sandbox*.

The repository (also called an *archive*) is the centralized storage area, managed by the version control system and the repository administrator, which stores the projects' files. The repository contains information required to reconstruct historical versions of the files in a project. An administrator sets up and controls the repository using the procedures and commands discussed later in the section "CVS Administrator Reference."

A *sandbox* (also called a *working directory*) contains copies of versions of files from the repository. New development occurs in sandboxes, and any number of sandboxes may be created from a single repository. The sandboxes are independent of one another and may contain files from different stages of the development of the same project. Users set up and control sandboxes, using the procedures and commands found in "CVS User Reference," later in this chapter.

In a typical interaction with the version control system, a developer checks out the most current code from the repository, makes changes, tests the results, and then commits those changes back to the repository when they are deemed satisfactory.

Locking and Merging

Some systems, including RCS, use a *locking model* to coordinate the efforts of multiple developers by serializing file modifications. Before making changes to a file, a developer must not only obtain a copy of it, but also request and obtain a lock on it from the system. This lock serves to prevent (really, dissuade) multiple developers from working on the same file at the same time. When the changes are committed, the developer unlocks the file, permitting other developers to gain access to it.

The locking model is pessimistic: it assumes that conflicts *must* be avoided. Serialization of file modifications through locks prevents conflicts. But it is cumbersome to have to lock files for editing when bug hunting. Often, developers will circumvent the lock mechanism to keep working, which is an invitation to trouble.

Unlike RCS and SCCS, CVS uses a *merging model* that allows everyone to have access to the files at all times and supports concurrent development. The merging model is optimistic: it assumes that conflicts are not common, and when they do occur, it *usually* isn't difficult to resolve them.

CVS is capable of operating under a locking model via the -L and -l options to the *admin* command. Also, CVS has special commands (*edit* and *watch*) for those who want additional development coordination support. CVS uses locks internally to prevent corruption when multiple people are accessing the repository simultaneously, but this is different from the user-visible locks of the locking model discussed here.

Conflicts and Merging

In the event that two developers commit changes to the same version of a file, CVS automatically defers the commit of the second committer's file. The second developer then issues the *cvs update* command, which merges the first developer's changes into the local file. In many cases, the changes are in different areas of the file, and the merge is successful. However, if both developers made changes to the same area of the file, the second to commit has to resolve the conflict. This involves examination of the problematic area(s) of the file and selection among the multiple versions, or making changes that resolve the conflict.

CVS detects only textual conflicts, but conflict resolution is concerned with keeping the project as a whole logically consistent. Therefore, conflict resolution sometimes involves changing files other than the one about which CVS complained.

For example, if one developer adds a parameter to a function definition, it may be necessary for all the calls to that function to be modified to pass the additional parameter. This is a logical conflict, so its detection and resolution is the job of the developers (with support from tools like compilers and debuggers); CVS won't notice the problem.

In any merge situation, whether or not there was a conflict, the second developer to commit will often want to retest the resulting version of the project because it has changed since the original commit. Once it passes, the developer needs to recommit the file.

Tagging

CVS tracks file versions by revision number, which can be used to retrieve a particular revision from the repository. In addition, it is possible to create symbolic tags so that a group of files (or an entire project) can be referred to by a single identifier, even when the revision numbers of the files are not the same (which is most often the case). This capability is often used to keep track of released versions or other important project milestones.

For example, the symbolic tag hello-1_0 might refer to revision number 1.3 of *hello.c* and revision number 1.1 of *Makefile* (symbolic tags are created with the *tag* and *rtag* commands).

Branching

The simplest form of development is *linear*, in which there is a succession of revisions to a file, each derived from the prior revision. Many projects can get by with a completely linear development process, but larger projects (as measured by number of files, number of developers, and/or the size of the user community) often run into maintenance issues that require additional capabilities. Sometimes it is desirable to do some speculative development while the main line of development continues uninterrupted. At other times bugs in the currently released version must be fixed while work on the next version is underway. In both of these cases, the solution is to create a branch (*fork*) from an appropriate point in the development of the project. If at a future point some or all of the changes on the branch are needed back on the main line of development (or elsewhere), they can be merged in (*joined*).

Branches are forked with the *tag -b* command; they are joined with the *update -j* command.

CVS Command Format

CVS commands are of the form:

```
cvs global_options command command_options
```

For example, here is a simple sequence of commands showing both kinds of options in the context of creating a repository, importing existing files, and performing a few common operations on them:

```
user@localhost$ cvs -d /usr/local/cvsrep init ⏎
user@localhost$ cd ~/work/hello
user@localhost$ cvs -d /usr/local/cvsrep import -m 'Import' hello vendor
start
user@localhost$ cd ..
user@localhost$ mv hello hello.bak
user@localhost$ cvs -d /usr/local/cvsrep checkout hello
user@localhost$ cd hello
user@localhost$ vi hello
user@localhost$ cvs commit -m 'Fixed a typo'
user@localhost$ cvs tag hello-1_0
user@localhost$ cvs remove -f Makefile
user@localhost$ cvs commit -m 'Removed old Makefile'
user@localhost$ cvs upd -r hello-1_0
user@localhost$ cvs upd -A
```

Some global options are common to both user and administrator commands, and some are specific to each of them. The common global options are described in the next section, and the user and administrator options are described in the "CVS User Reference" and "CVS Administrator Reference" sections, respectively.

Common Global Options

Table 18-1 lists the global options that apply to both user and administrator commands.

Table 18-1. Common global options

Option	Description
-b bindir	Location of external RCS programs. This option is obsolete, having been deprecated at CVS versions above 1.9.18.
-T tempdir	Absolute path for temporary files. Overrides the setting of TMPDIR.
-v --version	Display version and copyright information.

Gotchas

This section clarifies a few aspects of CVS that can sometimes cause confusion.

CVS's file orientation
> While directories are supported, they are not versioned in the same way as traditional files. This is particularly important in the early evolutionary stages of a project, when the structure may be in flux. Also, if the project is undergoing major changes, the structure is likely to change. See more later in "Hacking the Repository."

CVS's text-orientation
> There is no equivalent to *diff* for binary files, although CVS's support for binary files is usually sufficient. Use *admin -kb* to tell CVS a file is binary.

CVS's line-orientation
> Moving a segment of code from one place in a file to another is seen as one delete (from the old location) and an unrelated add (to the new location).

CVS is not syntax-aware
> As far as CVS is concerned, small formatting changes are equivalent to sweeping logic changes in the same line ranges.

RCS anachronisms
> CVS was originally built on top of RCS, but now all the RCS-related functionality is internal to CVS itself. RCS still shows up in the name of the RCSBIN environment variable and the description of the *-b* option, which are both now obsolete.

CVS Administrator Reference

This section provides details on creating and configuring repositories and performing other CVS administrative tasks. A single computer can run multiple copies of the CVS server, and each server can serve multiple repositories.

Creating a Repository

Select a directory that will contain the repository files (*/usr/local/cvsrep* is used in the following examples). Use the *init* command to initialize the repository. Either set the CVSROOT environment variable first:

```
user@localhost$ export CVSROOT=/usr/local/cvsrep
user@localhost$ cvs init
```

or use the *-d* option to specify the repository location:

```
user@localhost cvs -d /usr/local/cvsrep init
```

For information on importing code, see the section "CVS User Reference," later in this chapter—especially the "import" and "add" sections.

Setting up the password server

If you want users to access the repository from other computers, then configure the pserver by doing the following as root:

---

1. Make sure there is an entry in */etc/services* similar to the following:

```
cvspserver 2401/tcp
```

2. If you are not using `tcpwrappers`, then place a line like this in */etc/inetd.conf*:

```
cvspserver stream tcp nowait root /usr/bin/cvs cvs
--allow-root=/usr/local/cvsroot pserver
```

3. If you *are* using `tcpwrappers`, then use a line like this:

```
cvspserver stream tcp nowait root /usr/sbin/tcpd /usr/bin/cvs
--allow-root=/usr/local/cvsroot pserver
```

4. Once these changes are in place, restart *inetd* (or send it the appropriate signal to cause it to re-read *inetd.conf*).

Security Issues

The following are security issues that need to be considered when working with CVS:

- The contents of files will be transmitted in the open over the network with pserver and *rsh*. With pserver, passwords are transmitted in the open as well.
- When using a local repository (i.e., when CVS is not being used in client/ server mode), developers need write access to the repository, which means they can hack it.
- The CVS server runs as root briefly before changing its user ID.
- The *~/.cvspass* file must be kept unreadable by all users except the owner to prevent passwords from being accessible.
- A user who has authority to make changes to the files in the *CVSROOT* module can run arbitrary programs.
- Some of the options to the *admin* command are very dangerous, so it is advisable to restrict its use. This can be accomplished by creating a user group named cvsadmin. If this user group exists, then only users in that group can run the *admin* command (except *admin -k kflag*, which is available to everyone).

Repository Structure

The CVS repository is implemented as a normal directory with special contents. This section describes the contents of the repository directory.

The CVSROOT directory

The *CVSROOT* directory contains the administrative files for the repository; other directories in the repository contain the modules. The administrative files permit (and ignore) blank lines and comment lines in addition to the lines with real configuration information on them. Comment lines start with a hash mark (#).

Some of the administrative files contain filename patterns to match file and directory names. These patterns are regular expressions like those used in GNU Emacs. Table 18-2 contains the special constructions used most often.

Table 18-2. Filename pattern special constructions

Construction	Description
^	Match the beginning of the string.
$	Match the end of the string.
.	Match any single character.
*	Modify the preceding construct to match zero or more repetitions.

CVS performs a few important expansions in the contents of the administrative files before interpreting the results. First, the typical shell syntax for referring to a home directory is ~/, which expands to the home directory of the user running CVS; and ~*user* expands to the home directory of the specified user.

In addition, CVS provides a mechanism similar to the shell's environment variable expansion capability. Constructs such as ${*variable*} will be replaced by the value of the named variable. Variable names start with letters and consist entirely of letters, numbers, and underscores. Curly brackets may be omitted if the character immediately following the variable reference is not a valid variable name character. While this construct looks like a shell environment variable reference, the full environment is not available. Table 18-3 contains the built-in variables.

Table 18-3. Administrative file variables

Variable	Description
CVSEDITOR EDITOR VISUAL	The editor CVS uses for log file editing.
CVSROOT	The repository locator in use.
USER	The name of the user (on the server, if using a remote repository) running CVS.
=*var*	The value of a user-defined variable named *var*. Values for these variables are provided by the global -s option.

In order to edit these files, check out the *CVSROOT* module from the repository, edit the files, and commit them back to the repository. You must commit the changes for them to affect CVS's behavior.

Table 18-4 describes the administrative files and their functions.

Table 18-4. CVSROOT files

File	Description
checkoutlist	Extra files to be maintained in *CVSROOT*.
commitinfo	Specifications for commit governors.
config	Settings to affect the behavior of CVS.
cvsignore	Filename patterns of files to ignore.
cvswrappers	Specifications for *checkout* and *commit* filters.
editinfo	Specifications for log editors (obsolete).
history	Log information for the *history* command.
loginfo	Specify *commit* notifier program(s)

Table 18-4. CVSROOT files (continued)

File	Description
modules	Module definitions.
notify	Notification processing specifications.
passwd	A list of users and their CVS-specific passwords.
rcsinfo	Template form for log messages.
readers	A list of users having read-only access.
taginfo	Tag-processing specifications.
users	Alternate user email addresses for use with *notify*.
verifymsg	Specify log message evaluator program.
writers	A list of users having read/write access.

Since the *editinfo* file is obsolete, use the EDITOR environment variable (or the *-e* option) to specify the editor and the *verifymsg* file to specify an evaluator.

Each line of the *taginfo* file contains a filename pattern and a command line to execute when files with matching names are tagged.

The checkoutlist file

Whenever changes to files in the *CVSROOT* module are committed, CVS prints the message:

```
cvs commit: Rebuilding administrative file database
```

to inform you that the checked-out copy in the repository has been updated to reflect any changes just committed. As with any other module directory in the repository, the *CVSROOT* directory contains RCS (*,v) files that retain the history of the files. But to use the files, CVS needs a copy of the latest revision. So, when CVS prints this message, it is checking out the latest revisions of the administrative files.

If you have added files to the *CVSROOT* module (such as scripts to be called via entries in the *loginfo* file), you will need to list them in the *checkoutlist* file. This makes CVS treat them the same way as it treats the standard set of *CVSROOT* files.

Each line in this file consists of a filename and an optional error message that is displayed in case there is trouble checking out the file.

The commitinfo file

Whenever a *commit* is being processed, CVS consults this file to determine whether any precommit checking of the file is required. Each line of the file contains a directory name pattern, followed by the path of a program to invoke when files are commited in directories with matching names.

Aside from the usual filename-pattern syntax, there are two special patterns:

ALL

> If this pattern is present in the file, then all files are passed to the specified checking program. CVS then looks for a pattern that matches the name of each particular file and runs the additional checks found, if any.

DEFAULT

> If this pattern is present in the file, all files for which there was no pattern match are sent to the specified checking program. The automatic match of every file to the ALL entry, if any, does not count as a match when determining whether to send the file to the *DEFAULT* checking program.

CVS constructs the command line for the checking program by appending the full path to the directory within the repository and the list of files being committed (this means you can specify the first few command-line arguments to the program, if necessary). If the checking program exits with a nonzero status, the *commit* is aborted.

The programs that run via this mechanism run on the server computer when a remote repository is used. Here is an example of a *commitinfo* file:

```
ALL $CVSROOT/CVSROOT/commit-ALL.pl
DEFAULT $CVSROOT/CVSROOT/commit-DEFAULT.pl
CVSROOT$ $CVSROOT/CVSROOT/commit-CVSROOT.pl
```

This example assumes you will create the script files in the *CVSROOT* module and add them to the *checkoutlist* file.

The config file

Repository configuration is specified in the *config* administrative file.

LockDir=*dir*

> Directs CVS to put its lock files in the alternate directory given instead of in the repository itself, allowing users without write access to the repository (but with write access to *dir*) to read from the repository.
>
> Version 1.10 doesn't support alternate directories for lock files and reports an error if this option is set. Older versions of CVS (1.9 and older) don't support this option either and will not report an error. Do not mix versions that support alternate directories for lock files with versions that don't, since lock files in both places defeat the purpose of having them.

RCSBIN=*dir*

> Obsolete (used in Versions 1.9.12 to 1.9.18). This option was used to tell CVS where to find RCS programs. Since all RCS-related functions are now handled internally, this option does nothing.

SystemAuth=*value*

> CVS tries to authenticate users via the *CVSROOT/passwd* file first, and if that fails and this option is set to yes, CVS tries to authenticate via the system's user database. This option is used with the password server. The default is yes.

TopLevelAdmin=*value*

> If this option is set to yes, an additional *CVS* directory is created at the top-level directory when *checkout* is run. This allows the client software to detect the repository locator in that directory (see "Repository Locators" later in this chapter). The default is no.
>
> This option is useful if you check out multiple modules to the same sandbox directory. If it is enabled, you won't have to provide a repository locator after the first checkout; CVS infers it from the information in the top-level *CVS* directory created during the first checkout.

The cvsignore file

The *cvsignore* administrative file contains a list of filename patterns to ignore, just like the *.cvsignore* files that can appear in sandboxes and user home directories. Unlike the filename patterns in other administrative files, these patterns are in *sh* syntax; they are not GNU Emacs-style regular expressions. There can be multiple patterns on a line, separated by whitespace (consequently, the patterns themselves cannot contain whitespace).

Table 18-5 shows the most commonly used *sh*-style pattern constructs.

Table 18-5. Filename patterns for cvsignore

Construct	Description
?	Any one character.
*	Any sequence of zero or more characters.

Again, diverging from the standards used by the rest of the administrative files, the *cvsignore* file does not support comments.

The cvswrappers file

While the *cvsignore* file allows CVS to ignore certain files, the *cvswrappers* file allows you to give CVS default options for commands that work with files. Lines in this file consist of a *sh*-style filename pattern followed by a *-k* (keyword substitution mode) option and/or an *-m* (update method) option. The legal values for *-k* are described in Table 18-19. The legal values for *-m* are COPY and MERGE.

If *-m COPY* is specified, CVS does not attempt to merge the files. Instead, it presents the user with conflicting versions of the file, and he can choose one or the other or resolve the conflict manually.

For example, to treat all files ending in *.exe* as binary, add this line to the file:

```
*.exe -k b
```

The history file

If this file exists, CVS inserts records of activity against the repository. This information produces displays of the *cvs history* command. The history file is not intended for direct reading or writing by programs other than CVS.

A repository set up with *cvs init* automatically has a *history* file.

The loginfo file

The *loginfo* administrative file works much like the *commitinfo* file and can use the special patterns ALL and DEFAULT. This file allows you to do something with *commit* log messages and related information.

The programs called during *loginfo* processing receive the log message on standard input. Table 18-6 shows the three codes that can pass additional information to the called programs via command-line arguments.

Table 18-6. Special loginfo variables

Variable	Description
s	Filename
V	Pre-*commit* revision number
v	Post-*commit* revision number

If a percent sign (%) followed by the desired variable is placed after the command path, CVS inserts the corresponding information as a whitespace-separated list with one entry for each file, preceded by the repository path (as with *commitinfo*). There can be only one percent sign on the command line, so if you want information from more than one variable, place the variable names inside curly brackets: %{ }. In this case, each file-specific entry has one field for each variable, separated by commas. For example, the code %{sVv} expands into a list like this:

```
/usr/local/cvsrep/hello Makefile,1.1,1.2 hello.c,1.8,1.9
```

It can be helpful to send email notifications each time someone commits a file to the repository. Developers can monitor this stream of notices to determine when they should pull the latest development code into their private sandboxes. For example, consider a developer doing some preparatory work in his sandbox while he awaits stabilization and addition of another developer's new library. As soon as the new library is added and committed, email notification goes out, and the waiting developer sees the code is ready to use. So, he runs *cvs upd -d* in the appropriate directory to pull in the new library code and then sets about integrating it with his work.

It is simple to set up this kind of notification. Just add a line like this to the *CVSROOT/loginfo* file:

```
DEFAULT mail -s %s developers@company.com
```

Often, the email address is a mailing list, which has all the interested parties (developers or otherwise) on the distribution list. If you want to send messages to multiple email addresses, you can write a script to do that and have that script called via this file.

The modules file

The top-level directories in a repository are called *modules*. In addition to these physical modules, CVS provides a mechanism to create logical modules through the *modules* administrative file. Here are the three kinds of logical modules:

Alias
    Alias modules are defined by lines of the form:

```
module_name -a alias_module ...
```

    You can use the alias module name in CVS commands in the same way you use the modules named after the *-a* option.

Regular
    Regular modules are defined by lines of the form:

```
module_name [options] directory file ...
```

Checking out *module_name* results in the specified files from *directory* being checked out into a directory named *module_name*. The intervening directories (if any) are not reflected in the sandbox.

Ampersand

Ampersand modules are defined by lines of the form:

```
module_name [options] &other_module ...
```

Checking out such a module results in a directory named *module_name*, which in turn contains copies of the *other_module* modules.

Table 18-7 shows the options that can define modules.

Table 18-7. Module options

Option	Description
-d *name*	Overrides the default working directory name for the module.
-e *prog*	Runs the program *prog* when files are exported from the module; the module name is passed to *prog* as the sole argument.
-i *prog*	Runs the program *prog* when files are committed to the module; the repository directory of the committed files is passed in to *prog* as the sole argument.
-i *prog*	Runs the program *prog* when files are checked out from the module; the module name is passed in to *prog* as the sole argument.
-s *status*	Assigns a status descriptor to the module
-t *prog*	Runs the program *prog* when files are tagged in the module using *rtag*; the module name and the symbolic tag are passed to *prog*.
-u *prog*	Runs the program *prog* when files are updated in the module's top-level directory; the full path to the module within the repository is passed to *prog* as the sole argument.

Alias modules provide alternative names for other modules or shortcuts for referring to collections or subdirectories of other modules. Alias module definitions function like macro definitions in that they cause commands to run as if the expanded list of modules and directories were on the command line. Alias modules do not cause the modules of their definition to be grouped together under the alias name (use ampersand modules for that). For example, the definition:

```
h -a hello
```

makes the name *h* a synonym for the *hello* module. This definition:

```
project -a library client server
```

allows you to check out all three modules of the project as a unit. If an entry in the definition of an alias module is preceded by an exclamation point (!), then the named directory is excluded from the module.

Regular modules allow you to create modules that are subsets of other modules. For example, the definition:

```
header library library.h
```

creates a module that just contains the header file from the *library* module.

Ampersand modules are true logical modules. There are no top-level directories for them in the repository, but you can check them out to sandboxes and directories with their names will then appear. The modules listed in the definition are below that directory. For example:

```
project &library &client &server
```

is almost the same as the alias module example given earlier, except that the submodules are checked out inside a subdirectory named *project*.

In this file, long definitions may be split across multiple lines by terminating all but the last line with backslashes (\).

The notify file

This file is used in conjunction with the *watch* command. When notifications are appropriate, this file is consulted to determine how to do the notification.

Each line of the *notify* file contains a filename pattern and a command line. CVS's notification mechanism uses the command line specified to perform notifications for files having names that match the corresponding pattern.

There is a single special-purpose variable, %s, that can appear in the command specification. When the command is executed, the name of the user to notify replaces the variable name. If the *users* administrative file exists, the user names are looked up there, and the resulting values are used for %s instead. This allows emails to be sent to accounts other than those on the local machine. Details are sent to the notification program via standard input.

Typical usage of this feature is the single entry:

```
ALL mail %s -s "CVS notification"
```

In fact, this entry is present in the default *notify* file created when you run *cvs init* to create a repository (although it is initially commented out).

The passwd file

If you access the repository via a *pserver* repository locator (see the later section "Repository Locators"), then CVS can have its own private authentication information, separate from the system's user database. This information is stored in the *CVSROOT/passwd* administrative file.

This feature provides anonymous CVS access over the Internet. By creating an entry for a public user (usually *anoncvs* or *anonymous*), the *pserver* can be used by many people sharing the public account. If you don't want to create a system user with the same name as the public user, or if you have such a user but it has a different purpose, you can employ a user alias to map it to something else:

```
anonymous:TY7QWpLw8bvus:cvsnoname
```

Then, make sure you create the cvsnoname user on the system. You can use */bin/false* as the login shell and the repository's *root* directory as the home directory for the user.

To restrict the public user to read-only access, list it in the *CVSROOT/readers* administrative file.

Additionally, CVS's private user database is useful even if you don't want to set up anonymous CVS access. You can restrict access to a subset of the system's users, provide remote access to users who don't have general system access, or prevent a user's normal system password from being transmitted in the clear over the network (see the earlier section "Security Issues").

There is no *cvs passwd* command for setting CVS-specific passwords (located in the repository file *CVSROOT/passwd*). CVS-specific user and password management are manual tasks.

The rcsinfo file

CVS consults this file when doing a *commit* or *import* to determine the log message editor template. Each entry in the file consists of a filename pattern and the name of the file to use as the template for module directories with matching names.

The ALL and DEFAULT special patterns apply to this file.

The readers file

If this file exists, users listed in it have read-only access.

The taginfo file

CVS consults this file whenever the *tag* or *rtag* commands are used. Entries in this file are filename patterns and program specifications. The ALL special pattern applies to this file.

The *taginfo* file is called with the tag, the operation being performed, the module directory name (relative to the repository *root*), and the filename and revision number for each affected file. The valid operations are: add (for *tag*), del (for *tag -d*), and mov (for *tag -F*).

If the *taginfo* program returns a nonzero status, the *tag* or *rtag* command that caused its execution is aborted.

The users file

If this file exists, it is consulted during processing of the *notify* administrative file's contents. Entries in this file consist of two colon-separated fields on a single line. The first field is the name of a user, and the second field is a value (normally the user's email address on another machine). For example:

```
john:john@somecompany.com
jane:jane@anothercompany.com
```

The verifymsg file

CVS consults this file to determine if log messages should be validated. If the program returns a nonzero status, the commit is aborted. The *verifymsg* file is called with the full path to a file containing the log message to be verified.

The ALL special pattern is not supported for this file, although DEFAULT is. If more than one pattern matches, the first match is used.

The writers file

If this file exists, users listed in it have read/write access (unless they are also listed in the *readers* file, in which case they have read-only access).

Hacking the Repository

Since the repository is a normal directory, albeit one with special contents, it is possible to *cd* into the directory and examine its contents and/or make changes to the files and directories there. For each file that is added, there is a file with the same name followed by *,v* in a corresponding directory in the repository. These are RCS (the format, not the program) files that contain multiple versions of the file.

 Since the activities discussed in this section involve making changes directly to the repository instead of working through CVS commands, you should exercise extreme caution and have current backups when following these instructions.

Restructuring a project

Restructuring the project by moving files and directories around (and possibly renaming them) in the repository allows the files to retain their history. The standard way to rename a file when using CVS is to rename the file in the sandbox and do a *cvs remove* on the old name and a *cvs add* on the new name. This results in the file being disconnected from its history under the new name, so sometimes it is better to do the renaming directly in the repository, although doing this while people have active sandboxes is dangerous, since the sandboxes contain information about a file that is no longer in the repository.

Bulk importing

When importing an entire project, all of the project's files are added to the repository. But, if some of these files shouldn't have been added, you'll want to remove them. Doing a *cvs remove* accomplishes this, but copies of those files will remain in the repository's *.Attic* directory forever. To avoid this, you can delete the files from the repository directly before checking out sandboxes from it.

Importing

If you have an existing code base, you'll want to import it into CVS in a way that preserves the most historical information. This section provides instructions for importing projects into CVS from code snapshots or other version control systems. All of these, except the code snapshot import procedure, are based upon conversion to RCS files, followed by placing the RCS files in the proper location in the CVS repository.

Importing code snapshots

If you have maintained project history archives manually by taking periodic snapshots of the code, you can import the first snapshot, tag it with the date or version number, and then successively overlay the updated files from later archives. Each set can then be committed and tagged in order to bootstrap a repository that maintains the prior history.

For example, first unpack the distributions (this assumes they unpack to directories containing the version numbers):

```
user@localhost$ tar xvzf foo-1.0.tar.gz
user@localhost$ tar xvzf foo-1.1.tar.gz
user@localhost$ tar xvzf foo-2.0.tar.gz
```

Next, make a copy of the first version, import it into the CVS repository, check it out to make a sandbox (since importing doesn't convert the source directory into a sandbox), and use *cvs tag* to give it a symbolic name reflecting the project version:

```
user@localhost$ mkdir foo
user@localhost$ cp -R -p foo-1.0/* foo
user@localhost$ cd foo
user@localhost$ cvs import -m 'Imported version 1.0' foo vendor start
user@localhost$ cd ..
user@localhost$ mv foo foo.bak
user@localhost$ cvs checkout foo
user@localhost$ cd foo
user@localhost$ cvs tag foo-1_0
user@localhost$ cd ..
```

Now, apply the differences between Version 1.0 and 1.1 to the sandbox, commit the changes, and create a tag:

```
user@localhost$ diff -Naur foo-1.0 foo-1.1 | (cd foo; patch -Np1)
user@localhost$ cd foo
user@localhost$ cvs commit -m 'Imported version 1.1'
user@localhost$ cvs tag foo-1_1
user@localhost$ cd ..
```

Now, apply the differences between Version 1.1 and 2.0 to the sandbox, commit the changes, and create a tag:

```
user@localhost$ diff -Naur foo-1.1 foo-2.0 | (cd foo; patch -Np1)
user@localhost$ cd foo
user@localhost$ cvs commit -m 'Imported version 2.0'
user@localhost$ cvs tag foo-2_0
```

Now you can use the *log* command to view the history of the files, browse past versions of the files, and continue development under version control.

Importing from RCS

If you are migrating from RCS to CVS, following these instructions results in a usable CVS repository. This procedure involves direct modification of the CVS repository, so it should be undertaken with caution.

Before beginning, make sure none of the files to be imported into CVS are locked by RCS. Then create a new CVS repository and module (or a new module within an existing repository). Next, create directories in the CVS repository to mirror the project's directory structure. Finally, copy all the version files (*,v*) from the project (which may be in *RCS* subdirectories) into the appropriate directories in the repository (without *RCS* subdirectories).

For example, first move aside the directory under RCS control, create an empty directory to build the new CVS structure, import the directory, and then check it out to make a sandbox:

```
user@localhost$ mv foo foo-rcs
user@localhost$ mkdir foo
user@localhost$ cd foo
user@localhost$ cvs import -m 'New empty project' foo vendor start
user@localhost$ cd ..
user@localhost$ mv foo foo.bak
user@localhost$ cvs checkout foo
```

Next, make directories and add them to the repository to match the structure in the RCS project:

```
user@localhost$ cd foo
user@localhost$ mkdir dir
user@localhost$ cvs add dir
user@localhost$ cd ..
```

Now copy the ,v files from the RCS project into the *repository* for the CVS project:

```
user@localhost$ cp -p foo-rcs/*,v $CVSROOT/foo
user@localhost$ cp -p foo-rcs/dir/*,v $CVSROOT/foo/dir
```

Finally, issue the *cvs update* command in the sandbox directory to bring in the latest versions of all the files:

```
user@localhost$ cd foo
user@localhost$ cvs upd
```

Using an Interim Shared Sandbox

Sometimes projects will develop unintended environmental dependencies over time, especially when there is no pressure for the code to be relocatable. A project developed outside version control may even be initially developed in place (at its intended installation location). While these practices are not recommended, they do occur in real-world situations; CVS can be helpful in improving the situation, by encouraging relocatability from the beginning of a project.

The default mode of operation for CVS is multiple independent sandboxes, all coordinated with a central shared repository. Code that runs in this environment is necessarily (at least partially) relocatable. Thus, using CVS from the beginning of a project helps ensure flexibility.

However, if a project is already well underway, an interim approach can be used. For example, you could convert the development area to a single shared sandbox by importing the code into CVS and checking it back out again:

```
user@localhost$ cd /usr/local/bar
user@localhost$ cvs import bar vendor start
user@localhost$ cd ..
user@localhost$ mv bar bar.bak
user@localhost$ cvs checkout bar
```

Chances are good that this approach is too aggressive and checks in more files than absolutely necessary. You can either go back and hack the repository to remove the files that shouldn't be there or just issue the *cvs remove* command to delete them as you discover them.

In addition, there will probably be some binary files in the sandbox that were imported as text files. Wherever you see a binary file that needs to remain in the repository, you should issue the command *cvs admin -kb file*, and then make a fresh copy from the project backup. Finally, issue the command *cvs commit file* to commit the fixed file back to the repository.

Having version control in place before making flexibility enhancements is a good idea, since it makes it easier to find (and possibly reverse) changes that cause trouble.

The repository locator (see the later section "Repository Locators") is specified via the *-d* option or the $CVSROOT environment variable. It is stored in the various sandbox *CVS/root* files. If you are using the password server (*pserver*), the user ID of the person checking out the sandbox is remembered. If more than one person is working with a particular sandbox, they have to share an account for CVS access.

One way to do this is to have a neutral user account, with a password known by everyone with CVS access. Everyone can then issue the *cvs login* command with the same user ID and password and have access to the repository. Once you are no longer using a shared sandbox, this workaround won't be necessary. However, during the time you are using a shared sandbox, it is important that the developers type their real user IDs into their log messages, since all the changes will appear to be made by the common user.

Global Server Option

The server has one global option: *--allow-root=rootdir*. This option is used to tell the CVS server to accept and process requests for the specified repository.

Administrator Commands

Table 18-8 lists the commands that CVS administrators can use to manage their repositories.

Table 18-8. Administrator commands

Command	Description
admin adm rcs	Perform administrative functions.
init	Create a new repository.
server	Run in server mode.

admin

```
admin
        [ -b[rev] ]
        [ -cstring ]
        [ -kkflag ]
        [ -l[rev] ]
        [ -L ]
        [ -mrev:msg ]
        [ -nname[:[rev]] ]
        [ -Nname[:[rev]] ]
        [ -orange ]
        [ -q ]
        [ -sstate[:rev] ]
        [ -t[file] ]
        [ -t-string ]
        [ -u[rev] ]
        [ -U ]
        [ files  ]
```

The *admin* command is used to perform administrative functions. If a cvsadmin user group exists, then only those users in that group will be able to run *admin* with options other than -k. Additional options that may be used with the *admin* command are listed in Table 18-9.

Table 18-9. admin options

Option	Description
-b[rev]	Set the default branch.
-cstring	Obsolete. Set the comment leader.
-kkflag	Set the default keyword substitution mode.
-l[rev]	Lock the specified revision.
-L	Enable strict locking.
-mrev:msg	Change the revision's log message.
-nname[:[rev]]	Give the branch or revision specified the symbolic name *name*.
-Nname[:[rev]]	The same as -n, except that if *name* is already in use, it is moved.
-orange	Delete revisions permanently.
-q	Don't print diagnostics.
-sstate[:rev]	Change the state of a revision.
-t[file]	Set the descriptive text in the RCS file.
-t-string	Set the descriptive text in the RCS file to *string*.
-u[rev]	Unlock the specified revision.
-U	Disable strict locking.

If the revision specified for *-l* is a branch, the latest revision on that branch is used. If no revision is given, the latest revision on the default branch is used.

If the name given for *-n* is already in use, an error is generated. You can use *-N* to move a tag (change the revision associated with the tag); however, you should usually use *cvs tag* or *cvs rtag* instead.

The *-o* option is very dangerous and results in a permanent loss of information from the repository. Use it with extreme caution and only after careful consideration. See Table 18-10 for the various ways to specify ranges. There must not be any branches or locks on the revisions to be removed. Beware of interactions between this command and symbolic names.

If no *file* is specified to the *-t* option, CVS reads from standard input until it reaches the end of the file or a period on a line by itself.

The determination of the target revision for the *-u* option is the same as for *-l*.

Table 18-10. Range formats

Format	Description
rev1::rev2	Eliminate versions between *rev1* and *rev2*, retaining only enough information to go directly from *rev1* to *rev2*. The two specified versions are retained.
::rev	The same as *rev1::rev2*, except the first revision is the branchpoint revision.
rev::	The same as *rev1::rev2*, except the second revision is the end of the branch and is deleted instead of retained.
rev	Delete the specified revision.
rev1:rev2	The same as *rev1::rev2*, except the two named revisions are deleted as well.
:rev	The same as *::rev2*, except the named revision is deleted as well.
rev:	The same as *rev1::*, except the named revision is deleted as well.

The options in Table 18-11 are present in CVS for historical reasons and should not be used (using these options may corrupt the repository).

Table 18-11. Obsolete admin options

Option	Description
-alogins	Append the logins to the RCS file's access list.
-Aoldfile	Append the access list of *oldfile* to the access list of the RCS file.
-e[logins]	Erases logins from the RCS file's access list, or erases all if a list is not provided.
-i	Create and initialize a new RCS file. Don't use this option. Instead, use *add* to add files to a CVS repository.
-I	Run interactively. This option doesn't work with client/server CVS and is likely to be removed in a future version.
-Vn	Obsolete. This option was used to specify that the RCS files used by CVS should be made compatible with a specific version of RCS.
-xsuffixes	This option used to be described as determining the filename suffix for RCS files, but CVS has always only used *,v* as the RCS file suffix.

init

```
init
```

Initializes the repository. Use the global -d option to specify the repository's directory if $CVSROOT isn't set appropriately.

The newly initialized repository will contain a *CVSROOT* module, but nothing else. Once the repository is initialized, use other CVS commands to add files to it or to check out the *CVSROOT* module to make changes to the administrative files.

pserver

```
pserver
```

Operate as a server, providing access to the repositories specified before the command with the --allow-root option. This command is used in the *inetd.conf* file, not on the command line. Another global option frequently used with this command is -T (see Table 18-1).

CVS User Reference

This section provides details on connecting to a repository, the structure of sandboxes, and using the CVS commands.

Repository Locators

CVS currently supports five methods for the client to access the repository: local, external, a password server, a GSS-API (Generic Security Services API) server, and a Kerberos 4 server (most Kerberos users will want to use GSS-API). Table 18-12 describes the various repository locator types and their respective access methods.

Table 18-12. Repository access types and methods

Method	Locator format	Description
Local	`path`	If the repository directory is local to the computer from which you will access it (or appears local, such as an NFS or Samba mounted filesystem), the repository string is just the pathname of the repository directory, such as */usr/local/cvsrep*.
External	`:ext:user@host:path`	External repositories are accessed via a remote shell utility, usually *rsh* (the default) or *ssh*. The environment variable $CVS_RSH is used to specify the remote shell program.
Password server	`:pserver:user@host:path`	Password server repositories require authentication to a user account before allowing use of the repository. Public CVS servers are commonly configured this way so they can provide anonymous CVS access. See "The passwd file," earlier in this chapter, for more information on anonymous CVS.
GSS-API server	`:gserver:`	This locator type is used for servers accessible via Kerberos 5 or other authentication mechanisms supported by GSS-API.
Kerberos server	`:kserver:`	This locator type is used for servers accessible via Kerberos 4.

Configuring CVS

CVS's behavior can be influenced by two classes of settings other than the command-line arguments: the *environment variables* (see Table 18-13) and *special files* (see Table 18-14).

Table 18-13. Environment variables

Variable	Description
COMSPEC	Command interpreter on OS/2, if not *cmd.exe*.
$CVS_CLIENT_LOG	Client-side debugging file specification for client/server connections.
	$CVS_CLIENT_LOG is the basename for the *$CVS_CLIENT_LOG.in* and *$CVS_CLIENT_LOG.out* files, which are written in the current working directory at the time a command is executed.
$CVS_CLIENT_PORT	The port number for *:kserver:* locators.
$CVS_IGNORE_REMOTE_ROOT	$CVS_CLIENT_PORT doesn't need to be set if the *kserver* is listening on port 1999 (the default).
	According to the *ChangeLog*, this variable was removed from CVS with Version 1.10.3.
$CVS_PASSFILE	Password file for *:PSERVER:* locators. This variable must be set before issuing the *cvs login* to have the desired effect. Defaults to *$HOME/.cvspass*.
$CVS_RCMD_PORT	For non-Unix clients, the port for connecting to the server's *rcmd* daemon.
$CVS_RSH	Remote shell for *:ext:* locators, if not *rsh*.
$CVS_SERVER	Remote server program for *:ext:* locators, if not *cvs*.
$CVS_SERVER_SLEEP	Server-side execution delay (in seconds) to allow time to attach a debugger.
$CVSEDITOR	Editor used for log messages; overrides $EDITOR.
$CVSIGNORE	A list of filename patterns to ignore, separated by whitespace. (See also *cvsignore* in Table 18-4 and *.cvsignore* in Table 18-14.)
$CVSREAD	Determines read-only (if the variable is set) or read/write (if the variable is not set) for *checkout* and *update*.
$CVSROOT	Default repository locator.
$CVSUMASK	Used to determine permissions for (local) repository files.
$CVSWRAPPERS	A list of filename patterns for the *cvswrappers* function. See also "Repository Structure," earlier in this chapter.
$EDITOR	Specifies the editor to use for log messages; see notes for $CVSEDITOR earlier in this table.
$HOME	On Unix, used to find the *.cvsrc* file.
$HOMEDRIVE	On Windows NT, used to find the *.cvsrc* file.
$HOMEPATH	On Windows NT, used to find the *.cvsrc* file.
$PATH	Used to locate programs to run.
$RCSBIN	Used to locate RCS programs to run. This variable is obsolete.
$TEMP $TMP $TMPDIR	Location for temporary files. $TMPDIR is used by the server. On Unix, */tmp* (and TMP on Windows NT) may not be overridden for some functions of CVS due to reliance on the system's tmpnam( ) function.

Despite the similarity in names, the $CVSROOT environment variable and the *CVSROOT* directory in a repository are not related to each other.

The "RSH" in the name of the $CVS_RSH environment variable doesn't refer to the particular program (*rsh*), but rather to the program CVS is supposed to use for creating remote shell connections (which could be some program other than *rsh*, such as *ssh*).

Since there is only one way to specify the remote shell program to use ($CVS_RSH), and since this is a global setting, users that commonly access multiple repositories may need to pay close attention to which repository they are using. If one repository requires one setting of this variable and another requires a different setting, then you will have to change this variable between accesses to repositories requiring different settings. This aspect of the repository access method is not stored in the *CVS/Root* file in the sandbox (see "CVS directories," later in this chapter). For example, if you access some repositories via *rsh* and some via *ssh*, then you can create the following two utility aliases (*bash* syntax):

```
user@localhost$ alias cvs="export CVS_RSH=ssh; cvs"
user@localhost$ alias cvr="export CVS_RSH=rsh; cvs"
```

Table 18-14 shows the files used by the CVS command-line client for server connection and client configuration information. These files reside in the user's home directory.

Table 18-14. Client configuration files

Option	Description
~/.cvsignore	Filename patterns of files to ignore
~/.cvspass	Passwords cached by *cvs login*
~/.cvsrc	Default command options
~/.cvswrappers	User-specific *checkout* and *commit* filters

The ~/.*cvspass* file is really an operational file, not a configuration file. It is used by the *cvs* client program to store the repository user account password between *cvs login* and *cvs logoff*.

Some common .*cvsrc* settings are:

update -dP
  Brings in new directories and prunes empty directories on *cvs update*.

diff -c
  Gives output in context *diff* format.

Creating a Sandbox

In order to use CVS, you must create a sandbox or have one created for you. This section describes sandbox creation, assuming there is already a module in the repository you want to work with. See the section "import," later in this chapter, for information on importing a new module into the repository.

1. Determine the repository locator. Talk to the repository administrator if you need help finding the repository or getting the locator syntax right.

2. If this will be the main repository you use, set $CVSROOT; otherwise, use the -*d* option when running CVS commands that don't infer the repository from the sandbox files.

3. Pick a module to check out.

4. Pick a sandbox location and *cd* to the parent directory.

5. If the repository requires a login, use *cvs login*.

6. Run *cvs checkout module*.

For example:

```
export CVSROOT=/usr/local/cvsroot
cd ~/work
cvs checkout hello
```

Sandbox Structure

This section describes the files and directories that may be encountered in sandboxes.

.cvsignore files

Sandboxes may contain *.cvsignore* files. These files specify filename patterns for files that may exist in the sandbox but that normally won't be checked into CVS. This is commonly used to cause CVS to bypass derived files.

.cvswrappers files

Sandboxes may contain *.cvswrappers* files, which provide directory-specific file handling information like that in the repository configuration file *cvswrappers* (see "The cvswrappers file," earlier in this chapter).

CVS directories

Each directory in a sandbox contains a *CVS* directory. The files in this directory (see Table 18-15) contain metadata used by CVS to locate the repository and track which file versions have been copied into the sandbox.

Table 18-15. Files in the CVS directories

File	Description
Base Baserev Baserev.tmp	The *Base* directory stores copies of files when the *edit* command is in use. The *Baserev* file contains the revision numbers of the files in *Base*. The *Baserev.tmp* file is used in updating the *Baserev* file.
Checkin.prog Update.prog	The programs specified in the modules file for options *-i* and *-u*, respectively (if any).
Entries	Version numbers and timestamps for the files as they were copied from the repository when checked out or updated.
Entries. Backup Entries.Log Entries.Static	These are temporary and intermediate files used by CVS.
Notify Notify.tmp	These are temporary files used by CVS for dealing with notifications for commands like *edit* and *unedit*.
Repository	The name by which the directory is known in the repository.

Table 18-15. Files in the CVS directories (continued)

File	Description
Root	The repository locator in effect when the sandbox was created (via *cvs checkout*).
Tag	Information about sticky tags and dates for files in the directory.
Template	Used to store the contents of the *rcsinfo* administrative file from the repository for remote repositories.

Since each sandbox directory has one *CVS/Root* file, a sandbox directory corresponds to exactly one repository. You cannot check out some files from one repository and some from another into a single sandbox directory.

Client Global Options

Table 18-16 lists the global options that control the operation of the CVS client program.

Table 18-16. Client global options

Option	Description
-a	Authenticate (*gserver* only).
-d *root*	Locate the repository. Overrides the setting of $CVSROOT.
-e *editor*	Specify message editor. Overrides the settings of $CVSEDITOR and $EDITOR.
-f	Don't read ~/.cvsrc. Useful when you have .cvsrc settings that you want to forgo for a particular command.
-H [*command*] --help [*command*]	Display help. If no command is specified, general CVS help, including a list of other help options, is displayed.
-l	Don't log the command in history.
-n	Don't change any files. Useful when you want to know ahead of time which files will be affected by a particular command.
-q	Be quiet.
-Q	Be very quiet. Print messages only for serious problems.
-r	Make new working files read-only.
-s *variable=value*	Set the value of a user variable to a given value. User variables can be used in the contents of administrative files.
-t	Trace execution. Helpful in debugging remote repository connection problems and, in conjunction with *-n*, in determining the effect of an unfamiliar command.
-w	Make new working files read/write. Overrides $CVSREAD. Files are read/write unless $CVSREAD is set or *-r* is specified.
-x	Encrypt. (Introduced in Version 1.10.)
-z *gzip_level*	Set the compression level. Useful when using CVS in client/server mode across slow connections.

Common Client Options

Table 18-17 and Table 18-18 describe the options that are common to many CVS commands. Table 18-17 lists the common options with a description of their function, while Table 18-18 lists which options can be used with the user commands. In the sections that follow, details will be provided only for options that are not listed here and for those that do not function as described here.

Table 18-17. Common options

Option	Description
-D *date*	Use the most recent revision no later than *date*.
-f	For commands that involve tags (via -*r*) or dates (via -*D*), include files not tagged with the specified tag or not present on the specified date. The most recent revision will be included.
-k *kflag*	Determine how keyword substitution will be performed. The space between -*k* and *kflag* is optional. See Table 18-19 for the list of keyword substitution modes.
-l	Do not recurse into subdirectories.
-n	Don't run module programs.
-R	Do recurse into subdirectories (the default).
-r *rev*	Use a particular revision number or symbolic tag.

Table 18-18 shows which common options are applicable to each user command.

Table 18-18. Client common option applicability

User command	–D	–f	–k	–l	–n	–R	–r
add			✓				
annotate	✓	✓		✓		✓	✓
checkout	✓	✓	✓	✓	✓	✓	✓
commit				✓	✓	✓	✓
diff	✓		✓	✓		✓	✓
edit				✓		✓	
editors				✓		✓	
export	✓	✓	✓	✓	✓	✓	✓
help							
history	✓						✓
import			✓				
log				✓		✓	
login							
logout							
rdiff	✓	✓		✓		✓	✓
release							
remove				✓		✓	
rtag	✓	✓		✓		✓	✓
status				✓		✓	
tag				✓		✓	
unedit				✓		✓	
update	✓	✓	✓	✓		✓	✓
watch				✓		✓	
watchers				✓		✓	

Date formats

CVS can understand dates in a wide variety of formats, including:

ISO standard
> The preferred format is YYYY-MM-DD HH:MM, which reads as 2000-05-17 or 2000-05-17 22:00. The technical details of the format are defined in the ISO 8601 standard.

Email standard
> 17 May 2000. The technical details of the format are defined in the RFC 822 and RFC 1123 standards.

Relative
> 10 days ago, 4 years ago.

Common
> *month/day/year*. This form can cause confusion because not all countries use the first two fields in this order (1/2/2000 would be ambiguous).

Other
> Other formats are accepted, including YYYY/MM/DD and those omitting the year (which is assumed to be the current year).

Keyword substitutions

Table 18-19 describes the keyword substitution modes that can be selected with the *-k* option. CVS uses keyword substitutions to insert revision information into files when they are checked out or updated.

Table 18-19. Keyword substitution modes

Mode	Description
b	Binary mode. Treat the file the same as with mode o, but also avoid newline conversion.
k	Keyword-only mode. Flatten all keywords to just the keyword name. Use this mode if you want to compare two revisions of a file without seeing the keyword substitution differences.
kv	Keyword-value mode. The keyword and the corresponding value are substituted. This is the default mode.
kvl	Keyword-value-locker mode. This mode is the same as kv mode, except it always adds the lock holder's user ID if the revision is locked. The lock is obtained via the *cvs admin -l* command.
o	Old-contents mode. Use the keyword values as they appear in the repository rather than generate new values.
v	Value-only mode. Substitute the value of each keyword for the entire keyword field, omitting even the delimiters. This mode destroys the field in the process, so use it cautiously.

Keyword substitution fields are strings of the form $*Keyword*...$. The valid keywords are:

Author
> The user ID of the person who committed the revision.

Date
> The date and time (in standard UTC format) the revision was committed.

Header

> The full path of the repository RCS file, the revision number, the commit date, time, and user ID, the file's state, and the lock holder's user ID if the file is locked.

Id

> A shorter form of Header, omitting the leading directory name(s) from the RCS file's path, leaving only the filename.

Name

> The tag name used to retrieve the file, or empty if the no explicit tag was given when the file was retrieved.

Locker

> The user ID of the user holding a lock on the file, or empty if the file is not locked.

Log

> The RCS filename. In addition to keyword expansion in the keyword field, each commit adds additional lines in the file immediately following the line containing this keyword. The first such line contains the revision number, the commit date, time, and user ID. Subsequent lines are the contents of the commit log message. The result over time is a reverse-chronological list of log entries for the file. Each of the additional lines is preceded by the same characters that precede the keyword field on its line. This allows the log information to be formatted in a comment for most languages. For example:

```
#
# foo.pl
#
# $Log: ch18,v $
# Revision 1.2  2000/06/09 22:10:23  me
# Fixed the new bug introduced when the last one was fixed.
#
# Revision 1.1  2000/06/09 18:07:51  me
# Fixed the last remaining bug in the system.
#
```

> Be sure that you don't place any keyword fields in your log messages if you use this keyword, since they will get expanded if you do.

RCSfile

> The name of the RCS file (without any leading directories).

Revision

> The revision number of the file.

Source

> The full path of the RCS file.

State

> The file's state, as assigned by *cvs admin -s* (if you don't set the state explicitly, it will be Exp by default).

User Commands

The CVS client program provides the user commands defined in Table 18-20.

Table 18-20. User commands

Command	Description
ad add new	Indicate that files/directories should be added to the repository.
ann annotate	Display contents of the head revision of a file, annotated with the revision number, user, and date of the last change for each line.
checkout co get	Create a sandbox for a module.
ci com commit	Commit changes from the sandbox back to the repository.
di dif diff	View differences between file versions.
edit	Prepare to edit files. This is used for enhanced developer coordination.
editors	Display a list of users working on the files. This is used for enhanced developer coordination.
ex exp export	Retrieve a module, but don't make the result a sandbox.
help	Get help.
hi his history	Display the log information for files.
im imp import	Import new modules into the repository.
lgn login logon	Log in to (cache the password for) a remote CVS server.
lo log rlog	Show the activity log for the file(s).
logout	Log off from (flush the password for) a remote CVS server.
pa patch rdiff	Release diff. The output is the format of input to Larry Wall's *patch* command. Does not have to be run from within a sandbox.
re rel release	Perform a logged delete on a sandbox.
remove rm delete	Remove a file or directory from the repository.
rt rtag rfreeze	Tag a particular revision.

Table 18-20. User commands (continued)

Command	Description
st stat status	Show detailed status for files.
ta tag freeze	Attach a tag to files in the repository.
unedit	Abandon file modifications and make read-only again.
up upd update	Synchronize sandbox to repository.
watch	Manage the watch settings. This is used for enhanced developer coordination.
watchers	Display the list of users watching for changes to the files. This is used for enhanced developer coordination.

add

```
add

    [ -k kflag ]
    [ -m message ]
    file
```

Indicate that files/directories should be added to the repository. They are not actually added until they are committed via *cvs commit*. This command is also used to resurrect files that have been deleted with *cvs remove*.

The standard meaning of the common client that option *-k* applies. There is only one additional option that can be used with the *add* command: *-m message*. This option is used to provide a description of the file (which appears in the output of the *log* command).

annotate

```
annotate

    [ [ -D date | -r rev ] -f ]
    [ -l | -R ]
    file
```

CVS prints a report showing each line of the specified file. Each line is prefixed by information about the most recent change to the line, including the revision number, the user, and the date. If no revision is specified, then the head of the trunk is used.

The standard meanings of the common client options *-D*, *-f*, *-l*, *-r*, and *-R* apply.

checkout

checkout

```
[ -A ]
[ -c | -s ]
[ -d dir [ -N ] ]
[ [ -D date | -r rev ] -f ]
[ -j rev1 [ -j rev2 ] ]
[ -k kflag ]
[ -l | -R ]
[ -n ]
[ -p ]
[ -P ]
module
```

Copy files from the repository to the sandbox.

The standard meanings of the common client options -D, -f, -k, -l, -r, and -R apply. Additional options are listed in Table 18-21.

Table 18-21. Checkout options

Option	Description
-A	Reset any sticky tags or dates.
-c	Copy the *module* file to standard output.
-d *dir*	Override the default directory name.
-j *rev*	Join branches together.
-N	Don't shorten module paths.
-p	Pipe the files to standard output, with header lines between them showing the filename, RCS filename, and version.
-P	Prune empty directories.
-s	Show status for each module from the *modules* file.

commit

commit

```
[ -f | [ -l | -R ] ]
[ -F file | -m message ]
[ -n ]
[ -r revision ]
[ files ]
```

Commit the changes made to files in the sandbox to the repository.

The standard meanings of the common client options -l, -n, -r, and -R apply. Additional options are listed in Table 18-22.

Table 18-22. commit options

Option	Description
-f	Force commit, even if no changes were made.
-F *file*	Use the contents of the file as the message.
-m *message*	Use the message specified.

Use of the *-r* option causes the revision to be sticky, requiring the use of *admin -A* to continue to use the sandbox.

diff

```
diff
      [ -k kflag ]
      [ -l | -R ]
      [ format ]
      [ [ -r rev1 | -D date1 ] [ -r rev2 | -D date2 ] ]
      [ file  ]
```

The *diff* command compares two versions of a file and displays the differences in a format determined by the options. By default, the sandbox version of the file will be compared to the repository version it was originally copied from.

The standard meanings of the common client options *-D*, *-k*, *-l*, *-r*, and *-R* apply. All options for the *diff* command in Chapter 25 can also be used.

edit

```
edit
      [ -a action ]
      [ -l | -R ]
      [ file  ]
```

The *edit* command is used in conjunction with watch to permit a more coordinated (serialized) development process. It makes the file writable and sends out an advisory to any users who have requested them. A temporary *watch* is established and will be removed automatically when either the *unedit* or the *commit* command is issued.

The standard meanings of the common client options *-l* and *-R* apply. There is only one additional option that can be used with the *edit* command: *-a actions*. This option is used to specify the actions to watch. The legal values for actions are described in the entry for the *watch* command.

editors

```
editors
      [ -l | -R ]
      [ file  ]
```

Display a list of users working on the files specified. This is determined by checking which users have run the *edit* command on those files. If the *edit* command has not been used, no results are displayed.

The standard meanings of the common client options *-l* and *-R* apply.

See also the later section "watch."

export

export

```
      [ -d dir [ -N ] ]
      [ -D date | -r rev ]
      [ -f ]
      [ -k kflag ]
      [ -l | -R ]
      [ -n ]
      [ -P ]
      module
```

Export files from the repository, much like the *checkout* command, except that the result is not a sandbox (i.e., CVS subdirectories are not created). This can be used to prepare a directory for distribution. For example:

```
user@localhost$ cvs export -r foo-1_0 -d foo-1.0 foo
user@localhost$ tar czf foo-1.0.tar.gz foo-1.0
```

The standard meanings of the common client options *-D*, *-f*, *-k*, *-l*, *-n*, *-r*, and *-R* apply. Additional options are listed in Table 18-23.

Table 18-23. export options

Option	Description
-d *dir*	Use *dir* as the directory name instead of using the module name.
-n	Don't run any checkout programs.
-N	Don't shorten paths.

When checking out a single file located one or more directories down in a module's directory structure, the *-N* option can be used with *-d* to prevent the creation of intermediate directories.

help

help

Display helpful information about using the *cvs* program.

history

history

```
      [ -a | -u user ]
      [ -b string ]
      [ -c ]
```

```
[ -D date ]
[ -e | -x type ]
[ -f file | -m module | -n module | -p repository ]
[ -l ]
[ -o ]
[ -r rev ]
[ -t tag ]
[ -T ]
[ -w ]
[ -z zone ]
[ file  ]
```

Display historical information. To use the *history* command, you must first set up the *history* file in the repository. See "Repository Structure" for more information on this file.

> When used with the *history* command, the functions of *-f*, *-l*, *-n*, and *-p* are not the same as elsewhere in CVS.

The standard meanings of the common client options *-D* and *-r* apply. History is reported for activity subsequent to the date or revision indicated. Additional options are listed in Table 18-24.

Table 18-24. history options

Option	Description
-a	Show history for all users (default is current user).
-b str	Show history back to the first record containing *str* in the module name, filename, or repository path.
-c	Report each *commit*.
-e	Report everything.
-f file	Show the most recent event for *file*.
-l	Show the last event only.
-m module	Produce a full report on *module*.
-n module	Report the last event for *module*.
-o	Report on modules that have been checked out.
-p repository	Show the history for a particular repository directory.
-t tag	Show the history since the tag *tag* was last added to the history file.
-T	Report on all tags.
-u name	Show the history for a particular user.
-w	Show the history only for the current working directory.
-w zone	Display times according to the time zone *zone*.
-x type	Report on specific types of activity. See Table 18-25.

The *-p* option should limit the *history* report to entries for the directory or directories (if multiple *-p* options are specified) given, but as of Version 1.10.8, it doesn't seem to affect the output. For example, to report history for the *CVSROOT* and *hello* modules, run the command:

```
cvs history -p CVSROOT -p hello
```

Using *-t* is faster than using *-r* because it needs only to search through the history file, not all of the RCS files.

The record types shown in Table 18-25 are generated by *update* commands.

Table 18-25. Update-related history record types

Type	Description
C	Merge was necessary, but conflicts requiring manual intervention occurred.
G	Successful automatic merge.
U	Working file copied from repository.
W	Working copy deleted.

The record types shown in Table 18-26 are generated by *commit* commands:

Table 18-26. Commit-related history record types

Type	Description
A	Added for the first time
M	Modified
R	Removed

Each of the record types shown in Table 18-27 is generated by a different command.

Table 18-27. Other history Record Types

Type	Command
E	*only*
F	*release*
O	*checkout*
T	*rtag*

import

```
import
        [ -b branch ]
        [ -d ]
        [ -I pattern ]
        [ -k kflag ]
        [ -m message ]
        [ -W spec ]
        module
        vendor_tag
        release_tag
```

Import an entire directory into the repository as a new module. Used to incorporate code from outside sources or other code that was initially created outside the control of the CVS repository. More than one *release_tag* may be specified, in which case multiple symbolic tags will be created for the initial revision.

The standard meaning of the common client option *-k* applies. Additional options are listed in Table 18-28.

Table 18-28. import options

Option	Description
-b *branch*	Import to a vendor branch.
-d	Use the modification date and time of the file instead of the current date and time as the import date and time. For local repository locators only.
-I *pattern*	Filename patterns for files to ignore.
-m *message*	Use *message* as the log message instead of invoking the editor.
-W *spec*	Wrapper specification.

The *-k* setting applies only to those files imported during this execution of the command. The keyword substitution modes of files already in the repository are not modified.

When used with *-W*, the *spec* variable is in the same format as entries in the *cvswrappers* administrative file (see "The cvswrappers file").

Table 18-29 describes the status codes displayed by the *import* command.

Table 18-29. import Status Codes

Status	Description
C	Changed. The file is in the repository, and the sandbox version is different; a merge is required.
I	Ignored. The *.cvsignore* file is causing CVS to ignore the file.
L	Link. Symbolic links are ignored by CVS.
N	New. The file is new. It has been added to the repository.
U	Update. The file is in the repository, and the sandbox version is not different.

log

```
log
    [ -b ]
    [ -d dates ]
    [ -h ]
    [ -N ]
    [ -rrevisions ]
    [ -R ]
    [ -s state ]
    [ -t ]
    [ -wlogins ]
    [ file ]
```

Print an activity log for the files.

The standard meaning of the common client option -*l* applies. Additional options are listed in Table 18-30.

Table 18-30. log options

Option	Description
-b	List revisions on default branch.
-d *dates*	Report on these dates.
-h	Print header only.
-N	Don't print tags.
-r[*revisions*]	Report on the listed revisions. There is no space between -*r* and its argument. Without an argument, the latest revision of the default branch is used.
-R	Print RCS filename only. The usage of -*R* here is different than elsewhere in CVS (-*R* usually causes CVS to operate recursively).
-s *state*	Print only those revisions having the specified state.
-t	Print only header and descriptive text.
-w*logins*	Report on check-ins by the listed logins. There is no space between -*w* and its argument.

For -*d*, use the date specifications in Table 18-31. Multiple specifications separated by semicolons may be provided.

Table 18-31. log date range specifications

Specification	Description
d1<d2, or *d2>d1*	The revisions dated between *d1* and *d2*, exclusive
d1<=d2, or *d2>=d1*	The revisions dated between *d1* and *d2*, inclusive
<d, or *d>*	The revisions dated before *d*
<=d, or *d>=*	The revisions dated on or before *d*
d<, or *>d*	The revisions dated after *d*
d<=, or *>=d*	The revisions dated on or after *d*
d	The most recent revision dated *d* or earlier

For -*r*, use the revision specifications in Table 18-32.

Table 18-32. log revision specifications

Specification	Description
rev1:rev2	The revisions between *rev1* and *rev2*, inclusive.
:rev	The revisions from the beginning of the branch to *rev*, inclusive.
rev:	The revisions from *rev* to the end of the branch, inclusive.
branch	All revisions on the branch.
branch1:branch2	All revisions on all branches between *branch1* and *branch2* inclusive.
branch.	The latest revision on the branch.

For *rev1:rev2*, it is an error if the revisions are not on the same branch.

login

```
login
```

This command is used to log in to remote repositories. The password entered is cached in the *~/.cvspass* file, since a connection to the server is not maintained across invocations.

logout

```
logout
```

This command logs out of a remote repository. The password cached in the *~/.cvspass* file is deleted.

rdiff

```
rdiff
     [ -c | -s | -u ]
     [ { { -D date1 | -r rev1 } [ -D date2 | -r rev2 ] } | -t ]
     [ -f ]
     [ -l | -R ]
     [-V vn]
     file
```

The *rdiff* command creates a *patch* file that can be used to convert a directory containing one release into a different release.

The standard meanings of the common client options *-D, -f, -l, -r,* and *-R* apply. Additional options are listed in Table 18-33.

Table 18-33. rdiff options

Option	Description
-c	Use the *context diff* format (the default).
-s	Output a summary of changed files instead of a *patch* file.
-t	Show the differences between the two most recent revisions.
-u	Use *unidiff format*.
-V rcsver	Obsolete. Used to specify version of RCS to emulate for keyword expansion. (Keyword expansion emulates RCS Version 5.)

release

```
release
     [ -d ]
     directory
```

Sandboxes can be abandoned or deleted without using *cvs release* if desired; using the *release* command logs an entry to the history file (if this mechanism is configured) about the sandbox being destroyed. In addition, it checks the disposition (recursively) of each of the sandbox files before deleting anything. This can help prevent destroying work that has not yet been committed.

There is only one option that can be used with the release command, -d. The -d option deletes the sandbox copy if no uncommitted changes are present.

 New directories (including any files in them) in the sandbox are deleted if the -d option is used with *release*.

The status codes listed in Table 18-34 are used to describe the disposition of each file encountered in the repository and the sandbox.

Table 18-34. *release status codes*

Status	Description
A	The sandbox file has been added (the file was created and *cvs add* was run), but the addition has not been committed.
M	The sandbox copy of the file has been modified.
P	Update available. There is a newer version of the file in the repository, and the copy in the sandbox has not
U	been modified.
R	The sandbox copy was removed (the file was deleted and *cvs remove* was run), but the removal was not committed.
?	The file is present in the sandbox but not in the repository.

remove

remove
```
    [ -f ]
    [ -l | -R ]
    [ file ]
```

Indicate that files should be removed from the repository. The files will not actually be removed until they are committed. Use *cvs add* to resurrect files that have been removed, if you change your mind later.

The standard meanings of the common client options -l and -R apply. Only one other option may be used with the *remove* command: -f. When used, -f deletes the file from the sandbox first.

rtag

rtag
```
    [ -a ]
    [ -b ]
    [ -d ]
    [ -D date | -r rev ]
    [ -f ]
    [ -F ]
    [ -l | - R ]
    [ -n ]
    tag
    file
```

Assign a tag to a particular revision of a set of files. If the file already uses the tag for a different revision, *cvs rtag* will complain unless the -F option is used. This command does not refer to the sandbox file revisions (use *cvs tag* for that), so it can be run outside of a sandbox, if desired.

The standard meanings of the common client options -*D*, -*f*, -*l*, -*r*, and -*R* apply. Additional options are listed in Table 18-35.

Table 18-35. rtag options

Option	Description
-a	Search the *Attic* for removed files containing the tag.
-b	Make it a branch tag.
-d	Delete the tag.
-F	Force. Move the tag from its current revision to the one specified.
-n	Don't run any tag program from the *modules* file.

status

```
status
      [ -l | -R ]
      [ -v ]
      [ file  ]
```

Display the status of the files.

The standard meanings of the common client options -*l* and -*R* apply. The other option that can be used with the *status* command, -*v*, may be used to include tag information.

tag

```
tag
      [ -b ]
      [ -c ]
      [ -d ]
      [ -D date | -r rev ]
      [ -f ]
      [ -F ]
      [ -l | R ]
      tag
      [ file  ]
```

Assign a tag to the sandbox revisions of a set of files. You can use the *status -v* command to list the existing tags for a file.

The *tag* must start with a letter and must consist entirely of letters, numbers, dashes (-), and underscores (_). Therefore, while you might want to tag your *hello* project with 1.0 when you release Version 1.0, you'll need to tag it with something like hello-1_0 instead.

The standard meanings of the common client options -*D*, -*f*, -*l*, -*r*, and -*R* apply. Additional options are listed in Table 18-36.

Table 18-36. tag options

Option	Description
-b	Make a branch.
-c	Check for changes. Make sure the files are not locally modified before tagging.
-d	Delete the tag.
-F	Force. Move the tag from its current revision to the one specified.

Since the *-d* option throws away information that might be important, it is recommended that you use it only when absolutely necessary. It is usually better to create a different tag with a similar name.

unedit

unedit

```
    [ -l | -R ]
    [ file ]
```

Abandon file modifications and make the file read-only again. Watchers will be notified.

The standard meanings of the common client options *-l* and *-R* apply.

update

update

```
    [ -A ]
    [ -d ]
    [ -D date | -r rev ]
    [ -f ]
    [ -I pattern ]
    [ -j rev1 [ -j rev2 ] ]
    [ -k kflag ]
    [ -l | -R ]
    [ -p ]
    [ -P ]
    [ -W spec ]
    [ file ]
```

Update the sandbox, merging in any changes from the repository. For example:

```
cvs -n -q update -AdP
```

can be used to do a quick status check of the current sandbox versus the head of the trunk of development.

The standard meanings of the common client options *-D*, *-f*, *-k*, *-l*, *-r*, and *-R* apply. Additional options are listed in Table 18-37.

Table 18-37. update options

Option	Description
-A	Reset sticky tags.
-d	Create and update new directories.
-I *pattern*	Provide filename patterns for files to ignore.
-j *revision*	Merge in changes between two revisions. Mnemonic: *join*.
-p	Check out files to standard output.
-P	Prune empty directories.
-W *spec*	Provide wrapper specification.

Using -*D* or -*r* results in sticky dates or tags, respectively, on the affected files (using -*p* along with these prevents stickiness). Use -*A* to reset any sticky tags or dates.

If two -*j* specifications are made, the differences between them are computed and applied to the current file. If only one is given, then the common ancestor of the sandbox revision and the specified revision is used as a basis for computing differences to be merged.

For example, suppose a project has an experimental branch, and important changes to the file *foo.c* were introduced between revisions 1.2.2.1 and 1.2.2.2. Once those changes have proven stable, you want them reflected in the main line of development. From a sandbox with the head revisions checked out, we run:

```
user@localhost$ cvs update -j 1.2.2.1 -j 1.2.2.2 foo.c
```

CVS finds the differences between the two revisions and applies those differences to the file in our sandbox.

The *spec* used with -*W* is in the same format as entries in the *cvswrappers* administrative file (see "The cvswrappers file").

The status codes listed in Table 18-38 are used to describe the action taken on each file encountered in the repository and the sandbox.

Table 18-38. update status codes

Status code	Description
A	Added. Server took no action because there was no repository file. Indicates that *cvs add* (but not *cvs commit*) has been run.
C	Conflict. Sandbox copy is modified (it has been edited since it was checked out or last committed). There was a new revision in the repository, and there were conflicts when CVS merged its changes into the sandbox version.
M	Modified. Sandbox copy is modified (it has been edited since it was checked out or last committed). If there was a new revision in the repository, its changes were successfully merged into the file (no conflicts).
P	Patched. Same as U, but indicates the server used a *patch*.
R	Removed. Server took no action. Indicates that *cvs remove* (but not *cvs commit*) has been run.
U	Updated. The file was brought up to date.
?	File is present in sandbox, but not in repository.

watch

```
watch
      { { on | off } | { add | remove } [ -a action ] }
      [ -l | -R ]
      file
```

The *watch* command controls CVS's edit-tracking mechanism. By default, CVS operates in its concurrent development mode, allowing any user to edit any file at any time. CVS includes this *watch* mechanism to support developers who would rather be notified of edits made by others than discover them when doing an *update*.

The *CVSROOT/notify* file determines how notifications are performed.

Table 18-39 shows the *watch* subcommands and their uses.

Table 18-39. watch subcommands

Subcommand	Description
add	Start watching files.
off	Turn off watching.
on	Turn on watching.
remove	Stop watching files.

The standard meanings of the common client options *-l* and *-R* apply. The only other option that can be used with the *watch* command is *-a action*. The *-a* option is used in conjunction with one of the actions listed in Table 18-40.

Table 18-40. watch actions

Action	Description
all	All of the following.
commit	A user has committed changes.
edit	A user ran *cvs edit*.
none	Don't watch. Used by the *edit* command.
unedit	A user ran *cvs unedit*, *cvs release*, or deleted the file and ran *cvs update*, re-creating it.

See also the descriptions of the *edit*, *editors*, *unedit*, and *watchers* commands.

watchers

```
watchers
      [ -l | -R ]
      [ file ]
```

Display a list of users watching the specified files. This is determined by checking which users have run the *watch* command on a particular file (or set of files). If the *watch* command has not been used, no results are displayed.

The standard meanings of the common client options *-l* and *-R* apply.

See also "watch."

CVS in Project Builder

Project Builder has a CVS menu, though all of its options (even the tantalizing Enable CVS Integration) remain grayed out unless you set your project up as a CVS sandbox.

Activating the CVS Menu

If a project already exists in a repository—perhaps as a worldwide open source project,* or as part of an in-house repository at your company—then you need to run *cvs checkout* from within the Terminal to create a new sandbox directory containing your own personal copy of that project. See "checkout."

If you have an existing project not managed by CVS, then you must create a new CVS module for it inside an existing repository, through *cvs import* (see "import"), before you can use any CVS commands with it through Project Builder. If you lack access to a repository, you can simply make one on your machine through the commands described in "Creating a Repository."

Project Builder's CVS Menu

Most of Project Builder's CVS menu commands execute basic *cvs* commands (of the sort described earlier in "Basic Concepts") on the files or folders currently selected through the Files tab, and then display the results as described in the list below. The Files tab's CVS Status column (see the later section "The CVS Status Column") cues you as to which files you can run the following commands on:

Refresh Status
> This performs a *cvs status* on the selected files, updating the symbol displayed under the File tab's CVS status column as appropriate.

Update to Latest Revision
> Runs *cvs update* on the selected files, applying patches as necessary to bring them up to date.

Revert to Latest Revision
> Replaces the selected files (both on-disk an in-memory) with fresh copies of their most recent checked-in revisions (in other words, the result of performing a fresh *cvs checkout* on these files). This command is available only for locally modified files (with an M symbol in the CVS status column).
>
> Note that this is like the commonly seen File → Revert to Saved (⌘-U) menu command, except that instead of synching up the in-memory copy of the document with the on-disk version (wiping out any changes made since the file was last saved), *Revert to Latest Revision* synchs *both* the in-memory and local on-disk sandbox copies of the document with the CVS repository's version of it, erasing any local modifications made to them, even if they've been saved to disk.

---

* You can find some CVS-managed Mac OS X projects at SourceForge: *http://sourceforge.net/softwaremap/trove_list.php?form_cat=309*.

Compare with Base

Performs a *cvs diff* on the selected files, comparing them against the versions currently checked out in your sandbox. Differences detected are shown by the File Merge application (see "Using the FileMerge Application").

Compare/Merge with Latest Revision

Performs a *cvs diff* on the selected files, comparing them against their most recent revisions, as stored in the repository. Differences detected are shown by the File Merge application (see "Using the FileMerge Application").

Add to Repository

Adds an entry for each selected file to the repository. You will then be able to run CVS → Commit Changes on them.

Commit Changes

Commits all changes made with the selected files to the CVS repository.

At the time of this writing, this menu command seems to silently fail if you try committing a file before updating your sandbox copy to the latest revision, which causes the repository to refuse your commit request. To avoid this, run CVS → Refresh Status on files or folders before committing them, and then run CVS → Update to Latest Revision if needed. (This level of caution probably isn't necessary if you're the sole editor of these files.)

Disable CVS Integration

Disables all the options in the CVS menu, except for CVS → Enable CVS Integration, which replaces this command.

The CVS Status Column

When using CVS integration, Project Builder's File tab displays a CVS status column, headed with a yellow cylinder icon. This column displays one of the symbols listed in Table 18-41 for each file and group listed within the File tab (including no symbol at all for files and groups that are up to date with the project's CVS repository).

Table 18-41. CVS symbols in Project Builder

Symbol	File status
no symbol	Up to date
U	Needs an update
M	Locally modified
C	Contains conflicts
?	Not in repository
A	Added, but not yet committed

Using the FileMerge Application

The FileMerge application (which lives in */Developer/Applications/*) launches in order to display differences between your working copy of a file and the repository's version when you run CVS → Compare with Base or CVS → Compare/ Merge with Latest Revision. Figure 18-1 shows a file that has, through local editing, developed differences from its repository version.

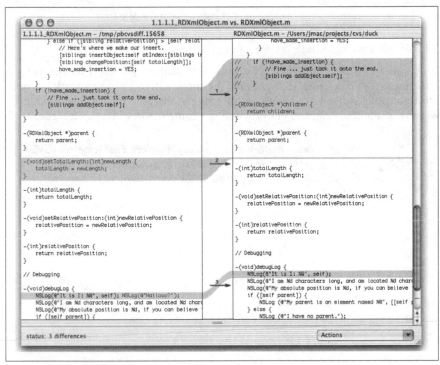

Figure 18-1. The FileMerge application

The FileMerge window displays both the repository's idea of the file in the frame on the left, and your local sandbox copy on the right. FileMerge pairs up the areas of difference between the file by highlighting them in gray, visually connecting them as Figure 18-1 shows. In the center column between each such difference lies a special control consisting of a number over an arrow. The arrow points to the area that, were you to select File → Save at that moment, would end up in the final, merged file.

To adjust the merge, click on a difference's arrow control; this selects that difference. You may now make a selection from the Actions pop-up menu, found in the window's lower-right corner, which changes the text you favor for going into the final merge. The selections are described in the following list.

Choose left
> Favor the text shown in the left pane.

Choose right
> Favor the text shown in the right pane (the default).

Choose both (left first)
> Put both sections into the merge, but place the left one first.

Choose both (right first)
> Put both sections into the merge, but place the right one first.

Choose neither
> Simply leave this whole section out of the merge.

When all the arrows correctly represent the text sections you favor for the merged outcome, select File → Save to perform the merge. If you want to work on your sandboxed file some more before performing the merge, just close the FileMerge window without saving, and perform another comparison when you feel ready.

> While Project Builder automatically invokes FileMerge for CVS merging, you can use on any two files in your filesystem, making it a useful graphical complement to the command-line `diff` and `merge` tools.

V

Under Mac OS X's Hood

Now it's time to roll up your sleeves. This part of the book goes deeper into the BSD Unix side of Mac OS X, introducing you to the Terminal application (your interface to Darwin), and covers topics on pattern matching, shells, using the *defaults* command, installing the X Window System, and installing Unix applications on your Mac.

This part wraps up with the most complete Unix command reference you'll find in print for Mac OS X. Every command and option has been verified against Jaguar; in many places, this reference is more accurate than the manpages installed on your system.

The chapters in this part include:

19

Using the Terminal

The Terminal application (*/Applications/Utilities*) is your gateway between the candy-coated Aqua graphical interface and the no-nonsense command-line interface that Darwin uses. This book (as well as a lot of Apple documentation) tends to use the terms *command-line* and *Terminal* interchangeably, since, with Mac OS X, to get to the former you must go through the latter. (Which is not to say there aren't alternatives for those willing to look; see "Terminal Alternatives," later in this chapter.)

Using the Terminal

Each window in the Terminal represents a separate *shell* process—a command-line interpreter ready to accept your instructions, as described in "Introduction to the Shell" in Chapter 21.

Terminal Preferences

The Terminal application's user settings control not just the application's look and feel, but the ways that you interact with your shells. This section covers the more important application preferences to know about.

Setting a default shell

There are two ways to set a default shell when using your system, suggested by the "When creating a new Terminal window" radio buttons found in Terminal's Terminal → Preferences window, seen in Figure 19-1. The lazier way involves activating the "Execute this command" button and typing a shell's path into the neighboring text field. Henceforth, whenever you open a new Terminal window, that shell will launch in place of your default login shell. This is a nice solution if you use only Terminal as a command line (as opposed to the alternatives noted in the section "Terminal Alternatives") and never log in remotely to your machine, or if you're not a member of the machine's admin group and hence can't set your login shell to something else.

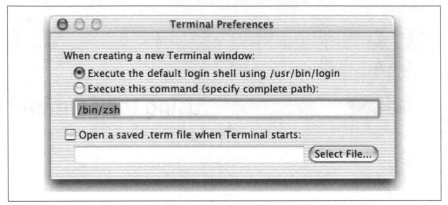

Figure 19-1. The Terminal Preferences dialog

A more permanent, but less obvious, way involves changing your account's default shell. This will affect not just the shell that Terminal opens by default, but the shell that appears when you use a different command-line access application, or log in to your machine from some other location via *ssh* (described in "The Secure Shell" in Chapter 13). If you have admin privileges, you can do this through the NetInfo database, adjusting your user account's low-level preferences. Launch NetInfo Manager and navigate to its */users/your-username* directory. (For a complete review of NetInfo, see Chapter 12.) Locate the *shell* property, double-click its value, and type some other shell's path in its place, as shown in Figure 19-2.

If you don't have admin access, you can ask someone who does to take these steps for you. Once your *shell* property under NetInfo has been reset one way or another, select the Terminal preferences' "Execute the default login shell using /usr/bin/login" radio button.

You can always change your shell on the fly by invoking it as a command. If you're running *zsh* and wish to temporarily drop into *tcsh* for some reason (perhaps you're following some Unix program's arcane installation instructions, which are written only in *tcsh*-ese), I can just type **tcsh** (or the full path, **/bin/tcsh**) at the command prompt.

A shell launched in this manner runs as a child to the Terminal window's main shell, so when you exit the second shell you'll pop safely back out to the first shell's command prompt again.

For a *really* lazy way to change your shell, you can make the first line of your default shell's *rc* file a command to switch to your shell of choice! This is a rather slovenly solution, and will probably cause you (or others) confusion later. Use one of the other solutions that this section presents, if at all possible.

The Terminal Inspector

Selecting File → Get Info (⌘-I) or Terminal → Window Settings calls up the Terminal Inspector window, shown in Figure 19-3. This window lets you set a

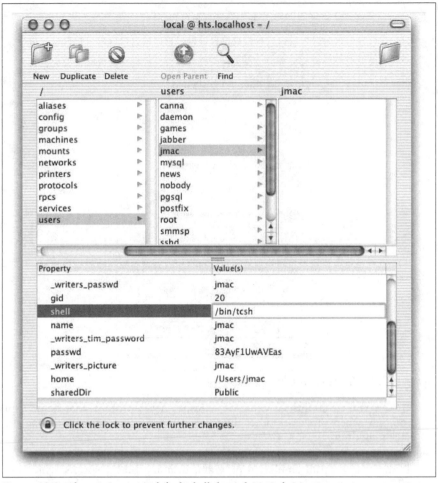

Figure 19-2. Changing a user's default shell through NetInfo Manager

variety of visual and shell-interaction options affecting the frontmost Terminal window. The pop-up menu at the top of the window lets you navigate between its many panes, summarized in the following list.

Shell

Lists the shell tied to this Terminal window, and lets you define the application's behavior when you exit a shell (through the *logout* or *exit* commands, or sending an EOF signal to the main shell through Control-D). See the earlier section "Setting a default shell" for information about changing shells.

Processes

Lists the processes running as children of this window's shell and lets you specify the Terminal's behavior if some processes are still running when you close a window, since closing a Terminal window kills its shell process and any non-backgrounded processes it may contain (see "Process Management" earlier in this chapter). As Figure 19-3 shows, you can have Terminal always

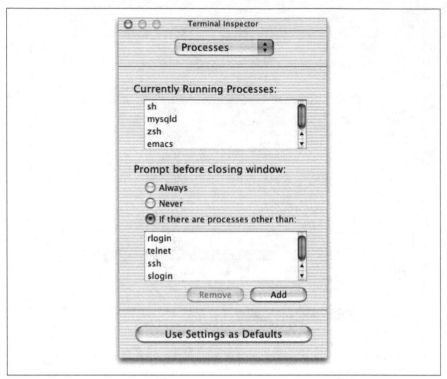

Figure 19-3. The Terminal Inspector window

prompt you to confirm a window's closure, never prompt you, or prompt you only when processes other than those in the given list exist among the shell's children.

Emulation

Terminal is a vt100 emulation program, meaning that it speaks a protocol originally conceived for a certain class of terminals made by (the now-defunct) Digital Equipment Corporation in the late 1970s and early 1980s. The Terminal's Emulation preferences pane gives you a list of checkboxes controlling high-level mapping between your Mac's keyboard and the underlying terminal protocol, as follows:

Delete key sends backspace

Some terminal or terminal programs make a distinction between the delete character (which your Delete key normally sends) and a backspace character. Try checking this box if you find that the Delete key is not doing what you expect.

Use option key as meta key

Some Terminal programs (such as the *Emacs* text editor—see "Emacs" in Chapter 17) define a "Meta" key for certain keystrokes. Since your Mac keyboard lacks such a thing, checking this box will have your Option key stand in for it.

Option click to position cursor

Though it may resemble an Aqua text view in some ways, a Terminal window is normally unresponsive to mouse clicks, making you use keyboard commands to move the cursor around. If you check this box, however, you can option-click a Terminal window to automatically reposition the cursor to that point. This can be a handy function when using Terminal-based text editors, such as *Emacs* or *vi* (see "Unix Text Editors" in Chapter 17).

Paste newlines as carriage returns

When this checkbox is active, then any newline characters within text you paste into a Terminal window—through the standard Edit → Paste (⌘-V) command—will be automatically converted to carriage return characters.

Strict VT-100 keypad behavior

When checked, the number keypad functions according to the VT-100 protocol.

Escape 8-bit chars with Control-V

Some Terminal shells and programs might react badly to your typing high-bit (accented) characters, interpreting them as control characters. If you find this happening, activate this checkbox. Henceforth, typing Control-V will tell the shell or program to literally interpret the next character you type.

Audible bell

Bell characters cause the Mac to sound its system beep.

Visual bell

Bell characters cause the Mac's screen to pulse.

Buffer

Lets you set how many lines of history the Terminal window remembers (and lets you scroll back to via the window's scrollbar), and how it handles line wrapping.

Display

Contains options for the cursor's shape and blinking pattern, as well as the text font and encoding to use. The Terminal uses Unicode UTF-8 as its default (see "Unicode on Mac OS X" in Chapter 17).

Color

Lets you set the window's text, background, cursor and text-selection colors. The Transparency slider sets the background color's opacity level; setting it to something less than full opacity (by dragging the slider to the right) lets you work with a Terminal window while keeping things behind it visible. This can prove useful when following instructions contained in another window without having to resize either.

Activating the pane's "Disable ANSI color" checkbox prevents your color choices from being overridden by ANSI color-setting instructions that the terminal might receive.

Window

> Lets you set the window's dimensions in terms of rows and columns of text, and assign it a title based on a number of checkbox-based criteria, as Figure 19-4 shows.

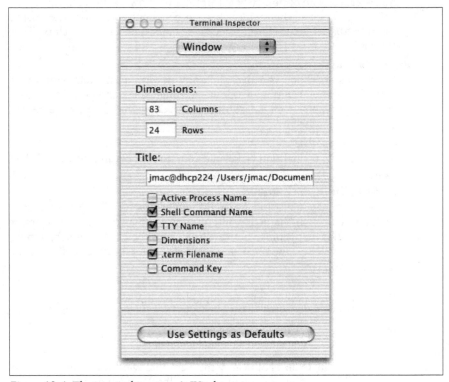

Figure 19-4. The terminal inspector's Window pane

Hitting the ever present Use Settings as Defaults button at the bottom of the inspector window saves all the panes' settings as your Terminal application defaults, affecting all future windows you open through File → New Shell (⌘-N). See the next section.

Saving and Loading Terminals

After you set up a Terminal window and shell via the terminal inspector window (see "The Terminal Inspector" later in this chapter), you have two ways of keeping these settings for future Terminal sessions: either click the Use Settings as Defaults to make them the Terminal applications' overall default settings, or save the frontmost window's settings to a file through File → Save (⌘-S). This creates a *.term* file that stores all the window's settings. (It uses the standard property list XML format described in "Property Lists" in Chapter 17, so you can manually browse these files if you wish.) When you want to open a new Terminal window with all those settings, select File → Open (⌘-O), and then navigate to and open that *.term* file.

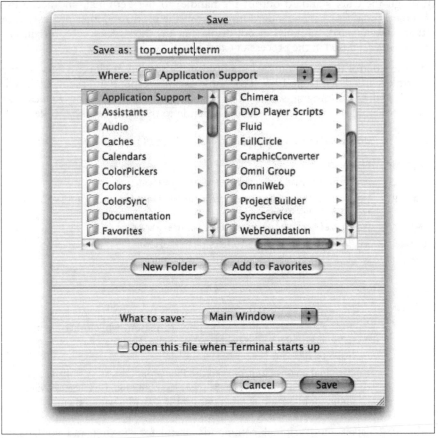

Figure 19-5. The Terminal's Save dialog

As Figure 19-5 shows, the dialog has two extra controls. If you select All Windows (rather than the default Main Window) from the "What to save" pop-up menu, then *all* the Terminal's open windows, including their on-screen positions, get stored to the resulting *.term* file. This is the option to choose if you like to arrange multiple Terminal windows, perhaps with different properties, in a "just-right" arrangement for a certain task.

Activating the "Open this file when Terminal starts up" checkbox will do just what it says. Note that you can set several *.term* files with this function, if you wish; if you wish to have a single such file as your default, and later change your mind about which *.term* file to use, you'd got to re-save the original window settings with File → Save As (Shift-⌘-S), and deactivate that checkbox.

Process Management

Each command you invoke or program that you run from a Terminal window becomes a child of that terminal's shell. The Terminal window can juggle many child processes at once, but only one at a time is *foregrounded*, writing its output (through the Unix standard output file handle) to the Terminal, and accepting keyboard input (via Unix standard input) from the user. Any other processes are either *backgrounded*, running but not displaying any interface or accepting input, or *suspended*, paused in the process of execution.

You can control the foregrounded application by sending it Unix signals via the keystrokes listed in Table 19-1. Programs usually respond to them as listed, though individual programs may interpret them differently. (The *Emacs* text editor, for example, ties a text-searching function to the Control-S keystroke.)

Table 19-1. Foreground process control keystrokes

Keystroke	Description
Control-C	Sends an interrupt signal, which usually causes the program to exit.
Control-D	Sends an end-of-file signal. If a program is accepting multiple lines of input from you, this signals that you're finished providing it.
Control-Z	Suspends the foregrounded process and returns you to the command line.
Control-S	Suspends the foregrounded process, but keeps it in the foreground.
Control-Q	Resumes a suspended, foregrounded process.

Control-Q is a good keystroke to try if a Terminal window ceases to update or accept input for no obvious reason, while other Terminal windows continue behaving normally. You may have hit Control-S by mistake.

Terminal aliases Control-C to the File → Send break (Control-C or ⌘-.) menu selection. The ⌘-. key combination is a legacy Mac idiom for interrupting programs (or the activities within them).

Table 19-2 lists some Terminal commands useful for viewing and controlling backgrounded processes. You can find complete references for all of them in Chapter 25. See the next section to find out a process's process ID number (*pid*), which many of these commands require. (You can also use the more convenient %N syntax described by that section when working with processes that are children of the current Terminal window's shell.)

Table 19-2. Process control commands

Command	Description
ps	List Terminal-based processes belonging to you.
jobs	List processes that are children of this terminal's shell process.
fg *pid*	Foregound (and resume, if suspended) the process with that pid.
bg *pid*	Background (and resume, if suspended) the process with that pid.
kill -*signal pid*	Send a signal (the terminate signal, by default) to the process with that pid.
killall -*signal process-name*	Send a signal (the terminate signal, by default) to all processes with that name.

Seeing processes

Typing *ps* by itself displays a simple list of all the shells you are running, as well as all their child processes:

```
[jmac@wireless251 jmac]% ps
  371 p1  Ss+   0:01.72 -zsh (zsh)
  454 p1  S     0:35.69 emacs reading/autohandler
  461 p2  Ss    0:00.04 -bin/tcsh -i (tcsh)
  462 p2  S+    0:18.11 tail -f /var/log/httpd/error_log
  463 p3  Ss    0:01.35 -zsh (zsh)
 1893 p3  S+    0:52.00 emacs xonx.xml
 2034 std Ss    0:00.07 -zsh (zsh)
[jmac@wireless251 jmac]%
```

Here we see that the user jmac owns four shell processes: three instances of the *zsh* shell, and one *tcsh*. (As it happens, there are three Terminal windows open and running the shell of choice, *zsh*, while in the background, a shell script that invokes *tcsh* is running—see Chapter 21.) Within these shells, there are two *Emacs* sessions active, and a *tail* program is dutifully running on my Apache web server's error log.

The numbers in the first column of the table show the PID (Process ID) number of each process. These are what you can feed to the commands listed in Table 19-2 in order to foreground, background, or send signals to them.

Alternatively, you can use shell-relative PIDs with these commands. Invoking *jobs* lists only those the processes running as children to the current shell:

```
[jmac@Jason-McIntoshs-Computer /Library]% jobs
[1]   running    sudo bin/safe_mysqld
[2] + suspended  emacs reading/autohandler
[jmac@Jason-McIntoshs-Computer /Library]%
```

The bracketed numbers leading each row of this output table can be used instead of PIDs when issuing process-control commands. The number can be prefaced with a percentage sign (%) to show that you're using a relative PID. So, to foreground that *Emacs* process, type **fg %2**. In this particular instance, you could also type **fg** for the same effect; the plus-sign symbol next to the number tells me that it's a child process, and hence the default target for commands like *fg* and *bg*.

> For another view of a Terminal window's child processes, select File → Get Info (⌘-I) and select the Processes choice from the resulting window's pop-up menu. See "The Terminal Inspector," later in this chapter, for more about this window's views and options.

To see a list of *all* the processes you're running on this machine, use *ps x*:

```
[jmac@Jason-McIntoshs-Computer /Library]% ps x
  PID  TT  STAT    TIME COMMAND
  175  ??  Ss   16:32.00 /System/Library/Frameworks/ApplicationServices.
framew
  184  ??  Ss   33:45.32 /System/Library/CoreServices/WindowServer -daemon
  336  ??  Ss    0:12.95 /System/Library/CoreServices/loginwindow.app/
Contents
```

```
  359 ??  Ss     0:02.63 /System/Library/CoreServices/pbs
  362 ??  S      1:37.68 /System/Library/CoreServices/Dock.app/Contents/
MacOS/
  367 ??  S      1:29.67 /System/Library/CoreServices/SystemUIServer.app/
Conte
  368 ??  S      3:00.47 /System/Library/CoreServices/Finder.app/Contents/
MacO
  370 ??  S     31:35.80 /Applications/Utilities/Terminal.app/Contents/
MacOS/T
  450 ??  S      0:08.37 /System/Library/Services/AppleSpell.service/
Contents/
  451 ??  S     16:24.86 /Applications/Mail.app/Contents/MacOS/Mail -psn_0_
117
  452 ??  S      0:03.63 /System/Library/CoreServices/SecurityAgent.app/
Conten
  944 ??  S      1:27.30 /Applications/OmniOutliner.app/Contents/MacOS/
OmniOut
  946 ??  S      0:09.72 /Applications/TextEdit.app/Contents/MacOS/TextEdit
-p
  995 ??  S      0:05.76 /Applications/System Preferences.app/Contents/
MacOS/S
 1155 ??  S      0:14.66 /Applications/ManOpen.app/Contents/MacOS/ManOpen -
psn
 1193 ??  S    137:16.24 /Applications/iTunes.app/Contents/MacOS/iTunes -
psn_0
 1623 ??  S     14:24.34 /System/Library/CoreServices/Classic Startup.app/
Cont
 1942 ??  Ss     0:00.15 /Applications/Utilities/Disk Copy.app/Contents/
MacOS/
 1995 ??  S      0:21.08 /Applications/OmniWeb.app/Contents/MacOS/OmniWeb -
psn
  371 std Ss     0:01.91 -zsh (zsh)
  454 std S      0:35.69 emacs reading/autohandler
  461 p2  Ss     0:00.04 -bin/tcsh -i (tcsh)
  462 p2  S+     0:18.33 tail -f /var/log/httpd/error_log
  463 p3  Ss     0:01.35 -zsh (zsh)
 1893 p3  S+     1:05.11 emacs xonx.xml
 2034 p4  Ss+    0:00.08 -zsh (zsh)
[jmac@Jason-McIntoshs-Computer /Library]%
```

This lists both the Terminal-controlled programs and the Aqua applications that are running, as well as the frameworks, system services, and plug-ins used by those applications. They are, after all, just Unix programs, all with their own pids.

Running *ps* with the *aux* options lists every single process running on the machine, regardless of context or user. This would, at a typical moment in any Mac OS X machine's life, be enough to fill a couple of pages of this book. You can pipe this output through the *grep* command to automatically filter the results: **ps ax | grep zsh** would show a table describing all the *zsh* processes every user is currently running, for example.

For a friendlier interface to browsing active processes, see the Process Viewer application, located at */Applications/Utilities/Process Viewer*.

Sending signals with kill and killall

As its name suggests, *kill*'s most common function involves terminating programs, through its default usage: `kill pid`. Actually, *kill* sends a Unix signal of some kind to the program, and the default happens to be the terminate (TERM) signal. You can send different signals through the `kill -signal pid` syntax, where *signal* is a signal name or number.

The even more violent-sounding *killall* is often more convenient than *kill* is. This really just lets you refer to processes by their name, saving you from having to look up their pids first. For example, `killall tail` sends the TERM signal to all *tail* processes that are running under one name.

killall -HUP process is a traditional Unix idiom for having a continually running process, such as a network daemon, reload its configuration information. However, if a Startup Script is available for this service, you should favor running that instead, even if they both ultimately have a similar effect; see "Configuring Startup Items" in Chapter 13.

Terminal Alternatives

Apple's Terminal application is good at what it does, but it doesn't always satisfy Unix veterans as they first explore Mac OS X. After all, they come from operating systems where the command line represents the primary user interface, even if the GUI-like X Windows are available to supplement it. To them, the Terminal application can seem serviceable but weak, with not nearly the amount of flexibility they're used to.

Alternatives to the Terminal come in two classes: native Aqua applications that replace the Terminal and bypass Aqua entirely by running genuine *xterm* windows in X.

GLterm

GLTerm, a shareware application by Michel Pollet available at *http://www.pollet. net/GLterm/*, represents (at the time of this writing) the only widely distributed, full-featured Mac OS X Terminal replacement application. It supports full vt102 emulation (which can be useful when *ssh*-ing to a machine that prefers it over Terminal's vt100 emulation), DEC function keys, and a wide array of customization options different than Terminal's. (And, it has a delightfully retro Finder icon: a photograph of an ancient vt100 terminal machine.)

On the other hand, GLTerm requires 3D-acceleration hardware to run well (its name comes from the fact that it's written with the OpenGL 3D graphics libraries, rather than the usual Quartz 2D libraries), and it supports only the Latin-1 character set, not Unicode. It also uses its own X11-based font set rather than the Mac's installed fonts.

xterm

If you've installed the X Windows system on your Mac, you can use the *xterm* program that comes with it, as well as a variety alternative terminals available for this windowing system. Consult Chapter 22 for full details.

Mac OS X's Console Mode

While not quite a Terminal alternative per se, Mac OS X's built-in console login mode lets you choose to use Darwin's command-line interface *instead of* the Aqua GUI for the length of a login session.

To enter console mode, identify yourself as >console at the Mac OS X login window, and then click Log In (or press Return) without providing a password. The Aqua interface vanishes, replaced by a standard Unix login prompt. Despite the vastly different appearance, it's the same old Mac OS X login procedure: type in your username and password as directed and you're in.

Once you log out (through the *logout* command, or by *exit*ing your shell program), the Aqua's login window will appear once more. You'll need to pull the >console trick again in order to re-enter console mode; otherwise, subsequent logins will launch the Finder, as usual.

See "Single-User Mode" in Chapter 11.

20

Pattern Matching

A number of Unix text-processing utilities let you search for, and in some cases change, text patterns rather than fixed strings. These utilities include the editing programs *vi* and *Emacs*, programming languages like Perl and Python, and the commands *grep* and *egrep*. Text patterns (formally called regular expressions) contain normal characters mixed with special characters (called metacharacters).

For more information on regular expressions, see *Mastering Regular Expressions* (O'Reilly & Associates, Inc.).

Filenames Versus Patterns

When you issue a command on the command line, special characters are seen first by the shell, and then by the program; therefore, unquoted metacharacters are interpreted by the shell for filename expansion. The command:

```
$ grep [A-Z]* chap[12]
```

could, for example, be transformed by the shell into:

```
$ grep Array.c Bug.c Comp.c chap1 chap2
```

and would then try to find the pattern Array.c in files Bug.c, Comp.c, chap1, and chap2. To bypass the shell and pass the special characters to *grep*, use quotes:

```
$ grep "[A-Z]*" chap[12]
```

Double quotes suffice in most cases, but single quotes are the safest bet.

Note also that in pattern matching, ? matches zero or one instance of a regular expression; in filename expansion, ? matches a single character.

Metacharacters, Listed by Unix Program

Some metacharacters are valid for one program but not for another. Those that are available to a Unix program are marked by a checkmark (✓) in Table 20-1.

Items marked with a P are specified by POSIX; double-check your system's version. Full descriptions are provided after the table.

Table 20-1. Unix metacharacters

Symbol	ed	ex	vi	sed	awk	grep	egrep	Action
.	✓	✓	✓	✓	✓	✓	✓	Match any character.
*	✓	✓	✓	✓	✓	✓	✓	Match zero or more preceding.
^	✓	✓	✓	✓	✓	✓	✓	Match beginning of line/string.
$	✓	✓	✓	✓	✓	✓	✓	Match end of line/string.
\	✓	✓	✓	✓	✓	✓	✓	Escape following character.
[ ]	✓	✓	✓	✓	✓	✓	✓	Match one from a set.
(\)	✓	✓	✓	✓		✓		Store pattern for later replay.[a]
\n	✓	✓	✓	✓		✓		Replay subpattern in match.
{ }					✓P		✓P	Match a range of instances.
\{ \}	✓			✓		✓		Match a range of instances.
\< \>	✓	✓	✓					Match word's beginning or end.
+					✓		✓	Match one or more preceding.
?					✓		✓	Match zero or one preceding.
|					✓		✓	Separate choices to match.
( )					✓		✓	Group expressions to match.

[a] Stored subpatterns can be replayed during matching. See Table 20-2.

Note that in *ed*, *ex*, *vi*, and *sed*, you specify both a search pattern (on the left) and a replacement pattern (on the right). The metacharacters in Table 20-1 are meaningful only in a search pattern.

In *ed*, *ex*, *vi*, and *sed*, the metacharacters in Table 20-2 are valid only in a replacement pattern.

Table 20-2. Metacharacters in replacement patterns

Symbol	ex	vi	sed	ed	Action
\	✓	✓	✓	✓	Escape following character.
\n	✓	✓	✓	✓	Text matching pattern stored in \(\).
&	✓	✓	✓	✓	Text matching search pattern.
~	✓	✓			Reuse previous replacement pattern.
%				✓	Reuse previous replacement pattern.
\u \U	✓	✓			Change character(s) to uppercase.
\l \L	✓	✓			Change character(s) to lowercase.
\E	✓	✓			Turn off previous \U or \L.
\e	✓				Turn off previous \u or \l.

Metacharacters

Search Patterns

The characters in the following table have special meaning only in search patterns.

Character	Pattern
.	Match any *single* character except newline. Can match newline in *awk*.
*	Match any number (or none) of the single character that immediately precedes it. The preceding character can also be a regular expression; e.g., since . (dot) means any character, .* means match any number of any character.
^	Match the following regular expression at the beginning of the line or string.
$	Match the preceding regular expression at the end of the line or string.
[ ]	Match any *one* of the enclosed characters. A hyphen (-) indicates a range of consecutive characters. A circumflex (^) as the first character in the brackets reverses the sense: it matches any one character *not* in the list. A hyphen or close bracket (]) as the first character is treated as a member of the list. All other metacharacters are treated as members of the list (i.e., literally).
{*n,m*}	Match a range of occurrences of the single character that immediately precedes it. The preceding character can also be a metacharacter. {*n*} matches exactly *n* occurrences, {*n*, } matches at least *n* occurrences, and {*n,m*} matches any number of occurrences between *n* and *m*. *n* and *m* must be between 0 and 255, inclusive.
\{*n,m*\}	Just like {*n,m*}, above, but with backslashes in front of the braces.
	Turn off the special meaning of the character that follows.
\(\)	Save the pattern enclosed between \(and \) into a special holding space. Up to nine patterns can be saved on a single line. The text matched by the subpatterns can be replayed in substitutions by the escape sequences \1 to \9.
\n	Replay the *n*th subpattern enclosed in \(and \) into the pattern at this point. *n* is a number from 1 to 9, with 1 starting on the left. See the section "Examples of Searching" later in this chapter.
\< \>	Match characters at beginning (\<) or end (\>) of a word.
+	Match one or more instances of preceding regular expression.
?	Match zero or one instances of preceding regular expression.
		Match the regular expression specified before or after.
( )	Apply a match to the enclosed group of regular expressions.

Many Unix systems allow the use of POSIX character classes within the square brackets that enclose a group of characters. These classes, listed here, are typed enclosed in [: and :]. For example, [[:alnum:]] matches a single alphanumeric character.

Class	Characters matched
alnum	Alphanumeric characters
alpha	Alphabetic characters
blank	Space or tab
cntrl	Control characters
digit	Decimal digits
graph	Nonspace characters
lower	Lowercase characters

Class	Characters matched
`print`	Printable characters
`space`	Whitespace characters
`upper`	Uppercase characters
`xdigit`	Hexadecimal digits

Replacement Patterns

The characters in this table have special meaning only in replacement patterns.

Character	Pattern
\	Turn off the special meaning of the character that follows.
\n	Restore the text matched by the nth pattern previously saved by \(and \). n is a number from 1 to 9, with 1 starting on the left.
&	Reuse the text matched by the search pattern as part of the replacement pattern.
~	Reuse the previous replacement pattern in the current replacement pattern. Must be the only character in the replacement pattern. (*ex* and *vi*)
%	Reuse the previous replacement pattern in the current replacement pattern. Must be the only character in the replacement pattern. (*ed*)
\u	Convert first character of replacement pattern to uppercase.
\U	Convert entire replacement pattern to uppercase.
\l	Convert first character of replacement pattern to lowercase.
\L	Convert entire replacement pattern to lowercase.
\e, \E	Turn off previous \u, \U, \l, and \L.

Examples of Searching

When used with *grep* or *egrep*, regular expressions should be surrounded by quotes. (If the pattern contains a $, you must use single quotes; e.g., *'pattern'*.) When used with *ed*, *ex*, *sed*, and *awk*, regular expressions are usually surrounded by /, although (except for *awk*) any delimiter works. The following tables show some example patterns.

General patterns

Pattern	What does it match?
bag	The string *bag*.
^bag	*bag* at the beginning of the line.
bag$	*bag* at the end of the line.
^bag$	*bag* as the only word on the line.
[Bb]ag	*Bag* or *bag*.
b[aeiou]g	Second letter is a vowel.
b[^aeiou]g	Second letter is a consonant (or uppercase or symbol).
b.g	Second letter is any character.
^...$	Any line containing exactly three characters.

Pattern	What does it match?
`^.`	Any line that begins with a dot.
`^\.[a-z][a-z]`	Same, followed by two lowercase letters (e.g., *troff* requests).
`^\.[a-z]\{2\}`	Same as previous; *ed*, *grep*, and *sed* only.
`^\[^.]`	Any line that doesn't begin with a dot.
`bugs*`	*bug, bugs, bugss*, etc.
`"word"`	A word in quotes.
`"*word"*`	A word, with or without quotes.
`[A-Z][A-Z]*`	One or more uppercase letters.
`[A-Z]+`	Same; *egrep* or *awk* only.
`[[:upper:]]+`	Same; POSIX *egrep* or *awk*.
`[A-Z].*`	An uppercase letter, followed by zero or more characters.
`[A-Z]*`	Zero or more uppercase letters.
`[a-zA-Z]`	Any letter.
`[^0-9A-Za-z]`	Any symbol or space (not a letter or a number).
`[^[:alnum:]]`	Same, using POSIX character class.

Egrep and awk Patterns

egrep or awk pattern	What does it Match?
`[567]`	One of the numbers *5*, *6*, or *7*.
`five|six|seven`	One of the words *five*, *six*, or *seven*.
`80[2-4]?86`	*8086, 80286, 80386*, or *80486*.
`80[2-4]?86|(Pentium(-II)?)`	*8086, 80286, 80386, 80486, Pentium*, or *Pentium-II*.
`compan(y|ies)`	*company* or *companies*.

Ex and vi Patterns

ex or vi pattern	What does it match?
`\<the`	Words like *theater* or *the*.
`the\>`	Words like *breathe* or *the*.
`\<the\>`	The word *the*.

Ed, sed and grep Patterns

ed, sed or grep pattern	What does it match?
`0\{5,\}`	Five or more zeros in a row.
`[0-9]\{3\}-[0-9]\{2\}-[0-9]{4\}`	U.S. Social Security number (*nnn-nn-nnnn*).

ed, sed or grep pattern	What does it match?
\(why\).*\1	A line with two occurrences of *why*.
\([[:alpha:]_][[:alnum:]_.]*\) = \1;	C/C++ simple assignment statements.

Examples of Searching and Replacing

The examples in Table 20-3 show the metacharacters available to *sed* or *ex*. Note that *ex* commands begin with a colon. A space is marked by a ".."; a tab is marked by an →.

Table 20-3. Searching and replacing

Command	Result
s/.*/(&)/	Redo the entire line, but add parentheses.
s/.*/mv & &.old/	Change a word list (one word per line) into *mv* commands.
/^$/d	Delete blank lines.
:g/^$/d	Same as previous, in *ex* editor.
/^→*$/d	Delete blank lines, plus lines containing only spaces or tabs.
:g/^→*$/d	Same as previous, in *ex* editor.
s/ ..*/ ./g	Turn one or more spaces into one space.
:%s/ ..*/ ./g	Same as previous, in *ex* editor.
:s/[0-9]/Item &:/	Turn a number into an item label (on the current line).
:s	Repeat the substitution on the first occurrence.
:&	Same as previous.
:sg	Same, but for all occurrences on the line.
:&g	Same as previous.
:%&g	Repeat the substitution globally (i.e., on all lines).
:.,$s/Fortran/\U&/g	On current line to last line, change word to uppercase.
:%s/.*/\L&/	Lowercase entire file.
:s/\<./\u&/g	Uppercase first letter of each word on current line. (Useful for titles.)
:%s/yes/No/g	Globally change a word to *No*.
:%s/Yes/~/g	Globally change a different word to *No* (previous replacement).

Finally, we have some *sed* examples for transposing words. A simple transposition of two words might look like this:

```
s/die or do/do or die/          Transpose words
```

The real trick is to use hold buffers to transpose variable patterns. For example:

```
s/\([Dd]ie\) or \([Dd]o\)/\2 or \1/     Transpose, using hold buffers
```

21

Shells and Shell Programming

As discussed in Chapter 19, a *shell* is a command-line interpreter program. It receives your typed-in commands when using the Terminal (or a similar program) and decides what to do with it. You can also use a shell in batch mode, treating it like an interpreted programming language and feeding it an entire scriptful of statements to execute, possibly including logic and flow control statements.

This chapter covers the shells included with Mac OS X, along with *tcsh*, its default shell program.

Introduction to the Shell

The shell is the user interface to Unix, and by the same token, several shells are available in Unix. Mac OS X provides you with more than one shell to choose from. Each shell has different features, but all of them affect how commands will be interpreted and provide tools to create your Unix environment.

Let's suppose that the Unix operating system is a car. When you drive, you issue a variety of "commands": you turn the steering wheel, press the accelerator, or press the brake. But how does the car translate your commands into the action you want? The car's drive mechanism, which can be thought of as the car's user interface, is responsible. Cars can be equipped with front-wheel drive, rear-wheel drive, four-wheel drive, and sometimes combinations of these.

The shell is simply a program that allows the system to understand your commands. (That's why the shell is often called a *command interpreter*.) For many users, the shell works invisibly—"behind the scenes." Your only concern is that the system does what you tell it to do; you don't care about the inner workings. In our car analogy, this is comparable to pressing the brake. Most of us don't care whether the user interface involves disk brakes, drum brakes, or anti-lock brakes, as long as the car stops.

There are three uses for the shell:

- Interactive use
- Customization of your Unix session
- Programming

Interactive Use

When the shell is used interactively, the system waits for you to type a command at the Unix prompt. Your commands can include special symbols that let you abbreviate filenames or redirect input and output.

Customization of Your Unix Session

A Unix shell defines variables to control the behavior of your Unix session. Setting these variables will tell the system, for example, which directory to use as your home directory, or the file in which to store your mail. Some variables are preset by the system; you can define others in startup files that are read when you log in. Startup files can also contain Unix commands or special shell commands. These are executed every time you log in.

Programming

Unix shells provide a set of special (or built-in) commands that let you create programs called *shell scripts*. In fact, many built-in commands can be used interactively like Unix commands, and Unix commands are frequently used in shell scripts. Scripts are useful for executing a series of individual commands. Scripts can also execute commands repeatedly (in a loop) or conditionally (if-else), as in many high-level programming languages.

Mac OS X Shells

In essence, all shells do the same thing; they just differ in the *way* they do it, the options and settings they recognize, and the special features they offer. The following list describes the Mac OS X shells, all of which are included with the */bin* directory, and are available to all users on the system.

tcsh

tcsh is an evolved version of *csh*, a shell whose syntax is based loosely on the C programming language. It's quite popular for interactive use, and is the default shell for new users on Mac OS X.

Mac OS X includes a */bin/csh* command, but it's really just an alias to */bin/ tcsh*.

bash

The Bourne Again Shell (a pun on the Bourne Shell, the very first Unix shell program) is, like *tcsh*, a conceptual child of the earlier *csh* shell, but it is more commonly used, and is probably the most popular shell in use across Unix systems today. Many Mac OS X newcomers will recognize it as the default shell on most Linux distributions.

bash is aliased to */bin/sh*, so that shell scripts run in Darwin will actually run through *bash*.

zsh

Among the popular shell programs in the whole Unix sphere, *zsh* is the newest. It attempts to meld the better features of *bash* and *tcsh* into a single shell, as well as add a lot more—one of its more well-known unique features is programmable tab completion.

For general information about changing and using shells, see "Setting a default shell" in Chapter 19.

Common Features

The following table displays features that are common to Mac OS X's shells.

Symbol/Command	Meaning/Action
>	Redirect output.
>>	Append to file.
<	Redirect input.
<<	Here document (redirect input).
|	Pipe output.
&	Run process in background.
;	Separate commands on same line.
*	Match any character(s) in filename.
?	Match single character in filename.
[ ]	Match any characters enclosed.
( )	Execute in subshell.
``	Substitute output of enclosed command.
" "	Partial quote (allows variable and command expansion).
' '	Full quote (no expansion).
\	Quote following character.
$var	Use value for variable.
$$	Process ID.
$0	Command name.
$n	*n*th argument ($0 < n \le 9$).
$*	All arguments as simple words.
#	Begin comment.
bg	Background execution.
break	Break from loop statements.
cd	Change directory.
continue	Resume a program loop.
echo	Display output.
eval	Evaluate arguments.
exec	Execute a new shell.
fg	Foreground execution.
jobs	Show active jobs.
kill	Terminate running jobs.
shift	Shift positional parameters.

Symbol/Command	Meaning/Action
stop	Suspend a background job.
suspend	Suspend a foreground job (such as a shell created by *su*).
time	Time a command.
umask	Set default file permissions for new files.
unset	Erase variable or function definitions.
wait	Wait for a background job to finish.

Differing Features

The following table is a sampling of features that are different among the three shells:

Meaning/Action	bash	csh	tcsh
Default prompt.	$	%	%
Force redirection.	>|	>!	>!
Force append.		>>!	>>!
Variable assignment.	*var=val*	set *var=val*	set *var=val*
Set environment variable.	**export** *var=val*	**setenv** *var val*	**setenv** *var val*
Number of arguments.	$#	$#argv	$#argv
Exit status.	$?	$status	$?
Execute commands in *file*.	. *file*	**source** *file*	**source** *file*
End a loop statement.	**done**	**end**	**end**
End *case* or *switch*.	**esac**	**endsw**	**endsw**
Loop through variables.	**for/do**	**foreach**	**foreach**
Sample if statement.	**if [$i -eq 5]**	**if ($i==5)**	**if ($i==5)**
End if statement.	**fi**	**endif**	**endif**
Set resource limits.	**ulimit**	**limit**	**limit**
Read from terminal.	**read**	$<	**set -r**
Make a variable read-only.	**readonly**		
File inquiry operator; tests for nonzero size.		-s	
Complete current word.	Tab		Tab
Ignore interrupts.	**trap 2**	**onintr**	**onintr**
Begin until loop.	**until/do**	**until**	**until**
Begin while loop.	**while/do**	**while**	**while**

Configuring Shells

All these shells get their startup configuration information from *rc-files*, which live in your Home folder and whose names take the form *.shell-namerc*. Your *tcsh* configuration, therefore, is at *~/.tcshrc*. These files are loaded and all their commands executed whenever you load the corresponding shell, making them a great place to initialize environment variables—see "Environment Variables" later in this chapter.

Note that the Terminal application also has a number of settings of its own, which are quite a bit easier to find and customize; see "Terminal Preferences."

tcsh in Detail

The default user shell on Mac OS X systems is *tcsh*. If you want to use *bash*, or *zsh*, you first need to change your default. Each user's shell preference is kept in the NetInfo database. Unlike other Unix systems, you cannot set the user's default shell when creating a new user account using the Accounts preferences panel (see Chapter 5). If the user account already exists, you can change the default shell using NetInfo Manager, or the *chsh* command (see Chapter 25) in the Terminal.

Syntax

This section describes the many symbols peculiar to *tcsh*. The topics are arranged as follows:

- Special files
- Filename metacharacters
- Quoting
- Command forms
- Redirection forms

Special Files

Filename	Description
~/.cshrc or ~/.tcshrc	Executed at each instance of shell startup. For *tcsh*, if there is no ~/.tcshrc, uses ~/.cshrc if present.
~/.login	Executed by login shell after .cshrc at login.
~/.cshdirs	Executed by login shell after .login (*tcsh*).
~/.logout	Executed by login shell at logout.
/etc/passwd	Source of home directories for ~*name* abbreviations.

Filename Metacharacters

Characters	Meaning
*	Match any string of 0 or more characters.
?	Match any single character.
[*abc*...]	Match any one of the enclosed characters; a hyphen can be used to specify a range (e.g., a–z, A–Z, 0–9).
{*abc,xxx*,...}	Expand each comma-separated string inside braces.
~	Home directory for the current user.
~*name*	Home directory of *username*.

Examples

```
% ls new*        Match new and new.1
% cat ch?        Match ch9 but not ch10
% vi [D-R]*      Match files that begin with uppercase D through R
% ls {ch,app}?   Expand, then match ch1, ch2, app1, app2
% cd ~tom        Change to tom's home directory
```

Quoting

Quoting disables a character's special meaning and allows it to be used literally, as itself. The following characters have special meaning to *tcsh*:

Characters	Description
;	Command separator
&	Background execution
( )	Command grouping
|	Pipe
* ? [ ] ~	Filename metacharacters
{ }	String expansion characters (usually don't require quoting)
> < & !	Redirection symbols
! ^	History substitution, quick substitution
" ' \	Used in quoting other characters
`	Command substitution
$	Variable substitution
newline space tab	Word separators

The characters that follow can be used for quoting:

" "

> Everything between " and " is taken literally, except for the following characters, which keep their special meaning:
>
> $ Variable substitution will occur.
>
> `   Command substitution will occur.
>
> "   Marks the end of the double quote.
>
> \   Escape next character.
>
> !   The history character.
>
> *newline*
>   The newline character.

' '

> Everything between ' and ' is taken literally except for ! (history), another ', and newline.

\

> The character following a \ is taken literally. Use within " " to escape ", $, and `. Often used to escape itself, spaces, or newlines. Always needed to escape a history character (usually !).

Examples

```
% echo 'Single quotes "protect" double quotes'
Single quotes "protect" double quotes

% echo "Well, isn't that "\""special?"\"
Well, isn't that "special"?
```

```
% echo "You have ls|wc -l files in `pwd`"
You have 43 files in /home/bob

% echo The value of \$x is $x
The value of $x is 100
```

Command Forms

Command	Action
cmd &	Execute *cmd* in background.
cmd1 ; *cmd2*	Command sequence; execute multiple *cmd*s on the same line.
(*cmd1* ; *cmd2*)	Subshell; treat *cmd1* and *cmd2* as a command group.
cmd1 | *cmd2*	Pipe; use output from *cmd1* as input to *cmd2*.
cmd1 *cmd2*	Command substitution; run *cmd2* first and use its output as arguments to *cmd1*.
cmd1 || *cmd2*	OR; execute either *cmd1* or (if *cmd1* fails) *cmd2*.
cmd1 && *cmd2*	AND; execute *cmd1* and then (if *cmd1* succeeds) *cmd2*.

Examples

% nroff file > output &	*Format in the background*
% cd; ls	*Execute sequentially*
% (date; who; pwd) > logfile	*All output is redirected*
% sort file | pr -3 | lp	*Sort file, page output, then print*
% vi grep -l ifdef *.c`	*Edit files found by grep*
% egrep '(yes|no)' `cat list`	*Specify a list of files to search*
% grep XX file && lp file	*Print file if it contains the pattern*
% grep XX file || echo XX not found	*Echo an error message if XX not found*

Redirection Forms

File descriptor	Name	Common abbreviation	Typical default
0	Standard input	stdin	Keyboard
1	Standard output	stdout	Screen
2	Standard error	stderr	Screen

The usual input source or output destination can be changed with redirection commands listed in the following sections.

Simple Redirection

Command	Action
cmd > *file*	Send output of *cmd* to *file* (overwrite).
cmd >! *file*	Same as preceding, even if *noclobber* is set.
cmd >> *file*	Send output of *cmd* to *file* (append).
cmd>>! *file*	Same as preceding, even if *noclobber* is set.

Command	Action
cmd < file	Take input for cmd from file.
cmd << text	Read standard input up to a line identical to text (text can be stored in a shell variable). Input usually is typed on the screen or in the shell program. Commands that typically use this syntax include cat, echo, ex, and sed. If text is enclosed in quotes, standard input will not undergo variable substitution, command substitution, etc.

Multiple redirection

Command	Action
cmd >& file	Send both standard output and standard error to file.
cmd >&! file	Same as preceding, even if noclobber is set.
cmd >>& file	Append standard output and standard error to end of file.
cmd >>&! file	Same as preceding, even if noclobber is set.
cmd1 |& cmd2	Pipe standard error together with standard output.
(cmd> f1) >& f2	Send standard output to file f1 and standard error to file f2.
cmd	tee files	Send output of cmd to standard output (usually the screen) and to files.

Examples

```
% cat part1 > book                         Copy part1 to book
% cat part2 part3 >> book                  Append parts 2 and 3 to same file as part1
% mail tim < report                        Take input to message from report
% cc calc.c >& error_out                   Store all messages, including errors
% cc newcalc.c >&! error_out               Overwrite old file
% grep Unix ch* |& pr                      Pipe all messages, including errors
% (find / -print > filelist) >& no_access  Separate error messages from list of files
% sed 's/^/XX /' << "END_ARCHIVE"          Supply text right after command
This is often how a shell archive is "wrapped",
bundling text for distribution. You would normally
run sed from a shell program, not from the command line.
"END_ARCHIVE"
```

Variables

This subsection describes the following:

- Variable substitution
- Variable modifiers
- Predefined shell variables
- Formatting for the *prompt* variable
- Sample *.cshrc* file
- Environment variables

Variable substitution

In the following substitutions, braces ({ }) are optional, except when needed to separate a variable name from following characters that would otherwise be considered part of the name:

Variable	Description
${*var*}	The value of variable *var*.
${*var*[*i*]}	Select word or words in position *i* of *var*. *i* can be a single number, a range *m*–*n*, a range –*n* (missing m implies 1), a range *m*– (missing *n* implies all remaining words), or * (select all words). *i* also can be a variable that expands to one of these values.
${#*var*}	The number of words in *var*.
${#argv}	The number of arguments.
$0	Name of the program.
${argv[*n*]}	Individual arguments on command line (positional parameters); 1≤*n*≤9.
${*n*}	Same as ${argv[*n*]}.
${argv[*]}	All arguments on command line.
$*	Same as {argv[*]}.
$argv[$#argv]	The last argument.
${?*var*}	Return 1 if *var* is set, 0 if *var* is not set.
$$	Process number of current shell; useful as part of a filename for creating temporary files with unique names.
${?name}	Return 1 if *name* is set, 0 if not.
$?0	Return 1 if input filename is known, 0 if not.

Examples

Sort the third through last arguments and save the output in a file whose name is unique to this process:

```
sort $argv[3-] > tmp.$$
```

Process *.cshrc* commands only if the shell is interactive (i.e., the prompt variable must be set):

```
if ($?prompt) then
    set commands,
    alias commands,
    etc.
endif
```

Variable Modifiers

Except for $?*var*, $$, and $?0, the variable substitutions in the preceding section may be followed by one of these modifiers (when braces are used, the modifier goes inside them):

:r   Return the variable's root (the portion before the last dot).

:e   Return the variable's extension.

:h   Return the variable's header (the directory portion).

:t   Return the variable's tail (the portion after the last slash).

:gr   Return all roots.

:ge   Return all extensions.

:gh   Return all headers.

:gt   Return all tails.

:q   Quote a wordlist variable, keeping the items separate. Useful when the variable contains filename metacharacters that should not be expanded.

:x   Quote a pattern, expanding it into a wordlist.

Examples using pathname modifiers

The following table shows the use of pathname modifiers on the following variable:

```
set aa=(/progs/num.c /book/chap.ps)
```

Variable portion	Specification	Output result
Normal variable	echo $aa	/progs/num.c /book/chap.ps
Second root	echo $aa[2]:r	/book/chap
Second header	echo $aa[2]:h	/book
Second tail	echo $aa[2]:t	chap.ps
Second extension	echo $aa[2]:e	ps
Root	echo $aa:r	/progs/num /book/chap.ps
Global root	echo $aa:gr	/progs/num /book/chap
Header	echo $aa:h	/progs /book/chap.ps
Global header	echo $aa:gh	/progs /book
Tail	echo $aa:t	num.c /book/chap.ps
Global tail	echo $aa:gt	num.c chap.ps
Extension	echo $aa:e	c /book/chap.ps
Global extension	echo $aa:ge	c ps

Examples using quoting modifiers

Unless quoted, the shell expands variables to represent files in the current directory:

```
% set a="[a-z]*" A="[A-Z]*"
% echo "$a" "$A"
[a-z]* [A-Z]*

% echo $a $A
at cc m4 Book Doc

% echo $a:x $A
[a-z]* Book Doc

% set d=($a:q $A:q)
% echo $d
at cc m4 Book Doc

% echo $d:q
[a-z]* [A-Z]*
```

```
% echo $d[1] +++ $d[2]
at cc m4 +++ Book Doc

% echo $d[1]:q
[a-z]*
```

Predefined Shell Variables

Variables can be set in one of two ways, by assigning a value:

> set *var=value*

or by simply turning the variable on:

> set *var*

In the following list, variables that accept values are shown with the equal sign followed by the type of value they accept; the value then is described. (Note, however, that variables such as argv, cwd, or status are never explicitly assigned.) For variables that are turned on or off, the table describes what they do when set. *tcsh* automatically sets (and, in some cases, updates) the variables addsuffix, argv, autologout, cwd, dirstack, echo-style, edit, gid, home, loginsh, logout, oid, owd, path, prompt, prompt2, prompt3, shell, shlvl, status, tcsh, term, tty, uid, user, and version. Variables in italics are specific to *tcsh*.

Variable	Description
addsuffix	Append / to directories and a space to files during tab completion to indicate a precise match.
ampm	Display all times in 12-hour format.
argv=(*args*)	List of arguments passed to current command; default is ( ).
autocorrect	Check spelling before attempting to complete commands.
autoexpand	Expand history (such as ! references) during command completion.
autolist[=ambiguous]	Print possible completions when correct one is ambiguous. If "ambiguous" is specified, print possible completions only when completion adds no new characters.
autologout=*logout-minutes* [*locking-minutes*]	Log out after *logout-minutes* of idle time. Lock the terminal after *locking-minutes* of idle time, requiring a password before continuing. Not used if the DISPLAY environment variable is set.
backslash_quote	Always allow backslashes to quote \, ', and ".
cdpath=*dirs*	List of alternate directories to search when locating arguments for cd, popd, or pushd.
color	Turn on color for ls-F, ls, or both. Setting to nothing is equivalent to setting for both.
command	If set, holds the command passed to the shell with the -c option.
complete=enhance	When enhance, ignore case in completion, treat ., -, and _ as word separators, and consider _ and - to be the same.
correct={cmd|complete|all}	When cmd, spellcheck commands. When complete, complete commands. When all, spellcheck whole command line.
cwd=*dir*	Full pathname of current directory.
dextract	When set, the *pushd* command extracts the desired directory and puts it at the top of the stack, instead of rotating the stack.
dirsfile=*file*	History file consulted by dirs -S and dirs -L. Default is ~/.cshdirs.

Variable	Description
dirstack	Directory stack, in array format. `dirstack[0]` is always equivalent to cwd. The other elements can be artificially changed.
dspmbyte=code	Enable use of multibyte code; for use with Kanji. See the *tcsh* manpage for details.
dunique	Make sure that each directory exists only once in the stack.
echo	Redisplay each command line before execution; same as `csh -x` command.
echo_ style={bsd|sysv|both|none}	Don't echo a newline with -n option (bsd) | parse escaped characters (sysv) | do both | do neither.
edit	Enable command-line editor.
ellipsis	For use with `prompt` variable. Represent skipped directories with . . . .
fignore=chars	List of filename suffixes to ignore during filename completion (see `filec`).
filec	If set, a filename that is partially typed on the command line can be expanded to its full name when Esc is pressed. If more than one filename matches, type EOF to list possible completions. Ignored in *tcsh*.
gid	User's group ID.
group	User's group name.
histchars=*ab*	A two-character string that sets the characters to use in history-substitution and quick- substitution (default is ! ^).
histdup={all|prev}	Maintain a record only of unique history events (all), or do not enter new event when it is the same as the previous one (prev).
histfile=file	History file consulted by `history -S` and `history -L`. Default is *~/.history*.
histlit	Do not expand history lines when recalling them.
history=*n format*	The first word indicates the number of commands to save in the history list. The second indicates the format with which to display that list (*tcsh* only; see the prompt section for possible formats).
home=*dir*	Home directory of user, initialized from HOME. The ~ character is shorthand for this value.
ignoreeof	Ignore an end-of-file (EOF) from terminals; prevents accidental logout.
implicitcd	If directory name is entered as a command, cd to that directory. Can be set to `verbose` to echo the cd to standard output.
inputmode={insert|overwrite}	Control editor's mode.
listflags=flags	One or more of the x, a, or A options for the `ls-F` built-in command. Second word can be set to path for `ls` command.
listjobs=long	When a job is suspended, list all jobs (in long format, if specified).
listlinks	In `ls -F` command, include type of file to which links point.
listmax=num	Do not allow `list-choices` to print more than *num* choices before prompting.
listmaxrows=num	Do not allow `list-choices` to print more than *num* rows of choices before prompting.
loginsh	Set if shell is a login shell.
logout	Indicates status of an imminent logout (normal, automatic, or hangup).
mail=(*n files*)	One or more files checked for new mail every 5 minutes or (if *n* is supplied) every *n* seconds.

Variable	Description
matchbeep={never|nomatch|ambiguous|notunique}	Specifies circumstances under which completion should beep: never, if no match exists, if multiple matches exist, or if multiple matches exist and one is exact.
nobeep	Disable beeping.
noclobber	Don't redirect output to an existing file; prevents accidental destruction of files.
noglob	Turn off filename expansion; useful in shell scripts.
nokanji	Disable Kanji (if supported).
nonomatch	Treat filename metacharacters as literal characters, if no match exists (e.g., vi ch* creates new file ch* instead of printing "No match").
nostat=directory-list	Do not stat directory-list during completion.
notify	Declare job completions when they occur.
owd	Old working directory.
path=(dirs)	List of pathnames in which to search for commands to execute. Initialized from PATH; the default is: . /usr/ucb /usr/bin.
printexitvalue	Print all nonzero exit values.
prompt='str'	String that prompts for interactive input; default is %. See "Formatting for the Prompt Variable" later in this chapter for formatting information.
prompt2='str'	String that prompts for interactive input in foreach and while loops and continued lines (those with escaped newlines). See "Formatting for the Prompt Variable" for formatting information.
prompt3='str'	String that prompts for interactive input in automatic spelling correction. See "Formatting for the Prompt Variable" for formatting information.
promptchars=cc	Use the two characters specified as cc with the %# prompt sequence to indicate normal users and the superuser, respectively.
pushdsilent	Do not print directory stack when pushd and popd are invoked.
pushdtohome	Change to home directory when pushd is invoked without arguments.
recexact	Consider completion to be concluded on first exact match.
recognize_only_executables	When command completion is invoked, print only executable files.
rmstar	Prompt before executing the command rm *.
rprompt=string	The string to print on the right side of the screen while the prompt is displayed on the left. Specify as for prompt.
savedirs	Execute dirs -S before exiting.
savehist=max [merge]	Execute history -S before exiting. Save no more than max lines of history. If specified, merge those lines with previous history saves, and sort by time.
sched=string	Format for sched's printing of events. See "Formatting for the Prompt Variable" for formatting information.
shell=file	Pathname of the shell program currently in use; default is /bin/csh.
shlvl	Number of nested shells.
status=n	Exit status of last command. Built-in commands return 0 (success) or 1 (failure).
symlinks={chase|ignore|expand}	Specify manner in which to deal with symbolic links. Expand them to real directory name in cwd (chase), treat them as real directories (ignore), or expand arguments that resemble pathnames (expand).
tcsh	Version of tcsh.

Variable	Description
term	Terminal type.
time='n %c'	If command execution takes more than n CPU seconds, report user time, system time, elapsed time, and CPU percentage. Supply optional %c flags to show other data.
tperiod	Number of minutes between executions of periodic alias.
tty	Name of tty, if applicable.
uid	User ID.
user	Username.
verbose	Display a command after history substitution; same as the command csh -v.
version	Shell's version and additional information, including options set at compile time.
visiblebell	Flash screen instead of beeping.
watch=([n] user terminal...)	Watch for user logging in at terminal, where terminal can be a tty name or any. Check every n minutes or 10 by default.
who=string	Specify information to be printed by watch.
wordchars=chars	List of all nonalphanumeric characters that may be part of a word. Default is *?_-.[ ]~=.

Formatting for the Prompt Variable

tcsh provides a list of substitutions that can be used in formatting the prompt. (*csh* allows only plain-string prompts and the ! history substitution shown in the following list.) The list of available substitutions includes:

%%

   Literal %

%/

   The present working directory

%~

   The present working directory, in ~ notation

%#

   # for the superuser, > for others

%?

   Previous command's exit status

%b

   End boldfacing

%c[[0]n], %.[[0]n]

   The last *n* (default 1) components of the present working directory; if 0 is specified, replace removed components with /<skipped>

%d

   Day of the week (e.g., Mon, Tues)

%h, %!, !

   Number of current history event

%l

   Current tty

%m
    First component of hostname
%n
    Username
%p
    Current time, with seconds (12-hour mode)
%s
    End standout mode (reverse video)
%t, %@
    Current time (12-hour format)
%u
    End underlining
%w
    Month (e.g., Jan, Feb)
%y
    Year (e.g., 99, 00)
%B
    Begin boldfacing
%C
    Similar to %c, but uses full pathnames instead of ~ notation
%D
    Day of month (e.g., 09, 10)
%M
    Fully qualified hostname
%P
    Current time, with seconds (24-hour format)
%S
    Begin standout mode (reverse video)
%T
    Current time (24-hour format)
%U
    Begin underlining
%W
    Month (e.g., 09, 10)
%Y
    Year (e.g., 1999, 2000)

Sample .cshrc File

The following is a sample *.cshrc* file. This should give you an idea of what the file contains and how the file is formatted:

```
# PREDEFINED VARIABLES

set path=(~ ~/bin /usr/ucb /bin /usr/bin . )
set mail=(/usr/mail/tom)
```

```
    if ($?prompt) then             # settings for interactive use
      set echo
      set noclobber ignoreeof

      set cdpath=(/usr/lib /usr/spool/uucp)
 # Now I can type cd macros
 # instead of cd /usr/lib/macros

      set history=100
      set prompt='tom \!% '        # includes history number
      set time=3

 # MY VARIABLES

      set man1="/usr/man/man1"     # lets me do   cd $man1, ls $man1
      set a="[a-z]*"               # lets me do   vi $a
      set A="[A-Z]*"               # or           grep string $A

 # ALIASES

      alias c "clear; dirs"        # use quotes to protect ; or |
      alias h "history|more"
      alias j jobs -l
      alias ls ls -sFC             # redefine ls command
      alias del 'mv \!* ~/tmp_dir' # a safe alternative to rm
    endif
```

Environment Variables

tcsh maintains a set of *environment variables*, which are distinct from shell variables and aren't really part of *tcsh*. Shell variables are meaningful only within the current shell, but environment variables are exported automatically, making them available globally. For example, C-shell variables are accessible only to a particular script in which they're defined, whereas environment variables can be used by any shell scripts, mail utilities, or editors you might invoke.

Environment variables are assigned as follows:

```
setenv VAR value
```

By convention, environment variable names are all uppercase. You can create your own environment variables, or you can use the predefined environment variables that follow.

The following environment variables have corresponding C-shell variables. When either one changes, the value is copied to the other (italics means the variable is specific to *tcsh*):

GROUP
    User's group name; same as *group*.

HOME
    Home directory; same as *home*.

PATH
    Search path for commands; same as *path*.

SHLVL

    Number of nested shell levels; same as *shlvl*.

TERM

    Terminal type; same as *term*.

USER

    User's login name; same as *user*.

Other environment variables, which do not have corresponding shell variables, include the following (italics means the variable is specific to *tcsh*):

COLUMNS

    Number of columns on terminal.

DISPLAY

    Identifies user's display for the X Window System. If set, the shell doesn't set *autologout*.

EDITOR

    Pathname to default editor. See also VISUAL.

HOST

    Name of machine.

HOSTTYPE

    Type of machine. Obsolete; will be removed eventually.

HPATH

    Colon-separated list of directories to search for documentation.

LANG

    Preferred language. Used for native language support.

LC_CTYPE

    The locale, as it affects character handling. Used for native language support.

LINES

    Number of lines on the screen.

LOGNAME

    Another name for the USER variable.

MACHTYPE

    Type of machine.

MAIL

    The file that holds mail. Used by mail programs. This is not the same as the C-shell `mail` variable, which only checks for new mail.

NOREBIND

    Printable characters that are not rebound. Used for native language support.

OSTYPE

    Operating system.

PWD

    The current directory; the value is copied from *cwd*.

REMOTEHOST

    Machine name of remote host.

SHELL

    Undefined by default; once initialized to *shell*, the two are identical.

The Shell

TERMCAP
> The file that holds the cursor-positioning codes for your terminal type. Default is */etc/termcap*.

VENDOR
> The system vendor.

VISUAL
> Pathname to default full-screen editor. See also EDITOR.

Expressions

Expressions are used in @, if, and while statements to perform arithmetic, string comparisons, file testing, and so on. exit and set also specify expressions, as can the *tcsh* built-in command filetest. Expressions are formed by combining variables and constants with operators that resemble those in the C programming language. Operator precedence is the same as in C but can be remembered as follows:

1. * / %
2. + -

Group all other expressions inside parentheses. Parentheses are required if the expression contains <, >, &, or |.

Operators

Operators can be one of the types listed in the following tables.

Assignment operators

Operator	Description
=	Assign value.
+= -=	Reassign after addition/subtraction.
*= /= %=	Reassign after multiplication/division/remainder.
&= ^= |=	Reassign after bitwise AND/XOR/OR.
++	Increment.
--	Decrement.

Arithmetic operators

Operator	Description
* / %	Multiplication; integer division; modulus (remainder)
+ -	Addition; subtraction

Bitwise and logical operators

Operator	Description
~	Binary inversion (one's complement).
!	Logical negation.

Operator	Description
<< >>	Bitwise left shift; bitwise right shift.
&	Bitwise AND.
^	Bitwise exclusive OR.
|	Bitwise OR.
&&	Logical AND.
||	Logical OR.
{ command }	Return 1 if command is successful, 0 otherwise. Note that this is the opposite of command's normal return code. The $status variable may be more practical.

Comparison operators

Operator	Description
== !=	Equality; inequality
<= >=	Less than or equal to; greater than or equal to
< >	Less than; greater than

File inquiry operators

Command substitution and filename expansion are performed on *file* before the test is performed. *tcsh* permits operators to be combined (e.g., -ef). The following is a list of the valid file inquiry operators:

Operator	Description
-d *file*	The file is a directory.
-e *file*	The file exists.
-f *file*	The file is a plain file.
-o *file*	The user owns the file.
-r *file*	The user has read permission.
-w *file*	The user has write permission.
-x *file*	The user has execute permission.
-z *file*	The file has 0 size.
!	Reverses the sense of any preceding inquiry.

Some additional operators specific to *tcsh* are:

Operator	Description
-b *file*	The file is a block special file.
-c *file*	The file is a character special file.
-g *file*	The file's set-group-ID bit is set.
-k *file*	The file's sticky bit is set.
-l *file*	The file is a symbolic link.
-L *file*	Applies any remaining operators to a symbolic link, not the file it points to.
-p *file*	The file is a named pipe (FIFO).

Operator	Description
-s *file*	The file has nonzero size.
-S *file*	The file is a socket special file.
-t *file*	*file* is a digit and is an open file descriptor for a terminal device.
-u *file*	The file's set-user-ID bit is set.
-X *file*	The file is executable and is in the path or is a shell built-in.

Finally, *tcsh* provides the following operators, which return other kinds of information:

Operator	Description
-A[:] *file*	Last time the file was accessed, as the number of seconds since the Epoch. With a colon (:), the result is in timestamp format.
-C[:] *file*	Last time the inode was modified. With a colon (:), the result is in timestamp format.
-D *file*	Device number.
-F *file*	Composite file identifier, in the form *device:inode*.
-G[:] *file*	Numeric group ID for the file. With a colon (:), the result is the group name if known; otherwise, the numeric group ID.
-I *file*	Inode number.
-L *file*	The name of the file pointed to by symbolic link *file*.
-M[:] *file*	Last time file was modified. With a colon (:), the result is in timestamp format.
-N *file*	Number of hard links.
-P[:] *file*	Permissions in octal, without leading 0. With a colon (:), the result includes a leading 0.
-P*mode*[:] *file*	Equivalent to -P *file* ANDed to *mode*. With a colon (:), the result includes a leading 0.
-U[:] *file*	Numeric user ID of the file's owner. With a colon (:), the result is the username if known, otherwise the numeric user ID.
-Z *file*	The file's size, in bytes.

Examples

The following examples show @ commands and assume n = 4:

Expression	Value of $x
@ x = ($n > 10 || $n < 5)	1
@ x = ($n >= 0 && $n < 3)	0
@ x = ($n << 2)	16
@ x = ($n >> 2)	1
@ x = $n % 2	0
@ x = $n % 3	1

The following examples show the first line of if or while statements:

Expression	Meaning
while ($#argv != 0)	While there are arguments
if ($today[1] == <">Fri<">)	If the first word is "Fri"
if (-f $argv[1])	If the first argument is a plain file
if (! -d $tmpdir)	If *tmpdir* is not a directory

Command History

Previously executed commands are stored in a history list. *tcsh* lets you access this list so you can verify commands, repeat them, or execute modified versions of them. The history built-in command displays the history list; the predefined variables histchars and history also affect the history mechanism. There are four ways to use the history list:

- Rerun a previous command.
- Make command substitutions.
- Make argument substitutions (replace specific words in a command).
- Extract or replace parts of a command or word.

The following subsections describe the *csh* tools for editing and rerunning commands. If you are running *tcsh*, you can use any of these features. In addition, you can use the arrow keys to move around in the command line and then use the editing features described later in "Command-Line Editing with tcsh" to modify the command. The *tcsh* arrow keys are described in the following table:

Key	Description
Up Arrow	Previous command.
Down Arrow	Next command.
Left Arrow	Move left in command line.
Right Arrow	Move right in command line.

Command Substitution

Command	Description
!	Begin a history substitution.
!!	Previous command.
!*N*	Command number *N* in history list.
!-*N*	*N*th command back from current command.
!*string*	Most recent command that starts with *string*.
!?*string*?	Most recent command that contains *string*.
!?*string*?%	Most recent command argument that contains *string*.
!$	Last argument of previous command.

Command	Description
`!!string`	Previous command, then append *string*.
`!N string`	Command *N*, then append *string*.
`!{s1}s2`	Most recent command starting with string *s1*, then append string *s2*.
`^old^new^`	Quick substitution; change string *old* to *new* in previous command; execute modified command.

Command Substitution Examples

The following command is assumed:

```
%3 vi cprogs/01.c ch002 ch03
```

Event number	Command typed	Command executed
4	`^00^0`	`vi cprogs/01.c ch02 ch03`
5	`nroff !*`	`nroff cprogs/01.c ch02 ch03`
6	`nroff !$`	`nroff ch03`
7	`!vi`	`vi cprogs/01.c ch02 ch03`
8	`!6`	`nroff ch03`
9	`!?01`	`vi cprogs/01.c ch02 ch03`
10	`!{nr}.new`	`nroff ch03.new`
11	`!!|lp`	`nroff ch03.new	lp`
12	`more !?pr?%`	`more cprogs/01.c`

Word Substitution

Colons may precede any word specifier.

Specifier	Description
`:0`	Command name
`:n`	Argument number *n*
`^`	First argument
`$`	Last argument
`:n-m`	Arguments *n* through *m*
`-m`	Words 0 through *m* same as :0–*m*
`:n-`	Arguments *n* through next-to-last
`:n*`	Arguments *n* through last; same as *n*–$
`*`	All arguments; same as ^–$ or 1–$
`#`	Current command line up to this point; fairly useless

Word Substitution Examples

The following command is assumed:

```
%13 cat ch01 ch02 ch03 biblio back
```

Event number	Command typed	Command executed
14	ls !13^	ls ch01
15	sort !13:*	sort ch01 ch02 ch03 biblio back
16	lp !cat:3*	more ch03 biblio back
17	!cat:0-3	cat ch01 ch02 ch03
18	vi !-5:4	vi biblio

History Modifiers

Command and word substitutions can be modified by one or more of the following modifiers:

Printing, substitution, and quoting

Modifier	Description
:p	Display command, but don't execute.
:s/old/new	Substitute string new for old; first instance only.
:gs/old/new	Substitute string new for old; all instances.
:&	Repeat previous substitution (:s or ^ command); first instance only.
:g&	Repeat previous substitution; all instances.
:q	Quote a word list.
:x	Quote separate words.

Truncation

Modifier	Description
:r	Extract the first available pathname root (the portion before the last period).
:gr	Extract all pathname roots.
:e	Extract the first available pathname extension (the portion after the last period).
:ge	Extract all pathname extensions.
:h	Extract the first available pathname header (the portion before the last slash).
:gh	Extract all pathname headers.
:t	Extract the first available pathname tail (the portion after the last slash).
:gt	Extract all pathname tails.
:u	Make first lowercase letter uppercase (tcsh only).
:l	Make first uppercase letter lowercase (tcsh only).
:a	Apply modifier(s) following a as many times as possible to a word. If used with g, a is applied to all words (tcsh only).

History Modifier Examples

From the preceding, command number 17 is:

%17 cat ch01 ch02 ch03

Event number	Command typed	Command executed
19	!17:s/ch/CH/	cat CH01 ch02 ch03
20	!17g&	cat CH01 CH02 CH03
21	!more:p	more cprogs/01.c *(displayed only)*
22	cd !$:h	cd cprogs
23	vi !mo:$:t	vi 01.c
24	grep stdio !$	grep stdio 01.c
25	^stdio^include stdio^:q	grep <">include stdio<"> 01.c
26	nroff !21:t:p	nroff 01.c *(is that what I wanted?)*
27	!!	nroff 01.c *(execute it)*

Special Aliases in tcsh

Certain special aliases can be set in *tcsh*. The aliases are initially undefined. Once set, they are executed when specific events occur. The following is a list of the special aliases:

beepcmd
> At beep.

cwdcmd
> When the current working directory changes.

periodic
> Every few minutes. The exact amount of time is set by the tperiod shell variable.

precmd
> Before printing a new prompt.

shell *shell*
> If a script does not specify a shell, interpret it with *shell*, which should be a full pathname.

Command-Line Manipulation

tcsh offers a certain amount of functionality in manipulating the command line. Both shells offer word or command completion, and *tcsh* allows you to edit a command line.

Completion

tcsh provides word completion when the Tab key is hit. If the completion is ambiguous (i.e., more than one file matches the provided string), the shell completes as much as possible and beeps to notify you that the completion is not finished. You may request a list of possible completions with Control-D. *tcsh* also notifies you when a completion is finished by appending a space to complete filenames or commands and a / to complete directories.

Both *csh* and *tcsh* recognize ~ notation for home directories. The shells assume that words at the beginning of a line and subsequent to |, &, ;, ||, or && are commands and modify their search paths appropriately. Completion can be done mid-word; only the letters to the left of the prompt are checked for completion.

Related Shell Variables

- `autolist`
- `fignore`
- `listmax`
- `listmaxrows`

Related Command-Line Editor Commands

- `complete-word-back`
- `complete-word-forward`
- `expand-glob`
- `list-glob`

Related Shell built-ins

- `complete`
- `uncomplete`

Command-Line Editing with tcsh

tcsh lets you move your cursor around in the command line, editing the line as you type. There are two main modes for editing the command line, based on the two most common text editors: *Emacs* and *vi*. *Emacs* mode is the default; you can switch between the modes with:

```
bindkey -e     Select Emacs bindings
bindkey -v     Select vi bindings
```

The main difference between the *Emacs* and *vi* bindings is that the *Emacs* bindings are modeless (i.e., they always work). With the *vi* bindings, you must switch between insert and command modes; different commands are useful in each mode. Additionally:

- *Emacs* mode is simpler; *vi* mode allows finer control.
- *Emacs* mode allows you to yank cut text and set a mark; *vi* mode does not.
- The command-history-searching capabilities differ.

Emacs mode

Tables 21-1 through 21-3 describe the various editing keystrokes available in *Emacs* mode.

Table 21-1. Cursor positioning commands (Emacs mode)

Command	Description
Ctrl-B	Move cursor back (left) one character.
Ctrl-F	Move cursor forward (right) one character.

Table 21-1. Cursor positioning commands (Emacs mode) (continued)

Command	Description
Esc b	Move cursor back one word.
Esc f	Move cursor forward one word.
Ctrl-A	Move cursor to beginning of line.
Ctrl-E	Move cursor to end of line.

Table 21-2. Text deletion commands (Emacs mode)

Command	Description
Del or Ctrl-H	Delete character to left of cursor.
Ctrl-D	Delete character under cursor.
Esc d	Delete word.
Esc Del or Esc Ctrl-H	Delete word backward.
Ctrl-K	Delete from cursor to end of line.
Ctrl-U	Delete entire line.

Table 21-3. Command control (Emacs mode)

Command	Description
Ctrl-P	Previous command.
Ctrl-N	Next command.
Up arrow	Previous command.
Down arrow	Next command.
cmd-fragment Esc p	Search history for *cmd-fragment*, which must be the beginning of a command.
cmd-fragment Esc n	Like Esc p, but search forward.
Esc *num*	Repeat next command *num* times.
Ctrl-Y	Yank previously deleted string.

vi mode

vi mode has two submodes, insert and command. The default mode is insert. You can toggle modes by pressing Esc; alternatively, in command mode, typing *a* (append) or *i* (insert) will return you to insert mode.

Tables 21-4 through 21-10 describe the editing keystrokes available in *vi* mode.

Table 21-4. Commands available (vi's insert and command mode)

Command	Description
Ctrl-P	Previous command
Ctrl-N	Next command
Up arrow	Previous command
Down arrow	Next command
Esc	Toggle mode

Table 21-5. Editing commands (vi insert mode)

Command	Description
Ctrl-B	Move cursor back (left) one character.
Ctrl-F	Move cursor forward (right) one character.
Ctrl-A	Move cursor to beginning of line.
Ctrl-E	Move cursor to end of line.
DEL or Ctrl-H	Delete character to left of cursor.
Ctrl-W	Delete word backward.
Ctrl-U	Delete from beginning of line to cursor.
Ctrl-K	Delete from cursor to end of line.

Table 21-6. Cursor positioning commands (vi command mode)

Command	Description
h or Ctrl-H	Move cursor back (left) one character.
l or SPACE	Move cursor forward (right) one character.
w	Move cursor forward (right) one word.
b	Move cursor back (left) one word.
e	Move cursor to next word ending.
W, B, E	Like w, b, and e, but treat just whitespace as word separator instead of as a nonalphanumeric character.
^ or Ctrl-A	Move cursor to beginning of line (first nonwhitespace character).
0	Move cursor to beginning of line.
$ or Ctrl-E	Move cursor to end of line.

Table 21-7. Text insertion commands (vi command mode)

Command	Description
a	Append new text after cursor until Esc.
i	Insert new text before cursor until Esc.
A	Append new text after end of line until Esc.
I	Insert new text before beginning of line until Esc.

Table 21-8. Text deletion commands (vi command mode)

Command	Description
x	Delete character under cursor.
X or Del	Delete character to left of cursor.
d*m*	Delete from cursor to end of motion command *m*.
D	Same as d$.
Ctrl-W	Delete word backward.
Ctrl-U	Delete from beginning of line to cursor.
Ctrl-K	Delete from cursor to end of line.

Table 21-9. Text replacement commands (vi command mode)

Command	Description
c*m*	Change characters from cursor to end of motion command *m* until Esc.
C	Same as c$.
r*c*	Replace character under cursor with character *c*.
R	Replace multiple characters until Esc.
s	Substitute character under cursor with characters typed until Esc.

Table 21-10. Character-seeking motion commands (vi command mode)

Command	Description
f*c*	Move cursor to next instance of *c* in line.
F*c*	Move cursor to previous instance of *c* in line.
t*c*	Move cursor just before next instance of *c* in line.
T*c*	Move cursor just after previous instance of *c* in line.
;	Repeat previous f or F command.
,	Repeat previous f or F command in opposite direction.

Job Control

Job control lets you place foreground jobs in the background, bring background jobs to the foreground, or suspend (temporarily stop) running jobs. *tcsh* provides the following commands for job control. For more information on these commands, see the later section "Built-in tcsh Commands."

bg
> Put a job in the background.

fg
> Put a job in the foreground.

jobs
> List active jobs.

kill
> Terminate a job.

notify
> Notify when a background job finishes.

stop
> Suspend a background job.

Ctrl-Z
> Suspend the foreground job.

Many job control commands take *jobID* as an argument. This argument can be specified as follows:

%*n*

> Job number *n*.

%*s*

> Job whose command line starts with string *s*.

%?*s*

> Job whose command line contains string *s*.

%%

> Current job.

%

> Current job (same as preceding).

%+

> Current job (same as preceding).

%-

> Previous job.

Built-in tcsh Commands

The Shell

@
> @ [*variable*[*n*]=*expression*]
>
> Assign the value of the arithmetic *expression* to *variable* or to the *n*th element of *variable* if the index *n* is specified. With no *variable* or *expression* specified, print the values of all shell variables (same as *set*). Expression operators as well as examples are listed under the section "Expressions" earlier in this chapter. Two special forms also are valid:
>
> @ *variable*++
> > Increment *variable* by 1.
>
> @ *variable*--
> > Decrement *variable* by 1.

#
> #
>
> Ignore all text that follows on the same line. # is used in shell scripts as the comment character and is not really a command.

#!
> #!*shell*
>
> Use as the first line of a script to invoke the named *shell* (with optional arguments). Not supported in all shells. For example:
>
> ```
> #!/bin/csh -f
> ```

:
> :
>
> Null command. Returns an exit status of 0. The colon command often is put as the first character of a Bourne- or Korn-shell script to act as a placeholder to keep a hash (#) from accidentally becoming the first character.

alias   alias [*name* [*command*]]

Assign *name* as the shorthand name, or alias, for *command*. If *command* is omitted, print the alias for *name*; if *name* also is omitted, print all aliases. Aliases can be defined on the command line, but more often they are stored in *.cshrc* so that they take effect upon logging in. (See the sample *.cshrc* file earlier in this chapter.) Alias definitions can reference command-line arguments, much like the history list. Use \!* to refer to all command-line arguments, \!^ for the first argument, \!\!:2 for the second, \!$ for the last, and so on. An alias *name* can be any valid Unix command; however, you lose the original command's meaning unless you type *name*. See also *unalias* and the "Special Aliases in tcsh" section.

Examples

Set the size for xterm windows under the X Window System:

alias R 'set noglob; eval `resize` unset noglob'

Show aliases that contain the string *ls*:

alias | grep ls

Run *nroff* on all command-line arguments:

alias ms 'nroff -ms \!*'

Copy the file that is named as the first argument:

alias back 'cp \!^ \!^.old'

Use the regular *ls*, not its alias:

% \ls

---

alloc   alloc

Print totals of used and free memory.

---

bg   bg [*jobIDs*]

Put the current job or the *jobIDs* in the background.

Example

To place a time-consuming process in the background, you might begin with:

4% nroff -ms report Ctrl-Z

and then issue any one of the following:

```
5% bg
5% bg %        Current job
5% bg %1       Job number 1
5% bg %nr      Match initial string nroff
5% % &
```

---

bindkey   bindkey [*options*] [*key*] [*command*]

tcsh only. Display all key bindings, or bind a key to a command.

Options

-a   List standard and alternate key bindings.

-b *key*
Expect *key* to be one of the following: a control character (in hat notation—e.g., ^B—or C notation—e.g., C-B); a meta-character (e.g., M-B); a function key (e.g., F-*string*); or an extended prefix key (e.g., X-B).

-c *command*
Interpret *command* as a shell, not editor, command.

-d *key*
Bind key to its original binding.

-e   Bind to standard *Emacs* bindings.

-k *key*
Expect *key* to refer to an arrow (left, right, up, or down).

-l   List and describe all editor commands.

-r *key*
Completely unbind *key*.

-s   Interpret *command* as a literal string and treat as terminal input.

-u   Print usage message.

-v   Bind to standard *vi* bindings.

---

break

`break`

Resume execution following the end command of the nearest enclosing while or foreach.

---

breaksw

`breaksw`

Break from a switch; continue execution after the endsw.

---

built-ins

`built-ins`

tcsh only. Print all built-in shell commands.

---

bye

`bye`

tcsh only. Same as *logout*.

---

case

`case pattern :`
Identify a *pattern* in a *switch*.

---

cd

`cd [dir]`

Change working directory to *dir*. Default is user's home directory. If *dir* is a relative pathname but is not in the current directory, the cdpath variable is searched. See the sample .*cshrc* file earlier in this chapter. *tcsh* includes some options for cd.

---

tcsh options

-     Change to previous directory.

-l   Explicitly expand ~ notation.

-n   Wrap entries before end-of-line; implies -p.

-p   Print directory stack.

-v   Print entries one per line; implies -p.

---

chdir

    chdir [*dir*]

    Same as cd. Useful if you are redefining cd.

---

complete

    complete [*string* [*word/pattern/list*[*:select*]/[*suffix*]]]

    tcsh only. List all completions or, if specified, all completions for *string* (which may be a pattern). Further options can be specified.

Options for word

c   Complete current word only and without referring to *pattern*.

C   Complete current word only, referring to *pattern*.

n   Complete previous word.

N   Complete word before previous word.

p   Expect *pattern* to be a range of numbers. Perform completion within that range.

Options for list

Various *list*s of strings can be searched for possible completions. Some *list* options include:

(string)
> Members of the list *string*

$variable
> Words from *variable*

`` `command` ``
> Output from *command*

a   Aliases

b   Bindings

c   Commands

C   External (not built-in) commands

d   Directories

D   Directories whose names begin with *string*

e   Environment variables

f   Filenames

F   Filenames that begin with *string*

g   Groups

j   Jobs

l   Limits

n	Nothing
s	Shell variables
S	Signals
t	Text files
T	Text files whose names begin with *string*
u	Users
v	Any variables
x	Like *n* but prints *select* as an explanation with the editor command *list-choices*
X	Completions

select

select should be a glob pattern. Completions are limited to words that match this pattern. *suffix* is appended to all completions.

---

continue

`continue`

Resume execution of nearest enclosing *while* or *foreach*.

---

default

`default :`

Label the default case (typically last) in a *switch*.

---

dirs

`dirs [options]`

Print the directory stack, showing the current directory first. See also *popd* and *pushd*. All options except -1, -n, and -v are *tcsh* extensions.

Options

-c   Clear the directory stack.

-1   Expand the home directory symbol (~) to the actual directory name.

-n   Wrap output.

-v   Print one directory per line.

-L *file*
    Re-create stack from *file*, which should have been created by dirs -S *file*.

-S *file*
    Print to *file* a series of *pushd* and *popd* commands, which can be invoked to replicate the stack.

---

echo

`echo [-n] string`

Write *string* to standard output; if *-n* is specified, the output is not terminated by a newline. Unlike the Unix version (*/bin/echo*) and the Bourne-shell version, *tcsh*'s *echo* doesn't support escape characters. See also *echo* in Chapter 25.

echotc

echotc [*options*] *arguments*

tcsh only. Display terminal capabilities, or move cursor on screen, depending on the argument.

Options

-s Return empty string, not error, if capability doesn't exist.

-v Display verbose messages.

Arguments

baud
    Display current baud.

cols
    Display current column.

cm *column row*
    Move cursor to specified coordinates.

home
    Move cursor to home position.

lines
    Print number of lines per screen.

meta
    Does this terminal have meta capacity (usually the Alt key)?

tabs
    Does this terminal have tab capacity?

else

else

Reserved word for interior of if ... endif statement.

end

end

Reserved word that ends a foreach or switch statement.

endif

endif

Reserved word that ends an if statement.

endsw

endsw

Reserved word that ends a switch statement.

eval

eval *args*

Typically, eval is used in shell scripts, and *args* is a line of code that may contain shell variables. eval forces variable expansion to happen first and then runs the resulting command. This "double scanning" is useful any time shell variables contain input/output redirection symbols, aliases, or other shell variables. (For example, redirection normally happens before variable expansion, so a variable containing redirection symbols must be expanded first using eval; otherwise, the redirection symbols remain uninterpreted.)

Examples

The following line can be placed in the *.login* file to set up terminal characteristics:

```
set noglob eval tset -s xterm unset noglob
```

The following commands show the effect of *eval*:

```
% set b='$a'
% set a=hello
% echo $b          Read the command line once
$a
% eval echo $b     Read the command line twice
hello
```

Another example of eval can be found under alias.

---

exec

exec *command*

Execute *command* in place of the current shell. This terminates the current shell, rather than create a new process under it.

---

exit

exit [*(expr)*]

Exit a shell script with the status given by *expr*. A status of zero means success; nonzero means failure. If *expr* is not specified, the exit value is that of the status variable. exit can be issued at the command line to close a window (log out).

---

fg

fg [*jobIDs*]

Bring the current job or the *jobIDs* to the foreground. *jobID* can be *%job-number*.

Example

If you suspend a *vi* editing session (by pressing Control-Z), you might resume *vi* using any of these commands:

```
% %
% fg
% fg %
% fg %vi          Match initial string
```

---

filetest

filetest -*op files*

tcsh only. Apply *op* file-test operator to *files*. Print results in a list. See the earlier section "File inquiry operators" for the list of file-test operators.

---

foreach

foreach *name (wordlist)*
    commands
end

Assign variable *name* to each value in *wordlist* and execute *commands* between foreach and end. You can use foreach as a multiline command issued at the C-shell prompt (see the first of the following examples), or you can use it in a shell script (see the second example).

Examples

Rename all files that begin with a capital letter:

```
% foreach i ([A-Z]*)
? mv $i $i.new
? end
```

Check whether each command-line argument is an option or not:

```
foreach arg ($argv)
   # does it begin with - ?
   if ("$arg" =~ -*) then
      echo "Argument is an option"
   else
      echo "Argument is a filename"
   endif
end
```

---

glob

`glob wordlist`

Do filename, variable, and history substitutions on *wordlist*. No \ escapes are recognized in its expansion, and words are delimited by null characters. glob typically is used in shell scripts to hardcode a value so that it remains the same for the rest of the script.

---

goto

`goto string`

Skip to a line whose first nonblank character is *string* followed by a colon and continue execution below that line. On the goto line, *string* can be a variable or filename pattern, but the label branched to must be a literal, expanded value and must not occur within a *foreach* or *while*.

---

hashstat

`hashstat`

Display statistics that show the hash table's level of success at locating commands via the path variable.

---

history

`history [options]`

Display the list of history events. (History syntax is discussed earlier in "Command History.")

Options

-c   *tcsh* only. Clear history list.

-h   Print history list without event numbers.

-r   Print in reverse order; show oldest commands last.

n   Display only the last *n* history commands, instead of the number set by the history shell variable.

-L *file*
   tcsh only. Load series of *pushd* and *popd* commands from *file* in order to re-create a saved stack.

-M *file*

> *tcsh* only. Merge the current directory stack and the stack saved in *file*. Save both, sorted by time, in *file*, as a series of *pushd* and *popd* commands.

-S *file*

> *tcsh* only. Print to *file* a series of *pushd* and *popd* commands that can be invoked to replicate the stack.

Example

To save and execute the last five commands:

```
history -h 5 > do_it
source do_it
```

hup

hup [*command*]

tcsh only. Start *command* but make it exit when sent a hangup signal, which is sent when shell exits. By default, configure shell script to exit on hangup signal.

if

if

Begin a conditional statement. The simple format is:

> if (*expr*) *cmd*

There are three other possible formats, shown side by side:

Example 1	Example 2	Example 3
if (*expr*) then	if (*expr*) then	if (*expr*) then
cmds	*cmds1*	*cmds1*
endif	else	else if (*expr*) then
	cmds2	*cmds2*
	endif	else
		cmds3
		endif

In the simplest form, execute *cmd* if *expr* is true; otherwise do nothing (redirection still occurs; this is a bug). In the other forms, execute one or more commands. If *expr* is true, continue with the commands after *then*; if *expr* is false, branch to the commands after *else* (or branch to after the *else if* and continue checking). For more examples, see "Expressions" earlier in this chapter, as well as the entries shift or while.

Example

Take a default action if no command-line arguments are given:

```
if ($#argv == 0) then
    echo "No filename given. Sending to Report."
    set outfile = Report
else
    set outfile = $argv[1]
endif
```

jobs   jobs [-l]

List all running or stopped jobs; -l includes process IDs. For example, you can check whether a long compilation or text format is still running. Also useful before logging out.

kill   kill [*options*] *ID*

Terminate each specified process *ID* or job *ID*. You must own the process or be a privileged user. This built-in is similar to */bin/kill* described in Chapter 25 but also allows symbolic job names. Stubborn processes can be killed using signal 9.

Options

-l   List the signal names. (Used by itself.)

-signal

The signal number or name, without the SIG prefix (e.g., HUP, not SIGHUP). The command kill -l prints a list of the available signal names. The list varies by system architecture; for a PC-based system, it looks like this:

```
% kill -l
HUP INT QUIT ILL TRAP ABRT BUS FPE KILL USR1 SEGV USR2
PIPE ALRM TERM STKFLT CHLD CONT STOP TSTP TTIN TTOU URG
XCPU XFSZ VTALRM PROF WINCH POLL PWR UNUSED
```

The signals and their numbers are defined in */usr/include/asm/ signal.h*; look in that file to find the signals that apply to your system.

Examples

If you've issued the following command:

44% **nroff -ms report &**

you can terminate it in any of the following ways:

45%	**kill 19536**	*Process ID*
45%	**kill %**	*Current job*
45%	**kill %1**	*Job number 1*
45%	**kill %nr**	*Initial string*
45%	**kill %?report**	*Matching string*

limit   limit [-h] [*resource* [*limit*]]

Display limits or set a *limit* on resources used by the current process and by each process it creates. If no *limit* is given, the current limit is printed for *resource*. If *resource* also is omitted, all limits are printed. By default, the current limits are shown or set; with -h, hard limits are used. A hard limit imposes an absolute limit that can't be exceeded. Only a privileged user may raise it. See also unlimit.

Option

-h   Use hard, not current, limits.

Resource

cputime
> Maximum number of seconds the CPU can spend; can be abbreviated as cpu.

filesize
> Maximum size of any one file.

datasize
> Maximum size of data (including stack).

stacksize
> Maximum size of stack.

coredumpsize
> Maximum size of a core dump file.

Limit

A number followed by an optional character (a unit specifier).

For cputime:	*n*h (for *n* hours)
	*n*m (for *n* minutes)
	mm:ss (minutes and seconds)
For others:	*n*k (for *n* kilobytes, the default)
	*n*m (for *n* megabytes)

---

log

log

tcsh only. Consult the watch variable for list of users being watched. Print a list of those who are presently logged in. If – is entered as an option, reset environment as if the user had logged in with a new group.

---

login

login [*user*|-p]

Replace *user*'s login shell with */bin/login*. -p is used to preserve environment variables.

---

logout

logout

Terminate the login shell.

---

ls-F

ls-F [*options*] [*files*]

tcsh only. Faster alternative to ls -F. If given any options, invokes *ls*.

---

newgrp

newgrp [-] [*group*]

tcsh only. Change user's group ID to specified group ID, or, if none is specified, to original group ID. If – is entered as an option, reset environment as if the user had logged in with a new group. Must have been compiled into the shell; see the version variable.

nice

`nice [+n] command`

Change the execution priority for *command*, or, if none is given, change priority for the current shell. (See also nice in Chapter 25.) The priority range is -20 to 20, with a default of 4. The range seems backward: -20 gives the highest priority (fastest execution); 20 gives the lowest. Only a privileged user may specify a negative number.

+n   Add *n* to the priority value (lower job priority).

-n   Subtract *n* from the priority value (raise job priority). Privileged users only.

nohup

`nohup [command]`

"No hangup signals." Do not terminate *command* after terminal line is closed (i.e., when you hang up from a phone or log out). Use without *command* in shell scripts to keep script from being terminated.

notify

`notify [jobID]`

Report immediately when a background job finishes (instead of waiting for you to exit a long editing session, for example). If no *jobID* is given, the current background job is assumed.

onintr

`onintr label`

`onintr -`

`onintr`

"On interrupt." Used in shell scripts to handle interrupt signals (similar to *bash*'s trap 2 and trap "" 2 commands). The first form is like a goto *label*. The script will branch to *label*: if it catches an interrupt signal (e.g., Control-C). The second form lets the script ignore interrupts. This is useful at the beginning of a script or before any code segment that needs to run unhindered (e.g., when moving files). The third form restores interrupt handling that was previously disabled with onintr -.

Example

onintr cleanup	*Go to "cleanup" on interrupt*
•	
•	*Shell script commands*
•	
cleanup:	*Label for interrupts*
onintr -	*Ignore additional interrupts*
rm -f $tmpfiles	*Remove any files created*
exit 2	*Exit with an error status*

popd

`popd [options]`

Remove the current entry from the directory stack, or remove the *n*th entry from the stack and print the stack that remains. The current entry has number 0 and appears on the left. See also *dirs* and *pushd*.

Options

+*n* Specify *n*th entry.

-1 Expand ~ notation.

-n Wrap long lines.

-p Override the `pushdsilent` shell variable, which otherwise prevents the printing of the final stack.

-v Print precisely one directory per line.

---

printenv

`printenv [`*variable*`]`

Print all (or one specified) environment variables and their values.

---

pushd

`pushd` *name*

`pushd [`*options*`]`

`pushd`

The first form changes the working directory to *name* and adds it to the directory stack. The second form rotates the *n*th entry to the beginning, making it the working directory. (Entry numbers begin at 0.) With no arguments, *pushd* switches the first two entries and changes to the new current directory. The +*n*, -1, -n, and -v options behave the same as in *popd*. See also `dirs` and *popd*.

Examples

```
% dirs
/home/bob /usr
% pushd /etc          Add /etc to directory stack
/etc /home/bob /usr
% pushd +2            Switch to third directory
/usr /etc /home/bob
% pushd               Switch top two directories
/etc /usr /home/bob
% popd                Discard current entry; go to next
/usr /home/bob
```

---

rehash

`rehash`

Recompute the internal hash table for the PATH variable. Use *rehash* whenever a new command is created during the current session. This allows the PATH variable to locate and execute the command. (If the new command resides in a directory not listed in PATH, add this directory to PATH before rehashing.) See also unhash.

---

repeat

`repeat` *n* *command*

Execute *n* instances of *command*.

Examples

Print three copies of *memo*:

% **repeat 3 pr memo | lp**

Read 10 lines from the terminal and store in *item_list*:

% **repeat 10 line > item_list**

Append 50 boilerplate files to *report*:

% **repeat 50 cat template >> report**

---

sched   sched [*options*]

sched *time command*

tcsh only. Without options, print all scheduled events. The second form schedules an event.

time should be specified in *hh:mm* form (e.g., 13:00).

Options

+*hh:mm*
> Schedule event to take place *hh:mm* from now.

-*n*   Remove *n*th item from schedule.

---

set   set *variable=value*

set [*option*] *variable[n]=value*

set

Set *variable* to *value*, or if multiple values are specified, set the variable to the list of words in the value list. If an index *n* is specified, set the *n*th word in the variable to *value*. (The variable must already contain at least that number of words.) With no arguments, display the names and values of all set variables. See also "Predefined Shell Variables" earlier in this chapter.

Option

-r   *tcsh* only. List only read-only variables, or set specified variable to read-only.

Examples

% **set list=(yes no maybe)**	*Assign a wordlist*
% **set list[3]=maybe**	*Assign an item in existing wordlist*
% **set quote="Make my day"**	*Assign a variable*
% **set x=5 y=10 history=100**	*Assign several variables*
% **set blank**	*Assign a null value to* blank

---

setenv   setenv [*name* [*value*]]

Assign a *value* to an environment variable *name*. By convention, *name* is uppercase. *value* can be a single word or a quoted string. If no *value* is given, the null value is assigned. With no arguments, display the names and values of all environment variables. setenv is not necessary for the PATH variable, which is automatically exported from path.

---

settc

settc *capability value*

tcsh only. Set terminal *capability* to *value*.

---

setty

setty [*options*] [+|-*mode*]

tcsh only. Do not allow shell to change specified tty modes. By default, act on the execute set.

Options

+*mode*
> Without arguments, list all modes in specified set that are on. Otherwise, set specified mode to on.

-*mode*
> Without arguments, list all modes in specified set that are off. Otherwise, set specified mode to on.

-a List all modes in specified set.

-d Act on the edit set of modes (used when editing commands).

-q Act on the quote of modes (used when entering characters verbatim).

-x Act on the execute set of modes (default) (used when executing examples).

---

shift

shift [*variable*]

If *variable* is given, shift the words in a wordlist variable (i.e., *name*[2] becomes *name*[1]). With no argument, shift the positional parameters (command-line arguments) (i.e., $2 becomes $1). shift is typically used in a while loop. See an additional example under while.

Example

```
while ($#argv)          While there are arguments
    if (-f $argv[1])
        wc -l $argv[1]
    else
        echo "$argv[1] is not a regular file"
    endif
    shift               Get the next argument
end
```

---

source

source [-h] *script* [*args*]

Read and execute commands from a C-shell script. With -h, the commands are added to the history list but aren't executed. For *tcsh* only, arguments can be passed to the script and are put in argv.

Example

```
source ~/.cshrc
```

stop

stop [*jobIDs*]

Suspend the current background jobs or the background jobs specified by *jobIDs*; this is the complement of Control-Z or suspend.

suspend

suspend

Suspend the current foreground job; same as Control-Z. Often used to stop an su command.

switch

switch

Process commands depending on the value of a variable. When you need to handle more than three choices, switch is a useful alternative to an if-then-else statement. If the *string* variable matches *pattern1*, the first set of *commands* is executed; if *string* matches *pattern2*, the second set of *commands* is executed; and so on. If no patterns match, execute commands under the default case. *string* can be specified using command substitution, variable substitution, or filename expansion. Patterns can be specified using the pattern-matching symbols *, ?, and [ ]. breaksw is used to exit the switch. If breaksw is omitted (which is rarely done), the switch continues to execute another set of commands until it reaches a breaksw or endsw. Following is the general syntax of switch, side by side with an example that processes the first command-line argument:

```
switch (string)          switch ($argv[1])
    case pattern1:           case -[nN]:
        commands                 nroff $file | lp
        breaksw                  breaksw
    case pattern2:           case -[Pp]:
        commands                 pr $file | lp
        breaksw                  breaksw
    case pattern3:           case -[Mm]:
        commands                 more $file
        breaksw                  breaksw
        .                    case -[Ss]:
        .                        sort $file
        .                        breaksw
    default:                 default:
        commands                 echo "Error—no such option"
                                 exit 1
        breaksw                  breaksw
endsw                    endsw
```

telltc

telltc

tcsh only. Print all terminal capabilities and their values.

time

time [*command*]

Execute a *command* and show how much time it uses. With no argument, *time* can be used in a shell script to time the script.

umask	`umask [nnn]`
	Display file creation mask or set file creation mask to octal *nnn*. The file creation mask determines which permission bits are turned off. With no *nnn*, print the current mask.
unalias	`unalias pattern`
	Remove all aliases whose names match *pattern* from the alias list. See *alias* for more information.
uncomplete	`uncomplete pattern`
	tcsh only. Remove completions (specified by complete) whose names match *pattern*.
unhash	`unhash`
	Remove internal hash table. The shell stops using hashed values and searches the path directories to locate a command. See also rehash.
unlimit	`unlimit [-h] [resource]`
	Remove the allocation limits on *resource*. If *resource* is not specified, remove limits for all resources. See limit for more information. With -h, remove hard limits. This command can be run only by a privileged user.
unset	`unset variables`
	Remove one or more *variables*. Variable names may be specified as a pattern, using filename metacharacters. Does not remove read-only variables. See set.
unsetenv	`unsetenv variable`
	Remove an environment variable. Filename matching is not valid. See setenv.
wait	`wait`
	Pause in execution until all child processes complete, or until an interrupt signal is received.
watchlog	`watchlog`
	tcsh only. Same as log. Must have been compiled into the shell; see the version shell variable.

where

where *command*

tcsh only. Display all aliases, built-ins, and executables named *command*.

which

which *command*

tcsh only. Report which version of command will be executed. Same as the executable which, but faster, and checks *tcsh* built-ins.

while

while *(expression)*

   commands

end

As long as *expression* is true (evaluates to nonzero), evaluate *commands* between while and end. break and continue can be used to terminate or continue the loop.

Example

```
set user = (alice bob carol ted)
while ($argv[1] != $user[1])     Cycle through each user, checking for a
    match
    shift user                        If we cycled through with no match...
    if ($#user == 0) then
        echo "$argv[1] is not on the list of users"
        exit 1
    endif
end
```

22
The Defaults System

Native Mac OS X applications store their preferences in the *defaults database*. This is made up of each application's property list (*plist*) file, which is an XML file consisting of key-value pairs that define the preferences for an application or service of the operating system.

If an application has a *plist* file, every time you change its preferences, the changes are saved back to the *plist* file. Also included in the defaults database system are the changes you make to your system via the panels found in System Preferences (*/Applications*).

As an administrator, you may need to access your or another user's preferences. This is done from the Terminal using the *defaults* command. This chapter covers Mac OS X's preferences system, including the format and location of application and system preference files, how they work, and how to view and adjust their settings using the Property List Editor and the Terminal.

Property Lists

User-defined property lists are stored in *~/Library/Preferences*, and the appropriate *plist* is called up when an application launches. Property lists can contain literal preferences set through the application's Application → Preferences dialog, or subtler things such as window coordinates or the state of an option (such as whether to display the battery menu extra in the menu bar, as shown in Example 22-1).

Example 22-1. The com.apple.menuextra.battery.plist file

```
<?xml version="1.0" encoding="UTF-8"?>
<!DOCTYPE plist PUBLIC "-//Apple Computer//DTD PLIST 1.0//EN" "http://www.apple.
com/DTDs/PropertyList-1.0.dtd">
<plist version="1.0">
<dict>
    <key>ShowPercent</key>
```

Example 22-1. The com.apple.menuextra.battery.plist file (continued)

```
        <string>YES</string>
        <key>ShowTime</key>
        <string>NO</string>
</dict>
</plist>
```

Each property list is named after its *domain*, the unique namespace that an application uses when working with its preference files. Domains can look like any string, but the Apple-recommended format is similar to a URL, just in reverse. The naming convention is based on your company or organization's name, using the application's name as the domain. All of the *plist* files for the System Preferences and other iApps use the syntax *com.apple.domain.plist*, where *domain* is the name of the service or application. For example, the *plist* file for the Dock's preferences is *com.apple.dock.plist*, while the preferences file for OmniGraffle (if you have it installed) is *com.omnigroup.OmniGraffle.plist*.

> Not all application preference files are part of the preferences system. Some applications may write their user preference files in a proprietary format to *~/Library/Preferences*. These are typically Carbon applications not packaged into bundles, and hence lacking the *Info.plist* files they need to claim a preferences domain. As such, these preference files cannot be read or altered by the *defaults* command (described later), even though they are stored in *~/Library/ Preferences*.
>
> Classic applications, on the other hand, are even more antisocial, always writing their preference files in opaque formats in Mac OS 9's */System Folder/Preferences* folder.

Table 22-1 lists the *com.apple.domain.plist* files in *~/Library/Preferences*.

Table 22-1. The com.apple property list files

Domain	Description
.GlobalPreferences	Lists the system's preferences as defined in NSGlobalDomain.
com.apple.desktop.plist	Contains the settings made in the Desktop preferences panel.
com.apple.digihub.plist	Contains the settings made in the CD & DVD preferences pane.
com.apple.dock.plist	Contains the settings made in the Dock preferences panel, as well as information about the application icons in the user's Dock.
com.apple.finder.plist	Contains the settings for the Finder, made via Finder → Preferences.
com.apple.iApps.plist	Contains information about where database files for the iApps are stored.
com.apple.ink.framework.plist	Contains the settings for the Ink preferences panel (available only if the user has installed the drivers for a graphics tablet).
com.apple.ink.inkpad.plist	Contains location information about the window placement for the Inkpad application (available only if the user has installed the drivers for a graphics tablet).
com.apple.internetconfig.plist	Contains details about how you've configured the settings in the Internet and Network preference panels, as well as some of the preferences you've set in Internet Explorer and other Internet-related applications.
com.apple.internetconnect.plist	Contains the settings you've entered in the Internet Connect application.

Table 22-1. The com.apple property list files (continued)

Domain	Description
com.apple.internetpref.plist	Points to another *plist*, found at *http://configuration.apple.com/ configurations/internetservices/idiskconfiguration/1/clientConfiguration.plist*.
com.apple.keychainaccess.plist	Contains the preferences you've set in the Keychain Access application (*/Applications/Utilities*).
com.apple.loginwindow.plist	Specifies the sound manager to use upon login.
com.apple.mail.plist	Contains your settings and defaults for the Mail application (*/Applications*).
com.apple.menuextra.battery.plist	Contains the settings for the menu bar's battery menu extra (only on laptop systems).
com.apple.print.PrintCenter.plist	Lists the settings for the printers you've specified using the Print Center (*/Applications/Utilities*).
com.apple.print.custompresets.plist	Lists any customized settings for your default printer.
com.apple.recentitems.plist	Contains the settings for the → Recent Items menu, along with a list of the applications and documents (and their respective aliases).
com.apple.scheduler.plist	Contains the settings for any scheduled system-related tasks, such as those for Software Update and automatic calendar synchronizations with iCal.
com.apple.security.plist	Contains the settings for the default keychains.
com.apple.speech.prefs.plist *com.apple.speech.recognition. AppleSpeechRecognition.prefs.plist* *com.apple.speech.recognition.feedback. prefs.plist* *com.apple.speech.synthesis.general. prefs.plist* *com.apple.speech.voice.prefs.plist*	Handle the settings made in the Speech preferences panel and its various panes.
com.apple.systempreferences.plist	Contains the settings for the main System Preferences application window, including which panels have icons in its toolbar.
com.apple.systemuiserver.plist	Contains settings for iChat and lists the various menu extras found in the menu bar.
com.apple.universalaccess.plist	Contains the settings made in the Universal Access preferences panel.

Looking at Example 22-1, you can see the basic structure of a *plist* file. At the most basic level, a *plist* file can be broken down into three parts: dictionaries, keys, and values for the keys. The dictionary sections, denoted with <dict/>, set the structure; keys (<key/>) define an available preference, and the values for the keys in this example are strings (<string/>).

NSGlobalDomain, the Master Domain

One special domain named NSGlobalDomain acts as a parent to all the other preferences domains on the system. They inherit its settings, which are all related to system-wide preferences that applications access frequently, such as localized time-format information and the currently selected system beep.

Run *defaults read NSGlobalDomain* or simply *defaults read -g* within the Terminal to see NSGlobalDomain's current settings.

The values for a key are defined within either a <data/>, <date/>, <boolean/>, <string/>, or <integer/> tag. Keys can also contain nested dictionary sections or arrays (<array/>) sections for holding encoded values or a series of strings. Nested dictionaries are referred to as children of the parent dictionary. For example, *com. apple.dock.plist* has a *persistent-apps* key, which contains an array for all of the applications in the Dock (to the left of the divider bar). Within the array, you'll see a number of nested dictionaries, which define the parameters for the application's icon in the Dock. Example 22-2 shows the array item for *Mail.app*'s Dock icon.

Example 22-2. Mail.app's array in com.apple.dock.plist

```
<key>persistent-apps</key>
<array>
    <dict>
        <key>GUID</key>
        <integer>1425994837</integer>
        <key>tile-data</key>
        <dict>
            <key>file-data</key>
            <dict>
                <key>_CFURLAliasData</key>
                <data>
                AAAAAAEkAAIAAQxNYWNpbnRvc2ggSEQAAAAA
                AAAAAAAAAAAAAAC4qhjeSCsAAAAAEb8ITWFp
                bC5hcHAAAAAAAAAAAAAAAAAAAAAAAAAAAAAAA
                AAAAAAAAAAAAAAAAAAAAAAAAAAAAAAAAAAAAA
                AAAAAAAAAAA+WLjTxXoAXgAcAMUAr/////8A
                AAAgAAAAAAAAAAAAAAAAAADEFwcGxpY2F0
                aW9ucwABAAQAABG/AAIAIk1khY2ludG9zaCBI
                RDpBcHBsaWNhdGlvbnM6TWFpbC5hcHAADgAS
                AAgATQBhAGkAbAAuAGEAcABwAA8AGgAMAE0A
                YQBjAGkAbgB0AG8AcwBoACAASABEABAACAAA
                uKpfLgAAABEACAAAuNQLygAA//8AAA==
                </data>
                <key>_CFURLString</key>
                <string>/Applications/Mail.app/</string>
                <key>_CFURLStringType</key>
                <integer>0</integer>
            </dict>
            <key>file-label</key>
            <string>Mail</string>
            <key>file-mod-date</key>
            <integer>-1185476103</integer>
            <key>file-type</key>
            <integer>9</integer>
            <key>parent-mod-date</key>
            <integer>-1176134759</integer>
        </dict>
        <key>tile-type</key>
        <string>file-tile</string>
    </dict>
    ...
</array>
```

Since a *plist* file is nothing more than text, you can use any text editor (such as *BBEdit*, *vi*, or *Emacs*) to view and edit its contents; however, the preferred method is using the Property List Editor (*/Developer/Applications*), described later. The Property List Editor application is installed when you install the Developer Tools. See Chapter 15 for details on how to install or obtain the Developer Tools.

Viewing and Editing Property Lists

There are two ways you can view and edit the contents of an application's preferences file:

- With the Property List Editor (*/Developer/Applications*)
- From the command line, using the *defaults* command

The Property List Editor is only available on your system after installing the Developer Tools; however, the *defaults* command is available with the base installation of Mac OS X, and doesn't require you to install any additional software.

Viewing is one thing, but knowing what you can enter into a *plist* file requires a bit of investigative work. An application asserts its domain through the *CFBundleIdentifier* key in its internal *Info.plist* file, which is stored in an application's */Contents* directory. For example, the *Info.plist* file for the Dock can be found in */System/Library/CoreServices/Dock.app/Contents*.

The preferences available to an application are defined via the *CFBundleExecutable* key in the *Info.plist* file. Typically, the string for *CFBundleExecutable* is the short name for the application (e.g., Dock). This executable can be found in an application's */Contents/MacOS* directory. For example, the Dock executable is located in */System/Library/CoreServices/Dock.app/Contents/MacOS*.

To see a listing of available keys and strings for an application, use the strings command in the Terminal, followed by the path to the application's short name as defined by *CFBundleExecutable*:

```
chuck% strings /System/Library/CoreServices/Dock.app/⏎
Contents/MacOS/Dock
```

Unfortunately, the output from *strings* doesn't have a discernible structure. You'll need to sift through the output to find hints about the preferences you can set and alter using the Property List Editor or the *defaults* command, defined in the following sections.

Using the Property List Editor

The Property List Editor, shown in Figure 22-1, is a GUI tool that lets you view and edit property list files.

At their base, every *plist* has a Root item, which contains all of the dictionaries, arrays, keys, and values that define the preferences for an application. When you initially open a *plist* file, all of its elements will be hidden inside the Root item. If you click on the disclosure triangle next to Root (this is similar to the List View of the Finder), the keys of the *plist* are revealed in the first column.

If you select a Dictionary or Array item in the Property List column that has a disclosure triangle next to it, you can use ⌘-Right (or Left) Arrow to respectively

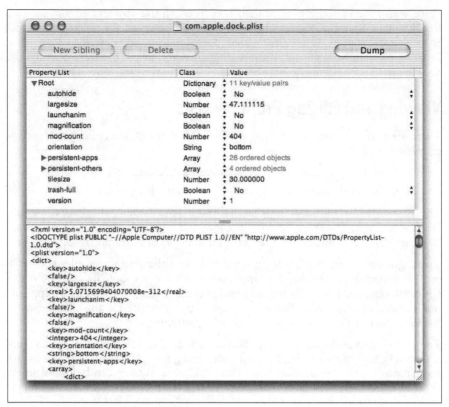

Figure 22-1. The Property List Editor

open or close a disclosure triangle. Likewise, Option-⌘-Right (or Left) Arrow will respectively open or close all of the disclosure triangles in the Property List Editor. For example, if you select Root and hit Option-⌘-Right Arrow, all of the contents of that *plist* file are shown in the upper display; Option-⌘-Left Arrow closes them up again.

As shown in Figure 22-1, there are three columns in the Property List Editor's display:

Property List

The Property List column lists the items seen in the <key/> tags of a *plist*'s XML file.

Class

The Class column lists the classes available for each key definition. Clicking on the set of up/down arrows next to a class reveals a pop-up menu, from which you can select from one of seven possible classes including:

String

A string can contain alphanumeric text, such as an application path (e.g., */Applications/Mail.app/*), a single-word response that defines the action of a key, or the default position of the application's window (e.g., {{125, 0}, {205, 413}}).

Dictionary

>Dictionary items are grayed out in the Property List Editor's display, and give you details on the number of key/value pairs listed in that dictionary item. Dictionaries are tagged as <dict/> in the XML file.

Array

>Like dictionaries, the Value column is grayed out for an Array, showing you the number of ordered objects available in that array. Within each array, you will find another Dictionary item listing its key/value pairs. Arrays are tagged as <array/> in the XML file.

Boolean

>Contains YES or NO responses as its value, and are tagged as <true/> or </false>, respectively, as the value in the XML file.

Number

>Contains a floating-point value for the key, such as a percentage value for the opaqueness of the Terminal application (e.g., 0.750000 for 75 percent), or the version number for an application. Values in the Number class are tagged in the *plist* file using <integer/>.

Date

>Contains the date in MM/DD/YY format. The Date Value can also include a time, in HH:MM:SS format.

Data

>Data information is stored as a string of encoded alphanumeric data, inside a set of opening and closing angle brackets. If you look closely at the Value, you'll see that the numbers are in blocks of eight characters (numbers and/or letters), which reveal its form as binary data. Example 22-3 shows the Data Value for *Mail.app*'s icon alias in the Dock.

Example 22-3. The Data Value for _CFURLAliasData as binary data

```
<00000000 01240002 00010c4d 6163696e 746f7368 20484400 00000000 00000000 00000000
0000b8aa 18de482b 00000000 11bf084d 61696c2e 61707000 00000000 00000000 00000000
00000000 00000000 00000000 00000000 00000000 00000000 00000000 00000000 00000000
00000000 00000000 3e58b8d3 c57a005e 001c00c5 00afffff ffff0000 00200000 00000000
00000000 00000000 000c4170 706c6963 6174696f 6e730001 00040000 11bf0002 00224d61
63696e74 6f736820 48443a41 70706c69 63617469 6f6e733a 4d61696c 2e617070 000e0012
0008004d 00610069 006c002e 00610070 0070000f 001a000c 004d0061 00630069 006e0074
006f0073 00680020 00480044 00100008 0000b8aa 5f2e0000 00110008 0000b8d4 0bca0000
ffff0000 >
```

Value

>Contains the value for the Class.

To view the XML source for the *plist* file, click on the Dump button in the upper-right corner of the Property List Editor's window. You cannot edit the XML source in the Property List Editor; edits to the *plist* file are made in the upper portion of the window.

You should avoid changing a *plist* file used by an application that's currently in use, as it could crash the application or cause it and your system to behave strangely.

To edit an item, double-click on the item you want to edit to select it, type in the new value, and then hit Return to accept the new value. If you want to see the change in the XML source, hit the Dump button again. After the changes have been entered, save the file before closing (File → Save, or ⌘-S).

The defaults Command

Another way to view and change the contents of a *plist* file is with the *defaults* command from the Terminal. The *defaults* command gives you an abstract way of reading from and writing to the preferences system. It lets you quickly modify any or all of an application's saved-state settings, which can prove quite handy when debugging your own applications. As with any command-line program, you can write shell scripts to run several invocations of *defaults* with a single command, letting you set the application's stage however you like in an instant.

If the preferences domain is bound to a specific host, then you must specify a host with the *-host* option, or refer to the current machine with the *-currentHost* option.

The following section contains a complete reference for the *defaults* command.

defaults

```
defaults [host] subcommand domain [option] [key]
defaults [-currentHost | -host hostname] read [domain [key]]
defaults [-currentHost | -host hostname] read-type domain key
defaults [-currentHost | -host hostname] write domain { 'plist' | domain key
'value' }
defaults [-currentHost | -host hostname] rename domain old_key new_key
defaults [-currentHost | -host hostname] delete [domain [key]]
defaults [-currentHost | -host hostname] { domains | find word | help }
```

Used to access Mac OS X's user defaults database to read, write (set or change), and delete system and application preferences.

The *defaults* command allows users and administrators to read, write, and delete Mac OS X user defaults from a command-line shell. An application's defaults belong to a *domain*, which typically correspond to individual applications; however, they can apply to system settings made via the System Preferences panels. Each domain has a dictionary of keys and values representing its defaults. Keys are always strings, but values can be complex data structures comprising arrays, dictionaries, strings, and binary data. These data structures are stored as XML property lists.

Though all applications, system services, and other programs have their own domains, they also share a domain named NSGlobalDomain. If a default isn't specified in the application's domain but is specified in NSGlobalDomain, then the application uses the value in that domain.

Host

-currentHost

Restricts the actions of the *defaults* command to the domains listed in *~/Library/ Preferences/ByHost*.

-host hostname

Used to specify the *hostname*, based on the Ethernet MAC address of the system the user is logged in to.

Subcommands

read

Prints all of the user's defaults, for every domain, to standard output.

read domain

Prints all of the user's defaults for domain to standard output.

read-type domain key

Prints the type of key for the given domain.

read domain key

Prints the value for the default of domain identified by key.

write domain key 'value'

Writes value as the value for key in domain. The *value* must be a property list, and must be enclosed in single quotes. For example:

    defaults write com.companyname.appname "Default Color" '(255, 0, 0)'

sets the application's *value* for the *key* (Default Color) to an array, which contains the string 255, 0, 0 (for the RGB values). Note that the *key* is enclosed in quotation marks because it contains a space.

write domain plist

Overwrites the defaults information in a domain with that given as *plist*. *plist* must be a property list representation of a dictionary and must be enclosed in single quotes. For example:

    defaults write com.companyname.appname '{ "Default Color" = (255, 0, 0);
    "Default Font" = Helvetica; }';

erases any previous defaults for *com.companyname.appname* and writes the values for the two names into the defaults system.

delete domain

Removes all default information for *domain*.

delete domain key

Removes the default named *key* from *domain*.

domains

Prints the names of all defaults domains on the user's system.

find word

Searches for *word* in the domain names, keys, and values of the user's defaults, and prints the results to standard output.

help

Prints a list of possible command formats.

-h

Prints an abbreviated list of possible command formats.

Options

-g

> Used as a synonym for the domain NSGlobalDomain. You can also use *"Apple Global Domain"* (including the quotation marks) as a synonym for the domain NSGlobalDomain. For example:
>
> `% defaults read "Apple Global Domain"`
>
> displays the same thing as:
>
> `% defaults read -g`
>
> or:
>
> `% defaults read NSGlobalDomain`
>
> or:
>
> `% defaults read -globalDomain`

Specifying values for preference keys:

-app

> Used to specify an application found in the */Applications* directory, rather than using its domain. For example:
>
> `% defaults read -app Mail`
>
> will output the defaults data for the Mail application.

-array

> Allows the user to specify an array as the value for the given preference key:
>
> `defaults write somedomain preferenceKey -array element1 element2 element3`
>
> The specified array overwrites the value of the *key* if the *key* was present at the time of the write. If the *key* was not present, it is created with the new value.

-array-add

> Allows the user to add new elements to the end of an array for a *key*, which has an array as its value. Usage is the same as *-array*. If the *key* was not present, it is created with the specified array as its value.

-dict

> Allows the user to add a dictionary to the defaults database for a domain. Keys and values are specified in order:
>
> `defaults write somedomain preferenceKey -dict key1 value1 key2 value2`
>
> The specified dictionary overwrites the *value* of the *key* if the *key* was present at the time of the write. If the *key* was not present, it is created with the new *value*.

-dict-add

> Allows the user to add new *key/value* pairs to a dictionary for a *key* that has a dictionary as its value. Usage is the same as *-dict*. If the *key* was not present, it is created with the specified dictionary as its value.

Host-Specific Preferences

A folder called *ByHost* can exist within *~/Library/Preferences*. *ByHost* contains property list files defining preferences specific to an application on a certain host. These files have filenames following the format of *com.apple.address.plist*, where *address* is the Ethernet MAC address associated with the *-currentHost*. Table 22-2 lists some of the more commonly found domains in the *ByHost* directory.

Table 22-2. Default domains found in ~/Library/Preferences/ByHost

Domain	Description
.GlobalPreferences.address.plist	Lists the global preference settings for various system services, including audio.
com.apple.Classic.address.plist	Lists the settings for the Classic environment.
com.apple.Flurry.address.plist	Lists the settings for the Flurry screen saver.
com.apple.HIToolbox.address.plist	Lists the input method settings for the keyboard and for Ink, if an input tablet is connected.
com.apple.ImageCapture2.address.plist	Lists the default application to be used when a digital camera is connected.
com.apple.ImageCaptureCamera.address.plist	Lists the settings for Image Capture and the digital camera connected to the system.
com.apple.MIDI.address.plist	Lists the settings for MIDI devices.
com.apple.PrefPane.Network.address.plist	Lists the previously selected port.
com.apple.SoftwareUpdate.address.plist	Displays whether the license agreement has been agreed to, and the number of inactive updates (if there are any).
com.apple.iToolsSlideSubscriptions.address.plist	Lists any .Mac slide shows that the user has subscribed to via System Preferences → Screen Effects → Screen Effects → Configure.
com.apple.iTunes.address.plist	Lists the settings for iTunes.
com.apple.preference.displays.address.plist	Shows the minimum recommended number of colors for the display (e.g., 256).
com.apple.print.PrintCenter.address.plist	Lists the printers supported by the Print Center application.
com.apple.screensaver..Mac.address.plist	Displays the settings for a .Mac screen saver, if the user has subscribed to one and if it has been set as the default screen saver.
com.apple.screensaver.address.plist	Lists the preference settings for the screen saver (as specified via System Preferences → Screen Effects).
com.apple.systempreferences.address.plist	Lists the system folder for the default startup disk.
com.apple.systemuiserver.address.plist	Lists the menu extras (i.e., menu extras) that shouldn't load at startup.
com.apple.windowserver.address.plist	Lists the settings for the display, including a second display if the user's computer has a second monitor connected (i.e., a dual-headed system).

To read the *plist* files located in the *ByHost* directory, you need to specify the *-currentHost* option, as follows:

```
% defaults -currentHost read com.apple.screensaver
```

Notice that you don't need to specify the Ethernet address that's part of the filename. The *-currentHost* option tells the *defaults* command to read the specified domain from the *ByHost* directory.

23

Running the X Windows System

The XFree86 project (*http://www.xfree86.org*) is an open source implementation of The X Window System—a.k.a., X Windows, or just X11 (X eleven)—which for many years has brought GUIs to all types of Unix. Less than a year after Apple's initial release of Mac OS X, the XFree86 team announced stable Darwin support.

The most significant thing X Windows can offer your Mac is the ability to run lots of Unix programs that require a GUI but are programmed using X11's own widget-working APIs, not Aqua's. Apple does not bundle X11 support with Mac OS X, however; you have to obtain it separately and install it yourself.

Installing the X Windows System

The XFree86 site contains instructions for downloading and installing the X11R6 binaries on a Mac OS X system. The site also provides instructions for compiling the X11R6 suite from source. The easiest way to get X11 for Mac OS X is through either XDarwin or GNU/Darwin, both of which contain easy-to-install binary distributions of X11. Alternatively, the Fink Project includes packages for the X11 server, software, and binaries. Fink also includes the system *xfree86* package, which is a placeholder package that lets you use the X11 distribution of your choice with Fink (the placeholder package satisfies the same dependencies as the Fink X11 package).

Manually Installing the X Window System

If you want to install the XFree86 distribution manually, download the XFree86 distribution (see the instructions on the XFree86 web site) and run the *Xinstall.sh* script to install the XFree86 suite.

This script will prompt you for some configuration details, although it includes defaults that should work for most Mac OS X users. The XFree86 web site has an extensive set of instructions for installing for the first time, installing over an older XFree86 installation, and for uninstalling XFree86. There are specific instructions for Mac OS X and Darwin.

This installer script installs the X11 binaries, libraries, header files, manpages, configuration files, etc., in */usr/X11R6* and */etc/X11*.

There is very little difference between manually installing XFree86 on Mac OS X and manually installing it on other Unix systems. One difference is that some files required on other Unix system are not required on Darwin; for example, there is no separate *Xvar.tgz* file to download. Another difference is that the double-clickable XDarwin application is placed in the */Applications* folder.

Running XDarwin

XDarwin can be run in two modes: full-screen or rootless. Either of these modes run side by side with Aqua, although full-screen mode hides the Finder Desktop. To launch the X server, double-click the XDarwin application (*/Applications*).

You will be prompted to choose which of these two modes to run. In rootless mode, X11 applications take up their own window on your Aqua Desktop. In full-screen mode, X11 takes over the entire screen and is suitable if you want to run an X11 Desktop environment (DTE) like GNOME, KDE, or Xfce. If you prefer rootless mode, you will probably want to run OroborOSX, an X window manager with an Aqua look and feel (see "Aqua-Like X Windows with OroborOSX," later in this chapter).

You can still access your Mac OS X Desktop while in full-screen mode by pressing Option-⌘-A. To go back to the X11 Desktop, press either Option-⌘-A, or click the XDarwin icon in the Dock.

Running XDarwin from the Console

XDarwin can also be run from the Darwin console. To do so, first shut down Core Graphics by logging into the machine as console. When the console prompt appears, log in with your normal username.

Once logged in, start the X11 server by entering the command *exec startx*. To quit X11, type *exit* from the main login Terminal window. If there is a long delay showing only the spinning beach ball cursor, type *logout* to return to console mode. Note that in this situation you will not see text appear on the screen as you type.

The normal user–level X window customization is possible with XDarwin. This typically starts with the *.xinitrc* script in the user */home* directory. A sample *.xinitrc* script is provided in */etc/X11/xinit/xinitrc*.

Using this as a starting point, you can specify which X11-based applications to start up when XDarwin is launched, including which window manager you'd like to have as your default. The default window manager for XDarwin is the tab window manager (or twm), but many other DTEs are available; see the next section.

Desktops and Window Managers

Once you have installed XFree86, you will probably want to install additional X11 applications, window managers, and perhaps other desktop environments.

One of the easiest ways to install additional window managers is to use Fink (described in Chapter 24). Table 23-1 lists some of the window managers and desktops that can be installed via Fink.

Table 23-1. Window managers available from Fink

Window manager	Fink package name
Enlightenment	enlightenment
FVWM	fvwm, fvwm2
GNOME	bundle-gnome
KDE	As of this writing, experimental support is available for KDE. See *http://fink.sourceforge.net/news/kde.php*
mwm	lesstif?
Oroborus	oroborus, oroborus2
Window Maker	windowmaker

Fink has an entire section devoted to GNOME, where you will find an extensive set of GNOME libraries, utilities, and plug-ins. Also included in the GNOME section are GTK+, glib, and Glade. You can use Fink to install an *xterm* replacement like *rxvt* or *eterm*.

X11-Based Applications and Libraries

Fink can also be used to install many X11-based applications like the *GNU Image Manipulation Program* (GIMP), *xfig/transfig*, *ImageMagick*, *nedit*, and many others. Since Fink understands dependencies, installation of some of these applications will cause Fink to install several other packages first. For example, since the text editor *nedit* depends on Motif libraries, Fink installs Lesstif first. (This also gives you the Motif window manager, *mwm*.) Similarly, when you install the GIMP via Fink, you also install the packages for *GNOME*, *GTK+*, and *glib*.

You can also use Fink to install libraries directly. For example:

```
fink install qt
```

installs the X11-based Qt libraries.

Aqua-Like X Windows with OroborOSX

OroborOSX, developed by Adrian Umpleby, is a modified version of the oroborus GNOME-compliant X11 window manager created by Ken Lynch. It is designed to make X11 windows look and behave as much like Aqua as possible. Although OroborOSX includes a copy of the XDarwin server, it does not include supporting files such as user binaries, headers, and libraries. So, you should install XFree86 before running OroborOSX. Aside from the prerequisite software, one of the most Mac-like features of OroborOSX is its installation. After unpacking the tarball, drag the OroborOSX folder to the */Applications* folder in the Finder. You might also consider adding its icon to the Dock.

To launch OroborOSX, double-click its icon. Launching OroborOSX also starts XDarwin in the background.

You will notice some differences immediately. The most obvious difference from other X11 window managers is that the *xterm* window frames look very similar to the Aqua Terminal windows. In particular, they have the Aqua-like buttons for closing, minimizing, and maximizing the window. Also, OroborOSX windows minimize to the Dock, just like other Aqua windows (other X11 window managers have their own locations for minimized windows). Figure 23-1 shows a Terminal window and an *xterm* side by side.

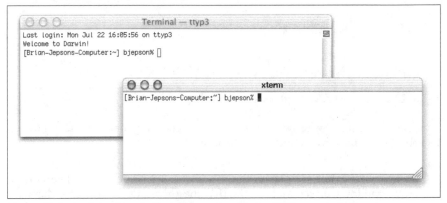

Figure 23-1. An Aqua Terminal window and an OroborOSX xterm window

Beyond simply looking the part, windows running under OroborOSX succeed in behaving as you'd expect ordinary Aqua windows to, even when it runs against default X11 window behavior. These windows interleave correctly with Aqua windows, for example, and clicking in a background window activates only that window (rather than the click being sent through to make something else happen in that window).

X11 applications are easy to launch under OroborOSX as well, either through its Launch menu or by using its *template* script to create X11 icons you can launch from the Finder. This script is located in the */Contents/Resources/Launch Menu Items* subdirectory of the OroborOSX application (*.app*) folder. Copy it to a file with an *.x11app* extension, edit it to suit your needs, and double-click it from the Finder to launch it under OroborOSX.

OroborOSX is a self-contained package. It does not interfere with any Unix-based software, although it can run X11 binaries that were installed by other packages.

By default, OroborOSX does not execute your *.xinitrc* script; however, this script can be run from OroborOSX's launch menu. If you want to use your *.xinitrc* script this way, be sure not to start some other window manager in it. This should be done by commenting out the line in your *.xinitrc* file that starts a window manager. For example, the following line:

```
exec mwm
```

should be changed to:

```
# exec mwm
```

One interesting Mac-like feature of OroborOSX is that double-clicking the titlebar of an OroborOSX window windowshades it. This feature gives OroborOSX something in common with Mac OS 9 that Mac OS X windows lack, since double-clicking a Mac OS X window's titlebar minimizes the window and places it in the Dock. The Window menu includes shortcuts for activating the windowshade feature, minimizing a window, or zooming it. Figure 23-2 shows a windowshaded *xterm* and a normal *xterm* next to each other.

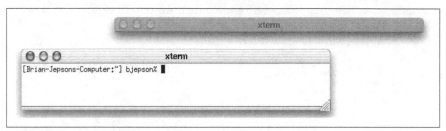

Figure 23-2. xterms with and without windowshading

You can customize windows' appearance by choosing one of the following OroborOSX themes from Options → Themes:

Eau
> This is the default, and styles the window and its titlebar just like normal Aqua windows under Mac OS X. (It's the theme used with this chapter's figures.)

Greyphite
> This gives the windows an Aqua-like look and feel, but with a graphite style, as per the "Graphite" style from Mac OS X's General preference pane (see "Personal" in Chapter 5).

Nextish
> This creates windows with a NeXTSTEP appearance.

Aqua-X11 Interactions

Since X11-based applications rely on different graphics systems even when running XDarwin in rootless mode, one would not necessarily expect that any GUI interactions between these two graphics systems are easily accomplished. There are several such easily accomplished interactions worth noting.

The first such interaction is to open X11-based applications from the Aqua terminal application. To allow an X11-based application to be launched from the Terminal application, you need to set the shell environment variable DISPLAY as follows (for *tcsh*):

```
setenv DISPLAY 0:0
```

If you are using *bash* or *zsh*, you could use the following shell environment:

```
DISPLAY="0:0"; export DISPLAY
```

You may choose to put the appropriate version of this in your startup configuration script (see "Configuring Shells" in Chapter 21).

You can also copy and paste between X11 and Mac OS X applications, though the mouse commands for using the clipboard on either side are different. Copying from or pasting to an Aqua window works the same no matter where the text came from, but X11 windows copy their text to the computer's clipboard *as soon as you select it*; X11 windows pastes text through a Command-click (or pressing the middle mouse button, if you have a three-button mouse).

 XDarwin allows you to configure key combinations that simulate two- and three-button mice. By default, Option-click simulates the middle mouse button, and z-click simulates the right mouse button. To configure this in XDarwin, choose Preferences from the XDarwin menu. In OroborOSX, choose XDarwin Preferences from the Options menu.

Connecting to Other X Window Systems

You can connect from Mac OS X to other X window systems using *ssh* with X11 forwarding. If you use OpenSSH (which is included with Mac OS X; see "Remote Logins" in Chapter 7), you must use the -*X* option to request X11 forwarding (the -2 option specifies the *ssh* Version 2 protocol, as opposed to the older Version 1 protocol). For example:

```
ssh -2 -X remotemachine -l username
```

As long as XDarwin is running, this can be entered in either an *xterm* window or in the Mac OS X Terminal. To have the X11 forwarding enabled in Terminal, you must have the DISPLAY variable set as noted earlier prior to making the connection. (This is always the case if the DISPLAY variable is set in your *.tcshrc* script.) It is also possible to make a double-clickable application that connects to a remote machine via *ssh2* with X11 forwarding enabled. For example, the following script can be used for this purpose:

```
#!/bin/sh
ssh -2 -X remotemachine -l username
```

If you've installed the commercial version of *ssh* from *http://www.ssh.com*, the equivalent of the preceding script is given with the following:

```
#!/bin/sh
ssh2 remotemachine -l username
```

Using OroborOSX, you can add a Launch menu item to accomplish the same task. To do this, start by copying the template file found in the directory *~/Library/Preferences/OroborOSX/Launch Menu Items* to whatever you'd like to call this application. For this example, suppose you want to connect to a remote machine named *chops* with a username of *sam*. Name the application *Connect2Chops*. Start by copying the template to *Connect2Chops.x11app*:

```
cp template Connect2Chops.x11app
```

Next you must edit this *Connect2Chops.x11app* file. You need only to change a couple of lines since you'll be using an *xterm*. In particular:

```
# ARGUMENTS FOR THE COMMAND GO HERE (can be left blank)
set argums="-geometry 80x25 -ls -sb -sl 5000 -e ssh -2 -X chops -l sam"
# OPTIONAL TITLE STRING GOES HERE (uncomment this if wanted)
# note that an ID number, sent from OroborOSX, will be added in
# brackets after this string [eg, below would give "xterm (3)"]
set titlenam="Connect2Chops"
```

Save this file (in *~/Library/Preferences/OroborOSX/Launch Menu Items*), then select Launch → Rebuild → Launch Menu.

That's it! Now you're ready to launch the connection to the remote machine via the menu bar. Once you've made such a connection to a machine running X Windows, you can start X11-based applications on the remote machine and display them on your Mac OS X machine. Figure 23-3 shows MATLAB running on a remote Sun workstation but displayed on the local Mac OS X machine.

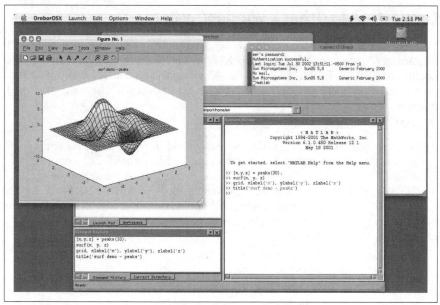

Figure 23-3. MATLAB running in a remote window on top of Mac OS X

24

Installing Unix Software

As "Installing Applications" in Chapter 6 describes, installing Mac OS X software is as easy as dragging an application's icon to your hard drive, or occasionally having to double-click a package icon and run through a few prompts in the Installer application. Thereafter, everything Just Works.

Installing software for Darwin, the Unix side of Mac OS X, is not always so easy. Since Mac OS X's graphical interface tends to keep Darwin and its activities invisible in the background, many Mac OS X users never need to worry about this. However, through Darwin, you have access to a whole world of largely open source software written for the Unix operating system. In Mac OS X's "factory" state (with the Developer Tools installed), you can immediately start installing and using Unix software that uses a command-line interface (or has no interface at all, as with system daemons; see Chapter 5). If you install the X Window System (as described in Chapter 23), you can start using all manner of GUI-using Unix software as well.

This chapter discusses the various strategies you have for Darwin-side software installation, including DIY-style compiling from raw source code and the rather friendlier use of package managers.

Package Managers

A *package management system* uses a local database to keep track of software packages installed on the machine and the dependencies that run among them. New packages consult this database to see if other packages whose presence they depend upon are already installed, and they assist with package uninstalls by remembering the location of all the files and directories involved during installation (as well as alerting you in case other installed packages depend upon this one, so that removing it would break all of them).

At the time of this writing, Mac OS X is still quite a young OS (despite its ancient Unix roots), so what few package management systems exist are still struggling down the road toward maturity. That said, users willing to spend a little extra time behind the Terminal can expand their Mac's software repetoire safely.

> Mac OS X has a native but rudimentary package management system, using a filesystem-based database stored in */Library/Receipts*. See "Uninstalling applications" in Chapter 6.

Fink

Fink is a package management system based on Debian GNU/Linux's (*http://www.debian.org*) popular *dpkg* and *apt-get* utilities, which let you easily sync a local package-information database with that of a central, Internet-based repository, as well as search for, install, and uninstall packages of ready-to-go binaries with single commands.

You can download Fink's essential command-line tools as a standard Mac OS X package by pointing your web browser to *http://fink.sourceforge.net* and following the instructions contained therein. (This book has left instructions purposefully vague to let the good Fink maintainers modify their online instructions with future releases.)

> At the time of this writing, Fink installs all of its packages (including *dpkg* and other essential tools) in a directory called */sw*, creating it in the (likely) event that it doesn't already exist. This is Fink's way of preventing any possible conflicts with software that you (or Mac OS X system CDs and upgrades) might install in more traditional Unix directories.
>
> You can, if you wish, take the road between caution and convenience by telling Fink to install its goodies into */usr/local*, the traditional Unix location for software accessible to all the system's users but not crucial to the system itself. (The distinction is similar between Mac OS X's demarcation of the */System/Library* and */Library* folders, as covered in Chapter 9).

Once Fink is installed, the following command-line programs becomes available to you. Consult their respective manpages for a full usage guide to each.

fink
> This command works as an abstract frontend to many of the commands below, including *apt-get* and *apt-cache*.

dpkg
> A lower-level interface to the package manager. You'll likely use *dselect* or *apt-get* more often, but this command gives you some functionality those programs don't. For example, you can see a list of what files a package installs by running *dpkg -L package-name*.

dselect
> A console-based browser of the Fink database and the system's installed and available packages.

apt-get command package

> This very handy utility lets you install and modify packages through single commands, including the following:
>
> *apt-get install package*
>> Install the named package.
>
> *apt-get remove package*
>> Uninstall the named package.
>
> *apt-get update*
>> Resynchronize the local Fink database with the central Fink repository via the Internet.

apt-cache

> You can use this program to comb through your local Fink database without changing or installing anything. With its *search* command, you can send keyword queries to the database. For example, to see all packages that might deal with XML:
>
> ```
> [jmac@Jason-McIntoshs-Computer jmac]% apt-cache search xml
> ant - Java based build tool.
> dia - Diagram drawing program
> expat - C library for parsing XML
> gnumeric - Spreadsheet program for gnome, reads many formats
> imagemagick - Tools and libs manipulate images in many formats.
> libxml - XML parsing library
> libxml2 - XML parsing library, version 2
> neon - HTTP/WebDAV client library with a C API
> [jmac@Jason-McIntoshs-Computer jmac]%
> ```

You could then, for example, run *apt-get install expat* and suddenly have the expat XML libraries installed on your machine.

> Fink Commander, a open source project led by Steve Burr, provides an Aqua-level GUI into your machine's Fink installation. Through this application, you can easily browse and search through Fink's available packages, search for packages, see which packages you have installed, and install or remove packages with one click.
>
> You can download Fink Commander from *http://finkcommander. sourceforge.net*.

GNU Mac OS X Packages

The GNU Mac OS X Public Archive (*http://www.osxgnu.org*) aims to create standard Mac OS X installer packages (of the sort described in "Software Installers" in Chapter 6) for the ever-growing wealth of software under the GNU open-source license, a staple of the Unix world. Unlike Fink, it doesn't provide its own package management framework, instead using and extending the bare-bones package management utilities that already ship as part of Mac OS X. In other words, you can install and manage packages without having to drop into the Terminal.

Unix Software

Where Fink has Fink Commander, the GNU Mac OS X archive has OS X Package Manager, an Aqua application that lets you view the packages you have installed on your Mac, and gives you an easy way to delete any you no longer need. (It also provides assistance in creating packages of your own, in keeping with the GNU Mac OS X project's goals.)

Unlike Fink Commander, the OS X Package Manager won't version-track and download packages for you—you've got to do that yourself, via the project's web site. Mac OS X's package manager just isn't as intertwined with the Internet as is the Debian package manager that Fink employs.

Installing from Source

Open source Unix software not available as Mac OS X packages exists as bundles of raw (usually C) source code and helper files. Fortunately, there are some long-standing traditions and idioms with Unix source installation that make this process somewhat easier, but there also remain many places to get stuck, which can bewilder those without C-programming experience (and bewilder those *with* experience if the source is messy enough).

The usual idiom for installing software from source runs as follows.

1. Obtain the source code as a *.tar.gz* file (a.k.a. a *tarball*). If you download it through a web browser, StuffIt Expander automatically inflates it into a folder within your browser's download folder (see "File Compression" in Chapter 6); otherwise, manually use StuffIt Expander or (since you're probably in the Terminal already) the *tar* command, with its *xzvf* (*tar*-extract, *gzip*-extract, verbose-mode, file-based) options, like so:

   ```
   [jmac]% tar xvzf something-i-just-downloaded.tar.gz
   ...output of list of files and directories extracted...
   [jmac]%
   ```

2. *cd* into the directory created through the previous step, and read the *README* and *INSTALL* files (and generally anything else with an all-caps filename), if they exist. These provide important information, including hints for installing the software on various systems—if Darwin or Mac OS X appear here, you're in luck. Also consult any information found on the web site for the *ftp* directory from which you obtained the source. Be generally suspicious of tarballs that didn't contain any of this documentation.

3. Run the software's *configure* script (by typing **./configure**). This script examines your computer, noting its processor type and the operating system that it runs, and tries to build a *Makefile* with commands and settings that will help the software compile correctly on it.

   You can feed the *configure* script some arguments to give it hints or force some of its settings. If it can't figure out what kind of OS you have (it will tell you as much, if so), you can help it out a little by copying the files */usr/share/libtool/config.guess* and */usr/share/libtool/config.sub* into the current directory and running *./configure* again. These two files, kindly provided by Apple, can give a helpful nudge to a Unix source that has never seen Darwin before, providing it with some introductory configuration information. (Alternately, you can try running it again, this time typing **./configure --with-host-type=powerpc-apple-darwin**version-number, where version-number is the number you see when you run uname -v.)

4. Run the system's *make* command. This will try building the software, based on the *Makefile* generated through the previous step.

   This is the do-or-die step of attempting to build from source. As the build process advances step by step, it echoes every compiler or shell command that it attempts to run. If everything compiles smoothly, the process silently exits, leaving the software ready to test and install. Otherwise, it will spew asterisk-studded error messages at you, leaving you to puzzle out what to do next.

   If the latter situation occurs, you have a few options. First, look at the first error message. If it complains about something obvious, like a missing file or directory, see if you can satisfy the problem by building symlinks, changing your working directory, or adjusting the *Makefile* and running *make* again. (Subsequent invocations of *make* will resume the build where it left off, unless you run *make clean* at some point to delete all the interim files and directories.) If it can't find a library, confirm that you have the library it's seeking, then try giving it a hint as to where it can find the library, either by manually re-running the last echoed compiler command with an additional *-L* argument, or by adjusting the *Makefile* to change or expand its library-path variables. If all else fails (which it often will), turn to a web-searching resource like Google.com, running a search query such as "mac os x" "software-name" "error-message", and seek wisdom from those who may have traveled this path before you.

   All this explains why prepackaged software is a good thing.

5. If you survived the *make* ordeal, congratulations. Try running *make test*. Not all source distributions include a test suite (ones that don't just return a message like Unable to make target "test") here, but if they do, it's worth running to see if everything works as it should.

6. Finally, run *make install*. This copies all the build binaries, libraries, and manpages into their permanent homes across the filesystem. In the likely event that the software in question installs in some place other than your home directory, you'll need to run *sudo make install*. Depending upon the software, you may be able to get away with a home-directory installation, but often you have to provide the configure script with an argument like *--prefix=/Users/username*. Consult the software's *README* file.

You should now be able to *cd* to some location other than the source directory (such as your home directory) and, if the freshly installed software included executables, invoke them from the command line.

25

Unix Command Reference

This chapter presents the Mac OS X user, programmer, and system administration commands available through the Terminal (see Chapter 19). Each entry is labeled with the command name on the outer edge of the page. The syntax line is followed by a brief description and a list of available options. Many commands come with examples at the end of the entry. If you need only a quick reminder or suggestion about a command, you can skip directly to the examples.

Typographic conventions for describing command syntax are in the Preface. For help in locating commands, see the index at the back of this book.

We've tried to be as thorough as possible in listing the options. The basic command information and most options should be correct; however, new options are added and sometimes old options are dropped. You may, therefore, find some differences between the options you find described here and the ones on your system. When there seems to be a discrepancy, check the manpage (by way of the man command). For most commands, you can also use the --help option to get a brief usage message. (Even when it isn't a valid option, it usually results in an "invalid option" error message, along with the usage message.)

Traditionally, commands take single-letter options preceded by a single hyphen, like -d. A more recent Unix convention allows long options preceded by two hyphens, like --debug. Often, a feature can be invoked through either the old style or the new style of options.

Some options can be invoked only by a user with root (superuser) privileges (see "Acting as Root" in Chapter 11).

There are 289 Unix Commands listed in this chapter, many of which don't have manpages, or worse—inaccurate manpages—on the system. These commands give you the basics of what you need to know to get under the hood of your Mac OS X system...and more.

Alphabetical Summary of Commands

ac

ac [*options*] [*users*]

Displays accumulative Aqua and shell login times for *users*, or for all users if none is specified. By default, ac reads from */var/log/wtmp* (see also last).

Options

-d   Show totals for each day.

-p   Show totals for each user.

-w *file*
    Read accounting data from *file* instead of */var/log/wtmp*.

---

addr

addr [-4 | -6] { -n | -p } *address*

Converts an IP address into both hexadecimal and dotted-decimal formats. The address is expected to be well-formed. An IPv4 address must be either 8 hexadecimal digits (with optional colons delimiting octets), or 4 dotted quads of decimal digits. An IPv6 address must be either 32 hexadecimal digits (with optional colons delimiting octets), or up to 4 octets of decimal or hexadecimal digits (delimited by dots or colons) preceded by a pair of colons and a possible prefix of several hexadecimal octets (e.g., ab:cd::12.34.56.78).

Options

-4   Specifies *address* as an IPv4 address. This is the default.

-6   Specifies *address* as an IPv6 address.

-n   Used when *address* is in hexadecimal format.

-p   Used when *address* is in dotted-decimal format, or abbreviated IPv6 format.

---

appleping

appleping *host* [*packet-size* [*npackets*]]

Sends AppleTalk Echo Protocol (AEP) request packets to *host* and displays transmission statistics if successful. The AppleTalk *host* is specified in either of the following ways:

name:type[*@zone*]
    The host's *name* and *type*, as shown by the atlookup command. If *zone* is not specified, the current zone is used.

network-node
    The host's network and node number in hexadecimal, as shown by the atlookup command.

Options

packet-size
    Send packets of *packet-size* bytes (a value between 14 and 599). The default value is 64.

npackets
> Send *npackets* number of packets before stopping. If *npackets* is not specified, appleping continues until you've sent an interrupt (using Control-C, for example).

---

appletalk

`appletalk` *options*

Displays or configures AppleTalk network interfaces. Any user may display settings, but only the superuser may change them. `appletalk` allows you to start and stop AppleTalk on a single port (network interface), or configure AppleTalk routing or multi-homing on multiple ports.

General options

`-d` Deactivate AppleTalk.

`-n` Show current AppleTalk interface, network number, node ID, and zone name.

`-p` Show AppleTalk information stored in parameter RAM (PRAM).

`-s` Show AppleTalk statistics.

Single port options

`-h` [*zone*]
> Change the default AppleTalk zone to *zone*, or if *zone* isn't specified, display the current zone.

`-q` Use with `-u` to start AppleTalk in quiet mode; doesn't prompt for zone selection.

`-u` *port*
> Start AppleTalk on the network interface *port* (en0, for example).

Multiple port options

`-c` Verify the AppleTalk configuration file, */etc/appletalk.cfg*, without starting AppleTalk. Use with `-r` or `-x`.

`-e` Same as `-c`, but also display the AppleTalk configuration.

`-f` *file*
> Use *file* instead of the default */etc/appletalk.cfg* to start Apple-Talk. Use with `-r` or `-x`.

`-j` Display AppleTalk router status.

`-m` *n*
> Limit routing speed to a maximum *n* packets per second.

`-q` Use with `-r` or `-x` to start AppleTalk in quiet mode; doesn't prompt for zone selection.

`-r` Start AppleTalk in routing mode.

`-t` Show the AppleTalk routing table.

`-v` *n*
> Set the maximum number of entries in the AppleTalk routing table to *n*. Use with `-r` or `-x`. Useful with large AppleTalk networks.

-w *n*

> Set the maximum number of entries in the Zone Information Protocol (ZIP) table to *n*. Use with -r or -x. Useful with large AppleTalk networks.

-x   Start AppleTalk in multihoming mode.

-z   List all AppleTalk zones.

Examples

Stop AppleTalk, using sudo to gain superuser privileges:

> **sudo appletalk -d**

Start AppleTalk on the en1 interface:

> **sudo appletalk -u en1**

Start an AppleTalk router in quiet mode:

> **sudo appletalk -q -r**

---

aexml

aexml -soap -SOAPAction *text* [-in *filename*] [-out *filename*] [-name *'App Name'* | -pid *pid* | psn *highPSN.lowPSN* | -sig *signature*] aexml -xmlrpc [-in *filename*] [-out *filename*] [-name *'App Name'* | -pid *pid* | psn *highPSN.lowPSN* | -sig *signature*]

Translates SOAP and XML-RPC requests into Apple Events understood by Mac OS X applications. The target application can be specified by name, process ID, process serial number, or signature. If no target is specified, a sandbox application is launched to handle the request. Output, if any, is in the form of XML or a one-line error.

Options

-soap

> Forwards a SOAP request to the target application.

-SOAPAction

> Provides the SOAPAction header. If specified as –, the header is read from input.

-xmlrpc

> Forwards an XML-RPC request to the target application.

-in

> Specifies source of input. Defaults to – (standard input).

-out

> Specifies location of output. Defaults to – (standard output).

-name

> Specifies target application by pathname.

-pid

> Specifies target application by Unix PID.

-psn

> Specifies target application by Carbon Process Manager process serial number.

-sig

> Specifies target application by signature. This is a four-character code unique to an application. The signature is usually the same as the application's creator code. In an application bundle, it is specified by the *CFBundleSignature* property in *Info.plist*.

appletviewer

`appletviewer [options] urls`

Connects to the specified *urls* and runs any Java applets they specify in their own windows, outside the context of a web browser.

Options

-debug

> Run the applet viewer from within the Java debugger, *jdb*.

-encoding name

> Specify the input HTML file encoding.

-J opt

> Pass *opt* on to the java command. *opt* should not contain spaces; use multiple -J options if necessary.

apply

`apply [options] command arguments`

Allows you to run a given command multiple times, each time with a different argument. By default, apply pairs and runs *command* followed by each argument listed in *arguments*. To place the argument elsewhere in *command*, mark that location in *command* with %*n*, where *n* is the *n*th unused item listed in *arguments* (see examples).

Options

-a*character*

> Use *character* instead of %.

-*number*

> Instead of pairing arguments one at a time with *command*, use them *number* at a time with *command*. If *number* is 0, none of the arguments will be used with *command*, but *command* will still run once for each item listed in *arguments*. If *command* contains %*n*, *number* is ignored.

Examples

Ping three different hosts, sending three packets to each:

```
apply 'ping -c3' host1.com host2.com host3.com
```

Ping three different hosts, sending a different number of packets to each:

```
apply -2 'ping -c' 3 host1.com 4 host2.com 5 host3.com
```

Ping three different hosts, and write output to file *pinglog*:

```
apply 'ping -c3 %1 >> pinglog' host1.com  host2.com⏎
host3.com
```

apropos	apropos *keywords*

Looks up one or more keywords in the online manpages. Same as man -k. See also whatis.

asr	asr -source *sourcepath* -target *targetpath* [*options*] asr -imagescan *imagepath*

Accurately copies the contents of a disk image or source volume onto a target volume. *asr* (Apple Software Restore) can also scan and prepare disk images when given the -imagescan option, allowing the images to be restored from more efficiently.

sourcepath can be the pathname of either a disk image or a volume, while *targetpath* can specify only a volume. Volumes can be specified by either their */dev* entries (e.g., */dev/disk0s10*) or mountpoints (e.g., */Volumes/Disk 2*).

For disk image creation, use either Disk Copy or the command line utility hdiutil. Once a volume has been restored, it might be necessary to use the bless utility to make it bootable. (See hdiutil and bless).

For a complete description of the imaging and restoration process, as well as tips on optimizing restores using the buffer settings, see the asr manpage.

Options
-buffers *n*
> During block-copies, use *n* number of buffers instead of the default eight.

-buffersize *n*
> During block-copies, use buffers of size n bytes instead of the default 1000. n can also be specified in bytes, kilobytes, megabytes, or gigabytes by appending it with b, k, m, or g, respectively.

-csumbuffers *n*
> Use *n* number of buffers specifically for checksumming. By default, checksumming is performed with the same buffers used for copying.

-csumbuffersize *n*
> Use checksum buffers of size *n* bytes. *n* can also be specified in bytes, kilobytes, megabytes, or gigabytes by appending it with b, k, m, or g, respectively.

-debug
> Print additional information during operation to assist in troubleshooting.

-disableOwners
> Don't enable the owners for the source and target. By default, asr ensures that all owners are enabled, allowing for more accurate file-by-file copying. If given, this option is ignored during block-copies.

As of asr Version 14.4, this option doesn't function as described; if given, -disableOwners behaves as if the -debug option were given instead.

-erase

Erase the target volume before copying to it. If this option is not used, asr will instead restore-in-place, overwriting only those files having the same name and location in both *sourcepath* and *targetpath*, and copying from *sourcepath* anything not already in *targetpath*. Using the -erase option allows asr to perform a block-copy restore, which can be faster than the file-by-file copying procedure used when restoring in place.

-h

Print a brief help message. This option can only be used by itself.

-imagescan *imagepath*

Scan disk image *imagepath* and generate checksums. Scanning optimizes images that asr will use as source images for restores. This option can only be used by itself.

-nocheck

Don't verify copied data. By default, asr uses checksums generated during the image scan for verification. This option will bypass that verification, allowing asr to restore from images that haven't first been scanned.

-noprompt

Don't prompt before erasing *targetpath* when the -erase option is used.

-rebuild

Rebuild the Classic system's desktop database on *targetpath*.

-v

Print version information. This option can only be used by itself.

Examples

Typically, asr requires root privileges, provided by the sudo command in these examples:

Clone one volume to another:

```
sudo asr -source /Volumes/Mac\HD -target /Volumes/Disk\↵
2 -erase
```

Restore-in-place from a disk image:

```
sudo asr -source /Volumes/Images/image1.dmg -target↵
/Volumes/Disk\ 2
```

at   at [*options*] [*time*] [*date*] [+ *increment*]

Executes commands entered on standard input at a specified *time* and optional *date*. (See also batch and crontab.) End input with *EOF*. *time* can be formed either as a numeric hour (with optional minutes and modifiers) or as a keyword. *date* can be formed either as a month and date, a day of the week, or a special keyword. *increment* is a positive integer followed by a keyword. See the following lists for details.

at will not run until you first enable atrun by uncommenting its line in */etc/crontab*.

Options

-f *file*

Execute commands listed in *file*.

-m Send mail to user after job is completed (if an MTA such as *sendmail* is configured to run).

-q *queuename*

Schedule the job in *queuename*. Values for *queuename* are the lowercase letters a through l. Queue a is the default queue for at jobs. Queue b is the queue for batch jobs. Queues with higher letters run with increased niceness (receive less priority).

Time

hh:mm [*modifiers*]

Hours can have one or two digits (a 24-hour clock is assumed by default); optional minutes can be given as one or two digits; the colon can be omitted if the format is *h*, *hh*, or *hhmm*; e.g., valid times are 5, 5:30, 0530, and 19:45. If modifier am or pm is added, *time* is based on a 12-hour clock.

midnight | noon | now | teatime

Use any one of these keywords in place of a numeric time. now must be followed by an *increment*. teatime is 4:00 PM.

Date

month num [*year*] | MM / DD / YY | DD . MM . YY

month is one of the 12 months, abbreviated to their first three letters; *num* is the calendar day of the month; *year* is the four-digit year. If the given *month* occurs before the current month, at schedules that month next year.

today | tomorrow

Indicate the current day or the next day. If *date* is omitted, at schedules today when the specified *time* occurs later than the current time; otherwise, at schedules tomorrow.

Increment

Supply a numeric increment if you want to specify an execution time or day *relative* to the current time. The number should precede any of the keywords minute, hour, day, or week (or their plural forms).

Examples

Note that the first two commands are equivalent:

```
at 1945 Dec 9
at 7:45pm Dec 9
at now + 5 hours
at noon tomorrow
```

---

at_cho_prn

at_cho_prn [*type*[@*zone*]]

Specifies the default AppleTalk printer be used with atprint. With no arguments, at_cho_prn prompts you to choose from the list of zones, and then from the list of network-visible entities (NVEs) of type LaserWriter and ImageWriter in the chosen zone. Use *type* to specify a different type of NVE to list. Use *zone* to specify a zone to search, bypassing the zone selection prompt. at_cho_prn requires superuser privileges to run.

---

atlookup

atlookup [*options*] [*scope*]

Lists network-visible entities (NVEs) on the AppleTalk network. If *scope* isn't specified, atlookup lists all NVEs in the current zone.

Options

-a Only show NVE names and types in the list; don't include network numbers.

-C When used with -z, display zones in several columns instead of one.

-d Print network numbers in decimal format instead of the default hexadecimal.

-r *n* Retry unsuccessful lookups *n* times. The default is 8.

-s *n* Retry unsuccessful lookups *n* seconds apart. The default is one second.

-x Convert nonprintable characters in lists to their hexadecimal equivalents, prefaced with /.

-z List all zones on the network. Used alone or with -C.

Scope

Specify the scope of the lookup by NVE *name*, *type*, and *zone* using this syntax:

[*name*[:*type*[@*zone*]]]

You can use the = wildcard anywhere in *name* or *type* to match zero or more characters, except with older AppleTalk Phase 1 nodes, which ignore such lookups. The = wildcard works with all Apple-Talk nodes, however, when used by itself to match all names or types. Lookups are not case-sensitive.

Examples

Display all NVEs of type darwin in the current zone:

    atlookup =:darwin

Display all NVEs on printers named with sales in the current zone (not AppleTalk Phase 1 compliant):

    atlookup sales=:=

---

atprint

atprint [*printer*]

Sends data from standard input to AppleTalk printer *printer*, or the printer chosen with at_cho_prn if no printer is specified. Specify *printer* using the [*name*[:*type*[@*zone*]]] syntax as described for atlookup. If the printer is a PostScript device, you must first reformat non-PostScript data, such as plain text, to PostScript before printing with atprint. You can do this easily using enscript, as shown in the first example.

Examples

Print text file *addresslist* to the AppleTalk PostScript printer sales:

    enscript -p- | atprint addresslist | sales

Print grep's manpage to the at_cho_prn chosen printer, using man's -t option to format it for PostScript printing:

    man -t grep| atprint

---

atq

atq [*options*]

Lists jobs created by the at command that are still in the queue. Normally, jobs are sorted by the order in which they execute.

Options

-q *queuename*
    Show jobs pending in queue *queuename*.

-v   Show jobs that have completed but not yet been deleted.

---

atrm

atrm *jobIDs*

Removes jobs queued with at that match the specified *jobIDs*.

---

atstatus

atstatus [*printer*]

Displays the status of AppleTalk printer *printer*, or the printer chosen with at_cho_prn if no printer is specified. Specify *printer* using the [*name*[:*type*[@*zone*]]] syntax as described for atlookup.

---

autodiskmount

autodiskmount [-d] [-v] [-a]

Automatically mounts filesystems from connected storage devices. Also performs consistency checks before mounting, and registers mounts with the Disk Arbitration framework to notify applications. If mount points are configured in */etc/fstab*, autodiskmount uses those; otherwise, it mounts filesystems under */Volumes*, on mount points named after the volume labels.

autodiskmount runs as a daemon, mounting filesystems as devices are added to the system. It stores its process ID in */var/run/autodiskmount.pid*, and responds to a SIGHUP by refreshing the Disk Arbitration tables, similar to running `disktool -r`.

Options

-a   Mounts filesystems from removable, as well as fixed, media.

-d   Enables debugging output, and prevents daemonization.

-v   After performing mounts, prints a list of all mounted filesystems to standard error, then exits.

---

automount

```
automount -help
automount -V
automount [-m map_directory map] [-1] [-a mount_directory] [-d]
[-D { mount | options | proc | select | all }] [-f] [-s] [-tcp]
[-tl timeout] [-tm timeout]
```

Provides transparent, automated access to NFS and AFP shares. When running, any filesystem access to *map_directory* is intercepted by automount. Typically, automount will then set up a symbolic link from *map_directory* or one of its subdirectories to a mount point under *mount_directory*, automatically creating directories and mounting remote volumes as needed. It will also unmount remote volumes that have been idle for too long. Directories or mounts set up by automount are removed when automount exits.

automount makes use of *maps* to determine how to mount volumes. When using a file as a map, the format is similar to that used by NFS automounters on other Unix platforms. Each entry in the file consists of a single line, either a comment beginning with a hash mark (#) or a mount directive of the form:

```
    subdirectory server:/pathname
```

If this line were included in a file named */etc/mountmaps*, and automount were called like so:

```
    # automount -m /mount_directory /etc/mountmaps
```

upon accessing */mount_directory*, automount would mount the NFS-exported *server:/pathname* on */private/mount_directory/subdirectory*, and create a symlink to that mount point from */mount_directory/subdirectory*.

At one time it was also possible to use a map stored in a NetInfo database under a */mountmaps* directory, but that functionality has apparently been deprecated in future versions of Mac OS X.

In addition to map files, there are several special maps available. Foremost among them are those used by default on Mac OS X systems, -fstab and -static. The following command is run from the NFS startup item (*/System/Library/StartupItems/NFS/NFS*):

```
    automount -m /Network/Servers -fstab -m /automount -static
```

Both maps use similar configuration formats, stored in an Open Directory database under the */mounts* directory. The following configuration line will trigger automount when using the -fstab map:

```
server:/subdirectory /mount_point url
net,url==afp://;AUTH=NO%20USER%20AUTHENT@server/share_name
0 0
```

The AFP mount will be the example used for the remainder of this section, but an equivalent NFS configuration would look like this:

```
server:/subdirectory /mount_point nfs net 0 0
```

There are several options for getting this configuration into Open Directory; one is to use niload fstab *domain*, then enter the configuration line, followed by Control-D. It will be stored in Open Directory like this (as displayed by nidump -r /mounts *domain*):

```
{
  "name" = ( "mounts" );
  CHILDREN = (
    {
      "dir" = ( "/mount_point" );
      "dump_freq" = ( "0" );
      "name" = ( "server:/subdirectory" );
      "opts" = ( "net", "url==afp://
;AUTH=NO%20USER%20AUTHENT@server/share_name" );
      "passno" = ( "0" );
      "vfstype" = ( "url" );
    }
  )
}
```

The net option is the signal for this configuration line to be used by automount with the -fstab map. Without the net option, this configuration line is picked up by the -static map.

With this configuration, and automount called like so:

```
# automount -m /Network/Servers -fstab
```

upon accessing */Network/Servers*, automount would mount the AFP *share_name* from *server* on */private/Network/Servers/server/ subdirectory*, and create a symlink from */Network/Servers/server*. The configured mount point (the value of the *dir* property) is ignored by the -fstab map.

Do not use a map_directory argument to *-m* that traverses a symlink, or any accesses to the mount will hang. For example, it's OK to do this:

```
# automount -m /private/tmp/map_dir -fstab
```

but not this:

```
# automount -m /tmp/map_dir -fstab
```

since */tmp* is a symlink to */private/tmp*.

While the -static map uses a configuration very much like that for -fstab, its mounting and linking behavior is significantly different. With a configuration like this (viewed as the output of nidump fstab *domain*):

```
server:/subdirectory /mount_point url
    url==afp://;AUTH=NO%20USER%20AUTHENT@server/share_name 0 0
```

and automount called like so:

```
# automount -m /automount -static
```

Upon accessing */mount_point*, automount would mount the AFP *share_name* from *server* on */private/automount/mount_point*, create a symlink to this from */automount/mount_point*, and then another from */mount_point* to */automount/mount_point*. The configured *server:/subdirectory* (the value of the *name* property) is ignored by the -static map for AFP shares. (Incidentally, the term "static" is a misnomer. Mounts are made dynamically when they're accessed, just as with the -fstab map.)

AFP URLs

The format of the AFP URLs in the automount examples is described in the manpage for mount_afp, but there are certain constraints you should be aware of.

- First, *server* must be a valid TCP/IP hostname or IP address, which may be different than the AFP name that shows up, for example, in a Connect to Server dialog window.

- Second, *share_name* is the AFP name for the share point, which is not necessarily the same as the full pathname to the share point on the server.

- Finally, there are a few ways to handle authentication to the AFP server. If guest access to the share is allowed, then you may use a URL like those in the examples for automount:

  ```
  afp://;AUTH=NO%20USER%20AUTHENT@server/share_name
  ```

  If user authentication is required, then you have two options. The first is to specify the necessary authentication information in the URL like so:

  ```
  afp://username:password@server/share_name
  ```

  However, this makes the authentication password available to anyone with access to Open Directory. The other option is to leave out the authentication parameters:

  ```
  afp://server/share_name
  ```

  In this case, the user logged into the graphical console should be presented with an authentication dialog to enable access to the share. Of course, if no one is logged into the GUI, then this won't work, and the mount attempt will fail.

Another special map is the -user map. It doesn't actually cause any remote filesystems to be mounted on its own; it merely sets up symlinks to every user account's home directory from the *map_directory*, which may be useful if you want a single place to look in for everyone's home directory. But proceed cautiously if you have a very large number of user accounts.

The -nsl map uses the Network Services Location service discovery API to automatically find available shares on the network (just as the Finder's Connect to Server menu item does) and create mounts for them. While this sounds like an idea with some potential, presently it doesn't seem to work quite right, resulting in I/O errors when trying to access the mounts.

The -host map is meant to automatically mount NFS exports from hosts listed in a NIS hosts map, when accessing a subdirectory of the *map_directory* with the same name as the host. For example, accessing */net/hostname/export* should mount *hostname:/export*, if */net* is the *map_directory*. This is similar to the -hosts map of other NFS automounters.

The -null map mounts well, nothing. It will, however, still intercept filesystem calls for the *map_directory*, thus effectively mounting an empty directory over whatever might have been there before. In the original automount, from which NeXT and Apple's versions are descended, this was meant to nullify configuration entries included from a network-wide NIS map.

When running in daemon mode, automount stores its process ID in */var/run/automount.pid* and responds to a SIGHUP by reloading its configuration.

Options

-1 Creates directories on the path to a -fstab mount point one at a time, as they're traversed, rather than creating the entire path to a mount point when the mount is accessed. However, using this option leads to I/O errors when trying to access the mount.

-a Specifies the directory in which mounts are made. Symbolic links from the directory specified in the -m option are used to access these mounts. The default is */private*.

-d Sends debugging output to standard error and prevents daemonization.

-D Outputs debugging messages of the specified type. If the -d option is used, output is to standard error; otherwise it's via *syslog*. Multiple occurrences of this option may be used to specify multiple types.

-f
     Runs the process in the foreground, preventing daemonization.

-help
     Prints a usage statement to standard output.

-m Uses the specified map to mount shares and create symlinks from the specified directory to the mount points. The map argument can be an absolute pathname to a file, a map in the /*mountmaps* directory of an Open Directory domain, or one of the special values -fstab, -host, -nsl, -null, -static, or -user. Multiple -m options enable the use of multiple maps. In the absence of a -m option, automount attempts to find maps in Open Directory.

-s Supposedly creates all mounts at startup and never unmounts them. However, mounts are still only attempted upon access, at which point automount prints a bus error and dumps core when using this option.

-tcp
    Attempts to mount NFS volumes over TCP, instead of the default UDP.

-tl Specifies a time-to-live for mount names, in seconds. After the timeout expires, mounts are rechecked. A timeout of 0 sets an infinite TTL. The default is 10000.

-tm
    Specifies a timeout to retry failing mounts, in seconds. The timeout roughly doubles with each mount attempt, until giving up after a few tries. The default is 20.

-V Prints version number and host information to standard output.

---

awk

awk [*options*] [*program*] [*var=value* …] [*files*]

Uses the pattern-matching program to process the specified files. awk has been replaced by nawk (there's also a GNU version called gawk). Program instructions have the general form:

> pattern { procedure }

pattern and *procedure* are optional. When specified on the command line, *program* must be enclosed in single quotes to prevent the shell from interpreting its special symbols. Any variables specified in *program* can be assigned an initial value by using command-line arguments of the form var = value. For more information on awk, see *sed & awk*, Second Edition (O'Reilly & Associates, Inc., 1997).

Options

-f *file*
    Use program instructions contained in *file*, instead of specifying *program* on the command line.

-F*c* Treat input *file* as fields separated by character *c*. By default, input fields are separated by runs of spaces and/or tabs.

---

banner

banner *characters*

Prints *characters* as a poster on the standard output.

---

basename   basename *pathname* [*suffix*]

Given a *pathname*, strips the path prefix and leave just the file-name, which is printed on standard output. If specified, a filename *suffix* (e.g., *.c*) is removed also. basename is typically invoked via command substitution ('...') to generate a filename. See also dirname.

Example

Given the following fragment from a Bourne shell script:

```
ofile=output_file
myname="`basename $0`"
echo "$myname: QUITTING: can't open $ofile" 1>&2
exit 1
```

If the script is called do_it, the following message is printed on standard error:

```
do_it: QUITTING: can't open output_file
```

---

batch   batch [*options*]

Executes commands entered on standard input. Ends with *EOF*. Unlike at, which executes commands at a specific time, batch executes commands one after another (waiting for each one to complete). This avoids the potentially high system load caused by running several background jobs at once. See also at.

batch is equivalent to issuing the command at -q b now.

Options

-f *file*
    Execute commands listed in *file*.

-m Send mail to user after job is completed (if an MTA such as *sendmail* is configured to run).

Example

```
% batch
sort in > out
troff -ms bigfile > bigfile.ps
EOF
```

---

bc   bc [*options*] [*files*]

Interactively performs arbitrary-precision arithmetic or convert numbers from one base to another. Input can be taken from *files* or read from the standard input. To exit, type **quit** or **EOF**.

Options

-c Do not invoke dc; compile only. (Since bc is a preprocessor for dc, bc normally invokes dc.)

-l Make available functions from the math library.

bc is a language (and compiler) whose syntax resembles that of C. bc consists of identifiers, keywords, and symbols, which are briefly described here. Examples follow at the end of this section.

Identifiers

An identifier is a single character, consisting of the lowercase letters a–z. Identifiers are used as names for variables, arrays, and functions. Within the same program, you may name a variable, an array, and a function using the same letter. The following identifiers would not conflict:

x Variable x.

$x[i]$
> Element i of array x. i can range from 0 to 2047 and can also be an expression.

$x(y,z)$
> Call function x with parameters y and z.

Input/Output keywords

ibase, obase, and scale each store a value. Typing them on a line by themselves displays their current value. More commonly, you would change their values through assignment. Letters A–F are treated as digits whose values are 10–15.

ibase = n
> Numbers that are input (e.g., typed) are read as base n (default is 10).

obase = n
> Numbers displayed are in base n (default is 10). Note: once ibase has been changed from 10, use digit "A" to restore ibase or obase to decimal.

scale = n
> Display computations using n decimal places (default is 0, meaning that results are truncated to integers). scale is normally used only for base-10 computations.

Statement keywords

A semicolon or a newline separates one statement from another. Curly braces are needed only when grouping multiple statements.

if (*rel-expr*) {*statements*}
> Do one or more *statements* if relational expression *rel-expr* is true; for example:

```
if (x == y) i = i + 1
```

while (*rel-expr*) {*statements*}
> Repeat one or more *statements* while *rel-expr* is true; for example:

```
while (i > 0) {p = p*n; q = a/b; i = i-1}
```

for (*expr1*; *rel-expr*; *expr2*) {*statements*}
> Similar to while; for example, to print the first 10 multiples of 5, you could type:

```
for (i = 1; i <= 10; i++) i*5
```

break
> Terminate a while or for statement.

quit
> Exit bc.

Function keywords

define j (k) {
> Begin the definition of function *j* having a single argument *k*. Additional arguments are allowed, separated by commas. Statements follow on successive lines. End with a }.

auto x , y
> Set up *x* and *y* as variables local to a function definition, initialized to 0 and meaningless outside the function. Must appear first.

return(*expr*)
> Pass the value of expression *expr* back to the program. Return 0 if (*expr*) is left off. Used in function definitions.

sqrt(*expr*)
> Compute the square root of expression *expr*.

length(*expr*)
> Compute how many digits are in *expr*.

scale(*expr*)
> Same as previous, but count only digits to the right of the decimal point.

Math library functions

These are available when bc is invoked with -1. Library functions set scale to 20.

s(*angle*)
> Compute the sine of *angle*, a constant or expression in radians.

c(*angle*)
> Compute the cosine of *angle*, a constant or expression in radians.

a(*n*)
> Compute the arctangent of *n*, returning an angle in radians.

e(*expr*)
> Compute e to the power of *expr*.

l(*expr*)
> Compute natural log of *expr*.

j(*n, x*)
> Compute Bessel function of integer order *n*.

Operators

These consist of operators and other symbols. Operators can be arithmetic, unary, assignment, or relational.

Arithmetic	+ - * / % ^
Unary	- ++ --
Assignment	=+ =- =* =/ =% =^ =
Relational	< <= > >= == !=

Other symbols

/* */ Enclose comments.

( ) Control the evaluation of expressions (change precedence). Can also be used around assignment statements to force the result to print.

{ } Used to group statements.

[ ] Array index.

"text"
> Use as a statement to print *text*.

Examples

Note that when you type some quantity (a number or expression), it is evaluated and printed, but assignment statements produce no display:

ibase = 8	*Octal input*
20	*Evaluate this octal number*
16	*Terminal displays decimal value*
obase = 2	*Display output in base 2 instead of base 10*
20	*Octal input*
10000	*Terminal now displays binary value*
ibase = A	*Restore base 10 input*
scale = 3	*Truncate results to three places*
8/7	*Evaluate a division*
1.001001000	*Oops! Forgot to reset output base to 10*
obase = 10	*Input is decimal now, so "A" isn't needed*
8/7	
1.142	*The Terminal displays result (truncated)*

The following lines show the use of functions:

define p(r,n){	*Function p uses two argument*
auto v	*v is a local variab*le
v = r^n	*r raised to the n power*
return(v)}	*Value returned*
scale = 5	
x = p(2.5,2)	*x = 2.5 ^ 2*
x	*Print value of x*
6.25	
length(x)	*Number of digits*
3	
scale(x)	*Number of places to right of decimal point*
2	

---

biff

biff [y | n]

Turns mail notification on or off. With no arguments, biff indicates the current status.

When mail notification is turned on, each time you get incoming mail, the bell rings, and the first few lines of each message are displayed. biff depends on the *comsat* daemon to be running.

bless

bless [*folder options* | *device options* | *info options*]

Enables a device containing a Mac OS 9, Darwin, or Mac OS X system folder to be bootable, and selects an enabled device or system folder to be the default boot system. bless can also report the current boot settings.

Folder options

Use bless's folder options to enable and select system folders.

-bootinfo *pathname*

> Enable a volume on New World Macintoshes to boot into Mac OS X by copying file *pathname* into the Mac OS X system folder (specified with -folder) to use as the BootX file. *pathname* is typically */usr/standalone/ppc/bootx.bootinfo*.

-bootBlocks

> Enable a volume to boot into Mac OS 9 by setting the required boot blocks.

-bootBlockFile *pathname*

> Enable a volume to boot into Mac OS 9 by setting the required boot blocks, which are extracted from the data fork of file *pathname*.

-folder *pathname*

> Bless a Mac OS X system for booting, identified by its Core-Services directory *pathname*. (See example.)

-folder9 *pathname*

> Bless a Mac OS 9 folder for booting or use by Classic, identified by its system folder *pathname*. (See example.)

-label *name*

> Use *name* as the system volume label used by the OS Picker, which appears when the Option key is held during startup.

-mount *pathname*

> Select to boot from volume *pathname* using its already blessed system folder, instead of selecting a specific folder. Specify a volume by its mount point pathname, such as */Volumes/Mac HD*.

-save9

> Retain the blessing of the blessed Mac OS 9 system folder when the -folder or -mount option is used, but the -folder9 option is not.

-saveX

> Retain the blessing of the blessed Mac OS X system folder when the -folder or -mount option is used, but the -folder option is not.

-setOF

> Set the computer to boot at next startup from the system specified by the -folder or -folder9 option. bless writes to Open Firmware's boot-device variable.

-system *pathname*

Enable a volume to boot into Mac OS 9 by setting the required boot blocks, which are extracted from the System file *pathname*.

-systemfile *pathname*

Insert the data fork of System file *pathname* into the System file of the Mac OS 9 system folder specified by the -folder9 option.

-use9

When both the -folder and -folder9 options are given, use the Mac OS 9 system as the default system for that volume.

Device options

Use bless's device options to set up new boot devices.

-bootBlockFile *pathname*

Enable the volume specified by -device to boot into Mac OS 9 by setting the required boot blocks, which are extracted from the data fork of file *pathname*.

-device *pathname*

Select an unmounted device for setup by opening its block file *pathname*

-format [*fstype*]

Use filesytem type *fstype* to format the device specified by the -device option. If *fstype* is not specified, bless formats the device using HFS+ with an HFS wrapper.

-fsargs *arguments*

Apply additional *arguments* when preparing the device specified by the -device option. *arguments* can be any options that exist for the newfs command.

-label *name*

Use *name* as the label for the new filesystem specified by the -device option.

-mount *pathname*

Use *pathname* as the temporary mount point for the HFS wrapper.

-setOF

Set the computer to boot at next startup from the device specified by the -device option. bless sets this by writing to Open Firmware's boot-device variable.

-system *pathname*

Use the file specifications from file *pathname* instead of from both the files specified by the -bootBlockFile and -wrapper options.

-wrapper *pathname*

Mount the HFS wrapper on the mount point specified by -mount and insert the System file *pathname* into the wrapper, making it the default System file.

-xcoff *pathname*

> Enable a volume on Old World Macintoshes to boot into Mac OS X by using file *pathname* as the HFS+ StartupFile. *pathname* is typically */usr/standalone/ppc/bootx.xcoff*.

Info options

-bootBlocks

> Display fields from the boot blocks of volume specified by -info.

-info [*pathname*]

> Display the blessed system folder(s) on volume *pathname*, or the default startup volume as set in Open Firmware, if *pathname* is not specified.

-plist

> Provide all information in *plist* format; used with -info.

General options

-quiet

> Operate in quiet mode; don't produce any output.

-verbose

> Be verbose; print extra output.

Examples

Bless a Mac OS X–only volume, and have it boot at next restart:

```
bless -folder "/Volumes/Mac  OS X/System/Library/⏎
CoreServices" -setOF
```

Set a current system volume that holds both a Mac OS X and a Mac OS 9 system to boot Mac OS 9 at next restart:

```
bless -folder9 "/Volumes/Mac  OS 9/System Folder" -saveX⏎
-use9 -setOF
```

See the bless manpage for more examples.

---

cal

cal [*options*] [[*month*] *year*]

With no arguments, prints a calendar for the current month. Otherwise, print either a 12-month calendar (beginning with January) for the given *year* or a one-month calendar of the given *month* and *year*. *month* ranges from 1 to 12; *year* ranges from 1 to 9999.

Options

-j   Print all days with Julian dates, which number from 1 (for January 1) to the last day of the year.

-y   Print the entire calendar for the current year.

Examples

```
cal -j 12 2003
cal 2003 > year_file
```

calendar   calendar [*option*]

Reads your *calendar* file and displays all lines that contain the current date. The *calendar* file is like a memo board. You create the file and add entries like the following:

```
5/4      meeting with design group at 2 pm
may 6    pick up anniversary card on way home
```

When you run calendar on May 4, the first line is displayed. calendar can be automated by using crontab or at, or by including it in your startup files *.profile* or *.login*.

Options

-a Allow a privileged user to invoke calendar for all users, searching each user's login directory for a file named calendar. Entries that match are sent to a user via mail. This feature is intended for use via cron. It is not recommended in networked environments with large user bases.

-d *MMDD* [[*YY*] *YY*]
Display lines for the given date.

-f *filename*
Display calendar items from file *filename* instead of the default *calendar* file in your home directory.

-l *n* Display calendar items up to *n* days ahead from the current date as well.

-w *n*
Forces calendar to skip over weekends. Display calendar items up to *n* days ahead from the current date only when the current day is a Friday. The default for *n* is 2.

---

cancel   cancel [*options*] [*printer*]

Cancels print requests made with lp. The request can be specified by its ID, by the *printer* on which it is currently printing, or by the username associated with the request (only privileged users can cancel another user's print requests). Use lpstat to determine either the *id* or the *printer* to cancel.

Options

-a Cancel all queued requests to the specified *printer*.

-h Specifies the hostname of the print server hostname, "local-host" by default.

id Cancel print request *id*.

---

cat   cat [*options*] [*files*]

Reads one or more files and print them on standard output. Reads standard input if no files are specified or if – is specified as one of the files; end input with EOF. Use the > shell operator to combine several files into a new file; >> appends files to an existing file.

Options

-b   Like -n, but don't number blank lines.

-e   Print a $ to mark the end of each line. Implies the -v option.

-n   Number lines.

-s   Squeezes out extra blank lines.

-t   Print each tab as ^I. Implies the -v option.

-u   Print output as unbuffered (default is buffered in blocks or screen lines).

-v   Display control characters and other nonprinting characters.

Examples

Display a file:

```
cat ch1
```

Combine files:

```
cat ch1 ch2 ch3 > all
```

Append to a file:

```
cat note5 >> notes
```

Create file at terminal; end with EOF:

```
cat > temp1
```

Create file at terminal; end with STOP:

```
cat > temp2 << STOP
```

---

cd9660.util

```
cd9660.util { -m | -M } device mount_point
cd9660.util { -p | -u } device
```

Mounts ISO 9660 (CD-ROM) filesystems into the directory hierarchy.

Options

-m

    Mounts the device.

-M

    Attempts to force the mount.

-p

    Probes the device, and prints the volume name to standard output.

-u

    Unmounts the device. This function doesn't appear to work.

device

    The CD device filename, e.g., *disk1s2*.

mount_point

    The directory on which the CD filesystem is mounted.

certtool   certtool c [h] [v] [k=*keychain* [c]]
                            certtool r *filename* [h] [v] [d] [k=*keychain* [c]]
                            certtool v *filename* [h] [v] [d]
                            certtool i *filename* [h] [v] [k=*keychain* [c]]
                            certtool d *filename* [h] [v]

Manages SSL/TLS certificates. It uses the Common Data Security Architecture (CDSA) in much the same way that */System/Library/ OpenSSL/misc/CA.pl* uses OpenSSL to ease the process of managing certificates.

As arguments, it takes a single-letter command, often a filename, and possibly some options.

Options

c   As a command, walks you through a series of interactive prompts to create a certificate and a public/private key pair to sign and possibly encrypt it. The resulting certificate is stored in your default Keychain. (Note that the first prompt, for a key and certificate label, is asking for two space-separated items. Common choices are an organization name for the key, and a label designating the purpose of the certificate.)

    As an option, instructs certtool to create a new Keychain by the name given in the k option.

d   As a command, displays the certificate contained in *filename*.

    As an option, indicates that the format of the CSR contained in *filename* is DER (a binary format), instead of the default PEM (an ASCII format).

h   Prints a usage statement to standard output, negating whichever command was given.

i   Imports the certificate contained in *filename* into the default Keychain.

k   Specifies the name of a Keychain to use other than the default.

r   Walks you through a series of interactive prompts to create a certificate-signing request (CSR) and a public/private key pair to sign and possibly encrypt it. The resulting CSR is stored in *filename*.

v   As a command, verifies the CSR contained in *filename*.

    As an option, should enable verbose output, but it doesn't actually seem to make a difference.

---

checkgid   checkgid *group_name*

Checks for the existence of the specified groups. If all groups exist, the return value is 0 and nothing is printed. If any groups do not exist, the return value is 255 and the following is printed to standard error for each nonexistent *group_name*:

    checkgid: group '*group_name*' not found

checkgid should be run with root privileges.

This tool is part of the Apache distribution.

Options

group_name

> Takes a list of group names as arguments. It should also be able to take numeric group IDs as *#groupID*, but checkgid always returns successful for arguments of that form.

---

chflags   chflags [*options*] flags *files*

Changes the file flags of one or more *files*. *flags* is a comma-separated list of file flags, described below. To unset a flag, use the same command but with no added to the front of the flag's name. To view a file's current flags, use the ls -lo command.

Options

-H   If any of the pathnames given in the command line are symbolic links, follow only those links during recursive operation. Works only with the -R option.

-L   Follow all symbolic links during recursive operation. Works only with the -R option.

-P   Follow no symbolic links during recursive operation. Works only with the -R option (the default).

-R   Recursively descend through the directory, including subdirectories and symbolic links, changing the specified file flags as it proceeds.

Flags

Flag name	Flag set	Who can change
arch	archived	Superuser only
opaque	opaque	Owner or superuser only
nodump	nodump	Owner or superuser only
sappend	system append-only	Superuser only
schg	system immutable	Superuser only
uappend	user append-only	Owner or superuser only
uchg	user immutable	Owner or superuser only

Though the system append-only (sappend) and system immutable (schg) flags can be set by the superuser in normal system mode, you can only *unset* them while in single-user mode.

Examples

Setting the user immutable (uchg) flag for a file prevents it from being deleted, changed, or moved. By locking a file in the Finder, you're actually setting its user immutable flag. Therefore, this command locks the file as well:

```
chflags uchg importantfile.doc
```

Unset the user immutable flag and thus unlock the file:

```
chflags nouchg importantfile.doc
```

chgrp

chgrp [options] newgroup files

Changes the ownership of one or more *files* to *newgroup*. *newgroup* is either a group ID number or a group name known to directory services. You must own the file or be a privileged user to succeed with this command.

Options

-f Force error messages to be suppressed.

-H If any of the pathnames given in the command line are symbolic links, follow only those links during recursive operation. Works only with the -R option.

-L Follow all symbolic links during recursive operation. Works only with the -R option.

-P Follow no symbolic links during recursive operation. Works only with the -R option (the default).

-R Recursively descend through the directory, including subdirectories and symbolic links, setting the specified group ID as it proceeds.

chkpasswd

chkpasswd [-c] [-i infosystem] [-l location] [username]

Useful for scripts, this prompts for a password that is then compared against the appropriate directory service for the user specified. If the password is incorrect, the string Sorry is output. (Strangely, *chkpasswd* appears to have a return value of 0 in either case.)

Options

-c User input is compared with the password hash directly, rather than running it through the *crypt* algorithm first.

-i Specifies the directory service to use, and may be *file*, *netinfo* (the default), or *nis*.

-l Depending on the directory service being used, it's either a filename (defaults to */etc/master.passwd*), a NetInfo domain name or server/tag combo, or an NIS domain name.

username
    Designates whose password will be checked. It defaults to that of the user running the command.

chmod

chmod [option] mode files

Changes the access *mode* of one or more *files*. Only the owner of a file or a privileged user may change its mode. Create *mode* by concatenating the characters from *who*, *opcode*, and *permission*. *who* is optional (if omitted, default is a); choose only one *opcode*.

Options

-f Suppress error message upon failure to change a file's mode.

-H If any of the pathnames given in the command line are symbolic links, follow only those links during recursive operation. Works only with the -R option.

-L   Follow all symbolic links during recursive operation. Works only with the -R option.

-P   Follow no symbolic links during recursive operation. Works only with the -R option (the default).

-R   Recursively descend directory arguments while setting modes.

Who

u   User

g   Group

o   Other

a   All (default)

Opcode

+   Add permission

-    Remove permission

=   Assign permission (and remove permission of the unspecified fields)

Permission

r   Read

w   Write

x   Execute (file) or search (directory)

X   Sets the execute bit for all *who* values if any of the execute bits are already set in the specified file; meaningful only in conjunction with the op symbol +

s   Set user (or group) ID

t   Sticky bit; save text mode (file) or prevent removal of files by nonowners (directory)

u   User's present permission

g   Group's present permission

o   Other's present permission

Alternatively, specify permissions by a 3-digit sequence. The first digit designates owner permission; the second, group permission; and the third, others permission. Permissions are calculated by adding the following octal values:

4   Read

2   Write

1   Execute

A fourth digit may precede this sequence. This digit assigns the following modes:

4   Set user ID on execution

2   Set group ID on execution or set mandatory locking

1   Sticky bit

Examples

Add execute-by-user permission to *file*:

```
chmod u+x file
```

Either of the following assigns read-write-execute permission by owner (7), read-execute permission by group (5), and execute-only permission by others (1) to *file*:

```
chmod 751 file
chmod u=rwx,g=rx,o=x file
```

Any one of the following assigns read-only permission to *file* for everyone:

```
chmod =r file
chmod 444 file
chmod a-wx,a+r file
```

Set the user ID, assign read-write-execute permission by owner, and assign read-execute permission by group and others:

```
chmod 4755 file
```

---

chown

```
chown [options] newowner[:newgroup] files
```

Changes the ownership of one or more *files* to *newowner*. *newowner* is either a user ID number or a login name known to directory services. The optional *newgroup* is either a group ID number (GID) or a group name known to directory services. When *newgroup* is supplied, the behavior is to change the ownership of one or more *files* to *newowner* and make it belong to *newgroup*.

Options

-f Force error messages to be suppressed.

-H If any of the pathnames given in the command line are symbolic links, follow only those links during recursive operation. Works only with the -R option.

-L Follow all symbolic links during recursive operation. Works only with the -R option.

-P Follow no symbolic links during recursive operation. Works only with the -R option (the default).

-R Recursively descend through the directory, including subdirectories, resetting the ownership ID.

---

cksum

```
cksum [files]
```

Calculates and prints a cyclic redundancy check (CRC) for each file. The CRC algorithm is based on the polynomial used for Ethernet packets. For each file, cksum prints a line of the form:

```
sum count filename
```

Here, *sum* is the CRC, *count* is the number of bytes in the file, and *filename* is the file's name. The name is omitted if standard input is used.

---

clear	`clear`
	Clear the Terminal display.

cmp	`cmp [options] file file2 [skip1 [skip2]]`

Compares *file1* with *file2*. Use standard input if *file1* or *file2* is −. To begin the comparison from byte offsets other than at the beginning of the files, use the optional arguments *skip1* and *skip2*, which specify the byte offsets from the beginning of each file. By default, the value is decimal. To use hexadecimal or octal values, precede them with a leading 0x or 0, respectively. See also comm and diff. The exit codes are as follows:

0   Files are identical.

1   Files are different.

2   Files are inaccessible.

Options

`-c, --print-chars`
Print differing bytes as characters.

`-i N, --ignore-initial= N`
Ignore differences in the first *N* bytes of input.

`-l`   For each difference, print the byte number in decimal and the differing bytes in octal.

`-s`   Work silently; print nothing, but return exit codes.

`-v, --version`
Output version info.

Example

Print a message if two files are the same (exit code is 0):

```
cmp -s old new && echo 'no changes'
```

colcrt	`colcrt [options] [files]`

A postprocessing filter that handles reverse linefeeds and escape characters, allowing output from tbl or nroff to appear in reasonable form on a terminal. Put half-line characters (e.g., subscripts or superscripts) and underlining (changed to dashes) on a new line between output lines.

Options

−   Do not underline.

`-2`   Double space by printing all half-lines.

colrm	`colrm [start [stop]]`

Removes specified columns from a file, where a column is a single character in a line. Read from standard input and write to standard output. Columns are numbered starting with 1; begin deleting columns at (including) the *start* column, and stop at (including) the *stop* column. Entering a tab increments the column count to the next multiple of either the *start* or *stop* column; entering a backspace decrements it by 1.

Example

```
colrm 3 5 < test1 > test2
```

---

column

column [*options*] [*files*]

Formats input from one or more *files* into columns, filling rows first. Read from standard input if no files are specified.

Options

-c *num*
> Format output into *num* columns.

-s *char*
> Delimit table columns with *char*. Meaningful only with -t.

-t   Format input into a table. Delimit with whitespace, unless an alternate delimiter has been provided with -s.

-x   Fill columns before filling rows.

---

comm

comm [*options*] *file1* *file2*

Compares lines common to the sorted files *file1* and *file2*. Three-column output is produced: lines unique to *file1*, lines unique to *file2*, and lines common to both *files*. comm is similar to diff in that both commands compare two files. In addition, comm can be used like uniq; that is, comm selects duplicate or unique lines between *two* sorted files, whereas uniq selects duplicate or unique lines within the *same* sorted file.

Options

-   Read the standard input.

-1   Suppress printing of Column 1.

-2   Suppress printing of Column 2.

-3   Suppress printing of Column 3.

-12   Print only lines in Column 3 (lines common to *file1* and *file2*).

-13   Print only lines in Column 2 (lines unique to *file2*).

-23   Print only lines in Column 1 (lines unique to *file1*).

Example

Compare two lists of top-10 movies and display items that appear in both lists:

```
comm -12 shalit_top10 maltin_top10
```

compress   compress [*options*] [*files*]

Reduces the size of one or more *files* using adaptive Lempel-Ziv coding and move to *file.Z*. Restore with uncompress or zcat.

With a filename of -, or with no *files*, compress reads standard input.

Unisys claims a patent on the algorithm used by compress. Today, gzip is generally preferred for file compression.

compress does not preserve resource forks or HFS metadata when compressing files that contain them.

Options

-b*n*

Limit the number of bits in coding to *n*; *n* is 9–16; 16 is the default. A lower *n* produces a larger, less densely compressed file.

-c   Write to the standard output (do not change files).

-f   Compress unconditionally; i.e., do not prompt before over-writing files. Also, compress files even if the resulting file would actually be larger.

-v   Print the resulting percentage of reduction for *files*.

---

configd   configd [-b] [-B *bundle_ID*] [-d] [-t *pathname*] [-v]
                             [-V *bundle_ID*]

This is the System Configuration Server. configd is normally started as a daemon during the boot process. It monitors changes to network-related items, such as link status, DHCP assignments, PPP connections, and IP configuration, and provides an API for applications to be notified of these changes. To monitor various items, it uses a set of plug-in configuration agents, including the Preferences Monitor, the Kernel Event Monitor, the PPP Controller Agent, the IP Configuration Agent, and the IP Monitor Agent. The agent plug-ins are located in */System/Library/SystemConfiguration*.

More information on the System Configuration framework can be found at *http:// developer.apple.com/techpubs/macosx/Networking/SysConfigOverview926/*.

Options

-b   Disables loading of all agents.

-B   Disables loading of the specified agent.

-d   Disables daemonization; runs process in foreground.

-t   Loads the agent specified by *pathname*.

-v   Enables verbose logging.

-V   Enables verbose logging for the specified agent.

cp   cp [*options*] *file1 file*
                          cp [*options*] *files directory*

Copies *file1* to *file2*, or copy one or more *files* to the same names
under *directory*. If the destination is an existing file, the file is overwritten; if the destination is an existing directory, the file is copied
into the directory (the directory is *not* overwritten). If one of the
inputs is a directory, use the -R option.

cp does not preserve resource forks or HFS metadata when copying
files that contain them. For such files, use CpMac or ditto instead.

Options

-f   Don't prompt for confirmation before overwriting an existing
     file.

-H   If any of the pathnames given in the command line are
     symbolic links, follow only those links during recursive opera-
     tion. Works only with the -R option.

-i   Prompt for confirmation (y for yes) before overwriting an
     existing file.

-L   Follow all symbolic links during recursive operation. Works
     only with the -R option.

-p   Preserve the modification time and permission modes for the
     copied file. (Normally cp supplies the permissions of the
     invoking user.)

-P   Follow no symbolic links during recursive operation. Works
     only with the -R option (the default).

-R   Recursively copy a directory, its files, and its subdirectories to a
     destination *directory*, duplicating the tree structure. (This
     option is used with the second command-line format when at
     least one of the source *file* arguments is a directory.)

Example

Copy two files to their parent directory (keep the same names):

     cp outline memo ..

---

cpio   cpio control_options [*options*]

Copies file archives in from or out to disk or to another location on
the local machine. Note that until native drivers for tape drives
exist for Mac OS X, cpio cannot write to tape. Each of the three
control options, -i, -o, or -p accepts different options. (See also
ditto, pax and tar.)

cpio does not preserve resource forks or metadata when copying
files that contain them. For such files, use ditto instead.

cpio -i [*options*] [*patterns*]
     Copy in (extract) files whose names match selected *patterns*.
     Each pattern can include filename metacharacters from the
     Bourne shell. (Patterns should be quoted or escaped so they are
     interpreted by cpio, not by the shell.) If no pattern is used, all
     files are copied in. During extraction, existing files are not over-
     written by older versions in the archive (unless -u is specified).

```
cpio -o [options]
```
Copy out a list of files whose names are given on the standard
input.

```
cpio -p [options] directory
```
Copy files to another directory on the same system. Destination pathnames are interpreted relative to the named *directory*.

Comparison of valid options

Options available to the -i, -o, and -p options are shown respectively in the first, second, and third row below. (The - is omitted
for clarity.)

```
i: 6   b B c C d E f H I    m   r s S t u v
o: a A   B c C        H   L  O            v
p: a          d          l L m        u v
```

Options

-a   Reset access times of input files.

-A   Append files to an archive (must use with -O).

-b   Swap bytes and half-words. Words are 4 bytes.

-B   Block input or output using 5120 bytes per record (default is
512 bytes per record).

-c   Read or write header information as ASCII characters; useful
when source and destination machines are different types.

-C *n*
    Like -B, but block size can be any positive integer *n*.

-d   Create directories as needed.

-E *file*
    Extract filenames listed in *file* from the archive.

-f   Reverse the sense of copying; copy all files *except* those that
match *patterns*.

-H *format*
    Read or write header information according to *format*. Values
for *format* are ustar (IEEE/P1003 Data Interchange Standard
header), or tar (tar header).

-I *file*
    Read *file* as an input archive.

-l   Link files instead of copying. Can be used only with -p.

-L   Follow symbolic links.

-m   Retain previous file-modification time.

-O *file*
    Direct the output to *file*.

-r   Rename files interactively.

-s   Swap bytes.

-S   Swap half-words.

-t   Print a table of contents of the input (create no files). When
used with the -v option, resembles output of ls -l.

-u   Unconditional copy; old files can overwrite new ones.

-v   Print a list of filenames.

-6   Process a PWB Unix 6th Edition archive format file. Useful only with the -i option, mutually exclusive with -c and -H.

Examples

Generate a list of old files using find; use list as input to cpio:

```
find . -name "*.old" -print | cpio -ocBvO ~/archive
```

Restore from a tape drive (if supported) all files whose name contains "save" (subdirectories are created if needed):

```
cpio -icdv "*save*" < /dev/rmt/0
```

To move a directory tree:

```
find . -depth -print | cpio -padml /mydir
```

CpMac

CpMac [-mac] [-p] [-r] *source_path* [*source_path*...] *dest_path*

Copies files, keeping multiple forks and HFS attributes intact.

Options

-mac

Arguments use legacy Mac OS pathname syntax (i.e., colons as path separators, paths as viewed from the Finder).

-p

Preserves file attributes.

-r

Recursively copies directory contents.

---

create_nidb

create_nidb [*tag* [*master_hostname* [*root_dir*]]]

Creates and populates an Open Directory database from the contents of flat files in */etc*. This may be especially useful if you have configuration information you wish to carry over from another Unix system. Currently create_nidb makes use of the following files:

> */etc/master.passwd*
> */etc/group*
> */etc/hosts*
> */etc/networks*

create_nidb should be run with root privileges.

Options

master_hostname

The name of the host serving the master copy of the Open Directory database. The default is localhost if the tag is local, otherwise it's the hostname of the system on which create_nidb is run.

root_dir
> The directory in which */var/db/netinfo/tag.nidb* will be created. The default is /.

tag
> The tag of the Open Directory database. The default is local.

crontab

```
crontab [file]
crontab options [user]
```

Runs crontab on your current crontab file, or specifies a crontab *file* to add to the crontab directory. A privileged user can run crontab for another user by supplying a *user* after any of the options.

A crontab file is a list of commands, one per line, that will execute automatically at a given time. Numbers are supplied before each command to specify the execution time. The numbers appear in five fields, as follows:

```
Minute        0-59
Hour          0-23
Day of month  1-31
Month         1-12
Day of week   0-6, with 0 = Sunday
```

Use a comma between multiple values, a hyphen to indicate a range, and an asterisk to indicate all possible values. For example, assuming the crontab entries below:

```
59 3 * * 5      find / -print | backup_program
0 0 1,15 * *    echo "Timesheets due" | mail user
```

The first command backs up the system files every Friday at 3:59 a.m., and the second command mails a reminder on the 1st and 15th of each month.

Options

-e   Edit the user's current crontab file (or create one).

-l   List the user's file in the crontab directory.

-r   Delete the user's file in the crontab directory.

csmount

```
csmount -help
csmount -m mount_point ftp://[username:password@]ftp_server
[/pathname] [-d] [-D { mount | options | proc | select | all }]
[-nodiskarb]
```

Mounts FTP archives as filesystem volumes.

Options

-d   Sends debugging output to standard error and prevents daemonization.

-D   Outputs debugging messages of the specified type. If the -d option is used, output is to standard error; otherwise via *syslog*. Multiple occurrences of this option may be used to specify multiple types.

-help

> Prints a usage statement for automount—on which the code for csmount is based—to standard output.

-m   Provides the mount point and the FTP URL.

-nodiskarb

> Neglects to inform Disk Arbitration of the presence of the mount so that it won't show up, for example, in the output of disktool -l (except as an "Unrecognized disk" after a refresh with disktool -r).

mount_point

> The directory on which the filesystem will be mounted. It must be an absolute pathname.

username

> The login name to use with an FTP server that requires authentication.

password

> The password to use with an FTP server that requires authentication. Note that this will leave the login password visible in a process listing.

ftp_server

> The hostname or IP address of an FTP server.

pathname

> The path to the directory you wish to access on the FTP server. If not provided, it defaults to the default FTP root directory (e.g., */Library/FTPServer/FTPRoot* on Mac OS X Server).

---

curl

curl [*options*] [*URL…*]

Transfers files to and from servers using one or more URLs. curl supports several common protocols specified in *URL*: HTTP, HTTPS, FTP, GOPHER, DICT, TELNET, LDAP, and FILE. The following descriptions and examples cover curl's basic operation; for a complete description, refer to curl's manpage.

The version of curl included with versions of Mac OS X at least up 10.2.1 can cause curl to display a "malloc" error after transfers finish. This error does not affect the success of the transfers, however, and in most cases can be ignored.

URL expressions

{*a, b, c, …*}

> Form multiple URLs, each using one of the alternate variables specified within the braces as part of its string. For example, this string will expand into three different URLs: *http://www.somesite.com/~{jonny,andy,miho}*.

[*n1–n2*]

> Form multiple URLs, each using one of the letters or numbers in the range specified within the brackets as part of its string. For example, this string will expand into five different URLs: *http://www[1–5].somesite.com/*. Note that brackets need to be escaped from the shell (i.e., preceded with a backslash or surrounded in quotes).

Selected options

-C *offset*, --continue-at *offset*

> Resume transfer after skipping the first *offset* bytes of the source file, for cases when the previous transfer attempt was interrupted.

-M, --manual

> Display a detailed usage manual.

-o *filename*, --output *filename*

> Save downloaded data to *filename* instead of standard output. If you specify multiple URLs using braces or brackets and use #*n* within *filename*, it will be replaced in each new filename by each of the multiple values inside the *n*th braces or brackets in the URL (see example.)

-O, --remote-name

> Save downloaded data to a local file of the same name as the remote file, instead of standard output.

-T *filename*, --upload-file *filename*

> Upload local file *filename* to *URL*. If *URL* ends with a slash, curl will use the local filename for the uploaded copy. Otherwise, the name at the end of *URL* will be used.

-#, --progress-bar

> Display a progress bar instead of the default statistics during transfers.

Examples

Perform an anonymous FTP download into the working directory:

> **curl -O ftp://ftp.xyzsite.com/installer.sit**

Download three sequentially named files from two different servers as user *jon*:

> **curl "ftp://jon@ftp.{abc,xyz}site.com/installer[1-3].sit"⏎**
> **-o "#1_installer#2.sit**

Upload a file to a public iDisk folder:

> **curl -T archive.tar http://idisk.mac.com/jon4738/Public/**

---

cut

cut *options* [*files*]

Selects a list of columns or fields from one or more files. Either -c or -f must be specified. *list* is a sequence of integers. Use a comma between separate values and a hyphen to specify a range (e.g., 1-10,15,20 or 50-). See also paste and join.

Options

-b *list*

> This *list* specifies byte positions, not character positions. This is important when multibyte characters are used. With this option, lines should be 1023 bytes or less in size.

-c *list*

> Cut the character positions identified in *list*.

-d *c*
>   Use with -f to specify field delimiter as character *c* (default is tab); special characters (e.g., a space) must be quoted.

-f *list*
>   Cut the fields identified in *list*.

-n   Do not split characters. When used with -b, cut doesn't split multibyte characters.

-s   Use with -f to suppress lines without delimiters.

Examples

Display only ping times while pinging a host:

> **ping 192.168.10.58 | cut -sd= -f4**

Find out who is logged on, but list only login names:

> **who | cut -d" " -f1**

Cut characters in the fourth column of *file*, and paste them back as the first column in the same file. Send the results to standard output:

> **cut -c4** *file* **| paste -** *file*

---

date

date [*option*] [+*format*]
date [*options*] [*string*]

In the first form, prints the current date and time, specifying an optional display *format*. In the second form, a privileged user can set the current date by supplying a numeric *string*. *format* can consist of literal text strings (blanks must be quoted) as well as field descriptors, whose values will appear as described below (the listing shows some logical groupings).

Format

%n   Insert a newline.

%t   Insert a tab.

%m   Month of year (01–12).

%d   Day of month (01–31).

%y   Last two digits of year (00–99).

%D   Date in %m/%d/%y format.

%b   Abbreviated month name.

%e   Day of month (1–31); pad single digits with a space.

%Y   Four-digit year (e.g., 1996).

%g   Week-based year within century (00–99).

%G   Week-based year, including the century (0000–9999).

%h   Same as %b.

%B   Full-month name.

%H   Hour in 24-hour format (00–23).

%M   Minute (00–59).

%S   Second (00–61); 61 permits leap seconds and double-leap seconds.

%R   Time in %H:%M format.

%T   Time in %H:%M:%S format.

%k   Hour (24-hour clock; 0–23); single digits are preceded by a space.

%l   Hour (12-hour clock; 1–12); single digits are preceded by a space.

%I   Hour in 12-hour format (01–12).

%p   String to indicate a.m. or p.m. (default is AM or PM).

%r   Time in %I:%M:%S %p format.

%a   Abbreviated weekday.

%A   Full weekday.

%w   Day of week (Sunday = 0).

%u   Weekday as a decimal number (1–7), Sunday = 1.

%U   Week number in year (00–53); start week on Sunday.

%W   Week number in year (00–53); start week on Monday.

%V   The ISO-8601 week number (01–53). In ISO-8601, weeks begin on a Monday, and week 1 of the year is the one that includes both January 4th and the first Thursday of the year. If the first Monday of January is the 2nd, 3rd, or 4th, the preceding days are part of the last week of the previous year.

%j   Julian day of year (001–366).

%Z   Time-zone name.

%x   Country-specific date format.

%X   Country-specific time format.

%c   Country-specific date and time format (default is %a %b %e %T %Z %Y; e.g., Mon Feb 1 14:30:59 EST 1993).

The actual formatting is done by the *strftime*(3) library routine.

Options

-r *seconds*
> Print the date and time that is *seconds* from the Epoch (00:00:00 UTC, January 1, 1970).

-u   Display or set the time using Greenwich Mean Time (UTC) .

Strings for setting the date

A privileged user can set the date by supplying a numeric *string*. *string* consists of time, day, and year concatenated in one of three ways: *time* or [*day*]*time* or [*day*]*time*[*year*]. Note: don't type the brackets.

time
> A two-digit hour and two-digit minute (*HHMM*); *HH* uses 24-hour format.

day

A two-digit month and two-digit day of month (*mmdd*); the default is current day and month.

year

The year specified as either the full four digits or just the last two digits; the default is current year.

Examples

Set the date to July 1 (0701), 4 a.m. (0400), 2003 (03):

date 0701040099

The command:

date +"Hello%t Date is %D %n%t Time is %T"

produces a formatted date as follows:

```
Hello       Date is 05/09/03
            Time is 17:53:39
```

---

dc

dc [*file*]

An interactive desk calculator program that performs arbitrary-precision integer arithmetic (input may be taken from a *file*). Normally you don't run dc directly, since it's invoked by bc (see bc). dc provides a variety of one-character commands and operators that perform arithmetic; dc works like a Reverse Polish calculator; therefore, operators and commands follow the numbers they affect. Operators include + - / * % ^ (as in C, although ^ means exponentiation); some simple commands include:

p   Print current result.

q   Quit dc.

c   Clear all values on the stack.

v   Take square root.

i   Change input base; similar to bc's ibase.

o   Change output base; similar to bc's obase.

k   Set scale factor (number of digits after decimal); similar to bc's scale.

!   Remainder of line is a Unix command.

Examples

3 2 ^ p	*Evaluate 3 squared, then print result*
9	
8 * p	*Current value (9) times 8, then print result*
72	
47 - p	*Subtract 47 from 72, then print result*
25	
v p	*Square root of 25, then print result*
5	
2 o p	*Display current result in base 2*
101	

Spaces are not needed except between numbers.

---

dd [*option = value*]

Makes a copy of an input file (if=), or standard input if no named input file, using the specified conditions, and send the results to the output file (or standard output if of is not specified). Any number of options can be supplied, although if and of are the most common and are usually specified first. Because dd can handle arbitrary block sizes, it is useful when converting between raw physical devices.

dd does not preserve resource forks or HFS metadata when copying files that contain them.

Options

bs=*n*

> Set input and output block size to *n* bytes; this option supersedes ibs and obs.

cbs=*n*

> Set the size of the conversion buffer (logical record length) to *n* bytes. Use only if the conversion *flag* is ascii, asciib, ebcdic, ebcdicb, ibm, ibmb, block, or unblock.

conv=*flags*

> Convert the input according to one or more (comma-separated) *flags* listed next. The first six *flags* are mutually exclusive. The next two are mutually exclusive with each other, as are the following two.

> ascii
>> EBCDIC to ASCII.

> asciib
>> EBCDIC to ASCII, using BSD-compatible conversions.

> ebcdic
>> ASCII to EBCDIC.

> ebcdicb
>> ASCII to EBCDIC, using BSD-compatible conversions.

> ibm
>> ASCII to EBCDIC with IBM conventions.

> ibmb
>> ASCII to EBCDIC with IBM conventions, using BSD-compatible conversions.

> block
>> Variable-length records (i.e., those terminated by a newline) to fixed-length records.

> unblock
>> Fixed-length records to variable length.

> lcase
>> Uppercase to lowercase.

> ucase
>> Lowercase to uppercase.

noerror
>   Continue processing when errors occur (up to five in a
>   row).

notrunc
>   Do not truncate the output file. This preserves blocks in
>   the output file that this invocation of dd did not write.

swab
>   Swap all pairs of bytes.

sync
>   Pad input blocks to ibs.

count=*n*
>   Copy only *n* input blocks.

files=*n*
>   Copy *n* input files (e.g., from magnetic tape), then quit.

ibs=*n*
>   Set input block size to *n* bytes (default is 512).

if=*file*
>   Read input from *file* (default is standard input).

obs=*n*
>   Set output block size to *n* bytes (default is 512).

of=*file*
>   Write output to *file* (default is standard output).

iseek=*n*
>   Seek *n* blocks from start of input file (like skip but more effi-
>   cient for disk file input).

oseek=*n*
>   Seek *n* blocks from start of output file.

seek=*n*
>   Same as oseek (retained for compatibility).

skip=*n*
>   Skip *n* input blocks; useful with magnetic tape.

You can multiply size values (*n*) by a factor of 1024, 512, or 2 by appending the letters k, b, or w, respectively. You can use the letter x as a multiplication operator between two numbers.

Examples

Convert an input file to all lowercase:

> **dd if=caps_file of=small_file conv=lcase**

Retrieve variable-length data; write it as fixed-length to out:

> *data_retrieval_cmd* | **dd of=out conv=sync,block**

---

defaults
defaults [-currentHost | -host *name*] *command*

Modifies the defaults system. When you customize your Mac using the System Preferences, all of those changes and settings are stored in the *defaults system*. Everything that you've done to make your Mac your own is stored as XML data in the form of a property list (or *plist*). This property list is, in turn, stored in *~/Library/Preferences*.

Every time you change one of those settings, that particular property list is updated. For the initiated, there are two other ways to alter the property lists. The first is by using the *Property List Editor* application (*/Developer/Applications*) and the other is by using the defaults command in the Terminal. Whether you use System Preferences, *Property List Editor*, or the defaults command, any changes you make affect the current user.

Options

-currentHost

> Performs operations on the local machine.

-host *name*

> Performs operations on the specified host.

Commands

read

> Prints out all of your current settings.

read *domain*

> Prints out your settings for the specified domain, such as *com. apple.dock*.

read *domain key*

> Prints out the value of the specified key. For example, to see the current Dock orientation, use:

    defaults read com.apple.dock orientation

read-type *domain key*

> Prints out the data type of the specified key. For example, defaults read-type com.apple.dock orientation tells you that the type of the *orientation* key is *string*.

write *domain key value*

> Writes a value to the specified key.

rename *domain old_key new_key*

> Renames the specified key.

delete *domain*

> Deletes the specified domain. So, if you issue the command defaults delete com.apple.dock, the Dock forgets everything. The next time you log in, the Dock's settings are set to the system default.

delete *domain key*

> Deletes the specified key. So, if you issue the command defaults delete com. apple.dock orientation, the Dock forgets its *orientation*. The next time you log in, the Dock's settings are set to the system default.

domains

> Lists all the domains in your defaults.

find *string*

> Searches all defaults for the specified string.

help

> Prints a list of options.

Values

A value may take one of the following forms:

string
> Specifies a string value. For example, defaults write com.
> apple.dock orientation right.

-type *value*
> Specifies a value of the specified type. The type may be *string*,
> *float*, or *boolean*. For example, defaults write com.apple.dock
> autohide -boolean true.

-array [-add] *value* [*value* ...]
> Creates or adds to a list of defaults. For example, you can
> create a list of your favorite colors with defaults write
> personal.favorites colors -array red, blue. Use -add to add
> values to an existing array.

-dict [-add] *key value* [*key value*...]
> Creates or adds to a dictionary list. For example, you can
> create a dictionary of preferred pet foods with defaults write
> personal.pets food -dict cat salmon dog steak.

> Using the defaults command is not for the foolhardy. If
> you manage to mangle your settings, the easiest way to
> correct the problem is to go back to that application's
> Preferences pane and reset your preferences. In some
> cases, you can use defaults delete, which will be reset to
> the same defaults when you next log in. Since the
> defaults command affects only the current user, you
> could also create a user just for testing random defaults
> tips you pick up on the Internet.

Examples

View all of the user defaults on your system:

> % **defaults domains**

This prints a listing of all of the *domains* in the user's defaults
system. The list you see is run together with spaces in between—
not quite the prettiest way to view the information.

View the settings for your Terminal:

> % **defaults read com.apple.Terminal**

This command reads the settings from the *com.apple.Terminal.plist*
file, found in *~/Library/Preferences*. This listing is rather long, so
you might want to pipe the output to *less* or *more* to view the
contents one screen at a time:

> % **defaults read com.apple.Terminal | more**

Change your Dock's default location to the top of the screen:

> % **defaults write com.apple.Dock orientation top**

This moves the Dock to the top of the screen underneath the menu
bar. After changing that setting, you'll need to logout from the
system and then log back in to see the Dock under the menu bar.

df
    df [*options*] [*name*]

Report the number of free disk blocks and inodes available on all mounted filesystems or on the given *name*. (Unmounted filesystems are checked with -F.) *name* can be a device name (e.g., */dev/disk0s9*), the directory name of a mount point (e.g., */Volumes/Drive2*), a directory name, or a remote filesystem name (e.g., an NFS filesystem). Besides the options listed, there are additional options specific to different filesystem types or df modules.

Options

-i   Report free, used, and percent-used inodes.

-k   Print sizes in kilobytes.

-l   Show local filesystems only.

-n   Print only the filesystem *type* name; with no other arguments, -n lists the types for all mounted filesystems.

-t *type1* [, *type2* , ...]
    Show only filesystem types specified.

---

diff
    diff [*options*] [*diroptions*] *file1 file2*

Compares two text files. diff reports lines that differ between *file1* and *file2*. Output consists of lines of context from each file, with *file1* text flagged by a < symbol and *file2* text by a > symbol. Context lines are preceded by the ed command (a, c, or d) that are used to convert *file1* to *file2*. If one of the files is -, standard input is read. If one of the files is a directory, diff locates the filename in that directory corresponding to the other argument (e.g., diff my_dir junk is the same as diff my_ dir/junk junk). If both arguments are directories, diff reports lines that differ between all pairs of files having equivalent names (e.g., olddir/program and newdir/program); in addition, diff lists filenames unique to one directory, as well as subdirectories common to both. See also cmp.

Options

Options -c, -C, -D, -e, -f, -h, and -n cannot be combined with one another (they are mutually exclusive).

-a, --text
    Treat all files as text files. Useful for checking to see if binary files are identical.

-b, --ignore-space-change
    Ignore repeating blanks and end-of-line blanks; treat successive blanks as one.

-B, --ignore-blank-lines
    Ignore blank lines in files.

-c   Context diff: print 3 lines surrounding each changed line.

-C *n*, --context[=*n*]
    Context diff: print *n* lines surrounding each changed line. The default context is 3 lines.

--changed-group-format=*format*
> Use *format* to output a line group containing differing lines from both files in if- then-else format.

-d, --minimal
> To speed up comparison, ignore segments of numerous changes and output a smaller set of changes.

-D *symbol*, --ifdef=*symbol*
> When handling C files, create an output file that contains all the contents of both input files, including #ifdef and #ifndef directives that reflect the directives in both files.

-e, --ed
> Produce a script of commands (a, c, d) to recreate *file2* from *file1* using the ed editor.

-f   Produce a script to recreate *file1* from *file2*; the script is in the opposite order, so it isn't useful to ed.

-F *regexp*, --show-function-line[=*regexp*]
> For context and unified diff, show the most recent line containing *regexp* before each block of changed lines.

--forward-ed
> Make output that looks vaguely like an ed script but has changes in the order they appear in the file.

-H   Speed output of large files by scanning for scattered small changes; long stretches with many changes may not show up.

-help
> Print brief usage message.

--horizon-lines=*n*
> In an attempt to find a more compact listing, keep *n* lines on both sides of the changed lines when performing the comparison.

-i, --ignore-case
> Ignore case in text comparison. Uppercase and lowercase are considered the same.

-I *regexp*, --ignore-matching-lines=*regexp*
> Ignore lines in files that match the regular expression *regexp*.

--ifdef=*name*
> Make merged if-then-else format output, conditional on the preprocessor macro *name*.

-L *label*, --label *label*, --label=*label*
> For context and unified diff, print *label* in place of the file-name being compared. The first such option applies to the first filename and the second option to the second filename.

--left-column
> For two-column output (-y), show only left column of common lines.

--line-format=*format*
> Use *format* to output all input lines in in-then-else format.

-n, -rcs
    Produce output in RCS diff format.

-N, --new-file
    Treat nonexistent files as empty.

--new-group-format=*format*
    Use *format* to output a group of lines taken from just the second file in if-then- else format.

--new-line-format=*format*
    Use *format* to output a line taken from just the second file in if-then-else format.

--old-group-format=*format*
    Use *format* to output a group of lines taken from just the first file in if-then-else format.

--old-line-format=*format*
    Use *format* to output a line taken from just the first file in if-then-else format.

-p, --show-c-function
    When handling files in C or C-like languages such as Java, show the function containing each block of changed lines. Assumes -c, but can also be used with a unified diff.

-P, --unidirectional-new-file
    If two directories are being compared and the first lacks a file that is in the second, pretend that an empty file of that name exists in the first directory.

-q, --brief
    Output only whether files differ.

--sdiff-merge-assist
    Print extra information to help sdiff. sdiff uses this option when it runs diff.

--suppress-common-lines
    Do not print common lines in side-by-side format.

-t, --expand-tabs
    Produce output with tabs expanded to spaces.

-T, --initial-tab
    Insert initial tabs into output to line up tabs properly.

--unchanged-group-format=*format*
    Use *format* to output a group of common lines taken from both files in if-then- else format.

-u   Unified diff: print old and new versions of lines in a single block, with 3 lines surrounding each block of changed lines.

-U *n*, --unified[=*n*]
    Unified diff; print old and new versions of lines in a single block, with *n* lines surrounding each block of changed lines. The default context is 3 lines.

-v, --version
    Print version number of this version of diff.

-w, --ignore-all-space
Ignore all whitespace in files for comparisons.

-W *n*, --width=*n*
For two-column output (-y), produce columns with a maximum width of *n* characters. Default is 130.

-x *regexp*, --exclude=*regexp*
Do not compare files in a directory whose names match *regexp*.

-X *filename*, --exclude-from=*filename*
Do not compare files in a directory whose names match patterns described in the file *filename*.

-y, --side-by-side
Produce two-column output.

-*n* For context and unified diff, print *n* lines of context. Same as specifying a number with -C or -U.

The following *diroptions* are valid only when both file arguments are directories.

Diroptions

-l, --paginate
Paginate output by passing it to pr.

-r, --recursive
Compare subdirectories recursively.

-s, --report-identical-files
Indicate when files do not differ.

-S *filename*, --starting-file=*filename*
For directory comparisons, begin with the file *filename*, skipping files that come earlier in the standard list order.

---

diff3   diff3 [*options*] *file1 file2 file3*

Compares three files and reports the differences. No more than one of the files may be given as − (indicating that it is to be read from standard input). The output is displayed with the following codes:

= = = =
All three files differ.

= = = =1
file1 is different.

= = = =2
file2 is different.

= = = =3
file3 is different.

diff3 is also designed to merge changes in two differing files based on a common ancestor file (i.e., when two people have made their own set of changes to the same file). diff3 can find changes between the ancestor and one of the newer files and generate output that adds those differences to the other new file. Unmerged

---

changes are places where both of the newer files differ from each other and at least one of them is from the ancestor. Changes from the ancestor that are the same in both of the newer files are called *merged changes*. If all three files differ in the same place, it is called an *overlapping change*.

This scheme is used on the command line with the ancestor being *file2*, the second filename. Comparison is made between *file2* and *file3*, with those differences then applied to *file1*.

Options

-3, --easy-only
> Create an ed script to incorporate into *file1* unmerged, nonoverlapping differences between *file1* and *file3*.

-a, --text
> Treat files as text.

-A, --show-all
> Create an ed script to incorporate all changes, showing conflicts in bracketed format.

-e, --ed
> Create an ed script to incorporate into *file1* all unmerged differences between *file2* and *file3*.

-E, --show-overlap
> Create an ed script to incorporate unmerged changes, showing conflicts in bracketed format.

-x, --overlap-only
> Create an ed script to incorporate into *file1* all differences where all three files differ (overlapping changes).

-X
> Same as -x, but show only overlapping changes, in bracketed format.

-m, --merge
> Create file with changes merged (not an ed script).

-L *label*, --label=*label*
> Use *label* to replace filename in output.

-i
> Append the w (save) and q (quit) commands to ed script output.

-T, --initial-tab
> Begin lines with a tab instead of two spaces in output to line tabs up properly.

-v, --version
> Print version information and then exit.

dig

dig [@*server*] *host* [*querytype*] [*queryclass*] [*options*]

Queries Internet domain name servers. Like the nslookup command, dig displays information about *host* as returned by the default or a specified name server. With dig, you specify all aspects of the query on the command line; there's no interactive mode as with nslookup.

Specifies the name server to query with @*server*, using either a domain name or an IP in *server*. The default is to query the name servers in *resolv.conf*. Specifies the type of query in *querytype*; the default is to look up address records. The supported types are:

A
: Host's Internet address

ANY
: Any available information (default)

AXFR
: Request zone transfer

HINFO
: Host CPU and operating system type

MX
: Mail exchanger

NS
: Nameserver for the named zone

SOA
: Domain start-of-authority

Use *queryclass* to specify query class of either IN (Internet) or ANY. Default is IN.

Options

The following descriptions cover dig's basic operation; for a complete description, refer to dig's manpage.

-x *address*
: Reverse map *address*, allowing you to locate a hostname when only an IP number is available. Implies ANY as the query type.

-p *port*
: Send queries to the specified port instead of port 53, the default.

+norec[urse]
: Turn off recursion (on by default).

+vc Send TCP-based queries (queries are UDP by default).

DirectoryService   DirectoryService [*options*]

This is the server process for the Directory Services framework.

Options

-h Prints a usage statement for the first form of command invocation to standard output.

-v Prints software release version to standard output.

-appledebug
: Runs service in debug mode.

-appleframework
: Starts service normally. This is the default.

-applenodaemon
: Disables daemonization; runs service in foreground.

-appleoptions

> Prints a usage statement for the second form of command invocation to standard output.

-appleperformance

> Runs service in foreground and logs extensively.

-appleversion

> Prints software build version to standard output.

dirname

dirname *pathname*

Prints *pathname*, excluding the last level. Useful for stripping the actual filename from a pathname. If there are no slashes (no directory levels) in *pathname*, dirname prints . to indicate the current directory. See also basename.

disktool

```
disktool [-l | -r | -x | -y]
disktool [-d | -e | -g | -m | -p | -u | -A | -D | -S] device
disktool [ -s ] device integer_flag
disktool -n device vol_name
disktool -a device vol_name vol_flags
disktool -c userID
```

Controls disks, including mounting, unmounting, ejecting, enabling permissions, and volume-naming. Most options require a device name argument (e.g., *disk0*), and some require additional parameters.

Options

-a   Adds disk to Disk Arbitration tables, to notify applications of a mounted volume. This is useful if you have forced a mount, thus bypassing standard notification.

-A   Activates permissions on the volume, adding an entry to */var/db/volinfo.database* if one does not already exist.

-c   Specifies user ID of account to use when mounting disks.

-d   Removes disk from Disk Arbitration tables, to notify applications of a dismount. This is useful if you have forced a dismount, thus bypassing standard notification.

-D   Deactivates permissions on the volume.

-e   Ejects disk.

-g   Prints HFS encoding on a volume to standard output.

-l   Lists disk volumes to standard output.

-m   Mounts disk.

-n   Names volume.

-p   Unmounts partition. Device name is that of a partition (e.g., *disk0s5*).

-r   Refreshes Disk Arbitration tables.

-s   Sets HFS encoding on a volume. Takes encoding as additional integer argument.

-S   Prints status of volume in */var/db/volinfo.database* to standard output.

-u   Unmounts disk.

-x   Disallows dismounts and ejects.

-y   Allows dismounts and ejects.

---

diskutil

```
diskutil list
diskutil mount[Disk] device
diskutil { info[rmation] | unmount[Disk] | eject | verifyDisk |
repairDisk | enableJournal | disableJournal | verifyPermissions
| repairPermissions } { mount_point | device }
diskutil rename { mount_point | device } vol_name
diskutil eraseVolume format vol_name [bootable] { mount_point |
device }
diskutil eraseDisk format vol_name [OS9Drivers] [bootable]
{ mount_point | device }
diskutil eraseOptical [quick] { mount_point | device }
diskutil partitionDisk device num_partitions [OS9Drivers]
[bootable] part1_format part1_name part1_size [part2_format
part2_name part2_size ]
diskutil checkRAID
diskutil createRAID { mirror | stripe } set_name [bootable]
{ HFS | HFS+ | UFS | BootableHFS+ } device1 device2 [device3]
diskutil destroyRAID { set_UUID | device }
diskutil repairMirror { set_UUID | device } partition_num from_
device to_device
```

Controls disk volumes, including mounting, unmounting, ejecting, erasing, journaling, partitioning, fixing permissions, and setting up RAIDs. This is a command-line analog of the Disk Utility application, and contains functionality beyond the somewhat less user-friendly disktool.

Volumes are specified by mount point (directory on which the volume is mounted) or device name (e.g., *disk0s1*).

Options

checkRAID
: Checks the status of RAID sets. Requires privileged access.

createRAID
: Creates a mirror (RAID 1) or a stripe (RAID 0) on a set of devices. Requires privileged access.

destroyRAID
: Destroys an existing mirrored or striped RAID set. Requires privileged access.

disableJournal
: Disables journaling on an HFS+ volume. Requires privileged access.

eject
: If a disk is ejectable, unmounts and ejects the disk. Requires privileged access, unless the user running diskutil is logged into the graphical console.

enableJournal

Enables journaling on an HFS+ volume. The journal keeps a record of all filesystem operations, which allows the system to roll back to a consistent filesystem state in the event of a crash. This eliminates the need for disk verification after a crash. Requires privileged access.

eraseDisk

Unmounts and reformats an entire disk. Requires privileged access.

eraseOptical

Unmounts and erases a read/write optical disk. Requires privileged access.

eraseVolume

Unmounts and reformats a disk partition. Requires privileged access.

information

Prints data about the device to standard output, including device name, volume name and mount point, filesystem format, disk hardware access protocol, total and free diskspace, and whether the device is read-only or ejectable.

list

Lists disk devices on the system, including device names, volume names, and sizes.

mount

Mounts the specified partition. Requires privileged access, unless the user running diskutil is logged into the graphical console.

mountDisk

Mounts all partitions on the specified disk. Requires privileged access, unless the user running diskutil is logged into the graphical console.

partitionDisk

Repartitions the specified disk. The number of partitions (*num_partitions*) is limited to 8. Partition sizes are given as a number concatenated with a letter, where the letter is B (bytes), K (kilobytes), M (megabytes), G (gigabytes), or T (terabytes). The current boot disk cannot be repartitioned. Requires privileged access.

rename

Gives the device a new volume name. For HFS, HFS+, and UFS partitions only.

repairDisk

Unmounts the device, attempts to repair any filesystem inconsistencies it finds, and remounts the device. Requires privileged access.

repairMirror

Repairs a mirrored RAID set. If checkRAID reports a problem with a mirrored partition, this lets you sync up the data for that partition from the good copy to the bad copy. Requires privileged access.

repairPermissions

Scans the *Archive.bom* files in */Library/Receipts* for installed software packages, and resets file permissions according to what they should have been upon installation. Requires privileged access.

unmount

Unmounts the specified partition. Requires privileged access, unless the user running `diskutil` is logged into the graphical console.

unmountDisk

Unmounts all partitions on the specified disk. Requires privileged access, unless the user running `diskutil` is logged into the graphical console.

verifyDisk

Unmounts the device, scans it for filesystem inconsistencies, and remounts the device. Requires privileged access.

verifyPermissions

Scans the *Archive.bom* files in */Library/Receipts* for installed software packages, and verifies whether file permissions are set according to what they should have been upon installation. Requires privileged access.

---

ditto

```
ditto [options] files directory
ditto [options] directory1 directory2
```

Copies files and directories while preserving most file information, including resource fork and HFS metadata information when desired. `ditto` preserves the permissions, ownership, and timestamp of the source files in the copies. `ditto` overwrites identically named files in the target directory without prompting for confirmation.

`ditto` works like `cp` in the first synopsis form. However, the second form differs in that `cp -r` copies the entire *directory1* into an existing *directory2*, while `ditto` copies the contents of *directory1* into *directory2*, creating *directory2* if it doesn't already exist.

Options

-arch *arch*

When copying fat binary files, copy only the code for chip type *arch*. Fat binary files contain different code for different chip architectures. The -arch flag allows you to "thin" the binary by copying only the code for the specified chip. Possible values for *arch* include ppc, m68k, i386, hppa, and sparc.

-bom *pathname*

When copying a directory, include in the copy only those items listed in bom file *pathname*. See also mkbom for information on making a BOM ("bill-of-materials") file.

-rsrcFork, -rsrc

When copying files, include any resource fork and HFS metadata information.

-v   Be verbose; report each directory copied.

-v   Be very verbose; report each file copied.

Example

Duplicate an entire home directory, copying the contents of directory */Users/chris* into the directory *Volumes/Drive 2/Users/chris*, and preserving resource forks and HFS metadata:

```
ditto -rsrc /Users/chris "/Volumes/Drive 2/Users/chris"
```

---

dmesg   dmesg [*options*]

Displays the system control messages from the kernel ring buffer. This buffer stores all messages since the last system boot or the most recent ones, if the buffer has been filled.

Options

-M *core*
> Use the specified *core* file from which to extract messages instead of */dev/kmem*.

-N *system*
> Use the specified *system* instead of the default */mach_kernel*.

---

dnsquery   dnsquery [*options*] *host*

Queries Internet domain name servers. A simpler alternative to nslookup, dnsquery displays information about *host* as returned by the default or a specified name server.

Options

-n *nameserver*
> Query server *namerserver* instead of the default name server specified in */etc/resolve.conf*.

-t *type*
> Change type of information returned from a query to one of the following:
>
> A
>> Host's Internet address
>
> AFSDB
>> DCE or AFS server
>
> ANY
>> Any available information (default)
>
> CNAME
>> Canonical name for an alias
>
> HINFO
>> Host CPU and operating system type
>
> MG
>> Mail group member
>
> MINFO
>> Mailbox or mail list information

MX

    Mail exchanger

NS

    Nameserver for the named zone

PTR

    Hostname or pointer to other information

RP

    Responsible person

SOA

    Domain start-of-authority

WKS

    Supported well-known services

-c *class*
: Set query class to IN (Internet), CHAOS, HESIOD, or ANY. Default is IN.

-r *number*
: Set number of retries to *number*.

-p *period*
: Set seconds to wait before retries to *period*.

-d   Turn on debugging mode.

-s, -v
: Connect with the name server using a TCP stream rather than a UDP datagram, the default.

---

du

du [*options*] [*directories*]

Prints disk usage (as the number of 512-byte blocks used by each named directory and its subdirectories; default is current directory).

Options

-a   Print usage for all files, not just subdirectories.

-c   In addition to normal output, print grand total of all arguments.

-H   Follow symbolic links, but only if they are command-line arguments.

-k   Print sizes in kilobytes.

-L   Follow symbolic links.

-P   Don't follow any symbolic links.

-s, --summarize
: Print only the grand total for each named directory.

-x, --one-file-system
: Display usage of files in current filesystem only.

| dynamic_pager | dynamic_pager [-F *filename*] [-H *hire_point*] [-L *layoff_point*] [-P *priority*] [-S *file_size*] |

Manages virtual memory swap files. This tool is started from */etc/rc* during the boot process.

Options

-F Specifies the base absolute pathname for swap files. Swap file-names consist of this base and a whole number suffix, starting at 0. The default is */private/var/vm/swapfile*.

-H Creates an additional swap file when free swap space drops below the *hire_ point* in bytes. The default is 0, which disables the use of this swap space.

-L Attempts to consolidate memory and remove a swap file when free swap space rises above the *layoff_point* in bytes. The *layoff_point* must be set higher than the sum of the swap file size and the *hire_point*, unless it is set to 0 (the default), which disables layoffs.

-P Determines the priority of this swap space. The default is 0.

-S Determines the size of swap files created, in bytes. The default is 20000000.

| echo | echo [-n] [*string*] |

Echoes arguments to standard output. Often used for producing prompts from shell scripts.

Option

-n Suppress printing of newline after text.

Example

```
echo "testing printer" | lp
```

| egrep | egrep [*options*] [*regexp*] [*files*] |

Searches one or more *files* for lines that match an extended regular expression *regexp*. egrep doesn't support the regular expressions \(, \), \n, \<, \>, \{, or \}, but does support the other expressions, as well as the extended set +, ?, |, and ( ). Remember to enclose these characters in quotes. Regular expressions are described in Chapter 20. Exit status is 0 if any lines match, 1 if none match, and 2 for errors.

See grep for the list of available options. Also see fgrep. egrep typically runs faster than those commands.

Examples

Search for occurrences of *Victor* or *Victoria* in *file*:

```
egrep 'Victor(ia)*' file
egrep '(Victor|Victoria)' file
```

Find and print strings such as *old.doc1* or *new.doc2* in *files*, and include their line numbers:

```
egrep -n '(old|new)\.doc?' files
```

---

enscript

enscript [*options*] [*files*]

Converts text files to PostScript for output to a printer or file. This converion is necessary when printing text files from the command line to most laser printers, for example, since most laser printers are PostScript devices. enscript is a feature-rich application that allows you to modfiy the printed output in many ways. The following descriptions and examples cover enscript's basic operation; for a complete description, refer to enscript's manpage.

Used with no arguments, enscript receives text from standard input and sends it to the default printer. Otherwise, enscript converts the text files specified in *files*, and directs output to a named printer, file, or standard output as specified by *options* (or the default printer if no options are specified).

Options

-# *n*, -n *n*, --copies=*n*
  Print *n* copies of every page.

-a *pages*, --pages=*pages*
  Print selected *pages*, as specified in the following format:

  begin-end
     Print from page number *begin* to page number *end*.

  -end
     Print until page number *-end*.

  begin-
     Print from page number *begin* to the last page.

  page
     Print only page number *page*.

  odd
     Print only the odd numbered pages.

  even
     Print only the even numbered pages.

--list-options
  List the current enscript option settings.

-r, --landscape
  Print the page in landscape mode, rotated 90 degrees.

-R, --portrait
  Print the page in portrait mode, the default.

-U *n*, --nup=*n*
  Print *n*-up; place *n* pages on each sheet of output.

--margins=*left*:*right*:*top*:*bottom*
  Print with margins of *left*, *right*, *top* and *bottom*, each specified in PostScript points. To use the default value for a margin, omit that argument.

Examples

Print pages 5 through 10, 2-up, of text document *notes.txt*:

```
enscript -a 5-10 -U 2 notes.txt
```

Print page 1 of text document *notes.txt*, setting a top margin of 50 points and a bottom margin of 25 points

```
enscript -a 1 --margins=::50:25 notes.txt
```

---

env

env [*options*] [*variable=value* …] [*command*]

Displays the current environment or, if environment *variables* are specified, sets them to a new *value* and displays the modified environment. If *command* is specified, executes it under the modified environment.

Options

-t *tablist*

Interpret tabs according to *tablist*, a space- or comma-separated list of numbers in ascending order, that describe the "tabstops" for the input data.

-*n*   Set the tabstops every *n* characters. The default is 8.

---

expand

expand [*options*] [*files*]

Expands tab characters into appropriate number of spaces. expand reads the named files or standard input if no files are provided. See also unexpand.

Options

-t *tablist*

Interpret tabs according to *tablist*, a space- or comma-separated list of numbers in ascending order, that describe the "tabstops" for the input data.

-*n*   Set the tabstops every *n* characters. The default is 8.

-*tablist*

Interpret tabs according to *tablist*, a space- or comma-separated list of numbers in ascending order, that describe the "tabstops" for the input data.

Example

Cut columns 10–12 of the input data, even when tabs are used:

```
expand data | cut -c 10-12 > data.col2
```

---

expr

expr *arg1 operator arg2* [*operator arg3* …]

Evaluates arguments as expressions and prints the result. Strings can be compared and searched. Arguments and operators must be separated by spaces. In most cases, an argument is an integer, typed literally or represented by a shell variable. There are three types of operators: arithmetic, relational, and logical. Exit status for expr is 0 (expression is nonzero and nonnull), 1 (expression is 0 or null), or 2 (expression is invalid).

expr is typically used in shell scripts to perform simple mathematics, such as addition or subtraction. It is made obsolete in the Korn shell by that program's built-in arithmetic capabilities.

Arithmetic Operators

Use the following operators to produce mathematical expressions whose results are printed:

+   Add *arg2* to *arg1*.

-     Subtract *arg2* from *arg1*.

*   Multiply the arguments.

/   Divide *arg1* by *arg2*.

%   Take the remainder when *arg1* is divided by *arg2*.

Addition and subtraction are evaluated last, unless they are grouped inside parentheses. The symbols *, (, and) have meaning to the shell, so they must be escaped (preceded by a backslash or enclosed in single or double quotes).

Relational operators

Use relational operators to compare two arguments. Arguments can also be words, in which case comparisons assume a < z and A < Z. If the comparison statement is true, the result is 1; if false, the result is 0. Symbols < and > must be escaped.

=   Are the arguments equal?

!=   Are the arguments different?

>   Is *arg1* greater than *arg2*?

>=   Is *arg1* greater than or equal to *arg2*?

<   Is *arg1* less than *arg2*?

<=   Is *arg1* less than or equal to *arg2*?

Logical operators

Use logical operators to compare two arguments. Depending on the values, the result can be *arg1* (or some portion of it), *arg2*, or 0. Symbols | and & must be escaped.

| *Logical OR*; if *arg1* has a nonzero (and nonnull) value, the result is *arg1*; otherwise, the result is *arg2*.

&   *Logical AND*; if both *arg1* and *arg2* have a nonzero (and nonnull) value, the result is *arg1*; otherwise, the result is 0.

:   Similar to grep; *arg2* is a pattern to search for in *arg1*. *arg2* must be a regular expression in this case. If the *arg2* pattern is enclosed in \(\), the result is the portion of *arg1* that matches; otherwise, the result is simply the number of characters that match. By default, a pattern match always applies to the beginning of the first argument (the search string implicitly begins with a ^). To match other parts of the string, start the search string with .*.

Examples

Division happens first; result is 10:

```
expr 5 + 10 / 2
```

Addition happens first; result is 7 (truncated from 7.5):

```
expr \( 5 + 10 \) / 2
```

Add 1 to variable i; this is how variables are incremented in shell scripts:

```
i=`expr $i + 1`
```

Print 1 (true) if variable a is the string "hello":

```
expr $a = hello
```

Print 1 (true) if variable b plus 5 equals 10 or more:

```
expr $b + 5 \>= 10
```

In the following examples, variable p is the string "version.100". This command prints the number of characters in p:

```
expr $p : '.*'          Result is 11
```

Match all characters and print them:

```
expr $p : '\(.*\)'      Result is "version.100"
```

Print the number of lowercase letters at the beginning of p:

```
expr $p : '[a-z]*'      Result is 7
```

Match the lowercase letters at the beginning of p:

```
expr $p : '\([a-z]*\)'  Result is "version"
```

Truncate $x if it contains five or more characters; if not, just print $x. (Logical OR uses the second argument when the first one is 0 or null; i.e., when the match fails.) Double-quoting is a good idea, in case $x contains whitespace characters.

```
expr "$x" : '\(.....\)' \| "$x"
```

In a shell script, rename files to their first five letters:

```
mv "$x" `expr "$x" : '\(.....\)' \| "$x"`
```

(To avoid overwriting files with similar names, use mv -i.)

---

false

false

A null command that returns an unsuccessful (nonzero) exit status. Normally used in bash scripts. See also true.

---

fdisk

fdisk [*device* { -diskSize | -isDiskPartitioned | -installSize |
-sizeofExtended | -freeSpace | -freeWithoutUFS |
-freeWithoutUFSorExt | -isThereExtendedPartition |
-isThereUFSPartition | -removePartitioning | -bootPlusUFS |
-dosPlusUFS *integer* | -setAvailableToUFS | -setExtendedToUFS |
-setExtAndAvailableToUFS | -setUFSActive | -script }]
[-bootsectorOnly] [-useAllSectors] [-useBoot0 [-boot0
filename]] [-heads *integer*] [-cylinders *integer*] [-sectors
integer]

Provides control over DOS partition maps on disk devices in Darwin *x*86 systems. Much of its functionality is devoted to managing an Apple UFS partition that Darwin uses as a boot volume. There can be only one Apple UFS partition on a disk.

When invoked without a device name argument, fdisk enters interactive mode, in which navigation is performed via a series of menus.

Options

`-boot0`

Specifies a nondefault file to use as the boot program for the -useBoot0 flag.

`-bootPlusUFS`

Repartitions the disk to include an 8-MB booter partition (which is set active) and the remainder as an Apple UFS partition.

`-bootsectorOnly`

Limits modification to include only the boot sector. Normally, the first sector of each new partition is erased, but this flag disables that behavior.

`-cylinders`

Forces an assumption of a disk geometry with the specified number of cylinders.

`-diskSize`

Prints the size of the specified device, in megabytes, to standard output.

`-dosPlusUFS`

Repartitions the disk to include a DOS partition of the specified size, in megabytes, and the remainder as an Apple UFS partition.

`-freeSpace`

Prints the size of the largest free area, in megabytes, to standard output.

`-freeWithoutUFS`

Prints the size of the largest free area, in megabytes, to standard output, as if there were no Apple UFS partition present.

`-freeWithoutUFSorExt`

Prints the size of the largest free area, in megabytes, to standard output, as if there were no Apple UFS or extended partitions present.

`-heads`

Forces an assumption of a disk geometry with the specified number of heads.

`-installSize`

Prints the size, in megabytes, of the area that would be taken by Darwin if it were to be installed. If the disk is partitioned, this is equal to the size of the Apple UFS partition; otherwise, it's equal to the size of the entire disk.

`-isDiskPartitioned`

Prints Yes to standard output if the disk has a DOS partition map on it, No if not.

-isThereExtendedPartition
> Prints Yes to standard output if the disk has a DOS extended partition on it, No if not.

-isThereUFSPartition
> Prints Yes to standard output if the disk has an Apple UFS partition on it, No if not.

-removePartitioning
> Erases the boot sector, which deletes the partition map and the boot program. After this, a Darwin installation will take the entire disk.

-script
> Reads in a new set of partition entries from standard input.

-sectors
> Forces an assumption of a disk geometry with the specified number of sectors per track.

-setAvailableToUFS
> After deleting any existing Apple UFS partition, creates a new Apple UFS partition taking up the largest free area on the disk.

-setExtAndAvailableToUFS
> After deleting any existing Apple UFS and extended partitions, creates a new Apple UFS partition taking up the largest free area on the disk.

-setExtendedToUFS
> Changes an existing extended partition to Apple UFS.

-setUFSActive
> Makes the Apple UFS partition the default boot partition on the disk.

-sizeofExtended
> Prints the size of the DOS extended partition, in megabytes, to standard output.

-useAllSectors
> Instructs fdisk to use all physical sectors on the disk, including those not seen by the BIOS.

-useBoot0
> Reads in a new boot program from */usr/standalone/i386/boot0*.

device
> The disk device filename, e.g., */dev/disk0*.

---

fetchmail

fetchmail [*options*] [*servers...*]

Retrieves mail from mail servers and forwards it to the local mail delivery system. fetchmail retrieves mail from servers that support the common mail protocols POP2, POP3, IMAP2bis, and IMAP4. Messages are delivered via SMTP through port 25 on the local host and through your system's mail delivery agent (such as *sendmail*), where they can be read through the user's mail client. fetchmail settings are stored in the *~/.fetchmailrc* file. Parameters and servers can also be set on the command line, which will override settings in the *.fetchmailrc* file.

Options

-a, --all

Retrieve all messages from server, even ones that have already been seen but left on the server. The default is to only retrieve new messages.

-A *type*, --auth *type*

Specify the type of authentication. *type* may be password, kerberos_v5, or kerberos. Authentication type is usually established by fetchmail by default, so this option isn't very useful.

-B *n*, --fetchlimit *n*

Set the maximum number of messages (*n*) accepted from a server per query.

-b *n*, --batchlimit *n*

Set the maximum number of messages sent to an SMTP listener per connection. When this limit is reached, the connection will be broken and reestablished. The default of 0 means no limit.

-c, --check

Check for mail on a single server without retrieving or deleting messages. Works with IMAP, but not well with other protocols, if at all.

-D [*domain*], --smtpaddress [*domain*]

Specify the *domain* name placed in RCPT TO lines sent to SMTP. The default is the local host.

-E *header*, --envelope *header*

Change the header assumed to contain the mail's envelope address (usually "X-Envelope-to:") to *header*.

-e *n*, --expunge *n*

Tell an IMAP server to EXPUNGE (i.e., purge messages marked for deletion) after *n* deletes. A setting of 0 indicates expunging only at the end of the session. Normally, an expunge occurs after each delete.

-F, --flush

For POP3 and IMAP servers, remove previously retrieved messages from the server before retrieving new ones.

-f *file*, --fetchmailrc *file*

Specify a nondefault name for the fetchmail configuration file.

-I *specification*, --interface *specification*

Require that the mail server machine is up and running at a specified IP address (or range) before polling. The *specification* is given as *interface/ipaddress/mask*. The first part indicates the type of TCP connection expected (*sl0*, *ppp0*, etc.), the second is the IP address, and the third is the bit mask for the IP, assumed to be 255.255.255.255.

-K, --nokeep

Delete all retrieved messages from the mail server.

-k, --keep

Keep copies of all retrieved messages on the mail server.

-l *size,* **--limit** *size*

Set the maximum message size that will be retrieved from a server. Messages larger than this size will be left on the server and marked unread.

-M *interface,* **--monitor** *interface*

In daemon mode, monitor the specified TCP/IP *interface* for any activity besides itself, and skip the poll if there is no other activity. Useful for PPP connections that automatically time out with no activity.

-m *command,* **--mda** *command*

Pass mail directly to mail delivery agent, rather than send to port 25. The *command* is the path and options for the mailer, such as */usr/lib/sendmail -oem*. A %T in the command will be replaced with the local delivery address, and an %F will be replaced with the message's From address.

-n, **--norewrite**

Do not expand local mail IDs to full addresses. This option will disable expected addressing and should only be used to find problems.

-P *n,* **--port** *n*

Specify a port to connect to on the mail server. The default port numbers for supported protocols are usually sufficient.

-p *proto,* **--protocol** *proto*

Specify the protocol to use when polling a mail server. *proto* can be:

POP2

Post Office Protocol 2.

POP3

Post Office Protocol 3.

APOP

POP3 with MD5 authentication.

RPOP

POP3 with RPOP authentication.

KPOP

POP3 with Kerberos v4 authentication on port 1109.

IMAP

IMAP2bis, IMAP4, or IMAP4rev1. fetchmail autodetects their capabilities.

IMAP-K4

IMAP4 or IMAP4rev1 with Kerberos v4 authentication.

IMAP-GSS

IMAP4 or IMAP4rev1 with GSSAPI authentication.

ETRN

ESMTP.

-Q *string,* **--qvirtual** *string*

Remove the prefix *string*, which is the local user's hostid, from the address in the envelope header (such as "Delivered-To:").

-r *folder,* --folder *folder*
    Retrieve the specified mail *folder* from the mail server.

-s, --silent
    Suppress status messages during a fetch.

-U, --uidl
    For POP3, track the age of kept messages via unique ID listing.

-u *name,* --username *name*
    Specify the user *name* to use when logging into the mail server.

-V, --version
    Print the version information for fetchmail and display the options set for each mail server. Performs no fetch.

-v, --verbose
    Display all status messages during a fetch.

-Z *nnn,* --antispam *nnn*
    Specify the SMTP error *nnn* to signal a spam block from the client. If *nnn* is -1, this option is disabled.

fgrep

fgrep [*options*] *pattern* [*files*]

Search one or more *files* for lines that match a literal text string *pattern*. Exit status is 0 if any lines match, 1 if not, and 2 for errors.

See *grep* for the list of available options. Also see *egrep*.

Examples

Print lines in *file* that don't contain any spaces:

    fgrep -v '' *file*

Print lines in *file* that contain the words in *spell_list*:

    fgrep -f spell_list *file*

file

file [*options*] *files*

Classify the named *files* according to the type of data they contain. file checks the magic file (*/etc/magic*) to identify some file types.

Options

-c   Check the format of the magic file (*files* argument is invalid with -c). Usually used with -m.

-f *file*
    Read the names of files to be checked from *file*.

-L   Follow symbolic links. By default, symbolic links are not followed.

-m *file*
    Search for file types in *file* instead of */etc/magic*.

-v   Print the version.

-z   Attempt checking of compressed files.

Many file types are understood. Output lists each filename, followed by a brief classification such as:

```
Apple QuickTime movie file (moov)
ASCII text
data
directory
gzip compressed data
empty
PDF document, version 1.4
Mach-O executable ppc
sticky symbolic link to private/tmp
```

Example

List all PDF Version 1.1 files:

```
file * | grep "PDF document, version 1.1"
```

---

find

find [*options*] [*pathnames*] [*conditions*]

An extremely useful command for finding particular groups of files (numerous examples follow this description). find descends the directory tree beginning at each *pathname* and locates files that meet the specified *conditions*. The default pathname is the current directory. The most useful conditions include -print (which is the default if no other expression is given), -name and -type (for general use), -exec and -size (for advanced users), and -mtime and -user (for administrators).

Conditions may be grouped by enclosing them in \(\) (escaped parentheses), negated with ! (use \! in the C shell), given as alternatives by separating them with -o, or repeated (adding restrictions to the match; usually only for -name, -type, -perm). Modification refers to editing of a file's contents. Change refers to modification, permission or ownership changes, and so on; therefore, for example, -ctime is more inclusive than -atime or -mtime.

Options

-d   Descend the directory tree, skipping directories and working on actual files first (and then the parent directories). Useful when files reside in unwritable directories (e.g., when using find with cpio).

-E   When used with the -regex or -iregex conditions, interpret the regular expression as extended instead of basic. For more information on regular expressions, see Chapter 20.

-H   If any of the pathnames given in the command line are symbolic links, consider the file information of the referenced files and not the links themselves. However, if the referenced file no longer exists, consider the link itself.

-L   If any of the files encountered during the search are symbolic links, consider the file information of the referenced files and not the links themselves. However, if the referenced file no longer exists, consider the link itself.

-P   If any of the files encountered during the search are symbolic links, consider the file information of the links themselves (the default behavior).

-s   Move through directory contents in alphabetical order.

-x   Don't scan filesystems (mounted volumes) other than the one that the command begins with.

-X   When used with the -xargs action, identify and skip any files whose names contain characters used by -xargs as delimiters (', ", \, space, tab and newline characters).

Conditions and actions

-amin +*n* | -*n* | *n*
> Find files last accessed more than *n* (+*n*), less than *n* (-*n*), or exactly *n* minutes ago. Note that find changes the access time of directories supplied as *pathnames*.

-anewer *file*
> Find files that were accessed after *file* was last modified.

-atime +*n* | -*n* | *n*
> Find files that were last accessed more than *n* (+*n*), less than *n* (-*n*), or exactly *n* days ago.

-cmin +*n* | -*n* | *n*
> Find files last changed more than *n* (+*n*), less than *n* (-*n*), or exactly *n* minutes ago. A change is anything that changes the directory entry for the file, such as a chmod.

-cnewer *file*
> Find files that were changed after they were last modified.

-ctime +*n* | -*n* | *n*
> Find files that were changed more than *n* (+*n*), less than *n* (-*n*), or exactly *n* days ago.

-delete +*n* | -*n* | *n*
> Delete found files and directories, operating as if the -d flag were being used as well (files first).

-empty
> Continue if file is empty. Applies to regular files and directories.

-exec *command* { } \;
> Run the Unix *command*, from the starting directory on each file matched by find (provided command executes successfully on that file; i.e., returns a 0 exit status). When command runs, the argument { } substitutes the current file. Follow the entire sequence with an escaped semicolon (\;).

-execdir *command* { } \;
> Same as -exec, but runs the Unix *command*, from the directory holding the file matched by find.

-flags [+ | -] *flags, notflags*
> Find files by their file flag settings (see chflags). To specify flags that are set, list them in *flags*. To specify flags that are not

set, list those flags (with their "no" prefixes) in *notflags*. To match files with at least all of the settings specified by both *flags* and *notflags*, use the - before *flags*. To match files with any of the flags specified in *flags* or *notflags*, use the + before *flags*. Without the - or the +, find will find only files with flag settings matching exactly with those in *flags* and *notflags*.

-fstype *fstype*
> Match files only on *type* filesystems. (Run sysctl vfs to view currently mounted filesystem types). You can also specify two pseudotypes, local and rdonly, allowing you to only match files on physically mounted volumes and read-only volumes, respectively.

-group *gname*
> Find files belonging to group *gname*. *gname* can be a group name or a group ID number.

-iname *pattern*
> A case-insensitive version of -name.

-inum *n*
> Find files whose inode number is *n*.

-ipath *pattern*
> A case-insensitive version of -path.

-iregex *pattern*
> A case-insensitive version of -regex.

-links *n*
> Find files having *n* links.

-ls Writes the list of found files to standard output as if provided by the ls -dgils command. Return true.

-maxdepth *num*
> Do not descend more than *num* levels of directories.

-mindepth *num*
> Begin applying tests and actions only at levels deeper than *num* levels.

-mmin +*n* | -*n* | *n*
> Find files last modified more than *n* (+*n*), less than *n* (-*n*), or exactly *n*.

-mtime +*n* | -*n* | *n*
> Find files that were last modified more than *n* (+*n*), less than *n* (-*n*), or exactly *n* days ago.

-name *pattern*
> Find files whose names match *pattern*. Filename metacharacters may be used but should be escaped or quoted.

-newer *file*
> Find files that have been modified more recently than *file*; similar to -mtime.

-nogroup
> The file's group ID does not correspond to any group.

-nouser
> The file's user ID does not correspond to any user.

-ok *command* { }\;
> Same as -exec, but prompts user to respond with y before *command* is executed.

-okdir *command* { } \;
> Same as -ok, but runs the Unix *command*, from the directory holding the file matched by find.

-path *pattern*
> Find files whose names match *pattern*. Expect full pathnames relative to the starting pathname (i.e., do not treat / or . specially).

-perm *nnn*
> Find files whose permission flags (e.g., rwx) match octal number *nnn* exactly (e.g., 664 matches -rw-rw-r--). Use a minus sign before *nnn* to make a "wildcard" match of any unspecified octal digit (e.g., -perm -600 matches -rw-******, where * can be any mode).

-print
> Print the matching files and directories, using their full pathnames. Return true.

-print0
> Print the matching files and directories, using their full pathnames and separating each with the ASCII NUL character. This allows find to properly work with the xargs utility and pathnames containing spaces, for example. Return true.

-prune
> Prevents find from descending into the directory found by the previous condition in the command line. Useful when used with an alternative condition (-o) that specifies which directories *must* be traversed. Return true.

-regex *pattern*
> Like -path but uses grep-style regular expressions instead of the shell-like globbing used in -name and -path.

-size *n*[c]
> Find files containing *n* blocks, or if c is specified, *n* characters long.

-type *c*
> Find files whose type is *c*. *c* can be b (block special file), c (character special file), d (directory), p (fifo or named pipe), l (symbolic link), s (socket), or f (plain file).

-user *user*
> Find files belonging to *user* (name or ID).

-xdev
> Search for files that reside only on the same filesystem as pathname.

Examples

List all files (and subdirectories) in your home directory:

```
find ~ -print
```

List all files named *chapter1* in the ~/*Documents* directory:

```
find /Documents -name chapter1 -print
```

List all files beginning with *memo* owned by *ann*:

```
find /Documents -name 'memo*' -user ann -print
```

Search the filesystem (begin at root) for manpage directories:

```
find / -type d -name 'man*' -print
```

Search the current directory, look for filenames that *don't* begin with a capital letter, and send them to the printer:

```
find . \! -name '[A-Z]*' -exec lpr { }\;
```

Find and compress files whose names *don't* end with *.gz*:

```
gzip `find . \! -name '*.gz' -print`
```

Remove all empty files on the system (prompting first):

```
find / -size 0 -ok rm { } \;
```

Search the system for files that were modified within the last two days (good candidates for backing up):

```
find / -mtime -2 -print
```

Recursively grep for a pattern down a directory tree:

```
find ~/Documents -print0 | xargs -0 grep '[Nn]utshell'
```

Search the system excluding all but the system volume:

```
find / -path '/Volumes/*' -prune -o -name "*.doc" -print
```

---

fixmount

```
fixmount [-q] [-a | -d | -e] [-v [-h hostname_or_IP] | -r | -A]
[-f] nfs_server
```

Communicates with the NFS mount daemon, *mountd*, to remove invalid records of client mounts from the NFS server. fixmount is run from the client, and when called without flags, prints the client's IP address to standard output if the server has a record of NFS mounts from the client.

mountd maintains records of which clients have mounted exports from the server, and writes the records to a file so that this information is retained through process or system restarts. (On most Unix platforms, this file is */etc/rmtab*; on Mac OS X, it's */var/db/ mountdtab*.) Over time, this file accumulates a lot of outdated information, primarily due to clients rebooting or otherwise dropping their mounts without properly informing the server, or changing their hostnames.

The primary purpose of fixmount is to clear out the bogus entries from the file kept by *mountd*. On most Unix systems, it does this by comparing the current set of mounts on the client, as listed in */etc/ mtab*, to the server's list of mounts from the client, and asking the server's *mountd* to remove any entries that don't match up.

However, a Mac OS X system keeps a current list of mounts in the kernel, and doesn't use */etc/mtab*. Therefore, when fixmount checks this file and finds it empty (or nonexistent), it perceives all of the server's entries as bogus, even those that do match up to current mounts on the client. This makes fixmount, at least as currently implemented, to be of very limited utility on Mac OS X.

Options

-a   Lists mounts from the client in the form *IP_addr:pathname*. This is similar to showmount -a, but limited to information about the client on which fixmount is run.

-A   Removes all of the entries for the client from the server's */var/db/mountdtab*.

-d   Lists exports that are mounted on the client, instead of the client's IP address. This is similar to showmount -d, but limited to information about the client on which fixmount is run.

-e   Prints the server's list of NFS exports to standard output. This is the same as showmount -e.

-f   Forces all entries for the client to be interpreted as bogus. This makes -f -r equivalent to -A. On a Mac OS X client, it's as if this flag is always set.

-h   Communicates with the server's *mountd* as if the client's hostname or IP address were that given by the argument to this option. This is useful when the client has changed its hostname or IP address, but the server retains invalid entries with the old information.

-q   Minimizes output from error messages.

-r   Removes bogus entries for the client from the server's */var/db/mountdtab*.

-v   Runs the verification procedure to determine the list of bogus entries for the client (which is printed to standard output), but doesn't actually remove anything from the server's */var/db/mountdtab*.

---

fixPrecomps

```
fixPrecomps -help
fixPrecomps [-checkOnly] [-force] [-relroot directory] [-all |
-precompsList filename] [-precomps filename] [-find_all_
precomps] [-gcc2 | -gcc3all] [-skipIfMissing] [-output
directory] [-precompFlags flag]
```

Compiles header files to improve performance for programs including them. When invoked without arguments, fixPrecomps reads any files in */System/Library/SystemResources/PrecompLists* in alphanumeric order by filename. Normally this includes *phase1.precompList* and *phase2.precompList*. These files are expected to consist of lists of precompiled header filenames to generate. fixPrecomps then runs cc -precomp on the ordinary header files where the precompiled headers are either out of date (i.e., have modification times less recent than the ordinary headers) or nonexistent.

The headers listed in the precompList files have filename extensions of either *.p* or *.pp*. fixPrecomps finds ordinary headers with the same base filenames but extensions of *.h*. The *.p* headers are compiled with GCC Version 2 for use with C and Objective-C programs, while the *.pp* headers are compiled with GCC Version 2 for C++ and Objective-C++ programs. By default, fixPrecomps compiles headers with GCC Version 3, in which case C/Objective-C precompiled header filenames end in *-gcc3.p*, and C++/Objective-C++ precompiled header filenames end in *-gcc3.pp*.

Options

-all

>   Uses all files contained in */System/Library/SystemResources/PrecompLists*. This is the default.

-checkOnly

>   For each header file listed in the *precompList* files, prints a status message to standard output indicating whether the precompiled header exists and is up to date with the ordinary header.

-find_all_precomps

>   Requires specification of -all, -precompList, or -precomps, but otherwise doesn't appear to do anything.

-force

>   Produces precompiled headers even if they're up to date. Using this flag causes the -checkOnly flag to be ignored.

-gcc2

>   Applies the command to GCC Version 2 C/Objective-C (*.p*) and C++/Objective-C++ (*.pp*) precompiled headers.

-gcc3all

>   Applies the command to GCC Version 3 C++/Objective-C++ (-gcc3.pp) precompiled headers, as well as to those for C/Objective-C (-gcc3.p).

-help

>   Prints a usage statement to standard error.

-output

>   Checks for and creates precompiled headers in locations relative to the specified directory. Intermediate directories must already exist or compilation will fail.

-precompFlags

>   Specifies additional cc command-line flags to use when compiling headers.

-precompList

>   Uses only the *precompList* files specified.

-precomps

>   Specifies a list of precompiled headers to check or create.

-relroot

Looks for */System/Library/SystemResources/PrecompLists* relative to the specified directory. The default is /.

-skipIfMissing

Compiles precompiled headers if they're out of date, but not if they don't exist. Using this flag causes the -checkOnly flag to be ignored.

FixupResource-Forks

FixupResourceForks [-nodelete] [-nosetinfo] [-q[uiet]] *pathname*

Recombines the resource fork and HFS metadata split out into a separate file (named *._filename*) with the file's data fork (in a file named *filename*), resulting in a single multiforked file (named *filename*) with HFS attributes. As such, this only works on HFS and HFS+ volumes. It reverses the effect of running SplitForks.

FixupResourceForks does a recursive descent into the directory specified by *pathname*, working on every file within it.

Options

-nodelete

Prevents deletion of *._filename* after recombination with *filename*.

-nosetinfo

Disables setting of HFS attributes on the recombined files.

-quiet

Suppresses printing the name of each recombined file to standard output.

---

fmt

fmt [*goal* [*maximum*]] [*files*]

Converts text to specified width by filling lines and removing newlines. Width is specified as being close to *goal* characters, but not over *maximum* characters wide (65 and 75 characters by default). Concatenate files on the command line, or read text from standard input if no file is specified. By default, preserve blank lines, spacing, and indentation. fmt attempts to break lines at the end of sentences and to avoid breaking lines after a sentence's first word or before its last.

---

fold

fold [*option*] [*files*]

Breaks the lines of the named *files* so they are no wider than the specified width (default is 80). fold breaks lines exactly at the specified width, even in the middle of a word. Reads from standard input when given - as a file.

Options

-b, --bytes

Count bytes, not columns (i.e., consider tabs, backspaces, and carriage returns to be one column).

-s, --spaces
    Break at spaces only, if possible.

-w, --width *width*
    Set the maximum line width to *width*. Default is 80.

---

fsck

fsck [-l *num_procs*] [-b *block_num*] [-m *mode*] [-c { 0 | 1 | 2 | 3 }] [-p | -n | -y] *device*

Performs consistency checks of UFS volumes, and attempts to fix any inconsistencies found.

Options

-b   Specifies an alternate super block for the filesystem.

-c   Converts the filesystem to the specified version level. See the fsck manpage for details.

-l   Limits the number of parallel fsck processes. Defaults to the number of disks.

-m   Specifies the permissions of the *lost+found* directory, where files that have become detached from their place in the directory hierarchy due to filesystem corruption can be located. The argument is an octal mode, as described in the chmod manpage. The default is 1777.

-n   Automatically answers "no" whenever fsck asks to resolve an inconsistency.

-p   Runs in preening mode, in which only purely innocuous inconsistencies are resolved.

-y   Automatically answers "yes" whenever fsck asks to resolve an inconsistency.

device
    The volume's device filename, e.g., */dev/disk1s2*.

---

fsck_msdos

fsck_msdos { -q | -p | [-n | -y] } *device*

Performs consistency checks of FAT volumes, and attempts to fix any inconsistencies found.

Options

-n   Automatically answers "no" whenever fsck_msdos asks to resolve an inconsistency.

-p   Runs in preening mode, in which only purely innocuous inconsistencies are resolved.

-q   Checks the filesystem but does not resolve any inconsistencies. Prints filesystem status to standard output.

-y   Automatically answers "yes" whenever fsck_msdos asks to resolve an inconsistency.

device
    The volume's device filename, e.g., */dev/disk1s2*.

fs_usage　　fs_usage [*options*] [*proccess*]

Shows a continuous display of filesystem-related system calls and page faults. You must run fs_usage as root. By default, it ignores anything originating from fs_usage, Terminal, telnetd, sshd, rlogind, tcsh, csh, or sh, but shows all other system processes. To have fs_usage track only specific processes, specify those process names or IDs (pids) in *processes*.

Options

-e [*processes*]
　　Exclude from tracking those processes specified in *processes*. If no processes are given, exclude only the current *fs_usage* process.

-w　　Display in a more detailed, wider format. Lines longer than the window width will be wrapped.

fsck_hfs　　fsck_hfs -u
　　fsck_hfs [-d] [-r] {-q | -p | [-n | -y]} *device*

Performs a consistency check of HFS and HFS+ volumes, and attempts to fix any inconsistencies found.

Options

-d　　Enables debugging output.

-f　　Forces check even if the volume is marked as clean.

-n　　Automatically answers "no" whenever *fsck_hfs* asks to resolve an inconsistency.

-p　　Runs in preening mode, in which only purely innocuous inconsistencies are resolved.

-q　　Checks the filesystem but does not resolve any inconsistencies. Returns filesystem status of clean, dirty, or failure to standard error.

-r　　Causes a rebuild of the volume's catalog btree to occur.

-u　　Prints a usage statement to standard output.

-y　　Automatically answers "yes" whenever *fsck_hfs* asks to resolve an inconsistency.

device
　　The volume's device filename, e.g., */dev/disk1s2*.

fstat　　fstat [*options*] [*files*]

Displays a list of open files and their status. By default, fstat lists all open files on the system. If any pathnames are specified in *files*, however, only those files are listed.

Options

-f [*pathname*]

> List open files residing only on the same filesystem as *pathname*, or if *pathname* is not specified, the current working directory.

-M *pathname*

> Extract values for the name list from core file *pathname* instead of */dev/kmem*, the default.

-N *pathname*

> Extract the name list from kernel file *pathname* instead of */mach_kernel*, the default.

-n Display data numerically. For filesystems, show the device number instead of mount point. For special files, show the device number instead of its */dev* filename. For regular files, show permissions in octal instead of symbolic format.

-p *pid*

> List only those files opened by the process whose ID is specified in *pid*.

-u *username*

> List only those files opened by the user *username*.

-v Be verbose.

---

ftp

ftp [*options*] [*hostname*]

Transfers files to and from remote network site *hostname*. ftp prompts the user for a command. Type **help** to see a list of known commands, and use the help command to view help on a specific command.

The *ftp* client included with Mac OS X supports auto-fetch, which allows you to perform a download with a single command line. To auto-fetch a file, supply its location as an argument to ftp in one of several formats:

- ftp [*user@*]*host*:[*path*][/]
- ftp [ftp://[*user*[:*password*]@]*host*[:*port*]/*path*[/]]
- ftp [http://[*user*[:*password*]@]*host*[:*port*]/*path*]

Options

-A Force active mode for use with older servers.

-a Perform anonymous login automatically.

-d Enable debugging.

-e Disable command-line editing.

-f Performs a forced reload of the cache. Useful when transferring through proxies.

-g Disable filename globbing.

-i Turn off interactive prompting.

-n No autologin upon initial connection.

-o *pathname*
> Save file as *pathname* when auto-fetching.

-p   Enable passive mode (the default).

-P *port*
> Specify alternate *port* number.

-r *wait*
> Attempt to connect again after *wait* seconds if initial attempt fails.

-R   When auto-fetching, resume incomplete transfers (if not transferring through a proxy).

-t   Enable packet tracing.

-T *direction, maximum [,increment]*
> Throttle transfer rates by specifying *direction* of transfer, *maximum* transfer speed in bytes/second, and an *increment* value that allows changing *maximum* on the fly. Direction can be get for incoming transfers, put for outgoing transfers, and all for both.

-u *url file [...]*
> Upload *file* to *url* from the command line.

-v   Verbose. Show all responses from remote server.

-V   Disable verbose.

---

gcc_select

```
gcc_select [-v | --version] [-nc | --no-color] [-h | --help]
gcc_select [-v | --version] [-nc | --no-color] [-n] [-force]
[-root] { 2 | 3 }
```

Sets the default major version of GCC (either 2 or 3) by creating various symlinks for compiler tools, libraries, and headers. With no arguments (or with just -v), the current default version is printed to standard output.

Options

-force
> Recreates symlinks for the specified version, even if it is already the current default version.

-h
--help
> Prints a usage statement to standard output.

-n   Prints the list of commands that would be executed to standard output, but does not actually execute them.

-nc
--no-color
> Disables color output.

-root
> Disables the initial check for root access before executing commands.

-v
-version
> Prints the version of gcc_select to standard output.

GetFileInfo   `GetFileInfo [options] pathname`

Displays HFS+ file attributes (metadata) of file *pathname*. If you specify no options, GetFileInfo will show all of the file's attributes. GetFileInfo is installed with the Developer Tools into */Developer/Tools*. Since this directory isn't in the shell's search path by default, you might to need to specify GetFileInfo's pathname to invoke it. See also SetFile.

Options

`-a[attribute]`

Display the settings for those attributes that toggle on or off (sometimes called "Finder flags"). If *attribute* is empty, the settings of all attributes are displayed as a series of letters. If the letter is shown in uppercase, that attribute is on (its bit is set). If the letter is shown in lowercase, that attribute is off. To view the setting for a single attribute (either 1 for on or 0 for off) specify that attribute by its letter in *attribute*. Refer to the following table for the specific attributes:

Attribute	Set | Unset	Meaning
Alias	A | a	File is/isn't an alias.
Bundle	B | b	File has/hasn't bundle resource.
Custom Icon	C | c	File has/hasn't a custom icon.
Desktop Item	D | d	File is/isn't on the desktop.
Extension	E | e	Filename extension is/isn't hidden.
Inited	I | i	File is/isn't inited.
Locked	L | l	File is/isn't locked.
Shared	M | m	Multiple users can/can't run a file at once (applies to application files).
INIT	N | n	File has/hasn't INIT resource .
System	S | s	File is/isn't a system file (locks name).
Stationary	T | t	File is/isn't a stationary file.
Invisible	V | v	File is/isn't invisible to Finder.

`-c` Display the file's 4-character creator code.

`-d` Display the file's creation date.

`-m` Display the file's modification date.

`-t` Display the file's 4-character type code.

Examples

Display all toggled attributes:

    /Developer/Tools/GetFileInfo -a Takashi&Junichi.jpg

Display only the locked setting:

    /Developer/Tools/GetFileInfo -aL Takashi&Junichi.jpg

gnutar

gnutar [*options*] [*tarfile*] [*other-files*]

Copies *files* to or restores *files* from an archive medium. An enhanced version of tar, gnutar is usually the preferred utility, since gnutar has the ability to handle much longer pathnames than tar, and gnutar's default omission of the leading slash in pathnames allows archives to be more easily opened on other systems. Note that until native drivers for tape drives exist for Mac OS X, gnutar cannot write to tape. Note also that gnutar does not preserve resource forks or HFS metadata when copying files that contain them.

gnutar is installed on Mac OS X as part of Apple's Developer Tools.

Function options

You must use exactly one of these, and it must come before any other options:

-A, --catenate, --concatenate
> Concatenate a second tar file on to the end of the first.

-c, --create
> Create a new archive.

-d, --diff, --compare
> Compare the files stored in *tarfile* with *other-files*. Report any differences, such as missing files, different sizes, different file attributes (such as permissions or modification time).

--delete
> Delete *other-files* from the archive.

-r, --append
> Append *other-files* to the end of an existing archive.

-t, --list
> Print the names of *other-files* if they are stored on the archive (if *other-files* are not specified, print names of all files).

-u, --update
> Add files if not in the archive or if modified.

-x, --extract, --get
> Extract *other-files* from an archive (if *other-files* are not specified, extract all files).

Options

--atime-preserve
> Preserve original access time on extracted files.

-b, --block-size=*n*
> Set block size to *n* 512 bytes.

-B, --read-full-blocks
> Form full blocks from short reads.

--backup
> If *tarfile* already exists, make a backup copy before overwriting.

-C, --directory=*directory*

    cd to *directory* before beginning tar operation.

--checkpoint

    List directory names encountered.

--exclude=*file*

    Remove *file* from any list of files.

-f *arch,* **--file=***filename*

    Store files in or extract files from archive *arch*. Note that *filename* may take the form *hostname:filename*. Also, since Mac OS X has no native tape drive support, gnutar will produce an error unless the -f option is used.

-F   *filename,*   **--info-script=***filename,*   **--new-volume-script=***filename*

    Run the script found in *filename* when tar reaches the end of a volume. This can be used to automatically swap volumes with a media changer. This option implies -M.

--force-loca*l*

    Interpret filenames in the form *hostname:filename* as local files.

-g, --listed-incremental

    Create new-style incremental backup.

-G, --incremental

    Create old-style incremental backup.

-h, --dereference

    Dereference symbolic links.

--help

    Display help information.

-i, --ignore-zeros

    Ignore zero-sized blocks (i.e., EOFs).

--ignore-failed-read

    Ignore unreadable files to be archived. Default behavior is to exit when encountering these.

-k, --keep-old-files

    When extracting files, do not overwrite files with similar names. Instead, print an error message.

-l, --one-file-system

    Do not archive files from other file systems.

-L, --tape-length=*length*

    Write a maximum of *length* 1024 bytes to each tape.

-m, --modification-time

    Do not restore file modification times; update them to the time of extraction.

-M, --multivolume

    Expect archive to multivolume. With -c, create such an archive.

--mode=*filemode*

    Set symbolic file mode (permissions) of added files to *filemode*.

-N *date*, --newer=*date*, --after-date=*date*
> Ignore files older than *date*.

--newer-mtime=*date*
> Ignore files whose modification times are older than *date*.

--no-recursion
> Do not descend into directories.

--null
> Allow filenames to be null-terminated with -T. Override -C.

--numeric-owner
> Use the ID numbers instead of names for file owners and groups.

-o, --old, old-archive, --portability
> Do not create archives with directory information that V7 tar would not be able to decode.

-O, --to-stdout
> Print extracted files on standard out.

--owner=*name*
> Set owner of added files to *name*.

-p, --preserver-permissions
> Keep ownership of extracted files same as that of original permissions.

-P, --absolute-paths
> Do not remove initial slashes (/) from input filenames.

--preserve
> Equivalent to invoking both the -p and -s options.

--posix
> Create archives that conform to POSIX standards. Such files are not readable by older versions of gnutar.

-R, --block-number
> Display record number with each file in the archive.

--record-size=*size*
> Set size of records to *size* bytes, with *size* a multiple of 512.

--recursive-unlink
> Remove directories and files prior to extracting over them.

--remove-files
> Remove originals after inclusion in archive.

--rsh-command=*command*
> Do not connect to remote host with rsh; instead, use *command*.

-s, --same-order, --preserve-order
> When extracting, sort filenames to correspond to the order in the archive.

-S, --sparse
> Treat short files specially and more efficiently.

--suffix=*c*
> If *tarfile* already exists, make a backup copy before over-writing. Name the backup file by appending the character *c* to *tarfile* instead of the default "~".

-T *filename*, --files-from *filename*
> Consult *filename* for files to extract or create.

--totals
> Print byte totals.

-U, --unlink-first
> Remove files prior to extracting over them.

--use-compress-program=*program*
> Compress archived files with *program*, or uncompress extracted files with *program*.

-v Verbose. Print filenames as they are added or extracted.

-V *name*, --label=*name*
> Name this volume *name*.

--version
> Show version of gnutar.

--volno-file=*n*
> Force decimal number *n* to be used in gnutar's prompt to change tapes.

-w, --interactive, --confirmation
> Wait for user confirmation (y) before taking any actions.

-W, --verify
> Check archive for corruption after creation.

-z Compress files with gzip before archiving them, or uncompress them with gunzip before extracting them.

-X *file*, --exclude *file*
> Consult *file* for list of files to exclude.

-z, --gzip, --ungzip
> Compress files with gzip before archiving them, or uncompress them with gunzip before extracting them.

-Z, --compress, --uncompress
> Compress files with compress before archiving them, or uncompress them with uncompress before extracting them.

[*drive*][*density*]
> Set drive (0–7) and storage density (1, m, or h, corresponding to low, medium, or high).

Examples

Create an archive of ~/*Documents* and ~/*Music* (c), show the command working (v), and write to an external volume, /*Volumes/Backups/archive.tar*, saving the previous backup file as *archive.tar~* (--backup):

```
gnutar cvf /Volumes/Backups/archive.tar --backup↵
~/Documents ~/Music
```

Extract only *~/Music* directory from *archive.tar* to the current directory:

gnutar xvf ~/archive.tar Music

Compare extracted files with those in the archive (d):

gnutar dvf ~/archive.tar Music

---

grep   grep [*options*] *pattern* [*files*]

Search one or more *files* for lines that match a regular expression *pattern*. Regular expressions are described in Chapter 20. Exit status is 0 if any lines match, 1 if none match, and 2 for errors. See also egrep and fgrep.

Options

-a, --text
> Don't suppress output lines with binary data; treat as text.

-A *num*, --after-context=*num*
> Print *num* lines of text that occur after the matching line.

-b, --byte-offset
> Print the byte offset within the input file before each line of output.

-B *num*, *--before-context=num*
> Print *num* lines of text that occur before the matching line.

--binary-files=*type*
> Treat binary files as specified. By default, grep treats binary files as such (*type* is binary). If a matching string is found within a binary file, grep reports only that the file matches; nothing is printed for nonmatching binary files. If *type* is without-match, grep assumes binary files don't match and skips them altogether. Same as -I. Using a *type* of text causes grep to treat binary files as text and print all matched lines. Same as -a.

-c, --count
> Print only a count of matched lines. With the -v or --invert-match option, count nonmatching lines.

-C*[num]*, --context=*[num]*, -*num*
> Print *num* lines of leading and trailing context. Default context is 2 lines.

-d *action*, --directories=*action*
> Define an *action* for processing directories. Possible actions are:

> read
>> Read directories like ordinary files (default).

> skip
>> Skip directories.

> recurse
>> Recursively read all files under each directory. Same as -r.

-e *pattern*, --regexp=*pattern*
> Search for *pattern*. Same as specifying a pattern as an argument, but useful in protecting patterns beginning with -.

-E, --extended-regexp
> Treat *pattern* as an extended regular expression. Same as using the egrep command.

-f *file*, --file=*file*
> Take a list of patterns from *file*, one per line.

-F *file*, --fixed-strings
> Treat *pattern* as a list of fixed strings. Same as using the egrep command.

-G *file*, --basic-regexp
> Treat *pattern* as a basic regular expression, the default behavior.

-h, --no-filename
> Print matched lines but not filenames (inverse of -1).

-H, --with-filename
> Print matched lines with filenames, the default behavior.

--help
> Display a help message.

-i, --ignore-case
> Ignore uppercase and lowercase distinctions.

-I   Skip binary files. Same as --binary-files=without-match.

-l, --files-with-matches
> List the names of files with matches but not individual matched lines; scanning per file stops on the first match.

-L, --files-without-match
> List files that contain no matching lines.

--mmap
> For possibly better performance, read input using the mmap system call, instead of read, the default. Can cause unexpected system behavior.

-n, --line-number
> Print lines and their line numbers.

-q, --quiet, --silent
> Suppress normal output in favor of quiet mode; the scanning stops on the first match.

-r, --recursive
> Recursively read all files under each directory. Same as -d recurse.

-s, --no-messages
> Suppress error messages about nonexistent or unreadable files.

-v, --revert-match
> Print all lines that don't match pattern.

-V, --version
> Print the version number and then exit.

-w, --word-regexp
> Match on whole words only. Words are divided by characters that are not letters, digits, or underscores.

-x, --line-regexp
> Print lines only if pattern matches the entire line.

-Z, --null
> Print the matching files using their full pathnames and separating each with the ASCII NUL character instead of the newline character. This allows grep to properly work with the xargs utility and pathnames that contain spaces, for example.

Examples

List the number of email messages from a specific domain:

```
grep -c '^From .*@mac\.com' mbox
```

List files that have at least one URL:

```
grep -Eil '*p:\/\/*' *
```

List files that don't contain *pattern*:

```
grep -c pattern files | grep :0
```

---

gunzip

gunzip [gzip *options*] [*files*]

Identical to gzip -d. Provided as a hard link to gzip. The -1 ... -9 and corresponding long-form options are not available with gunzip; all other gzip options are accepted. See gzip for more information.

---

gzcat

gzcat [gzip *options*] [*files*]

A link to gzip instead of using the name zcat, which preserves zcat's original link to compress. Its action is identical to gunzip -c. Also installed as zcat. See gzip for more information.

---

gzip

gzip [*options*] [*files*]
gunzip [*options*] [*files*]
zcat [*options*] [*files*]

Compresses specified files (or read from standard input) with Lempel-Ziv coding (LZ77). Rename compressed file to *filename.gz*; keep ownership modes and access/modification times. Ignore symbolic links. Uncompress with gunzip, which takes all of gzip's options, except those specified. zcat is identical to gunzip -c and takes the options -fhLV, described here. Files compressed with the compress command can be decompressed using these commands.

gzip does not preserve resource forks or HFS metadata when compressing files that contain them.

Options

-*n*, --fast, --best
> Regulate the speed of compression using the specified digit *n*, where -1 or --fast indicates the fastest compression method (less compression) and -9 or --best indicates the slowest compression method (most compression). The default compression level is -6.

`-c, --stdout, --to-stdout`
Print output to standard output, and do not change input files.

`-d, --decompress, --uncompress`
Same as gunzip.

`-f, --force`
Force compression. gzip normally prompts for permission to continue when the file has multiple links, its *.gz* version already exists, or it is reading compressed data to or from a terminal.

`-h --help`
Display a help screen and then exit.

`-l, --list`
Expects to be given compressed files as arguments. Files may be compressed by any of the following methods: gzip, deflate, compress, lzh, and pack. For each file, list uncompressed and compressed sizes (the latter being always -1 for files compressed by programs other than gzip), compression ratio, and uncompressed name. With -v, also print compression method, the 32-bit CRC of the uncompressed data, and the timestamp. With -N, look inside the file for the uncompressed name and timestamp.

`-L, --license`
Display the gzip license and quit.

`-n, --no-name`
When compressing, do not save the original filename and timestamp by default. When decompressing, do not restore the original filename if present, and do not restore the original timestamp if present. This option is the default when decompressing.

`-N, --name`
Default. Save original name and timestamp. When decompressing, restore original name and timestamp.

`-q, --quiet`
Print no warnings.

`-r, --recursive`
When given a directory as an argument, recursively compress or decompress files within it.

`-S suffix, --suffix suffix`
Append *.suffix*. Default is gz. A null suffix while decompressing causes gunzip to attempt to decompress all specified files, regardless of suffix.

`-t, --test`
Test compressed file integrity.

`-v, --verbose`
Print name and percent size reduction for each file.

`-V, --version`
Display the version number and compilation options.

halt

halt [*options*]

Prepares the system and then terminates all processes, usually ending with a hardware power-off. During preparation, all filesystem caches are flushed and running processes are sent SIGTERM followed by SIGTERM.

Options

-l Do not log the halt via syslog (i.e., mach_kernel: syncing disks...).

-n Do not flush filesystem caches. Should not be used indiscriminately.

-q The filesystem caches are flushed but the system is otherwise halted ungracefully. Should not be used indiscriminately.

-y Halts the system from a dial-up operation.

hdid

hdid -help
hdid *image_file* [*options*]

Loads disk images, attaches them to device nodes (files in */dev*), and signals Disk Arbitration to mount them into the directory hierarchy.

Option

hdid

    A synonym for hdiutil -attach, and takes the same set of options and arguments. See the hdid manpage for more details.

hdiutil

hdiutil *command* [*cmd-specific_args_and_opts*] [-quiet | -verbose | -debug] [-plist]

Essentially the command-line equivalent of the Disk Copy application, hdiutil manages disk images. The following list highlights some common uses, but the full set of commands (and associated arguments and options) is extensive, and will not be detailed here. See the hdiutil manpage or run hdiutil help for more information.

Options

attach

    Attaches a disk image to a device node and mounts it. As arguments, it takes the filename of a disk image and a possible list of options, some of which are:

    -help

        Prints a usage summary to standard output.

    -nomount

        Creates device nodes in */dev* and attaches the image or its partitions to them, but doesn't mount them.

`-readonly`

Disables write access to the mounted image.

`-shadow`

Passes modifications to the disk image through to a shadow image. Subsequent access to the modified data will be from the shadow, which allows effective read/write access to data on a disk image, which should not or cannot be modified. This option takes the filename of a shadow disk image as an argument, but defaults to the name of the attached image with a *.shadow* extension. The shadow image is created if it doesn't already exist.

`burn`

Burns a disk image to an optical disk (a writable CD or DVD). As arguments, it takes the filename of a disk image and a possible list of options, some of which are:

`-erase`

Erases an optical disk if the drive and media support erasure.

`-forceclose`

Closes the optical disk after burning the image, preventing any future burns to the disk.

`-fullerase`

Performs a sector-by-sector erasure of an optical disk if the drive and media support it.

`-noeject`

Disables ejection of the disk after burning.

`-optimizeimage`

Optimize the size of the image for burning, reducing the size of HFS and HFS+ volumes to the size of the data on them.

`create`

Creates a blank disk image. It takes the filename for the disk image as an argument. One of the following options is required to specify the size of the image:

`-megabytes`

Specifies the size of the image in megabytes. Takes an integer argument.

`-sectors`

Specifies the size of the image in 512-byte sectors. Takes an integer argument.

`-size`

Specifies the size of the image with a choice of unit. Takes an argument consisting of an integer concatenated with a letter, where the letter is b (for bytes), k (for kilobytes), m (for megabytes), g (for gigabytes), t (for terabytes), p (for petabytes), or e (for exabytes).

Finally, create can take a list of discretionary options, some of which are:

-fs

> Formats the disk image with a filesystem, the format being given as an argument to this option. Possible formats are HFS+, HFS, UFS, and MS-DOS. After the image is created, it's attached, formatted, and detached.

-stretch

> If creating an HFS+ filesystem, initializes it so that it can later be stretched with hdiutil resize. Takes an argument with the same format as the -size option, which determines the maximum size to which the filesystem can be stretched.

-volname

> Specifies the volume name for the image. Takes a string argument; the default volume name is *untitled*.

detach

> Unmounts an image or its partitions and detaches them from their device nodes. Takes a device name (e.g., disk1) as an argument.

eject

> Same as detach.

header

> Prints the disk image header to standard output. Takes the filename of a disk image as an argument.

help

> Prints an extensive usage summary to standard output.

imageinfo

> Prints information about a disk image or device to standard output, including properties (such as whether the image is compressed, encrypted, or partitioned), format, size, and checksum. As arguments, it takes a device name (e.g., /dev/disk1) or the filename of a disk image, and a possible list of options, some of which are:

-checksum

> Displays only the checksum.

-format

> Displays only the image format.

info

> Prints the version of the DiskImages framework to standard output, as well as information about mounted images (such as image filename, format, associated device node, mount point, and mounting user's identity).

mount

> Same as attach.

mountvol

Mounts a device into the filesystem hierarchy using Disk Arbitration (similar to diskutil mount). Takes a device name (e.g., disk1) as an argument. This can be used to complete the process of mounting a disk image after using hdiutil attach -nomount.

plugins

Prints information about plug-ins for the DiskImages framework to standard output.

pmap

Prints the partition map of a disk image or device to standard output. As arguments, it takes a device name (e.g., /dev/disk1) or the filename of a disk image, and a possible list of options.

testfilter

Tests whether a file is a valid disk image, and returns Yes or No to standard error.

unmount

Unmounts an image or its partitions without detaching them from their device nodes. Takes a device name (e.g., disk1) or a mount point as an argument.

-debug

Enables debugging output to standard error.

-plist

Displays output in XML property list format, if the command is capable of it.

-quiet

Minimizes output.

-verbose

Enables verbose output.

---

head

head [*options*] [*files*]

Prints the first few lines of one or more *files* (default is 10).

Options

-*n*   Print the first *n* lines of the file.

-n *n* Print the first *n* lines of the file.

Example

Display the first 20 lines of phone_list:

    head -20 phone_list

---

hfs.util

hfs.util { -m | -M } *device mount_point* { fixed | removable }
{ readonly | writable } { suid | nosuid } { dev | nodev }
hfs.util -p *device* { fixed | removable } { readonly |
writable }
hfs.util { -a | -k | -s | -u } *device*
hfs.util { -J | -U } *mount_point*

Mounts HFS and HFS+ filesystems into the directory hierarchy.

Options

-a   Enables (adopts) permissions on the volume, creating an entry for it in */var/db/volinfo.database* if one does not already exist. Unlike disktool -A or vsdbutil -a, this functions only on an unmounted volume.

-J   Enables journaling on the volume.

-k   Reads the disk's UUID key and prints it to standard output. Functions only on an unmounted volume.

-m   Mounts the device.

-M   Attempts to force the mount.

-p   Probes the device, and prints the volume name to standard output.

-s   Generates a new disk UUID key and sets it on the volume. Functions only on an unmounted volume.

-u   Unmounts the device. This function doesn't appear to work.

-U   Disables journaling on the volume.

device
> The disk device filename, e.g., disk0s5.

mount_point
> The directory on which the filesystem is mounted.

---

host

    host [options] host [server]
    host [options] domain [server]

Prints information about specified hosts or zones in DNS. Hosts may be IP addresses or hostnames; host converts IP addresses to hostnames by default and appends the local domain to hosts without a trailing dot. Default servers are determined in */etc/resolv.conf*. For more information about hosts and zones, try Chapters 1 and 2 of *DNS and BIND* (O'Reilly & Associates, Inc., 2001).

Options

-a   all, same as -t ANY.

-c *class*
> Search for specified resource record class (in[ternet], cs[net], ch[aos], hs/hesiod, or any). Default is in. The *chaos* and *csnet* classes, although defined in RFC1035, are rejected as invalid classes by the host command.

-d   Debugging mode. -dd is a more verbose version.

-l *domain*
> List all machines in *domain*.

-r   No recursion. Do not ask contacted server to query other servers, but require only the information that it has cached.

-s   Chase signatures back to parent key (DNSSEC).

-t *type*

Look for *type* entries in the resource record. Acceptable values for *type* are: a, ns, md, mf, cnames, soa, mb, mg, mr, null, wks, ptr, hinfo, minfo, mx, any, and * (careful, the shell loves those asterisks; be sure to escape them).

-v

Verbose. Include all fields from the resource record, even time-to-live and class, as well as "additional information" and "authoritative nameservers" (provided by the remote nameserver).

-w

Wait forever for a response from a queried server.

hostinfo

hostinfo

Outputs system hardware and OS specifications and statistics, as in this example:

```
Mach kernel version:
    Darwin Kernel Version 6.1:
Fri Sep  6 23:24:34 PDT 2002; root:xnu/xnu-344.2.obj~2/
RELEASE_PPC
Kernel configured for up to 2 processors.
1 processor is physically available.
Processor type: ppc7400 (PowerPC 7400)
Processor active: 0
Primary memory available: 512.00 megabytes.
Default processor set: 61 tasks, 142 threads, 1 processors
Load average: 1.62, Mach factor: 0.43
```

hostname

hostname [*option*] [*nameofhost*]

Sets or prints name of current host system. A privileged user can temporarily set the hostname with the *nameofhost* argument. Edit */etc/hostconfig* to make a permanent change.

Option

-s, --short

Trim domain information from the printed name.

id

id [*options*] [*username*]

Displays information about yourself or another user: user ID, group ID, effective user ID and group ID if relevant, and additional group IDs.

Options

-g   Print group ID only.

-G   Print supplementary groups only.

-n   With -u, -g, or -G, print user or group name, not number.

-p   Print the output in a more easily read format. Not used with other options.

-r   With -u, -g, or -G, print real, not effective, user ID or group ID.

-u   Print user ID only.

---

ifconfig

ifconfig [*options*] [*interface address_family address parameters*]

Assigns an address to a network interface and/or configure network interface parameters. ifconfig is typically used at boot time to define the network address of each interface on a machine. It may be used at a later time to redefine an interface's address or other parameters. Without arguments, ifconfig displays the current configuration for a network interface. Used with a single *interface* argument, ifconfig displays that particular interface's current configuration.

Display Options

-a   Display information about all configured interfaces. This is the default when no options and arguments are specified.

-d   Display information about interfaces that are down.

-L   Display address lifetime for IPv6 addresses.

-l   Display all configured interfaces names only.

-m   Display all supported media for specified interface.

-u   Display information about interfaces that are up.

Arguments

interface
String of the form *name unit*—for example, en0.

address
Hostname or address in "dotted-octet" notation—for example, 172.24.30.12.

address_family
Since an interface may receive transmissions in differing protocols, each of which may require separate naming schemes, you can specify the *address_family* to change the interpretation of the remaining parameters. You may specify inet (the default; for TCP/IP) or inet6.

dest_address
Specify the address of the correspondent on the other end of a point-to-point link.

The following parameters may be set with ifconfig:

add/delete
[-]alias
Create/delete an additional/existing network address for this interface.

anycast
Specify address as an anycast address (inet6 only).

[-]arp

Enable/disable use of the Address Resolution Protocol in mapping between network-level addresses and link-level addresses.

broadcast

Specify address to use to represent broadcasts to the network (inet only.). The default is the address with a host part of all 1s (i.e., x.y.z.255 for a class C network).

create/plumb *and* **destroy/unplumb**

These commands perform operations related to interface cloning. However, Mac OS X itself does not support interface cloning. Therefore, the manpage descriptions of these parameters are of historical significance only.

[-]debug

Enable/disable driver-dependent debugging code.

down

Mark an interface "down" (unresponsive).

ether

Same as lladdr.

[-]link[0-2]

Enable/disable special link level processing modes. Refer to driver manpage for more information.

lladdr *addr*

Set the link-level *addr*ess on an interface as a set of colon-separated hex digits—for example, 00:03:93:67:7a:4a.

media *type*

Set the interface media type to *type*—for example, 10base5/AUI.

[-]mediaopt *opts*

Comma separated list of media options for a supported media selection system.

metric *n*

Set routing metric of the interface to *n*. Default is 0.

mtu *num*

Set the interface's Maximum Transfer Unit (MTU) to *mtu*.

netmask *mask*

Specify how much of the address to reserve for subdividing networks into subnetworks ((inet only). *mask* can be specified as a single hexadecimal number with a leading 0x, with a dot notation Internet address, or with a pseudonetwork name listed in the network table */etc/networks*.

up

Mark an interface "up" (ready to send and receive).

info   info [*options*] [*topics*]

Info files are arranged in a hierarchy and can contain menus for subtopics. When entered without options, the command displays the top-level info file (usually */usr/local/info/dir*). When *topics* are specified, find a subtopic by choosing the first *topic* from the menu in the top-level info file, the next *topic* from the new menu specified by the first *topic*, and so on. The initial display can also be controlled by the -f and -n options.

Options

-d *directories*, --directory *directories*
> Search *directories*, a colon-separated list, for info files. If this option is not specified, use the INFOPATH environment variable or the default directory (usually */usr/local/info*).

--dribble *file*
> Store each keystroke in *file*, which can be used in a future session with the --restore option to return to this place in info.

-f *file*, --file *file*
> Display specified info *file*.

-h, --help
> Display brief help.

--index-search=*string*
> Go to node pointed to by index entry *string*.

-n *node*, --node *node*
> Display specified *node* in the info file.

-O, --show-options, --usage
> Don't remove ANSI escapes from manpages.

-o *file*, --output *file*
> Copy output to *file* instead of displaying it at the screen.

-R, --raw-escapes
> Don't remove ANSI escapes from manpages.

--restore=*file*
> When starting, execute keystrokes in *file*.

--subnodes
> Display subtopics recursively.

--version
> Display version.

--vi-keys
> Use vi-like key bindings.

install   install [*options*] *file1* *file2*
                                install [*options*] *files* *directory*
                                install -d [*options*] [*file*] *directory*

Used primarily in makefiles to update files. install copies files into user-specified directories. Similar to cp, with additional functionality regarding inode-based information like uid, gid, mode, flags, etc.

Options

-b Create backup copies of existing target files by renaming existing *file* as *file.old*. See -B for specifying extension name (i.e., default is *.old*)

-B *suffix*
Use *suffix* as a filename extension when -b is in effect.

-c Copy the specified file(s). This is the default behavior of the install command.

-C Copy the file. Don't change the modification timestamp if the target exists and is the same as the source.

-d Create any missing directories.

-f *flags*
Set the file flags of the target file(s). Flags are a comma-separated list of keywords. See the chflags(1) manpage for further details.

-g *gid or groupname*
Set group ID of target file to *group* (privileged users only or user is member of specified group).

-m *mode*
Set the mode of the target files to *mode*. The default is 0755, or rwxr-xr-x.

-M Don't use mmap(2).

-o *uid or username*
Set ownership to *uid or username* or, if unspecified, to root (privileged users only).

-s Strip binaries to enhance portability.

-S Safe copy. The source file is copied to temp file and then renamed. The default behavior is to first unlink the existing target before the source is copied.

-v Verbose. Install will print symbolic representations for each copy action.

---

installer

installer *options* -pkg *pkgpath* -target *volpath*

Installs standard Mac OS X package files from the command line. install is an alternative to the *Installer.app* GUI application.

Options

-allow
Install over an existing version of the software, even when the version being installed is older. The package must have special support for this option.

-config
Send the list of installer command-line arguments, formatted in *plist* XML, to standard output without performing the installation. If you direct the output to a file, you can use that file with the -file option to perform multiple identical installations.

-dumplog
> Log installer's messages to standard output.

-file *pathname*
> Read arguments from file *pathname*. The file needs to be a product of the -config option, or a file of the same format.

-help
> Display a help screen and then exit.

-lang *language*
> Identify *language* (specified in ISO format) as the default language of the target system. Used only with OS installations.

-pkginfo
> List the packages to be installed without performing the installation. Metapackages contain multiple subpackages; this option will list those subpackages as well.

-plist
> When used with -pkginfo and -volinfo, format the output into plist XML.

-verbose
> Print more package and volume information. Used with -pkginfo and -volinfo.

-verboseR
> Print more package and volume information, formatted for parsing. Used with -pkginfo and -volinfo.

-vers
> Display the version of installer and then exit.

-volinfo
> List the volumes mounted at the time the command is run without performing the installation.

Examples

Only list available packages and target volumes:

> % **installer -volinfo -pkginfo -pkg newpkg.pkg**

Install newpkg.pkg on the current system volume:

> % **installer -pkg newpkg.pkg -target /**

Install newpkg.pkg, using arguments from installfile:

> % **installer -pkg newpkg.pkg -file installfile**

---

ipconfig

```
ipconfig getifaddr interface
ipconfig getoption { interface | "" } { option_name | option_
code }
ipconfig getpacket interface
ipconfig ifcount
ipconfig set interface { BOOTP | DHCP }
ipconfig set interface { INFORM | MANUAL } IP_addr netmask
ipconfig waitall
```

Interacts with the IP Configuration Agent of configd to manage network configuration changes.

Options

getifaddr
> Prints the specified network interface's IP address to standard output.

getoption
> Prints the value of the specified DHCP option to standard output. If *interface* is specified, the option is interface-specific. If empty quotes are used instead, the option is global. Option names and numeric codes are DHCP-standard (such as host_ name, domain_name, netinfo_server_ address, etc.).

getpacket
> Prints DHCP-transaction packets to standard output.

ifcount
> Prints the number of network interfaces to standard output.

set
> Sets the method by which the specified network interface is assigned an IP address. Using BOOTP or DHCP causes the system to attempt to contact a server of the appropriate type to obtain IP configuration information. Using INFORM sets the IP address locally, but initiates a DHCP request to obtain additional IP configuration information (DNS servers, default gateway, etc.). Using MANUAL indicates that all IP configuration information is set locally.

waitall
> Sets the configurations of all network interfaces according to the specifications in */etc/iftab*.

---

join

join [*options*] *file1* *file2*

Joins the common lines of sorted *file1* and sorted *file2*. Reads standard input if *file1* is -. The output contains the common field and the remainder of each line from *file1* and *file2*. In the options below, *n* can be 1 or 2, referring to *file1* or *file2*.

Options

-a[*n*]
> List unpairable lines in file *n* (or both if *n* is omitted).

-e *s*
> Replace any empty output field with the string *s*.

-j*n* *m*
> Join on the *m*th field of file *n* (or both files if *n* is omitted).

-o *n.m*
> Each output line contains fields specified by file number *n* and field number *m*. The common field is suppressed unless requested.

-t*c*
> Use character *c* as field separator for input and output.

-v *n*
> Print only the unpairable lines in file *n*. With both -v 1 and -v 2, all unpairable lines are printed.

-1 *m*
> Join on field *m* of file 1. Fields start with 1.

-2 *m*
> Join on field *m* of file 2. Fields start with 1.

Examples

Assuming the following input files:

```
% cat score
olga     81      91
rene     82      92
zack     83      93
% cat grade
olga     B       A
rene     B       A
```

List scores followed by grades, including unmatched lines:

```
% join -a1 score grade
olga 81 91 B A
rene 82 92 B A
zack 83 93
```

Pair each score with its grade:

```
% join -o 1.1 1.2 2.2 1.3 2.3 score grade
olga 81 B 91 A
rene 82 B 92 A
```

---

jot

jot [*option*] [*repetitions* [*begin* [*end* [*seed*]]]]

Generates a list of random or sequential data *repetitions* lines long. Sequential lists start from the number given in the *begin* value and finish with the *end* value. Random data is generated using the seed value *seed*.

Options

-r Generate random data. jot generates sequential data by default.

-b *word*
> Print *word* only.

-w *word*
> Print *word* along with the other generated data.

-c Print ASCII character equivalents instead of numbers.

-s *string*
> Print the list separated by *string* instead of by newlines, the default.

-n Don't print a trailing newline character at the end of the list.

-p *precision*
> Print the data using the number of digits or characters specified by the number *precision*.

Examples

Return a list of sequentially numbered names:

```
% jot -w box- 20 1 20
```

Return the ASCII values of numbers 43 to 52:

```
% jot -c 10 43 52
```

---

kdump

kdump [*option*]

Decode and display a kernel trace file produced by ktrace. By default, kdump processes any ktrace.out file found in the current working directory.

Options

-d   Show all numbers in decimal format.

-f *tracefile*
    Process the file *tracefile* instead of ktrace.out.

-l   Continue to read and display the trace file as new trace data are added.

-m *maxdata*
    When decoding I/O data, show no more than *maxdata* bytes.

-n   Don't decode completly; display some values, such as those from ioctl and errno, in their raw format.

-R   With each entry, show time since previous entry (relative timestamp).

-t *tracepoints*
    Show only the traces specified in *tracepoints* (see kdump's -t option).

-T   With each entry, show seconds since the epoch (absolute timestamp).

---

kill

kill [*option*] *IDs*

This is the /bin/kill command; there is also a shell command of the same name that works similarly. Send a signal to terminate one or more process *IDs*. You must own the process or be a privileged user. If no signal is specified, TERM is sent.

Options

-l   List the signal names. (Used by itself.)

-s *signal*
    Send signal *signal* to the given process or process group. The signal number (from /usr/include/sys/signal.h) or name (from kill -l). With a signal number of 9, the kill is absolute.

-*signal*
    Send signal *signal* to the given process or process group.

killall
killall [*options*] *procname* …

Kills processes specified by command or pattern match. The default signal sent by killall is TERM but may be specified on the command line. killall assembles and executes a set of kill commands to accomplish its task.

Options

-d   Prints diagnostic info only about targeted processes; does not send signal.

-l   Lists known signal names.

-m   Interprets the *procname* as a case-insensitive regular expression for selecting real process names to send a signal to.

-s   Shows the kill command lines that would be used to send the signal but do not actually execute them.

-*signal*
   Sends specified *signal* to process. *signal* may be a name (see -l option) or number.

-t *tty*
   May be used to further select only those processes attached to the specified *tty* (procname ∩ tty), or to select all processes attached to the specified *tty* (i.e., no *procname* specified).

-u *user*
   May be used to further select only those processes owned by the specified *user* (procname ∩ user), or to select all processes owned by the specified *user* (i.e., no *procname* specified).

-c *procname*
   Use with the -t or -u options to limit processes that sent a signal to those matching *procname*.

-v   Verbose output. Print the kill command lines that are used to send the signal.

ktrace
ktrace [*options*] *command*

Trace kernel operations for process *command* and log data to file ktrace.out in the current working directory. The tracing will continue until you either exit *command* or clear the trace points (with the -c or -C options). Use kdump to view the trace log.

Options

-a   Append new data to the trace file instead of overwriting it.

-C   Stop tracing of all processess run by a user invoking ktrace. If this option is used with superuser privileges, the tracing of all processes will be stopped.

-c   Stop tracing of process *command*.

-d   Also trace any current child processes of the specified process.

-f *file*
   Log to *file* instead of *ktrace.out*, the default.

-g *pgid*
  Toggle tracing of all processes that are part of the process group *pgid*.

-i Also trace any future child processes of the specified process.

-p *pid*
  Toggle tracing of process *pid*.

-t *tracepoints*
  Trace only kernel operations specified in *tracepoints*. Use the appropriate letters from this list to indicate which type of operation(s) to trace:

  c System calls

  i I/O

  n Name translations

  s Signal processing

  u Userland operations

  w Context switches

Examples

Trace only system calls and I/O on process 489:

  ktrace -t ci -p 489

Run the atlookup command and trace all of its kernel operations:

  ktrace atlookup

Turn off tracing for all user processes:

  ktrace -C

---

last

last [*options*] [*users*]

Lists information about current and previous login sessions, including username and duration of each session. Sessions are listed one per line, newest first. To view only sessions from select users, specify those usernames in *users*.

Options

-f *file*
  Read from log *file* instead of */var/log/wtemp*, the default.

-h *host*
  Report only on those sessions initiated from machine *host*.

-*n* Display only the first *n* lines of output.

-t *tty*
  Report only on those sessions initiated from device *tty*. To list Aqua logins, for example, specify console for *tty*.

---

leave

leave [[+]*time*]

Sets a time to be reminded that it's "time to leave." leave will remind you with a message at the command prompt five minutes, and then one minute, before the specified time. You'll be reminded again at the specified time and then every minute after until you either log out of that shell session, or kill leave with kill -9 *pid.* Specify the time in the *hhmm* format. Use + before *time* to specify a relative time, hours, and minutes from the current time. Without any arguments, leave will prompt you to enter a time in the same format.

less

less [*options*] [*filename*]

less is a program for paging through files or other output. It was written in reaction to the perceived primitiveness of more (hence its name). Some commands may be preceded by a number.

Options

-[z]*num*
> Set number of lines to scroll to *num*. Default is one screenful. A negative *num* sets the number to *num* lines less than the current number.

+[+]*command*
> Run *command* on startup. If *command* is a number, jump to that line. The option ++ applies this command to each file in the command-line list.

-? Print help screen. Ignore all other options; do not page through file.

-a When searching, begin after last line displayed. (Default is to search from second line displayed.)

-b*buffers*
> Use *buffers* buffers for each file (default is 10). Buffers are 1 kilobyte in size.

-c Redraw screen from top, not bottom.

-d Suppress dumb-terminal error messages.

-e Automatically exit after reaching EOF twice.

-f Force opening of directories and devices; do not print warning when opening binaries.

-g Highlight only string found by past search command, not all matching strings.

-h*num*
> Never scroll backward more than *num* lines at once.

-i Make searches case-insensitive, unless the search string contains uppercase letters.

-j*num*
> Position target line on line *num* of screen. Target line can be the result of a search or a jump. Count lines beginning from 1 (top line). A negative *num* is counted back from bottom of screen.

-k*file*
> Read *file* to define special key bindings.

-m Display a more-like prompt, including percent of file read.

-n   Do not calculate line numbers. Affects -m and -M options and = and v commands (disables passing of line number to editor).

-o*file*

When input is from a pipe, copy output to *file* as well as to screen. (Prompt for overwrite authority if *file* exists.)

-p*pattern*

At startup, search for first occurrence of *pattern*.

m   Set medium prompt (specified by -m).

M   Set long prompt (specified by -M).

=   Set message printed by = command.

-q   Disable ringing of bell on attempts to scroll past EOF or before beginning of file. Attempt to use visual bell instead.

-r   Display "raw" control characters, instead of using ^x notation. Sometimes leads to display problems.

-s   Print successive blank lines as one line.

-t*tag*

Edit file containing *tag*. Consult *./tags* (constructed by ctags).

-u   Treat backspaces and carriage returns as printable input.

-w   Print lines after EOF as blanks instead of tildes (~).

-x*n*   Set tab stops to every *n* characters. Default is 8.

-y*n*   Never scroll forward more than *n* lines at once.

-B   Do not automatically allocate buffers for data read from a pipe. If -b specifies a number of buffers, allocate that many. If necessary, allow information from previous screens to be lost.

-C   Redraw screen by clearing it and then redrawing from top.

-E   Automatically exit after reaching EOF once.

-G   Never highlight matching search strings.

-I   Make searches case-insensitive, even when the search string contains uppercase letters.

-M   Prompt more verbosely than with -m, including percentage, line number, and total lines.

-N   Print line number before each line.

-O*file*

Similar to -o but does not prompt when overwriting file.

-P[m,M,=]*prompt*

Set *prompt* (as defined by -m, -M, or =). Default is short prompt (-m).

-Q   Never ring terminal bell.

-S   Cut, do not fold, long lines.

-T*file*

With the -t option or :t command, read *file* instead of *./tags*.

-U   Treat backspaces and carriage returns as control characters.

-V   Display the lesser version number and a disclaimer.

-X   Do not send initialization and deinitialization strings from termcap to terminal.

Commands

Many commands can be preceded by a numeric argument, referred to as *number* in the command descriptions.

SPACE, ^V, f, ^F

> Scroll forward the default number of lines (usually one window).

z

> Similar to SPACE, but allows the number of lines to be specified, in which case it resets the default to that number.

RETURN, ^N, e, ^E, j, ^J

> Scroll forward. Default is one line. Display all lines, even if the default is more lines than the screen size.

d, ^D

> Scroll forward. Default is one-half the screen size. The number of lines may be specified, in which case the default is reset.

b, ^B, ESC-v

> Scroll backward. Default is one windowful.

w

> Like b, but allows the number of lines to be specified, in which case it resets the default to that number.

y, ^Y, ^P, k, ^K

> Scroll backward. Default is one line. Display all lines, even if the default is more lines than the screen size.

u, ^U

> Scroll backward. Default is one-half the screen size. The number of lines may be specified, in which case the default is reset.

r, ^R, ^L

> Redraw screen.

R

> Like r, but discard buffered input.

F

> Scroll forward. When an EOF is reached, continue trying to find more output, behaving similarly to tail -f.

g, <, ESC-<

> Skip to a line. Default is 1.

G, >, ESC->

> Skip to a line. Default is the last one.

p, %

> Skip to a *position number* percent of the way into the file.

{

> If the top line on the screen includes a {, find its matching }. If the top line contains multiple {s, use *number* to determine which one to use in finding a match.

}

> If the bottom line on the screen includes a }, find its matching {. If the bottom line contains multiple }s, use *number* to determine which one to use in finding a match.

(

> If the top line on the screen includes a (, find its matching). If the top line contains multiple (s, use *number* to determine which one to use in finding a match.

)   If the bottom line on the screen includes a), find its matching
     (. If the bottom line contains multiple)s, use *number* to deter-
     mine which one to use in finding a match.

[If the top line on the screen includes a [, find its matching]. If
     the top line contains multiple [s, use *number* to determine
     which one to use in finding a match.

]   If the bottom line on the screen includes a], find its matching
     [. If the bottom line contains multiple]s, use *number* to deter-
     mine which one to use in finding a match.

ESC-^F
     Behave like {, but prompt for two characters, which it substi-
     tutes for { and } in its search.

ESC-^B
     Behave like }, but prompt for two characters, which it substi-
     tutes for { and } in its search.

m   Prompt for a lowercase letter and then use that letter to mark
     the current position.

'   Prompt for a lowercase letter and then go to the position
     marked by that letter. There are some special characters:

     '   Return to position before last "large movement."

     ^   Beginning of file.

     $ End of file.

^X^X
     Same as '.

/*pattern*
     Find next occurrence of *pattern*, starting at the second line
     displayed. Some special characters can be entered before
     pattern:

     !   Find lines that do not contain pattern.

     *   If current file does not contain *pattern*, continue through
          the rest of the files in the command-line list.

     @   Search from the first line in the first file specified on the
          command line, no matter what the screen currently
          displays.

?*pattern*
     Search backward, beginning at the line before the top line.
     Treats !, *, and @ as special characters when they begin
     pattern, as / does.

ESC-/*pattern*
     Same as /*.

ESC-?*pattern*
     Same as ?*.

n   Repeat last pattern search.

N   Repeat last *pattern* search, in the reverse direction.

ESC-n
> Repeat previous search command but as though it were prefaced by *.

ESC-N
> Repeat previous search command but as though it were prefaced by * and in the opposite direction.

ESC-u
> Toggle search highlighting.

:e [*filename*]
> Read in *filename* and insert it into the command-line list of filenames. Without *filename*, reread the current file. *filename* may contain special characters:
>
> %   Name of current file.
>
> #   Name of previous file.

^X^V, E
> Same as :e.

:n   Read in next file in command-line list.

:p   Read in previous file in command-line list.

:x   Read in first file in command-line list.

:f, =, ^G
> Print filename, position in command-line list, line number on top of window, total lines, byte number, and total bytes.

-
> Expects to be followed by a command-line option letter. Toggles the value of that option or, if appropriate, prompts for its new value.

-+
> Expects to be followed by a command-line option letter. Resets that option to its default.

--
> Expects to be followed by a command-line option letter. Resets that option to the opposite of its default, where the opposite can be determined.

_
> Expects to be followed by a command-line option letter. Display that option's current setting.

+*command*
> Execute *command* each time a new file is read in.

q, :q, :Q, ZZ
> Exit.

v
> Not valid for all versions. Invoke editor specified by $VISUAL or $EDITOR, or vi if neither is set.

! [*command*]
> Not valid for all versions. Invoke $SHELL or sh. If *command* is given, run it and then exit. Special characters:
>
> %   Name of current file.
>
> #   Name of previous file.
>
> !!   Last shell command.

| *mark-letter* command

Not valid for all versions. Pipe fragment of file (from first line on screen to *mark-letter*) to *command*. *mark-letter* may also be:

^   Beginning of file.

$ End of file.

., newline

Current screen is piped.

Prompts

The prompt interprets certain sequences specially. Those beginning with % are always evaluated. Those beginning with ? are evaluated if certain conditions are true. Some prompts determine the position of particular lines on the screen. These sequences require that a method of determining that line be specified. See the -P option and the manpage for more information.

---

ln

ln [*options*] *file1 file2*
ln [*options*] *files directory*

Creates pseudonyms (links) for files, allowing them to be accessed by different names. In the Finder, links appear and work as aliases. In the first form, link *file1* to *file2*, where *file2* is usually a new filename. If *file2* is an existing file, it is removed first; if *file2* is an existing directory, a link named *file1* is created in that directory. In the second form, create links in *directory*, each link having the same name as the file specified.

Options

-f   Force the link to occur (don't prompt for overwrite permission).

-n, -h

Do not overwrite existing files.

-s   Create a symbolic link. This lets you link across filesystems and also see the name of the link when you run ls -l. (Otherwise, you have to use find -inum to find any other names a file is linked to.)

---

lnresolve

lnresolve *pathname*

Resolves symbolic links.

Option

lnresolve

Takes a pathname as an argument. If the pathname refers to a symlink, the target of the symlink is printed to standard output. If not, the original pathname is printed to standard output. If the pathname doesn't exist, no result is printed.

locate
    locate *pattern*

Searches a database of filenames and print matches. *, ?, [, and] are treated specially; / and . are not. Matches include all files that contain *pattern*, unless *pattern* includes metacharacters, in which case locate requires an exact match.

The locate database file is */var/db/locate.database*, which by default is updated as part of the weekly system maintenance cron job.

lock
    lock [*options*]

Place a lock on the current shell session, preventing anyone from typing to the prompt without first entering a password or waiting until the end of the timeout period.

Options

-p Use the user's system password instead of prompting to create a new one-time password.

-t *timeout*
    Unlock the prompt in *timeout* minutes instead of the default 15 minutes.

lockfile
    lockfile [*options*] *filenames*

Creates semaphore file(s), used to limit access to a file. When lockfile fails to create some of the specified files, it pauses for 8 seconds and retries the last one on which it failed. The command processes flags as they are encountered (i.e., a flag that is specified after a file will not affect that file).

Options

-sleeptime
    Time lockfile waits before retrying after a failed creation attempt. Default is 8 seconds.

-! Invert return value. Useful in shell scripts.

-l *lockout_time*
    Time (in seconds) after a lockfile was last modified at which it will be removed by force. See also -s.

-ml, -mu
    If the permissions on the system mail spool directory allow it or if lockfile is suitably setgid, it can lock and unlock your system mailbox with the options -ml and -mu, respectively.

-r *retries*
    Stop trying to create *files* after *retries* retries. The default is -1 (never stop trying). When giving up, remove all created files.

-s *suspend_time*
    After a lockfile has been removed by force (see -1), a suspension of 16 seconds takes place by default. (This is intended to prevent the inadvertent immediate removal of any lockfile newly created by another program.) Use -s to change the default 16 seconds.

logger

logger [options] [messages]

Logs messages to the system log (/var/log/system.log). Command-line messages are logged if provided. Otherwise, messages are read and logged, line-by-line, from the file provided via -f. If no such file is given, logger reads messages from standard input.

Options

-f file

Read and log messages from file.

-i   Log the process ID of the logger process with each message.

-p priority

Log each message with the given priority. Priorities have the form facility.level. The default is user.notice. See syslog(3) for more information.

-s   Also log messages to standard error.

-t tag

Add tag to each message line.

Example

Warn about upcoming trouble:

    logger -p user.emerg 'Incoming Klingon battleship!'

look

look [options] string [file]

Looks through a sorted file and prints all lines that begin with string. Words may be up to 256 characters long. This program is potentially faster than fgrep because it relies on the file being already sorted, and can thus do a binary search through the file, instead of reading it sequentially from beginning to end.

With no file, look searches /usr/share/dict/words (the spelling dictionary) with options -df.

Options

-d   Use dictionary order. Only letters, digits, space, and tab are used in comparisons.

-f   Fold case; ignore case distinctions in comparisons.

-t char

Use char as the termination character, i.e., ignore all characters to the right of char.

lp

lp [options] [files]

Sends files to the printer. With no arguments, prints standard input. Part of the Common Unix Printing System (CUPS).

Options

-c   Copy files to print spooler; if changes are made to file while it is still queued for printing, the printout is unaffected. This option has no effect when used with a CUPS server, which performs in a similar manner already.

-d *dest*
> Send output to destination printer named *dest*.

-E Force an encrypted connection if supported by the print server.

-h *host*
> Send print job to to print server *host*, localhost by default.

-H *action*
> Print according to the named *action*: hold (notify before printing), resume (resume a held request), immediate (print next; privileged users only).

-i *IDs*
> Override lp options used for request *IDs* currently in the queue; specify new lp options after -i. For example, change the number of copies sent.

-m Send mail after files are printed (not supported in CUPS as of Version 1.1.15).

-n *number*
> Specify the *number* of copies to print.

-o *options*
> Set one or more printer options. CUPS documentation describing these options is included with Mac OS X and viewable via a web browser using *http://127.0.0.1:631/sum.html#STANDARD_OPTIONS*.

-P *list*
> Print only the page numbers specified in *list*.

-q *n* Print request with priority level *n*, increasing from 1 to 100. The default is 50.

-s Suppress messages.

-t *title*
> Use *title* for the print job name.

Example

Print five copies of a formatted manpage:

    man -t niutil | lp -n 5

---

lpc

lpc [*command*]

Controls line printer; CUPS version. If executed without a command, lpc will generate a prompt (lpc>) and accept commands from standard input.

Commands

?, help [*commands*]
> Get a list of commands or help on specific commands.

exit, quit
> Exit lpc.

status *queue*
> Return the status of the specified print queue.

lpq   lpq [options]

Shows the printer queue. Part of the Common Unix Printing System (CUPS).

Options

+interval
  Repeat the lpq command every *interval* seconds until the queue is empty.

-a   Shows the jobs in the queues for all printers.

-E   Forces an encrypted connection if supported by the print server.

-l   Be verbose.

-P *printer*
  Show queue for the specified *printer*.

---

lpr   lpr [options] files

Sends *files* to the printer spool queue. Part of the Common Unix Printing System (CUPS).

Options

-C, -J, -T *title*
  Use *title* for the print job name.

-E   Forces an encrypted connection if supported by the print server.

-l   Assume print job is preformatted for printing and apply no further filtering. Same as -o raw.

-o *options*
  Set one or more printer options. CUPS documentation describing these options is included with Mac OS X and viewable via a web browser using *http://127.0.0.1:631/sum.html#STANDARD_OPTIONS*.

-p   Print text files with pretty printing, adding a shaded header with date, time, job name, and page number. Same as -o prettyprint.

-P *printer*
  Output to *printer* instead of system default.

-r   Remove the file upon completion of spooling

-#*num*
  Print *num* copies of each listed file (100 maximum).

---

lprm   lprm [options] [jobnum]

Remove a print job from the print spool queue. You must specify a job number or numbers, which can be obtained from lpq. Used with no arguments, lprm removes the current job. Part of the Common Unix Printing System (CUPS).

Options

-E Forces an encrypted connection if supported by the print server.

-P *printer*
    Specify printer name. Normally, the default printer or printer specified in the PRINTER environment variable is used.

-   Remove all jobs in the spool

---

lpstat

lpstat [*options*]

Prints the lp print queue status. With options that take a *list* argument, omitting the list produces all information for that option. *list* can be separated by commas or, if enclosed in double quotes, by spaces.

Options

-a [*list*]
    Show whether the *list* of printer or class names is accepting requests.

-c [*list*]
    Show information about printer classes named in *list*.

-d Show the default printer destination.

-E Forces an encrypted connection if supported by the print server.

-h *host*
    Communicate with print server *host*, localhost by default.

-l Shows a long listing of classes, jobs, or printers when used before -c, -o, or -p, respectively.

-o [*list*]
    Show job queues for printers in *list*, or all printers if *list* isn't given.

-p [*list*]
    Show the status of printers named in *list*, or all printers if *list* isn't given.

-r Show whether the print scheduler is on or off.

-R Show the job's position in the print queue when used before -o.

-s Summarize the print status (shows almost everything). Same as -d -c -v.

-t Show all status information (reports everything). Same as -r -d -c -v -a -p.

-u *user*
    Show request status for *user*, or all users if user isn't given.

-v [*list*]
    Show device associated with each printer named in *list*, or all printers if *list* isn't given.

ls   ls [*options*] [*names*]

List contents of directories. If no *names* are given, list the files in the current directory. With one or more *names*, list files contained in a directory *name* or that match a file *name*. *names* can include filename metacharacters. The options let you display a variety of information in different formats. The most useful options include -F, -R, -l, and -s. Some options don't make sense together (e.g., -u and -c).

Options

-1   Print one entry per line of output.

-a   List all files, including the normally hidden files whose names begin with a period.

-A   List all files, including the normally hidden files whose names begin with a period. Does not include the . and . directories.

-c   List files by status change time (not creation/modification time).

-C   List files in columns (the default format).

-d   Report only on the directory, not its contents.

-f   Print directory contents in exactly the order in which they are stored, without attempting to sort them.

-F   Flag filenames by appending / to directories, * to executable files, @ to symbolic links, | to FIFOs, = to sockets, and % to whiteouts.

-i   List the inode for each file.

-k   If file sizes are being listed, print them in kilobytes

-l   Long format listing (includes permissions, owner, size, modification time, etc.).

-L   Used with -l. List the file or directory referenced by a symbolic link rather than the link itself.

-n   Used with -l. Displays group ID and user ID numbers instead of owner and group names.

-o   Used with -l. Shows file flags (see chflags).

-p   Mark directories by appending / to them.

-q   Show nonprinting characters as ? (the default when printing to the terminal).

-r   List files in reverse order (by name or by time).

-R   Recursively list subdirectories as well as the specified (or current) directory.

-s   Print size of the files in blocks.

-S   Sort by file size, largest to smallest.

-t   Sort files according to modification time (newest first).

-T   Used with -l. Show complete time and date information.

-u   Sort files according to the file access time.

-x   List files in rows going across the screen.

-v   Don't edit nonprinting characters for output (the default when not printing to the terminal).

-W   Show whiteouts when listing directories on mounted filesystems.

Examples

List all files in the current directory and their sizes; use multiple columns and mark special files:

    ls -asCF

List the status of directories /bin and /etc:

    ls -ld /bin /etc

List C-source files in the current directory, the oldest first:

    ls -rt *.c

Count the nonhidden files in the current directory:

    ls | wc -l

---

lsbom

lsbom [options] bomfile

Prints the contents of a binary BOM ("bill of materials") file (bomfile) in human-readable format. By default, lsbom prints a line of information for each file listed in the BOM, as in this example:

    ./Documents/Install Log.txt 100664 0/80 1182 4086739704

This line shows, in order, the plain file's pathname, permissions (modes) in octal format, owner and group IDs, size, and checksum. When listing symbolic links, lsbom reports the size and checksum of the link itself, and also lists the pathname of the linked file. Device file listings include the device number but not the file size or checksum.

Options

-b   List only block devices.

-c   List only character devices.

-d   List only directories.

-f   List only files.

-l   List only symbolic links.

-m   When listing plain files, also display their modification dates.

-s   Print only the file pathnames.

-x   Don't show the permissions of directories and symbolic links.

-arch arch
     When listing fat binary files, show only the size and checksums of the code for chip type arch. Possible values for arch include ppc, m68k, i386, hppa, and sparc.

-p *parameters*

Limit the content of each line as specified by *parameters*, which you can compose using any of the options in this list (but none more than once):

c   Show the checksum.

f   Show the filename.

F   Show the filename within quotes.

g   Show the group ID.

G   Show the group name.

m   Show the octal file mode.

M   Show the symbolic file mode.

s   Show the file size.

S   Show the file size, formatted with commas.

t   Show the modification date in Posix format (seconds since the epoch).

T   Show the modification date in human-readable format.

u   Show the user ID.

U   Show the username.

/   Show the user ID and group ID, separated with a slash.

?   Show the user name and group name, separated with a slash.

Examples

List the contents of BOM file *Installer.bom*:

```
lsbom Installer.bom
```

List only the paths of the directories in the bom:

```
lsbom -s -d Installer.bom
```

Format lines similar to those shown by the ls -l command:

```
lsbom -p MUGsTf Installer.bom
```

---

lsof

lsof [*options*] [*pathname*]

List open files, including regular files, directories, special files, libraries, network files, and others. The following descriptions and examples cover lsof's basic operation; for a complete description, refer to lsof's manpage.

Used without arguments, lsof will list all files opened by all active processes. Used with *pathname*, lsof will list the open files in the given file system mount point. If *pathname* is a file, lsof will list any processes having the given file open.

Selected Options

-a   Recognize all list options as joined with "and" instead of the default "or."

-c *chars*

List files opened by processes whose command names begin with characters *chars*. *chars* can contain a regular expression if put between slashes (/). You can further define the expression by following the closing slash with b, to denote a basic expression, i to denote a case-insensitive expression, or x to denote an extended expression (the default).

+d *pathname*

List all open instances of the files and directories in *pathname*, including the directory *pathname* itself. This option does not search below the level of *pathname*, however.

+D *pathname*

List all open instances of the files and directories in *pathname*, including directory *pathname* itself, searching recursively to the full depth of directory *pathname*.

-i [*address*]

List all Internet files, or if specified, those with a Internet address matching *address*. Specify *address* as [*protocol*][@*host*][:*port*].

version

Specify IP version; 4 for IPv4, the default. IPv6 is not supported in this version of lsof.

protocol

Specify TCP or UDP.

host

Specify a host by name or numerically.

port

Specify a port number or service name.

-p [*pid*]

List files opened by processes whose IDs are specified in the comma-separated list *pid*.

+|-r [*n*]

Operate in repeat mode. lsof will list open files as specified by the other options, and then repeat the listing every 15 seconds (or *n* seconds, if specified). If r is prefixed with +, lsof will repeat until the selection options produce no files to list. If r is prefixed with -, lsof will repeat until the process is terminated with an interrupt or quit signal.

-u [*user*]

List files opened by users whose login names or user IDs are in the comma separated list *user*. You can also specify a user whose files *aren't* to be listed by prefixing *user* with ^.

Examples

List processes that have your home directory opened:

    lsof ~

List all open files in your home directory:

    lsof +D

List the files opened by processes whose names begin with "i" and whose owner is "bob":

```
lsof -a -c i -u bob
```

List files using TCP port 80, repeating every two seconds until `lsof` is terminated:

```
lsof -i TCP:80 -r 2
```

---

machine

machine

Returns the system's processor type. A returned value of ppc750 indicates a PowerPC G3 chip, and ppc7400 indicates a PowerPC G4, for example.

---

mailq

mailq [*option*]

Lists all messages in the sendmail mail queue. Equivalent to sendmail -bp.

Option

-v   Verbose mode.

---

mailstat

mailstats [*options*] [*logfile*]

Displays mail-arrival statistics. Parses a procmail-generated log file and displays a summary about the messages delivered to all folders (total size, average size, etc.). The log file will be renamed as *logfile. old* and a new *logfile* of size 0 will be created.

Options

-k   Keep log file intact.

-l   Long display format.

-m   Merge any errors into one line.

-o   Use the old log file.

-s   Silent in case of no mail.

-t   Terse display format.

---

makekey

makekey

Produces *crypt* password hashes. This could be used to automatically populate a password database from known passwords, or to make hashes of prospective passwords that could be subjected to cracking attempts before being put into use.

makekey takes no command-line arguments. It accepts a character string on standard input, consisting of an eight-character password combined with a two-character *salt*, which is used to permute the DES password encryption algorithm. (Use man crypt for more information.) It prints a thirteen-character string to standard output, with the first two characters being the salt, and the other eleven characters being the password hash. The entire string is suitable for use as the password field in a standard Unix /etc/passwd-format file, or as the value of the passwd property in an Open Directory entry for a user employing Basic authentication.

Example

```
% echo password12 | /usr/libexec/makekey
12CsGd8FRcMSM
```

---

man   man [options] [section] [title]

Displays information from the online reference manuals. man locates and prints the named *title* from the designated reference *section*.

Options

-a   Show all pages matching title.

-b   Leave blank lines in output.

-d   Display debugging information. Suppress actual printing of manual pages.

-f   Same as whatis command.

-k   Same as apropos command.

-m *systems*, --systems=*systems*
     Search *systems'* manual pages. *systems* should be a comma-separated list.

-p *preprocessors*, --processor=*processors*
     Preprocess manual pages with *preprocessors* before turning them over to nroff, troff, or groff. Always runs soelim first.

-t   Format the manual page with troff.

-w   Print pathnames of entries on standard output.

-M *path*, --manpath=*path*
     Search for manual pages in *path*. Ignore -m option.

-P *pager*, --pager=*pager*
     Select paging program *pager* to display the entry.

Section names

Manual pages are divided into sections, depending on their intended audience:

1   Executable programs or shell commands

2   System calls (functions provided by the kernel)

3   Library calls (functions within system libraries)

4   Special files (usually found in /dev)

5   File formats and conventions

6   Games

7   Macro packages and conventions

8   System administration commands (usually only for a privileged user)

9   Kernel routines (nonstandard)

---

md5

md5 [*options*] [-s *string*] [*files*]

Calculates an md5 checksum value of the text provided in *string*, *files*, or from standard input. By default, when *string* or *files* is given, md5 prints those values first, followed by the checksum.

Options

-s *string*
  Calculate a checksum of the text in *string*.

-p   Print the standard input followed by the checksum.

-q   Operate in quiet mode. Print only the checksum.

-r   Reverse the order of the output when *string* or *files* is given (checksum first).

-t   Run the built-in speed test, which calculates a checksum from 100 MB of data.

-x   Run the built-in test suite, which calculates checksums from seven short strings.

---

merge

merge [*options*] *file1 file2 file3*

Performs a three-way file merge. merge incorporates all changes that lead from *file2* to *file3* and puts the results into *file1*. merge is useful for combining separate changes to an original. Suppose *file2* is the original, and both *file1* and *file3* are modifications of *file2*. Then merge combines both changes. A conflict occurs if both *file1* and *file3* have changes in a common segment of lines. If a conflict is found, merge normally outputs a warning and puts brackets around the conflict, with lines preceded by <<<<<<< and >>>>>>>. A typical conflict looks like this:

```
<<<<<<< file1
```
relevant lines from file1
```
=======
```
relevant lines from file3
```
>>>>>>> file3
```

If there are conflicts, the user should edit the result and delete one of the alternatives.

Options

-e   Don't warn about conflicts.

-p   Send results to standard output instead of overwriting *file1*.

-q   Quiet; do not warn about conflicts.

-A   Output conflicts using the -A style of diff3. This merges all changes leading from *file2* to *file3* into *file1*, and generates the most verbose output.

-E   Output conflict information in a less verbose style than -A; this is the default.

-L *label*
       Specify up to three labels to be used in place of the corresponding filenames in conflict reports. That is:

       merge -L x -L y -L z file_a file_b file_c

       generates output that looks as if it came from *x*, *y*, and *z* instead of from *file_a*, *file_b*, and *file_c*.

-V   Print version number.

---

mkbom

mkbom [*option*] *sourcedir bomfile*

Creates a bill-of-materials, or *BOM* file. The new *BOM*, named in *bomfile*, lists the full contents of directory *sourcedir*. Included with each listing in the bom is information about the listed file or directory, such as its permissions, size, and checksum. The Mac OS X Installer uses boms to determine what files to install, delete, or upgrade. See also ditto and lsbom for more information about working with BOM files.

Option

-s   Create a simplified *bom*, which includes only the pathnames of the listed files and directories.

---

mkdir

mkdir [*options*] *directories*

Creates one or more *directories*. You must have write permission in the parent directory in order to create a directory. See also rmdir. The default mode of the new directory is 0777, modified by the system or user's umask.

Options

-m   Set the access *mode* for new directories. See chmod for an explanation of acceptable formats for *mode*.

-p   Create intervening parent directories if they don't exist.

Examples

Create a read-only directory named *personal*:

    mkdir -m 444 personal

The following sequence:

    mkdir work; cd work
    mkdir junk; cd junk
    mkdir questions; cd ../..

can be accomplished by typing this:

    mkdir -p work/junk/questions

more
more [*options*] [*files*]

Displays the named *files* on a terminal, one screenful at a time. See less for an alternative to more. Some commands can be preceded by a number.

Options

+num
> Begin displaying at line number *num*.

-num
> Set screen size to *num* lines.

+/pattern
> Begin displaying two lines before *pattern*.

-c Repaint screen from top instead of scrolling.

-d Display the prompt "Press space to continue, 'q' to quit" in response to illegal commands.

-f Count logical rather than screen lines. Useful when long lines wrap past the width of the screen.

-l Ignore form-feed (Control-L) characters.

-p Page through the file by clearing each window instead of scrolling. This is sometimes faster.

-r Force display of control characters, in the form ^x.

-s Squeeze; display multiple blank lines as one.

-u Suppress underline characters.

Commands

All commands in more are based on vi commands. An argument can precede many commands.

*num*SPACE
> Display next screen of text, or *num* more lines.

*num*z
> *Display next lines of text, and redefine a screenful to num lines. Default is one screenful.*

*num*RETURN
> *Display num lines of text, and redefine a screenful to num lines. Default is one line.*

*num*d, ^D
> Scroll *num* lines of text, and redefine scroll size to *num* lines. Default scroll is eleven lines.

q, Q,
> Quit.

*num*s
> Skip forward *num* lines of text.

*num*f
> Skip forward *num* screens of text.

numb, ^B
> Skip backward *num* screens of text.

'   Return to point where previous search began.

=   Print number of current line.

/pattern
> Search for *pattern*, skipping to *num*th occurrence if an argument is specified.

n   Repeat last search, skipping to *num*th occurrence if an argument is specified.

!*cmd,*
> Invoke shell and execute *cmd* in it.

v   Invoke *vi* editor on the file, at the current line.

h   Display the help information.

:n   Skip to next file, *skipping to num*th file if an argument is specified.

:p   Skip to previous file, *skipping to num*th file if an argument is specified.

:f   Print current filename and line number.

.   Re-execute previous command.

Examples

Page through *file* in "clear" mode and display prompts:

```
more -cd file
```

Format *doc* to the screen, removing underlines:

```
nroff doc | more -u
```

View the manpage for the grep command; begin near the word "BUGS" and compress extra whitespace:

```
man grep | more /BUGS -s
```

---

mount

```
mount [-t type]
mount [-d] [-f] [-r] [-u] [-v] [-w] { [-t types] -a | special |
mount_point | [-o mount_options] special mount_point]
```

Integrates volumes on local storage devices and network file servers into the system's directory hierarchy.

The first form of the command merely lists currently mounted volumes.

The second form of the command mounts volumes, with one of four possible sets of arguments. The -a flag causes all filesystems (possibly limited to those of a certain *type*) listed in */etc/fstab* or in the */mounts* directory of an Open Directory domain to be mounted, with the options given in the configuration. If only *special* or *mount_point* is provided, the associated fstab or Open Directory entry is used to determine what's mounted. The final alternative specifies both *special* and *mount_point*, and a possible list of options.

Options

-a   Attempts to mount all filesystems listed in fstab or Open Directory, other than those marked with the noauto option.

-d   Disables the actual mount, but does everything else. May be useful when used with the -v flag in a troubleshooting situation.

-f   When using the -u flag and changing the status of a read-write filesystem to read-only, forces the revocation of write access. Normally the change is denied if any files are open for writing at the time of the request.

-o   Takes a comma-separated list of options, which may include async, noauto, nodev, noexec, nosuid, union, and others. See the mount manpage for details.

-r   Mounts the filesystem for read-only access.

-t   Restricts the use of the command to filesystems of the specified types presented in a comma-separated list, which may include hfs, ufs, afp, nfs, or others.

-u   When used with -o, -r, or -w, changes the status of a currently mounted filesystem to match the newly provided options.

-v   Enables verbose output.

-w   Mounts the filesystem for read-write access.

special
> The form of this argument is particular to the type of filesystem being mounted, and could be a disk device name, a fixed string, or something involving a server name and directory. See the individual mount_type entries for details.

mount_point
> The directory on which the filesystem will be mounted.

---

mount_afp

mount_afp [-i] [-o *mount_options*]
afp:/[at]/[*username*[;AUTH=*auth_method*][:*password*]@]*afp_server*[:*port_or_zone*]
/*share_name mount_point*

Mounts Apple Filing Protocol (AFP) shares as filesystem volumes. It takes an AFP URL and a mount point as arguments.

Options

-i   Prompts for password if not specified in the AFP URL.

-o   Takes -o options as listed in the mount manpage.

username
> The name to use for authentication to the AFP server. *username* may be null if the NO%20USER%20AUTHENT authentication method is used.

auth_method
> The name of the authentication method used. Examples include NO%20USER%20AUTHENT (no authentication required for guest-accessible shares), CLEARTXT%20PASSWRD (cleartext password), 2-WAY%20RANDNUM (two-way random number exchange), and CLIENT%20KRB%20V2 (Kerberos).

password
> The password to use for authentication. Note that specifying this on the command line exposes the password in a process listing.

afp_server
> The hostname or IP address of an AFP server.

port_or_zone
> A TCP port number if accessing the share over TCP/IP, or a zone name if accessing it over AppleTalk.

share_name
> The name of the AFP share you wish to access.

mount_point
> The directory on which the filesystem will be mounted.

---

mount_cd9660

mount_cd9660 [-e] [-g] [-j] [-r] [-o *mount_options*] *device* *mount_point*

Mounts ISO-9660 CD-ROM filesystems into the directory hierarchy.

Options

-e   Enables extended attributes.

-g   Disables stripping version numbers from files, making all versions visible.

-j   Disables Joliet extensions.

-o   Takes -o options as listed in the mount manpage.

-r   Disables Rockridge extensions.

device
> The CD device filename, e.g., */dev/disk1s2*.

mount_point
> The directory on which the filesystem will be mounted.

---

mount_cddafs

mount_cddafs [-o *mount_options*] *device* *mount_point*

Mounts CDDAFS audio CD filesystems into the directory hierarchy.

Options

-o   Takes -o options as listed in the mount manpage.

device
> The CD device filename, e.g., */dev/disk1s2*.

mount_point
> The directory on which the filesystem will be mounted.

---

mount_devfs

mount_devfs [-o *mount_options*] devfs *mount_point*

Mounts the *devfs* filesystem in */dev*, where block and character device special files exist.

Options

-o   Takes -o options as listed in the mount manpage. Not normally used for mount_devfs.

mount_point

The directory on which the filesystem will be mounted, normally */dev*.

---

mount_fdesc   mount_fdesc [-o *mount_options*] fdesc *mount_point*

Mounts the *fdesc* filesystem in */dev*. It contains the *fd* subdirectory, which contains one entry for each file descriptor held open by the process reading the contents of the directory. It also contains *stdin*, *stdout*, and *stderr*, which are symlinks to *fd/0*, *fd/1*, and *fd/2*, respectively; and *tty*, which is a reference to the controlling terminal for the process.

Options

-o   Takes -o options as listed in the mount manpage. Normally includes the union option, which prevents mounting over and obscuring the *devfs* filesystem in */dev*.

mount_point

The directory on which the filesystem will be mounted, normally */dev*.

---

mount_ftp   mount_ftp ftp://[*username:password@*]*ftp_server*[/*pathname*] *mount_point*

Mounts FTP archives as filesystem volumes. It takes an FTP URL and a mount point as an argument. In actuality, this is a Perl script that passes its arguments to csmount as:

/System/Library/Filesystems/ftp.fs/csmount -m *mount_point*↵
FTP_URL

Options

username

The login name to use with an FTP server that requires authentication.

password

The password to use with an FTP server that requires authentication. Note that this will leave the login password visible in a process listing.

ftp_server

The hostname or IP address of an FTP server.

pathname

The path to the directory you wish to access on the FTP server. If not provided, it defaults to the default FTP root directory (e.g., */Library/FTPServer/FTPRoot* on Mac OS X Server). Defaults to /.

mount_point

The directory on which the filesystem will be mounted. It must be an absolute pathname.

mount_hfs

mount_hfs [-w] [-o *mount_options*] *device mount_point*
mount_hfs [-e] [-x] [-u *user_ID*] [-g *group_ID*] [-m *mode*] [-o
mount_options] *device mount_point*

Mounts HFS and HFS+ filesystems into the directory hierarchy.
The first form is applicable to HFS+ volumes, the second to HFS.

Options

-e   Sets the character set encoding. Defaults to Roman.

-g   Sets group ownership on files. Defaults to the mount point's
      group owner.

-m   Sets the maximum permissions for files. The argument is an
      octal mode, as described in the chmod manpage.

-o   Takes -o options as listed in the mount manpage.

-u   Sets ownership on files. Defaults to the mount point's owner.

-w   Mounts an HFS+ volume with its HFS wrapper, if one exists.
      An HFS wrapper is required for the volume to boot Mac OS 9.

-x   Disables execute permissions.

device
      The disk device filename, e.g., /dev/disk0s5.

mount_point
      The directory on which the filesystem will be mounted.

---

mount_msdos

mount_msdos [-l | -s | -9] [-W *filename*] [-L *locale*] [-u *user_
ID*] [-g *group_ID*] [-m *mode*] [-o *mount_options*] *device mount_
point*

Mounts HFS and HFS+ filesystems into the directory hierarchy.

Options

-9   Ignores files with Win95 long filenames and special attributes.
      This option may result in filesystem inconsistencies, so it's
      better to use -s.

-g   Sets group ownership on files in the volume. Defaults to the
      mount point's group owner.

-l   Lists and generates long filenames and separate creation,
      modification, and access dates on files. This is the default if
      any long filenames exist in the volume's root directory, and
      neither -s nor -9 have been specified.

-L   Sets the locale for character set conversions. Defaults to ISO
      8859-1.

-m   Sets the maximum permissions for files in the volume. The
      argument is an octal mode, as described in the chmod manpage.

-o   Takes -o options as listed in the mount manpage.

-s   Ignores and disables generation of long filenames and sepa-
      rate creation, modification, and access dates on files. This is
      the default if no long filenames exist in the volume's root
      directory, and -l has not been specified.

-u   Sets ownership on files in the volume. Defaults to the mount point's owner.

-W   Specifies a file containing character set conversion tables.

device
> The disk device filename, e.g., /dev/disk0s5.

mount_point
> The directory on which the filesystem will be mounted.

---

mount_nfs

mount_nfs [*nfs_mount_options*] [-o *mount_options*] *nfs_server:pathname mount_point*

Mounts Network File System (NFS) exports as filesystem volumes. mount_nfs can take a large number of options, most of which offer knobs to tune the performance of NFS mounts. Only a few are described in the following list; see the manpage for full details.

Options

-b   After an initial mount attempt fails, forks off a background process to continue trying the mount.

-i   Makes the mount interruptible, so that processes failing to access the mount can be terminated, instead of getting stuck in an uninterruptible state waiting on I/O.

-K   Enables Kerberos authentication.

-m   Specifies a Kerberos realm to use with the -K option. Takes a realm name as an argument.

-o   Takes -o options as listed in the mount manpage.

-s   Makes the mount soft, so that processes failing to access the mount will eventually receive an error, instead of getting interminably stuck waiting on I/O.

-T   Enables the use of TCP as the underlying network transport protocol, instead of the default UDP.

nfs_server
> The hostname or IP address of an NFS server.

pathname
> The pathname of the NFS export you wish to access.

mount_point
> The directory on which the filesystem will be mounted.

---

mount_smbfs

mount_smbfs { -h | -v }
mount_smbfs [-u *username_or_ID*] [-g *groupname_or_ID*] [-f *mode*]
[-d *mode*] [-I *hostname_or_IP*] [-n long] [-N] [-U *username*]
[-W *workgroup_name*] [-O *c_user*[:*c_group*]/*s_user*[:*s_group*]]
[-M *c_mode*[/*s_mode*]] [-R *num_retries*] [-T *timeout*]
[-o *mount_options*] [-x *max_mounts*] //
[*workgroup*;][*username*[:*password*]@]*smb_server*[/*share_name*]
mount_point

Mounts Server Message Block (SMB) shares as filesystem volumes. It takes a share UNC and a mount point as arguments.

---

mount_smbfs can make use of the same configuration files used by smbutil: either *.nsmbrc* in the user's home directory, or the global */usr/local/etc/nsmb.conf*, which overrides per-user files. The following example *.nsmbrc* demonstrates some of the parameters available:

```
[default]
username=leonvs
# NetBIOS name server
nbns=192.168.1.3

[VAMANA]
# server IP address
addr=192.168.1.6
workgroup=TEST

[VAMANA:LEONVS]
password= $$178465324253e0c07
```

The file consists of sections, each with a heading in brackets. Besides the [default] section, headings have a server name to which the parameters in the section apply, and can also include a username and a share name.

 Sections of the configuration file may not be read properly unless the hostnames and usernames in the section headings are rendered in uppercase characters.

All sections and parameter definitions in *.nsmbrc* are optional; everything can be specified right on the mount_smbfs command line. It may come in handy for providing passwords for automated connections, when prompting for a password (which is the most secure method of providing it) is impractical. The value of the password parameter can be a cleartext password, but in this example is derived from the output of smbutil crypt password. While that's better than cleartext, don't trust the encryption too much, as it's fairly weak. Make sure you restrict permissions on *.nsmbrc* to prevent anyone reading your passwords.

Options

-d   Specifies directory permissions on the mounted volume, which default to the same as file permissions, plus an execute bit whenever a read bit is set. The argument is an octal mode, as described in the chmod manpage.

-f   Specifies file permissions on the mounted volume, which default to the same as those set on the mount point. The argument is an octal mode, as described in the chmod manpage.

-g   Specifies group ownership for files and directories on the mounted volume, which defaults to the same as that set on the mount point.

-h   Prints a brief usage statement to standard error.

-I   Avoids NetBIOS name resolution, connecting directly to the hostname or IP address specified as an argument.

-M   Assigns access rights to the SMB connection.

-n   With an argument of long, disables support for long file-names, restricting them to the "8.3" naming standard.

-N   Suppresses the prompt for a password. Unless a password is specified in a configuration file, authentication will fail for non-guest users.

-o   Takes -o options as listed in the mount manpage.

-O   Assigns owner attributes to the SMB connection.

-R   Specifies the number of times to retry a mount attempt. The default is 4.

-T   Specifies the connection request timeout (in seconds). The default is 15.

-u   Specifies ownership for files and directories on the mounted volume, which defaults to the same as that set on the mount point.

-U   Specifies a username for authentication. This may also be part of the UNC.

-v   Prints software version to standard error.

-W   Specifies an SMB workgroup or NT domain for authentication. This may also be part of the UNC.

-x   Automatically mounts all shares from the SMB server. The argument specifies a maximum number of shares that mount_ smbfs is willing to mount from a server, to forestall resource starvation when the server has a very large number of shares. If the server has more shares than max_mounts, the mount attempt is cancelled.

workgroup
> The name of the SMB workgroup or NT domain to use for authentication to the SMB server.

username
> The name to use for authentication to the SMB server.

password
> The password to use for authentication. Note that specifying this on the command line exposes the password in a process listing.

smb_server
> The NetBIOS name of an SMB server.

share_name
> The name of the SMB share you wish to access.

mount_point
> The directory on which the filesystem will be mounted.

mount_synthfs   mount_synthfs [-o *mount_options*] synthfs *mount_point*

Mounts a synthfs filesystem, which is a simple mapping of memory into the filesystem hierarchy (i.e., the contents of a synthfs filesystem are contained in memory). While creation of files in the filesystem is prevented (in fact, you may cause the system to hang after attempting to create files), directory hierarchies are allowed. This could be used as transient mount points for other volumes, for example, read-only media with a shortage of spare directories to serve as mount points (like an installation CD).

Options

-o   Takes -o options as listed in the mount manpage.

mount_point
    The directory on which the filesystem will be mounted.

---

mount_udf   mount_udf [-e] [-o *mount_options*] *device mount_point*

Mounts Universal Disk Format (UDF) DVD-ROM filesystems into the directory hierarchy.

Options

-e   Enables extended attributes.

-o   Takes -o options as listed in the mount manpage.

device
    The DVD device filename, e.g., /dev/disk1.

mount_point
    The directory on which the filesystem will be mounted.

---

mount_volfs   mount_volfs [-o *mount_options*] *mount_point*

Mounts the *volfs* filesystem in /.*vol*. The *volfs* filesystem enables the Carbon File Manager API to map a file ID to a file, without knowing the BSD path to it. Thus, HFS aliases, which use file IDs, remain consistent, even if the targets of the aliases move around within the volume.

The /.*vol* directory contains subdirectories named with numeric IDs, each associated with a volume on the system. While the directories appear empty if listed, with a file or directory ID one can access any object on those volumes. A file ID is a unique number associated with each file on a volume (analogous to an inode number on a UFS-formatted filesystem), and can be viewed with the -i option of ls.

If you know a file's ID, you can access it as /.*vol*/*vol_ID*/*file_ID*. If you know the ID of the directory the file is in, you can also access it as /.*vol*/*vol_ID*/*dir_ID*/*filename*. The root directory of a volume always has a directory ID of 2, so you can map volume IDs to volumes with:

```
% cd /.vol/vol_ID/2; pwd
```

Options

-o   Takes -o options as listed in the mount manpage. Not normally used for mount_volfs.

mount_point
    The directory on which the filesystem will be mounted, normally */.vol*.

---

mount_udf   mount_udf [-e] [-o *mount_options*] *device mount_point*

Mounts Universal Disk Format (UDF) DVD-ROM filesystems into the directory hierarchy.

Options

-e   Enables extended attributes.

-o   Takes -o options as listed in the mount manpage.

device
    The DVD device filename, e.g., */dev/disk1*.

mount_point
    The directory on which the filesystem will be mounted.

---

mv   mv [*option*] *sources target*

Moves or renames files and directories. The source (first column) and target (second column) determine the result (third column):

Source	Target	Result
File	*name* (nonexistent)	Rename file to *name*.
File	Existing file	Overwrite existing file with source file.
Directory	*name* (nonexistent)	Rename directory to *name*.
Directory	Existing directory	Move directory to be a subdirectory of existing directory.
One or more files	Existing directory	Move files to directory.

mv does not preserve resource forks or HFS metadata when moving files that contain them. For such files, use MvMac instead.

Options

-f   Force the move, even if target file exists; suppress messages about restricted access modes.

-i   Query user before removing files.

MvMac   MvMac *sources target*

Moves or renames files while preserving resource forks and HFS metadata. MvMac works like mv, but doesn't have any of mv's options. MvMac is installed with the Developer Tools into */Developer/Tools*. Since this directory isn't in the shell's search path by default, you might to need to specify MvMac's pathname to invoke it.

nice

nice [option] [command [arguments]]

Executes a *command* (with its *arguments*) with lower priority (i.e., be "nice" to other users). With no arguments, nice prints the default scheduling priority (niceness). If nice is a child process, it prints the parent process's scheduling priority. Niceness has a range of -20 (highest priority) to 19 (lowest priority).

Option

-n *adjustment*, -*adjustment*, --adjustment=*adjustment*
    Run *command* with niceness incremented by *adjustment* (1–19); default is 10. A privileged user can raise priority by specifying a negative *adjustment* (e.g., -5).

---

nicl

nicl [options] datasource [command]

Modifies entries in the NetInfo database. You can manipulate directories and properties with *nicl*. The *datasource* may be the path to a NetInfo directory (such as /_) or the filesystem path of a NetInfo database (you must use the -*raw* option for this). Use -raw to work directly with the NetInfo database, such as */var/db/netinfo/local.nidb*. This is useful in cases when the NetInfo daemon is down (such as when you boot into single-user mode).

Options

-c   Create a new data source.

-p   Prompt for a password. You can use this instead of prefixing the command with *sudo*.

-P *password*
    Use the specified password.

-q   Be quiet.

-raw
    Indicates that the *datasource* is a filesystem path to a NetInfo database.

-ro
    Open *datasource* as read-only.

-t   Treats the domain as a tagged domain, which includes a machine name and a tagged NetInfo database.

-u *user*
    Use the specified user's identity when running the command. You'll be prompted for a password.

-v   Be verbose.

-x500
    Use X.500 names (see the nicl manpage for more details).

Commands

-append *path key val ...*
    Appends a value to an existing property. The property is created if it does not already exist.

-copy *path newparent*
    Copies the specified *path* to a new parent path.

-create *path* [*key* [*val* ...]]
>   Creates a NetInfo directory specified by *path*.

-delete *path* [*key* [*val* ...]]
>   Destroys the specified path and all its contents. If you specify a key and/or value, only the specified key is deleted.

-domainname
>   Prints the NetInfo domain name of *datasource*.

-flush
>   Flushes the directory cache.

-insert *path key val index*
>   Operates like -append, but instead of placing the value at the end, it inserts it at the specified index.

-list *path* [*key* ...]
>   Lists all the NetInfo directories in the specified path. For example, to list all users, use nicl / -list /users.

-merge *path key val* ...
>   Operates like -append, but if the value already exists, it is not duplicated.

-move *path newparent*
>   Moves the specified *path* to a new parent path.

-read *path* [*key* ...]
>   Displays all the properties of the specified path. For example, to see root's properties, use nicl / -read /users/root.

-search *arguments*
>   Performs a search within the NetInfo database. For complete details, see the nicl manpage.

-rename *path oldkey newkey*
>   Renames a property.

-resync
>   Resynchronizes NetInfo.

-rparent
>   Prints the NetInfo parent of *datasource*.

-statistics
>   Displays NetInfo server statistics.

netstat

netstat [*options*]

Shows network status. For all active sockets, prints the protocol, the number of bytes waiting to be received, the number of bytes to be sent, the port number, the remote address and port, and the state of the socket.

Options

-A   Show the address of any protocol control blocks associated with sockets.

-a   Show the state of all sockets, including server sockets (not displayed by default).

-b   Modify the -i option display by providing bytes in and bytes out.

-d   Modify the -i and -w options' display by providing dropped packets.

-f *address_family*
      Limit displayed information to the specified *address_family* where legitimate families are [inet, inet6, unix].

-g   Display group address (multicast routing) information.

-I *interface*
      Display information for the specified *interface*.

-i   Display state and packet transfer statistics for all auto-config-ured interfaces.

-L   Display curerent listen queue sizes.

-l   Modifies display of -r option to include mtu information. As a standalone option, prints full IPv6 address.

-M *core*
      Extract information from specified *core* file instead of */dev/kmem*.

-m   Display statistics related to network memory management routines

-N *system*
      Extract the name list from specified *system* instead of */kernel*.

-n   Display network addresses using dotted octet notation (i.e., 172.24.30.1).

-p *protocol*
      Display statistics about *protocol* (see */etc/protocols* for names and aliases).

-r   Display routing tables.

-s[s]
      Display per protocol statistics. Use of double s filters zero count statistics.

-W   Don't truncate addresses.

-w *wait*
      Display network statistics every *wait* seconds.

---

nidomain   nidomain *options*

Creates or destroys NetInfo databases. nidomain can also list which databases on a particular computer are serving which domains.

Options

-l [*host*]
      List which domains are served by machine *host*, or the local host if *host* is not specified.

-m *tag*
      Create a new local database to serve the NetInfo domain *tag*.

-d *tag*
>   Destroy the local database serving domain *tag*.

-c *tag master/remotetag*
>   Create the local database *tag*, cloned from the remote machine *master*'s database *remotetag*.

---

nidump

nidump [-T *timeout*] (-r *directory|format*) [-t] *domain*

Dumps NetInfo information in a flat file format (such as the */etc/hosts* format) or in a raw format that uses a C-like syntax:

```
{
  "name" = ( "localhost" );
  "ip_address" = ( "127.0.0.1" );
  "serves" = ( "./local" );
}
```

Options

-T *timeout*
>   Specifies a timeout in seconds.

-t   Treats the domain as a tagged domain, which includes a machine name and a tagged NetInfo database. For example, *abbot/local* refers to the local NetInfo domain of the machine named *abbot*.

-r *directory*
>   Dumps the directory in raw format. Directory should be a path to a NetInfo directory, such as */users/root* or */machines*.

format
>   Specifies a format corresponding to a Unix flat file of the same name. Can be: *aliases, bootptab, bootparams, ethers, exports, fstab, group, hosts, networks, passwd, printcap, protocols, resolv.conf, rpc, services,* or *mountmaps*.

domain
>   Specifies a NetInfo domain. For standalone machines, use a dot (.), which refers to the local domain.

---

nifind

nifind [*options*] nidir [*domain*]

Searches the root domain for the NetInfo directory *nidir*, and returns the location and ID of the found directories. If *domain* is specifed, searches the hierarchy only up to that domain.

Options

-a   Search the entire NetInfo directory.

-n   Don't search local directories.

-p   Display the contents of the directories.

-t *n*   Set the connection timeout to *n* seconds (default is 2).

-v   Be verbose.

nigrep

nigrep *regx* [*option*]*domain* [*nidir*]

Searches the specified NetInfo domain using the regular expression *regx* and return the location and ID of the found directories. If *nidir* is specifed, starts the search from that directory.

Option

-t   Identify *domain* by a specified IP number or hostname and tag.

---

niload

niload   [-v] [-T *timeout*] [(-d|-m)] [(-p|-P *password*)]
[-u *user*] {-r *directory*|*format*} [-t] *domain*

Reads the Unix flat file format from standard input and loads it into the NetInfo database.

Options

-v   Selects verbose mode.

-T *timeout*
  Specifies a timeout in seconds.

-d   Specifies that if a duplicate entry already exists, NetInfo deletes that entry before adding the new one. This can cause you to lose data if NetInfo is tracking information that isn't represented in the flat file. For example, if you dump the */users* directory to a flat *passwd* file format and load it back in with niload -d, you will lose the *picture*, *hint*, and *sharedDir* properties for every user on your system because the *passwd* file does not have a field for those properties. Most of the time, the -m option is what you want.

-m   Specifies that if a duplicate entry already exists, niload will merge the changes. So, if you dump the */users* directory to a flat *passwd* file format, change a user's shell, and load that file back in with niload, NetInfo will keep the old shell. If you use the -m option, NetInfo will accept the new shell without the destructive side effects of the -d option.

-p   Prompts for a password. You can use this instead of prefixing the command with *sudo*.

-P *password*
  Uses the specified password.

If your shell history file is enabled, the -P option presents a security risk, since the password will be stored, along with the history of other shell commands. It is best to avoid using this option.

-u *user*
  Uses the specified user's identity when running the command. You'll be prompted for a password.

-t   Treats the domain as a tagged domain, which includes a machine name and a tagged NetInfo database.

---

domain
Specifies a NetInfo domain.

directory
Denotes a path to a NetInfo directory.

format
Specifies a format corresponding to a Unix flat file of the same name. Can be: *aliases, bootptab, bootparams, exports, fstab, group, hosts, networks, passwd, printcap, protocols, rpc,* or *services*.

nireport

nireport [-T *timeout*] [-t] *domain directory* [*property* ...]

Lists all NetInfo groups.

Options

-T *timeout*
Specifies a timeout in seconds.

-t   Treats the domain as a tagged domain, which includes a machine name and a tagged NetInfo database.

domain
Specifies a NetInfo domain.

directory
Denotes a path to a NetInfo directory.

property ...
Specifies one or more NetInfo properties. For example, each user listed in the */users* directory has *name, passwd, uid,* and *gid* properties (as well as a few other properties). Every directory has a *name* property that corresponds to the directory name. For example, the */machines* directory's *name* property is machines.

You can use nireport to list any portion of the NetInfo directory. For example, to list the top-level directory, specify the local domain, the / directory, and the *name* property, as in nireport . / *name*.

niutil

niutil *command* [-T *timeout*] [(-p|-P *password*)]
[-u *user*] [-R] [-t] *arguments*

Use niutil to modify entries in the NetInfo database. You can manipulate directories and properties with niutil.

Options

-T *timeout*
Specifies a timeout in seconds.

-p   Prompts for a password. You can use this instead of prefixing the command with sudo.

-P *password*
Uses the specified password.

-u *user*

Uses the specified user's identity when running the command. You'll be prompted for a password.

-R   Retries the operation if the NetInfo server is busy.

-t   Treats the domain as a tagged domain, which includes a machine name and a tagged NetInfo database.

Commands and arguments

niutil -create *options domain path*

Creates a NetInfo directory specified by *path*. For example, the first step in creating a user is to create their directory with niutil -create . /users/username.

niutil -destroy *options domain path*

Destroys the specified path and all its contents.

niutil -createprop *options domain path   propkey* [*val*...]

Creates a property (specified by *propkey*) under the NetInfo directory specified by *path*. You can create a list by specifying multiple values.

niutil -appendprop *options domain path propkey val*...

Appends a value to an existing property. The property is created if it does not already exist.

niutil -mergeprop *options domain path propkey val*...

This is like -appendprop, but if the value already exists, it is not added.

niutil -insertval *options domain path propkey   val index*

This is like -appendprop, but instead of placing the value at the end, it inserts it at the specified index.

niutil -destroyprop *options domain path propkey*...

Deletes the specified property. For an example, see "Modifying a User" later in this chapter.

niutil -destroyval *options domain path propkey val*...

Deletes one or more values from a property.

niutil -renameprop *options domain path oldkey newkey*

Renames a property.

niutil -read *options domain path*

Displays all the properties of the specified path. For example, to see root's properties, use niutil -read . /users/root.

niutil -list *options domain path* [*propkey*]

Lists all the NetInfo directories in the specified path. For example, to list all users, use niutil -list . /users

niutil -readprop *options domain path propkey*

Displays the values of the specified property.

niutil -readval *options domain path propkey index*

Displays the value of the specified property at the given index. For example, to list the first member of the writers group, use niutil -readval . /groups/writers users 0.

niutil -rparent *options domain*
> Prints the NetInfo parent of the specified domain.

niutil -resync *options domain*
> Resynchronizes NetInfo.

niutil -statistics *options domain*
> Displays NetInfo server statistics.

niutil -domainname *options domain*
> Prints the NetInfo domain name of the specified domain.

---

nslookup

nslookup [-option...] [*host_to_find* | - [*server*]]

Queries Internet domain name servers. nslookup has two modes: interactive and noninteractive. Interactive mode allows the user to query name servers for information about various hosts and domains or to print a list of hosts in a domain. Interactive mode is entered when either no arguments are provided (the default name server will be used) or the first argument is a hyphen and the second argument is the hostname or Internet address of a name server. Noninteractive mode is used to print just the name and requested information for a host or domain. It is used when the name of the host to be looked up is given as the first argument. Any of the *keyword=value* pairs listed under the interactive set command can be used as an option on the command line by prefacing the keyword with a −. The optional second argument specifies a name server.

Options

All of the options under the set interactive command can be entered on the command line, with the syntax -*keyword*[=*value*].

Interactive commands

exit
> Exit nslookup.

finger [*name*] [>|>>*filename*]
> Connect to finger server on current host, optionally creating or appending to *filename*.

help, ?
> Print a brief summary of commands.

host [*server*]
> Look up information for *host* using the current default server or using *server* if specified.

ls -[adhs] -[t *querytype*] *domain* [>|>>*filename*]
> List information available for *domain*, optionally creating or appending to *filename*. The -a option lists aliases of hosts in the domain. -d lists all contents of a zone transfer. -h lists CPU and operating system information for the domain. -s lists well-known services for the domain. -t lists all records of the specified type (see type table).

Unix Command
Reference

lserver *domain*
> Change the default server to *domain*. Use the initial server to look up information about *domain*.

root
> Change default server to the server for the root of the domain namespace.

server *domain*
> Change the default server to *domain*. Use the current default server to look up information about *domain*.

set *keyword*[*=value*]
> Change state information affecting the lookups. Valid keywords are:

all Print the current values of the frequently used options to set.

class=*name(upper or lower class)*
> Set query class to IN (Internet; default), CHAOS, HESIOD/HS, or ANY.

domain=*name*
> Change default domain name to *name*.

[no]debug
> Turn debugging mode on or off.

[no]d2
> Turn exhaustive debugging mode on or off.

[no]defname
> Append default domain name to a single-component lookup name.

[no]ignoretc
> Ignore truncate error.

[no]recurse
> Tell name server to query or not query other servers if it does not have the information.

[no]search
> With defname, search for each name in parent domains of current domain.

[no]vc
> Always use a virtual circuit when sending requests to the server.

port=*port*
> Connect to name server using *port*.

querytype=*value*
> See type=*value*.

retry=*number*
> Set number of retries to *number*.

root=*host*
> Change name of root server to *host*.

srchlist=*domain-list*
> Where *domain-list* is a maximum of six slash (/) separated domain names.

timeout=*number*
> Change timeout interval for waiting for a reply to *number* seconds.

type=*value*
> Change type of information returned from a query to one of:

A
> Host's Internet address

ANY
> Any available information

CNAME
> Canonical name for an alias

HINFO
> Host CPU and operating system type

MD
> Mail destination

MG
> Mail group member

MINFO
> Mailbox or mail list information

MR
> Mail rename domain name

MX
> Mail exchanger

NS
> Nameserver for the named zone

PTR
> Hostname or pointer to other information

SOA
> Domain start-of-authority

TXT
> Text information

UINFO
> User information

WKS
> Supported well-known services

view *filename*
> Sort and list output of previous ls command(s) with more. This appears to be nonfunctional in Mac OS X Version 10.2

nvram   nvram [-p] [-f *filename*] [*name*] [= *value*] ...

Modifies Open Firmware variables, which control the boot-time behavior of your Macintosh. To list all Open Firmware variables, use nvram   -p. The Apple Open Firmware page is *http://bananajr6000.apple.com*.

To change a variable, you must run nvram as root or as the superuser. To set a variable, use *variable=value*. For example, to configure Mac OS X to boot verbosely, use nvram boot-args=-v. (Booting into Mac OS 9 or earlier will reset this.) The following table lists Open Firmware variables. Some variables use the Open Firmware Device Tree notation (see the technotes available at the Apple Open Firmware page).

 Be careful changing the nvram utility, since incorrect settings can turn a G4 iMac into a $2000 doorstop. If you render your computer unbootable, you can reset Open Firmware by zapping the PRAM. To zap the PRAM, hold down Option-⌘-P-R as you start the computer, and then release the keys when you hear a second startup chime. (If your two hands are busy holding down the other buttons and you have trouble reaching the power button, remember that you can press it with your nose.)

Options

-f *filename*
> Read the variables to be set from *filename*, a text file of *name=value* statements.

-p   Display all Open Firmware variables.

Variable	Description
auto-boot?	The automatic boot settings. If true (the default), Open Firmware will automatically boot an operating system. If false, the process will stop at the Open Firmware prompt. Be careful using this with Old World (unsupported) machines and third-party graphics adapters, since the display and keyboard may not be initialized until the operating system starts (in which case you will not have access to Open Firmware).
boot-args	The arguments that are passed to the boot loader.
boot-command	The command that starts the boot process. The default is *mac-boot*, an Open Firmware command that examines the boot-device for a Mac OS startup.
boot-device	The device to boot from. The syntax is *device*: [*partition*],*path*:*filename*, and a common default is hd:,\\:tbxi. In the path, \\ is an abbreviation for */System/Library/CoreServices*, and tbxi is the file type of the *BootX* boot loader. (Run */Developer/Tools/GetFileInfo* on *BootX* to see its type.)
boot-file	The name of the boot loader. (This is often blank, since boot-command and boot-device are usually all that are needed.)
boot-screen	The image to display on the boot screen.
boot-script	A variable that can contain an Open Firmware boot script.

Variable	Description
console-screen	A variable that specifies the console output device, using an Open Firmware Device Tree name.
default-client- ip	An IP address for diskless booting.
default-gateway- ip	A gateway address for diskless booting.
default-mac-address?	Description not available at time of writing; see errata page at *http://www. oreilly.com/catalog/mosxian?*.
default-router- ip	A router address for diskless booting.
default-server- ip	An IP address for diskless booting.
default-subnet-mask	A default subnet mask for diskless booting.
diag-device	A private variable; not usable for security reasons.
diag-file	A private variable; not usable for security reasons.
diag-switch?	A private variable; not usable for security reasons.
fcode-debug?	A variable that determines whether the Open Firmware Forth interpreter will display extra debugging information.
input-device	The input device to use for the Open Firmware console.
input-device-1	A secondary input device (so you can have a screen and serial console at the same time). Use *scca* for the first serial port.
little-endian?	The CPU endian-ness. If `true`, initializes the PowerPC chip as little-endian. The default is `false`.
load-base	A private variable; not usable for security reasons.
mouse-device	The mouse device using an Open Firmware Device Tree name.
nvramrc	A sequence of commands to execute at boot time (if *use-nvramc?* is set to `true`).
oem-banner	A custom banner to display at boot time.
oem-banner?	The oem banner settings. Set to `true` to enable the oem banner. The default is `false`.
oem-logo	A 64-by-64 bit array containing a custom black-and-white logo to display at boot time. This should be specified in hex.
oem-logo?	The oem logo settings. Set to `true` to enable the oem logo. The default is `false`.
output-device	The device to use as the system console. The default is `screen`.
output-device-1	A secondary output device (so you can have everything go to both the screen and a serial console). Use *scca* for the first serial port.
pci-probe-mask	A private variable; not usable for security reasons.
ram-size	The amount of RAM currently installed. For example, 256 MB is shown as `0x10000000`.
real-base	The starting physical address that is available to Open Firmware.
real-mode?	The address translation settings. If `true`, Open Firmware will use real-mode address translation. Otherwise, it uses virtual-mode address translation.
real-size	The size of the physical address space available to Open Firmware.
screen-#columns	The number of columns for the system console.
screen-#rows	The number of rows for the system console.
scroll-lock	Set by page checking output words to prevent Open Firmware text from scrolling off the top of the screen.
selftest-#megs	The number of MB of RAM to test at boot time. The default is `0`.

Variable	Description
use-generic?	The device node naming settings. Specifies whether to use generic device node names such as "screen," as opposed to Apple hardware code names.
use-nvramrc?	The command settings. If this is true, Open Firmware uses the commands in *nvramrc* at boot time.
virt-base	The starting virtual address that is available to Open Firmware.
virt-size	The size of the virtual address space Open Firmware.

open

open *file*
open [-a *application*] *file*
open [-e] *file*

The open command can be used to open files and directories, and to launch applications from the Terminal application.

Options

-a *application*
    Uses *application* to open the file.

-e *file*
    Forces the use of Mac OS X's TextEdit application to open the specified *file*.

Examples

To open a directory in the Finder, use open, followed by the name of the directory. For example, to open the current directory, type:

    open .

To open your */Public* directory:

    open ~/Public

To open the */Applications* directory:

    open /Applications

To open an application, you need only its name. For example, you can open Project Builder (*/Developer/Applications*) with this command:

    open -a "Project Builder"

 You are not required to enter the path for the application—only its name—even if it is a Classic application. The only time you are required to enter the path is if you have two different versions of applications with similar names on your system.

You can also supply a filename argument with the -a option, which launches the application and open the specified file with that application. You can use this option to open a file with something other than the application with which it's associated. For example, to open an XML file in Project Builder instead of the default text editor, TextEdit, you could use the following command:

```
open -a "Project Builder" data.xml
```

To open multiple files, you can use wildcards:

```
open *.c
```

To force a file to be opened with TextEdit, use -e:

```
open -e *.c
```

The -e option will only open files in the TextEdit application; it cannot be used to open a file in another text editor, such as BBEdit. If you want to use TextEdit on a file that is owned by an administrator (or root), open -e will not work. You'll need to specify the full executable path, as in:

```
% sudo /Applications/TextEdit.app/Contents⏎
MacOS/TextEdit filename
```

---

opendiff

opendiff file1 file2 [-ancestor ancestor_file] [-merge merge_file]

Opens the two designated files in the FileMerge application.

Options

-ancestor
> Compares the two files against a common ancestor file.

-merge
> Merges the two files into a new file.

---

osacompile

osacompile [-l language] -e command] -o name] [-d] [-r typeid] [-t type] -c creator] [file...]

Compiles into a new script file one or more text or compiled OSA script files or standard input.

Options

-c creator
> Assign the four-character file-creator code creator to the new script (the default is osas).

-e command
> Use command as a line of script to be compiled. You can use more than one -e option; each will specify a new line of script.

-i pathname
> Use the dictionary from the application pathname when compiling.

-l OSAlang
> Use OSA language OSAlang instead of the default Apple-Script. Use the osalang command (described later in this chapter) to get information on all of the system's OSA languages.

-o name
> Use name as a filename for the new script instead of the default a.scpt.

-r *type:id*
> Place the resulting script in the resource fork of the output file, in the resource specified by *type:id*.

-t *type*
> Assign the four-character file-type code *type* to the new script (the default is osas).

-x Save file as execute only. This doesn't produce an applet, but a compiled script file that can't be viewed in Script Editor.

Examples

Use the filename *newscript* for a new script file, compiled from the source in *scripttext.txt*:

```
osacompile -o newscript scripttext.txt.
```

Compile the file *scripttext.txt* into a compiled script called *newscript* (assuming that a JavaScript OSA scripting component exists on the system):

```
osacompile -l JavaScript rawscript.txt
```

---

osalang   osalang [*options*]

Lists the computer's installed OSA-compliant languages (i.e., languages that use Apple Events to communicate among applications). In the newness of Mac OS X, this command may only return "AppleScript" and "Generic Scripting System."

Options

-d Print only the default language.

-l List the name and description for each installed language.

-L List the name and a longer description for each installed language.

---

osascript   osascript [*options*] [*files*]

Executes an OSA script from *files*, or from standard input if *files* is not specified.

Options

-e *command*
> Use *command* as a line of script to be compiled. You can use more than one -e option; each will specify a new line of script.

-l *OSAlang*
> Use OSA language *OSAlang* instead of the default AppleScript. Use the osalang command (described previously) to get information on all of the system's OSA languages.

-s *options*
> Provide output as specifed in *options* with one or more of the following flags:
>
> h   Human readable (default).

---

s   Recompilable source.

e   Send errors to standard error (default).

o   Send errors to standard output.

Examples

To run a script that displays a dialog window from the Finder, first run osascript with no arguments, which allows you to enter the script into standard input:

```
% osascript
tell app "Finder"
    activate
    display dialog "Hi there"
end tell
```

Press Control + D to send an EOF, at which point osascript executes the script and prints the value returned:

```
button returned:OK
```

Run with the -s s option, the output is better formatted for subsequent parsing:

```
% osascript -s s
tell app "Finder"
    activate
    display dialog "Hi there"
end tell
{button returned:"OK"} or argument/switch mismatch
```

---

passwd

passwd [-i *infosystem*] [-l *location*] [*username*]

Sets a user password in the designated directory service.

Options

-i   Specifies the directory service to use, which may be file, netinfo (the default), or nis.

-l   Depending on the directory service being used, it's either a filename (defaults to */etc/master.passwd*), a NetInfo domain name or server/tag combo, or a NIS domain name.

username
    Designates whose password will be set. It defaults to that of the user running the command.

---

paste

paste [*options*] *files*

Merges corresponding lines of one or more *files* into vertical columns, separated by a tab. See also cut, join, and pr.

Options

−   Replace a filename with the standard input.

−d'*char*'
    Separate columns with *char* instead of a tab. *char* can be any regular character or the following escape sequences:

You can separate columns with different characters by supplying more than one char.

\n   Newline

\t   Tab

\   Backslash

\0   Empty string

-s   Merge subsequent lines from one file.

Examples

Create a three-column file from files *x*, *y*, and *z*:

paste x y z > file

List users in two columns:

who | paste - -

Merge each pair of lines into one line:

paste -s -d"\t\n" list

---

pax   pax [*options*] [*patterns*]

Portable Archive Exchange program. When members of the POSIX 1003.2 working group could not standardize on either tar or cpio, they invented this program. (See also cpio and tar.) Note that until native drivers for tape drives exist for Mac OS X, pax cannot write to tape. Note also that pax does not preserve resource forks or HFS metadata when copying files that contain them.

pax operates in four modes, depending on the combinations of -r and -w:

List mode
No -r and no -w. List the contents of a pax archive. Optionally, restrict the output to filenames and/or directories that match a given pattern.

Extract mode
-r only. Extract files from a pax archive. Intermediate directories are created as needed.

Archive mode
-w only. Archive files to a new or existing pax archive. The archive is written to standard output; it may be redirected to an appropriate tape device if needed for backups.

Pass-through mode
-r and -w. Copy a directory tree from one location to another, analogous to cpio - p.

Options

Here are the options available in the four modes:

```
None:       c d f     n   s   v               U G   T
-r:           c d f i k   n o p s   u v   D       Y Z E U G   T
-w:       a b   d f i         o   s t u v x   H L P X       U G B T
-rw:          d   i k l n     p s t u v   D H L P X Y Z   U G   T
```

-a   Append files to the archive. This may not work on some tape devices.

-b *size*
> Use *size* as the blocksize, in bytes, of blocks to be written to the archive.

-c   Complement. Match all file or archive members that do not match the patterns.

-d   For files or archive members that are directories, extract or archive only the directory itself, not the tree it contains.

-f *archive*
> Use *archive* instead of standard input or standard output.

-i   Interactively rename files. For each file, pax writes a prompt to */dev/tty* and reads a one-line response from */dev/tty*. The responses are as follows:

Return
> Skip the file.

A period
> Take the file as is.

new name
> Anything else is taken as the new name to use for the file.

EOF
> Exit immediately with a nonzero exit status.

-k   Do not overwrite existing files.

-l   Make hard links. When copying a directory tree (-rw), make hard links between the source and destination hierarchies wherever possible.

-n   Choose the first archive member that matches each pattern. No more than one archive member will match for each pattern.

-o *options*
> Reserved for format-specific options specified by the -x option.

-p *privs*
> Specify one or more privileges for the extracted file. *privs* specify permissions or other characteristics to be preserved or ignored.
>
> a   Do not preserve file-access times.
>
> e   Retain the user and group IDs, permissions (mode), and access and modification time.
>
> m   Do not preserve the file modification time.
>
> o   Retain the user and group ID.
>
> p   Keep the permissions (mode).

-r   Read an archive and extract files.

-s *replacement*
> Use *replacement* to modify file or archive member names. This is a string of the form - s/*old*/*new*/[gp]. This is similar to the substitution commands in ed, ex, and sed. *old* is a regular expression, and *new* may contain & to mean the matched text

and \n for subpatterns. The trailing g indicates the substitution should be applied globally. A trailing p causes pax to print the resulting new filename. Multiple -s options may be supplied. The first one that works is applied. Any delimiter may be used, not just /, but in all cases, it is wise to quote the argument to prevent the shell from expanding wildcard characters.

-t   Reset the access time of archived files to what they were before being archived by pax.

-u   Ignore files older than preexisting files or archive members. The behavior varies based on the current mode.

Extract mode
> Extract the archive file if it is newer than an existing file with the same name.

Archive mode
> If an existing file with the same name as an archive member is newer than the archive member, supersede the archive member.

Pass-through mode
> Replace the file in the destination hierarchy with the file in the source hierarchy (or a link to it) if the source hierarchy's file is newer.

-v   In list mode, print a verbose table of contents. Otherwise, print archive member names on standard error.

-w   Write files to standard output in the given archive format.

-x *format*
> Use the given format for the archive. The value of format is either cpio or ustar. The details of both formats are provided in the IEEE 1003.1 (1990) POSIX standard. The two formats are mutually incompatible; attempting to append using one format to an archive while using the other is an error.

-B   Sets the number of bytes that can be written to one archive volume. This option can only be used by a device that supports an end-of-file read condition such as a file or tape drive. This option should not be used with a floppy or hard disk.

-D   The file inode change time is checked to see if it is a newer version of the file.

-E *limit,*
> Sets the number of read errors that can occur before pax will stop. *limit* can be from 0 to none. 0 will cause pax to stop after the first read error; none will keep pax form stopping on any amount of errors. Caution should be used with none as it could put pax into an infinite loop if the archive is severely flawed

-G   The group is used to select the file. To select by group number instead of group name, use a # in front of the number; to escape the #, use \.

-H If any of the pathnames given in the command line are symbolic links, follow only those links.

-L Follow all symbolic links.

-P Do not follow symbolic links. This is the default.

-T *[from_date][, to_date][/[c][m]]*
Uses either file modification date[*m*] or inode change time[*c*] to select files in a specified date range. The options c and m can be used together. The default option is m.

-U The user is used to select the file. To select by user ID instead of username, use a # in front of the number; to escape the #, use \.

-X When traversing directory trees, do not cross into a directory on a different device (the st_dev field in the stat structure, see stat(2); similar to the -mount option of find).

-Y Similar to the -D option, with the exception that pax checks the inode change time after it has completed the filename modifications and a pathname has been generated.

-Z Similar to the -u option, with the exception that pax checks the modification time after it has completed the filename modifications and a pathname has been generated.

Example

Copy a home directory to a different directory (presumably on a bigger disk):

```
# cd /Users
# pax -r -w arnold /newhome
```

---

pbcopy   pbcopy [-help]

Copies standard input to the pasteboard buffer. The Clipboard is used to implement GUI copy, cut, and paste operations, drag-and-drop operations, and the Cocoa Services menu.

Option

-help
Prints a usage statement to standard output.

---

pbpaste   pbpaste[-help] [-Prefer { ascii | rtf | ps }]

Prints the contents of the Clipboard to standard output. The combination of pbcopy and pbpaste may be an interesting tool to use in scripting. However, the Clipboard can be modified by other processes at any time, which limits the tool's actual usefulness.

Options

-help
Prints a usage statement to standard output.

-Prefer

> Specifies the output format to use if the desired format (ASCII, Rich Text Format, or PostScript) is available in the Clipboard.

---

pdisk

pdisk

pdisk *device* { -diskSize | -isDiskPartitioned | -dump | -blockSize | -initialize }
pdisk *device* { -partitionEntry | -partitionName | -partitionType | -partitionBase | -partitionSize | -deletePartition } *part_num*
pdisk *device* { -setWritable | -setAutoMount } *part_num* { 0 | 1 }
pdisk *device* -makeBootable *part_num boot_addr boot_bytes load_ addr goto_addr*
pdisk *device* -createPartition *part_name part_type part_base part_size*
pdisk *device* -splitPartition *part_num part1_size part2_name part2_type*
pdisk *device* -getPartitionOfType *part_type instance_num*
pdisk *device* -getPartitionWithName *part_name instance_num*

Provides control over Apple partition maps on disk devices in Macintosh systems.

Options

-blockSize

> Prints the block size of the specified device, in bytes, to standard output.

-createPartition

> Adds a partition to the partition map with the specified name, type (such as Apple_HFS or Apple_UFS), base (i.e., starting block number), and size (in blocks).

-deletePartition

> Deletes the specified partition from the partition map.

-diskSize

> Prints the size of the specified device, in megabytes, to standard output.

-dump

> Prints the partition map on the specified device to standard output.

-getPartitionOfType

> Prints the number of a partition with the specified type to standard output. An *instance_num* of 0 refers the lowest-numbered partition of the specified type, 1 refers to the second partition of that type, etc.

-getPartitionWithName

> Prints the number of a partition with the specified name to standard output. An *instance_num* of 0 refers the lowest-numbered partition with the specified name, 1 refers to the second partition of that name, etc.

-initialize
> Creates a partition map on the device.

-isDiskPartitioned
> Returns 0 if the device has an Apple partition map on it, 1 if not.

-makeBootable
> Sets the startup bit on a partition. This is unused by Mac OS X.

-partitionBase
> Prints the starting block number of the specified partition to standard output.

-partitionEntry
> Prints a line to standard output containing the name, type, base, and size of the specified partition.

-partitionName
> Prints the name of the specified partition to standard output.

-partitionSize
> Prints the size of the specified partition, in blocks, to standard output.

-partitionType
> Prints the type of the specified partition to standard output.

-setAutoMount
> Sets (1) or clears (0) the automount bit on a partition. This is unused by Mac OS X.

-setWritable
> Sets (1) or clears (0) the writable bit on a partition.

-splitPartition
> Splits an existing partition in two. The arguments include the size (in blocks) of the first partition formed from the split, and the name and type of the second partition.

device
> The disk device filename, e.g., /dev/disk0.

Commands

pdisk enters interactive mode when invoked without arguments. Interactive commands that take arguments will prompt for any that are missing.

?   Displays a summary list of commands.

a
> Toggles the abbreviate flag. When in abbreviate mode, partition type names are shortened. For example, Apple_HFS is displayed as HFS.

d   Toggles the debug flag. When in debug mode, some extra commands are enabled, including commands to display block contents and partition map data structures.

e *device*
> Edits the partition map on a device.

E *device*
> Should open a partition map for editing after prompting for a redefinition of the logical block size from the default 512 bytes, but this doesn't appear to work at present.

h
> Displays a summary list of commands.

l *device*
> Displays the partition map on a device.

L
> Displays the partition maps on all devices.

p
> Toggles the physical flag. When in physical mode, block positions and sizes are reported according the physical limits of the partitions, which may not be the same as their logical limits.

q
> Quits interactive mode.

r
> Toggles the readonly flag. When in read-only mode, changes to the partition map are disallowed.

v
> Prints the version number and release date of pdisk. (The output is currently far out of date, listing a release in 1997, when it was still used for MkLinux.)

x *device block_num*
> Displays the contents of the block given by *block_num*. While it always appears to produce a bus error when called at this level, the same functionality is available from an expert level while editing a map, where it does work.

---

periodic

periodic *name*

Serves as a method of organizing recurring administrative tasks. periodic is used in conjunction with the cron facility, called by the following three entries from */etc/crontab*:

```
1   3   *   *   *   root    periodic daily
15  4   *   *   6   root    periodic weekly
30  5   1   *   *   root    periodic monthly
```

The facility is controlled by the */etc/defaults/periodic.conf* file, which specifies its default behavior. periodic runs all of the scripts that it finds in the directory specified in *name*. If *name* is an absolute pathname, there is no doubt as to which directory is intended. If simply a name—such as daily—is given, the directory is assumed to be a subdirectory of */etc/periodic* or of one of the alternate directories specified in the configuration file's *local_periodic* entry.

periodic can also be executed from the command line to run the administrative scripts manually. For example, to run the daily script, run periodic as root using *daily* as its argument:

sudo periodic daily

The configuration file contains several entries for valid command arguments that control the location and content of the reports that periodic generates. Here are the entries related to daily:

```
# Daily options
...
daily_output="/var/log/daily.out"Append report to a file.
```

```
           daily_show_success="YES"        Include success messages.
           daily_show_info="YES"           Include informational
             messages.
           daily_show_badconfig="NO"       Exclude configuration error
             messages.
```

ping   ping [options] host

Confirms that a remote host is online and responding. ping is
intended for use in network testing, measurement, and management. Because of the load it can impose on the network, it is
unwise to use ping during normal operations or from automated
scripts.

Options

-c count
: Stop after sending (and receiving) *count* ECHO_RESPONSE
  packets.

-d   Set the SO_DEBUG option on the socket being used.

-f   Flood ping-output packets as fast as they come back or 100
     times per second, whichever is more. This can be very hard on
     a network and should be used with caution; only a privileged
     user may use this option.

-i wait
: Send a packet every *wait* seconds. Default is to wait 1 second
  between each packet. *Wait* must be a positive integer value.
  This option is incompatible with the -f option.

-l preload
: Send *preload* number of packets as fast as possible before
  changing to default packet dispatch frequency. High packet
  losses are to be expected during preload delivery.

-n   Numeric output only. No attempt will be made to look up
     symbolic names for host addresses.

-p digits
: Specify up to 16-pad bytes to fill out packet sent. This is useful
  for diagnosing data-dependent problems in a network. The 32
  most significant hexadecimal *digits* are used for the pattern.
  For example, -p ff will cause the sent packet to be filled with
  all 1s, as will -p ffffffffffffffffffffffffffffffff0001.

-q   Quiet output—nothing is displayed except the summary lines
     at startup time and when finished.

-r   Bypass the normal routing tables and send directly to a host
     on an attached network.

-s packetsize
: Specify number of data bytes to be sent. Default is 56, which
  translates into 64 ICMP data bytes when combined with the 8
  bytes of ICMP header data. Maximum *packetsize* is
  $8192(2^{13}) - 8 = 8184$.

-v   Verbose—list ICMP packets received other than ECHO_ RESPONSE.

-R   Set the IP record route option, which will store the route of the packet inside the IP header. The contents of the record route will be printed if the -v option is given, and will be set on return packets if the target host preserves the record route option across echoes or the -l option is given. Currently does not work in Mac OS X 10.2.1 (gets invalid argument error)

---

pl

pl [-input *input_binary_file* | -output *output_binary_file*]

Translates XML property list files into the more compact and readable "key=value" NeXT format. Also translates between this and a serialized binary format, in either direction. XML is read from standard input, NeXT-format data is read from standard input and written to standard output, and serialized binary data is read from and written to files specified with arguments.

Also see the manpage for plutil, which can check a file's property list syntax and translate directly between XML and binary (but not NeXT) formats.

Options

-input
    Specifies a serialized binary file as input.

-output
    Specifies a serialized binary file as output.

Examples

Translate XML property list to NeXT format:

    cat *foo.plist* | **pl**

Translate XML property list to serialized binary format:

    cat *foo.plist* | **pl** | **pl -output** *foo.bin*

Translate serialized binary file to NeXT format:

    pl -input *foo.bin*

---

pmset

pmset [-a | -b | -c] *action(s)*

Modifies the system's power management settings. pmset is a command-line alternative to the Energy Saver System Preferences (Chapter 5). The settings apply system-wide and across reboots. Therefore, pmset requires root privileges to run.

Options

-a   Use the settings that follow this flag when only the battery is in use and also when the power adapter is plugged in (the default).

-b   Use the settings that follow this flag when only the battery is in use.

-c   Use the settings that follow this flag only when the power
      adapter is plugged in.

Actions

dim *n*
> Dim the display after *n* minutes of idle time.

sleep *n*
> Put the computer to sleep after *n* minutes of idle time.

slower 1 | 0
> Set the processor performance setting to "reduced" (1) or
> "highest" (0).

spindown *n*
> Spin down the hard drive after *n* minutes of idle time.

womp 1 | 0
> Set the wake on magic packet ("wake for network adminis-
> trator access") setting to on (1) or off (0).

Examples

Set the system to dim the display after 3 minutes and go to sleep
after 10 minutes when using the battery:

    pmset -b dim 3 sleep 10

Set both the battery-only and power adapter settings at once:

    pmset -b dim 3 sleep 10 slower 1 -c dim 20 sleep 60↵
    slower
        0

---

pr

pr [*files*]

Converts a text file or files to a paginated, columned version, with
headers. If – is provided as the filename, read from standard input.

Options

+*beg_pag*
> Begin printing on page *beg_pag*.

-*num_cols*
> Print in *num_cols* number of columns, balancing the number
> of lines in the columns on each page.

-a   Print columns horizontally, not vertically.

-d   Double space.

-e[*tab-char*[*width*]]
> Convert tabs (or *tab-chars*) to spaces. If *width* is specified,
> convert tabs to *width* characters (default is 8).

-F   Separate pages with form feeds, not newlines.

-h *header*
> Use *header* for the header instead of the filename.

-i[out-tab-char[out-tab-width]]
> Replace spaces with tabs on output. Can specify alternative tab character (default is tab) and width (default is 8).

-l lines
> Set page length to *lines* (default 66). If *lines* is less than 10, omit headers and footers.

-m   Print all files, one file per column.

-n[delimiter[digits]]
> Number columns, or, with the -m option, number lines. Append *delimiter* to each number (default is a tab) and limit the size of numbers to *digits* (default is 5).

-o width
> Set left margin to *width*.

-r   Continue silently when unable to open an input file.

-s[delimiter]
> Separate columns with *delimiter* (default is a tab) instead of spaces.

-t   Suppress headers, footers, and fills at end of pages.

-v   Convert unprintable characters to octal backslash format.

-w page_width
> Set the page width to *page_width* characters for multicolumn output. Default is 72.

---

printenv

printenv [variables]

Print values of all environment variables or, optionally, only the specified *variables*.

---

ps

ps [options]

Reports on active processes. Note that you do not need to include a - before options. In options, *list* arguments should either be separated by commas or be put in double quotes.

Options

a   List all processes.

c   List the command name without the path.

e   Include environment.

h   Includes a header with each page of information.

j   List information for keywords: user, pid, ppid, pgid, sess, jobc, state, tt, time, and command.

L   List all keywords.

l   List information for keywords: uid, pid, ppid, cpu, pri, nice, vsz, rss, wchan, state, tt, time, and command.

M   List each tasks threads.

m   Sort by memory usage.

0   Appends the *keywords* that are in a list after the process ID. The title of the *keyword* can be changed by using an = sign after the *keyword*. (*keyword=newtitle*)

o   Same as 0 except it uses only the supplied keywords for the output of ps.

p   List information for the supplied PID.

r   List by cpu rather than by PID.

S   Include child processes' CPU time and page faults.

T   List information for standard input process.

t*tty* Display only processes running on *tty*.

U   List processes belonging to *username*.

u   List information for keywords: user, pid, %cpu, %mem, vsz, rss, tt, state, start, time, and command. The listing will be as if the -r option was supplied to ps.

v   List information for keywords: pid, state, time, sl, re, pagein, vsz, rss, lim, tsiz, %cpu, %mem, and command. The listing will be as if the -m option was supplied to ps.

w   Wide format. Don't truncate long lines.

x   Include processes without an associated terminal.

Keywords

If there is an alias for the keyword it is listed next to it.

Keyword	Description
%cpu,pcpu	Percentage of CPU used
%mem,pmem	Percentage of memory used
acflag,acflg	Accounting flag
command	Command and arguments
cpu	Short-term factor of CPU use
flags,f	Hexadecimal representation of process flags
inblk,inblock	Total amount of blocks read
jobc T	Count for job control
ktrace	Tracing flags
ktracep	Tracing vnode
lim	Limit of memory usage
logname	Username of user that started the command
lstart	Start time
majflt,pagein	Page fault totals
minflt	Page reclaim totals
msgrcv	Messages received total
msgsnd	Messages sent total
nice,ni	Value of nice
nivcsw	Involuntary context switches total

Keyword	Description
nsigs,nsignals	Signals taken total
nswap	Swap in/out totals
nvcsw	Voluntary context switch totals
nwchan	Wait channel
oublk,oublock	Blocks written total
p_ru	Amount of resources used out of resources used
padd	Address of swap
pgid	Group number for the process
pid	ID number of the process
poip	Progress of current pageouts
ppid	ID number of the parent process
pri	Scheduling priority
re	Core residency time
rgid	The real group ID
rlink	Reverse link on run queue
rss	Resident set size
rsz	Resident set size + (text size/text use count) (alias rssize)
rtprio	Priority in real time
ruid	ID of the real user
ruser	Name of the user
sess	Pointer for the session
sig ,penging	Signals that are pending
sigcatch,caught	Signals that have been caught
sigignore,ignored	Signals that have been ignored
sigmask,blocked	Signals that have been blocked
sl	Sleep time
start	Start time
state,stat	Sate of symbolic process
svgid	An executable setgid's saved gid
svuid	An executable setuid's saved uid
tdev	Device number of the control terminal
time,cputime	Total of user + system cpu time
tpgid	Group ID of the control terminal process
tsess	Pointer session of the control terminal
tsiz	Size of the text
tt	Name of control terminal
tty	The control terminals full name
uprocp	Pointer of the process

Keyword	Description
ucomm	Accounting name
uid	ID of the user
upr,usrpri	The scheduling priority after a system call as been made
user	Name of the user from uid
Vsz,vsize	Listed in Kbytes the virtual size
wchan	Wait channel
xstat	Status of a zombie or stopped process; exit or stop

pwd

pwd [options]

Print the full pathname of the current working directory.

Options

-L   Write the full pathname of the current working directory without resolving symbolic links.

-P   Write the full pathname of the current working directory with resolving symbolic links (-P is the default behavior).

rcp

rcp [options] file1 file2
rcp [options] file ... directory

Copies files between two machines. Each *file* or *directory* is either a remote filename of the form *rname@rhost:path* or a local filename.

rcp does not preserve resource forks or metadata when copying files that contain them.

Options

-K   Suppress all Kerberos authentication.

-k   Attempt to get tickets for remote host; query krb_realmofhost to determine realm.

-p   Preserve modification times and modes of the source files.

-r   If any of the source files are directories, rcp copies each subtree rooted at that name. The destination must be a directory.

-x   Turns on DES encryption for all data passed by rcp.

reboot

reboot [options]

Prepares the system, terminates all processes, and then reboots the operating system. During preparation, all filesystem caches are flushed and running processes are sent a SIGTERM followed by SIGKILL.

Options

-l   Do not log the halt via syslog (i.e., mach_kernel, syncing disks, etc.).

-n   Do not flush filesystem caches. Should not be used indiscriminately.

-q   The filesystem caches are flushed but the system is otherwise halted ungracefully. Should not be used indiscriminately.

-y   Reboots the system from a dialup operation.

---

renice

renice [*priority*] [*options*] [*target*]

Controls the scheduling priority of various processes as they run. May be applied to a process, process group, or user (*target*). A privileged user may alter the priority of other users' processes. *priority* must, for ordinary users, lie between 0 and the environment variable PRIO_MAX (normally 20), with a higher number indicating increased niceness. A privileged user may set a negative priority, as low as PRIO_MIN, to speed up processes.

Options

+*num*

    Specify number by which to increase current priority of process, rather than an absolute priority number.

-*num*

    Specify number by which to decrease current priority of process, rather than an absolute priority number.

-g   Interpret *target* parameters as process group IDs.

-p   Interpret *target* parameters as process IDs (default).

-u   Interpret *target* parameters as usernames.

---

rev

rev [*files*]

Prints each line of each specified file. The order of the characters in each line is reversed. If no file is specified, rev reads from standard input.

---

rlogin

rlogin *rhost* [*options*]

Remote login. rlogin connects the terminal on the current local host system to the remote host system *rhost*. The remote terminal type is the same as your local terminal type. The terminal or window size is also copied to the remote system if the server supports it.

Options

-8   Allow an 8-bit input data path at all times.

-e*c*   Specify escape character *c* (default is ~).

-d   Debugging mode.

-k   Attempt to get tickets from remote host, requesting them in the realm as determined by krb_realm-ofhost.

-l *username*

   Specify a different *username* for the remote login. Default is the same as your local username.

-x Turns on DES encryption for all data passed via the rlogin session.

-E Do not interpret any character as an escape character.

-K Suppress all Kerberos authentication.

-L Allow rlogin session to be run without any output postprocessing (i.e., run in litout mode).

---

rm

rm [*options*] *files*

Deletes one or more *files*. To remove a file, you must have write permission in the directory that contains the file, but you need not have permission on the file itself. If you do not have write permission on the file, you will be prompted (y or n) to override.

Options

-d Remove directories, even if they are not empty.

-f Remove write-protected files without prompting.

-i Prompt for y (remove the file) or n (do not remove the file).

-P Causes rm to overwrite files three different times before deleting them.

-r, -R

   If *file* is a directory, remove the entire directory and all its contents, including subdirectories. Be forewarned: use of this option can be dangerous.

-v Turn on verbose mode. (rm prints the name of each file before removing it.)

-W Undelete files on a union filesystem that whiteouts have been applied over.

---

rmdir

rmdir [*options*] *directories*

Deletes the named *directories* (not the contents). *directories* are deleted from the parent directory and must be empty (if not, rm -r can be used instead). See also mkdir.

Option

-p Remove *directories* and any intervening parent directories that become empty as a result; useful for removing subdirectory trees.

---

rsync

rsync [*options*] *source destination*

Transfers files from *source* to *destination*. rsync is a synchronization system that uses checksums to determine differences (instead of relying on modification dates) and does partial file transfers (transferring only the differences instead of the entire files).

rsync can use a remote shell (rsh by default) as a transport, in which case the remote host must have rsync installed as well. You can use a remote shell like ssh instead of the default by specifying that in *options*.

You can also use rsync without a remote shell, in which case rsync requires that the remote host run an rsync server daemon. For details on the advanced features of rsync, including running an rsync server, refer to rsync's manpage. The following descriptions and examples cover rsync's basic operation.

rsync does not preserve resource forks or HFS metadata when copying files that contain them.

The rsync *source* and *destination* arguments can be specified in several ways, as shown in the following table.

Source	Destination	Description
srcpath [...]	[user@]host:destpath	Transfer local directory *srcpath* to remote directory *destpath*.[a]
[user@]host: srcpath	destpath	Transfer remote directory *srcpath* to local directory *destpath*.[a]
[user@]host:srcpath		List contents of *srcpath* without transfering anything.[a]
srcpath [...]	[user@]host::destpath	Transfer local directory *srcpath* to remote directory *destpath*. [b]
[user@]host::srcpath	[destpath]	Transfer remote directory *srcpath* to local directory *destpath*, or list *srcpath* if *destpath* is not specified.[b]
rsync:// [user@]host[:port]:/ srcpath	[destpath]	Transfer remote directory *srcpath* to local directory *destpath*, or list *srcpath* if *destpath* is not specified.[b]
srcpath [...]	destpath	Transfer local directory *srcpath* to local directory *destpath*.

a. Uses a remote shell as the transport and requires rsync on the remote host.
b. Doesn't use a remote shell but requires an rsync server running on thbe remote host. Note the double colons (::), except for the URL format.

Selected options

-a, --archive

Copies *source* recursively and save most file metadata in the copies, including owner, group, permissions, and modification times. Also copies symlinks (but not hard links). Equivalent to using -rlptgoD.

-b, --backup

If a file in *source* already exists in *destination*, make a backup copy before overwriting. Name the backup file by appending ~ to the original filename.

-D, --devices

Copy any character and block device files in *source* to *destination*.

`--delete`
> Delete any files in *destination* that aren't in *source*.

`-e` *command,* `--rsh=`*command*
> Use the remote shell *command* as the transport instead of the default rsh. The usual alternative is ssh.

`--existing`
> Don't add any new files to *destination*; update only what's there with any newer versions in *source*.

`--exlude=`*pattern*
> Exclude from transfer those files in *source* that match *pattern*. See rsync's manpage for details on constructing exclude patterns.

`-g, --group`
> Preserve the groups of the source files in the copies.

`-I, --ignore-times`
> Transfer source files that have the same name, length, and date stamp as files in *destination*. The default behavior is to skip transfer of such files.

`-l, --links`
> Copy any symbolic links in *source* to *destination*.

`-o, --owner`
> Preserve the owners of the source files in the copies.

`-p, --perms`
> Preserve the permissions of the source files in the copies.

`--partial`
> Don't remove partially transferred files from *destination*. If a transfer is interrupted, this option allows a retried transfer to resume from where the failed attempt ended, instead of starting again from the beginning.

`-r, --recursive`
> Copy recursively. If any of the source files are directories, rsync copies each subtree rooted at that name.

`-t, --times`
> Preserve the modification times of the source files in the copies. Use this option whenever you want identical files excluded from subsequent transfers to the same directory.

`-u, --update`
> Don't transfer a file if it has a newer copy already existing in *destination*.

`-v, --verbose`
> Be verbose. Add vs for increased verbosity.

`-z, --compress`
> Compress data before transfer, which helps decrease transfer time over slower connections.

Examples

Transfer the entire local ~/*Documents* directory into *Backups* on the machine at 192.168.2.56, using rsh as the transport:

```
rsync ~/Documents fred@192.168.2.56:Backups
```

Perform the same transfer using the archive and compress options as well as ssh as the transport:

```
rsync -aze ssh ~/Documents fred@192.168.2.56:Backups
```

A trailing slash on the source pathname causes rsync to transfer only the *contents* of that directory into the destination directory. This example transfers the contents of the remote */Backups/Documents* directory int the local ~/*Temp* directory:

```
rsync -aze ssh fred@192.168.2.56:Backups/Documents/ ~/Temp
```

---

scp

```
scp [options] file1 file2
scp [options] file ... directory
```

Securely copies files between two machines, using ssh as the transport. Each *file* or *directory* is either a remote filename of the form *rname@rhost:path* or a local filename.

scp does not preserve resource forks or metadata when copying files that contain them.

Options

-B   Run in batch mode; don't prompt for passwords.

-c *cipher*
    Use the specified type of encryption, either blowfish, des, or 3des. (3des is the default.)

-C   Turn on compression.

-F *filename*
    Use specified *ssh* configuration file.

-i *keyfile*
    Specify an identity file to use for authentication. The default is *$HOME/.ssh/identity*.

-o *keyword*
    Set configuration keyword.

-p   Preserve modification times and modes of the source files.

-P *port*
    Select TCP port number.

-r   If any of the source files are directories, scp copies each subtree rooted at that name. The destination must be a directory.

-S *pathname*
    Use the local *ssh* executable located at *pathname*.

-q   Run in quiet mode.

-v   Be verbose.

-4   Use only IPv4 addresses.

-6   Use only IPv6 addresses.

---

screencapture screencapture [-i [-s | -w | -W] | -m] [-x] { -c | *pathname* }

Saves the contents of the screen to a PDF file or to the Clipboard. Unless you are using the -i option to start an interactive screen capture, the contents of the entire display are captured.

Options

-c Saves screenshot to the Clipboard for later pasting.

-i Initiates interactive screen capture using these keys:

- The mouse is used to select a region of the screen to capture.
- Pressing the spacebar toggles between this mouse selection mode and a window selection mode, in which clicking on a window captures the portion of the screen taken up by that window.
- Pressing the Control key saves the screenshot to the Clipboard.
- Pressing the Escape key cancels the interactive screen capture.

-m Captures only the main display, if multiple displays are in use.

-s Disables window selection mode in an interactive screen capture; only mouse selection is allowed.

-w Disables mouse selection mode in an interactive screen capture; only window selection is allowed.

-W Starts an interactive screen capture in window selection mode instead of mouse selection mode.

-x Disables sound effects.

pathname
> The name of a file in which to save the screenshot. You should terminate the filename with a *.pdf* extension.

---

script script [*option*] [*file*]

Forks the current shell and makes a typescript of a terminal session. The typescript is written to *file*. If no *file* is given, the typescript is saved in the file *typescript*. The script ends when the forked shell exits, usually with Control-D or exit.

Option

-a Append to file or typescript instead of overwriting the previous contents.

---

scselect scselect [[-n] *location*]

Changes active network Location. With no arguments, a usage statement and a list of defined Locations (or "sets") is printed to standard output, along with an indication of which Location is currently active. Locations can be referred to by name or by integer ID.

At the time of publication, scselect exhibits a minor bug. Network configuration information is stored in */var/db/SystemConfiguration/ preferences.xml*. When scselect is used to modify the configuration, it removes read permissions to this file for non-root users. While this doesn't break networking, it does make the configuration invisible from within Network Preferences, until the permissions are reset to allow world read access.

Option

-n   Changes the active network Location, but does not apply the change.

---

scutil

scutil [-r *node_or_address* | -w *key* [-t *timeout*]]

Provides control of the System Configuration framework's dynamic store. scutil opens an interactive session with configd, in which various commands are available to view and modify System Configuration keys.

As a quick sample run-through, invoke scutil. You will be placed at the scutil prompt. Enter open to start the session with configd, then enter list. You will see a set of keys, some of which are provided by the System Configuration framework (such as the keys in the File: domain), some of which are obtained from the preferences file */var/db/SystemConfiguration.xml* (the Setup: keys), and some of which are published by the configuration agents (the State: keys). Enter **get State:/Network/Global/DNS** to load the dictionary associated with that key. Then run d.show to display it. You should see a list of DNS servers and search domains configured on your system. Finally, run close, then quit.

Options

-r   Checks for reachability of the node or address. (Any numerical argument seems to result in Reachable status.)

-t   Specifies the timeout to wait for the presence of a data store key, in seconds. The default is 15.

-w   Exits when the specified key exists in the data store or when the timeout has expired.

Commands

scutil enters interactive mode when it is invoked with no arguments.

add *key [temporary]*
> Adds a key to the data store with the value of the current dictionary. The temporary keyword causes it to be flushed when the session to configd is closed.

close
> Closes a session with configd.

d.add key [* | ? | #] *value*...
> Adds an entry to the current dictionary. The optional type specifier can designate the values as arrays (*), booleans (?), or numbers (#).

---

d.init
Creates an empty dictionary.

d.remove *key*
Removes the specified key from the current dictionary.

d.show
Displays the contents of the current dictionary.

f.read *file*
Reads prepared commands from a file.

get *key*
Causes the value of the specified key to become the current dictionary.

help
Prints a list of available commands.

list *[key_pattern]*
Lists keys in the System Configuration data store. The *key_ pattern* can restrict which keys are output, but *key_pattern* appears to be quite limited.

n.add *{ key | key_pattern }*
Requests notification of changes to the specified keys.

n.cancel
Cancels n.watch settings.

n.changes
Lists changed keys that have been marked with notification requests.

n.list *[key_pattern]*
Lists keys upon which notification requests have been set.

n.remove *{ key | key_pattern }*
Removes notification requests for the specified keys.

n.watch *[verbose]*
Causes changes to keys marked with notification requests to issue immediate notices, obviating the need to use n.changes to serve notice that the change has occurred.

notify *key*
Sends a notification for the specified key.

open
Opens a session with configd.

quit
Exits the scutil session.

remove *key*
Removes the specified key from the data store.

set *key*
Sets the specified key to the value of the current dictionary.

sdiff

sdiff [*options*] *file1* *file2*

Compares two files to find differances and interactivly merges them. Without the -o option, sdiff behaves like diff-side-by-side.

Options

-a, --text

Treat all files as text files. Useful for checking to see if binary files are identical.

-b, --ignore-space-change

Ignore repeating blanks and end-of-line blanks; treat successive blanks as one.

-B, --ignore-blank-lines

Ignore blank lines in files.

-d, --minimal

Ignore segments of numerous changes and output a smaller set of changes.

-H Speed output of large files by scanning for scattered small changes; long stretches with many changes may not show up.

--help

Print brief usage message.

-i, --ignore-case

Ignore case in text comparison. Upper- and lowercase are considered the same.

-I *regexp*, --ignore-matching-lines=*regexp*

Ignore lines in files that match the regular expression *regexp*.

-l,--left-column

For two-column output (-y), show only left column of common lines.

-s, --suppress-common-lines

For two-column output (-y), do not show common lines.

-t, --expand-tabs

Produce output with tabs expanded to spaces to line up tabs properly in output.

-v, --version

Print version number of this version of sdiff.

-W, --ignore-all-space

Ignore all whitespace in files for comparisons.

-w *n*, --width=*n*

For two-column output (-y), produce columns with a maximum width of *n* characters. Default is 130.

-o *outfile*

Send identical lines of *file1* and *file2* to *outfile*; print line differences and edit *outfile* by entering, when prompted, the following commands:

e   Edit an empty file.

e b   Edit both left and right columns.

e l	Edit left column.	
e r	Edit right column.	
l	Append left column to *outfile*.	
q	Exit the editor.	
r	Append right column to *outfile*.	
s	Silent mode; do not print identical lines.	
v	Turn off "silent mode."	

Example

Show differences using 80 columns and ignore identical lines:

```
sdiff -s -w80 list.1 list.2
```

---

sed

sed [*options*] [*files*]

Streams editor. Edits one or more *files* without user interaction. For more information on sed, see *sed & awk*, Second Edition (O'Reilly & Associates, Inc., 1997). The -e and -f options may be provided multiple times, and they may be used with each other.

Options

-a   Treat all files as text and compare them.

-e '*instruction*'
     Apply the editing *instruction* to the files.

-f *script*
     Apply the set of instructions from the editing *script*.

-n   Suppress default output.

SetFile

SetFile [*options*] *files*

Sets the HFS+ file attributes (metadata) of *files*. SetFile is installed with the Developer Tools into /Developer/Tools. Since this directory isn't in the shell's search path by default, you might to need to specify SetFile's pathname to invoke it. See also GetFileInfo.

Options

-a *attribute*
     Set those file attributes that toggle on or off (sometimes called "Finder flags"). To set an attribute, provide that attribute's letter as uppercase in *attribute*. To unset an attribute, provide the letter in lowercase. You can specify multiple attributes at once; any not specified will retain their current setting in *files*. Refer to this table for the specific attributes:

Attribute	Set | Unset	Meaning
Alias	A | a	File is/isn't an alias.
Bundle	B | b	File has/hasn't a bundle resource.
Custom Icon	C | c	File has/hasn't a custom icon.
Desktop Item	D | d	File is/isn't on the Desktop.

Attribute	Set | Unset	Meaning
Extension	E | e	Filename extension is/isn't hidden.
Inited	I | i	File is/isn't inited.
Locked	L | l	File is/isn't locked.
Shared	M | m	Multiple users can/can't run file at once (applies to application files).
INIT	N | n	File has/hasn't INIT resource.
System	S | s	File is/isn't a system file (locks name).
Stationary	T | t	File is/isn't a stationary file.
Invisible	V | v	File is/isn't invisible to Finder.

-c *creator*
> Set the file's four-character creator code to *creator*.

-d *date*
> Set the file's creation date to date. Specify *date* in this format: **"mm/dd[yy]yy [hh:mm:[:ss] [AM | PM]]"**. Enclose *date* in quotes if it contains spaces.

-m *date*
> Set the file's modification date to *date*, specified as for -d.

-t *type*
> Set the file's four-character type code to *type*.

Example

Set the attributes of all files in the working directory whose names end with "jpg" to those of an unlocked GraphicConverter JPEG file, and give them all the same creation date:

```
/Developer/Tools/SetFile -a l -c GKON -t JPEG -d↲
"07/01/03 00:00" *jpg
```

---

sftp

sftp [*options*] [*hostname*]
sftp [*user@*]hostname:[*pathname*]

Secure FTP. Transfer files to and from remote network site *hostname* using *ssh* as the transport. Once an *sftp* connection is made, sftp becomes interactive, prompting the user for a command. Type **help** to see a list of known commands,

If *pathname* is a directory, it will become the initial remote working directory once the connection is made. If *pathname* is a file, sftp will transfer that file into the local working directory, close the connection, and exit without entering interactive mode.

Options

-b *filename*
> Run in batch mode, reading commands from *filename* instead of standard input.

-B *buffersize*
> Use a buffer size of *buffersize* bytes when transferring files instead of the default 32768 bytes.

-C Turn on compression.

-F *filename*
> Use specified *ssh* configuration file.

-o *keyword*
> Set configuration keyword.

-P *sftp-server_path*
> Connect to the local *sftp-server* program at *sftp-server_path*, instead of using *ssh* (for debugging purposes). The default location for the program on Mac OS X is */usr/libexec/sftp-server*.

-R *n*
> Allow up to *n* outstanding requests, instead of the default, 16.

-s *subsystem*
> Invoke remote subsystem.

-S *pathname*
> Use local *ssh* executable located at *pathname*.

-v Be verbose.

-1 Attempt a Version 1 connection.

---

showmount

showmount [-a | -d | -e] [-3] [*nfs_server*]

Queries the NFS mount daemon, *mountd*, to show which clients have mounted which directories from the NFS server. Called without flags, showmount prints a list of NFS client IP addresses to standard output; *nfs_server* defaults to localhost.

See the fixmount entry for more information.

Options

-3 Uses NFS Version 3.

-a Lists clients with the exports they're mounting, in the form *IP_addr:pathname*.

-d Lists exports that are mounted on clients, instead of client IP addresses.

-e Prints the server's list of NFS exports to standard output.

---

shutdown

shutdown [*options*] *when* [*message*]

Terminate all processing. *when* may be a specific time (in *hh*:*mm* format), a number of minutes to wait (in +*m* format), or now. A broadcast *message* notifies all users to log off the system. Processes are signaled with SIGTERM, to allow them to exit gracefully. Only privileged users can execute the shutdown command. Broadcast messages, default or defined, are displayed at regular intervals during the grace period; the closer the shutdown time, the more frequent the message.

Options

-c Cancel a shutdown in progress.

-f Reboot fast, by suppressing the normal call to fsck when rebooting.

-h	Halt the system when shutdown is complete.
-k	Print the warning message, but suppress actual shutdown.
-n	Perform shutdown without a call to sync.
-r	Reboot the system when shutdown is complete.

slogin See ssh. (The slogin command file is a symbolic link to the *ssh* executable.)

sort sort [*options*] [*files*]

Sort the lines of the named *files*. Compare specified fields for each pair of lines, or, if no fields are specified, compare them by byte, in machine collating sequence. See also uniq, comm, and join.

Options

-b	Ignore leading spaces and tabs.
-c	Check whether *files* are already sorted, and if so, produce no output.
-d	Sort in dictionary order.
-f	Fold—ignore uppercase/lowercase differences.
-i	Ignore nonprinting characters (those outside ASCII range 040–176).
-m	Merge (i.e., sort as a group) input files.
-n	Sort in arithmetic order.

-o*file*
> Put output in *file*.

-r	Reverse the order of the sort.
-t*c*	Separate fields with *c* (default is a tab).
-u	Identical lines in input file appear only one (unique) time in output.

-z*recsz*
> Provide *recsz* bytes for any one line in the file. This option prevents abnormal termination of sort in certain cases.

+*n* [-*m*]
> Skip *n* fields before sorting, and sort up to field position *m*. If *m* is missing, sort to end of line. Positions take the form *a.b*, which means character *b* of field *a*. If *.b* is missing, sort at the first character of the field.

-k *n[,m]*
> Similar to +. Skip *n*–1 fields and stop at *m*–1 fields (i.e., start sorting at the *n*th field, where the fields are numbered beginning with 1).

-M
> Attempt to treat the first three characters as a month designation (JAN, FEB, etc.). In comparisons, treat JAN < FEB and any valid month as less than an invalid name for a month.

-T *tempdir*
> Directory pathname to be used for temporary files.

Examples

List files by decreasing number of lines:

```
wc -l * | sort -r
```

Alphabetize a list of words, remove duplicates, and print the frequency of each word:

```
sort -fd wordlist | uniq -c
```

---

slp_reg

```
slp_reg -l
slp_reg { -r | -d } URL [-a attribute_list]
```

Communicates with *slpd* to register services with the Service Location Protocol. Services are designated by SLP URLs.

Options

-a Specifies an SLP attribute list.

-d Deregisters the given service.

-l Lists registered services. This option is currently unimplemented.

-r Registers the given service.

---

softwareupdate

```
softwareupdate [package_ID]
```

A command-line version of the Software Update application, this checks for and installs Apple software updates. When invoked without arguments, it prints a list of uninstalled updates (if any) to standard output, each labeled with a numeric ID.

Option

package_ID
   The numeric ID of a software update package to install.

---

split

```
split [option] [infile] [outfile]
```

Split *infile* into equal-sized segments. *infile* remains unchanged, and the results are written to *outfile*aa, *outfile*ab, and so on. (Default is xaa, xab, etc.). If *infile* is (or missing and default *outfile* is used), standard input is read.

Options

-n, -l *n*
   Split *infile* into *n*-line segments (default is 1000).

-b *n[km]*
   Split *infile* into *n*-byte segments. Alternate blocksizes may be specified:

k 1 kilobyte

m 1 megabyte

— Take input from the standard input.

Examples

Break *bigfile* into 1000-line segments:

```
split bigfile
```

Join four files, then split them into 10-line files named *new.aa*, *new.ab*, and so on. Note that without the -, *new.* would be treated as a nonexistent input file:

```
cat list[1-4] | split -10 - new.
```

SplitForks

SplitForks { -u | [-v] *pathname* }

Copies the resource fork and HFS attributes from a file named *filename* into a separate file named *._filename*, equivalent to an AppleDouble Header file. The original file retains the resource fork and HFS metadata as well.

If *pathname* refers to a file, that file's resource fork and metadata are split out. If *pathname* is a directory, SplitForks does a recursive descent into the directory, working on every file within it.

FixupResourceForks undoes the actions of SplitForks.

Options

-u   Prints a usage statement to standard output.

-v   Enables verbose output.

---

spray

spray [*options*]

Similar to ping, spray sends RPC packets to a host and determines how many were received and their transit time. spray can cause a lot of network traffic, so use it cautiously.

Options

-c *count*
    Specifies *count* packets to send.

-d *delay*
    Allows for *delay* microseconds between each packet.

-l *length*
    Sets the RPC call message packet length to *length* bytes. Since all values are not possible, spray rounds to the nearest possible value.

---

ssh

ssh [-l *user*] *host* [*commands*]
ssh [*options*] [*user@*]*host*

Secures shell. This is a secure replacement for the rsh, rlogin, and rcp programs. ssh uses strong public-key encryption technologies to provide end-to-end encryption of data. There may be licensing/patent issues restricting the use of the software in some countries.

Options

-a   Turn off authentication agent connection forwarding.

-A   Turn on authentication agent connection forwarding.

-b *interface*
: Use the specified network interface (on a multiple interface machine).

-c *cipher*
: Use the specified type of encryption, either blowfish, des or 3des. 3des is the default.

-C Turn on compression.

-D Behave like a SOCKS4 server.

-ec Specify escape character *c*. Use the word "none" to disable any escape character.

-f Send ssh to the background.

-F *filename*
: Use specified configuration file.

-g Accept connections to local forward ports from remote hosts.

-i *keyfile*
: Specify an identity file to use for authentication. The default is *$HOME/.ssh/identity*.

-I *device*
: Used smartcard *device*.

-k Turn off Kerberos ticket forwarding.

-l *user*
: Log in as *user*.

-L *port1:host2: port2*
: Set up port forwarding from a local host to a remote host.

-m *algorithm*
: Use specifed MAC algorithm(s).

-n Does not allow reading form stdin.

-N Turn off remote command execution.

-o *keyword*
: Set configuration keyword.

-p *port*
: Select TCP port number.

-P Use a nonprivileged port is for outgoing connections.

-q Run in quiet mode.

-R *port1:host2: port2*
: Set up port forwarding from a remote host to a local host.

-s *subsystem*
: Invoke remote subsystem.

-t Turn on pseudo-tty distribution.

-T Turn off pseudo-tty distribution.

-v Be verbose.

-x Turn off X11 forwarding.

-X Turn on X11 forwarding.

-1	Attempt a Version 1 connection.
-2	Attempt a Version 2 connection.
-4	Use only IPv4 addresses.
-6	Use only IPv6 addresses.

strings

strings [*options*] *files*

Searches object or binary files for sequences of four or more printable characters that end with a newline or null.

Options

-a   Search entire file, not just the initialized data portion of object files. Can also specify this option as –.

-o   Display the string's offset position before the string.

-*num*
    Minimum string length is *num* (default is 4). Can also specify this option as -*n*.

stty

stty [*options*] [*modes*]

Set terminal I/O options for the current device. Without options, stty reports the terminal settings, where a ^ indicates the Control key, and ^' indicates a null value. Most modes can be switched using an optional preceding – (shown in brackets). The corresponding description is also shown in brackets. As a privileged user, you can set or read settings from another device using the syntax:

stty [*options*] [*modes*] < *device*

stty is one of the most complicated Unix commands. The complexity stems from the need to deal with a large range of conflicting, incompatible, and nonstandardized terminal devices—everything from printing teletypes to CRTs to pseudoterminals for windowing systems. Only a few of the options are really needed for day-to-day use. stty sane is a particularly valuable one to remember.

Options

-a   Report all option settings.

-e   Report current settings in BSD format.

-f *file*
    Use file instead of standard input.

-g   Report current settings in stty format.

Control modes

0   Hang up connection (set the baud rate to zero).

n   Set terminal baud rate to *n* (e.g., 19200).

[-]clocal
    [Enable] disable modem control.

[-]cread
> [Disable] enable the receiver.

[-]crtscts
> [Disable] enable output hardware flow control using RTS/ CTS.

csn Select character size in bits (5 *n* 8).

[-]cstopb
> [One] two stop bits per character.

[-]hup
> [Do not] hang up connection on last close.

[-]hupcl
> Same as [-]hup.

ispeed *n*
> Set terminal input baud rate to *n*.

[-]loblk
> [Do not] block layer output. For use with shl; obsolete.

ospeed *n*
> Set terminal output baud rate to *n*.

[-]parenb
> [Disable] enable parity generation and detection.

[-]parext
> [Disable] enable extended parity generation and detection for mark and space parity.

[-]parodd
> Use [even] odd parity.

speed *num*
> Set ispeed and opseed to the same *num*.

Input modes

[-]brkint
> [Do not] signal INTR on break.

[-]icrnl
> [Do not] map carriage return (^M) to newline (^J) on input.

[-]ignbrk
> [Do not] ignore break on input.

[-]igncr
> [Do not] ignore carriage return on input.

[-]ignpar
> [Do not] ignore parity errors.

[-]imaxbel
> [Do not] echo BEL when input line is too long.

[-]inlcr
> [Do not] map newline to carriage return on input.

[-]inpck
> [Disable] enable input parity checking.

[-]istrip
> [Do not] strip input characters to 7 bits.

[-]iuclc
> [Do not] map uppercase to lowercase on input.

[-]ixany
> Allow [only XON] any character to restart output.

[-]ixoff
> [Do not] send START/STOP characters when the queue is nearly empty/full.

[-]ixon
> [Disable] enable START/STOP output control.

[-]parmrk
> [Do not] mark parity errors.

Output modes

[-]ocrnl
> [Do not] map carriage return to newline on output.

[-]olcuc
> [Do not] map lowercase to uppercase on output.

[-]onlcr
> [Do not] map newline to carriage return-newline on output.

[-]onlret
> [Do not] perform carriage return after newline.

[-]onocr
> [Do not] output carriage returns at column zero.

[-]opost
> [Do not] postprocess output; ignore all other output modes.

[-]oxtabs
> [Do not] on output expand tabs to spaces.

Local modes

[-]echo
> [Do not] echo every character typed.

[-]echoctl
> [Do not] echo control characters as ^*char*, DEL as ^?.

[-]echoe
> [Do not] echo ERASE character as BS-space-BS string.

[-]echok
> [Do not] echo newline after KILL character.

[-]echoke
> [Do not] erase entire line on line kill.

[-]echonl
> [Do not] echo newline (^J).

[-]echoprt
> [Do not] echo erase *character* as *retcaeahc*/. Used for printing terminals.

[-]flusho

Output is [not] being flushed.

[-]icanon

[Disable] enable canonical input (ERASE and KILL processing).

[-]iexten

[Disable] enable extended functions for input data.

[-]isig

[Disable] enable checking of characters against INTR, QUIT, and SWITCH.

[-]lfkc

Same as [-]echok. Obsolete.

[-]noflsh

[Enable] disable flush after INTR, QUIT, or SWITCH.

[-]pendin

[Do not] retype pending input at next read or input character.

[-]stappl

[Line] application mode on a synchronous line.

[-]stflush

[Disable] enable flush on synchronous line.

[-]stwrap

[Enable] disable truncation on synchronous line.

[-]tostop

[Do not] send SIGTTOU when background processes write to the terminal.

[-]altwerase

[Do not] use a different erase algorithm when processing WERASE characters.

[-]mdmbuf

Carrier Detect condition determines flow control output if on. If off, low Carrier Detect writes, return an error.

[-]xcase

[Do not] change case on local output.

Control assignments

ctrl-char c

Set control character to *c*. *ctrl-char* is one of the following: dsusp, eof, eol, eol2, erase, intr, kill, lnext, quit, reprint, start, status, stop, susp, switch, or werase.

min n

With -icanon, *n* is the minimum number of characters that will satisfy the read system call until the timeout set with time expires.

time n

With -icanon, *n* is the number of tenths of seconds to wait before a read system call times out. If the minimum number of characters set with min is read, the read can return before the timeout expires.

Combination modes

[-]evenp
> Same as [-]parenb and cs7[8].

ek   Reset ERASE and KILL characters to # and @.

[-]nl
> [Un] set icrnl and onlcr. -nl also unsets inlcr, igncr, ocrnl, and onlret.

[-]oddp
> Same as [-]parenb, [-]parodd, and cs7[8].

[-]parity
> Same as [-]parenb and cs7[8].

[-]raw
> [Disable] enable raw input and output (no ERASE, KILL, INTR, QUIT, EOT, SWITCH, or output postprocessing).

sane
> Reset all modes to reasonable values.

tty
> Line discipline is set to TTYDISC.

[-]crt
> [Do not] set all CRT display modes.

[-]kerninfo
> [Do not] allow a STATUS character to display system information.

columns num, cols num,
> Terminal size is set to num columns.

rows num
> Terminal size is set to num rows.

dec
> Digital Equipment Corporation mode set.

[-]extproc
> [Is not] Terminal hardware is doing some of the terminal processing.

size
> Terminal size is output as row number and column number.

---

su

su [option] [user] [shell_args]

Creates a shell with the effective user-ID user. If no user is specified, creates a shell for a privileged user (that is, becomes a superuser). Enter EOF to terminate. You can run the shell with particular options by passing them as shell_args (e.g., if the shell runs sh, you can specify -c command to execute command via sh or -r to create a restricted shell).

Options

-l   Go through the entire login sequence (i.e., change to user's environment).

-c *command*
> Execute *command* in the new shell and then exit immediately. If *command* is more than one word, it should be enclosed in quotes—for example:

> **su -c 'find / -name *.c -print' nobody**

-f   Start shell with -f option. In *csh* and *tcsh*, this suppresses the reading of the *.cshrc* file. In *bash*, this suppresses filename pattern expansion.

-m   Do not reset environment variables.

---

sudo

sudo [*options*] *command*

Executes a command as the superuser or as another user on the system. Before sudo executes *command*, it will prompt for the current account password (*not* root's).

sudo determines who is an authorized user by consulting the file */etc/sudoers*. If the current user account is listed in */etc/sudoers* and is authorized there to run *command*, that user can then run subsequent sudo commands without being prompted for a password. However, if five minutes (the default value) passes between sudo commands, the user will be prompted again for a password at the next sudo attempt, and given another five minute window.

By default, Mac OS X includes the *admin* group in the sudoers file and gives that group authorization to run any command with sudo. Mac OS X accounts given administrator privileges become members of the *admin* group, and thereby receive complete sudo privileges.

All attempts to use the sudo command are logged to the system log.

Options

-V   Print the version number. When run by root, also list the options used at sudo's compilation.

-l   List the commands that the current user is authorized to run with sudo.

-L   List all option settings that can be used in the *Defaults* section of the *sudoers* file.

-h   Print a usage statement.

-v   Reset the timestamp, giving the user a new five-minute window to use sudo without being prompted for a password.

-k   Kill the timestamp by setting it past the default timeout value. A password is not needed to use this option.

-K   Kill the timestamp by removing it. A password does not need to be supplied.

-b   Run *command* in the background, but do not allow use of shell job control to manipulate the process.

-p *prompt*
    Use *prompt* instead of the default password prompt. Within *prompt*, you can specify %*u* and %*h* to have them replaced by the current account name and local hostname, respectively

-u *user*
    Run the command as *user*, specified by either name or UID.

-s   Begin a shell session as root or *user*, if -u is specified.

-H   Set the HOME environment variable to the target user's home directory path. By default, sudo does not modify HOME.

-P   Preserve the user's group vector instead of changing it to that of the target user.

-S   Read password from standard input instead of prompting for it.

--   Stop processing command line arguments. This option makes the most sense when run with -s.

Examples

These examples assume that an appropriate sudoers file is in place. Refer to the sudoers manpage for more information on modifying the file.

List an otherwise protected directory:

    sudo ls /Users/brick

Edit the hostconfig file.:

    sudo vi /etc/hostconfig

Edit a another user's *.login* file:

    sudo -u jax vi ~jax/.login

---

sw_vers   sw_vers

Displays the product name, version, and build version for the OS; for example:

```
% sw_vers -h
ProductName:    Mac OS X
ProductVersion: 10.2.2
BuildVersion:   6F21
```

SystemStarter   SystemStarter [*options*] [*action* [*service*]]

Utility to control the starting, stopping, and restarting of system services. The services that can be affected are described in the */Library/StartupItems* and */System/Library/StartupItems/* paths.

The action and service arguments are optional. If no service argument is specified, all startup items will be affected. When a specific startup item is given, that item and all the items that it depends upon, or that are dependent on it, will be affected.

Currently, rc calls SystemStarter at boot time. Since SystemStarter may eventually take over the role of rc, it is advisable to create custom startup items rather than to continue to modify rc.

Options

-g   Graphical startup

-v   Verbose startup

-x   Safe mode startup (a basic startup that only runs Apple items)

-d   Prints debugging output

-D   Prints debugging output and shows dependencies

-q   Quiet mode that silences debugging output

-n   A pretend run mode that doesn't actually perform actions on any items

---

tail

tail [*options*] [*file*]

Prints the last ten lines of the named file. Use either -f or -r, but not both.

Options

-f   Don't quit at the end of file; "follow" file as it grows. End with an INTR (usually ^C).

-F   Behaves the same as the -f option with the exception that it checks every five seconds to see if the filename has changed. If it has, it will close the file and open the new file.

-r   Copy lines in reverse order.

-c *num*
> Begin printing at *num*th byte from the end of file.

-b *num*
> Begin printing at *num*th block from the end of file.

-n *num*
> Start at *num*th line from the end of file. -n is the default and does not need to be specified.

[+/-]
> To start from the beginning of the file, use + before *num*. The default is to start from the end of the file; this can also be done by using a - before *num*.

Examples

Show the last 20 lines containing instances of .Ah:

> **grep '\.Ah' file | tail -20**

Continually track the system log:

> **tail -f /var/log/system.log**

Show the last 10 characters of variable name:

> **echo "$name" | tail -c -10**

Reverse all lines in list:

> **tail -r list**

talk   talk *user* [*@hostname*] [*tty*]

Exchanges typed communication with another *user* who is on the local machine or on the machine *hostname*. talk might be useful when you're logged in via modem and need something quickly, making it inconvenient to telephone or send email. talk splits your screen into two windows. When a connection is established, you type in the top half while *user*'s typing appears in the bottom half. Type ^L to redraw the screen and ^C (or interrupt) to exit. If *user* is logged in more than once, use *tty* to specify the terminal line. The *user* needs to have used mesg y.

Notes

- There are different versions of talk that use different protocols; interoperability across different Unix systems is very limited.

- talk is also not very useful if the remote user you are "calling" is using a windowing environment, since there is no way for you to know which *tty* to use to get their attention. The connection request could easily show up in an iconified window! Even if you know the remote *tty*, the called party must have done a mesg y to accept the request.

---

tar   tar [*options*] [*tarfile*] [*other-files*]

Copy *files* to or restore *files* from an archive medium. If any *files* are directories, tar acts on the entire subtree. Options need not be preceded by – (though they may be). Note that until native drivers for tape drives exist for Mac OS X, tar cannot write to tape. Note also that tar does not preserve resource forks or metadata when copying files that contain them.

Function options

You must use exactly one of these, and it must come before any other options:

-c   Create a new archive.

-r, u
    Append *other-files* to the end of an existing archive.

-t   Print the names of *other-files* if they are stored on the archive (if *other-files* are not specified, print names of all files).

x   Extract *other-files* from an archive (if *other-files* are not specified, extract all files).

Options

-b   Set block size to 512 bytes.

-e   If there is an error, stop.

-f *arch*
    Store files in or extract files from archive *arch*. The default is */dev/rst0*. Since Mac OS X has no native tape drive support, tar produces an error unless the -f option is used.

-h   Dereference symbolic links.

-m   Do not restore file modification times; update them to the time of extraction.

-0   Create non-POSIX archives.

-o   Do not create archives with directory information that v7 tar would not be able to decode.

-p   Keep ownership of extracted files the same as that of original permissions.

-s *regex*
      Using ed-style regular expressions, change filenames in the archive.

-v   Verbose. Print filenames as they are added or extracted.

-w   Rename files with user interaction.

-z   Compress files with gzip before archiving them, or uncompress them with gunzip before extracting them.

-C   cd to *directory* before beginning tar operation.

-H   If any of the pathnames given in the command line are symbolic links, follow only those links.

-L   Follow all symbolic links.

-P   Do not remove initial slashes (/) from input filenames.

-X   Mount points will not be crossed.

-Z   Compress files with compress before archiving them, or uncompress them with uncompress before extracting them.

Examples

Create an archive of */bin* and */usr/bin* (c), show the command working (v), and write to the file in your home directory, ~/archive. tar:

    tar cvf ~/archive.tar /bin /usr/bin

List the the files contents in a format like ls -1:

    tar tvf ~/archive.tar

Extract only the */bin* directory from archive.tar to the current directory:

    tar xvf ~/archive.tar bin

---

tee

tee [*options*] *files*

Accepts output from another command and send it both to the standard output and to *files* (like a T or a fork in a road).

Options

-a   Append to *files*; do not overwrite.

-i   Ignore interrupt signals.

Example

View listing and save for later:

    ls -1 | tee savefile

telnet   telnet [*options*] [*host* [*port*]]

Accesses remote systems. telnet is the user interface that communicates with another host using the Telnet protocol. If telnet is
invoked without *host*, it enters command mode, indicated by its
prompt, telnet>, and accepts and executes the commands listed
after the following options. If invoked with arguments, telnet
performs an open command (shown in the following list) with those
arguments. *host* indicates the host's official name. *port* indicates a
port number (default is the Telnet port).

Options

-a   Automatic login into the remote system.

-b *alias*
      Used to connect to an *alias* setup by ifconfig or another inter-
      face as the local address to bind to.

-c   Tells telnet not to use a users *.telnetrc* file.

-d   Turn on socket-level debugging.

-e [*escape_char*]
      Set initial telnet escape character to *escape_char*. If *escape_
      char* is omitted, there will be no predefined escape character.

-k   Attempt to get tickets for remote host; query krb_realmofhost
      to determine realm.

-l *user*
      When connecting to remote system, and if remote system
      understands ENVIRON, send *user* to the remote system as the
      value for variable USER.

-n *tracefile*
      Open *tracefile* for recording the trace information.

-r   Emulate rlogin. The default escape character is a tilde (~); an
      escape character followed by a dot causes telnet to discon-
      nect from the remote host; a ^Z instead of a dot suspends
      telnet; and a] (the default telnet escape character) generates
      a normal telnet prompt. These codes are accepted only at the
      beginning of a line.

-x   Encryption will be used if possible.

-8   Request 8-bit operation.

-E   Disable the escape character functionality.

-F, -f Forward kerberos authentication criteria if kerberos is being
      used.

-K   Disable automatic login to remote systems

-L   Specify an 8-bit data path on output.

-S *tos*
      Set the IP type-of-service (TOS) option for the Telnet connec-
      tion to the value *tos*.

-X *type*
      Turns off the *type* of authentication.

Commands

CTRL-Z
> Suspend telnet.

! [*command*]
> Execute a single command in a subshell on the local system. If *command* is omitted, an interactive subshell will be invoked.

? [*command*]
> Get help. With no arguments, print a help summary. If a command is specified, print the help information for just that command.

auth *argument* ...
> Controls information sent through the TELNET AUTHENTICATION option.
>
> disable *type*
>> Authentication *type* is turned off.
>
> enable *type*
>> Authentication type is turned on.
>
> status
>> Status of authentucation type is displayed.

close
> Close a Telnet session and return to command mode.

display *argument* ...
> Display all, or some, of the set and toggle values.

encrypt *arguments* ...
> Controls information sent through the TELNET ENCRYPT option.
>
> disable *type* [input|output]
>> Encryption *type* is turned off.
>
> enable *type* [*input*|*output*]
>> Encryption *type* is turned on.
>
> start [*input*|*output*]
>> Encryption will be turned on if it can be. If neither input or output is given both will be started.
>
> status
>> Encryption status will be displayed.
>
> stop [*input*|*output*]
>> Encryption will be turned off. If neither input or output is given, both will be stopped.
>
> type *type*
>> Encryption *type* will be set.

environ [*arguments* [...]]
> Manipulate variables that may be sent through the TELNET ENVIRON option. Valid arguments for environ are:
>
> ?   Get help for the environ command.
>
> define *variable* *value*
>> Define *variable* to have a value of *value*.

undefine *variable*
> Remove *variable* from the list of environment variables.

export *variable*
> Mark *variable* to have its value exported to the remote side.

unexport *variable*
> Mark *variable* to not be exported unless explicitly requested by the remote side.

list
> Display current variable values.

logout
> If the remote host supports the logout command, close the telnet session.

mode [*type*]
> Depending on state of Telnet session, *type* is one of several options:

> ?   Print out help information for the mode command.

> character
>> Disable TELNET LINEMODE option, or, if remote side does not understand the option, enter "character-at-a-time" mode.

> [-]edit
>> Attempt to [disable] enable the EDIT mode of the TELNET LINEMODE option.

> [-]isig
>> Attempt to [disable]enable the TRAPSIG mode of the LINEMODE option.

> line
>> Enable LINEMODE option, or, if remote side does not understand the option, attempt to enter "old line-by-line" mode.

> [-]softtabs
>> Attempt to [disable] enable the SOFT_TAB mode of the LINEMODE option.

> [-]litecho
>> [Disable] enable LIT_ECHO mode.

open[-l *user*] *host* [*port*]
> Open a connection to the named *host*. If no *port* number is specified, attempt to contact a Telnet server at the default port.

quit
> Close any open Telnet session and then exit telnet.

status
> Show current status of telnet. This includes the peer you are connected to, as well as the current mode.

send *arguments*

> Send one or more special character sequences to the remote host. Following are the arguments that may be specified:
>
> ?　　Print out help information for send command.
>
> abort
>> Send Telnet ABORT sequence.
>
> ao
>> Send Telnet AO sequence, which should cause the remote system to flush all output from the remote system to the user's terminal.
>
> ayt
>> Send Telnet AYT (Are You There) sequence.
>
> brk
>> Send Telnet BRK (Break) sequence.
>
> do *cmd*
>
> dont *cmd*
>
> will *cmd*
>
> wont *cmd*
>> Send Telnet DO *cmd* sequence, where *cmd* is a number between 0 and 255 or a symbolic name for a specific telnet command. If *cmd* is ? or help, this command prints out help (including a list of symbolic names).
>
> ec
>> Send Telnet EC (Erase Character) sequence, which causes the remote system to erase the last character entered.
>
> el
>> Send Telnet EL (Erase Line) sequence, which causes the remote system to erase the last line entered.
>
> eof
>> Send Telnet EOF (End Of File) sequence.
>
> eor
>> Send Telnet EOR (End Of Record) sequence.
>
> escape
>> Send current Telnet escape character (initially ^).
>
> ga
>> Send Telnet GA (Go Ahead) sequence.
>
> getstatus
>> If the remote side supports the Telnet STATUS command, getstatus sends the subnegotiation request that the server sends to its current option status.
>
> ip
>> Send Telnet IP (Interrupt process) sequence, which causes the remote system to abort the currently running process.
>
> nop
>> Send Telnet NOP (No operation) sequence.

susp

Send Telnet SUSP (Suspend process) sequence.

synch

Send Telnet SYNCH sequence, which causes the remote system to discard all previously typed (but not read) input.

set *argument value*
unset *argument value*

Set any one of a number of telnet variables to a specific value or to TRUE. The special value off disables the function associated with the variable. unset disables any of the specified functions. The values of variables may be interrogated with the aid of the display command. The variables that may be specified are:

?   Display legal set and unset commands.

ayt

If telnet is in LOCALCHARS mode, this character is taken to be the alternate AYT character.

echo

This is the value (initially ^E) that, when in "line-by-line" mode, toggles between doing local echoing of entered characters and suppressing echoing of entered characters.

eof

If telnet is operating in LINEMODE or in the old "line-by-line" mode, entering this character as the first character on a line will cause the character to be sent to the remote system.

erase

If telnet is in LOCALCHARS mode or operating in the "character-at-a-time" mode, then when this character is entered, a Telnet EC sequence will be sent to the remote system.

escape

This is the Telnet escape character (initially ^[), which causes entry into the Telnet command mode when connected to a remote system.

flushoutput

If telnet is in LOCALCHARS mode and the flushoutput character is entered, a Telnet AO sequence is sent to the remote host.

forw1

If Telnet is in LOCALCHARS mode, this character is taken to be an alternate end-of- line character.

forw2

If Telnet is in LOCALCHARS mode, this character is taken to be an alternate end-of- line character.

interrupt

If Telnet AO is in LOCALCHARS mode and the interrupt character is entered, a Telnet IP sequence is sent to the remote host.

kill

If Telnet IP is in LOCALCHARS mode and operating in the "character-at-a-time" mode, then when this character is entered, a Telnet EL sequence is sent to the remote system.

lnext

If Telnet EL is in LINEMODE or in the old "line-by-line" mode, then this character is taken to be the terminal's lnext character.

quit

If Telnet EL is in LOCALCHARS mode and the quit character is entered, a Telnet BRK sequence is sent to the remote host.

reprint

If Telnet BRK is in LINEMODE or in the old "line-by-line" mode, this character is taken to be the terminal's reprint character.

rlogin

Enable rlogin mode. Same as using -r command-line option.

start

If the Telnet TOGGLE-FLOW-CONTROL option is enabled, this character is taken to be the terminal's start character.

stop

If the Telnet TOGGLE-FLOW-CONTROL option is enabled, this character is taken to be the terminal's stop character.

susp

If Telnet is in LOCALCHARS mode, or if the LINEMODE is enabled and the suspend character is entered, a Telnet SUSP sequence is sent to the remote host.

tracefile

The file to which output generated by netdata is written.

worderase

If Telnet BRK is in LINEMODE or in the old "line-by-line" mode, this character is taken to be the terminal's worderase character. Defaults for these are the terminal's defaults.

slc [*state*]

Set the state of special characters when Telnet LINEMODE option has been enabled.

?   List help on the slc command.

check

Verify current settings for current special characters. If discrepancies are discovered, convert local settings to match remote ones.

export
> Switch to local defaults for the special characters.

import
> Switch to remote defaults for the special characters.

toggle *arguments* [...]
> Toggle various flags that control how Telnet responds to events. The flags may be set explicitly to true or false using the set and unset commands listed previously. The valid arguments are:

? Display legal toggle commands.

autoflush
> If autoflush and LOCALCHARS are both true, then when the ao or quit characters are recognized, Telnet refuses to display any data on the user's terminal until the remote system acknowledges that it has processed those Telnet sequences.

autosynch
> If autosynch and LOCALCHARS are both true, then when the intr or quit characters are entered, the resulting Telnet sequence sent is followed by the Telnet SYNCH sequence. The initial value for this toggle is false.

binary
> Enable or disable the Telnet BINARY option on both the input and the output.

inbinary
> Enable or disable the Telnet BINARY option on the input.

outbinary
> Enable or disable the Telnet BINARY option on the output.

crlf
> If this toggle value is true, carriage returns are sent as CR-LF. If it is false, carriage returns are sent as CR-NUL. The initial value is false.

crmod
> Toggle carriage return mode. The initial value is false.

debug
> Toggle socket level debugging mode. The initial value is false.

localchars
> If the value is true, then flush, interrupt, quit, erase, and kill characters are recognized locally, and then transformed into appropriate Telnet control sequences. Initial value is true.

netdata
> Toggle display of all network data. The initial value is false.

Toggle display of some internal telnet protocol processing that pertains to Telnet options. The initial value is false.

prettydump

When netdata is enabled, and if prettydump is enabled, the output from the netdata command is reorganized into a more user-friendly format, spaces are put between each character in the output, and an asterisk precedes any Telnet escape sequence.

skiprc

Toggle whether to process ~/.telnetrc file. The initial value is false, meaning the file is processed.

termdata

Toggle printing of hexadecimal terminal data. Initial value is false.

Verbose_enrypt

When encryption is turned on or off, TELNET displays a message.

z   Suspend telnet; works only with csh.

---

test

test *expression*
[*expression*]

Also exists as a built-in in most shells.

Evaluates an *expression* and, if its value is true, returns a zero exit status; otherwise, return a nonzero exit status. In shell scripts, you can use the alternate form [*expression*]. This command is generally used with conditional constructs in shell programs.

File testers

The syntax for all of these options is test *option file*. If the specified file does not exist, the testers return false. Otherwise, they test the file as specified in the option description.

-b   Is the file block special?

-c   Is the file character special?

-d   Is the file a directory?

-e   Does the file exist?

-f   Is the file a regular file?

-g   Does the file have the set-group-ID bit set?

-k   Does the file have the sticky bit set?

-L,-h
     Is the file a symbolic link?

-p   Is the file a named pipe?

-r   Is the file readable by the current user?

-s   Is the file nonempty?

-S   Is the file a socket?

-t *[file-descriptor]*
     Is the file associated with *file-descriptor* (or 1, which is standard output, by default) connected to a terminal?

-u   Does the file have the set-user-ID bit set?

-w   Is the file writable by the current user?

-x   Is the file executable?

-O   Is the file owned by the process's effective user ID?

-G   Is the file owned by the process's effective group ID?

File comparisons

The syntax for file comparisons is *test file1 option file2*. A string by itself, without options, returns true if it's at least one character long.

-nt
     Is *file1* newer than *file2*? Check modification, not creation, date.

-ot
     Is *file1* older than *file2*? Check modification, not creation, date.

-ef
     Do the files have identical device and inode numbers?

String tests

The syntax for string tests is test *option string*.

-z   Is the string 0 characters long?

-n   Is the string at least 1 character long?

= *string*
     Are the two strings equal?

!= *string*
     Are the strings unequal?

<   Does *string1* come before *string2*, based on their ASCII values?

>   Does *string1* come after *string2*, based on their ASCII values?

Expression tests

Note that an expression can consist of any of the previous tests.

! *expression*
     Is the expression false?

expression -a *expression*
     Are the expressions both true?

expression -o *expression*
     Is either expression true?

Integer tests

The syntax for integer tests is test *integer1 option integer2*. You may substitute -l *string* for an integer; this evaluates to *string*'s length.

-eq

    Are the two integers equal?

-ne

    Are the two integers unequal?

-lt

    Is integer1 less than integer2?

-le

    Is *integer1* less than or equal to *integer2*?

-gt

    Is integer1 greater than integer2?

-ge

    Is *integer1* greater than or equal to *integer2*?

---

tftp

tftp [*host* [*port*]]

User interface to the TFTP (Trivial File Transfer Protocol), which allows users to transfer files to and from a remote machine. The remote *host* may be specified, in which case tftp uses *host* as the default host for future transfers.

Commands

Once tftp is running, it issues the prompt:

    tftp>

and recognizes the following commands:

? [*command-name*...]
    Print help information.

ascii
    Shorthand for mode ASCII.

binary
    Shorthand for mode binary.

connect *hostname* [*port*]
    Set the *hostname*, and optionally the *port*, for transfers.

get *filename*
get *remotename localname*
get *filename1 filename2 filename3...filenameN*
    Get a file or set of files from the specified remote sources.

mode *transfer-mode*
    Set the mode for transfers. *transfer-mode* may be ASCII or binary. The default is ASCII.

put *filename*
put *localfile remotefile*
put *filename1 filename2...filenameN remote-directory*
    Transfer a file or set of files to the specified remote file or directory.

quit
    Exit tftp.

rexmt *retransmission-timeout*
> Set the per-packet retransmission timeout, in seconds.

status
> Print status information: whether `tftp` is connected to a remote host (i.e., whether a host has been specified for the next connection), the current mode, whether verbose and tracing modes are on, and the values for retransmission timeout and total transmission timeout.

timeout *total-transmission-timeout*
> Set the total transmission timeout, in seconds.

trace
> Toggle packet tracing.

verbose
> Toggle verbose mode.

---

tiff2icns

tiff2icns [-noLarge] *input_filename* [*output_filename*]

Converts TIFF image files to Apple icon (ICNS) files. If *output_filename* is not specified, the output file receives the same name as the input file, with the filename extension changed to *.icns*.

Option
-noLarge
> Prevents the creation of the highest resolution icons.

---

tiffutil

tiffutil { -dump | -info | -verboseinfo } *input_file…*
tiffutil { -extract *number* | -jpeg [-f*N*] | -lzw | -none | -packbits } *input_file* [-out *output_file*]
tiffutil -cat *input_file…* [-out *output_file*]

Manipulates TIFF image files.

Options
-cat
> Concatenates multiple input files.

-dump
> Prints a list of all tags in the input file to standard output.

-extract
> Extracts an individual image from the input file, with 0 designating the first image in the file.

-f Specifies the compression factor to use with JPEG compression. The value can range from 1 to 255. The default is 10.

-info
> Prints information about images in the input file to standard output.

-jpeg
> Specifies the use of JPEG compression when producing the output file.

-lzw
>Specifies the use of Lempel-Ziv-Welch compression when producing the output file.

-none
>Specifies the use of no compression when producing the output file.

-output
>Specifies the name of the output file; defaults to *out.tiff*.

-packbits
>Specifies the use of PackBits compression when producing the output file.

-verboseinfo
>Prints lots of information about images in the input file to standard output.

---

time

time [*option*] *command* [*arguments*]

Executes a *command* with optional *arguments* and print the total elapsed time, execution time, process execution time, and system time of the process (all in seconds). Times are printed on standard error.

Option

-p   Print the real, user, and system times with a single space separating the title and the value, instead of a tab.

---

top

top [*options*] [*number*]

Full screen, dynamic display of global and per process resource usage by descending PID order.

Options

number
>top limits the total processes displayed to *number*.

-a   Cumulative event counting mode. Counts are cumulative from top start time. -w and -k are superceded and ignored while -a is in effect

-d   Delta event counting mode. Counts are deltas relative to a previous sample. -w and -k are superceded and ignored while -d is in effect.

-e   Absolute event counting mode. Counts are absolute values from process start times. -w and -k are superceded and ignored while -e is in effect.

-k   Report *kernal_task* memory map parameters: #MREGS, RPRVT, and RSHRD (and VPRVT with -w). Normally unreported and displayed as –.

-l *samples*
>Logging mode. Changes display mode from periodic full screen updating to a sequential line mode output suitable for output redirection. The number of sequential snapshots is specified as *samples*.

-s *interval*
> Sampling interval. Default one second sample interval is replaced by *interval*.

-u   Sort processes by decreasing cpu usage instead of by descending PID order.

-w   Changes the memory map and memory size parameters for all processes from counts to deltas, and adds a VPRVT column.

touch

touch [*options*] *files*

For one or more *files*, updates the access time and modification time (and dates) to the current time and date. touch is useful in forcing other commands to handle files a certain way; e.g., the operation of make, and sometimes find, relies on a file's access and modification time. If a file doesn't exist, touch creates it with a file size of 0.

Options

-a   Update only the access time.

-c   Do not create any file that doesn't already exist.

-f   Try to update even if you do not have permissions.

-h   The access or modification times of a symbolic link are changed. Access and modification time can be changed at the same time. The -c option is also applied.

-m   Update only the modification time.

-r *file*
> Change times to be the same as those of the specified *file*, instead of the current time.

-t *time*
> Use the time specified in *time* instead of the current time. This argument must be of the format: *[[cc]yy]mmddhhmm[.ss]*, indicating optional century and year, month, date, hours, minutes, and optional seconds.

tr

tr [*options*] [*string1* [*string2*]]

Translates characters—copies standard input to standard output, substituting characters from *string1* to *string2*, or deleting characters in *string1*.

Options

-c   Complement characters in *string1* with respect to ASCII 001-377.

-d   Delete characters in *string1* from output.

-s   Squeeze out repeated output characters in *string2*.

Special characters

Include brackets ([ ]) where shown.

\a   ^G (bell)

\b   ^H (backspace)

\f   ^L (form feed)

\n   ^J (newline)

\r   ^M (carriage return)

\t   ^I (tab)

\v   ^K (vertical tab)

nnn
>   Character with octal value *nnn*.

\\   Literal backslash.

char1-char2
>   All characters in the range *char1* through *char2*. If *char1* does not sort before *char2*, produce an error.

[*char1-char2*]
>   Same as *char1-char2* if both strings use this.

[*char**]
>   In *string2*, expand *char* to the length of *string1*.

[*char*number*]
>   Expand *char* to number occurrences. [x*4] expands to xxxx, for instance.

[:*class*:]
>   Expand to all characters in *class*, where *class* can be:
>
>   alnum
>   >   Letters and digits
>
>   alpha
>   >   Letters
>
>   blank
>   >   Whitespace
>
>   cntrl
>   >   Control characters
>
>   digit
>   >   Digits
>
>   graph
>   >   Printable characters except space
>
>   lower
>   >   Lowercase letters
>
>   print
>   >   Printable characters
>
>   punct
>   >   Punctuation
>
>   space
>   >   Whitespace (horizontal or vertical)
>
>   upper
>   >   Uppercase letters
>
>   xdigit
>   >   Hexadecimal digits

[=*char*=]
>   The class of characters in which *char* belongs.

Examples

Change uppercase to lowercase in a file:

    cat file | tr '[A-Z]' '[a-z]'

Turn spaces into newlines (ASCII code 012):

    tr ' ' '\012' < file

Strip blank lines from *file* and save in *new.file* (or use 011 to change successive tabs into one tab):

    cat file | tr -s "" "\012" > new.file

Delete colons from *file*; save result in *new.file*:

    tr -d : < file > new.file

---

traceroute

traceroute [*options*] *host* [*packetsize*]

Traces route taken by packets to reach network host. traceroute attempts tracing by launching UDP probe packets with a small TTL (time to live), then listening for an ICMP "time exceeded" reply from a gateway. *host* is the destination hostname or the IP number of host to reach. *packetsize* is the packet size in bytes of the probe datagram. Default is 38 bytes.

Options

-d   Turn on socket-level debugging.

-m *max_ttl*
      Set maximum time-to-live used in outgoing probe packets to *max-ttl* hops. Default is 30 hops.

-n   Show numerical addresses; do not look up hostnames. (Useful if DNS is not functioning properly.)

-p *port*
      Set base UDP port number used for probe packets to *port*. Default is (decimal) 33434.

-q *n*
      Set number of probe packets for each time-to-live setting to the value *n*. Default is 3.

-r   Bypass normal routing tables and send directly to a host on an attached network.

-s *src_addr*
      Use *src_addr* as the IP address that will serve as the source address in outgoing probe packets.

-t *tos*
      Set the type-of-service in probe packets to *tos* (default 0). The value must be a decimal integer in the range 0 to 255.

-v   Verbose—received ICMP packets (other than TIME_ EXCEEDED and PORT_ UNREACHABLE) will be listed.

-w *wait*
      Set time to wait for a response to an outgoing probe packet to *wait* seconds (default is 3 seconds).

---

true   true

A null command that returns a successful (0) exit status. See also false.

tset   tset [*options*] [*type*]

Set terminal modes. Without arguments, the terminal is reinitialized according to the TERM environment variable. tset is typically used in startup scripts (*.profile* or *.login*). *type* is the terminal type; if preceded by a ?, tset prompts the user to enter a different type, if needed. Press the Return key to use the default value, *type*.

Options

-q,- Print terminal name on standard output; useful for passing this value to TERM.

-e*c* Set erase character to *c*; default is ^H (backspace).

-i*c* Set interrupt character to *c* (default is ^C).

-I Do not output terminal initialization setting.

-k*c* Set line-kill character to *c* (default is ^U).

-m[*port*[*baudrate*]:*type*]

Declare terminal specifications. *port* is the port type (usually dialup or plugboard). *tty* is the terminal type; it can be preceded by ? as above. *baudrate* checks the port speed and can be preceded by any of these characters:

>   Port must be greater than baudrate.

<   Port must be less than baudrate.

@   Port must transmit at baudrate.

!   Negate a subsequent >, <, or @ character.

?   Prompt for the terminal type. With no response, use the given type.

-Q Do not print "Erase set to" and "Kill set to" messages.

-r Report the terminal type.

-s Return the values of TERM assignments to the shell environment. This is commonly done via eval \'tset -s\' (in the C shell, surround this with the commands set noglob and unset noglob).

-V Prints the version of ncurses being used.

Examples

Set TERM to wy50:

    eval `tset -s wy50`

Prompt user for terminal type (default is vt100):

    eval `tset -Qs -m '?vt100'`

Similar to above, but the baudrate must exceed 1200:

    eval `tset -Qs -m '>1200:?xterm'`

Set terminal via modem. If not on a dial-in line, the ?$TERM causes tset to prompt with the value of $TERM as the default terminal type:

```
eval `tset -s -m dialup:'?vt100' "?$TERM"`
```

tty

tty [*option*]

Prints the device name for your terminal. This is useful for shell scripts and commands that need device information. tty exits 0 if the standard input is a terminal, 1 if the standard input is not a terminal, and >1 if an error occurs.

Option

-s   Suppress the terminal name.

udf.util

udf.util -m *device mount_point*
udf.util { -p | -u } *device*

Mounts UDF (DVD) filesystems into the directory hierarchy.

Options

-m   Mounts the device.

-p   Probes the device, and prints the volume name to standard output.

-u   Unmounts the device.

device
   Specifies the DVD device filename; for example, disk1.

mount_point
   Specifies the directory on which the DVD filesystem is mounted.

umount

umount [-f] [-v] [-t *types*] { -a | -A | -h *hostname* }
umount [-f] [-v] { *special* | *mount_point* }

Removes mounted volumes from the directory hierarchy.

Options

-a   Unmounts all filesystems listed in *fstab* or Open Directory.

-A   Unmounts all currently mounted filesystems, other than the root.

-f   Attempts to force the unmount.

-h
   Unmounts all filesystems currently mounted from the specified server.

-t   Restricts the use of the command to filesystems of the specified types presented in a comma-separated list, which may include hfs, ufs, afp, nfs, or others.

-v   Enables verbose output.

special
> The form of this argument is particular to the type of filesystem being mounted, and could be a disk device name, a fixed string, or something involving a server name and directory. See the individual *mount_type* entries for details.

mount_point
> The directory on which the filesystem is mounted.

uname

uname [*options*]

Prints information about the machine and operating system. Without options, prints the name of the operating system.

Options

-a, --all
> Combine all the system information from the other options.

-m, --machine
> Print the hardware the system is running on.

-n, --nodename
> Print the machine's hostname.

-r, --release
> Print the release number of the kernel.

-s, --sysname
> Print the name of the operating system.

-p, --processor
> Print the type of processor.

-v
> Print build information about the kernel.

uncompress

uncompress [*option*] [*files*]

Restores the original file compressed by compress. The .Z extension is implied, so it can be omitted when specifying *files*.

The -b, -c, -f, and -v options from compress are also allowed. See compress for more information.

unexpand

unexpand [*options*] [*files*]

Converts strings of initial whitespace, consisting of at least two spaces and/or tabs to tabs. Reads from standard input if given no file or a given file named –.

Option

-a
> Convert all, not just initial, strings of spaces and tabs.

uniq

uniq [*options*] [*file1* [*file2*]]

Removes duplicate adjacent lines from sorted *file1*, sending one copy of each line to *file2* (or to standard output). Often used as a filter. Specify only one of -c, -d, or -u. See also comm and sort.

Options

-c Print each line once, counting instances of each.

-d Print duplicate lines once, but no unique lines.

-f *n* Ignore the first *n* fields of a line. Fields are separated by spaces or by tabs.

-s *n* Ignore the first *n* characters of a field.

-u Print only unique lines (no copy of duplicate entries is kept).

-n Ignore the first *n* fields of a line. Fields are separated by spaces or by tabs.

+*n* Ignore the first *n* characters of a field. Both [-/+]*n* have been depricated but are still in this version.

Examples

Send one copy of each line from *list* to output file *list.new* (list must be sorted):

uniq list list.new

Show which names appear more than once:

sort names | uniq -d

Show which lines appear exactly three times:

sort names | uniq -c | awk '$1 == 3'

---

units

units [*options*]

Interactively supply a formula to convert a number from one unit to another. A complete list of the units can be found in */usr/share/ misc/units.lib*.

Options

-f *filename*
    Use the units data in *filename*.

-q The prompts for "you have" and "you want" will not appear.

-v The version of units is listed.

[*have-unit want-unit*]
    A unit conversion can be entered from the command line instead of using the interactive interface.

---

unzip

unzip [*options*[*modifiers*]] *zipfile* ... [*extraction options*]
unzip -Z [*zipinfo options*] *zipfile* ...

Unzip prints information about or extracts files from ZIP format archives. The *zipfile* is a ZIP archive whose filename ends in *.zip*. The .zip can be omitted from the command line; unzip supplies it. *zipfile* may also be a shell-style wildcard pattern (which should be quoted); all matching files in the ZIP archive will be acted upon. The behavior of *options* is affected by the various *modifiers*.

In the second form, the *options* are taken to be zipinfo options; unzip performs like that command.

Options may also be included in the UNZIP environment variable, to set a default behavior. Options on the command line can override settings in $UNZIP by preceding them with an extra minus. See the Examples.

When extracting files, if a file exists already, unzip prompts for an action. You may to choose to overwrite or skip the existing file, overwrite or skip all files, or rename the current file.

Notes

- unzip and its companion program zip are part of the InfoZIP project. InfoZIP is an open collaborative compressed archive format, and implementations exist for Unix, Amiga, Atari, DEC VAX and Alpha VMS, OpenVMS, MS-DOS, Macintosh, Minix, OS/2, Windows NT, and many others. It is the *only* similar format one can expect to port to all of these systems without difficulty.

- Unlike most Unix tar implementations, zip removes leading slashes when it creates a ZIP archive, so there is never any problem unbundling it at another site.

- The Java Archive format (*.jar*) is based on ZIP; zip and unzip can process *.jar* files with no trouble.

- unzip is installed on Mac OS X as part of Apple's Developer Tools.

Extraction options

-d *dir*
Extract files in *dir* instead of in the current directory. This option need not appear at the end of the command line.

-x *files*
Exclude. Do not extract archive members that match *files*.

Options

-c   Print files to standard output (the CRT). Similar to -p, but a header line is printed for each file, it allows -a, and automatically does an ASCII to EBCDIC conversion. Not in the unzip usage message.

-f   Freshen existing files. Only files in the archive that are newer than existing disk files are extracted. unzip queries before overwriting, unless -o is used.

-l   List archived files, in short format (name, full size, modification time, and totals).

-p   Extract files to standard output (for piping). Only the file data is printed. No conversions are done.

-t   Test the archived files. Each file is extracted in memory, and the extracted file's CRC is compared to the stored CRC.

-u   Same as -f, but also extract any files that don't exist on disk yet.

-v   Be verbose or print diagnostic information. -v is both an
       option and a modifier, depending upon the other options. By
       itself, it prints the unzip ftp site information, details on how it
       was compiled, and what environment variable settings are in
       effect. With a zipfile, it adds compression information to that
       provided by -l.

-z   Print only the archive comment.

-Z   Run as zipinfo.

Modifiers

-a[a]
       Convert text files. Normally, files are extracted as binary files.
       This option causes text files to be converted to the native
       format (e.g., adding or removing CR characters in front of LF
       characters). EBCDIC-to-ASCII conversion is also done as
       needed. Use -aa to force all files to be extracted as text.

-b   Treat all files as binary.

-C   Ignore case when matching filenames. Useful on non-Unix
       systems where filesystems are not case-sensitive.

-j   "Junk" paths. Extract all files in the current extraction direc-
       tory, instead of reproducing the directory tree structure stored
       in the archive.

-L   Convert filenames to lowercase from archives created on
       uppercase-only systems. By default, filenames are extracted
       exactly as stored in the archive.

-M   Pipe output through the internal pager, which is similar to
       more. Press the Return key or spacebar at the --More-- prompt
       to see the next screenful.

-n   Never overwrite existing files. If a file already exists, don't
       extract it, just continue on without prompting. Normally,
       unzip prompts for an action.

-o   Overwrite existing files without prompting. Often used
       together with -f. Use with care.

-q[q]
       unzip will use quiet mode. A second q is a quieter mode.

-Z zipinfo Options

-x files
       Exclude. Do not extract archive members that match files.

-1   List only filenames, one per line. Nothing else is printed. For
       use in shell scripts.

-2   Like -1, but also permit headers, trailers, and ZIP archive
       comments (-h, -t, -z).

-h   Print a header line with the archive name, size in bytes, and
       total number of files.

-l   Use "long" format. Like -m, but also print the compressed size
       in bytes, instead of the compression ratio.

-m   Use "Medium" format. Like -s, but also include the compression factor (as a percentage).

-M   Pipe output through the internal pager, which is similar to more. Press the Return key or spacebar at the --More-- prompt to see the next screenful.

-s   Use "short" format, similar to ls -l. This is the default.

-t   Print totals for all files (number of files, compressed and uncompressed sizes, overall compression factor).

-T   Print times and dates in a decimal format (*yymmdd.hhmmss*) that can be sorted.

-v   Use verbose, multipage format.

-z   Print the archive comment.

Examples

List the contents of a ZIP archive:

```
unzip -lv whizprog.zip
```

Extract C source files in the main directory, but not in subdirectories:

```
unzip whizprog.zip '*.[ch]' -x '*/*'
```

---

uptime   uptime

Prints the current time, amount of time the system has been up, number of users logged in, and the system-load averages over the last one, five, and fifteen minutes. This output is also produced by the first line of the w command.

---

users   users [*file*]

Prints a space-separated list of each login session on the host. Note that this may include the same user multiple times. Consult *file* or, by default, */var/run/utmp*.

---

uudecode   uudecode [*file*]

Reads a uuencoded file and re-creates the original file with the permissions and name set in the file (see uuencode).

---

uuencode   uuencode[*file*] *name*

Encodes a binary *file*. The encoding uses only printable ASCII characters and includes the permissions and *name* of the file. When *file* is reconverted via uudecode, the output is saved as *name*. If the *file* argument is omitted, uuencode can take standard input, so a single argument is taken as the name to be given to the file when it is decoded.

uuencode does not preserve resource forks or metadata when copying files that contain them.

Examples

It's common to encode a file and save it with an identifying extension, such as *.uue*. This example encodes the binary file *flower12.jpg*, names it *rose.jpg*, and saves it to a *.uue* file:

```
% uuencode flower12.jpg rose.jpg > rose.uue
```

Encode *flower12.jpg* and mail it:

```
% uuencode flower12.jpg flower12.jpg | mail jax@ora.com
```

---

uuidgen

uuidgen

Sends to standard output a generated Universally Unique Identifier (UUID). A UUID is a 128-bit value guaranteed to be unique. This is achieved by combining a value unique to the computer, such as the MAC Ethernet address, and a value representing the number of 100-nanosecond intervals since a specific time in the past.

---

vi

vi [*options*] [*files*]

A screen-oriented text editor based on ex. See Chapter 17 for more information on vi and ex. Options -c, -C, -L, -r, -R, and -t are the same as in ex.

Options

-c *command*
   Enter vi and execute the given vi *command*.

-e   Edit in ex mode.

-F   Do not make a temporary backup of the entire file.

-l   Run in LISP mode for editing LISP programs.

-r *file*
   Recover and edit *file* after an editor or system crash.

-R   Read-only mode. Files can't be changed.

-S   No other programs can be run, vi is put in secure edit mode.

-s   This option works only when ex mode is being used. It enters into batch mode.

-t *tag*
   Edit the file containing *tag*, and position the editor at its definition.

-w*n*
   Set default window size to *n*; useful when editing via a slow dial-up line.

+   Start vi on last line of file.

+*n*   Start vi on line *n* of file.

+/*pat*
   Start vi on line containing pattern *pat*. This option fails if nowrapscan is set in your *.exrc* file.

view	view [*options*] [*files*]
	Same as vi -R.

vm_stat	vm_stat [*interval*]
	Displays Mach virtual memory statistics. The default view, without a specified interval, shows accumulated statistics. If interval is specified, vm_stat will list the changes in each statistic every interval seconds, showing the accumulated statistics for each item in the first line.

vmmap	vmmap *PID*
	Displays the virtual memory regions associated with *PID*. vmmap displays the starting address, region size, read/write permissions for the page, sharing mode for the page, and the page purpose. This can be useful information for programmers especially, who often need to understand the memory allocation of a given process.

vndevice	vndevice { attach | shadow } *device pathname* vndevice detach *device*
	Attaches or detaches a virtual device node to or from a disk image file. (Note that the functionality of vndevice is incorporated within hdiutil.)

Options

attach

> Attaches a device node to a disk image designated by *pathname*.

detach

> Detaches a device node from a disk image.

shadow

> Associates an attached device node to a "shadow" disk image designated by *pathname*. Modifications to data on the attached disk image will instead be written to the shadow image, and subsequent access to that data will be from the shadow. This allows effective read/write access to data on a disk image which should not or cannot be modified.

device

> The device node filename; e.g., */dev/vn0*.

Examples

Create a disk image, attach a virtual device node to it, and mount it:

```
% hdiutil create test.dmg -volname test -size 5m -fs↵
HFS+ -layout NONE
% sudo vndevice attach /dev/vn0 test.dmg
% mkdir mount_point
% sudo mount -t hfs /dev/vn0 mount_point
```

Wait a minute, and then:

```
% touch mount_point/test_file
% ls -l test.dmg
```

Note that the modification time on the disk image is current, reflecting the change you made by creating a test file.

Now set up shadowing. Unmount the volume first, then create the shadow disk image, attach the virtual node to it, and mount it again:

```
% sudo umount /dev/vn0
% hdiutil create shadow.dmg -volname shadow -size 5m↵
-fs HFS+ -layout NONE
% sudo vndevice shadow /dev/vn0 shadow.dmg
% sudo mount -t hfs /dev/vn0 mount_point
```

Wait a minute, and then:

```
% rm mount_point/test_file
% ls -l test.dmg; ls -l shadow.dmg
```

The modification time on the test image wasn't updated, but the shadow image reflects the change you just made, indicating that writes are being passed through to the shadow.

Finish up by unmounting the volume and detaching the virtual node:

```
% sudo umount /dev/vn0
% sudo vndevice detach /dev/vn0
```

---

vsdbutil

```
vsdbutil { -a | -c | -d } pathname
vsdbutil -i
```

Enables or disables the use of permissions on a disk volume. This is equivalent to using the Ignore Privileges checkbox in the Finder's Info window for a mounted volume. The status of permissions usage on mounted volumes is stored in the permissions database, */var/db/ volinfo.database*.

Options

-a Activates permissions on the volume designated by *pathname*.

-c Checks the status of permissions usage on the volume designated by *pathname*.

-d Deactivates permissions on the volume designated by *pathname*.

-i Initializes the permissions database to include all mounted HFS and HFS+ volumes.

---

w

```
w [options] [user]
```

Prints summaries of system usage, currently logged-in users, and what they are doing. w is essentially a combination of uptime, who, and ps -a. Display output for one user by specifying *user*.

Options

-h   Suppress headings and uptime information.

-i   List by idle time.

-M *file*
> Use data from the supplied *file*.

-N *sysname*
> Use data from the supplied *sysname*.

-n   List IP address as numbers.

---

wall

wall [*file*]

Writes to all users. wall reads a message from the standard input until an end-of-file. It then sends this message to all users currently logged in, preceded by "Broadcast Message from..." If *file* is specified, read input from that, rather than from standard input.

---

wc

wc [*options*] [*files*]

Prints byte, character, word, and line counts for each file. Prints a total line for multiple *files*. If no *files* are given, read standard input. See other examples under ls and sort.

Options

-c   Print byte count only.

-l   Print line count only.

-m   Print character count only.

-w   Print word count only.

Examples

Count the number of users logged in:

> **who | wc -l**

Count the words in three essay files:

> **wc -w essay.[123]**

Count lines in the file named by variable *$file* (don't display the filename):

> **wc -l < $file**

---

whatis

whatis *keywords*

Searches the short manual page descriptions in the *whatis* database for each *keyword* and print a one-line description to standard output for each match. Like apropos, except that it searches only for complete words. Equivalent to man -f.

---

whereis

whereis *files*

Checks the standard binary directories for the specified programs, printing out the paths of any it finds.

Compatibility

The historic flags and arguments for the whereis utility are no longer available in this version.

---

which

which [*commands*]

Lists which files are executed if the named *commands* are run as a command. which reads the user's *.cshrc* file (using the source built-in command), checking aliases and searching the path variable. Users of the Bourne or Korn shells can use the built-in type command as an alternative.

Example

```
$ which file ls
/usr/bin/file
ls:      aliased to ls -sFC
```

---

who

who [*options*] [*file*]

Displays information about the current status of the system. With no options, list the names of users currently logged in to the system. An optional system file (default is */var/run/utmp*) can be supplied to give additional information. who is usually invoked without options, but useful options include am i and -u. For more examples, see cut, line, paste, tee, and wc.

Options

-H   Print headings.

-m   Report only about the current terminal.

-T   Report whether terminals are writable (+), not writable (–), or unknown (?).

-u   Report terminal usage (idle time). A dot (.) means less than one minute idle; old means more than 24 hours idle.

am i
   Print the username of the invoking user. (Similar to results from id.)

Example

This sample output was produced at 8 a.m. on April 17:

```
% who -uH
NAME   LINE   TIME          IDLE   PID  COMMENTS
martha ttyp3  Apr 16 08:14  16:25  2240
george ttyp0  Apr 17 07:33   .     15182
```

The output shows that the user martha has beenidle for 16 hours and 25 minutes (16:25, under the IDLE column).

---

whoami

whoami

Prints current user ID. Equivalent to id -un.

---

whois

whois [*option*] *name*

Queries the Network Information Center (NIC) database to display registration records matching *name*. Multiple *names* need to be separated by whitespace. The special *name* "help" will return more information on the command's use.

Option

-h   Use to specify a different whois server to query. The default is *whois.internet.net*.

---

window

window [*options*]

Instantiates multiple (two by default), virtual, ASCII-based windows on a single terminal window. I

A window is a user-configurable, rectangular area located on the terminal and provides the STDIN, STDOUT, and STDERR bindings for an associated set of processes. The STDIN file handle of only one window may actively communicate with the keyboard at any given time, but all windows may utilize their STDOUT and STDERR simultaneously.

window is bimodal and operates by establishing an association between the keyboard and STDIN of the current window (conversation mode), or between the keyboard and the window command processor (command mode).

Options

-t   Enter terse command mode; doesn't display command window.

-f   Fast startup; create command window only.

-d   Start with default number of windows (2) and ignore any *.windowrc* file.

-e *char*

Set the escape charter is to *char*. The default is ^P.

-c *command*

Run the long *command* prior to creating any windows.

Short commands

Short commands are used in the conversation mode of window. To enter conversation mode, press the Escape key.

num

Change current window to *num* and return to conversation mode.

%*num*

Change current window to *num* and stay in command mode.

^^   Toggle between two windows in conversation mode.

escape

Enter conversation mode.

^P   Enter into conversation mode and write ^P to the current window. If the window escape is changed to some other character, that character takes the place of ^P here.

?   List a summary of short commands.

^L   Refresh the display.

q   Exit.

^Z   Suspend.

w   Create a new window, to be sized interactively. Use keys "h," "j," "k," and "l" move the cursor left, down, up, and right, respectively. The keys "H," "J," "K," and "L" move the cursor to the respective limits of the screen. Typing a number before the movement keys repeats the movement that number of times. Press Return to mark when each corner is done. To cancel the command, press the Escape key.

cnum
Close the window *num*.

mnum
Move window *num* to another location.

Mnum
Move window *num* to its previous position.

snum
Change the size of window *num*.

Snum
Change the size of the window *num* to its previous size.

^Y   Scroll the current window up by one line.

^E   Scroll the current window down by one line.

^U   Scroll the current window up by half the window size.

^D   Scroll the current window down by half the window size.

^B   Scroll the current window up by the full window size.

^F   Scroll the current window down by the full window size.

y   Yank the contents of the current window between two points. The info will be saved in the yank buffer.

p   Put the content of the yank buffer in the current window.

^S   Stop output to the current window.

^Q   Start output to the current window.

:   Enter a line to be executed as long commands. Refer to the window manpage for details.

---

write   write *user* [*tty*] *message*

Initiates or responds to an interactive conversation with *user*. A write session is terminated with *EOF*. If the user is logged in to more than one terminal, specify a *tty* number. See also talk; use mesg to keep other users from writing to your terminal.

---

xargs

xargs [*options*] [*command*]

Executes *command* (with any initial arguments), but reads remaining arguments from standard input instead of specifying them directly. xargs passes these arguments in several bundles to *command*, allowing *command* to process more arguments than it could normally handle at once. The arguments are typically a long list of filenames (generated by ls or find, for example) that get passed to xargs via a pipe.

Options

-0 Expect filenames to be terminated by NULL instead of whitespace. Do not treat quotes or backslashes specially.

-n *args*
    Allow no more than *args* arguments on the command line. May be overridden by -s.

-s *max*
    Allow no more than *max* characters per command line.

-t Verbose mode. Print command line on standard error before executing.

-x If the maximum size (as specified by -s) is exceeded, exit.

Examples

grep for *pattern* in all files on the system, including those with spaces in their names:

    find / -print0 | xargs -0 grep *pattern* **> out &**

Run diff on file pairs (e.g., *f1.a* and *f1.b*, *f2.a*, and *f2.b* ...):

    echo $* | xargs -n2 diff

The previous line would be invoked as a shell script, specifying filenames as arguments. Display *file*, one word per line (same as deroff -w):

    cat *file* **| xargs -n1**

yes

yes [*strings*]

Prints the command-line arguments, separated by spaces and followed by a newline, until killed. If no arguments are given, print y followed by a newline until killed. Useful in scripts and in the background; its output can be piped to a program that issues prompts.

zcat

zcat [*options*] [*files*]

Reads one or more *files* that have been compressed with gzip or compress and write them to standard output. Read standard input if no *files* are specified or if - is specified as one of the files; end input with *EOF*. zcat is identical to gunzip -c and takes the options -fhLV described for gzip/gunzip.

zcmp

`zcmp [options] files`

Reads compressed files and passes them, uncompressed, to the cmp command, along with any command-line options. If a second file is not specified for comparison, looks for a file called *file.gz*.

zdiff

`zdiff [options] files`

Reads compressed files and passes them, uncompressed, to the diff command, along with any command-line options. If a second file is not specified for comparison, looks for a file called *file.gz*.

zgrep

`zgrep [options] [files]`

Uncompresses files and passes to grep, along with any command-line arguments. If no files are provided, reads from (and attempts to uncompress) standard input. May be invoked as zegrep or zfgrep; in those cases, invokes egrep or fgrep.

zip

`zip [options] zipfile [files]`

Archives files in InfoZIP format. These files can be retrieved using unzip. The files are compressed as they are added to the archive. Compression ratios of 2:1 to 3:1 are common for text files. zip may also replace files in an existing archive. With no arguments, display the help information. See also unzip.

Default options may be placed in the ZIPOPT environment variable, with the exceptions of -i and -x. Multiple options may be included in ZIPOPT.

zip does not preserve resource forks or metadata when copying files that contain them. zip is installed on Mac OS X as part of Apple's Developer Tools. There are a number of other important notes in the unzip entry; go there for more information.

Options

-b *path*

Use *path* as the location to store the temporary ZIP archive while updating an existing one. When done, copy the temporary archive over the new one. Useful primarily when there is not enough disk space on the filesystem containing the original archive.

-c   Add one-line comments for each file. zip first performs any file operations and then prompts you for a comment describing each file.

-d   Delete entries from a ZIP archive. Filenames to be deleted must be entered in uppercase if the archive was created by PKZIP on an MS-DOS system.

-D   Don't create entries in the archive for directories. Usually entries are created so that attributes for directories may be restored upon extraction.

-f   Freshen (replace) an existing entry in the ZIP archive if the file has a more recent modification time than the one in the archive. This doesn't add files that are not already in the archive: use -u for that. Run this command from the same directory where the ZIP archive was created, since the archive stores relative path names.

-F, -FF
      Fix the ZIP archive. This option should be used with care; make a backup copy of the archive first. The -FF version does not trust the compressed sizes in the archive, and instead scans it for special "signatures" that identify the boundaries of different archive members. See the manpage for more information.

-g   Grow the archive (append files to it).

-h   Display the zip help information.

-i *files*
      Include only the specified *files*, typically specified as a quoted shell wildcard-style pattern.

-j   "Junk" the path; i.e., store just the name of the saved file, not any directory names. The default is to store complete paths, although paths are always relative.

-J   Strip any prepended data (e.g., an SFX stub for self-extracting executables) from the archive.

-k   Create an archive that (attempts to) conform to the conventions used under MS-DOS. This makes it easier for PKUNZIP to extract the archive.

-l   For text files only, translate the Unix newline into a CR-LF pair. Primarily for archives extracted under MS-DOS.

-ll   For text files only, translate the MS-DOS CR-LF into a Unix newline.

-L   Display the zip license.

-m   "Move" the files into the ZIP archive. This actually deletes the original files and/or directories after the archive has been created successfully. This is somewhat dangerous; use -T in conjunction with this option.

-n *suffixlist*
      Do not compress files with suffixes in *suffixlist*. Useful for sound or image files that often have their own, specialized compression method.

-o   Set the modified time of the ZIP archive to be that of the youngest file (most recently modified) in the archive.

-q   Quiet mode. Don't print informational messages and comment prompts. Most useful in shell scripts.

-r   Recursively archive all files and subdirectories of the named files. The -i option is also useful in combination with this one.

-t *mmddyy*
      Ignore files modified prior to the date given by *mmddyy*.

-T Test the new ZIP archive's integrity. If the test fails, an existing ZIP archive is not changed, and with -m, no files are removed.

-u Update existing entries in the ZIP archive if the named files have modification dates that are newer than those in the archive. Similar to -f, except that this option adds files to the archive if they aren't already there.

-v As the only argument, print help and version information, a pointer to the home and distribution Internet sites, and information about how zip was compiled. When used with other options, cause those options to print progress information and provide other diagnostic information.

-x *files*
Exclude the specified *files*, typically specified as a quoted shell wildcard-style pattern.

-X Do not save extra file attributes (extended attributes on OS/2, user ID/group ID, and file times on Unix).

-y Preserve symbolic links in the ZIP archive, instead of archiving the file the link points to.

-z Prompt for a (possibly multiline) comment describing the entire ZIP archive. End the comment with line containing just a period, or EOF.

-n Specify compression speed: *n* is a digit between 0 and 9. 0 indicates no compression, 1 indicates fast but minimal compression, 9 indicates slowest but maximal compression. Default is -6.

-@ Read standard input for names of files to be archived. Filenames containing spaces must be quoted using single quotes.

Examples

Archive the current directory into *source.zip*, including only C source files:

```
zip source -i '*.[ch]'
```

Archive the current directory into *source.zip*, excluding the object files:

```
zip source -x '*.o'
```

Archive files in the current directory into *source.zip*, but don't compress *.tiff* and *.snd* files:

```
zip source -z '.tiff:.snd' *
```

Recursively archive the entire directory tree into one archive:

```
zip -r /tmp/dist.zip .
```

---

zprint

zprint [*options*] *name*

Displays information in columnar output about all memory zones. Using command-line switches, you can alter the formatting and amount of information displayed.

Options

-w Display the space allocated, but not in use, for each memory zone. The output for each zone is displayed in the right-most column.

-s Produces a sorted output of the memory zones in descending order beginning with the zone that wastes the most memory.

-C Overrides the default columnar format with a row-based display that also reduces the information fields shown.

-H Hides the default columnar headings. This may be useful when sorting output by column.

name is a substring of one or more memory zone names. Only memory zones matching this substring will be included in the output.

---

zmore zmore [*files*]

Similar to more. Uncompress files and print them, one screenful at a time. Works on files compressed with compress, gzip, or pack, and with uncompressed files.

Commands

space
> Print next screenful.

i[*number*]
> Print next screenful, or *number* lines. Set *i* to *number* lines.

d, ^D
> *Print next i*, or 11, lines.

iz Print next *i* lines or a screenful.

is Skip *i* lines. Print next screenful.

if Skip *i* screens. Print next screenful.

q, Q, :q, :Q
> Go to next file, or, if current file is the last, exit zmore.

e, q Exit zmore when the prompt "--More--(Next file: *file*)" is displayed.

s Skip next file and continue.

= Print line number.

i/expr
> Search forward for *i*th occurrence (in all files) of *expr*, which should be a regular expression. Display occurrence, including the two previous lines of context.

in Search forward for the *i*th occurrence of the last regular expression searched for.

!*command*
> Execute *command* in shell. If *command* is not specified, execute last shell command. To invoke a shell without passing it a command, enter \!.

. Repeat the previous command.

znew   znew [*options*] [*files*]

Uncompresses .Z files and recompress them in .*gz* format.

Options

-9   Optimal (and slowest) compression method.

-f   Recompress even if *filename.gz* already exists.

-t   Test new .*gz* files before removing .Z files.

-v   Verbose mode.

-K   If the original .Z file is smaller than the .*gz* file, keep it.

-P   Pipe data to conversion program. This saves disk space.

Resources

The following is a list of resources for Mac OS X users, including books, magazines, mailing lists, and web sites.

Books

The following books are available for Mac users, administrators, and developers:

AppleScript in a Nutshell
    By Bruce Perry (O'Reilly & Associates, Inc., 2001)

AppleScript for Applications: Visual QuickStart Guide
    By Ethan Wilde (Peachpit Press, 2001)

AppleWorks 6: The Missing Manual
    By Jim Elferdink and David Reynolds (Pogue Press/O'Reilly & Associates, Inc., 2001)

Building Cocoa Applications: A Step-by-Step Guide
    By Simson Garfinkel and Michael Mahoney (O'Reilly & Associates, Inc., 2002)

Carbon Programming
    By K. J. Bricknell (Sams, 2001)

Cocoa Programming
    By Scott Anguish, Erik Buck, and Donald Yacktman (Sams, 2002)

Cocoa Programming for Mac OS X
    By Aaron Hillegass (Addison-Wesley, 2001)

Cocoa Recipes for Mac OS X: The Vermont Recipes
    By Bill Cheeseman (Peachpit Press, 2003)

iMovie 2: The Missing Manual
    By David Pogue (Pogue Press/O'Reilly & Associates, Inc., 2001)

iMovie 2 Solutions: Tips, Tricks, and Special Effects
    By Erica Sadun (Sybex, 2002)

iPhoto: The Missing Manual
By David Pogue, Joseph Schorr, and Derrick Story (Pogue Press/O'Reilly & Associates, Inc., 2002)

Learning Carbon
By Apple Computer, Inc. (O'Reilly & Associates, Inc., 2001)

Learning Cocoa with Objective-C, Second Edition
By James Duncan Davidson and Apple Computer, Inc. (O'Reilly & Associates, Inc., 2002)

Learning Unix for Mac OS X
By Dave Taylor and Jerry Peek (O'Reilly & Associates, Inc., 2002)

The Little Mac OS X Book
By Robin Williams (Peachpit Press, 2001)

The Macintosh Bible, Eighth Edition
By Clifford Colby, Marty Cortinas, et al. (Peachpit Press, 2002)

Macintosh Troubleshooting Pocket Guide for Mac OS 9 and Mac OS X
By David Lerner, Aaron Freimark, Tekserve Corporation (O'Reilly & Associates, Inc., 2002)

Mac 911
By Christopher Breen (Peachpit Press, 2002)

Mac OS 9: The Missing Manual
By David Pogue (Pogue Press/O'Reilly & Associates, Inc., 2000)

Mac OS X: The Missing Manual, Second Edition
By David Pogue, (Pogue Press/O'Reilly & Associates, Inc., 2002)

Mac OS X Disaster Relief
By Ted Landau and Dan Frakes (Peachpit Press, 2002)

Mac OS X Java: Early Adopter
By Murray Todd Williams et al. (Wrox Press, 2001)

Mac OS X Killer Tips
By Scott Kelby (New Riders Publishing, 2003)

Mac OS X Pocket Guide, Second Edition
By Chuck Toporek (O'Reilly & Associates, Inc., 2002)

Mac OS X for Unix Geeks
By Brian Jepson and Ernest E. Rothman (O'Reilly & Associates, Inc., 2002)

Mac OS X Unleashed
By John Ray and William C. Ray (Sams, 2002)

Objective-C Pocket Reference
By Andrew M. Duncan (O'Reilly & Associates, Inc., 2002)

Office 2001 for Macintosh: The Missing Manual
By Nan Barber and David Reynolds (Pogue Press/O'Reilly & Associates, Inc., 2001)

Office X for Macintosh: The Missing Manual
By Nan Barber, David Reynolds, Tonya Engst (Pogue Press/O'Reilly & Associates, Inc., 2002)

REALbasic: The Definitive Guide, Second Edition
By Matt Neuburg (O'Reilly & Associates, Inc., 2001)

Secrets of the iPod
By Christopher Breen (Peachpit Press, 2002)

Switching to the Mac: The Missing Manual
By David Pogue (Pogue Press/O'Reilly & Associates, Inc., 2001)

Using csh & tcsh
By Paul DuBois (O'Reilly, 1995)

Magazines

The following print magazines are available for Mac users:

MacAddict
Published monthly, *MacAddict* is a magazine for users and power users. each issue contains hardware and software reviews, and is accompanied with a CD containing free and shareware applications, as well as demo versions games and most popular graphics applications.

http://www.macaddict.com

Mac Design
Published monthly, *Mac Design* is a magazine for Mac-based graphic designers.

http://www.macdesignonline.com

macHOME
Published monthly, *macHOME* is a magazine for home-based Mac users. Each issue contains articles and tutorials on how to use your Mac.

http://www.machome.com

MacTech
Published monthly, *MacTech* is a magazine for Macintosh developers. Each issue contains articles and tutorials with code examples.

http://www.mactech.com

Macworld
Published monthly, each issue contains hardware and software reviews, as well as tutorials and how-to articles.

http://www.macworld.com

Mailing Lists

The following mailing lists can help you learn more about the Mac.

Apple-Run Mailing Lists

The following mailing lists are run by Apple:

applescript-studio
For scripters and developers who are using AppleScript Studio to build AppleScript-based applications for Mac OS X.

applescript-users
> For scripters who are working with AppleScript.

carbon-development
> For Carbon developers.

cocoa-dev
> For Cocoa developers.

java-dev
> For Java developers.

mac-games-dev
> For Mac-based game developers.

mac-opengl
> For Mac-based OpenGL developers.

macos-x-server
> For network and system administrators who are running the Mac OS X Server.

rendezvous
> Discussions on how to develop applications and devices that use Rendezvous.

scitech
> Discussions on Apple's support for science and technology markets.

studentdev
> For student developers.

weekly-kbase-changes
> Keep informed of weekly changes to Apple's Knowledge Base (KB).

> For information on how to subscribe to these and other Apple-owned mailing lists, see *http://lists.apple.com*.

Apple also maintains a listing of miscellaneous Mac-related mailing lists at *http://lists.apple.com/cgi-bin/mwf/forum_show.pl*; click on the "Non-Apple Mailing Lists" link.

Omni Group's Mailing Lists

The following mailing lists are run by the Omni Group:

macosx-admin
> A technical list for Mac OS X system administrators.

macosx-dev
> A moderated list for Mac OS X application developers.

macosx-talk
> A list for general discussions about the Mac OS X operating system.

> For more information on how to subscribe to these and other Omni lists, see *http://www.omnigroup.com/developer/mailinglists*.

Web Sites

These are just a few of the many URLs every Mac user should have bookmarked.

Apple Sites

Apple's Mac OS X page
   http://www.apple.com/macosx

Software Downloads page
   http://www.apple.com/downloads/macosx

Apple's Support page
   http://www.info.apple.com

Apple's Knowledge Base
   http://kbase.info.apple.com

Apple Developer Connection (ADC)
   http://developer.apple.com

Apple Store Locator
   http://www.apple.com/retail

Bug Reporting
   http://developer.apple.com/bugreporter

.Mac page
   http://www.mac.com

Developer

Cocoa Dev Central
   http://www.cocoadevcentral.com

Cocoa Dev Wiki
   http://www.cocoadev.com

Mac DevCenter (by O'Reilly Network)
   http://www.macdevcenter.com

Stepwise
   http://www.stepwise.com

Discussions and News

Applelust
   http://www.applelust.com

Apple Slashdot
   http://apple.slashdot.org

MacCentral
   http://www.maccentral.com

MacInTouch
   http://www.macintouch.com

Mac Minute
    http://www.macminute.com

Mac News Network
    http://www.macnn.com

MacSlash
    http://www.macslash.org

Rumor Sites

Apple Insider
    http://www.appleinsider.com

MacRumors
    http://www.macrumors.com

RumorTracker
    http://www.rumortracker.com

SpyMac
    http://www.spymac.com

Think Secret
    http://www.thinksecret.com

Software

AquaFiles
    http://www.aquafiles.com

Bare Bones Software
    http://www.barebones.com

Fun with Fink
    http://www.funwithfink.com

The Omni Group
    http://www.omnigroup.com

Sherlockers
    http://www.sherlockers.com

Version Tracker
    http://www.versiontracker.com/macosx

Tips, Tricks, Advice

Mac OS X FAQ
    http://www.osxfaq.com

Mac OS X Hints
    http://www.macosxhints.com

Index

graphical text editors, 368
graphical user interface (GUI) (see Aqua)
GraphicConverter application, 198
Graphing Calculator, 86, 190
grayscale, changing display to
    color, 100
Greenspun, Philip, 402
grep command, 622
    examples, 624
    finding files with, 80
    patterns, 467
    searching with, 466
Greyphite (OroborOSX theme), 530
grid layout, 48
GROUP environment variable
    (tcsh), 484
groups, 112, 261
    adding, 102
    creating, 283
    managing, 279–283
    NetInfo and, 313
GTK+, 528
GUI Emacs, 400
gunzip command, 624
.gz files, 208
gzcat command, 624
gzip command, 624
Gzip files, 208

H

halt command, 626
handwriting recognition, 159
hard drive
    erasing, 108
    partitioning, 107
    spindown time, 151
hardware
    address (see MAC address)
    identifying, 122
    preferences panels, 144–161
hashstat command (csh/tcsh), 504
hdid command, 626
hdiutil command, 626
head command, 629
    example, 629
/Headers folder (/Developer folder), 338
hearing impairments
    alert cue for users with, 100
    (see also accessibility)
Hearing pane (Universal Access
    panel), 179

Help menu, 17, 61
    Mac Help option, 61
hexadecimal value for a color, 106
HFS filesystem, 248
    identify whether a drive is formatted
        as, 107
HFS+ filesystem, 246–248
    differences between UFS and, 246
hfs.util command, 629
hidden files, 255–260
    changing Finder preferences, 255
    Darwin, 259
    dotfiles, 256
    Mac OS 9, 258
    seeing, 255
Hide Application Name option
    (Application menu), 14
Hide Extension checkbox, 38
Hide Finder option (Application
    menu), 58
Hide Others option (Application
    menu), 15, 58
Hide Toolbar option (View menu), 59
Hide/Show Status Bar option (View
    menu), 59
HIG (Aqua Human Interface
    Guidelines), 6
Hill, Brian, 291
hints, password, 102, 282
history command (csh/tcsh),
    example, 504
history file for shell, 123
history substitution (tcsh), 474
HOME environment variable
    (tcsh), 484
Home folder, 22
Home (From pull-down menu), 36
Home option (Go menu), 60
host command, 630
HOST environment variable (tcsh), 485
host specific application
    preferences, 524
hostinfo command, 631
hostname command, 631
HOSTTYPE environment variable
    (tcsh), 485
HPATH environment variable
    (tcsh), 485
.hqx files, 208
.html files, 367
hup command (tcsh), 505

L

S

Sampler (Aqua application), 341
sandbox (see CVS, sandbox)
Save As... option (File menu), 16, 38
Save option (File menu), 16
Save window, 38
saving documents, 36–38
/sbin directory, 260
scanning ports, 286
scanning (see port scanning)
sched command (tcsh), 510
scheduled times, running scripts and
        programs at, 298
scitech mailing list, 766
scp command, 706
Scrapbook, 86
Screen Effects panel (System
        Preferences), 141–144
Screen Saver (plug-in), 347
screen savers, 119, 143
screencapture command, 707
screenshots, 119, 197
    with the keyboard, 198
script command, 707
Script Editor, 361–363
Script Menu, enabling and
        removing, 104
Script Menu Extra, 355
scripting
    Terminal, 365
    (see also AppleScript, programming)
Scripting Additions, 104
/Scripting Additions folder (/Library
        folder), 254
scripts
    creating, compiling, and
        running, 361
    locating, 104
    recording, 362
    running at scheduled times, 298
    saving, 362
    testing, 363
/Scripts folder (/Library folder), 254
scrollbar controls together, placing, 100
scselect command, 707
scutil command, 708
sdiff command, 710
    example, 711
Search Domains (Network pane), 212
Search in (pop-up menu), 77

searching and replacing examples, 468
searching for files (see finding files;
        pattern matching)
secure FTP, 712
secure Internet protocols, 224
Secure Shell (see SSH)
Secureit (Perl script), 297
security, 121
    AirPort networks, 296
    AirPort-enabled Macs and, 224
    network disks and, 224
security tips
    AirPort network, 296
    AirPort networks, 224
    CVS, 407
    deactivate Show password hint, 283
    FTP, 227, 321
    network disks, 224
    NFS, 290
    print servers, 243
    Telnet, 228
sed command, 467, 711
sed, metacharacters, 464
Seeing pane (Univeral Access
        panel), 177
Select All option (Edit menu), 16, 59
sendmail, 318
Server Message Block (SMB), 220
service discovery, 301
Service Location Protocol (SLP), 302
/services directory and NetInfo, 314
Services menu, 39
Services option (Application menu), 14,
        58
Services (Sharing panel), 169
Set Autologin... (Accounts preference
        pane), 281
:set command, 381
set command (tcsh), examples, 510
setenv command (csh/tcsh), 510
SetFile command, 711
    example, 712
settc command (tcsh), 511
Settings for (Energy Saver panel), 151
setty command (tcsh), 511
sftp command, 712
/Shared directory (user directory), 251
shared domains, 304
shared folder, displaying contents, 107

About the Authors

Jason McIntosh lives in Somerville, Massachusetts, and works as a senior web programmer with the Institute for Chemistry and Cellular Biology at Harvard Medical School in Boston. Previous technical publications include *Perl and XML* (coauthored with Erik T. Ray and published by O'Reilly), and an occasional series of columns and weblog entries on XML or Mac OS X for the O'Reilly Network, particularly *http://www.macdevcenter.com*. His primary hobby is playing and designing obscure board and card games. All these things, as well as other inventions and reflections, may be found at his online home at *http://www.jmac.org*. Jason has worked with Macintosh computers (selling them, administrating them, programming them, and writing about them) since 1991. He agrees that, yes, that is pretty funny about his name, now that you mention it.

Chuck Toporek (*chuckdude@mac.com*) is a Mac Head, through and through. He has used Macs since 1988, when he first cut his teeth on a Mac II system, and is now the Macintosh editor for O'Reilly & Associates. He is a coauthor of *Hydrocephalus: A Guide for Patients, Families, and Friends*, and author of the *Mac OS X Pocket Guide*, portions of which were borrowed for this book. Originally from a small town in Michigan, Chuck has lived in various places on the west coast of the United States and Canada, and at sea, when he proudly served as a yeoman in the United States Naval Service. He now lives in Arlington, Massachusetts, with his wife, Kellie Robinson (coauthor of the *Hydrocephalus* book), and their cat, Max. In a former life, Chuck worked for print and online magazines, wrote numerous articles and tutorials on Mac software and web design, and used Linux and Windows machines when required. In a future life, he hopes to come back as a cat so he can sleep 18 hours a day. To find out more about him and see the Pez collection Chuck and Kellie have amassed, go to *http://homepage.mac.com/chuckdude*. Unlike Jason, there is nothing funny about his name (unless, of course, you consider that "Toporek" in Polish means "little hammer," and is also rumored to mean "assassin.")

Chris Stone (*cjstone@mac.com*) is a senior systems administrator (the Mac guy) at O'Reilly & Associates. He's written several Mac OS X-related articles for the O'Reilly MacDevCenter (*http://www.macdevcenter.com*) and contributed to *Mac OS X: The Missing Manual*, published by O'Reilly and Pogue Press. Chris lives in Petaluma, California, with his wife, Miho, and two sons, Andrew and Jonathan.

Colophon

Our look is the result of reader comments, our own experimentation, and feedback from distribution channels. Distinctive covers complement our distinctive approach to technical topics, breathing personality and life into potentially dry subjects.

The animal on the cover of *Mac OS X in a Nutshell* is a German shepherd. The model for this picture was Vinny, a search and rescue dog for the King County (Washington) Sheriff's department. The German shepherd was hand-drawn from photographs of Vinny by his aunt, Lorrie LeJeune, an editor at O'Reilly.

Search and rescue dogs are in quite a stressful field of work. In order for the dogs to be able to perform well, it must adapt to many different things—for example, modes of travel, new people, all kinds of weather, and various types of terrain. Often, search and rescue dogs are medium to large in size. They are expected to be intelligent, strong, and generally even-tempered. The German shepherd is by no means the only breed of dog who takes on this line of work. Ultimately, search and rescue dogs must have a strong nose and be physically fit. It is a difficult job that requires the dedication and commitment of both the dog and its owner/partner.

Mary Brady was the production editor and copyeditor for *Mac OS X in a Nutshell*. Ann Schirmer was the proofreader. Sarah Sherman and Claire Cloutier provided quality control. Genevieve d'Entremont, Judy Hoer, Andrew Savikas, and Reg Aubry provided production assistance. Julie Hawks wrote the index.

Emma Colby designed the cover of this book, based on a series design by Edie Freedman. The cover image is an original illustration created by Lorrie LeJeune. Emma Colby produced the cover layout with QuarkXPress 4.1 using Adobe's ITC Garamond font.

David Futato designed the interior layout. Joe Wizda and Mike Sierra converted the files from Microsoft Word to FrameMaker 5.5.6 using tools created by Mike Sierra. The text font is Linotype Birka; the heading font is Adobe Myriad Condensed; and the code font is LucasFont's TheSans Mono Condensed. The illustrations that appear in the book were produced by Robert Romano and Jessamyn Read using Macromedia FreeHand 9 and Adobe Photoshop 6. The tip and warning icons were drawn by Christopher Bing. This colophon was written by Mary Brady.

Other Titles Available from O'Reilly

Macintosh Users

Mac OS X: The Missing Manual, 2nd Edition

By David Pogue
2nd Edition October 2002
728 pages, ISBN 0-596-00450-8

David Pogue applies his scrupulous objectivity to this exciting new operating system, revealing which new features work well and which do not. This second edition offers a wealth of detail on the myriad changes in OS X 10.2. With new chapters on iChat (Apple's new instant-messaging software), Sherlock 3 (the Web search tool that pulls Web information directly onto the desktop), and the new Finder (which reintroduces spring-loaded folders).

Office X for Macintosh: The Missing Manual

By Nan Barber, Tonya Engst & David Reynolds
1st Edition July 2002
728 pages, ISBN 0-596-00332-3

This book applies the urbane and readable Missing Manuals touch to a winning topic: Microsoft Office X for Apple's stunning new operating system, Mac OS X. In typical Missing Manual style, targeted sidebars ensure that the book's three sections impart business-level details on Word, Excel, and the Palm-syncable Entourage, without leaving beginners behind. Indispensable reference for a growing user base.

iPhoto: The Missing Manual

By David Pogue, Joseph Schorr & Derrick Story
1st Edition July 2002
350 pages, ISBN 0-596-00365-x

With this guide, Macintosh fans can take their digital photos to the screen, to the Web, to print-outs, to hardbound photo books, even to DVDs. And they'll learn how to take iPhoto far beyond its seemingly simple feature list. But the software is just the beginning. The book also covers choosing and mastering a digital camera, basic photographic techniques, and tips for shooting special subjects like kids, sports, nighttime shots, portraits, and more.

Macintosh Troubleshooting Pocket Guide

By David Lerner & Aaron Freimark, Tekserve Corporation
1st Edition November 2002
80 pages, ISBN 0-596-00443-5

Tekserve Corporation, the distinctive Macintosh repair store in New York City, has long provided its customers with a free "Frequently Asked Questions" document to cover the most common troubleshooting questions. We recently discovered this FAQ sheet and realized that—like New York itself—it was too good to leave just for the New Yorkers. With the help of Tekserve's owners, we turned this FAQ sheet into the *Macintosh Troubleshooting Pocket Guide*.

iMovie 2: The Missing Manual

By David Pogue
1st Edition January 2001
420 pages, ISBN 0-596-00104-5

iMovie 2: The Missing Manual covers every step of iMovie video production, from choosing and using a digital camcorder to burning the finished work onto CDs. Far deeper and more detailed than the meager set of online help screens included with iMovie, the book helps iMovie 2 users realize the software's potential as a breakthrough in overcoming the cost, complexity, and difficulty of desktop video production.

AppleScript in a Nutshell

By Bruce W. Perry
1st Edition June 2001
528 pages, ISBN 1-56592-841-5

AppleScript in a Nutshell is the first complete reference to AppleScript, the popular programming language that gives both power users and sophisticated enterprise customers the important ability to automate repetitive tasks and customize applications. *AppleScript in a Nutshell* is a high-end handbook at a low-end price—an essential desktop reference that puts the full power of this user-friendly programming language into every AppleScript user's hands.

Macintosh Developers

Learning Cocoa with Objective-C, 2nd Edition

By James Duncan Davidson & Apple Computer, Inc.
2nd Edition September 2002
384 pages, ISBN 0-596-00301-3

Based on the Jaguar release of Mac OS X 10.2, this new edition of *Learning Cocoa* covers the latest updates to the Cocoa frameworks, including examples that use the Address Book and Universal Access APIs. Also included with this edition is a handy quick reference card, charting Cocoa's Foundation and AppKit frameworks, along with an Appendix that includes a listing of resources essential to any Cocoa developer—beginning or advanced.

Learning Carbon

By Apple Computer, Inc.
1st Edition May 2001
368 pages, ISBN 0-596-00161-4

Get up to speed quickly on creating Mac OS X applications with Carbon. You'll learn the fundamentals and key concepts of Carbon programming as you design and build a complete application under the book's guidance. Written by insiders at Apple Computer, *Learning Carbon* provides information you can't get anywhere else, giving you a head start in the Mac OS X application development market.

Learning Unix for the Mac OS X

By Dave Taylor & Jerry Peek
1st Edition May 2002
160 pages, ISBN 0-596-00342-0

This concise introduction offers just what readers need to know for getting started with Unix functions on Mac OS X. Mac users have long been comfortable with the easy-to-use elegance of the Mac GUI, and are loathe to change. With Mac OS X, they can continue using their preferred platform and explore powerful capabilities of Unix at the same time. *Learning Unix for the Mac OS X* tells readers how to use the Terminal application, become functional with the command interface, explore many Unix applications, and—most important—how to take advantage of the strengths of both interfaces.

Building Cocoa Applications: A Step-by-Step Guide

By Simson Garfinkel & Mike Mahoney
1st Edition May 2002
648 pages, ISBN 0-596-00235-1

Building Cocoa Applications is a step-by-step guide to developing applications for Apple's Mac OS X. It describes, in an engaging tutorial fashion, how to build substantial, object-oriented applications using Cocoa. The primary audience for this book is C programmers who want to learn quickly how to use Cocoa to build significant Mac OS X applications. The book takes the reader from basic Cocoa functions through the most advanced and powerful facilities.

AppleScript in a Nutshell

By Bruce W. Perry
1st Edition June 2001
528 pages, ISBN 1-56592-841-5

AppleScript in a Nutshell is the first complete reference to AppleScript, the popular programming language that gives both power users and sophisticated enterprise customers the important ability to automate repetitive tasks and customize applications. *AppleScript in a Nutshell* is a high-end handbook at a low-end price—an essential desktop reference that puts the full power of this user-friendly programming language in every AppleScript user's hands.

Mac OS X for Unix Geeks

By Brian Jepson & Ernest E. Rothman
1st Edition September 2002
216 pages, 0-596-00356-0

If you're one of the many Unix developers drawn to Mac OS X for its BSD core, you'll find yourself in surprisingly unfamiliar territory. Even if you're an experienced Mac user, Mac OS X is unlike earlier Macs, and it's radically different from the Unix you've used before, too. Their new book is your guide to figuring out the BSD Unix system and Mac-specific components that are making your life difficult and to help ease you into the Unix inside Mac OS X.

O'REILLY®

To order: *800-998-9938* • *order@oreilly.com* • *www.oreilly.com*
Online editions of most O'Reilly titles are available by subscription at *safari.oreilly.com*
Also available at most retail and online bookstores.

How to stay in touch with O'Reilly

1. Visit our award-winning web site

http://www.oreilly.com/

★ "Top 100 Sites on the Web"—PC Magazine
★ CIO Magazine's Web Business 50 Awards

Our web site contains a library of comprehensive product information (including book excerpts and tables of contents), downloadable software, background articles, interviews with technology leaders, links to relevant sites, book cover art, and more. File us in your bookmarks or favorites!

2. Join our email mailing lists

Sign up to get email announcements of new books and conferences, special offers, and O'Reilly Network technology newsletters at:

http://elists.oreilly.com

It's easy to customize your free elists subscription so you'll get exactly the O'Reilly news you want.

3. Get examples from our books

To find example files for a book, go to:

http://www.oreilly.com/catalog

select the book, and follow the "Examples" link.

4. Work with us

Check out our web site for current employment opportunites:

http://jobs.oreilly.com/

5. Register your book

Register your book at:
http://register.oreilly.com

6. Contact us

O'Reilly & Associates, Inc.
1005 Gravenstein Hwy North
Sebastopol, CA 95472 USA
TEL: 707-827-7000 or 800-998-9938
(6am to 5pm PST)
FAX: 707-829-0104

order@oreilly.com
For answers to problems regarding your order or our products. To place a book order online visit:

http://www.oreilly.com/order_new/

catalog@oreilly.com
To request a copy of our latest catalog.

booktech@oreilly.com
For book content technical questions or corrections.

corporate@oreilly.com
For educational, library, government, and corporate sales.

proposals@oreilly.com
To submit new book proposals to our editors and product managers.

international@oreilly.com
For information about our international distributors or translation queries. For a list of our distributors outside of North America check out:

http://international.oreilly.com/distributors.html

adoption@oreilly.com
For information about academic use of O'Reilly books, visit:

http://academic.oreilly.com

O'REILLY®